Language and Cul

THE FRENCH OF ENGLAND *c*.1100–*c*.1500

Language and Culture in Medieval Britain

THE FRENCH OF ENGLAND *c*.1100–*c*.1500

Edited by
Jocelyn Wogan-Browne

with Carolyn Collette, Maryanne Kowaleski, Linne Mooney,
Ad Putter and David Trotter

YORK MEDIEVAL PRESS

First published 2009
Paperback edition 2013

ISBN 978 1 903153 27 7 hardback
ISBN 978 1 903153 47 5 paperback

Transferred to digital printing

A York Medieval Press publication
in association with The Boydell Press
an imprint of Boydell & Brewer Ltd
PO Box 9   Woodbridge   Suffolk IP12 3DF   UK
and of Boydell & Brewer Inc.
668 Mt Hope Avenue   Rochester   NY 14620–2731   USA
website: www.boydellandbrewer.com
and with the
Centre for Medieval Studies, University of York

The publisher has no responsibility for the continued existence or accuracy
of URLs for external or third-party internet websites referred to in this book,
and does not guarantee that any content on such websites is,
or will remain, accurate or appropriate

A CIP catalogue record for this book is available
from the British Library

This publication is printed on acid-free paper

CONTENTS

ILLUSTRATIONS AND TABLES

Illustrations

Tables

CONTRIBUTORS

Henry Bainton's research interests centre on the historical writing of England and northern France in the twelfth century. In his Ph.D. research in Medieval Studies at the University of York, he is exploring how changing attitudes towards the written word in the late twelfth century affected Latin and vernacular historical writing.

Michael Bennett is Professor of History at the University of Tasmania. The author of four books and many articles on late medieval and early Tudor England, he has made a number of contributions to literary studies, including most recently and relevantly 'Mandeville's Travels and the Anglo-French moment' in *Medium Aevum* (2006). He is currently researching and writing on the global spread of vaccination in the early nineteenth century.

Julia Boffey is Professor of Medieval Studies at Queen Mary, University of London. Her research involves writings of all kinds in English c.1350–1550, especially their transmission and reception. She has edited a collection of *Fifteenth-Century English Dream Visions* (Oxford, 2003), co-produced *A New Index of Middle English Verse* (London, 2005), and published articles on Middle English lyrics, on fourteenth- and fifteenth-century poetry, on women's literacy and reading in the Middle Ages, and on early printing in England.

Richard Britnell, who specializes in the social and economic history of the Middle Ages, was successively a lecturer, reader and professor of History at Durham University, but is now retired. His most recent book is an edition of *Records of the Borough of Crossgate, Durham, 1312–1531*, published by the Surtees Society (Durham, 2008).

Carolyn Collette is Professor of English Language and Literature on the Alumnae Foundation at Mount Holyoke College and a Research Associate at the Centre for Medieval Studies at the University of York. Her recent publications, which centre on Anglo-French court culture, include *Performing Polity: Women and Agency in the Anglo-French Tradition, 1350–1620* (Turnhout, 2006) and *The Legend of Good Women: Context and Reception* (Cambridge, 2006).

Godfried Croenen is Senior Lecturer and Director of the Centre for Medieval and Renaissance Studies at the University of Liverpool. His current research focuses on Jean Froissart, in particular the chronicler's biography and the manuscript tradition of his work. He is also Associate Director of the AHRC-funded Online Froissart Project (Universities of Sheffield and Liverpool). He has published two books on the medieval nobility of the Low Countries.

Helen Deeming is a Lecturer in the Department of Music, Royal Holloway, University of London. She has published on the manuscript contexts of medieval music in England and France, and has a particular interest in manuscripts that contain music alongside other, non-musical materials. She is currently completing a book on miscellany manuscripts in twelfth- and thirteenth-century Britain, as well as an edition of Latin, French and English songs recorded in English manuscripts of the same period.

Stephanie Downes is completing a Ph.D. thesis at the University of Sydney, Australia, on the reception of Christine de Pizan in England. She has taught English literature at the University of Paris VII, France, and teaches in the department of English at the University of Sydney. She has published articles on responses to Christine and her works in England from the early fifteenth through to the late nineteenth centuries.

Martha W. Driver is Distinguished Professor of English and Women's and Gender Studies at Pace University in New York City. A co-founder of the Early Book Society for the study of manuscripts and printing history, she has published numerous articles and has also edited fourteen journals over eleven years. Her books include *The Image in Print: Book Illustration in Late Medieval England* (London, 2004) and *The Medieval Hero on Screen: Representations from Beowulf to Buffy*, edited with Sid Ray (Jefferson NC, 2004).

Monica Green is Professor of History at Arizona State University. She has published extensively on various aspects of the history of women's medicine in pre-modern Europe, her most recent book being *Making Women's Medicine Masculine: The Rise of Male Authority in Pre-Modern Gynecology* (Oxford, 2008). She is currently working on a general study of the medical school of Salerno in the twelfth century, and another on aspects of surgery in pre-modern Europe.

Richard Ingham has held teaching and research posts at the University of Reading, and is now Senior Lecturer in English in the School of English, Birmingham City University. He is the author of numerous articles on the syntactic development of Middle English, as well as on the use of French in England and France between 1200 and 1400. He has edited *The Anglo-Norman Language and its Contexts* (York, forthcoming).

Rebecca June is a Ph.D. candidate at Fordham University, New York, and is currently writing a dissertation titled 'Mothers of Exile: Gender and Identity in Medieval Narratives of Foundation'. Much of her research addresses Anglo-Norman (or French of England) texts and the issue of multilingualism in medieval England, her specific interest being the intersection of gender and vernacular language in the construction of communal identity.

Maryanne Kowaleski is Joseph Fitzpatrick S. J. Distinguished Professor of History and Director of the Center for Medieval Studies at Fordham University. Her publications include *Local Markets and Regional Trade in Medieval Exeter* (Cambridge, 1995), and *Medieval Towns: A Reader* (Peterborough ON, 2007). Her most recent book is a co-edited volume of essays: *Medieval Domesticity: Home, Housing, and Household in Medieval England* (Cambridge, 2009). She has published articles on medieval towns, women and work, overseas trade, and maritime history.

Pierre Kunstmann, Emeritus Professor at the University of Ottawa, started his career as a philologist and published several critical editions of Old French Miracles of the Virgin. He then turned to diachronic linguistics and published in 1990 a monograph on *Le relatif-interrogatif en ancien français*. Working presently as a lexicographer, he heads the *Dictionnaire Électronique de Chrétien de Troyes* project (LFA, Ottawa and ATILF, Nancy).

Françoise H.M. Le Saux is Professor of Medieval Languages and Literatures at the University of Reading. She has worked extensively on issues of translation and cultural adaptation, in particular of Arthurian texts.

Serge Lusignan is Professor of Medieval History at the Université de Montréal and Associate Researcher at the Laboratoire de médiévistique occidentale (Université de Paris I – CNRS). Most of his research deals with sociolinguistic history of medieval French. He is the author of *Parler vulgairement. Les intellectuels et la langue française aux XIIIe et XIVe siècles* (2e éd., Paris, 1987) and of *La langue des rois au Moyen Âge. Le français en France et en Angleterre* (Paris, 2004).

Tim William Machan is Professor of English at Marquette University, where his teaching and research focus on historical English linguistics and medieval literature. His most recent books are *Language Anxiety: Conflict and Change in the History of English* (Oxford, 2009), an edition of Chaucer's 'Boece' (Heidelberg, 2008) and an edition of the Eddic poem 'Vafþrúðnismál' (Durham, 2008)

Julia Marvin studies the historical writing and literature of late medieval England, with particular interest in the French of England, manuscript studies, and the prose *Brut* tradition. Educated at Princeton, she is associate professor in the Program of Liberal Studies and fellow of the Medieval Institute at the University of Notre Dame. Among her publications is *The Oldest Anglo-Norman Prose 'Brut' Chronicle: An Edition and Translation* (Woodbridge, 2006).

Brian Merrilees is Professor Emeritus of French at the University of Toronto and is the editor of *Le Petit Plet* (Oxford, 1970) and *La Vie des Set Dormanz* (London, 1977) in the ANTS series and the *Liber Donati* (with Beata FitzPatrick) in the Plain Texts Series (London, 1993). With Ian Short he has published three editions of the *Voyage de saint Brendan*, and is also the editor of three substantial Latin–French dictionaries from the fifteenth century, the *Dictionnaire de Firmin Le Ver* (Turnhout, 1994) and the *Dictionnaire latin–français de Guillaume Le Talleur* (with William Edwards) (Louvain-la-Neuve, 1995) and the *Glossarium gallico-latinum* (with Jacques Monfrin) (Turnhout, 1998). He is the author of some fifty articles on Anglo-Norman language and literature and medieval lexicography.

Ruth Nisse is an Associate Professor in the Department of English, Wesleyan University. She has written on Middle English theatre, alliterative poetry, Lollardy and apocalypse. Her current book project, *Jacob's Shipwreck: Diaspora in the Literature of the Jewish and Christian Middle Ages*, deals with the reception of ancient post-biblical texts in the Latin and Hebrew traditions of medieval Europe.

Marilyn Oliva is an adjunct professor at Fordham University, New York. Her area of special interest is medieval English religious women, particularly nuns. Her publications include *The Convent and the Community in Late Medieval England* (Woodbridge, 1998) and 'Nuns at Home: The Domesticity of Sacred Space', in *Medieval Domesticity: Home, Housing and Household in Medieval England*, edited by Maryanne Kowaleski and Jeremy Goldberg (Cambridge, 2009).

W. Mark Ormrod is Professor of History at the University of York. He is the author of *The Reign of Edward III* (New Haven CT, 1990), *Political Life in Medieval England* (New York, 1995) and (with Anthony Musson) *The Evolution of English Justice* (Basingstoke, 1999). He was a member of the editorial team for *The Parliament Rolls of Medieval England* (Woodbridge, 2005), and has published many articles on the government, politics and political culture of fourteenth-century England.

Heather Pagan obtained her Ph.D. at the University of Toronto in 2006. She is currently working as Assistant Editor for the *Anglo-Norman Dictionary* (www.anglo-norman.net) and preparing an edition of the *Anglo-Norman Prose Brut* for publication with the ANTS.

Laurie Postlewate is Senior Lecturer of French at Barnard College of Columbia University. In addition to a number of publications on the Franciscan poet Nicole Bozon, she has published articles on medieval lives of the saints and their reception, both in the Middle Ages and in nineteenth-century France. She is the co-editor of a volume of articles entitled *Acts and Texts: Performance and Ritual in the Middle Ages and the Renaissance* (Amsterdam, 2007).

Jean-Pascal Pouzet is a Lecturer in English at the University of Limoges, and a Research Fellow at the Centre d'Études Supérieures de Civilisation Médiévale (Poitiers). His research interests and publications fall within three main interlocking areas: vernacular book production in Medieval England, contacts between Insular French and Middle English languages and literatures, and literary theory (poetics).

Ad Putter is Professor of Medieval English at the University of Bristol. His publications include *Sir Gawain and the Green Knight and French Arthurian Romance* (Oxford, 1995), *An Introduction to the Gawain Poet* (London, 1996), and, with J. Jefferson and M. Stokes, *Studies in the Metre of Alliterative Verse* (Oxford, 2007). His essay on 'Multilingualism in England and Wales, c.1200: The Testimony of Gerald of Wales' is soon to be published in *Medieval Multilingualism in England, France, and Italy: The Francophone World and its Neighbors*, edited by K. Busby and C. Kleinhenz.

Geoff Rector is an Assistant Professor in the English Department at the University of Ottawa. He works on twelfth- and thirteenth-century English literary culture, with particular emphasis on Anglo-Norman literature. He has published on Jordan Fantosme's *Chronicle* and the Oxford Psalter, and is currently working on two related projects: *L'Escole des Letres: Pedagogy and Formation in Anglo-Norman Literature (1100–1215)*, which considers the ways in which education shaped twelfth-century vernacular literary culture, and *Emergence and Formation in Early Anglo-Norman Literature*, which expands on the first project's idea to consider the processes that drove the emergence of a francophone literature in England in the century after the Conquest.

Delbert W. Russell is Professor of French at the University of Waterloo, Canada. His medieval publications include critical editions of Anglo-Norman hagiographical texts, and he is currently preparing a new edition of the *Vie de seint Edmund le rei* by Denis Piramus for the Anglo-Norman Text Society, as well as collaborating on a French of England literary theory anthology (with Jocelyn Wogan-Browne and Thelma Fenster). Recent publications include a critical edition, in collaboration with Tony Hunt, of the Anglo-Norman prose *Seth and the Holy Rood* and the verse *Debate Humility and Pride*, 'Two Anglo-Norman *inedita* from MS Douce d.6', *Florilegium* 24 (2007), 55–79.

Thea Summerfield is a former lecturer in Old and Middle English literature in the English Department of the University of Utrecht, The Netherlands and is currently an affiliated researcher there. She also works as a translator of primary and secondary medieval literature. Recent work includes a chapter in *The Oxford History of Literary Translation in English*, vol. I: *to 1550*, ed. Roger Ellis (2008). Forthcoming are a translation into English of *Van den Vos Reynaerde* and an article on multilingualism in the

Auchinleck Manuscript in *Medieval Multilingualism in Later Medieval Britain: Sources and Analysis*, ed. Ad Putter and Judith Jefferson (Turnhout, forthcoming).

Andrew Taylor is Associate Professor in the Department of English at the University of Ottawa. His publications include *Textual Situations: Three Medieval Manuscripts and Their Readers* (Philadelphia, 2002) and, with Godfried Croenen and Kristen Figg, 'Authorship, Patronage, and Literary Gifts: The Books Froissart Brought to England in 1381', *Journal of the Early Book Society* (2008).

David Trotter is Professor of French at Aberystwyth University, and currently directs the AHRC-funded revision of the Anglo-Norman Dictionary. His other research interests include medieval translation (Anglo-Norman and also continental French), administrative and scientific language, textual editing, and medieval French dialectology (eastern France). He has also published on language use in medieval Gascony.

Elizabeth M. Tyler is a Reader in Medieval English Literature at the University of York. Her research and teaching focuses on English literary culture from the end of the ninth through to the twelfth century. She is the author of *Old English Poetics: The Aesthetics of the Familiar in Anglo-Saxon England* (York, 2006) and is completing a book, *Crossing Conquests: Women and the Politics of Literature in Eleventh-Century England* (Toronto). Her work emphasizes the international nature of English literature well before the Conquest, and draws attention to the key role England plays in the flourishing of European literary culture in the High Middle Ages.

Nicholas Watson is Professor of English at Harvard University. His publications include *The Idea of the Vernacular: An Anthology of Middle English Literary Theory 1280–1520*, co-edited with Ruth Evans, Andrew Taylor and Jocelyn Wogan-Browne (University Park PA, 1999), *Writings of Julian of Norwich: 'A Vision Showed to a Devout Woman' and 'A Revelation of Love'*, co-edited with Jacqueline Jenkins (University Park PA, 2006), as well as numerous articles on related topics. At present he is completing a monograph, *Balaam's Ass: Vernacular Theology and the Secularization of England, 1050–1550*, and co-editing, with Claire Fanger, John of Morigny's *Liber florum doctrine celestis*.

Jocelyn Wogan-Browne is Professor of Medieval Literature at the Centre for Medieval Studies, University of York, and was formerly professor in the English Department at Fordham University, New York. With Thelma Fenster, she co-edits the French of England Translation Series, in which they have co-written *Matthew Paris: The History of St Edward the King*, FRETS 1 (Tempe AZ, 2008); *Matthew Paris: The Life of St Alban*, FRETS 2 (forthcoming) and published Judith Weiss, *Boeve de Haumtone and Gui de Warewic*, FRETS 3 (2008): further volumes are forthcoming. With Delbert Russell, Fenster and Wogan-Browne are working on a large anthology of medieval discussions of textual and literary practice, entitled *French Vernacular Literary Theory and Practice in Medieval England, c.1100–c.1500*.

Robert F. Yeager is Professor of English and chair of the Department of English and Foreign Languages at the University of West Florida. He is president of the John Gower Society, and has written extensively on Gower and Chaucer, as well as on Shakespeare and on Old English literature. His facing-page edition and translation of Gower's *Traitié pour essampler les amantz marietz* and *Cinkante Balades* will be published as a TEAMS volume by the Medieval Institute Press of Kalamazoo, Michigan, in the spring of 2009.

ACKNOWLEDGEMENTS

The French of England teaching and research program initiated by Thelma Fenster and Jocelyn Wogan-Browne has been generously supported by Fordham University, NY, and the University of York, UK. A special debt is owed to Professor Maryanne Kowaleski, Joseph Fitzpatrick S. J. Distinguished Professor of History and Director of the Center for Medieval Studies at Fordham: every aspect of the French of England program from its conception onwards has benefited from her scholarship, generosity, vision, and organizational genius.

In 2007 three international conferences were held (in New York and York) on the French of England, supported in New York by Fordham University, especially by Dr Kowaleski and by Dr Nancy Busch, Dean of the Graduate School of Arts and Sciences and Associate Vice President for Academic Affairs, and in the UK by the Modern Humanities Research Association, the British Academy, the Leverhulme Trust and its International Network Award funding for the project *Multilingualism in the Middles Ages* (through the good offices of Professor Ad Putter), Boydell & Brewer and the Centre for Medieval Studies, University of York. Professor Linne Mooney generously made 'French in English Manuscripts and French Manuscripts in England' the theme of her 2007 Eleventh York Manuscripts Conference, thus creating the third conference in the series: this conference was supported by the British Academy.

Half of the sixty papers given in these three conferences have been selected and revised for this volume in the light of its intellectual and strategic goals. Many other papers will appear in other publications, some directly related to the French of England program, such as the French of England Translation Series (FRETS). We remain deeply grateful to all conference contributors and participants, and thank the contributors to this volume for the good cheer and professionalism with which they have co-operated with the general editor and the editorial committee. All conference and initial volume planning was done jointly with Thelma Fenster, although our current sharing of the academic editing work in the French of England project means that she is working on other publications than the present one. Special thanks go to Dr Cathy Hume, who, as part of her year's Research Associateship in the French of England at York, played a major role in organizing the French of England conference there and contributed to the conference Round Table from her own work on a forthcoming French of England publication.

The editor of the volume owes a great debt to the volume's Editorial Committee, Carolyn Collette, Maryanne Kowaleski, Linne Mooney, Ad Putter and David Trotter. Their advice and expertise in reading contributions at the edge of or outside her competence has been as generously and unstintingly given as their support for the French of England conferences. The Board of York

Medieval Press is also gratefully acknowledged for much helpful discussion and backing. Caroline Palmer of Boydell & Brewer has given her usual excellently informed and far-sighted support to the organization and publishing of the volume: as always it has been a pleasure to work with her and with her production team, led by Vanda Andrews with much efficiency and graciousness. Judith Everard brought her very helpful historian's expertise to the making of the Indices. Helen Barber designed the beautiful jacket for the volume. Claire Ruben provided supportive copy-editing at a time when the editor was disabled from typing. Thanks are also due to Christopher Baswell, Thelma Fenster, Mark Ormrod and Craig Taylor for extra help most generously given. Initial external review for the volume's proposal was undertaken by Professor Robert M. Stein of Purchase College of the State University of New York and Columbia University, whose encouragement and constructive criticism was invaluable. The completed typescript was reviewed by Derek Pearsall, Professor Emeritus, Harvard University and Honorary Professor in English and the Centre for Medieval Studies, University of York: his generously detailed and characteristically acute commentary has much improved the final version and is deeply appreciated.

ABBREVIATIONS

AF	Anglo-French
AL	Anglo-Latin
AN	Anglo-Norman
AND	*Anglo-Norman Dictionary* (unless otherwise specified this refers to the 2nd edn, available at http://www.anglo-norman.net)
ANS	*Anglo Norman Studies* (*Proceedings of the Battle Abbey Conference*)
ANTS	Anglo-Norman Text Society
ANTS OPS	Anglo-Norman Text Society Occasional Publication Series
AS	Anglo-Saxon
ASC	Anglo-Saxon Chronicle
Baker, *Inscribing the Hundred Years War*	*Inscribing the Hundred Years War in French and English Culture*, ed. D. N. Baker (Albany NY, 2000)
Bell, *What Nuns Read*	D. N. Bell, *What Nuns Read: Books and Libraries in Medieval English Nunneries*, Cistercian Studies Series 158 (Kalamazoo MI, 1995)
BJRL	*Bulletin of the John Rylands Library*
BL	British Library
BNF	Bibliothèque nationale de France
CBMLC	Corpus of British Medieval Library Catalogues
CF	Continental French or Central French
CL	Classical Latin
CUL	Cambridge University Library
DEAF	*Dictionnaire étymologique de l'ancien français*, ed. K. Baldinger et al., Tübingen & Québec, 1971–
Dean	R. J. Dean with M. B. M. Boulton, *Anglo-Norman Literature: A Guide to Texts and Manuscripts*, ANTS OPS 3 (London, 1999)
DMF	*Dictionnaire du Moyen Français*, CNRS 2003, 2007 (http://atilf.atilf.fr/dmf.htm)
DMLBS	*Dictionary of Medieval Latin from British Sources prepared by R. E. Latham under a Committee appointed by the British Academy* (London, 1975–)
EETS ES	Early English Text Society Extra Series
EETS OS	Early English Text Society Original Series
EETS SS	Early English Text Society Supplementary Series
EHR	*English Historical Review*

EME	*Early Medieval Europe*
FMLS	*Forum for Modern Language Studies*
FRETS	French of England Translation Series
FRETS OPS	French of England Translation Series Occasional Publication Series
Gee, *Women, Art and Patronage*	L. L. Gee, *Women, Art and Patronage from Henry III to Edward III, 1216–1377* (Woodbridge, 2002)
Godefroy	F. Godefroy, *Dictionnaire de l'ancienne langue française et de tous ses dialectes du IXe au XVe siècle*, 10 vols. (Paris, 1880)
Gregory and Trotter, *De mot en mot*	*De mot en mot: Aspects of Medieval Linguistics. Essays in Honour of William Rothwell*, ed. S. Gregory and D. A. Trotter (Cardiff, 1997)
IMEV	J. Boffey and A. S. G. Edwards, *A New Index to Middle English Verse* (London, 2005)
Ingham, *Anglo Norman Language*	*The Anglo-Norman Language and its Contexts*, ed. R. Ingham (York, forthcoming)
ISTC	Incunabula Short Title Catalogue (http://www.bl.uk/catalogues/istc/)
JEBS	*Journal of the Early Book Society*
JWCI	*Journal of the Warburg and Courtauld Institutes*
JMH	*Journal of Medieval History*
Ker, *MLGB*	N. R. Ker, *Medieval Libraries of Great Britain: A List of Surviving Books*, 2nd edn (London, 1964)
Ker, *MMBL*	N. R. Ker and A. J. Piper, *Medieval Manuscripts in British Libraries*, 4 vols. with vol. 5, *Indexes and Addenda*, ed. A. J. Piper, A. G. Watson and I. C. Campbell (Oxford, 1969–2002)
Legge, *Anglo-Norman in the Cloisters*	M. D. Legge, *Anglo-Norman in the Cloisters: The Influence of the Orders upon Anglo-Norman Literature* (Edinburgh, 1950)
Lusignan, *Langue des rois*	S. Lusignan, *La langue des rois au Moyen Âge: Le français en France et en Angleterre* (Paris, 2004)
LSE	*Leeds Studies in English*
ME	Middle English
MED	*Middle English Dictionary*, ed. H. Kurath and S. M. Kuhn (Michigan, 1956–) (http://quod.lib.umich.edu)
MGH SS	Monumenta Germaniae Historica Scriptores
MLR	*Modern Language Review*
Morgan, *EGM*	N. J. Morgan, *Early Gothic Manuscripts I (1190–1250) and II (1250–1285)*, Survey of Manuscripts Illuminated in the British Isles, 4 (London, 1982 and 1988)
NF	Northern French
NMS	*Nottingham Medieval Studies*

ODNB	*Oxford Dictionary of National Biography* (Oxford, 2004; online version 2008 at http://www.oxforddnb.com unless otherwise specified)
OE	Old English
OED	*Oxford English Dictionary*, 2nd edn (http://dictionary.oed.com)
OF	Old French
ONF	Old Northern French
OP	Order of Preachers (Dominican Friars)
Ormrod, 'Use of English'	W. M. Ormrod, 'The Use of English: Language, Law, and Political Culture in Fourteenth-Century England', *Speculum* 78 (2003), 750–87
PL	*Patrologia Latina cursus completus ... Series latinus*, ed. J.-P. Migne 217 vols. (Paris, 1844–55)
PMLA	*Publications of the Modern Language Association of America*
Pr	Provençal
PRO	London, The National Archives, Public Record Office
PROME	*Parliament Rolls of Medieval England*
Rothwell, 'Sugar and Spice'	W. Rothwell, 'Sugar and Spice and All Things Nice: From Oriental Bazaar to English Cloister in Anglo-Norman', *MLR* 94:3 (1999), 647–59
RS	Rolls Series
Salter, *English and International*	E. Salter, *English and International: Studies in the Literature, Art and Patronage of Medieval England*, ed. D. Pearsall and N. Zeeman (Cambridge, 1988)
SATF	Société des anciens textes français
Scott, *LGM*	K. L. Scott, *Later Gothic Manuscripts 1390–1490: A Survey of Manuscripts Illuminated in the British Isles*, 6, 2 vols. (London, 1996)
Short, 'Patrons and Polyglots'	I. Short, 'Patrons and Polyglots: French Literature in Twelfth-Century England', *ANS* 14 (1991), 229–49
Short, '*Tam Angli quam Franci*'	I. Short, '*Tam Angli quam Franci*: Self-definition in Anglo-Norman England', *ANS* 18 (1995), 153–75
STC	*A Short-Title Catalogue of Books Printed in England, Scotland and Ireland and of English Books Printed Abroad 1475–1640*, ed. A. W. Pollard and G. R. Redgrave; 2nd edn, W. A. Jackson, F. S. Ferguson and K.F. Pantzer (London, 1976–91)
TL	A. Tobler, rev. E. Lommatzsch, *Tobler–Lommatzsch Altfranzösisches Wörterbuch* (Berlin, 1925–76 and Stuttgart, 1989–)
TNA	The National Archives (Public Record Office)
TRHS	*Transactions of the Royal Historical Society*
Trotter, *Multilingualism*	*Multilingualism in Later Medieval Britain*, ed. D. A. Trotter (Cambridge, 2000)

Tyler, *Conceptualizing Multilingualism*	*Conceptualizing Multilingualism in England, 850–1250*, ed. E. M. Tyler (Turnhout, forthcoming)
VCH	*Victoria County History* (http://www.victoriacountyhistory.ac.uk/)
Wallace, *Medieval English Literature*	*The Cambridge History of Medieval English Literature*, ed. D. Wallace (Cambridge, 1999)
ZfSL	*Zeitschrift für französische Sprache und Literatur*

General Introduction: What's in a Name: The 'French' of 'England'

Jocelyn Wogan-Browne

The 'French' of 'England'

'The French of England' is a term designed to embrace medieval francophony in England, from the eleventh century to the fifteenth. In previous study of insular medieval culture, French has usually been divided into two periods and fields labelled respectively 'Anglo-Norman' and 'Anglo-French'. The problem lies not in the inappropriateness of either term but in the division itself and the separateness and self-enclosure of the categories they have come to signify. 'Anglo-Norman', a coinage first found in the eighteenth century, generally denotes French texts composed in the British Isles from the Conquest to the early fourteenth century. 'Anglo-French', a usage from the nineteenth century, frequently refers to textual imports from the continent into England and to contacts between England and the continent in the later fourteenth and early fifteenth centuries (though, confusingly, it is also sometimes used of the texts more usually called 'Anglo-Norman').[1]

The division has fostered notions of discontinuity in the French of England that fit comfortably with nineteenth- and early twentieth-century anglocentric periodizations of vernacular literary history and of the languages of record in England. The two terms, Anglo-Norman and Anglo-French, helped consolidate a model in which English lies dormant after the Conquest, having been overwhelmed and replaced by Anglo-Norman, but rises again in a late fourteenth century efflorescence (by which time England's French is supposed to be chiefly

---

[1] See OED *s.v.* Anglo-French, Anglo-Norman. Linguistically, as W. Rothwell points out in his introduction to the online AND, 'the term "Anglo-Norman" harks back to the time when the language was regarded as being the regional dialect of the Norman invaders who came across the Channel with William the Conqueror. Yet when account is taken of the heterogeneous composition of William's army, which included many men from different regions of France, together with the fact that over the following three centuries [French] must have been used in Britain by all manner of people from dissimilar ethnic backgrounds and whose linguistic competence, to judge by the writings which have survived, may be readily seen to have varied from a native mastery of French down to an elementary acquaintance with it, the generic term "Anglo-French", the French of England, perhaps reflects the reality of the situation better than the more restrictive "Anglo-Norman"' (http://www.anglo-norman.net/sitedocs/main-intro.html).

1

a matter of importation from and communication with the Continent). Between the twelfth and the early fourteenth centuries, in this model, there is an early period of composition in Anglo-Norman as a mother tongue, followed by writing in an Anglo-Norman acquired as a second language. After the early fourteenth century, Anglo-Norman becomes orphaned and ossified, a language cut off from its tap-root in continental French; English triumphs in the fourteenth century; and the French language of England, along with its texts, continues its decline to the status of a relic, principally surviving in the fixed and archaic register of law French.

In addition to this literary–linguistic narrative, some long-held assumptions in modern political historiography of the Middle Ages reinforce notions of French as always already in decline and always to be construed as an oppositional partner in the development of English traditions and institutions. The enduring tendency of historians to see the loss of Normandy in 1204 as an event as momentous as the Conquest assumes two mutually exclusive ethnicities, states and languages (and so lays an apparently plausible foundation for the fourteenth-century 'triumph of English'). 'When the Normans became French they did a great deal more than bring their national epic to a close. They permitted the English once more to become a nation, and they established the French state for all time,' concludes Powicke in 1913.[2] But even as late as 1997, the work of Rees Davies, historian of the *British* Isles, joins with the *English* linguistic nationalism posited by a literary scholar, Thorlac Turville-Petre, to assume that English 'triumphed' over Anglo-Norman by the early fourteenth century.[3] Such linguistic assumptions are deeply embedded in modern models of medieval state-building (understood as a matter of naturalized and inevitable 'English' emancipation and self-definition against the French) and they also play a role in cultural history.

There is of course much that is valuably addressed by such older models (themselves evolved in the interests of discerning major literary works and traditions and significant political and cultural change), just as there is in the terms 'Anglo-Norman' and 'Anglo-French', but there are also omissions and obfuscations. For one thing, the idea that post-Conquest Anglo-Saxon texts should be seen as survivals dispossessed by French culture has been challenged by recent work on manuscripts produced in England in the late eleventh to thirteenth centuries.[4] For another, it is not the case that texts in continental French

2   F. M. Powicke, *The Loss of Normandy 1189–1204* (Manchester, 1913), p. 449.
3   See T. Turville-Petre, *England the Nation: Language, Literature and National Identity 1290–1340* (Oxford, 1996), and for Rees Davies's sense that the loss of the French provinces in 1204–59 allowed the development of a much greater assertion of English political (and cultural) authority over Wales, Ireland and Scotland, culminating in the English supremacy of Edward I, see e.g. R. R. Davies, *Domination and Conquest: The Experience of Ireland, Scotland and Wales 1100–1300* (Cambridge, 1990), ch. 6, esp. pp. 114–15, 123–8; and his 'The Peoples of Britain and Ireland, 1100–1400: IV Language and Historical Mythology', *TRHS* 6th series 7 (1997), 1–24. I thank Mark Ormrod for these references.
4   *Rewriting English in the Twelfth Century*, ed. M. Swan and E. M. Treharne (Cambridge, 2000); E. M. Treharne, M. Swan, O. Da Rold and J. Story, *The Production and Use of*

did not circulate in twelfth and thirteenth-century England: to take just one example, there were early copies in the monastic library at Durham, and one at Hereford, of the twelfth-century psalter commentary made on the Continent for Laurette, countess of Alsace (a commentary in fact principally represented in Anglo-Norman manuscripts).[5] Unlike later fourteenth-century texts, however, this psalter commentary is not usually classified among 'Anglo-French' works. By the same token, texts in 'Anglo-Norman' continued to be produced in the later Middle Ages, even though most uses of the term 'Anglo-French' silently omit such texts.[6] (It is true that the composition, though not the copying, of most kinds of French literary texts ceases in England, but it does so at the turn of the fifteenth century rather than in the early fourteenth century – unless one refuses to count the particular types of devotional, doctrinal and historiographical texts that continued to be produced.) But the most serious effect of the two terms Anglo-Norman and Anglo-French has been artificially to sunder, contain, even ghettoize the actual continuities and discontinuities of French in England and so to muffle its importance and value in the study of insular culture and its internal and external relations.[7]

A great deal of further enquiry is needed in which the narratives of historians and literary and linguistic scholars cross-fertilize each other, rather than simply co-exist without challenging each others' assumptions and frameworks. Legal historians and literary critics, examining one another's material, have for some time demonstrated the usefulness of considering their evidence together.[8]

English Manuscripts 1060–1220 at http://www.le.ac.uk/english/em1060to1220/index. html project, B. Millett, 'The Pastoral Context of the Trinity and Lambeth Homilies', in *Manuscript Geography of the West Midlands*, ed. W. Scase (Turnhout, 2007), pp. 43–64; E. M. Treharne, 'Periodization and Categorization: The Silence of (the) English in the Twelfth Century', *New Medieval Literatures* 8 (2006), 247–73. See also the essays by Tyler and Green in this volume.

[5] See *The Twelfth-Century Psalter Commentary in French for Laurette d'Alsace: an Edition of Psalms I–L*, ed. S. Gregory, 2 vols., MHRA Texts and Dissertations 29 (London, 1990).

[6] See further the essay by Bennett in this volume for a more inclusive sense of 'Anglo-French' and for *Mandeville's Travels* as an (initially) insular French text of *c.*1360.

[7] Study has been further fragmented by the construction of French and English as nationalizing disciplines. Though work in Anglo-Norman has been vigorous in departments of French outside France, scholars of French literature and culture from continental France have only exceptionally perceived the French of England as part of their discipline. Current interest in extending the canon and linguistic range of French studies to embrace francophone cultures outside France and the rising numbers of studies by continental French scholars of insular medieval French works suggests that this situation is about to change. For new approaches to *francophonie*, see e.g. K. Busby and A. Putter, Introduction to *Medieval Multilingualism: The Francophone World and Its Neighbours*, Texts and Cultures of Northern Europe, ed. K. Busby and C. Kleinhenz (Turnhout, forthcoming); *Cultural Traffic in the Medieval Romance World*, ed. S. Gaunt and J. Weiss, *Journal of Romance Studies* 4.3, special issue (Winter 2004).

[8] For example, P. Hyams, 'Henry II and Ganelon', *The Syracuse Scholar* 4 (1983), 23–35 and idem, 'Warranty and Good Lordship in Twelfth-Century England', *Law and History Review* 2 (1987), 437–503; E. A. Francis, 'The Trial in *Lanval*', in *Studies in French Language*

Medical writing is another area with implications for language and literature: Linda Voigts has drawn attention to bilingualism in medical texts as a practice that challenges any notions of fixed and universal hierarchies and class status among England's languages.[9] More recently, historians have shown how important it is in dealing with administrative records to distinguish between the languages in which a process or decision is recorded and the languages in which it was actually carried out. Such work has the potential to transform our understanding of the motivations and contexts for the alleged milestones on the road to banishing French and (re-)instating English by showing how much longer and how much more variously French functioned for specific procedures and text-types than was previously thought.[10] So, for example, the long-standing, though queried account of fifteenth-century 'standardization' of English, purportedly driven by the Lancastrian crown and disseminated by chancery, has been steadily crumbling away under historians' and linguists' investigations. Instead, new specificities of English, French and Latin usage in the written and oral forms of the processes and records of documentary culture are emerging, together with many surprising and long-lived uses of French.[11] A complex linguistic story emerges, where the written language and the oral performance of different kinds of records and different legal and administrative processes continue to be hugely various and often francophone, and where, as Mark Ormrod has argued, there is no single 'great linguistic shift among the secular elites (whether gentle or bourgeois) that provided the market and audience for Middle English literature'.[12] If historians are currently providing some of the most interesting work on language, literary scholars' attention to French in England helps to reconceive the

---

and *Medieval Literature presented to Prof. Mildred K. Pope by pupils, colleagues and friends*, ed. anon (Manchester, 1939), pp. 115–24; *The Letter of the Law: Legal Practice and Literary Production in Medieval England*, ed. E. Steiner and C. Barrington (Ithaca NY, 2002); D.A. Trotter, 'Language and Law in the Anglo-French *Mirror of Justices*', in *L'Art de la Philologie: Mélanges en l'honneur de Leena Löfsted*, ed. J. Härmä, E. Suomela-Härmä and O. Välikangas (Helsinki, 2007), pp. 257–70.

9   L. E. Voigts, 'What's the Word? Bilingualism in late-Medieval England', *Speculum* 71 (1996), 813–26, and see T. Hunt, 'Code-Switching in Medical Texts', in Trotter, *Multilingualism*, pp. 131–47; D. A. Trotter, 'Translation and the Development of Scholarly and Scientific Discourse: Early Medical Translations and Multilingual Lexicography', in *International Encyclopedia of Translation Studies*, ed. H. Kittel et al. (Berlin, 2007), pp. 1073–81. On medical literature, see further the essay by Green in this volume.

10 Ormrod, 'Use of English'. For a fascinating demonstration that an English historian's textual policies for Anglo-Norman are arguably more suitable than the traditions of continental French scholarship in shaping literary work in the French of England, see J. Marvin, 'The Unassuming Reader: F. W. Maitland and the Editing of Anglo-Norman', in *The Book Unbound: Editing and Reading Medieval Manuscripts and Texts*, ed. S. Echard and S. Partridge (Toronto, 2004), pp. 14–36.

11 In addition to Ormrod's landmark study, 'The Use of English', see the important essay by G. Dodd, 'The Spread of English in the Records of Central Government, 1400–1430', in *Vernacularity in England and Wales, c. 1300–1550*, ed. E. Salter and H. Wicker (Turnhout, forthcoming), and the essay by Ormrod in the present volume.

12 Ormrod, 'Use of English', p. 751.

4

francophony of Anglo-Latin histories as part of their writers' working cultural
and intellectual *habitus* and so to further the integration of vernacular and Latin
in modern assessments of medieval historiography.[13] So too, linguistic work such
as Trotter's on French before the Conquest or Machan's on the role (or absence
of role) for French in the early modern narratives of English and French national
identity has much to say to historiographical and literary assumptions regarding
linguistic nationalism.[14]

Nor can it any longer be a matter of conceptualizing two separate vernacular
languages and traditions, the English of England and the French of England. The
idea of a culture as a monoglot entity proceeding in organic linearity through time
and within the territories of a modern nation state cannot adequately represent
medieval textual production and linguistic and cultural contacts.[15] Linguistically
aware literary criticism in English has always challenged a bounded perception of English cultural and political tradition: so, for example, the final, still
indispensable book by Elizabeth Salter (d. 1980) on the literary culture of medieval England was published as *English and International*, while Derek Pearsall
has argued that Chaucer chooses English not to assert an independent national
identity, but for the creation of an 'illustrious vulgar tongue' among others in
Europe.[16] We could indeed turn to Dante, as several essays in this volume do, for
his demonstration in his *De vulgari eloquentia* that, in Carolyn Collette's words,
'what is now marked as inter-linguistic borrowing could well be understood as
a normal function of vernaculars, which were inherently unstable because they

---

[13] See e.g. H. Blurton, 'From *Chanson de Geste* to Magna Carta: Genre and the Barons in
Matthew Paris's *Chronica majora*', *New Medieval Literatures* 9 (2007), 113–78; M. Otter,
'La Vie des deux Offa, l'Enfance de Saint Edmund, et la logique des "antecedents"', in
Médiévales: Langue, Textes, Histoires 38 (2000), 17–34. Although the francophone working
environment of many Anglo-Latin writers (as of other socio-linguistic configurations,
such as Latin and Anglo-Norse and Anglo-Welsh) has been implicitly recognized from
at least the Rolls Series onwards in the inclusion of multilingual records, it has taken
time in some cases for vernacular texts to be studied as intensively for their historiographical value as their Latin counterparts. For Matthew Paris, for instance, Blurton's study is one of the few to examine the interplay of Latin and French traditions
in Paris's Latin historiography, while work on Paris's vernacular compositions has
been the province of art historians rather than of historians: see P. Binski, 'Reflections
on *La Estoire Seint Aedward le rei*: Hagiography and Kingship in Thirteenth-Century
England', *JMH*, 16 (1990), 333–50, and idem, *Westminster Abbey and the Plantagenets:
Kingship and the Representation of Power, 1200–1400* (New Haven CT, 1995).

[14] See the essays by Trotter and Machan in this volume: also T.W. Machan, *English in the
Middle Ages* (Oxford, 2003); Trotter, *Multilingualism*; idem, 'Language Contact, Multilingualism, and the Evidence Problem', in *The Beginnings of Standardization: Language
and Culture in Fourteenth-Century England*, ed. Ursula Schaefer (Frankfurt, 2006), pp.
73–90.

[15] For a valuable statement of this case, see R. M. Stein, 'Multilingualism', in *Oxford
Twenty-First Century Approaches to Literature: Middle English*, ed. P. Strohm (Oxford,
2007), pp. 23–37.

[16] Salter, *English and International*; D. Pearsall, 'Chaucer and Englishness', *Proceedings of
the British Academy* 101 (1998), 77–99 (p. 90).

were responsive to changing circumstances, constantly adding and dropping vocabulary'.[17] Scholars of modern linguistics have in any case long argued that a monoglot culture with clearly defined boundaries between languages (and hence between itself and other languages and cultures) is exceptional: most language acquisition proceeds in multilingual and more permeable ways.[18] This does not mean that languages cannot be differentiated from each other, or indeed that particular images of social class and linguistic hierarchy cannot be attached to particular languages, but it does mean that such distinctions are as much situational as essential or automatically present. In trilingual England, where three major languages co-existed (to say nothing of cultural contacts and interchanges with other languages in the British Isles, such as Norse, Welsh, Gaelic, Cornish, Hebrew, Flemish),[19] linguists and lexicographers studying medieval English and medieval French in England have shown that complex models of language contact are needed to account for their characteristics. There is, for instance, a deeply interwoven lexical borrowing back and forth from English to French and from French to English that makes the boundaries of our modern dictionaries of 'Middle English' and 'Anglo-Norman' themselves problematic.[20] In phraseology as well as lexis, many medieval texts interchange their languages in ways that cannot serve as straight socio-linguistic history but require contextualizing analysis.

In his classic study of medieval linguistic code-switching, Herbert Schendl quotes a letter from Richard Kingston, Dean of Windsor, to Henry IV in 1403:

> Please a vostre tresgraciouse Seignourie entendre que a jour-duy... furent venuz deinz nostre countie pluis de .cccc. des les rebelz. ... leueth nought that ye ne come for no man that may counsaille yowe the contrarie. ...
>
> Tresexcellent, trespuissant, et tresredouté Seignour, autrement say a present nieez. ... In god fey I hope to almighty god that, yef ye come youre owne persone, ye shulle haue the victorie of alle youre enemyes ... escript a Here-

---

17 See p. 374 below and see also the essay by Rector in this volume.
18 S. Romaine, *Bilingualism* (Oxford, 1989; 2nd edn 1995).
19 See e.g. M. Townend, 'Contacts and Conflicts: Latin, Norse, and French', in *The Oxford History of English*, ed. L. *The Oxford History of English*, ed. L. Mugglestone (Oxford, 2006), pp. 61–85.
20 See especially the work of W. Rothwell, including the AND and numerous articles (listed to 1996 in Gregory and Trotter, *De mot en mot*). Texts of selected lexicographical articles by Professor Rothwell are currently available at The Anglo-Norman On-Line Hub (http://www.anglo-norman.net/articles/): for a list of works cited in the present volume, see the Bibliography. For further important lexicographical work, see studies by the current AND editor, D. A. Trotter, including most recently 'Words, words, words ... but what exactly is a "word" in Anglo-Norman?', in *Essays in Honour of Brian Merrilees*, « *Queil boen professeur, mult enseinné, queil boen collegue* » : *Mélanges offerts à Brian Merrilees*, ed. C. Harvey, *Florilegium* 24 (2007), 109–23; '*Pur meuz acorder en parlance E descorder en variaunce*: convergence et divergence dans l'évolution de l'anglo-normand', in *Sprachwandel und (Dis-) Kontinuität in der Romania*, ed. S. Heinemann and P. Videsott (Tübingen, 2008), pp. 87–95; 'Intra-textual Multilingualism and Diaphasic/Diastratic Variation in Anglo-Norman', in Tyler, *Conceptualizing Multilingualism*, forthcoming.

ford, en tresgraunte haste, a trois de la clocke apres noone le tierce jour de Septembre.[21]

A number of words in this letter can be found in both the Middle English *and* the Anglo-Norman Dictionary.[22] The elite and literate status of the letter is clear: its linguistic switching is not driven by lack of resource (either in the linguistic competence of the people involved or in their access to clerisy). At the same time the pragmatic function of the letter would inhibit immediately seeing it as an example of macaronic art, as in, for instance, the exquisite English, French and Latin Harley Lyrics of the great early fourteenth-century trilingual manuscript Harley 2253, or of fifteenth-century love-letter poems.[23] Yet the switching here is nonetheless expressive: the letter distributes its French and English preponderantly between formality and narrative on the one hand and urgent wishes and injunctions on the other. There is an effect both of appropriate elevation and of urgency and intimacy, such as can be found in other letters of the period.[24]

How different is an apparently specialized letter like this, with its intercalation of French and English lexis and syntax between the dean of Windsor and Henry IV, from the multilingual vocabulary and varying linguistic substrata of medieval writing in England? One general answer to this question is 'Not very different'. This perspective comes from Michelle Warren's illuminating work on a related issue, the medieval practice of translation. No medieval text, she argues, is ever

---

[21] H. Schendl, 'Linguistic Aspects of Code-switching in Medieval English Texts', in Trotter, *Multilingualism*, pp. 77–92 (p. 81).

[22] For example, in this extract: *please, countie, rebelz, counsaille, contrarie, present, trinite, fey, persone, victorie, enemyes, haste, clocke, noone, Septembre*. See further D. A. Trotter, 'Language Contact and Lexicography: The Case of Anglo-Norman', in *The Origins and Development of Emigrant Languages: Proceedings from the Second Rasmus Rask Colloquium, Odense University, November 1994*), ed. H.-F. Nielsen and L. Schøsler (Odense, 1996), pp. 1–39. There is also of course the further question of the diachronic assimilation of 'French' words as 'English': see e.g. W. Rothwell's argument it is 'virtually impossible to state categorically in many cases whether a word is intended to be French or English': Rothwell, 'Sugar and Spice', p. 659.

[23] See S. G. Fein, *Studies in the Harley Manuscript: The Scribes, Contents and Social Contexts of BL MS Harley 2253* (Kalamazoo MI, 2000). On the late medieval love-letter poem and its macaronics, see the essay by Putter in this volume.

[24] H. Schendl, 'Code-Choice and Code-Switching in Some Early Fifteenth-Century Letters', in *Middle English from Tongue to Text: Selected Papers from the Third International Conference on Middle English*, ed. P. Lucas et al. (Frankfurt, 2002), pp. 247–62. The use of English for intimacy and urgency is specific to the text-type, and has varying effects. When petitions to late medieval kings were endorsed in English, for instance, this was 'personal' in the sense that the recording clerks were demonstrating that the king himself rather than his officers had dealt with the petition (the latter conventionally using French as the normal and formulaic response), so that English signified both the king's personal attention and the exact recording of the royal response: see the essay by Ormrod in this volume, p. 39.

truly monoglot: all are composed and received in a multilingual network of allusions, undergirdings, expectations, resonances.[25] Translation is at once highly pragmatic, pervasive, central to medieval literary aesthetics, and undertaken in a multitude of ways: oral, literate, carefully prepared, *ex tempore*. The languages even of apparently monoglot medieval texts are always in varying relation with other languages – substrate, authorizing, subverting.

A second answer might come from Christopher Baswell's recent argument that the overt language of a text on its manuscript page may be pierced by other languages so as to reveal the surface language as but a particular coding: in the Middle English *Alexander* narratives, for instance, French emerges into the English matrix, 'with key leaders speaking in the recognizably authentic voice of the antique aristocrat'.[26] Of this French example Baswell asks: 'given these brief but intense emergences of the Anglo-French language of aristocratic authenticity, is the reader invited to experience these poems primarily as English, or rather as fundamentally French but largely coded in a more accessible tongue through which there emerges, at intense moments, its genuine, underlying voice?'[27]

A third important perspective arises from consideration of text-type. Medieval letters, to take the genre of Schendl's example cited above, may belong both to literature and administration and can be hard to classify. Attention to the compositional practices and text-types of medieval administrative and professional cultures shows, firstly, that binary oppositions between the literary and the documentary oversimplify the interrelations of the two, and secondly, that the study of non-literary compositional, translation and rhetorical practices has much to tell us about the cultural assumptions of the texts we identify as literary.[28] Linguistic permeability, code-switching and the other phenomena currently studied as part of contemporary interest in multilingualism may be a wider and more normative cultural practice than the construction of nationalizing literary canons has suggested.

A fourth new perspective comes from current developments in the linguistic study of French in England in the later Middle Ages. Previously seen as a degenerate and deracinated language and no longer a mother tongue, later Anglo-Norman or Anglo-French has been relatively little attended to (though the medi-

25 M. R. Warren, 'Translation', in Strohm, ed., *Middle English*, pp. 51–67.

26 C. Baswell, 'Multilingualism on the Page', in Strohm, ed., *Middle English*, pp. 38–50 (p. 43).

27 Baswell, 'Multilingualism', pp. 43–4: and see further R. Hanna, 'Pepys 2498: Anglo-Norman Audiences and London Biblical Texts', ch. 4 of his *London Literature 1300–1380* (Cambridge, 2005), pp. 148–221.

28 E. Steiner, *Documentary Culture and the Making of English Literature* (Cambridge, 2003); M. Otter, Inventiones: *Fiction and Referentiality in Twelfth-Century English Historical Writing* (Chapel Hill NC, 1996): see also A. Hiatt, *The Making of Medieval Forgeries: False Documents in Medieval England* (London, 2004); J. Crick, 'St. Albans, Westminster, and Some Twelfth-Century Views of the Anglo-Saxon Past', *ANS* 25 (2003 for 2002), 65–83.

eval conduct and language learning guides produced in later medieval England are an exception here).[29] But, as regards the wider use of late Anglo-Norman in administrative records of all kinds, Richard Ingham and others are currently showing that reports of the fourteenth-century death of Anglo-Norman have been exaggerated and the phenomenon conceived without sufficient subtlety. The title of Ingham's essay in this volume, 'The Persistence of Anglo-Norman', speaks for a rapidly developing field of study in later French language in England, with the potential to override the linguistic division of French in England into Anglo-Norman and Anglo-French mentioned at the outset here, and to open the way to mapping the linguistic continuities of francophony in England, as well as to securing greater respect and attention for the later periods of the language.[30]

At the moment, 'French of England' is pre-eminently a working term, designed to draw attention to the French literary texts (numbering nearly a thousand) composed or circulating in and out of medieval Britain from the eleventh to the later fifteenth centuries, and also to occupational, civic, professional, administrative and governmental French records.[31] In the current ferment of thought and investigation concerning francophony and the multilingualism of England, 'French of England' may well be modified or replaced as new directions of research and thought develop: without denying the existence of appeals to national feeling (which certainly do occur on particular occasions in medieval texts and records), it seems we need a new post-national vocabulary – and that it is not easy to find.[32] There is however, lingering still, a mnemonically useful

---

[29] *Manières de langage, 1396, 1399, 1415*, ed. A. Kristol, ANTS 53 (London, 1995); see also W. Rothwell's ongoing edition of all manuscripts of Walter Bibbesworth's *Tretiz*, of which the *Femina* version is currently available at http://www.anglo-norman.et/txts/femina.pdf.

[30] See further Ingham, *Anglo-Norman Language*, and see the essays by Ingham and Kunstmann in this volume.

[31] Most of the literary texts are documented in R. J. Dean with M. B. M. Boulton, *Anglo-Norman Literature: A Guide to Texts and Manuscripts*, ANTS OPS 3 (London, 1999), henceforth cited as Dean by item number. For an initial bibliography of French records, see M. Kowaleski and R. Slitt, 'Bibliography', under 'Primary Sources: History' at http://www.fordham.edu/frenchofengland. For an overview of documentary sources see W. Rothwell, Introduction to the On-Line AND, 'Anglo-French and the AND' (http://www.anglo-norman.net/sitedocs/main-intro.html). Other resources such as the *Parliament Rolls of Medieval England* (PROME), ed. C. Given-Wilson et al., and the *Ancient Petitions* (some 17,000 medieval petitions mostly datable between the late thirteenth and the mid-fifteenth centuries), ed. W. M. Ormrod et al (online at the UK National Archives respectively since 2005 and 2007) have still to be fully exploited for their linguistic distribution and properties: see further http://www.sd-editions.com/PROME/home.html, and *Ancient Petitions* at http://www.nationalarchives.gov.uk/catalogue and http://www.nationalarchives.gov.uk/documentsonline. See also *Medieval Petitions: Grace and Grievance*, ed. W. M. Ormrod, G. Dodd and A. Musson (York, 2009).

[32] Linguistically, as Serge Lusignan points out in his essay in this volume, the French of England can be seen as part of a wider Anglo-French, encompassing, for instance, the

frisson to 'French of England', since it is a name that links two nationalizing terms in what would once have been regarded as a perverse coupling.

Changing the narrative

The present volume seeks to articulate something of the difference it makes if we re-position what has been often treated as a monoglot English culture within its multilingual actualities, and use more open and less prescriptive models of language and language-contact for thinking about the French of England. The Latin of England has tended to receive more attention than the French: both in its own right and in its relation with Middle English, Latin is relatively integrated as part of the cultural landscape of medieval Britain (though, among other issues, its relations with insular vernaculars remains an ongoing area of reassessment).[33] But the French of England is less recognized both in its relation to the Latin of England and to the English of England.

This volume is not a handbook or a survey, of which excellent examples already exist: the monumental labours of Dean and Boulton have given us a very full guide to texts and manuscripts: a recent manual of Anglo-Norman by Ian Short gives us a lucid and authoritative guide to the language and an important account of its phonology.[34] Susan Crane's excellent chapter on Anglo-Norman cultures in the 1999 *Cambridge History of Medieval English Literature* exemplifies the best of what can be done through general accounts and

French used in the English settlement of Gascony, as well as of the British Isles (p. 000 below). Literary texts and documents in insular and continental French were produced in and about Ireland, Wales and Scotland: for the French of Wales, see D. A. Trotter, 'L'anglo-français au Pays de Galles: une enquête préliminaire', *Revue de Linguistique romane* 58 (1994), 461–88; and for Irish Anglo-Norman texts, see E. Mullally, 'Hiberno-Norman Literature and Its Public', in *Settlement and Society in Medieval Ireland: Studies Presented to F.X. Martin, O.S.A.*, ed. J. Bradley (Kilkenny, 1988), pp. 327–43. For some Anglo-Norman texts produced in or concerned with Scotland, see Dean nos. 28, 74, 75, 86. For the use of continental French in Scotland, see further the essay by Lusignan in this volume, p. 23. In the aftermath of Anglo-Germanic philology's treatment of the Celtic as the subaltern, 'French of Britain', a more obviously inclusive term, seems not so useful at the moment, though it may well become so.

33 See e.g. A.G. Rigg, *A History of Anglo-Latin Literature, 1066–1422* (Cambridge, 1992); C.Baswell, 'Latinitas', in Wallace, *Medieval English Literature*, pp. 122–51; and for the role of Latin in relation to Middle English, J. Catto, 'Written English: The Making of the Language, 1370–1400', *Past and Present* 179 (2003), 24–59.

34 Dean with Boulton, cited in n. 31 above. For discursive surveys, see M. D. Legge, *Anglo-Norman Literature and its Background* (Oxford, 1963) and her *Anglo-Norman in the Cloisters*; W. Calin, *The French Tradition and the Literature of Medieval England* (Toronto, 1994). The greatest lack at the moment is in francophone insular palaeography: this will be remedied for the twelfth century at least by the *Catalogue illustré des manuscrits de la littérature française et occitane: le XIIᵉ siècle*, ed. M. Careri, T. Nixon, C. Ruby and I. Short (Rome, forthcoming).

overviews.[35] What is urgent at the moment is that we start exploring the ways in which the French of England and the English of England, as well as the Latin of England, affect each other and their neighbours so that the interrelations and not just the co-presence of languages and texts are addressed.

As a result, the organization of this volume is both purposeful and eclectic. Its chronological span deliberately addresses the entire medieval period of England's French culture, part of the point here being that the French of England is not something to be closed off, something that happened 'before' Middle English. Culture in medieval England remains multilingual and, as the title and arrangement of this volume insist, the French of England is integral to our *entire* narrative of medieval insular culture: it cannot be bracketed off as a separate and therefore optional study.

Through the essays and the brief section introductions, this volume pursues a narrative stretching from the eleventh to the sixteenth centuries, a narrative of five medieval francophone centuries in England, not two. In pursuing this chronological span, the volume necessarily emphasizes, at the expense of well-established fields, those areas in which new connections and questions are opening up. There is, for instance, no study here of the acknowledged glories of twelfth-century Anglo-Norman literature – of the great romances, the *chansons de geste* and the sophisticated and vital hagiography – of insular literary culture.[36] These are relatively well known and feature in most literary histories: they do not need resurveying here, although they are assumed as an absent presence. So too, thirteenth- and fourteenth-century Middle English romance studies have long been in dialogue with French. The study of pastoralia and devotional writing has not, however: it is accordingly the latter that is given particular attention here.

More detailed rationales will be found in the brief section introductions, but it is worth explaining here that the volume begins with a section on *Language and Socio-Linguistics* in order to demonstrate the foundational importance of our linguistic models for how we conceive literary and historical texts and textual cultures at large. The possibility of new linguistic histories and socio-linguistics, especially for the fourteenth and early fifteenth centuries, is opened up in this first section. In the sections that follow, the volume moves chronologically, with appropriately varying themes and issues in each subdivision and with a continuing linguistic as well as literary emphasis. Section II, *Crossing the Conquest: New Linguistic and Literary Histories* looks at Anglo-Norman and its co-eval languages

---

[35] S. Crane, 'Anglo-Norman Cultures in England, 1066–1460', in Wallace, *Medieval English Literature*, pp. 35–60. The attention given Anglo-Norman in this volume is of course very welcome, though, as so often, and in spite of the chronological range of Crane's article, 'the Anglo-Norman chapter' is here positioned as preliminary to the main business of the history.

[36] The most recent full-length study is L. Ashe, *Fiction and History in England, 1066–1200* (Cambridge, 2007). See also on twelfth-century romance, R. Field, 'Children of Anarchy: Anglo-Norman Romance in the Twelfth Century', in *Writers of the Reign of Henry II*, ed. R. Kennedy and S. Meecham Jones (Houndmills, 2006), pp. 249–62.

to trace some of the linguistic, cultural and literary continuities across the pre-Conquest period and the later eleventh and twelfth centuries. So too Section III, *After Lateran IV: Francophone Devotions and Histories*, does not work through the well-known landmarks of English thirteenth- and fourteenth-century literary history, but looks to those areas where new narratives with the power to impact on our general sense of this period are beginning to be shaped. The fourth and final section on *England and French in the late Fourteenth and Fifteenth Centuries* opens with a reminder of the teleology we too readily apply to the socio-linguistic history of French and English in the late medieval and early modern period, before exploring the specificities of multilingualism and manuscript culture in later medieval England.

For the reasons noted earlier in this Introduction, we hope that the term 'French of England' will be useful, especially as a newly inclusive name for its field of enquiry, but it has not solved all the terminological problems even of this present volume. Where contributors are contrasting continental French with the French of England or the French of Britain, for instance, or dealing with texts composed on one side of the Channel and circulated on the other, 'insular French' has sometimes been the more convenient term; while the older names Anglo-Norman and Anglo-French have been sometimes necessarily used precisely because of their existing currency. A variety of terminology has therefore been retained, though every effort has been made to ensure that usage is clear in the context of each essay. Given the rich complexities of linguistic and cultural contact in medieval England and medieval Britain, a single term is unlikely to be able to do all the work, though 'French of England' perhaps does more than most.

Despite Chaucer's importance in both anglophone and francophone accounts of literary culture, his French is not explicitly dealt with as a separate entity in this volume. This is partly because Chaucer has been well served elsewhere.[37] It is well known that his writing is seamed with French lexis (much of it from the French of England, not just from the Continent), and with French sources and French intertexts – and that he was as happy to use French as a crib or an interlanguage as any merchant or administrator (it is not the Prioress's adminstrative French that Chaucer satirizes but her Parisian ambitions). But it would also be fallacious to suppose that in some simple way by adding the French of England we can get a different Chaucer. What is important is that if we integrate the French of England as an area of enquiry in a multilingual landscape, *everything* becomes different – a different literary, cultural and linguistic history, a different

---

[37] See e.g. C. Cannon, *The Making of Chaucer's English: A Study of Words* (Cambridge, 1998); J. I. Wimsatt, *Chaucer and the French Love Poets: The Literary Background of the Book of the Duchess* (Chapel Hill NC, 1968) and *Chaucer and his French Contemporaries: Natural Music in the Fourteenth Century* (Toronto, 1991); *Chaucer and the City*, ed. A. Butterfield (Cambridge, 2006); eadem, *The Familiar Enemy: Chaucer, Language and Nation in the Hundred Years War* (Oxford, 2009). Chaucer is, however, treated in the context of late fourteenth-century international francophone culture in England and seen against some contemporary continental French writers in the essays by Bennett and Collette respectively in this volume.

relation to the languages of record and of particular occupations, and to the interactions of all these, to say nothing of a different sense of how we think language
works in and as literature. We have much to gain by taking Chaucer and all our
other texts out of monoglottism and into the multilingualism of which the francophone presence throughout medieval English culture is so important a strand.

Section I
Language and Socio-Linguistics

INTRODUCTION

This section offers a series of linguistic and socio-linguistic forays revitalizing the existing accounts of how French was used in England and showing how its history is longer, its class range wider, and its uses more specific, more part of particular linguistic politics, than is allowed for by the reflex conservatism often assumed to explain continuing composition in Anglo-Norman.

The section opens with further reflections by Serge Lusignan on his important work on royal and administrative French in England, whose linguistic situation, he concludes, may be typical rather than unusual in medieval Europe. Mark Ormrod shows the continuing value of studying documentary records and the importance of such work for linguistic and cultural history: linguistic changes in petitions to the crown, he argues, are a function not of global shifts towards English in royal administration and the legal system, but of specific usages as between oral and written forms, with exceptional uses of English being explicitly defended and explained by clerks and others as against the more usual French. Richard Ingham's study confirms from a linguistic point of view the living status of such clerical Anglo-Norman, still evolving as part of a French dialect continuum late in the fourteenth century. His essay signals an important shift in the study of later Anglo-Norman, now to be taken seriously as a language and not as a decayed remnant of one. Pierre Kunstmann offers an equally important model for earlier Anglo-Norman: the linguistic development of French in England early shows changes that happen later in continental French. In other words, the French of England can be regarded as advanced – 'avant-gardiste' is Kunstmann's term – rather than degenerate.

The next four essays look at various uses of French in multilingual environments: Thea Summerfield studies the implications of language-mixing in vernacular historiography; Richard Britnell surveys the uses of French in town records and practices into the fifteenth century; Marilyn Oliva examines the French account-keeping of late medieval nunneries and uses the example of Campsey Priory to argue that these communities, still important consumers and sometimes producers of French texts, may be less elite than commonly supposed; Maryanne Kowaleski reveals sailors and merchants as a community still using French, an early maritime *lingua franca*, into the fifteenth century, and using it certainly for written records and codes, and very probably for oral communication. To these linguistic communities can be added the Anglo-French one of the English soldiers in the Hundred Years War.[1] Gower, traditionally the last major

---

[1] See A. Bell and A. Curry, *The Soldier in Later Medieval England*, http://www.medieval-soldier.org/ and A. Curry, A. Bell et al., 'Languages in the Military Profession in Later Medieval England', in Ingham, *Anglo-Norman Language*, forthcoming.

Anglo-Norman writer in England, is the subject of two studies updating existing accounts: Brian Merrilees and Heather Pagan show that, even though Gower claimed one version of his *Confessio amantis* as 'a bok for Engelondes sake', his French is not Anglo-Norman's last gasp, but, like Chaucer's English, a new departure – for Gower's French is deliberately not *anglo-normanisant*. Robert Yeager's lively account of Gower's linguistic decisions reveals them as a series of political choices. Gower's, then, is one French idiolect in a landscape of varying Frenches – literary, administrative, professional, insular and continental in varying shades – practised in England, in different multilingual situations and for differing and specific reasons.

1

French Language in Contact with English:
Social Context and Linguistic Change
(mid-13th–14th centuries)

Serge Lusignan*

The presence of French in England, especially from 1066 onwards, created one of the most intricate linguistic situations in medieval Europe. Certainly, no society is ever truly monolingual, and England was already a meeting place for Anglo-Saxon, Celtic and Scandinavian. Moreover England, and most other societies elsewhere in Europe, relied on Latin, a living language for clerics but the mother tongue of no one. With the arrival of the Normans, French asserted itself as the language of the ruling elites in society and the vernacular of a prolific written culture. Over time it became the second language for the greater portion of its users, which meant that in some ways it resembled Latin.[1] I would like to analyse this situation from a historical sociolinguistic perspective. Administrative sources, rather than literary ones, seem most promising for this approach. The French that is of greatest interest for social history is that which was used in royal administration and judicial processes, since it concerns, directly or indirectly, all inhabitants of the realm.[2]

Although the archives contain tens of thousands of documents that confirm the strong vitality of French in medieval England, it remains very difficult to evaluate the proportion of people who were able to read or to speak the language.[3] Several institutional factors contributed directly to the diffusion of both oral and written forms of French within English society. The first of these was the royal court itself. The Plantagenets succeeded the first Norman kings in 1154. With the

---

*   I would like to express my gratitude to Dr Emily Hutchison who translated this article into English, and to David Trotter for his constructive suggestions.

1   French was the only vernacular language which could be learned with the help of a didactic literature in the same way as Latin: A. M. Kristol, 'L'enseignement du français en Angleterre (XIIIe–XVe siècles): Les sources manuscrites', *Romania* 111 (1990), 289–330; A. M. Kristol, 'Le ms. 188 de Magdalen College Oxford: une "pierre de Rosette" de l'enseignement médiéval du français en Angleterre', *Vox Romanica* 60 (2001), 149–67.

2   The general considerations that follow draw on my book *La langue des rois au Moyen Âge. Le français en France et en Angleterre* (Paris, 2004), ch. IV.

3   For arguments for a wider range of users in specific groups than previously thought, see the essays by Kowaleski and Oliva in this volume.

sole exception of Henry IV, the first Lancastrian king, every king from Henry III until Henry VI had a wife in their first or second marriage whose first language was French. The mothers of kings were thus almost entirely French-speaking. The court was therefore a centre where French prospered from 1066 until the beginning of the fifteenth century at least. It is no surprise that Jean Froissart, who was eager to document the feats and to record the testimonies of English knights, appears to have communicated with them almost entirely in French.

The development of institutions contributed to the permeation of French beyond court circles. From the start of the fourteenth century, administrative officers in London and in other counties were frequently required to execute the royal mandates written in French. The use of French was, moreover, indispensable for all that pertained to justice. A solid command of French was required of all professionals in the field of law, including judges and lawyers.[4] The same linguistic competence was certainly very useful for participation in Parliament, which, among other things, provided advice to the king on statutes. In the fourteenth century and the beginning of the fifteenth, these were more often than not written in French. French was also of great importance for the merchant bourgeoisie, who traded with the cloth towns in Picardy and Flanders. Therefore, we must conclude that in order to participate in the smooth running of royal government or in their own day-to-day affairs, a large number of the urban elite and the rural gentry had to possess some French. Such factors contributed to the growth and diffusion of French well beyond the exclusive circle of the royal court and of the high nobility.

An interesting source studied by Michael Richter seems to confirm that there was indeed a fairly broad diffusion of the French language.[5] This document relates to the canonization trial of Thomas Cantilupe, the bishop of Hereford, held in Hereford in 1307. It provided the testimony of 203 witnesses, in which the language of each deposition was generally recorded. It reveals that not a single cleric used English in their testimonials. Interestingly, they were almost evenly divided between those who provided their testimony in Latin and those who provided it in French. Among the laymen, almost half of the inhabitants of the towns chose French, and the other half English.[6] On the other hand, the great majority of rural inhabitants chose English. Remarkably, some laymen used Latin in addition to French. This admittedly small sample of English society demonstrates that at the beginning of the fourteenth century, there was a significant group of people who had some competence in French in the county of Hereford. This is all the more important considering that Hereford is 150 miles away from London, on the periphery of the area in which the strongest Norman presence was felt.

---

4 P. Brand, 'The Languages of the Law in Later Medieval England', in Trotter, *Multilingualism*, pp. 63–76.
5 M. Richter, 'Collecting Miracles along the Anglo-Welsh Border in the Early Fourteenth Century', in Trotter, *Multilingualism*, pp. 53–61.
6 On French in towns, see further the essay by Britnell in this volume.

The chronological background

During the decades after 1066, French was the first language of the ruling elites, the more important barons, bishops and abbots. It remained, for the following centuries, the language of kings and queens. For this reason it asserted itself as the second language of the higher nobility and other frequenters of the court, who had been progressively anglicized over the course of the twelfth century. But what appears most interesting to me with regard to the diffusion of French into English society was the emergence of French as the language of administration and of law.[7]

It is not until the end of the reign of Edward I that we observe the king using French in his royal charters under the privy seal. This practice increased with time. Under Edward II, we find as many royal acts in the vernacular as in Latin. French dominated under Edward III, Richard II and Henry IV. However, we must remember that the vernacular was reserved only for acts sealed under the privy seal or the signet; all acts sealed with the chancery's great seal remained in Latin until the arrival of Henry VIII. The first official act written in English and sealed with the signet is dated to 1417, when Henry V was undertaking the campaign that won him the north of France. Afterwards, acts written in English increased in number, with a declining number being written in French.

In the legislative field, the first statute written in French can be dated to 1275. Under Edward II French statutes were more numerous than those in Latin, and from Edward III they were almost exclusively in French. English began to make its appearance in this area only at the beginning of the fifteenth century, and it was not until 1488 that it replaced French entirely in its function as a legislative language. With regard to the Parliamentary Rolls it is notable that from the reign of Edward I to the reign of Henry IV, French and Latin were the only languages used. English finally appeared during the reigns of Henry V and Henry VI.

The status of French within the realm of justice was reinforced by the professionalization of law under Edward I.[8] It became the technical language of a group of professionals who thus sought to protect their prerogatives. The importance of French for the mastery of common law was strengthened with the development of the Year Books. Essentially, these were elaborate summaries of significant cases pleaded before royal courts over the course of a year, and they served in the teaching and interpretation of common law. The practice of compiling these synopses seems to have begun at the end of the reign of Henry III. For the reign

[7] For this section, see E. Déprez, *Études de diplomatique anglaise: De l'avènement d'Édouard Ier à celui d'Henri VII (1272–1485). Le sceau privé, le sceau secret, le signet* (Paris, 1908); W. Rothwell, 'Language and Government in Medieval England', *ZfSL* 93 (1983), 258–70; D. A. Kibbee, *For to Speke Frenche Trewely. The French Language in England, 1000–1600: Its Status, Description and Instruction* (Amsterdam, 1991); Brand, 'The Languages of the Law'; Lusignan, *Langue des rois*, pp. 163–85, and the essay by Ormrod in this volume.

[8] P. Brand, *The Origin of the English Legal Profession* (Oxford, 1992).

of Edward I, we know of more than 8,000 summaries, almost all in French. In fact French dominates the almost 20,000 pieces that have been edited thus far, from the period ending in 1535.[9] French was, clearly, an essential language for lawyers.

Participation in public administration and justice required a certain command of French. This requirement was manifest from the last decades of the thirteenth century until the first decades of the fifteenth and, for jurists, until the end of the Middle Ages and beyond. The Golden Age of the king's French spanned a long fourteenth century. Most strikingly, it began at the time when the great period of Anglo-Norman literature was reaching its end. Well-entrenched in the curial milieu since the end of the eleventh century, French became important for the rural gentry and urban bourgeoisie at the end of the thirteenth century. It appears that as time passed the social basis of the language spread from the royal court and the nobility to the gentry and the urban elites.

Up to this point, I have used the word 'French' to identify the language. Yet when we examine the administrative documents of the fourteenth century, we are clearly faced with Anglo-French.

The geographical diffusion of the English king's French

Having outlined the chronology of the penetration of French into English society, let us turn to how royal authority contributed to its spread in parts of England that seemed, at times, remote. William Rothwell has argued that French was used mostly in the south of England, in the Home Counties, around London and in the south-east. He points to Andover, Coventry, Leicester, King's Lynn, Reading, Southampton and Winchester, all of which are within one hundred miles or so from London, as the only towns for which merchant guild regulations were drawn up in Anglo-French.[10]

Royal government did, however, export its French into other parts of the British Isles. David Trotter has identified a significant number of documents written in Anglo-French in Wales.[11] In many cases, these documents were very probably written by Welsh people themselves, and some of them contained words the origins of which were Celtic. Ireland also was dominated by England during our period, and several clues reveal that Anglo-French was used in Irish administrative and literary documents between the thirteenth and fifteenth centuries.[12]

---

9 Lusignan, *Langue des rois*, p. 175.
10 Rothwell, 'Language and Government'. A discussion with Maryanne Kowaleski during the French of England conference at York convinced me that the question of the use of French in municipal administration should be fully re-examined. Such investigation may well show that the use of French extended far beyond those limits. See further the essay by Britnell in this volume.
11 D. A. Trotter, 'L'anglo-français au pays de Galles: une enquête préliminaire', *Revue de linguistique romane* 58 (1994), 461–87.
12 R. Hickey, 'Assessing the Relative Status of Languages in Medieval Ireland', in *Studies in Middle English Linguistics*, ed. J. Fisiak (Berlin, 1997), pp. 181–205; G. Mac Niocaill,

Scotland was an independent realm that frequently allied itself with France against England. Its chancery typically used Latin before it eventually turned to English at the very end of the Middle Ages. In a recent study, Cynthia Neville demonstrates that there was a significant Anglo-Norman emigration into the southern part of Scotland, which had been encouraged by the king from around 1125.[13] Michael Richter has noted that many Scottish kings and the courts were very much at ease using French.[14] According to Jean Froissart, David II 'sçavoit parler moult biau françois, car il fu de sa jonece nourris en France' ('could speak French very well, for in his youth he was raised in France').[15] In my own work, *La langue des rois*, I established that between 1300 and 1392 nearly twenty treaties between Scotland and England were drawn up in French.

The king of England also exported French into Gascony. Indeed, the king and his administration in England used Anglo-French in their correspondence with subjects in the south-west of France; and their subjects often responded in the same Anglo-French. Likewise, the Black Prince used Anglo-French in that same region, where he spent much of his active life.[16] David Trotter has identified Jean Aymeri and Guillaume Sériz as two Gascon notaries in the service of the prince.[17] I would also add to this list Piers Maderan, who accompanied the Black Prince during the latter's journey across Gascony between 1363 and 1364 to receive oaths of homage from all the lords of the region.[18] These Gascons mastered perfectly the art of writing French in the style of the English.

Thus it appears that Anglo-French was written by people having a wide variety of mother tongues, ranging from the various forms of English spoken all through the kingdom to Celtic and Occitan languages. Anglo-French was more than the French of England.

ed., 'Gnathaimh Bhaile Atha Cliath', *Na Buirgeisi XII–XIV Aois* (Dublin, 1964), vol. 1, pp. 3–59.

[13] C. J. Neville, *Native Lordship in Medieval Scotland: The Earldom of Strathearn and Lennox c.1140–1365* (Dublin, 2005).

[14] M. Richter, *Sprache und Gesellschaft im Mittelalter: Untersuchungen zur mündlichen Kommunikation in England von der Mitte des elften bis zum Beginn des vierzehnten Jahrhunderts* (Stuttgart, 1979), pp. 123–5.

[15] J. Froissart, *Chroniques, Livre 1, Le manuscrit d'Amiens, Bibliothèque municipale no 486*, ed. G. T. Diller (Geneva, 1991), pp. 779–80.

[16] On the French of English military campaigners in France, see further A. Curry, A. Bell, et al., 'Languages in the Military Profession in Later Medieval England', in Ingham, *Anglo-Norman Language*.

[17] D. A. Trotter, '"Mossenhor, fet metre aquesta letra en bon francés": Anglo-French in Gascony', in Gregory and Trotter, *De mot en mot*, pp. 199–222.

[18] Lusignan, *Langue des rois*, p. 183.

Serge Lusignan

The king's French: a language in contact

The geographical and social expansion of the king's French had an immediate effect on its contact with other languages, such as English and Occitan, and with other forms of French, such as Picard and Parisian French. Considering that there is so much work yet to do in this area, I will concentrate on two of the most important points: the influence of French on English, and the meeting of the French of England with Parisian French.

The French influence on the English language
The first locus of contact between French and English was certainly within the minds of individual royal courtiers, royal officers and jurists, members of the urban elites and of the gentry, who were required to use it either by necessity or through ambition. We can confidently claim that nearly all authors of documents drafted in French, in England, between the thirteenth and the fifteenth centuries, had English as their mother tongue.[19]

The most obvious influence that French had on English was on its vocabulary. It is a commonplace of the history of English to recall that thousands of French words were absorbed into the English language in the later Middle Ages. Frequently, a word of Romance origin simply took the place of an already existing Anglo-Saxon word. In other cases, the French word was juxtaposed to the Anglo-Saxon one, expressing a new meaning or nuance. In some circumstances, a French word was used to name something entirely new or unknown, as was the case for words relating to the nobility, such as *count*, *duke*, or *peer*; or in the lexicon associated with justice, such as *court*, *crime*, or *judge*; or that relating to politics, such as *chancellor*, *government*, or *nation*. Generally, the accepted view has been that vocabulary that was borrowed from French was applied to the semantics of culture, and to the life of the aristocracy, of social elites, and of political and religious powers; whereas the semantics of daily life, popular culture, emotions, and indeed the basic vocabulary of the English language, remained Anglo-Saxon.[20]

But what factors explain French's influence on English? Specialists repeatedly emphasize that the integration of a Romance vocabulary into English began in the second half of the thirteenth century, intensifying in the fourteenth, at the very same time that the production of Anglo-Norman literature in England was slackening. There are two complementary explanations for this phenomenon.

The first of these is approached from a literary perspective. As summarised by Charles Barber, the phenomenon developed at the very moment when English began to be used as a language of literary culture. Barber explains:

---

[19] For this section, see Lusignan, *Langue des rois*, pp. 210–17.

[20] W. Rothwell challenges this generally accepted view in showing that some vulgar English terms are of Anglo-French origin: 'Adding Insult to Injury: The English who Curse in Borrowed French', in *The Origins and Development of Emigrant Languages*, ed. H.-F. Nielsen and L. Schøsler (Odense, 1996), pp. 41–54: see also the essays by Kowaleski and Oliva in this volume.

this is not surprising: when bilingual speakers were changing over to English for such purposes as government and literature, they felt the need for the specialized terms that they were accustomed to in those fields, and brought them over from French.[21]

In the eyes of the first professional writers of the fourteenth century, such as Geoffrey Chaucer, French was well established as the language of 'culture'. The English in which Chaucer eventually chose to write already included many French (including Anglo-French and continental French) terms and Chaucer added still more, as part of a long career of 'cultural importation' and translation in the widest medieval senses, in which works from several languages were translated or used as sources by him in the creation of an extended and internationalized Middle English.[22]

The second explanation takes its inspiration from sociolinguistic research. James Milroy has shown that social groups who benefit from strong internal cohesion and maintain few links with other groups within society are less likely to experience an evolution in their language.[23] Change typically comes from individuals who diversify their social relations, and who become the intermediaries between their milieu and the new social circles in which they operate.

Using this model, we can suggest that, although there was always necessarily much interaction between lords and their servants, bailiffs and manorial stewards, the absorption of French words into English first greatly intensified with the development of professional administrative classes in institutions relating to justice, administration and representation. It was then that lawyers, royal officers and parliamentary representatives proliferated, and were obliged to learn to communicate in French. Milroy's model suggests that it was this group that introduced the characteristics of the language spoken by the Norman nobility – the elites of their society, with whom they interacted – into their own social milieu. For a language to evolve, it is not necessary that a particularly large group act as agents of linguistic change, but it is necessary for the changes to appeal to a broad audience. The Anglo-French words that the above individuals found particularly efficient or pleasing were doubtless used by them in their conversations with their English peers, thereby beginning to percolate into their spoken language. This hypothesis suggests then, that in 'Frenchifying' the language, these royal officers, parliamentarians and lawyers were the mediators of an important modification of English. Indeed, the penetration of French into the English language

---

[21] C. Barber, *The English Language: A Historical Introduction* (Cambridge, 2002), pp. 145–6. The question of what proportion of such terms would already have been integrated into English, is, as Rothwell has shown in his many articles on the lexical interchanges of English and French (see above, General Introduction, n. 20) an extremely complicated matter.

[22] See further C. Cannon, *The Making of Chaucer's English* (Cambridge, 1998); B. Windeatt, 'Geoffrey Chaucer', in *The Oxford History of Literary Translation in English*, ed. Roger Ellis (Oxford, 2008), pp. 137–48.

[23] J. Milroy, *Linguistic Variation and Change* (Oxford, 1992).

and the professionalization of law in the second half of the thirteenth century occurred in time to coincide with the growing reliance on French by the royal administration at the beginning of the fourteenth century, followed by the institutionalization of Parliament a little later. From this perspective, the first agents of the Frenchification of the English language were the urban bourgeoisie and the gentry.

The meeting between the French of England and France
The last three centuries of the Middle Ages brought the English and the French into constant, but not always peaceful, contact with one another. The French language seems continuously to have dominated their relations, though Latin remained an important language of written documents between the two realms. These systems of communication were, however, called into question in the three decades between 1390 and 1420.[24]

According to Froissart, during the 1392 negotiations between the highest representatives of the English and French royal families at Leulinghen, held halfway between Calais and Boulogne, the English indicated that written documents rather than oral discussions were the preferred way to communicate. Both parties submitted their requests in written form, which were then available for counter-discussion. Froissart explains this way of doing things in the following manner:

> car en parlure françoise a mots soubtils et couvers et sur double entendement, et les tournent les François, là où ils veulent, à leur prouffit et avantage: ce que les Anglois ne sçauroient trouver, ne faire, car euls ne le veulent entendre que plainement. ('for the French language has subtleties and hidden meanings, and where there are double meanings, the French manipulate them the way they want to, for their own profit and advantage: which the English do not realize, nor can they do it themselves, for they only want to understand it clearly and plainly.')

The English claim that they are not equipped to understand the rhetorical subtleties of the oral form of the French language, and that the French took advantage of this to mislead them. Froissart takes their linguistic manoeuvering literally and constructs an explanation for their apparent difficulty:

> le françois que ils [les Anglais] avoient apris chiés eulx d'enfance, n'estoit pas de telle nature et condition que celluy de France estoit, et duquel les clers de droit en leurs traittiés et parlers usoient.[25] ('the French that they [the English] had learned in England during their childhood was not the same as that of France in terms of its nature and structure, and which the law clerks used in their treaties and speech.')

---

24 For this section, see Lusignan, *Langue des rois*, pp. 240–7.
25 For the two quotations, see J. Froissart, *Chroniques*, ed. J. B. C. Kervyn de Lettenhove, 25 vols. (Brussels, 1867–77), XV, pp. 114–15.

The English, Froissart claims, had learned French within a rigid framework, linked directly to law and administration.

This was not the end of the English demands. After their crushing victory at Agincourt and their conquest of the north of France, they undertook negotiations culminating in the Treaty of Troyes, which recognized the king of England as the heir to the French crown. Sources tell us that during one of the preliminary meetings, held in Normandy in December 1418, the English insisted that they would not use French as the language of exchange in either written or oral form. They demanded that the negotiations be held in Latin, a language that *est indifferens omni nationi*.[26] Moreover, they even threatened to use the only other language that they knew: English. After a series of exchanges coordinated by the papal legate, Giordano Orsini, it was agreed that the final treaty was to be drafted in Latin. The French were permitted to translate the document into French, but when it came to interpreting the document, only the Latin text would be referred to.

At the end of the Middle Ages, just as today, the choice of language is based as much on its functionality as on its symbolic value. Throughout their negotiations, the French and English were attentive to two fundamental realities. English could not be used because communication would have been impossible between the two parties. French was understood by both sides, but the English claimed that the French had a greater mastery than they did. But the sources also reveal that the English reticence with regard to French stemmed from the need felt by both realms to strengthen their own identity: to assert the English language in England, and the French language in France. Only Latin, the linguistic symbol of their shared Christianity, was an appropriate common ground for the two realms.

The isolated case of English?

The growing interest in the question of the languages of England may, however, lead us to overlook the appropriate socio-political dimensions of the situation, which go far beyond the English phenomenon. I would like to conclude by extending the parameters of our present perspective and by examining, however briefly, an issue that has, to date, been largely ignored: the linguistic usage in the county of Flanders during the same period.[27] I must admit at the start that I am completely ignorant of the Flemish language and that I must rely on what I have been able to read on this subject in secondary sources.[28]

---

6 For the documents related to this event, see T. Rymer, *Foedera, Conventiones, Literae*, 7 vols. (London, 1816–69), IV, 2, pp. 79–80.

7 For the history of Flanders with some considerations about the linguistic situation see D. Nicholas, *Medieval Flanders* (London, 1992); see also E. E. Kadens, 'The Vernacular in a Latin World: Changing the Language of Record in Thirteenth-Century Flanders' (Ph.D. dissertation, Princeton, 2001, to be published in the monograph series *Mediaevalia Lovaniensia*).

8 J. J. Salverda de Grave, *L'influence de la langue française en Hollande d'après les mots empruntés* (Paris, 1913); B. C. Donaldson, *Dutch. A Linguistic History of Holland and*

With the exception of the people inhabiting the area around the cities of Lille and Douai, the greater part of the population in Flanders spoke Flemish, one of the dialects of the Dutch language. The counts of Flanders who took over the county in the thirteenth century were French-speaking. As was the case for the other great barons of the north of France, their chancery progressively changed over from Latin to French and, from 1277, almost all of their charters were exclusively in Picard French. This situation persisted until the entry of Louis de Male on the scene in 1346. He was the first to open his administration to the Flemish language. For example, his cartulary reveals that in 1349, 50 per cent of his acts were drawn up in Flemish. This increased to 70 per cent between 1357 and 1358. However, this was short-lived for Flanders, which came under the control of Philip the Bold, duke of Burgundy, in 1382. He and his successors reinstated French as the language of their administration.

It should also be noted that the county of Flanders did not contain a single bishopric, but was dotted with dioceses associated with Thérouanne, Tournay, Arras and Cambrai, towns that were located in the French linguistic domain. Only a small area in the north was part of the Dutch diocese of Utrecht. This situation was the cause of many tensions throughout the Middle Ages that were not resolved until 1559, when the Church reorganized these dioceses with consideration of the linguistic boundaries of the country.

The third important power in Flanders was the towns themselves, of which the most important were Bruges, Ghent, Ypres, Lille and Douai. All the towns whose language was Flemish retained this language in their written documents with the exception of Ypres, which used French from the middle of the thirteenth century until the 1380s. However, the towns used French as their second language, and employed it whenever corresponding with France or England.[29]

Beneath the veneer of the French language, the sources sometimes disclose details about the extent to which the relationship between the people and the authorities was influenced by the linguistic manoeuvring between French and Flemish. This situation led to frequent conflicts between the two groups regarding the use of the two languages.[30]

In much the same way as in England, French was an elite language in Flanders

Belgium (Leiden, 1983). I owe much to discussions with Professor Jacques Van Keymeulen from the University of Ghent who is currently working on a dictionary of the Flemish dialects. On French in Flanders, see R. Mantou, *Actes originaux rédigés en français dans la partie flamingante du comté de Flandre (1250–1350), Étude linguistique* (Liège, 1972); R. Mantou, *Documents linguistiques de la Belgique romane. 2, Chartes en langue française antérieures à 1271 conservées dans les provinces de Flandre orientale et de Flandre occidentale* (Paris, 1987).

[29] For examples of correspondence between Flanders and London, see G. F. Chapple 'Correspondence of the City of London 1298–1370' (unpublished Ph.D. thesis, London 1938).

[30] C. A. Armstrong, 'The Language Question in the Low Countries: The Use of Dutch by the Dukes of Burgundy and their Administration', in *Europe in the Late Middle Ages* ed. J. R. Hale, J. R. L. Highfield and B. Smalley (Evanston IL, 1965), pp. 386–409.

insofar as it was used for communicating with society's ruling groups. For those who intended to nourish their ambition by finding employment in the count's service or by becoming involved in international trade, mastery of French was a prerequisite. It is interesting that the same socio-political situation produced similar effects on the native language. Flemish, like English, was subject to a substantial influence from French, particularly with regard to vocabulary. Regrettably there are very few studies on this phenomenon. It seems to specialists in the field that the influence of French over Dutch increases to the south-west of this linguistic domain.[31] Flemish integrated numerous words borrowed from Picard. For instance, French words with a -*té* ending, such as *activité*, *neutralité*, or *souveraineté*, developed into their Dutch counterparts in -*teit*, betraying their Picard origin. Likewise, the French words ending in -*er*, such as *cocher*, ended in -*ier* as Picard. But in the present state of research, we cannot provide a clear evaluation of the medieval linguistic situation that would permit us to pursue detailed comparisons with that of French and English.

Conclusion

The similarities between England and Flanders nevertheless invite us to reconsider the position of the language of royalty within a far more general context. The situation in the Middle Ages was starkly different from that of the modern nation state, where the ambition is to impose a cohesive language, the language of political authority, upon the inhabitants of the entire realm. Nowhere in medieval Europe did the language of the ruling class become the predominant language of all its subjects. Thus, the king of France used Parisian French to communicate with the various Romance languages area of France, and the count of Flanders and the king of England borrowed French to communicate with peoples whose languages were Germanic in origin.

At the end of the Middle Ages, language became a strong means of identification, though I refuse to characterize language as 'national'. The word 'nation' did not yet exist in its present sense, meaning 'a political community living in one single State'. The Franco-English negotiations to which I referred earlier suggest that French became an important emblem of the king of France, rather like the colour blue, or the fleur-de-lys. At the same time, the king of England doubtless wished to impose a language that would help bolster his arsenal of symbols, such as the colour red, the cross of Saint George and the lion. As for the Flemish, I would argue that their promotion of their own language was linked to their desire to protect their urban liberties, something that had an impact on their relationship with the count of Flanders during the entire period under consideration here.

However, we must not minimize the significant communication problems that

---

[31] Information gathered from an informal discussion with Jacques Van Keymeulen.

inevitably occurred. Evidently, it was easier to impose a common language on a territory that shared dialects of the same language, as was the case for the *pays d'oïl*, the north-west of modern France, than over a territory in which people spoke several entirely different languages. We know that written instruments were more often than not read aloud in public spaces. Where dialects of the same language dominated a region, these public readings would only require slight adaptations of the text for the sake of local phonetic particularities. Where the language was entirely different, a complete translation was required. Yet in all cases the language of the ruling elite had a major impact on the language of the localities. It inevitably contributed over the very long term to the creation of a common language, as was the case for French in France and later, for English in England. The language of the elites may also have contributed to the profound alteration of the common language of the population, as was the case for the Romanization of Germanic languages in both England and Flanders. Viewed from that perspective, I would be tempted to conclude that the linguistic situation in England was not as unique as is often implicitly postulated.

2

The Language of Complaint:
Multiligualism and Petitioning in
Later Medieval England

W. Mark Ormrod*

This study focuses on the three 'official' languages of later medieval law and government – Latin, French and English – and their particular usage in relation to petitions to the crown. It aims to reconsider the influences that drove the initial choice of French as the language of petitioning in the late thirteenth century and led to the adoption of English as a valid alternative for these documents by the mid-fifteenth century. It also addresses the oral/aural qualities of the petition and attempts to rationalize the relationship between written and spoken forms through analysis of the language employed by the authors of these texts.

My sources are derived from two important collections: the parliament rolls and the Ancient Petitions, both held in the National Archives and both now available in searchable electronic form.[1] Between them, the parliament rolls

I am grateful to participants in the 'French of England' project and conferences for much stimulating exchange, to Gwilym Dodd, Simon Harris, Lisa Liddy and Shelagh Sneddon for advice and references, and to Maryanne Kowaleski and Jocelyn Wogan-Browne for much useful editorial input. For the purposes of this essay I use 'French' to denote the generic language, and restrict my use of 'Anglo-Norman' and 'law French' to the description of specific texts and traditions. Since this essay is about petitions, it ought to be stressed that both private and common petitions demonstrate a significant range of linguistic variation within the catch-all of 'French', not least because the English crown received petitions from its subjects in Aquitaine and Calais and from many residents of the kingdom of France (particularly merchants) involved in disputes in England. For the use of Languedocian forms in petitions from Gascony, see G. Pépin, 'Petitions from Gascony: Testimonies of a Special Relationship', in *Medieval Petitions: Grace and Grievance*, ed. W. M. Ormrod, G. Dodd and A. Musson (York, 2009), pp. 120–34.

Parliament rolls: *The Parliament Rolls of Medieval England*, ed. C. Given-Wilson, P. Brand, A. Curry, R. Horrox, G. H. Martin, W. M. Ormrod and J. R. S. Phillips (CD ROM version, Leicester, 2005; print edition, 16 vols., Woodbridge, 2006) cited hereafter as *PROME* (references are to the printed edition). Ancient Petitions: Kew, The National Archives, SC 8 (Ancient Petitions) cited hereafter as TNA, SC 8. Indexes and calendars are available in TNA online Catalogue at http://www.nationalarchives.gov.uk/catalogue and digitized images are available via TNA Documents Online service at http://www.nationalarchives.gov.uk/documentsonline. The project that generated the entries from the Ancient Petitions in TNA Catalogue was directed by the present

and the Ancient Petitions provide us with access to a large body (though not it must be emphasized, all) of the extant petitions made to the English crown during the later Middle Ages. These petitions come in two main forms: 'private petitions', which express the concerns of individuals or specific interest groups, and 'common petitions', which are either articulations of general concerns of the kingdom as a whole put together by the commons in parliament or private petitions 'adopted' by the commons because they raise issues perceived to be of general interest to the realm.[2]

Petitions in the form in which they are discussed here were a product of the 'bill revolution' of the later thirteenth century and played a very important part in the evolution of parliament, where, from Edward I's reign onwards, supplicants were provided with special access to the king's grace and common petitions came to form much of the basis of statutory legislation.[3] Petitions have attracted a good deal of attention of late as part of a revived interest in the archival footprint and the political and cultural dimensions of parliament in the later Middle Ages.[4] They are different from so many of the other Public Records because they express not a government-authored outcome to a case but the substance of a plaintiff's grievance or request. This in itself should not lead us to suppose that they capture the unmediated, authentic voices of the king's subjects: petitions were written on behalf of the plaintiffs by experts – scriveners, legal attorneys, men of law and sometimes king's clerks – who set the complainant's narrative into a more specialist discourse of remedy that was designed to prompt particular actions by the crown.[5] Nevertheless, their narrative and descriptive forms contrast markedly with the terseness of many of the other administrative and judicial records in the National Archives, and they provide a particularly rich 'worm's eye' view both of social conditions and of political expectations in the later Middle Ages. The fact that they were composed and committed to record outside the confines of the offices of government is also an important issue in relation to the language choices made by their authors.

A discussion of the relationship between the spoken and written languages of law and government may fruitfully begin with the document set out in Appendix 1 to this chapter. This is a private petition from one Alexander Mering, which was supported by the commons and written up on the parliament roll for 1416.[6]

author and funded by two grants under the Arts and Humanities Research Council's Resource Enhancement Scheme in 2003–7.

2   G. Dodd, *Justice and Grace: Private Petitioning and the English Parliament in the Late Middle Ages* (Oxford, 2007), pp. 1–15.

3   A. Harding, *Medieval Law and the Foundations of the State* (Oxford, 2002), pp. 109–90.

4   P. Brand, 'Petitions and Parliament in the Reign of Edward I', in *Parchment and People. Parliament in the Middle Ages*, ed. L. Clark (Edinburgh, 2004), pp. 14–38; Dodd, *Justice and Grace*; W. Scase, *Literature and Complaint in England, 1272–1553* (Oxford, 2007); M. Giancarlo, *Parliament and Literature in Late Medieval England* (Cambridge, 2007); and *Medieval Petitions*, ed. Ormrod, Dodd and Musson.

5   Dodd, *Justice and Grace*, pp. 302–16.

6   The original of the petition has not survived.

The narrative elements of the petition, as was still usual in the early fifteenth century, are in Anglo-Norman. The petition also makes two direct quotations, one (recounting an oral exchange) in English and the other (claiming to represent a piece of written text) in Latin. Mering contends that the jury, assembled on a case of novel disseisin, when asked the date at which the alleged disseisin had taken place, had replied *viva voce*, in English, 'The disseisin was made on St Bartholomew's day two years ago.' However, the clerk of the court (who, we should realize, kept his official records in Latin) had rendered the date incorrectly, representing it as St Bartholomew's day 1412 when it ought to have been 1411.

The seriousness of this case, and the reason why it was sponsored by the commons as a matter of more general concern, is evident from the request clause, 'Plese a voz tressages discrecions …', and particularly from the crown's response provided at the end. Resolving the case involved a change to the Latin text of the relevant official record of the court, and this could only be done with the express permission of the king and the 'authority of this parliament'.[7] For present purposes, however, it is the shifts in language within the document that create most interest. The moves successively into English and Latin are, of course, quite self-conscious: the petitioner's legal adviser, in drafting the statement of grievance, has taken care to convey the authenticity of what was said by the jurors and written by the clerk. Many a common law action in this period foundered on technicalities arising from inadvertent inaccuracies in the written documents that formed the basis of legal process, and it is hardly surprising in itself that Alexander Mering's attorney explicitly referred to the clerk's error of dating in transferring spoken English into written Latin. The case is instructive in allowing us to rationalize the often misunderstood relationship between the spoken vernacular and the written proceedings of the king's court after the famous Statute of Pleading of 1362 had required the use of English in the oral proceedings of the courts.[8] Here, though, I want to concentrate on what is at once a more obvious and a more curious point: that the petition within which these English and Latin phrases occur is itself written in Anglo-Norman. Why, two generations after the Statute of Pleading and in the reign of a king – Henry V – who carries such a reputation for the nurturing of the English language,[9] would one go to the bother of arguing the faulty relationship between spoken English and written Latin through the medium of French?

Because petitions are an invention of the thirteenth century, legal historians have tended to be content to explain the use of French as the normal language of petitioning from its inception to at least the end of the fourteenth century simply

---

[7] In another context, see the charge against Richard II in 1399 that he had 'erased and altered' the roll of the parliament of Shrewsbury: C. Given-Wilson, *Chronicles of the Revolution, 1397–1400* (Manchester, 1993), p. 175.

[8] *Statutes of the Realm*, ed. S. Raith, A. Luders and T. E. Tomlins, 11 vols. (London, 1810–28), I, 375–6; and Ormrod, 'Use of English'.

[9] See, for example, C. Allmand, *Henry V* (London, 1992), pp. 421–5.

in terms of the general expansion of French written forms in English government during this period.[10] The danger here, of course, is that the argument becomes circular: petitions become evidence of a phenomenon that they themselves helped to generate. What other explanations might we propose for the characteristic use of French as the language of petitioning during and after the reign of Edward I?

One way to approach this subject is to see the petition as part of a wider set of changes that took place in royal justice in the second half of the thirteenth century. Up until this time, common law process in the central courts was almost always begun by writ (the 'original' writ, issued by chancery, which provided the authority for the case to be opened) and proceeded by a set process, each stage of which was in turn regulated by writs (that is, 'judicial' writs, issued under the deputed great seals of the king's bench and common pleas).[11] All such writs were in Latin. Similarly, as Alexander Mering's petition reminds us, the record of the resulting proceedings was entered on the plea roll of the relevant court in Latin. Petitions sat at a distance from common law process: they derived their force and popularity from the notion that they addressed the king and his council directly and were concerned with matters that could only be resolved by the application of his grace. Wherever possible, however, petitioners to the crown were redirected to the common law courts, and would then have to obtain original writs allowing them to proceed with their allegations against opponents.[12] Petitioning was thus seen to supplement, rather than replace, the common law, and its own origins were in turn profoundly shaped by contemporary changes in common law procedure.

The later thirteenth century witnessed the emergence of an important alternative to the original writ as a means of beginning legal process, in the procedure based on the bill in eyre.[13] The bill or plaint (the terms are interchangeable) was

---

10 For which see M. T. Clanchy, *From Memory to Written Record: England, 1066–1307*, 2nd edn (Oxford, 1993), pp. 197–223. For quantitative evidence of French (originally alongside some Latin) as the language of early petitioning, see Brand, 'Petitions and Parliament', pp. 24–5.

11 See, among much else, B. Wilkinson, 'The Seals of the Two Benches under Edward III', *EHR* 42 (1927), 397–401; J. C. Davies, 'Common Law Writs and Returns, Richard I to Richard II', *Bulletin of the Institute of Historical Research* 26 (1953), 125–56; 27 (1954), 1–34; *Early Registers of Writs*, ed. E. de Haas, Selden Society 87 (London, 1970); and L. C. Hector, 'Reports, Writs and Records in the Common Bench in the Reign of Richard II', in *Medieval Legal Records Edited in Memory of C. A. F. Meekings*, ed. R. F. Hunnisett and J. B. Post (London, 1978), pp. 267–88.

12 Private petitions were often turned down with the response that the supplicant should sue at common law. For examples, see: TNA, SC 8/3/143; SC 8/14/676; SC 8/41/2003; SC 8/74/3668; SC 8/111/5112; and SC 8/128/6400.

13 For what follows, see *Select Cases of Procedure without Writ under Henry III*, ed. H. G. Richardson and G. O. Sayles, Selden Society 60 (London, 1941); and A. Harding, 'Plaints and Bills in the History of English Law, Mainly in the Period 1250–1350', in *Legal History Studies 1972*, ed. D. Jenkins (Cardiff, 1975), pp. 63–86. The early bills in eyre that have survived are listed by D. Crook, *Records of the General Eyre*, Public Record Office Handbooks 20 (London, 1982), pp. 41–2. Several additional bills in eyre of 1293 have come to light as strays in the cataloguing project for the Ancient Peti-

a simple written statement of the grievance of the plaintiff which, if accepted for prosecution, would allow the eyre to take cognizance of the case and pursue it under common law process. By avoiding the logistical and financial challenge of having to obtain a writ out of chancery, the bill allowed ready and cheap access to justice within the locality where the eyre sat. This convention continued after the abandonment of the general eyre in 1330, and bills became a particular feature of the provincial sessions of the court of king's bench in the fourteenth century.[14] On some occasions, bills may well have been written by the cluster of royal clerks who serviced the eyre and the king's bench. More usually, though, they must have been the work of attorneys and scriveners in private practice.[15]

The linguistic distinction between writs and bills can thus be explained in relation to the different contexts in which they were written. Whereas the crown maintained the tradition of committing legal process to writing in Latin, the attorneys and paralegals who compiled bills for their plaintiffs used French: that is, the language in which the oral elements of the case would proceed in the king's courts.[16] If this scenario is credible, then it also naturally helps to explain why petitions, which developed at the same time as the bill in eyre, were also written in French, while the chancery instruments in which they often resulted were still composed in Latin. I am suggesting that the adoption of Anglo-Norman as the language of the written bill and petition is to be attributed primarily to the legal advisers who served and represented private parties in the king's courts. And the reason why the lawyers promoted written French in these contexts (and why the crown acceded to it) is, I would now argue, to be explained specifically in terms of the complex relationship that both sides worked out between the oral and the written in proceedings on bills and petitions.

Probably from the time of Henry II, and certainly from that of Henry III, the formal spoken language of the king's courts was Anglo-Norman (itself developing over the later Middle Ages into a specialized language usually referred to as law French).[17] Whether procedure was by writ or bill, legal counsel working

---

tions: TNA, SC 8/89/4449; SC 8/134/6687; SC 8/134/6688; SC 8/134/6691; and SC 8/134/6695.

[14] *Select Cases in the Court of King's Bench under Edward II*, ed. G. O. Sayles, Selden Society 74 (1957), pp. lxvii–lxxxvi; and W. M. Ormrod, 'Edward III's Government of England, c.1346–1356' (unpublished Ph.D. thesis, University of Oxford, 1984), pp. 187–93.

[15] N. Ramsay, 'Scriveners and Notaries as Legal Intermediaries in Later Medieval England', in *Enterprise and Individuals in Fifteenth-Century England*, ed. J. Kermode (Stroud, 1991), pp. 118–31.

[16] Previous explanations of the adoption of French in bill forms seem inadequate in this respect. *Select Cases in Eyre, AD 1292–1333*, ed. W. C. Bolland, Selden Society 30 (London, 1914), p. xix, offered the rather curious observation that writing bills in French was a matter of 'custom'. Harding, 'Plaints and Bills', pp. 74–5, commented equally contentiously that plaints were 'in French, the litigant's [sic] vernacular'.

[17] G. E. Woodbine, 'The Language of English Law', *Speculum* 18 (1943), 395–436; and P. Brand, 'The Languages of the Law in Later Medieval England', in Trotter, *Multilingualism*, pp. 63–76. This is not to say that English was not used in the lower courts or that it was not sometimes employed pragmatically in the king's courts. For further

in the common law courts would, at least until 1362, undertake all oral pleadings in Anglo-Norman/law French, which was also the language in which their own profession compiled the case reports written up in the year books.[18] We know very little about the language employed in the oral business of parliament and council prior to the 1360s, but it seems highly likely that this, too, was almost invariably French.[19] The relationship of bills and petitions both to oral process and to the resulting written records of the courts was, however, rather different from that of proceedings begun by writ. Whereas each stage of procedure instigated by an original (Latin) writ was recorded in the (Latin) plea rolls, cases brought by (French) bill were only committed to (Latin) record if and when they were brought successfully to final judgment.[20] And because parliament and council dispensed the king's prerogative or discretionary justice and were not classified as courts of record, no written statements were normally kept as to the discussion and debating of petitions: all we generally have are the decisions written on the dorses of the petitions themselves and the substantive outcomes in the form of letters patent or close written up in chancery. It is arguable, then, that one of the reasons why both bills and petitions were written by lawyers, and accepted by the crown, in French was that these documents themselves substituted for the intermediate (mesne) stages of process through which the case would pass in the oral business of the court before final judgment.

In the case of petitions, the inclusion of these written substitutes for oral proceedings was all the more pertinent since neither the parties nor their legal counsel would be present when the petition was read aloud (by the clerks who received and sorted them) before king and council.[21] Furthermore, because the petition could be subject to summary decision and justice, it had ideally to contain within it all of the necessary details of the case that would otherwise be accounted for in oral proceedings: the stages of plea, count, defence, answer and debate which, in the common pleas, were conducted by oral exchange between

discussion, see Ormrod, 'Use of English', pp. 763–72. For an overview, see the essay by Lusignan in this volume.

[18] *Year Books of Edward II: 1 & 2 Edward II*, ed. F. W. Maitland, Selden Society 17 (London, 1904), pp. xxxiii–xxxvi; and J. H. Baker, *Manual of Law French*, 2nd edn (Aldershot, 1990), pp. 9–14.

[19] See, for example, the surviving script (or transcript) of the king's speech to the parliament of 1324: *PROME*, III, 444. For further discussion and detailed analysis of the position in the 1360s, see Ormrod, 'Use of English', pp. 777–81.

[20] *Select Cases in the Court of King's Bench under Edward II*, pp. lxvii–lxxxvi.

[21] For the receivers of petitions in parliament, see Brand, 'Petitions and Parliament', pp. 33–7; and, more generally, G. P. Cuttino, 'King's Clerks and the Community of the Realm', *Speculum* 29 (1954), 395–409. Outside times of parliament, the position is less secure, but the general absence of the named petitioners can be inferred from those cases where plaintiffs were subsequently summoned before the council: W. M. Ormrod, 'Murmur, Clamour and Noise: Voicing Complaint and Remedy in Petitions to the English Crown, c.1300–c.1460', in *Medieval Petitions*, ed. Ormrod, Dodd and Musson, pp. 135–55 (pp. 137–8).

serjeants-at-law.[22] From a late thirteenth-century perspective, then, I think it is possible to argue that the essential reason why the petition emerged in French is precisely because this substituted for the oral pleadings that, under common law, would have been undertaken as part of the live 'performance' of the case before the bench.

Taking this hypothesis about the conscious and rational choice of French as the language of petitioning in the reign of Edward I, I would now like to offer some commentary and explanation on the perpetuation of the practice through the fourteenth and on into the early fifteenth centuries, and then turn to the implications of the shift to petitioning in English that occurred by the mid-fifteenth century.

Proponents of the 'triumph of English' in the age of Chaucer have long pointed to the precedents in the Ancient Petitions for the adoption of Middle English as a language of communication between subjects and king in later medieval England.[23] Recent work, however, has strongly suggested that the earliest such documents – the petition of John Drayton and Margery King (1344) and that of the Mercers of London (1387–8) – were altogether exceptional in term both of form and (in the latter case) of political context and intention.[24] Similarly, although petitions in English occur during the reigns of Henry IV and Henry V, they are still the exception to the rule and often, indeed, exceptional in themselves: take the example of the long petition of Thomas Paunfield of 1414, written not only in English but also (an even more unusual phenomenon) in the first-person singular, and having a complex relationship to a related and much more conventional Anglo-Norman petition from the same petitioner on the same subject.[25] A parallel point might be made about the new form of petition that developed at the end of the fourteenth century, known as the chancery bill. This was addressed not to the king and council but to the chancellor, and it became

---

[22] This does not, of course, preclude the fact that the audience of many petitions led to demands for further information. See G. Dodd, 'Thomas Paunfield, the "heye Court of rightwisnesse" and the Language of Petitioning in the Fifteenth Century', in *Medieval Petitions*, ed. Ormrod, Dodd and Musson, pp. 222–41 (pp. 232–9).

[23] For example, J. Coleman, *English Literature in History, 1350–1400: Medieval Readers and Writers* (London, 1981), pp. 51–2.

[24] SC 8/192/9580, partly transcribed in *A Book of London English, 1384–1425*, ed. R. W. Chambers and M. Daunt (Oxford, 1931), p. 272; and SC 8/20/997, transcribed in *Rotuli Parliamentorum*, 7 vols. (London, 1783), III, 225–6, and in J. H. Fisher, M. Richardson and J. L. Fisher, *An Anthology of Chancery English* (Knoxville TN, 1984), pp. 194–7. The exceptional forms and contexts of both petitions are emphasized by Scase, *Literature and Complaint*, pp. 91–2. For the hand of SC 8/20/997, see L. Mooney, 'Chaucer's Scribe', *Speculum* 81 (2006), 97–138.

[25] SC 8/23/1143A–B, transcribed in *Rotuli Parliamentorum*, IV, 57–61b. The English text is also provided in Fisher, Richardson and Fisher, *Anthology of Chancery English*, pp. 198–204. For discussions, see Giancarlo, *Parliament and Literature*, pp. 222–7; and Dodd, 'Thomas Paunfield'. I hope in due course to undertake a more detailed quantitative study of the adoption of English in petitions over the late fourteenth and fifteenth centuries.

the basis for what is later referred to as the so-called 'English' side of chancery proceedings. Here again, later practice has tended to colour our assumptions about the language of early petitions to chancery: in fact, these were originally written in Anglo-Norman, and although English begins to appear in the 1410s it is not until the 1430s that it becomes the norm.[26]

In emphasizing the slowness and uncertainty of the shift from French to English in government records over the fourteenth and fifteenth centuries, it is easy to see a number of administrative, judicial and cultural forces at work. As I have emphasized elsewhere, resistance to change in language was part of a wider conservatism in royal government driven both by institutional inertia and by contemporary concerns over the subversive nature of vernacular literacy and texts.[27] Here, I want to focus that wider debate back on to private and common petitions and pursue the relationship between the written language of supplication and oral language of process and judgment as a means of rationalizing some of the shifts in writing practice during the first decades of the fifteenth century.

If the arguments set out above about the petition replacing some of the oral forms spoken in court have validity, then we need first to address why the Statute of Pleading of 1362 apparently had no immediate effect on the language of petitioning. The answer seemingly lies, once more, in the distinction between spoken and written language. In the common law courts, the effect of the statute was to create a separation between the language of oral pleading (which, contrary to widespread assumption, did indeed move to English after 1362) and that of the case reports compiled in the written year books (which remained, enduringly, in law French).[28] The very fact that the elements of pleadings were replaced in petitions by written text helps us to understand why, even if the king and council may sometimes have been given English translations or summaries of the content of petitions in the late fourteenth and early fifteenth centuries, the written version itself remained quite firmly in Anglo-Norman. In fact, the evidence – such as it is – suggests that down to the late fourteenth century the audience of petitions

---

[26] M. E. Avery, 'The History of the Equitable Jurisdiction of Chancery before 1460', *Bulletin of the Institute of Historical Research* 42 (1969), 129–44; and T. S. Haskett, 'Country Lawyers? The Composers of English Chancery Bills', in *The Life of the Law*, ed. P. Birks (London, 1993), pp. 9–23 (p. 14).

[27] Ormrod, 'Use of English', pp. 781–7. For the connections made in this period between vernacularity and religious/political subversion, see (among much else), S. Justice, *Writing and Rebellion: England in 1381* (Berkeley CA, 1994); N. Watson, 'Censorship and Cultural Change in Late-Medieval England: Vernacular Theology, the Oxford Translation Debate, and Arundel's *Constitutions* of 1409', *Speculum* 70 (1995), 822–64; and D. Aers, '*Vox populi* and the Literature of 1381', Wallace, *Medieval English Literature*, pp. 432–53.

[28] J. H. Baker, *The Common Law Tradition: Lawyers, Books and the Law* (London, 2000), pp. 225–46. The widely cited work of M. D. Legge, 'Anglo-Norman and the Historian', *History* 26 (1941–2), 163–75, which appears to assume (p. 167) that French written in the year books denotes French spoken in the courts, has created a great deal of misunderstanding. See Ormrod, 'Use of English', pp. 751–2.

lso continued to be conducted in French.[29] From Henry IV's reign, however, the
vidence begins to change, and in a way that we might not expect. When English
rst begins to appear in relation to petitions on the parliament rolls during this
eriod, it is found not in the texts of the petitions themselves (which are still
lmost always in Anglo-Norman) but in the royal responses given to them. This
rst occurred in 1404 and set a trend that continued into the reign of Henry V.[30]
he recording of royal responses in this fashion suggests a concern to preserve
s accurately as possible the actual words spoken or chosen by the king and his
nner circle of advisers in addressing and replying to the common petitions, and
herefore provides the vital clue that, by this point at least, the oral discussion of
etitions was indeed conducted in English.[31]

This emphasis on preserving as much as possible of the substance and nuances
f the royal response also chimes with the tradition, discernible from Henry IV's
rst parliament, whereby the king's words spoken publicly in parliament 'in
he mother tongue' (as in 1399) were self-consciously written up in English on
he roll. The king's pronouncements, after all, were always important and often
olitically charged: in 1399 the English text on the roll preserves Henry's formal
tatement of his controversial claim to the throne.[32] Writing such statements up
n the language in which they were spoken removed the ambiguity or blame that
night arise if the clerk of parliament were to translate them into French or Latin
nd thus inadvertently modify their meaning. Beyond this point about political
ensitivity is also the more general sense that the use of written English in royal
ommunication denoted an immediate, intimate and privileged relationship:
nglish, as the brewers' guild of London famously put it, was a 'common idiom'
etween the king and his subjects.[33] The use of English forms in responses to
ommon petitions by Henry IV and Henry V, which heralded the occasional use
f English in endorsements to private petitions at least by the reign of Henry VI,[34]
nay therefore be said to have had some influence on the slow process of change

---

Among the scraps of evidence available, one might cite the French response written
at the foot of the petition in SC 8/246/12268, which appears to preserve a decision
spoken by the king, and *PROME*, III, V, 128, where the petition of the king's cousin,
Blanche, Lady Wake, was read out in full parliament, and the king replied in his
own words, 'Jeo prenk la querele en ma main.' The possibility that either of these
written responses could, in turn, be translations of spoken English cannot, of course,
be discounted, and the subject awaits further investigation.

PROME, VIII, 285.

For other uses of spoken English in parliament before this date, see Ormrod, 'Use of
English', pp. 750, 777–9.

PROME, VIII, 25. Another example, from 1397, of a controversial text left in English
when it was transcribed onto the official record of the parliament roll is the account of
William Rickhill of the confession of Thomas of Woodstock: *PROME*, VII, 413–14; and
Book of London English, ed. Chambers and Daunt, p. 278. The 1397 text is actually the
first use of English on a parliament roll: Ormrod, 'Use of English', p. 777, n. 108.

Book of London English, ed. Chambers and Daunt, p. 16; and Fisher, Richardson and
Fisher, *Anthology of Chancery English*, p. xvi.

TNA, SC 8/121/6035; SC 8/195/9733; etc.

whereby petitions themselves came to be rendered and submitted in the vernac
ular.

The argument presented above suggests that the language of petitioning
moved into English as part of a logical process which, in the first quarter of th
fifteenth century, re-established the linguistic correlation between the written
form of the petition and the oral processes surrounding its audience before king
and council. The process was never fully established because, despite the genera
movement of private and common petitions into English, the crown continued to
be locked into a repertoire of stock Anglo-Norman phrases: royal assent to parlia
mentary bills is even today written in the form 'La reine le veult'. But an impor
tant and perhaps self-conscious precedent was struck in 1414 in the common
petition preserved on the parliament roll for that year, transcribed in Appendi
2 below. The constitutional implications of this statement by the commons, and
of the king's response, have been much discussed,[35] but the implications of th
use of English have thus far been ignored. The text under scrutiny sits within th
larger sequence of common petitions entered by the knights and burgesses in
this parliament. The usual practice was for the clerk of the commons to compil
a schedule of the common petitions for the attention of the king and counci
and for this schedule, with the answers provided to each request, to be written
up in fair copy by the clerk of parliament on the parliament roll. The common
petitions in the form in which they come down to us are therefore the product o
several stages of drafting and copying, and it is evident that changes (both acci
dental and deliberate) could occur in the written record as the compilation of th
records proceeded.[36] Though positive evidence is difficult to come by, it might
be possible to argue that one part of the harmonization that clerks of parliamen
imposed in their fair copies of the common petitions during the late fourteenth
and early fifteenth centuries was to translate English petitions into the defaul
language of record of the parliament rolls, Anglo-Norman.[37] The 1414 example
provides some indirect evidence towards that thesis, since the preservation of th
English form of the petition is so self-consciously rationalized: this, the clerk i
telling us, is a special case.

As the text makes clear, this particular request arose from the commons

---

[35] See the references to earlier debates on the significance of the petition by A. L. Brown
'Parliament, c.1377–1422', in *The English Parliament in the Middle Ages*, ed. R. G. Davie
and J. H. Denton (Manchester, 1982), pp. 109–40 (p. 128).

[36] W. M. Ormrod, 'On – and Off – the Record: The Rolls of Parliament, 1337–1377', in
Parchment and People, ed. Clark, pp. 39–56.

[37] It was only from 1423 that the clerks of parliament generally felt it appropriate to leav
common petitions in their original language of formulation, so that for a while unde
Henry VI the common petitions become a hybrid of French and English: Ormrod, 'Us
of English', p. 777 n. 108. One effect of this hybridization is to point up the linguisti
variations between petition and response, with petitions in English sometime
receiving French answers, and *vice versa*. See A. Curry, '"A Game of Two Halves"
Parliament, 1422–1454', in *Parchment and People*, ed. L. Clark (Edinburgh, 2004), pp
73–102 (p. 98).

concern over the possible subversion of their original intentions when the crown used their petitions as the basis of formal legislation. They asked 'that no law should ever be made thereon and engrossed as statute and law which changes the sense or meaning of what is requested by the common speaker or of the aforesaid petitions proffered in writing'. The petition was itself very obviously about words and meanings expressed both in writing, in the common petitions, and in oral form, in requests communicated *viva voce* by the speaker. It was also something that could be interpreted as an exceptionally bold and confrontational demand, either deliberately or (more likely) inadvertently challenging the crucial legislative freedom claimed by king and council throughout the Middle Ages. It is therefore evident why the clerk of parliament chose, in this case, not to render the commons' request in Anglo-Norman like the rest of their business but to transcribe it, as he puts it in the preamble, 'word for word' (*de mote a mote*). What is equally striking, of course, is the crown's response, which engages in the same process of plain speaking by committing, in English, to both the spirit and the letter of the commons' request. Here again, then, I would argue, the precedents for a future in which common petitions written in English would became the norm are to be located not in some generalized process of the Englishing of parliament but in terms of very deliberate and coherent justifications, by the crown and its agents, of the use of the vernacular in written forms.

This discussion has suggested some of the ways in which we can use the surviving paper-trail of petitioning in later medieval England to elucidate the relationship between Latin, French and English in the context of written and spoken language in the courts, council and parliament between the reigns of Edward I and Henry VI. Much remains to be done on this subject, with respect both to petitions and to records generated in the departments of central government. For the present, however, I have tried to suggest that there may have been distinct forms of agency at work in the adoption first of French and then of English petitioning. When they were first invited, petitions were written in French in such a way as to denote their authorship outside the royal chancery and to reflect the spoken language in which their authors, the lawyers, operated in the courts. There was thus a sense in which the use of French was promoted 'from below'. Petitions then continued in French until the early fifteenth century because the king and council did not feel themselves bound by the requirements of the Statute of Pleading and still predominantly used Anglo-Norman as their language of spoken communication. And, because of the prejudices in elite and official circles against the use of written English, it took a 'top-down' initiative from the crown, in the form of English responses to common petitions, to facilitate a more general move into the use of English in private and common petitions under Henry IV, V and VI. From the new emphasis placed here on the oral/aural qualities of the text contained in petitions, there naturally spring many more questions about the political and legal culture of late medieval England. It is hoped that the enhanced access now provided to crucial documentary sources such as the parliament rolls and the Ancient Petitions will in turn encourage further such work on the multilingualism of medieval English government.

Appendix 1

Item, mesmes les communes bailleront une peticione en le dit parlement, pur Alisaundre Meryng, en la forme ensuant:

Item, priount les communes: qe come Alisaundre Meryng ad suye un especialle assise du novelle disseisyn envers Johan Tuxford et Katerine sa femme, des tenementz en Petyt Markham, Tuxford, Mylton, et Bevercote, devant Robert Tyrwhyt et autres justices, a ceo assignez, processe taunt suye en la dit assise, qe les ditz Johan Tuxford et Katerine, en la dit assise, prierent eyde du nostre seignur le roy pur diversez causez, le qelle eyde par les ditz justicez fuist graunte, et tant avaunt fuist suye apres a nostre seignur le roy en sa chauncerie, que le dit suppliaunt avoyt brief nostre dit seignur le roy, direct as ditz justicez, pur proceder pluys avaunt en la dit assise, paryssynt qe lez ditz justices ne procederent a juggement en la dit assise, le dit nostre seignur le roy ent nyent counseille, et en la dit assise sy avaunt fuist pursue devant les ditz justices, tanqe qe la dit assise passa, et trove fuist par verdit del dit assise, que le dit suppliaunt fuist seyse, et disseise par les ditz Johan et Katerine, et assesserocount les damagez a cinqaunt marcez, et lez ditz justices apres enquysterount des ditz assises come longe temps fuist puys qe le dit disseisyn fuyst fait, lez queux disoient qe la disseisyn fuyst fait par tieux paroles: 'The dissesyn was donne on Seynt Bartilmewe day was two yer'. Et le clerk des ditz justices, par negligencez et mesprisione, fyst une note du dit verdit, et escryva les ditz parolles avaunt escryez en Engelysch, par teux parolex en Latyn: 'Quod Johannes Tuxford et Katerina uxor ejus, disseiserunt predictum Alexandrum, in festo Sancti Bartholomei anno regni Regis Henrici quarti terciodecimo', la oue il dussoyt avoir fait anno duodecimo. Et issint par sa mesprision et negligence par la dit note fuyt suppose, qe disseisyn fuyt fait puys la date del purchace du dit assise, issint par celles negligence et mesprision, le dit suppliaunt estoyt tant outrement en poynt d'estre disherite, et jammez d'avoir juggement sur le verdit du dit assise.

Please a voz tressagez discrecions, considerez lez negligencez et mesprisions du dit clerk ensy fait, a fynale desheritaunce del dit suppliaunt, et qe saunz vostre bone supplicacione en cest present parlement, le dit suppliant unqes avera juggement en la dit assise, du prier a nostre tressoveraigne seignur le roy, et a toutz ses seignurs temporelx et espirituales en cest present parlement, du charger le dit Robert Tyrwhit et sez compaignons justicez en la dite assise, du faire la recorde du dit assise, acordaunt a ceo qe fuyst trove et dit par la dite assise, par issint qe le dit suppliaunt poet avoir soun brief du procedendo en la dite assise, etc.

La quele peticione leeu overtement en cest parlement, et bien entendu, fuist respondu en le manere q'ensuyt:

Le roy, del assent des seignurs espirituelx et temporelx esteantz en mesme le parlement, et a le requeste des communes suisditz, voet qe les justices de mesme l'assise, facent le recorde d'ycelle, quant a celle point tant solement, et ceo en la presence du chaunceller d'Engleterre pur le temps esteant, par auctorite de celle parlement.

ource: *PROME*, IX, pp. 141–2, with facing-page translation.

Appendix 2

em, fait a remembrer, qe les communes baillerent a roi nostre seignur tresso-rain en cest present parlement une peticion, dont le tenure ensuyt de mote a ote.

Oure soverain lord, youre humble and trewe lieges that ben come for the commune of youre lond by sechyn on to youre rizt riztwesnesse, that so as hit hath evere be thair liberte et fredom, that thar sholde no statut no lawe be made of lasse than they yaf ther to their assent: consideringe that the commune of youre lond, the whiche that is, et evere hath be, a membre of youre parle-ment, ben as well assentirs as peticioners, that fro this tyme foreward, by compleynte of the commune of eny myschief axkynge remedie by mouthe of their speker for the commune, other ellys by peticione writen, that ther never be no lawe made theruppon, et engrosed as statut et lawe, nother by addi-cions, nother by diminucions, by no maner of terme ne termes, the whiche that sholde chaunge the sentence, et the entente axked by the speker mouthe, or the peticions biforesaid yeven up yn writyng by the manere forsaid, withoute assent of the forsaid commune. Consideringe oure soverain lord, that it is not in no wyse the entente of youre communes, zif hit be so that they axke you by spekyng, or by writyng, too thynges or three, or as manye as theym lust: but that evere it stande in the fredom of your hie regalie, to graunte whiche of thoo that you luste, et to werune the remanent.
Responsio: The kyng of his grace especial, graunteth that fro hens forth no thyng be enacted to the peticions of his comune, that be contrarie of hir askyng, wharby they shuld be bounde withoute their assent. Savyng alwey to our liege lord his real prerogatif, to graunte and denye what him lust of their peticions and askynges a foresaide.

ource: *PROME*, IX, p. 52, with facing-page translation.

3

The Persistence of Anglo-Norman 1230–1362: A Linguistic Perspective

Richard Ingham

Introduction

The issue addressed in this essay is whether later Anglo-Norman (AN) was n
more than a fossilized version of the French brought over with the Conquero
or whether it continued to evolve as part of the French dialect continuum. Muc
has been made of what, according to Kibbee,[1] was a 'fundamental differenc
between the French used in England and that used on the Continent by virtue c
the fact that there it was a mother tongue, whereas in England, after the initi
few generations following the Conquest, it was not. But that does not mean tha
later AN can be treated as a foreign language barely understood by its user
the position seemingly taken by Pope[2] and roundly condemned by Rothwe
and Trotter.[3] It is true that AN had features that seemed to make it distinct fror
those of continental French. Continental French scribes of the thirteenth centur
corrected AN manuscripts on grammatical points such as the use of *a les* fc
aux, de les for *des*, and *que* for *qui* as a subject relative pronoun.[4] It is therefor
easy to conclude that AN was 'une langue à part',[5] cut off from the mainstrear
development of the French language, and to agree with Kibbee, who called lat
AN an 'artificial language'.[6] It will be argued here, however, that later AN wa

---

1   D. Kibbee, *For to Speke Frenche Trewely: The French Language in England, 1000–1600: I
    Status, Description and Instruction* (Amsterdam, 1991).

2   M. K. Pope, *From Latin to Modern French with especial consideration of Anglo-Norma
    (Manchester, 1934).

3   W. Rothwell, 'From Latin to Modern French: Fifty Years On', *BJRL* 68 (1985), 179–20
    D. A. Trotter, 'Not as Eccentric as It Looks: Anglo-French and French French', *FML*
    39 (2003), 427–38; D. A. Trotter, 'L'anglo-normand: variété insulaire ou variété isolée?
    Grammaires du vulgaire. Médiévales 45 D (2003), 43–54.

4   G. Brereton, 'Some Grammatical Changes Made by Two Revisers of the Anglo-Norma
    Version of *Des Grantz Geantz*', in *Studies in French Language and Mediæval Literatu
    presented to Mildred K. Pope by Pupils, Colleagues and Friends*, ed. anon. (Mancheste
    1939), pp. 21–8.

5   C. Bruneau, *Petite histoire de la langue française*, tome 1 (Paris, 1955).

6   D. Kibbee, 'Emigrant Languages and Acculturation: the Case of Anglo-French', in *T
    Origins and Development of Emigrant Languages*, ed. H. Nielsen and L. Schøsler (Odens
    1996), pp. 1–20 (p. 9).

in key respects evolving in parallel with continental French, and that the notion that it was 'artificial' cannot be accepted as it stands.

In general this essay assumes the standpoint of Rothwell's more recent work on the survival of insular French in the later fourteenth century and beyond, taking up his observation that French continued to flourish at a later stage than conventional textbook accounts suggest.[7] Our focus will be on the quality of the French that was being used during the roughly one hundred-year period in which French flourished as a language of administrative record in England, beginning in the mid-thirteenth century. During this period it extended its use across numerous different written genres, such as legal and other treatises, royal and municipal administration, charters, and business correspondence in various professional spheres, as well as maintaining its strong presence in religious and secular imaginative literature. This extension of a language across a range of written language functions is, according to sociolinguists, part of the process by which a language becomes standardized.[8]

Pope distinguished earlier and later periods of Anglo-Norman, putting the demarcation roughly around 1230–50.[9] Prior to that time, according to her, it was 'still possible to regard AN as a dialect of French', and 'to trace a real development of linguistic usage'. Thereafter, Pope talked of a 'period of degeneracy', once insular French had supposedly been cut off from its Norman base by the loss of Angevin lands on the Continent. As will be seen in this essay, this position seems to have been overstated: it is somewhat remarkable, for instance, that when, according to Pope, insular French was 'degenerating' into a 'poorly understood jargon', it was showing signs of behaving as a standard language capable of performing the sophisticated functions required of a written code.

The rather arbitrary endpoint used in the title of this chapter is that of 1362, when Parliament approved the Statue of Pleading, so called as it was intended to ban pleading in French in English law courts on the grounds that French was not very well known. Although its practical significance has been played down by Rothwell,[10] it may surely be taken as indicating that contemporaries were aware of a reduction in the extent of knowledge of French in England. This study, however, is not so much concerned with the extent to which French was known, but rather seeks to establish certain indicators of the *quality* of French used in England between those time points. What can it tell us about the status of AN vis-à-vis the medieval francophone dialect area? It is of particular interest to consider what happened when continental French underwent system changes: if AN did not adopt them, we may be fairly confident that AN was indeed cut off

---

7 W. Rothwell, 'English and French in England after 1362', *English Studies* 82 (2001), 539–59.
8 See e.g. E. Haugen, 'Dialect, Language, Nation', *American Anthropologist* 58 (1966), 922–35.
9 Pope, *From Latin*, p. 424.
10 Rothwell, 'English and French'.

from its Romance roots, as Pope claimed.[11] Conversely, if it did adopt them, that would certainly cast doubt on the isolation of AN from the French dialect area. To this end, three grammatical changes will be considered, specifically matters of syntax, that occurred in continental French (henceforth CF) around 1300–50, and to what extent they were adopted in AN.

As noted by Lusignan, the advantage of using syntax or lexis as a research variable in historical linguistic enquiry is that it allows us to get around difficulties in identifying spoken-language dialects of past states of language.[12] In particular we sidestep issues of what spelling forms might or might not tell us about phonological and morphological systems. The evidential base is more direct. The downside of this is that contexts are much less frequent for a particular item of syntax or lexis than for a given spelling form or morpheme. But that is a restriction that can in principle be circumvented by the use of a large electronic corpus such as those that are now becoming available for historical language study. This is not yet the case for those studying insular French, hence sample sizes in this study will be relatively limited by comparison.

Analysis

Object pronouns in infinitive clauses
The first of the three types of grammar change in CF to be studied concerns object pronouns depending on an infinitive governed by a preposition, as in:

(1) a. ... por doner le au chien   *Dits* SQ P, 108[13]

In Old French only tonic, or strong form, object pronouns could precede a verb in the infinitive:

(2) c. Il se doit presenter ... et <u>soi</u> ofrir contre cex a qui...
                              Beaumanoir, *Coutumes de Beauvaisis*, p. 61

Tonic forms could also follow the infinitive:

(3) A demain por convertir lui/ atant li mauveés   *BibleM, Genèse* 1041–2[14]
('The devil waits till tomorrow to seduce him')

---

[11] A reviewer points out that this did not logically have to be the case: AN might have retained substantial links with CF, yet for some reason, such as a desire on the part of insular speakers to preserve their distinctive language identity in French, it might not have followed developments in CF. However, there are numerous well-known references in AN texts to continental (especially Parisian) French as a desirable variety to use. It therefore seems to us unlikely that if AN had not followed continental usage, this could be attributed to a deliberate aversion to continental forms.

[12] Lusignan, *Langue des rois*, p. 158.

[13] C. Buridant, *Grammaire nouvelle de l'ancien français* (Paris, 2000), p. 443.

[14] Buridant, *Grammaire nouvelle*, p. 444.

Atonic forms could not do so, that is, the modern French order, corresponding to *ror le veoir*, was not normally used in Old French. The Old French atonic pronoun pattern with infinitives gave way in the early fourteenth century to the modern preverbal order,[15] variably at first, while the syntax of strong form pronouns did not change until much later: strong form pronouns are still found accompanying infinitives in Rabelais, for example. Did AN show the same evolution? To answer that question, an analysis was carried out of object pronouns in infinitive clauses in a large body of chronicles, correspondence, and administrative and legal texts dating from between the mid-thirteenth century and the mid-fourteenth century.[16] The results show that it did. As seen in Table 3.1 the syntax of tonic object pronouns showed no change across that time span, whereas the atonic object pronouns went from being almost always postverbal before 1320 to being, in the majority of cases, preverbal, as was happening in CF:

Table 3.1: Syntax of object pronouns in AN non-finite clauses, 1250–1362

	1250–1319	1320–1362
Clitic preverbal (*les voir*)	1 (4%)	36 (61%)
Clitic postverbal (*voir les*)	27 (96%)	23 (39%)
Total	28	59
Strong form preverbal (*eux voir*)	17 (85%)	39 (89%)
Strong form postverbal (*voir eux*)	3 (15%)	5 (11%)
Total	20	44

The data size is relatively modest, but infinitive clauses are rather rare events in running text, and given the absence of a parsed electronic corpus of Anglo-

---

[15] A. de Kok, *La place du pronom personnel régime conjoint en français: Une étude diachronique* (Amsterdam, 1985).

[16] Primary sources used for this study are: 'AR': *The English Text of the* Ancrene Riwle, ed. E. J. Dobson, EETS OS 267 (London, 1972); 'Beaumanoir': *Les coutumes de Beauvaisis*, ed. J. Renouard (Paris, 1842); 'Brembre, Usk': Appeal of Thomas Usk, *English Gilds*, ed. L. T. Smith, EETS OS 40 (London, 1870); 'GCF VII': *Les Grandes Chroniques de France*, publiées pour la Société de l'Histoire de France par J. Viard, t. 7 (Paris, 1932); 'H. III': *Royal and Other Historical Letters Illustrative of the Reign of Henry III*, Vol. III, 1236–1272, ed. W. Shirley (London, 1866); 'Lanc.': *Le livre de seyntz medicines: The Unpublished Devotional Treatise of Henry of Lancaster*, ed. E. Arnould, ANTS 2 (Oxford, 1940) [Book I only]; 'LC': *Literae Cantuarienses, the Letter Books of the Monastery of Christ Church, Canterbury*, ed. J. B. Sheppard, 3 vols. (London, 1887–9); 'Pir.': H. Pirenne, *Le soulèvement de la Flandre maritime de 1323–1328: documents inédits publiés avec une introduction* (Brussels, 1900); 'PROME': *Parliament Rolls of Medieval England* ed. C. Given-Wilson et al. (Scholarly Digital Editions, 2005); 'RAM': *Règlements sur les arts et métiers de Paris rédigés au XIIIᵉ siècle, Collection de documents inédits sur l'histoire de France*, ed. G.-B. Depping (Paris, 1837); 'Reims': *Documents relatifs au comté de Champagne et de Brie, 1172–1361*, publiés par A. Longnon, t. II [enquêtes et prisées du domaine] (Paris, 1904); 'Sen.': *Seneschaucie*, in *Walter of Henley and other Treatises on Estate Management and Accounting*, ed. D. Oschinsky (Oxford, 1971).

Norman such as those available to Anglicists, scope for quantitative research is currently limited. Nevertheless, the almost total absence of clitic pronouns preceding an infinitive until 1320 is unlikely to be the effect of insufficient sampling. There can be little doubt that a change was taking place in AN at this time, and that it was in line with what was happening on the continent.

Also noteworthy was the fact that almost all the preverbal atonic forms were third-person singular or plural personal pronouns, conforming to the findings of Marchello-Nizia that in continental Old French change took place first with these forms,[17] for example:

Pre-1320
(4)a. ... ke jeo asuase par deboneirete de treiter <u>les</u> en amur   *H. III* 2, 321 (1268)
(4)b. Len a mester de prendre <u>le</u>   *Sen.* c.41 (c.1280)
Post-1320
(5)a. ... qe ascun s'entremet de <u>les</u> faire entrer   *LC II* 62 (1334)
(5)b. ... de ensi <u>le</u> faire   *Lanc.* p. 29 (c.1354)

Preverbal first-person singular and third-person singular reflexive pronouns tended to remain as strong forms for longer, for example:

(6)a. ... q'il vous plese <u>moy</u> aver excuse en ceste chose   *LC I* 464 (1332)
(6)b. ... et <u>soi</u> garder   *Lanc.* p. 82 (c.1354)

Only a single case of *se*, and none of *me*, preceding infinitives were noted in the later AN data. Even down to this level of detail, then, we find AN behaving as would be expected of a francophone dialect in touch with mainstream developments.

A sceptic might say that these data from a rather obscure corner of syntax do not necessarily tell us very much about the big picture of AN, but in fact this particular trait is highly significant. It is an area where French syntax and English syntax behaved quite differently, since by the fourteenth century English had lost the Old English clitic pronoun constructions, and was tending towards modern verb–object order. If, as maintained by Kibbee and others, AN was artificial because it was influenced by English, the last thing we would expect is that it changed its object pronoun order in a way that went in the opposite direction from English, yet that is what happened. Object pronouns in English by the fourteenth century were tending to be placed postverbally, so since the trend in AN was going against the grain of English, we can take this as a clear demonstration of the absence of grammatical influence from English, at least in this respect.

Aucun *as a negative polarity item*
The second change to be considered here is perhaps as much lexical as syntactic. It concerns the use of indefinite noun modifiers in negative clauses. Late Old French regularly used the word *nul* for this purpose, for example:

---

17 C. Marchello-Nizia, *La langue française aux XIVe et XVe siècles* (Paris, 1997).

(7)a. Mes <u>nul</u> frepier ne puet partir a <u>nul</u> home qu'il achate pour son user

RAM 200 (*c.*1280)

('But no clothes merchant may distribute to anyone what he buys for his own use')

(7)b … que l'on ne retiengne <u>nulles</u> causes es Parlemenz

Philippe III p. 429 (1278)

Indefinites in negated clauses in north-eastern France 1300–50 showed a sharp increase in the use of the modifier *aucun*. In administrative documents from Reims, Abbeville and Amiens, *aucun* is very common in negated contexts by the mid-fourteenth century, for example:

(8)a. Et ne pourra <u>aucun</u> eslu reffuser qu'il ne soit mestre…

Reims II 847 (1340)

('And no chosen member shall refuse to be master…')

(8)b. … que lidis visconte ne peut gaigier … <u>aucuns</u> bourgois dudit eschevinage qui seroit…   Reims II 939 (1345)

('And the said sheriff shall not engage any townsman of the said eschevins who would be…')

(8)c. Et ne sera tenus de recevoir <u>aucun</u> apel contre…   Reims II 1173 (1348)

('And will not be required to receive any appeal against…')

This innovation is not limited to administrative prose texts from north-eastern France, but is found at around the same time in Parisian miracle plays, written in the mid-fourteenth century,[18] for example:

(9)a. … non pas par nature ne par <u>aucune</u> autre reson. Et en ce jour que…

S. Louis (p.74)

(9)b. … a nul fuer Qu'il n'ait <u>aucuns</u> charnelz amis / par qui…

MirPer24 (p. 109)

(9)c. … ne onques, selon ses misericordes, ses loenges et ses beneurtés, a <u>aucun</u> ne deffailli.   *Miracle de la femme que nostre* … (p. 182)

How was *aucun* used in AN? This question was addressed by using an electronic data source that allows lexical searches by lexical item.[19] We used the AN petitions in PROME[20] in order to see whether they reflected CF developments. The data showed that in general *nul* continued to be used in most of the *PROME* data in much the same ways as before, until around the mid-fourteenth century, for example:

(10) Et si <u>nul</u> de la commune sache enfourmer le roi pur son profit

PROME Jan. 1348

---

18 P. Kunstmann, *Miracles de Notre-Dame* (Ottawa, 1991).

19 Bearing in mind alternative spelling forms, a particularly important consideration in AN. These were identified from L. Stone, T. Reid and W. Rothwell, eds., *An Anglo-Norman Dictionary* (1977–92).

20 *Parliament Rolls of Medieval England*, ed. C. Given-Wilson, P. Brand, A. Curry, R. Horrox, G. Martin, S. Philips and M. Ormrod (Scholarly Digital Editions, 2005).

However, *aucun* emerged in negative clauses in the 1340s:

(11)a. ... qe riens qe purreit tourner en blemissement de sa roiale dignitee, ou en prejudice des nobles, ou de son poeple, ils **ne** attempteroient ou feissent en **ascune** manere estre attemptez. PROME Apr. 1343

('So that anything that could turn to the detriment of his royal dignity or in prejudice of the nobles or his people, they would not attempt or cause to be attempted in any manner.')

(11)b. Acorde est qe ceux qi tiegnent les fees des queux les services dues ne serront rien tenuz affaire le service acustume et due, ne y ceux **ne ascun** autre du dit pais. PROME Sept. 1346.

('It is agreed that those who hold fees from which services are due should not be bound to make the service accustomed and due, nor should those or any other of the said region')

Thus shortly after the time when *aucun* starts to establish itself in CF negative clauses, at the expense of *nul*, AN displays the same incipient trend. Furthermore, the first example of *aucun* in a negative clause in the AN correspondence edited by Tanquerey dates from precisely this time, 1351.[21] Again, this forms a significant development in that Middle English was still a negative concord (multiple negation) language, which did not yet allow the English counterpart of *aucun* in negative clauses, that is, the word *any*.[22] Instead the *no* series of indefinites was used, for example:

(12)a. ... þe feont *ne* mei neden *nan* mon. to *na* sunne. AR II.224.3246 (a.1220)
('The devil may not compel any man to any sin.')

(12)b. The aduersairs of John Northampton should noght have be in non offices
Usk, 121 (1384)

('The opponents of JN should not have held any offices.')

(13)c. ... that no man make none congregaciouns Brembre I, 4 (1384)
('... that no-one should make any public gatherings.')

Middle English up to the time of Chaucer and Gower did not allow *any* in negative clauses. In later fifteenth-century texts we begin to get some use of *any*, in negative clauses as well as in non-assertive declaratives.[23] But it is not until the sixteenth century that the *any* series develops productively as an indefinite in a negative clause; English influence as a source of the use of *aucun* in AN can therefore be fairly confidently ruled out.

---

21 F. Tanquerey, *Receuil de lettres anglo-françaises 1265–1399* (Paris, 1916).
22 R. Ingham, 'On Two Negative Concord Dialects in Early English', *Language Variation and Change* 18 (2006), 241–66; R. Ingham, 'Negative Concord and the Loss of the Negative Particle *ne* in Late Middle English', *Studia Anglica Posnaniensia* 42 (2006), 77–96.
23 Y. Iyeiri, *Negative Constructions in Middle English* (Kyushu, 2001); A. Kallel, 'The Loss of Negative Concord in English' (unpublished Ph.D. thesis, University of Reading, 2005).

'S order

A third piece of evidence to support the proposal that AN participated in the mainstream of language evolution in French comes from the syntax of subjects and verbs, where changes occurred to the Old French pattern around 1300. In Classical Old French, as shown by early thirteenth-century prose, inversion of subject and verb normally takes place if a non-subject constituent stands at the beginning of the clause. By the early fourteenth century, this was still the case if the proposed element was a direct object, but if it was a circumstantial adverbial, inversion often failed to apply, for example:

(14)a. Grant partie des prisonniers envoia le roy a Paris   *GCF VII* 93 (*c.*1300)
('The king sent a large part of the prisoners to Paris')
(14)b. En cel an meismes messires Jacques roys d'Arragon tint son parlement...   *GCF VII* 48 (c.1300)
('In that year Sire J. King of Aragon held his parliament')

Research into the syntax of inversion in later Old French and Middle French using data from a series of chronicles shows a sharp decline in inversion with time adverbials at the end of the thirteenth century, giving rise to an asymmetry in inversion between preposed objects and proposed time adverbials.[24] Anglo-Norman chronicles from the later thirteenth century onwards also showed a clear asymmetry, of the same type. In Tables 3.2 and 3.3 we present the Anglo-Norman chronicle results, supplemented by data we have subsequently analysed from the *Oldest Prose Brut Chronicle*.[25] With full noun phrase subjects, inversion after time adjuncts was found to occur only about a quarter of the time, as compared with 83 per cent inversion after preposed object constituents.

Table 3.2: Frequency of VS versus SV order with full NP subjects
in AN chronicles, c.1280–1350

	VS	%	SV	%	Total
Preposed time adverbials	40	24	128	76	168
Preposed dir./ind. objects	13	87	2	13	15

With pronoun subjects, although numbers are small, there is a strong indication that the asymmetry was present here too. After time adjuncts, inversion took

---

R. Ingham, 'Syntactic Change in Anglo-Norman and Continental French Chronicles: Was There a "Middle" Anglo-Norman?', *Journal of French Language Studies* 16:1 (2006), 25–49; R. Ingham, 'The Status of French in Medieval England: Evidence from the Use of Object Pronoun Syntax', *Vox Romanica* 65 (2006), 1–22.

The Oldest Anglo-Norman Prose 'Brut' Chronicle: An Edition and Translation, ed. J. Marvin, Medieval Chronicles 4 (Woodbridge, 2006).

place a little under half the time, whereas after preposed objects, it was almos
categorical.

Table 3.3: Frequency of VS versus SV order with pronoun subjects
in AN chronicles, c.1280–1350

	VS	%	SV	%	Total
Preposed time adverbials	6	43	8	57	14
Preposed dir./ind. objects	21	96	1	4	22

Once again, our choice of this particular corner of AN syntax is not random
Old and Early Middle English had a strong tendency to subject–verb inversion
after any kind of proposed non-subject constituent, regardless of whether i
was an adjunct or a preposed object. But inversion usually took place only i
the subject was a full noun phrase;[26] subject pronouns did not normally shov
inversion. The interesting outcome with later AN, then, is that it followed th
pattern developing in CF, rather than using inversion in accordance with medi
eval English syntax. Once again, AN demonstrates its independence of Englis
grammar, and its adherence to the mainstream of CF language change.

Discussion

What can we glean from this syntactic micro-analysis? First, it gives an inter
estingly different picture from the extensive micro-analysis of phonology an
morphology undertaken by Pope, Tanquerey and others, in particular th
editors of ANTS volumes, who seem to be among the few to have taken u
the challenge of any detailed systematic description of AN.[27] It shows later AN
continuing to evolve in company with CF. So the answer to the question 'Wa
AN isolated from the mainstream of CF?' may depend on what kind of evidenc
we decide to evaluate, and then on how we interpret the results that we ge
Instead of contenting ourselves with the surface differences noted by medieva
contemporaries,[28] we may seek to distinguish on the one hand phonological an
morphological differences in a language variety that are quite compatible wit

[26] E. Haeberli, 'Observations on the Loss of Verb-second in the History of English', i
  Studies in Comparative Germanic Syntax. Proceedings from the 15th Workshop on Compara
  tive Germanic Syntax, ed. C. Zwart and W. Abraham (Amsterdam, 2002), pp. 245–72.
[27] See e.g. Fouke Le Fitz Waryn, ed. E. Hathaway, P. Ricketts, C. Robson and A. Wilshere
  ANTS 26, 27, 28 (Oxford, 1975).
[28] See Brereton, Grammatical Changes.

its being part of a dialect area, and on the other hand underlying differences relating to syntactic rules that all, or most, varieties tend to share.[29]

Secondly, none of the three changes features in discussions of the supposed teaching of French in medieval England.[30] This is not surprising, for one thing because they are not very salient and also because medieval grammarians might not have had the technical vocabulary with which to explain them. So it seems highly doubtful that they would have figured on any language syllabus used by putative instructors of French in England.[31] It is worth stating that the changes to AN discussed here are not matters of stylistic preference or literary fashion. They are just basic points of core syntax, the sort of feature that is normally an unconscious part of sentence construction, and belong to the areas of grammar that are learned instinctively in early childhood, but with difficulty by second-language learners in adulthood.

Conclusion

Around the beginning of the fourteenth century, AN showed the same syntactic trends as CF: it retained VS order after an initial direct object, but not regularly after a time adjunct. In step with CF, it shifted the order of atonic object pronouns governed by an infinitive, against the direction being taken by English at this time. Later in the fourteenth century, AN began to follow the development of *aucun* in continental French, at a period before the Middle English negative concord rule weakened to allow 'any' as a negative polarity item. The new form arises first in the genre most closely and regularly in touch with the upper levels of society in France, that is, the records written by royal clerks. Later it spreads to other levels of English society not in regular contact with continental developments.

Perhaps the most significant overall conclusion from this study is that for AN to have adopted CF changes means sustained contact with CF during the decades before and after 1300, in a form substantial enough for semantico-grammatical structures to change in line with CF developments. These developments took place exactly as we should expect if AN was part of a dialect continuum in which innovations spread outward from an innovative central zone. The kind of language transmission that accounts for this parallel evolution of grammar in

---

[29] For example, the syntactic changes discussed in this study may have taken place concurrently in all the pre-modern dialects of French despite their surface phonological differences. Given the dearth of Old and Middle French syntax studies that control for dialect variation, we do not know whether this was the case.

[30] W. Rothwell, 'The Role of French in Thirteenth-Century England', *BJRL* 58 (1976), 445–66.

[31] We make this point purely for the sake of argument: we do not in fact subscribe to the position that regular formal instruction in French would have taken place until after the period covered by this study.

later Anglo-Norman and continental French may therefore have been the same as elsewhere, that is, contact between speakers/writers.

For all its well-known eccentricities, AN belonged to the French language family at the level of the evolution of its basic grammar. If we had found that AN came adrift from changing continental usage, then surely we would have wanted to say that it was becoming isolated from the native-speaker French mainstream, but that was not the finding obtained. This finding does not disprove the position taken by some earlier scholars that French was an instructed L2, but it does set the bar somewhat higher for those who wish to make that claim. That is, we now see very specifically how good the instructors, and the learners, had to be, to perform as well as they did. Protagonists of the 'French as an instructed L2' position need to explain how these putatively first-rate medieval pedagogues and their star pupils managed to achieve continental native speaker proficiency on say, atonic object pronoun position, but apparently failed to convey, or comprehend, when to use *un* or *une*, or that *de le* is contracted to *du*. This comment is of course ironic, but this is a field that has been bedevilled by simplistic solutions and unsupported claims that themselves invite irony. What is surely apparent from this study is that, qualitatively speaking, the grammar of AN cannot be said to have 'declined' in the respects studied during the period investigated, but rather to have maintained the characteristics that would be expected of an evolving variety of medieval French at that time. The so-called 'final decline' of insular French, we would argue, did not occur much before the end of the fourteenth century,[32] after which plain evidence of collapse of its formal systems becomes apparent in the Law French used in the later fifteenth century and thereafter.[33]

In consequence, we wish to hypothesize a transmission system for the survival of these grammatical systems as far as the mid-fourteenth century, long beyond the period of time when scholars assumed French was anybody's native language. The nature of this transmission system, which it seems clear to us cannot have been a matter of classroom teaching, is a topic we hope to elaborate in future research.

---

[32] R. Berndt, 'The Period of the Final Decline of French in Medieval England (14th and early 15th centuries)', *Zeitschrift für Anglistik und Amerikanistik* 20 (1972), 341–69.

[33] See http://www.richardingham.com/id20.html.

4

Syntaxe anglo-normande : étude de certaines caractéristiques du XIIe au XIVe siècle

Pierre Kunstmann

Dans le domaine de la morphosyntaxe anglo-normande on peut constater, en ancien français, trois points qui caractérisent nettement, dès le XIIe siècle, cette variété de la langue française et la distinguent des dialectes en usage sur le continent. Il s'agit, d'une part, de ce qu'on appelle communément la disparition de la déclinaison, d'autre part de l'apparition précoce de la forme *lequel*, pronom relatif, dans les textes religieux ainsi que de l'usage croissant du relatif *que* sujet avec pour antécédent un nom de personne. Je ne m'attarderai pas sur le premier point, car il est trop connu ; je m'attacherai, par contre, aux deux autres, auxquels on a prêté jusqu'à récemment moins d'attention, au moins pour ce qui est de l'usage généralisé du relatif composé dans un secteur particulier de la production littéraire.

Dans l'introduction de sa seconde édition de la *Vie de saint Alexis*, Christopher Storey écrivait en 1968 : 'Grâce à l'influence anglaise, la désintégration de la vieille déclinaison française commença de bonne heure en anglo-normand.'[1] C'est effectivement le cas des deux plus anciens textes continentaux copiés en Angleterre : dans le texte d'*Alexis* que présente le manuscrit de Hildesheim (copie c.1120 d'une œuvre de la fin du XIe siècle),[2] 'la confusion est considérable' ;[3] dans celui de la *Chanson de Roland* conservé dans le manuscrit d'Oxford (copie du deuxième quart du XIIe siècle, l'œuvre originale ayant été composée vers 1100), '26% des substantifs déclinables n'observent pas la déclinaison théoriquement attendue', comme le constate C. Buridant dans sa *Grammaire nouvelle de l'ancien français*.[4] Dans sa thèse fondamentale sur *La déclinaison bicasuelle de l'ancien français*,[5] L. Schøsler, ayant procédé à des dépouillements, complet pour *Alexis*, partiel (une centaine de vers pour le *Roland*), précise que dans le premier texte '147 sur 221, soit 66,5% des masculins déclinables apparaissant dans les fonctions de prime actant, d'attribut, etc. [apposition, apostrophe] revêtent la

---

[1] *La Vie de Saint Alexis*, éd. C. Storey (Geneva, 1968), p. 52.
[2] Les datations mentionnées dans cette étude sont empruntées au *Complément bibliographique* du DEAF.
[3] Loc. cit.
[4] C. Buridant, *Grammaire nouvelle de l'ancien français* (Paris, 2000), p. 75.
[5] L. Schøsler, *La déclinaison bicasuelle de l'ancien français. Son rôle dans la syntaxe de la phrase, les causes de sa disparition* (Odense, 1984), p. 101.

forme du cas sujet' ; par contre, dans le second texte, ces masculins ne sont que 28 sur 59 (47,5%).

Dans les premiers textes anglo-normands rédigés en Angleterre, la confusion entre cas sujet et cas complément est fréquente : ainsi dans l'œuvre de Philippe de Thaon (*Comput* composé en 1119, copie du 3e quart du XIIe siècle), dans l'*Estoire des Engleis* de Geoffroy Gaimar (texte de 1139, ms. D du 1er tiers du XIIIe siècle), et dans les psautiers d'Oxford et de Cambridge (dont il sera question plus loin). Il faut cependant noter une grosse exception, celle du *Voyage de saint Brendan* (1er quart du XIIe siècle, ms. A de la 2e moitié du XIIIe siècle) ; ses derniers éditeurs (I. Short et B. Merrilees) concluent d'un examen des rimes : 'Syntactically Benedeit's rhymes indicate relatively careful observance of the two-case declension system for nouns and adjectives, and despite a score of cases of non-adherence [...], there is no clear evidence that the system was breaking down to any significant extent.'[6] Cette constatation contraste fortement avec celle de l'éditeur de Gaimar (A. Bell) : 'The two-case declension has broken down completely in the *Estoire*.'[7] Il s'agit pourtant, dans les deux cas, de textes narratifs que ne sépare qu'un quart de siècle. En bonne méthode, je ne tiens évidemment compte que de la langue des auteurs et pas de celle des manuscrits. Cela n'apparaît pas toujours clairement dans les ouvrages de synthèse ; ainsi quand, dans sa grammaire,[8] C. Buridant note que dans le *Protheselaus* de Hue de Rotelande (texte de *c*.1185, ms. A du XIIIe siècle), le cas sujet se trouve couramment en fonction de cas complément d'après l'observation de l'éditeur du texte,[9] le lecteur ne peut savoir, sans recourir à l'édition critique, s'il s'agit de la langue de l'auteur ou de celle du manuscrit (les remarques sur la déclinaison concernant l'auteur figurent à la p. 16), ce qui fausse la perspective.

Faut-il vraiment voir une influence de l'anglais, comme l'a soutenu Storey dans cette négligence apparente du système bicasuel de l'ancien français ? Personnellement, je ne le pense pas : je doute que la langue des vaincus ait pu influer de façon si déterminante sur celle des vainqueurs dans des œuvres ou des manuscrits écrits cinquante ou soixante ans après la conquête. De toute façon, la même situation apparaît sur le continent, dans les dialectes de l'Ouest, à partir de 1200. Comment parler alors d'influence anglaise ou même anglo-normande ? On cite souvent les vers de la religieuse de Barking (*une Deu ancele de Berkinges*) qui, dans le prologue de sa *Vie de saint Édouard le Confesseur* (*c*.1170), reconnaît le caractère spécial de son dialecte :

---

6 Benedeit, *The Anglo-Norman Voyage of St Brendan*, éd. I. Short et B. S. Merrilees (Manchester, 1979), pp. 14–15.

7 Geffrei Gaimar, *L'Estoire des Engleis*, éd. A. Bell, ANTS 14, 15 et 16 (Oxford, 1960) p. xxvii.

8 Buridant, *Grammaire nouvelle*, p. 75.

9 A. J. Holden, *Protheselaus by Hue de Rotelande*, ANTS 47, 48, 49, vol. 3 (London, 1993) p. 26.

Si joe l'ordre des cases ne gart
Ne ne juigne part a sa part,
Certes n'en dei estre reprise,
Ke nel puis faire en nule guise.
Qu'en latin est nominatif,
Ço frai romanz acusatif.
Un faus franceis sai d'Angletere,
Ke ne l'alai ailurs quere.
Mais vus ki ailurs apris l'avez,
La u mester iert, l'amendez. (Éd. Södergård, v. 1–10) [10]

La situation est bien décrite. Il faut, d'ailleurs, voir là une *captatio benevolentiae*, plutôt que l'aveu d'un complexe d'infériorité. Comme l'indique l'éditeur, 'la langue de notre poème est remarquablement pure. Si ce n'était la désorganisation de la déclinaison et quelques synérèses, on pourrait même croire avoir affaire à un texte continental.'[11]

Pour L. Schøsler (position reprise par C. Buridant dans son manuel), le système bicasuel s'est désagrégé car il servait très peu : citant la thèse de E. R. Daniels qui avait observé que, dans le *Lancelot* de Chrétien de Troyes, le système était fonctionnel ou efficace (c'est-à-dire essentiel pour l'interprétation de la phrase) dans 1% des cas, elle n'hésite pas à le trouver 'redondant, pour ne pas dire superflu' ;[12] les fonctions, dans 99% des cas, sont déjà suffisamment marquées par des facteurs syntaxiques et/ou contextuels, ce qui lève quasiment toute ambiguïté.

Dans les textes (œuvres ou manuscrits) écrits en Angleterre dans la première moitié du XIIe siècle, je pense donc que, plutôt qu'une marque de faiblesse ou un signe de confusion, la tendance à la désagrégation de la déclinaison procède du caractère linguistiquement (et littérairement) avant-gardiste de la production insulaire. Libre et foncièrement innovateur, l'anglo-normand annonce souvent des caractéristiques qui n'apparaîtront qu'un siècle plus tard, de l'autre côté de la Manche. Il est vrai que pour la France, à pareille époque, nous ne disposons que de très peu de témoins : le fragment de *Gormont et Isambart* (ms. anglo-normand du 1er quart du XIIIe siècle), la *Chanson de Guillaume* (ms. unique anglo-normand, également du 1er quart du XIIIe siècle) le fragment d'un *Roman d'Alexandre* d'Alberic de Briançon (mais le ms., du XIIe siècle, est franco-provençal ou toscan),

---

[10] ('Si je n'observe pas l'ordre des cas et que je n'accorde pas tel élément avec celui qui lui correspond, certes je ne dois pas en être reprise, car je ne puis le faire en aucune façon. Ce qui est en latin au nominatif, je le mettrai à l'accusatif en langue romane. Je sais un faux français d'Angleterre, car je ne suis pas allé le chercher ailleurs. Mais vous qui l'avez appris ailleurs, corrigez-le là où il le faudra.') Voir sur ce passage les remarques de W. Rothwell, 'Playing "follow my leader" in Anglo-Norman Studies', dans *Journal of French Language Studies*, 1996, vol. 6, n° 2, pp. 186–90. Ce dernier propose, pour le v. 7, la traduction suivante : 'My French is not genuine native French (literally: I know [only] a second-hand Anglo-French).'

[11] *La Vie d'Édouard le Confesseur: Poème anglo-normand du XIIe siècle*, éd. Ö. Södergård (Uppsala, 1948), p. 102.

[12] *La Vie d'Édouard le Confesseur*, éd. Södergård, p. 60.

tous textes difficiles à utiliser pour une étude linguistique. La situation est assurément différente pour la seconde moitié du siècle : si l'on met en parallèle deux auteurs contemporains s'étant illustrés dans le même type de littérature, l'un anglo-normand, Hue de Rotelande, l'autre champenois, Chrétien de Troyes, on pourrait, de ce point de vue, qualifier le premier de progressiste et le second de conservateur ...

Ce caractère indépendant et novateur est particulièrement remarquable dans le second domaine que je vais aborder, celui du relatif/interrogatif. Je reprendrai certains des traits que j'avais observés, il y a vingt ans, dans ma thèse d'État qui portait sur la question,[13] mais je les présenterai ici de façon plus détaillée et élargie.

Les deux tableaux suivants présentent les formes du relatif en ancien français et leurs valeurs.

Tableau 4.1: Les formes simples du relatif

	+ antécédent +/- animé		- antécédent + animé	- animé
cas sujet	qui		qui	
cas objet direct	que		cui	que
cas obliques	dont, ou		dont, ou	
- (") -	cui	quoi	cui	quoi
- (") -	+ animé	- animé	+ animé	- animé

Tableau 4.2 : Les formes composées du relatif

		masculin	féminin
singulier	sujet	li quels	la quel/quele
- (") -	complément	le quel	- (") -
pluriel	sujet	li quel	les quels/queles
- (") -	complément	les quels	- (") -

Le tableau 4.1 est celui des formes simples. Les colonnes de droite donnent les formes qui introduisent les propositions relatives sans antécédent exprimé ; ces formes fonctionnent aussi en emploi interrogatif. La colonne de gauche présente les formes qu'on trouve en tête des relatives à antécédent exprimé. On voit nettement la dissymétrie entre la série *qui/que* indiquant la fonction (sujet/objet direct) et l'axe *cui/quoi* marquant le genre naturel (animé/inanimé).

Le tableau 4.2 est celui des formes composées (à partir des pronoms latins *ille* et *qualis*). Ces formes varient en genre (grammatical : masculin/féminin) et en nombre (singulier/pluriel) ; pour le masculin, elles varient aussi suivant la fonction (sujet/complément).

Le point remarquable dans certains des premiers textes anglo-normands est l'apparition d'un nouveau paradigme, celui du tableau 4.2, et la généralisation

13 P. Kunstmann, *Le relatif-interrogatif en ancien français* (Genève, 1990).

le l'emploi des formes composées au détriment des formes simples (sans pour utant les faire disparaître – tant s'en faut !). Ce paradigme est attesté depuis l'ori- ine : je veux parler du premier manuscrit anglo-normand ayant reproduit une euvre littéraire, le fameux manuscrit de Hildesheim mentionné plus haut, où la *'ie de saint Alexis* précède le *Psautier de Saint-Albans*. La chanson est introduite ar un prologue, qui ne figure que dans ce manuscrit. Si le prologue est l'œuvre lu copiste (scribe 3), il se peut que l'auteur soit l'abbé Geoffrey de Gorrham lui- même, destinant la chanson à sa protégée, Christine de Markyate.[14]

Ici cumencet amiable cançun espiritel raisun d'iceol noble barun Eufemien par num. e de la vie de sum filz boneü-
rét *del quel* nus avum oït lire et canter. par le divine
volentét. il desirrables icel sul filz angendrat. Après le naisance
ço fut emfes de Deu methime amét. e. de pere e de mere
par grant certét nurrit. La sue juvente fut honeste e spiritel.
Por l'amistét del surerain pietét la sue spuse juvene cuman-
dat al spus vif de veritét *ki* est un sul faitur e regnet
en trinitiet. Icesta istorie est amiable grace e suverain
consulaciun a cascun memorie spiritel. *les quels* vivent
purement sulunc castethét. e dignement sei delitent
es goies del ciel & es noces virginels.[15]

Dans les douze lignes du texte, écrites en alternance en rouge et en bleu, on ompte trois occurrences de relatif : deux relèvent du nouveau paradigme (*del uel*, *les quels*), la troisième (*ki*) de l'ancien. La première forme composée entre lans un tour prépositionnel en tête d'une proposition relative non restrictive explicative, appositive) ; ce pourrait être pratiquement du français moderne : a vie de son fils bienheureux, duquel nous avons entendu déclamer et chanter'. La seconde forme composée, par contre, en fonction sujet (même si elle est mise, lans le manuscrit, au cas complément)[16] introduit une relative restrictive (qui estreint la portée de l'antécédent et en détermine la signification) – tour impos- ible de nos jours : 'chacun qui vit purement en chasteté...' Précisons que la *Vie e saint Alexis* en tant que telle (l'original ayant été composé sur le continent) ne résente pas d'occurrence de relatif composé.

---

[14] Voir à ce sujet http://www.abdn.ac.uk/stalbanspsalter/english/essays/introduction. shtml.

[15] ('Ici commence une agréable chanson, un pieux discours, du noble baron appelé Eufémien et de la vie de son fils bienheureux, *duquel* nous avons entendu déclamer et chanter. Par la divine volonté, lui, dans son désir, engendra ce seul fils. Après la nais-sance, ce fut un enfant aimé de Dieu même et élevé par son père et sa mère avec une grande affection. Sa jeunesse fut honorable et pieuse. Par amitié pour la souveraine pitié, il recommanda sa jeune épouse au vivant époux de vérité, *qui* est créateur unique et règne en trinité. Cette histoire est une douce grâce et une consolation souveraine, un pieux souvenir pour tous ceux *qui* vivent purement en chasteté et font dignement leurs délices des joies du ciel et des noces virginales' *Alexis* quire, p. 57.)

[16] À noter aussi le passage du singulier distributif (antécédent) au pluriel (relatif).

Le paradigme de *le quel* réapparaît quelques années plus tard, dans toute sa splendeur, dans toute son expansion (qu'il ne retrouvera jamais plus), dans le psautier en prose dit *Psautier d'Oxford* (l'œuvre appartient à la première moitié du XIIe siècle, remontant peut-être même à 1100 ;[17] le manuscrit de la Bodléienne est du milieu du siècle). J'y ai compté soixante-dix-sept occurrences du relatif composé ;[18] le tableau 4.3 en indique la distribution ; on trouvera en note les références (psaume et verset).

Tableau 4.3: La distribution des formes composées du relatif

Avec antécédent		Avec antécédent intégré		Sans antécédent	
Sujet[19]	9	suj.	1	suj.	
objet direct[20]	30	obj. dir.		obj. dir.	2
objet indirect[21]	1	obj. indir.		obj. indir.	1
complément déterminatif[22]	14	Comp. dét.		comp. dét.	
complément circonstanciel[23]	17	Comp. circ.	2	comp. circ.	

Voici un exemple pour chacun de ces cas :

1. Avec antécédent :
   sujet :
   > ... Que il ne seient fait sicume li peres d'els, generaciuns felunesse e enasprissante, Generaciun *laquele* n'adreceat sun cuer [LXXVII, 11][24]
   objet direct :
   > La pierre *laquele* reproverent li edifiant, iceste faite est el chief del angle. [CXVII, 21][25]
   objet indirect :
   > Beneeuré cil *asquels* sunt pardunées lur felunies, e desquels sunt cuvert pechet. [XXXI, 1][26]

---

17 B. Merrilees, 'Oxford Psalter', dans *Dictionary of the Middle Ages*, ed. R. J. Strayer, vol IX (New York, 1987), p. 319.

18 En utilisant les outils de requête que l'Anglo-Norman On-Line Hub met à la disposi tion des internautes : www.anglo-norman.net/texts/oxfps-contents.html.

19 XXX 21 ; LVII 4 ; LXV 12 ; LXXIII 23 ; LXXVII 10 ; CXXI 3 ; CXXVIII 5 ; CXXXII 2, 3.

20 XX 11 ; XXI 34 ; XXX 23 ; LV 12 ; LXXIII 2 ; LXXVII 14, 59, 74 ; LXXIX 16, 16, 18 ; LXXX 26 ; XCIII 12 ; CIII 10, 18, 26, 28 ; CIV 4, 7, 24 ; CV 32, 35 ; CVI 2 ; CXVII 21, 23 ; CXVII 47, 48 ; CXXXVI 11 ; CXXXVIII 14 ; CXL 10.

21 J'y inclus, pour des raisons pratiques, le complément d'attribution. XXXI 1.

22 XIII 5 ; XXV 32 ; XXXI 1 ; XXXII 12 ; XXXIX 6, 16 ; LXXXIII 6 ; LXXXVII 5 ; CIV 32 CXXI 3 ; CXLIII 9, 12, 13, 18.

23 IX 23 ; XVIII 3 (mais sous la forme simple *quels*, sans article) ; XXVI 12 ; XLIV 10 ; XLIX 24 ; LXVII 17 ; LXXIII 3 ; LXXVII 47 ; LXXXIX 17, 17, CVIII 18, 18, CXVIII 49 ; CXXVII 6 ; CXLI 4 ; CXLII 9 ; CXLV 2.

24 ('... Qu'ils ne soient faits comme leurs pères, génération félonne et rebelle, génération qui n'a pas redressé son cœur.')

25 ('La pierre *qu'*ont rejetée les bâtisseurs est devenue la tête de l'angle.')

26 ('Bienheureux ceux *dont* les félonies ont été pardonnées, et dont les péchés sont couverts.')

complément déterminatif :
> beneuré li poples *delquel* li sire est li suens Deus. [CXLIII, 18][27]

complément circonstanciel :
> Coneude fai à mei la veie *en laquele* je voise [CXLII, 9][28]

2. Avec antécédent intégré :

sujet :
> Fus, gresille, neif, glace, espiriz de tempestez, *lesquels* choses funt la parole de lui [CXLVIII, 8][29]

complément circonstanciel :
> Empurice amai-je les tuens comandemenz, sur or e topaze. *Pur laquel* chose à tuz les tuens comandemenz esteie adreciez [CXVIII, 128][30]

3. Sans antécédent :

objet direct :
> Beneurez *lequel* tu eslesis e prisis; enhabiterat en tes aitres. [LXIV, 4][31]

objet indirect :
> Beneurez *alquel* li Deus de Jacob est li ajuere de lui, l'esperance de lui, el Segnor, sun Deu. [CXLV, 4][32]

Le relatif issu de *ille qualis* est donc utilisé essentiellement en fonction d'objet direct, de complément circonstanciel et de complément déterminatif. Il est d'ailleurs à noter que pour le relatif en fonction de sujet, les quatre occurrences de formes masculines[33] ne respectent pas les règles de la déclinaison ; on trouve, en effet, *lequel* et *lesquels* pour, respectivement, *liquels* et *liquel*. En bonne méthode, il convient aussi de préciser que le relatif composé reste, dans ce psautier, bien moins fréquent que le relatif simple.

Le paradigme tiré de *ille qualis* sert aussi en français (au moyen âge comme de nos jours) à l'emploi interrogatif : le morphème *lequel* se caractérise par sa valeur partitive et son statut de représentant. Il s'emploie lorsqu'on doit choisir entre plusieurs éléments (personnes ou choses) connus et se trouve alors en relation avec un terme de la phrase précédente ou de celle qu'il introduit. C'est dans la *Chanson de Roland* qu'il apparaît pour la première fois en français, mais déjà avec une fréquence aussi forte que dans les œuvres de la seconde moitié du XIIIᵉ siècle. Or dans les psautiers anglo-normands, *lequel* n'est pas employé avec cette valeur, mais comme un *qui* non partitif et en concurrence avec lui. On en compte treize occurrences dans le psautier d'Oxford, toujours en fonction de sujet et, cette fois-ci, à la bonne forme casuelle (cas sujet masculin) *liquels* :

---

[27] ('Bienheureux le peuple *dont* le seigneur est son Dieu.')
[28] ('Fais-moi connaître la voie *dans laquelle* j'aille')
[29] ('Feu, grêle, neige, glace, vent de tempête, choses par *lesquelles* il parle')
[30] ('C'est pourquoi j'aimai tes commandements, plus qu'or et topaze. Chose *pour laquelle* j'étais tourné vers tous tes commandements')
[31] ('Bienheureux celui *que* tu as choisi et pris; il habitera dans ta demeure.')
[32] ('Bienheureux celui pour *lequel* le Dieu de Jacob est auxiliaire, espérance, seigneur, Dieu.')
[33] LXV 12, CXXVIII 5, CXXXII 2, 3.

Liquels s'esdrecerad à mei envers les malignanz? u *liquels* estrad ot mei encontre les ovranz felunie? [XCIII, 16][34]

Le contraste avec le relatif sujet *lequel* est on ne peut plus net. À quoi cela tient-il? Peut-être au fait qu'il s'agit ici d'un sujet animé + humain en position d'agent antéposé au verbe (contrairement aux quatre occurrences de relatif susmentionnées); comme l'indique C. Buridant, c'est une 'des zones de résistance tendant à maintenir la marque du CS'.[35]

Il importe de remarquer que, dans le manuscrit de la Bodléienne, ces traits langagiers se rencontrent aussi dans les poèmes qui suivent le livre des psaumes; ainsi dans l'exemple suivant :

Kiqueunkes veolt estre salf, devant tutes choses li est mestier que il tienge veire creance. *Laquele chose* si chascuns entiere e nient malmise ne guarderat, senz dutance pardurablement perirat. [*Sancti Athanasii Credo*, 1][36]

particulièrement intéressant vu que le relatif à antécédent intégré est, en fait, extraposé par rapport à la proposition hypothétique qui suit et dans laquelle il exerce la fonction de complément d'objet direct et où il se trouve qualifié par les deux attributs *entiere e nient malmise* – construction enchâssée dont, dans mes dépouillements, je n'ai pas rencontré d'équivalent jusqu'au XIVe siècle.[37]

Il convient aussi de noter que ces traits s'observent également dans les autres manuscrits qui ont conservé le psautier d'Oxford, comme l'indique l'apparat critique de l'édition Michel. Ils se retrouvent dans l'autre grand psautier anglo-normand de cette époque, celui de Cambridge (œuvre de la première moitié du XIIe siècle, ms. A de Canterbury avant 1160).[38] Dans le vieux manuel de Menger,[39] qui se termine par un choix de textes, on peut lire en parallèle les psaumes I et

---

34 (*'Qui* se dressera pour moi contre les méchants? ou *qui* se tiendra avec moi contre les malfaisants?') Autres occurrences : XXIII 3, LVIII 8, LXXV 7, LXXXVIII 7, LXXXIX 13, CV 2, CVI 43, CVII 11, CXII 5.

35 Buridant, *Grammaire nouvelle*, pp. 77–8.

36 ('Quiconque veut être sauvé doit avoir, avant tout, une croyance vraie. *Cette chose*, si on ne *la* garde pas entière et intacte, on périra sans doute définitivement.')

37 Kunstmann, *Le relatif-interrogatif*, p. 474.

38 Comme l'indique B. Merrilees ('Cambridge Psalter', dans *Dictionary of the Middle Ages*, vol. III (New York, 1983), p. 57), le manuscrit a été copié par un certain Eadwine et contient aussi la version romaine des *Psaumes* avec une version interlinéaire en anglo-saxon. Le psautier est une glose intégrale, transformée en 'texte' par son éditeur moderne (voir les remarques de D. Trotter, '*Tutes choses en sapience*: la transmission du lexique biblique dans les psautiers anglo-normands', dans V. Bubenicek et al., éds., *Gouvernement des hommes, gouvernement des âmes : Mélanges Charles Brucker* (Nancy, 2007), pp. 508–9).

39 L. E. Menger, *The Anglo-Norman Dialect* (New York, 1904). Au paragraphe 60, consacré au pronom relatif, il constate curieusement : 'Our texts offer nothing extraordinary here' ; il ne mentionne pas le relatif composé et se contente de quelques remarques banales d'ordre graphique.

XXXVI dans la version d'Oxford et celle de Cambridge et constater ainsi un passé-croisé entre les formes des deux paradigmes : tableau 4.4.

Tableau 4.4: Les formes des deux paradigmes du relatif

	Psautier d'Oxford	Psautier de Cambridge
3	les decurs des ewes, *chi*...	les ruisals des ewes, *lequel*...
5	cume la puldre *que*...	cume puldre, *lequel*...
XXXVI, 11	la tue gueredunance, *laquele*...	la twe feiede, *ke*...

ans son *Fragment d'une traduction en prose française du Psautier*,[40] C. Samaran publié ce qui reste d'une traduction (produite en Angleterre, ms. du XIIe ècle) de la version dite gallicane des psaumes[41] avec, en regard, les passages orrespondants des psautiers d'Oxford et de Cambridge. On y trouve le même passé-croisé : tableau 4.5.

Tableau 4.5: La distribution des paradigmes entre les psautiers

	Psautier d'Oxford	Psautier de Cambridge	Fragment de l'Orne
XXVII, 47	el jurn *elquel* il raenst...	el jurn *que* les reeinst...	el jur *k'*il reienst...
XXVII, 59	el mont *lequel* aquist...	icest munt *que*...	munt *lequel* aquist...
XXXVIII, 7	Kar *liquels*[42] es nues sera...	Kar *ki* serad es nues...	Ker *qui* es nues sera...

Ces formes perdurent chez les clercs anglo-normands, essentiellement dans les œuvres religieuses traduites du latin. Nous en avons un témoignage net et bien ocumenté, cent ans après le Psautier d'Oxford, dans l'œuvre de frère Angier. Je m'attacherai à sa *Vie de saint Grégoire*, le seul texte de lui qui nous soit facilement ccessible. L'auteur était moine au prieuré de Sainte Frideswide à Oxford, dont église est devenue plus tard la cathédrale Christ Church. Le grand intérêt du xte est qu'il est parfaitement daté (terminé le 30 avril 1214) et conservé dans un manuscrit probablement autographe. Le tableau 4.6 montre l'emploi que notre moine d'Oxford faisait du paradigme du relatif composé.

C. Samaran, 'Fragment d'une traduction en prose française du Psautier', *Romania* 55 (1929), 161–73.
Précisons que le *Psautier d'Oxford* est aussi une traduction de la version gallicane, tandis que celui de Cambridge provient de la version hébraïque.
Cette forme est ici en emploi interrogatif, contrairement à la ponctuation de C. Samaran, qui en fait un relatif sans antécédent.

Tableau 4.6: Les formes du relatif chez Angier

objet direct[43]	19
objet indirect[44]	4
complément déterminatif[45]	3
complément circonstanciel[46]	3

Toutes ces occurrences se trouvent dans des relatives avec antécédent. À titr d'exemple, voici une phrase (longue de quinze vers, il est vrai) qui ne compt pas moins de trois occurrences de relatifs composés :

Sis preechot haut et clerment
Com evangelien bedel
Qui la meistrie e le cembel
Enportot de toz les pastors
Q'onc fussent ainz n'après ses jors,
Sanz les apostres principaus
As quels nul seint n'est paregaus,
Car sor trestoz les seinz del mont
Meistres e princes sanz per sont,
Si com cil *les quels* Deu meïsme
En sa persone demeinisme,
Veirs oem de la virge Marie,
Espirtaument en ceste vie
Sa seinte doctrine enseingna,
Com ceus *les quels* sor toz ama. [1258–72][47]

Proposition non restrictive pour la première occurrence; restrictive pour les deu autres, où le relatif détermine le démonstratif antécédent.[48]

Notons aussi qu'Angier semble ignorer, dans son œuvre, l'usage de *lequ* comme interrogatif non partitif.

Le relatif composé se retrouve dans d'autres œuvres insulaires au XIIIᵉ siècl quoiqu'avec une fréquence moindre (par exemple, dans les *Vitas Patrum*, écrite pour le templier Henri d'Arci – œuvre et manuscrit du milieu du siècle), mais

43 Aux vers 124, 173, 253, 354, 449, 866, 896, 1267, 1272, 1460, 1463, 1516, 1731, 1876, 228! 2543, 2732, 2821, 2863.
44 Aux vers 1324, 1868, 1897, 1985.
45 Aux vers 833, 1264, 2101.
46 Aux vers 1468, 2642, 2942.
47 ('Il les prêchait haut et clairement comme un héraut de l'Évangile, supérieur à tous le pasteurs qui aient jamais été avant ou après son époque, à l'exception des principau apôtres *auxquels* aucun saint n'est égal, car au-dessus de tous les saints du monde i sont maîtres et princes sans pairs, comme ceux *à qui* Dieu même en sa propre personn vrai homme de la vierge Marie, enseigna sa sainte doctrine spirituellement en cette vi comme ceux *qu'*il aima par-dessus tous.')
48 Ce texte présente dix-sept occurrences de *lequel* en relative restrictive contre douze e non restrictive.

reste très rare sur le continent, où il ne se répand avec une certaine fréquence que dans les textes didactiques, administratifs et juridiques de la seconde moitié du siècle.[49] Je dois cependant faire exception pour certains textes de dialecte lorrain du tournant du siècle (le *Dialogue de l'âme* de saint Isidore, par exemple, avec versions latines et françaises copiées dans le même manuscrit de *c*.1200) où *lequel* relatif est particulièrement fréquent.

Quelles sont les raisons de cette innovation morphosyntaxique au début du XIIe siècle? La raison se trouve dans la diglossie fonctionnelle de l'occident médiéval. Les clercs, plongés dans une situation de bilinguisme, étaient amenés, dans la vie courante, à changer constamment de code, s'exposant à de multiples inter-férences. Ils pouvaient comparer les codes et aspirer, pour telle différence struc-turelle gênante, à une certaine convergence. C'est ce qui explique l'apparition de *lequel*, une forme souple articulée en genre grammatical, en nombre et, dans une certaine mesure, en cas, à la façon du paradigme latin (masculin/féminin : *qui/quae*; singulier/pluriel : *quem, quam/quos, quas*; nominatif/accusatif : *qui, quae/quem, quam*). Frustrés par le flou et l'incomplétude des avatars français (notre tableau 4.1) du relatif latin, ils ont ainsi trouvé une forme neuve, répondant à leurs attentes. *Qualis* employé pour *quis* relatif s'observe en latin médiéval (chez Bède, par exemple, au VIIIe siècle); *quel* adjectif relatif est attesté en français autour de l'an 1000 (deux exemples dans la *Vie de saint Léger*,[50] texte aux nombreux occitan-ismes). Mais l'élément central du relatif composé est l'article dérivé de *ille* (ce que prouve, dans les textes espagnols du XIIIe siècle, *el qui/el que* alternant avec *el cual* en relative avec antécédent). Les premiers exemples du dérivé de **ille qualis* dans les langues romanes apparaissent en langue d'oc,[51] quelques décennies avant nos textes anglo-normands.

La seconde caractéristique de l'anglo-normand pour la morphosyntaxe du relatif est mieux connue et souvent signalée : il s'agit de l'apparition précoce et du développement considérable de l'emploi de la forme *que* sujet animé (au lieu de *qui*). On a avancé plusieurs raisons pour ce passage de *qui* à *que*, la plus impor-tante et la plus convaincante étant l'abandon du cadre strict de la déclinaison bicasuelle.[52] L'anglo-normand est le premier dialecte à présenter cet emploi,[53] celui aussi où il est le plus répandu. Comme pour le relatif composé, c'est encore le manuscrit de Hildesheim qui offre la première attestation; on trouve, en effet, dans sa copie de la *Vie de saint Alexis*, le vers suivant :

49 Kunstmann, *Le relatif-interrogatif*, pp. 472–3.
50 Dans la structure à antécédent incorporé; il est attesté à la même époque, dans cet environnement syntaxique, en ancien occitan et en ancien italien: voir P. Kunstmann, 'Création et diffusion du relatif/interrogatif *lequel* en ancien français. Comparaison avec d'autres langues romanes', dans *Actes du XVIIIe Congrès International de Linguis-tique et de Philologie Romanes* publ. par D. Kremer (Tübingen, 1991), pp. 660–70.
51 À la fin du XIe siècle, dans la traduction de l'*Évangile de saint Jean*.
52 Kunstmann, *Le relatif-interrogatif*, pp. 206–7.
53 Si l'on excepte les textes à formes occitanes de la fin du Xe siècle, *Vie de saint Léger* et *Passion*.

... E la pulcele *quet* li ert espusede [v. 237][54]

occurrence escamotée par Storey, qui, dans son édition, corrige, sans état d'âme, en *quet il out* (c'est-à-dire un emploi objet direct), sans même mentionner cet escamotage dans le passage de son introduction consacré aux pronoms relatifs dans la langue du scribe. Les psautiers d'Oxford et de Cambridge en offrent d'autres exemples. Au XIIIe siècle, cet emploi se répand, en particulier dans les textes de théâtre; c'est la version de la *Sainte Résurrection* (milieu du siècle) conservée dans le manuscrit de Canterbury (écrit peu après 1275) qui en présente le plus d'occurrences : pour les relatives à antécédent, on y relève vingt-sept occurrences de *que* sujet contre une seule de *qui*. Au siècle suivant, dans *Fouke Le Fitz Waryn* (œuvre en prose du début du XIVe siècle, ms. de *c.*1335), comme le remarquent les éditeurs, 'the subject form of the relative, *qui*, has been completely replaced by *que, qe*'.[55] C'est aussi pratiquement le cas de la prose de Nicole Bozon : les vingt premières pages de ses *Contes Moralisés*, présentent trente-sept occurrences de *que* sujet contre simplement cinq de *qui*.

Je soulignerai, en conclusion, que les trois phénomènes étudiés, qu'on observe dans le français d'Angleterre dès la première moitié du XIIe siècle, sont reliés entre eux non tant par une relation de cause à effet que par une relation de nature : une tendance lourde à l'abandon du système des cas. Ce qui, dans le domaine du morphème relatif, produit deux résultats en apparence opposés, mais en fait complémentaires : d'un côté, une nouvelle variabilité (en genre grammatical et en nombre) avec le paradigme de *lequel* ; de l'autre, un penchant pour l'invariabilité avec *que* sujet animé, qui rentre dans le cadre plus général de *que* relatif universel.[56] Le français d'Angleterre est, dans ce domaine, en avance sur les dialectes du continent, ce qui en rend l'étude particulièrement importante pour les linguistes et les historiens de la langue.

English summary

This essay discusses three morphosyntactic features generally recognized as characteristic of Anglo-Norman: confusion between subject and object cases in nouns and adjectives, the early appearance of the relative/interrogative pronoun *lequel* and the increasing use of the pronoun *que* as subject.

Briefly reviewing theories about, and evidence for, the loss of declension (Storey, Schøsler, Buridant, Daniels), the essay argues against the theory of English-language influence as the cause of Anglo-Norman's loss of subject/object distinctions, pointing out that the same phenomena appear in Western continental dialects around 1200 and that the distinction is in fact not useful

---

54 Littéralement : '... Et la jeune fille *qui* lui était conjointe.'
55 *Fouke le Fitz Waryn*, éd. E. J. Hathaway, P. T. Ricketts, C. A. Robson et A. D. Wilshere, Oxford, ANTS 26–28 (Oxford, 1975), p. lxxxvii.
56 Voir Kunstmann, *Le relatif-interrogatif*, pp. 206 et ss.

n the great majority of instances, since other syntactic and contextual features preclude ambiguity. The loss of declension in insular French is to be seen not as a sign of confusion but of the innovative nature of Anglo-Norman, which often displays characteristics appearing only much later in continental French.

The essay then presents detailed evidence for the early occurrence of the relative/interrrogative pronoun *lequel* (together with its paradigm) in place of the Old French relative (*qui, que* etc.) in twelfth-century Anglo-Norman texts (for example, the prologue to the Hildesheim manuscript of *La Vie de saint Alexis* and the Oxford manuscript of the prose psalter, Bodleian Library MS Douce 320). *lequel* and its various forms are also deployed in Anglo-Norman as interrogatives (a use continuing to this day in modern French) and with more consistent use of subject and object cases than when *lequel* is used as a relative pronoun. Other twelfth-century psalter texts (the Cambridge psalter by the scribe Eadwine, the Orne psalter) continue to deploy the compound relative *lequel* (always in the position of relative with antecedent), as do some insular thirteenth-century texts but less frequently). The form remains very rare in continental French (though it is more frequent in some late twelfth-century didactic, administrative and juridical texts, notably in a group of didactic/religious works from Lorraine where Latin and French versions of the text are present together in the manuscripts). The appearance of *lequel* in insular texts, it is argued here, is an instance of code convergence in a diglossic situation. The crucial element in the development of the compound relative pronoun is the derivation of the article (*le* and forms) from the *ille* of **ille qualis* and the flexibility of use this bestowed.

The third Anglo-Norman feature, the use of the relative *que* for animate subjects instead of *qui*, has been often commented on: it is found in early and widespread use in Anglo-Norman. It is probably best seen as part of the abandonment of strict declension of subject and object. Again, the Hildesheim *Alexis* offers the earliest occurrence, closely followed by the Oxford and Cambridge Psalters, and subsequently by a widening array of thirteenth- and fourteenth-century texts (for example, *Fouke le Fitz Waryn* and Bozon's *Contes Moralisés*), to the point where the use of *que* is almost universal.

Taken together, these three features are related through Anglo-Norman's strong tendency to abandon the case system, even though this produces apparently contradictory results (flexibility in gender and number in the *lequel* paradigm and invariability in the use of the relative *que* for animate subjects). The French of England precedes continental French in this development and is thereby all the more important as a field of linguistic study.

5

'"Fi a debles," quath the king': Language-mixing in England's Vernacular Historical Narratives, *c.*1290 – *c.*1340

Thea Summerfield*

Historically and ethnically wide-ranging narratives like the extensively dissem-inated *Brut* chronicles in English and Anglo-Norman vibrate with countless largely implicit voices speaking a range of languages. The kings, their subjects and their enemies who people these works and speak in them – Trojans, Saxons, Danes, Normans, and many others, including people of different social status – do so most often, but not always, in the language of their authors, who themselves were writing at a time (the reign of Edward I) when the variety of languages in use in England was much discussed. The use of French especially had long been associated with political issues such as the hatred of Henry III's Savoyards, the fear of invasion from France, and the beginning of the Hundred Years' War.

This essay presents an investigative survey of the extent to which this variety in language is reflected in six *Bruts* written between *c.*1290 and *c.*1340, three in Middle English and three in Anglo-Norman.[1] I shall be concerned with the extent and effect of switches of language between English and Anglo-Norman or Latin in the utterances of individuals featured in these works, often presented by the author through direct speech. The decision to present an actor on the historical

---

* I should like to thank Ad Putter for his comments on an earlier version of this article

1 The following representative *Brut* chronicles are investigated in this essay: *The Metrical Chronicle of Robert of Gloucester*, RS 86, ed. W. A. Wright (London, 1887); Robert Mannyng's *Chronicle*, ed. I. Sullens (Binghamton NY, 1996); Thomas Castleford's *Chronicle or the Boke of Brut*, ed. C. Eckhardt, 2 vols., EETS OS 305 and 306 (London, 1996); *The Oldest Anglo-Norman Prose 'Brut' Chronicle*, ed. J. Marvin (Woodbridge, 2006); Rauf de Boun, *Le Petit Bruit*, ed. D. Tyson, ANTS Plain Text Series 4 (London, 1987); Pierre de Langtoft's *Chronicle*, ed. T. Wright (London, 1866); Pierre de Langtoft, *Le Règne d'Edouard* Ier, ed. J.-C. Thiolier (Paris, 1989). All references are to these editions by line number, unless otherwise stated. All references to Thiolier's edition of Langtoft are to his 'Rédaction II'. On the authorship of text and continuations of Robert of Gloucester's *Chronicle*, see O. Pickering, 'South English Legendary Style in Robert of Gloucester's *Chronicle*', *Medium Aevum* 70/1 (2001), 1–18. For a discussion of language-switching in the *Anonymous Short English Metrical Chronicle*, see my article in Putter and Jefferson, *Medieval Multilingualism* (forthcoming). For an account of the *Brut* and its Anglo-Norman manuscript tradition, see the essay by Marvin in this volume.

stage offered by these *Bruts* as switching to a language different from that in which the work itself is written – or alternatively to be consistently monolingual – is never an arbitrary one.

Authors in a multilingual society are constrained to write their works in the language of their target audiences who are likely to be, in sociolinguistic terms, members of the same speech community. However, as the sociolinguist Gumperz points out, '[M]embers of the same speech community need not all speak the same language. [...] All that is required is that there be at least one language in common and that rules governing basic communicative strategies be shared so that speakers can decode the social meanings carried by alternative modes of communication.'[2] If, therefore, authors include passages, phrases or words from other languages than their own, they need to be acutely aware of 'any limitations [that] the environment imposes on [their] choice of interactional strategies'.[3] However, language-switching may also be used as a literary tool. Thus a focus on language-mixing offers researchers possibilities for getting closer to the author's primary audience, but also for studying the effect of language-switching in a work as a whole or in a particular passage. In addition, the linguistic mixture – or the absence of mixture – within these texts may reveal insights into feelings of linguistic and resulting social inclusion/exclusion, of performance potential and of the assumed multilingual capabilities of the people for whom the work was first written.

The derivative nature of *Brut* chronicles may at first sight appear to make these texts an odd choice for such an investigation. However, although they all derive ultimately from the base texts of the *Brut* genre, Geoffrey of Monmouth's *Historia Regum Britanniae* and Wace's translation of that work, *Le Roman de Brut*, and are in essence translations, their authors work according to normal, medieval practice; that is, adapting, amplifying, abbreviating, elaborating – as well as often translating faithfully and skilfully – their source text(s) as they saw fit. They are *appropriators*, creating a new work for a new linguistic community. Their interest in linguistic matters is evident from their comments on the contemporary linguistic situation and their emphasis on the onomastic evidence of regime change. However, although they write with considerable freedom, they do so within the constraints of the generic tradition, which occasionally appears to govern the switches to a different language. Thus language-switching in *Brut* chronicles is often found in specific *loci*, notably on the occasions of Brutus' prayer to Diana and the goddess's answer, the meeting of the British king Vortigern and the Saxon princess Rowena, and the treacherous attack of the Saxons.[4]

In the description of Brutus' visit to Diana's temple,[5] prayer and answer may

---

2 J. J. Gumperz, 'Introduction', *Directions in Sociolinguistics: The Ethnography of Communication*, ed. J. J. Gumperz and D. Hymes (New York, 1972), p. 16.
3 Gumperz, 'Introduction', *Directions in Sociolinguistics*, p. 15.
4 Among the texts studied here, Rauf de Boun's *Le Petit Bruit* omits these episodes.
5 In Robert of Gloucester's *Chronicle* Brutus finds a prophesying, English-speaking idol in the temple (318–37).

be entirely in the text's overall language, whether that is Latin,[6] French,[7] or, in the later chronicles, English[8] or Anglo-Norman.[9] However, probably from a desire to add authenticity to the episode, Mannyng's chronicle in English inserts a two-line incantation by Brutus in Latin, while Diana speaks English in octosyllabic couplets.[10] In Langtoft's Anglo-Norman *Chronicle* both incantation and answer are given as six and eight lines respectively of elegiac Latin verse among the stately monorhymed *laisses* used by this author. However, Brutus' subsequent explanation in Anglo-Norman to his followers of what the goddess has said will have served to inform any non-Latinists in Langtoft's audience of the drift of the goddess's words.[11]

In the episodes relating the encounter of Vortigern and Rowena and in that of Hengist's treachery, almost all chroniclers follow Geoffrey of Monmouth in his use of the Germanic terms that these invaders are said to have used: Rowena's 'Lauerd king, wassheil' and 'drincheil', which need to be translated for Vortigern by an interpreter,[12] and Hengist's battle cry 'nimet oure saxas'.[13] In this way the contemporary way of proposing a toast, which, according to Castleford, was normal practice in England in the fourteenth century ('þis custom vses yitte þe housbandes / þorout Britaine')[14] was given ancient, 'English', roots. It was also frequently used, and exploited as such by authors, as a defiant (and riotous) identification of Englishness, especially when used among foreigners.[15] In the Anglo-Norman Prose *Brut*, however, the story of Hengist's treachery is very different.

---

6 Geoffrey of Monmouth, *The History of the Kings of Britain*, ed. M. D. Reeve, trans. N. Wright (Woodbridge, 2007), 18–21. Text and translation will be referred to as *HRB*.

7 Wace's *Roman de Brut. A History of the British*, ed. and trans. J. Weiss, 2nd rev. edn (Exeter, 2002), 633–702. In a later passage on naming the island, both Geoffrey and Wace mention that originally Brutus and his followers spoke Trojan (Geoffrey adds 'or Crooked Greek': 'troiana siue curuum greca'), but that this language was later called British. *HRB*, pp. 28–9; *Roman de Brut*, 1189–91.

8 Castleford's *Chronicle*, 1468–84; 1510–28.

9 Anglo-Norman Prose *Brut*, pp. 76–9.

10 R. Mannyng's *Chronicle*: 'Diua potens nemore terror siluestribus / apris. Cui licet amfractus', I, 1363–4, 1379–92.

11 Langtoft's *Chronicle*, ed. Wright I, pp. 12–13. Langtoft quotes Geoffrey of Monmouth, as does Robert Mannyng, possibly from Langtoft's *Chronicle*, as it was certainly in his possession, thus supplementing Wace's *Roman de Brut*, his exemplar for this section of his work.

12 *HRB*, pp. 128–9.

13 *HRB*, pp. 134–5.

14 See for this episode *The Oldest Anglo Norman Prose 'Brut' Chronicle*, p. 134; Langtoft's *Chronicle*, ed. Wright, I, p. 102; Robert of Gloucester's *Chronicle*, 2514–17; Castleford's *Chronicle*, 14184–5; 14144.

15 As, for example, by English students in Paris according to N. Longchamps' *Speculum Stultorum*, ed. J. H. Mozley and R. R. Raymo (Berkeley, 1960), 1521; King Richard I in *Der Mittelenglische Versroman über Richard Löwenherz*, ed. K. Brunner (Vienna, 1913), 6816; and the feasting English before the Battle of Hastings as described in *Le Roman de Rou de Wace*, ed. A. J. Holden, 3 vols., SATF (Paris, 1970–3), 7357–60, translated by G. S. Burgess as *The History of the Norman People: Wace's Roman de Rou* (Woodbridge, 2004), p. 173.

here, the knives are to be pulled from each man's boot when Hengist incongru-
usly says, 'Fair lords, now is the time to speak of love' ('Beaus seignurs, ore est
mps de parler de amour'; pp. 138–9).[16]

Although, as we shall see, chronicle authors often exploited for their own
ids the possibilities of England's complex linguistic situation, this was not a
ven; Thomas of Castleford does not introduce any French or Latin at all into his
ironicle of 39,500 words, not even, as we have seen, in episodes where this was
onventional. Even his rubrics are in English, which is unusual.[17]

In Robert Mannyng's *Chronicle* all language switches are towards Latin.
Iannyng, like Castleford, may have had a pedagogical purpose, but his manner
very different. He seems keen to share his linguistic interest with his audi-
ice, regularly explaining hard words and commenting on aspects of language
se: the proficiency in Latin of the messengers to Rome, Gawain among them
, 12214), the precise meaning of the toponym Cirencister and its equivalents in
nglish, French and Latin (I, 14084), the meaning of the name of Julius Caesar's
vord Crucia Mors (I, 4452), and many others. Longer stretches of Latin, like
ie anthem sung by St Augustine's followers, are translated in the immediately
illowing two lines,[18] but the simple benediction received by young Constant,
Christus vincit, Christus regnat; / Christus vincit, Christus imperat' (I, 6862–3) is
it. It is, however, stated specifically that these are Latin words (6861). Mannyng
so displays interlinguistic ingenuity, as when the Latin text of Psalm 43, *Deus
iribus nostris*, sung by Cawaladre and those of his followers 'þat lered were
..] with o tunge' (I, 15703–4) is cleverly integrated into the octosyllabic couplet
irmat of the *Chronicle* and woven into the action described:

> 'Deus auribus nostris' *hate* þat psalme   *is called*
> þat þei said for þat *qualme*;   *killing*
> at a verse þat is þerin,
> pleynt to gun (L: Pleynyng to god þus) þei bigyn:
> 'Vendidisti populum tuum sine precio',
> toward þer schippes þei song so.
> 'Dedisti nos tanquam oues escarum
> & cetera per totum psalmum'.   (I, 15705–12)[19]

In the English-language texts we find 'Nimeþ ʒour soxes' (Robert of Gloucester, 2658),
'Takis oute ʒour sexis whan I seie' (Mannyng, I, 7753), and 'Nimid our saxes!' (Castleford, 14,815).

R. Allen in T. Summerfield, with R. Allen, 'Chronicles and Historical Narratives', in
The Oxford History of Translation into English, ed. R. Ellis (Oxford, 2008), pp. 340–1.

'Deprecamur te Domine in omni misericordia tua / vt auferatur furor tuus & ira tua
/ a ciuitate ista & de domo tua / sancta quia peccauimus Alleluya.' ('Of mercie, Lord,
we pray þe, do þi wreth fro þis cite, & fro þi holy house alsua, for we have synned,
Alleluya'), I, 11457–64.

The relevant lines from Psalm 43 are lines 12 and 13; sections used by Mannyng have
been underlined: 43:12. '<u>Dedisti nos</u> quasi gregem ad vorandum et in gentibus disper-
sisti nos' ('Thou hast given us up like sheep to be eaten: thou hast scattered us among
the nations'); 43:13: '<u>Vendidisti populum tuum sine pretio</u> nec grandis fuit commutatio

Mannyng's incorporation of Latin suggests an audience associated with one ⸤ the houses of his Order, but without great proficiency in Latin.[20] French is virtu ally absent, with the curious single instance of one short French phrase in direc speech in the single surviving manuscript for this part of the story: 'Þe kyn said on hie: "Symon, ieo vous defie!"' (II, 5322).[21] Perhaps it is an echo of a son that was sung about Simon de Montfort, who became a popular martyr after hi death at the Battle of Evesham in 1265.[22]

Linguistic aspects of the Barons' War led by Montfort certainly play a part i Robert of Gloucester's *Chronicle*, which has Latin rubrics and includes Frenc phrases prominently in a small number of passages. The use of French is ofte found in terms of address or common phrases.[23] My first example is taken fro an episode in the reign of William Rufus. Rufus's personality is described i violently negative terms by the chronicler: Rufus destroyed abbeys and prie ries, was wicked, foolishly extravagant, and never had mercy on anyone; he i said to have acted 'as a tirant tormentor in speche & ek in dede' (8005). Thi opinion is consistent with that in the sources used for this episode: the Peterbor ough manuscript of the Anglo-Saxon Chronicle, William of Malmesbury's *Ges* *Regum Anglorum* and Henry of Huntingdon's *Historia Anglorum*. To illustrate an emphasize the king's prodigality Robert of Gloucester borrows the followin exemplum from William of Malmesbury:[24]

---

20 eorum' ('Thou hast sold thy people for no price: [and there was no reckoning in th exchange of them]').

20 Suggestions as to Mannyng's audience have ranged from master of novices (R. Crosb 'Robert Mannyng of Brunne: A New Biography', *PMLA* 57 (1942), 15–28 (p. 27)); baron (T. Turville-Petre, 'Politics and Poetry in the Early Fourteenth Century: The Case ⸤ Robert Manning's *Chronicle*', *Review of English* Studies, n.s. 39 (1988), 1–29); lay brother and 'the mixed, rural community centred around a Gilbertine house' (T. Summerfiel *The Matter of Kings' Lives: The Design of Past and Present in the Early Fourteenth-centur Verse Chronicles by Pierre de Langtoft and Robert Mannyng* (Amsterdam, 1998), pp. 144– (p. 146)); and guests in houses of the order (Joyce Coleman, 'Handling Pilgrims: Robe Mannyng and the Gilbertine Cult', *Philological Quarterly* 81 (2004 for 2002), 311–26 Some of these suggestions need not be mutually exclusive.

21 This is a translation, with direct speech added, from two lines in the Langtoft MS B (B Royal 20 A.xi) used by Mannyng. Cf. 'Þe kyng said on hie: "*Symon, ieo vous defie!*" Edward was hardie, þe Londres gan he ascrie' (II, 5322/3) and 'Le dragon est levé, ⸤ rei le quens defie / Sir Edduard, fiz le rays, les Loudrays escrye' ('The dragon is raise the king defies the earl; Sir Edward, the king's son, gets sight of the Londoners'), e⸤ Wright, II, pp. 142–3.

22 See C. Valente, 'Simon de Montfort, Earl of Leicester, and the Utility of Sanctity in Thi teenth-century England', *JMH* 21 (1995), 27–49. The phrase is not used in the Angl⸤ Norman 'Lament of Simon de Montfort' in T. Wright, *The Political Songs of Englan* (London, 1837), pp. 125–7.

23 In a number of cases French terms of address (Madame, Damaisele) are used, alway exclusively for persons of high social status, like Queen Maud (8968), the girl wh bargains with King Henry I before accepting his illegitimate son Robert of Glouceste as her husband (8892, 8902), and King Arviragus' daughter (1492).

24 In William of Malmesbury's story it is boots that are bought; the exchange is entire in Latin. The chamberlain is there called 'fili meretricis' ('you son of a bitch'). Willia

One day William Rufus's chamberlain brings the king a new pair of hose to wear:

> He esste wat hii costnede – þre ssillinges þe oþer sede.
> *Fi a debles* quaþ þe king – wo sey a so vil dede
> King to werye eny cloþ – bote hit costnede more
> Buy a peire of a marc – oþer þou ssalt acorie sore
> A worse peire of inou – þe oþer suþþe him broȝte
> & sede hii were of a marc – & vnneþ so ibouȝte
> ȝe *belamy* quaþ þe king – þes were wel iboȝt
> In þis manere serue me – oþer þou ssalt me serue noȝt.

He asked what they cost; three shillings, the other said. 'Go to the devil,' said the king, 'who ever saw anything so demeaning as a king wearing any clothing unless it was more costly than that? Buy a pair [of hose] worth a mark, or you shall regret it sorely.' The other then brought him a worse (quality) pair, worth quite enough, and said they had cost a mark, and that he had barely had enough to buy them. 'Yes, indeed, *fair friend*,' said the king, 'these were well bought; serve me in this manner, or don't serve me at all.'

> (8014–21; my italics)

What prompted the author to add the French phrases? They are too ordinary to attribute to a source, and virtually self-explanatory: no real knowledge of French is needed to understand the phrases – a mere recognition of them as being, or, perhaps as important, as sounding French would suffice.[25] Both are in frequent use in English contexts in the Middle Ages. *Fi a debles* gives a marked quality to the king's swearing and characterizes him as violent and forceful. The original French meaning of *bel amy* and its negative connotation in English usage as a way of addressing inferiors held in contempt[26] here converge to express the king's approval of his servant at the same time as the contempt in which the author holds the king.

The use of French thus enhances the contrast between the high social position of the king and the low level of his morality, integrity and common sense. It also, of course, gives the story greater credibility and authority; here we hear the king actually speaking in his own language – if only for a few phrases that suggest, however, that the complete exchange was in French.

Rufus was not the only historical figure that roused the author to anger – and

---

of Malmesbury, *Gesta Regum Anglorum. The History of the English Kings*, ed. and trans. R. A. B. Mynors, completed by R. M. Thomson and M. Winterbottom, 2 vols. (Oxford, 1998), I, 556–9.

25 '*Bel amy*' is used elsewhere to suggest that French is being spoken; see, for example, *Richard Löwenherz*, ed. K. Brunner, 3276.

26 The MED glosses *bel-ami* as '(a) fair friend; *iron.* rascal, knave; (b) in direct address [often to enemies or inferiors as an expression of contempt]: fair friend.' According to the OED the term was used as a form of address until 1596 (in Spenser's *Fairie Queen*); the form 'pseudo-bellamy' was recorded as late as 1689.

to French. The empress Maude, too, is consistently presented as a hateful person, who threw good nobles into prison (9480), but whose worst crime seems to have been, in the eyes of the author, that she was a woman ambitious to be *maistre* of all (9487). Fortunately, says Robert, the people recognize her wickedness and turn against her. The author adds that once she had returned home (i.e. to Anjou) she might talk how she liked of the king's coronation: 'segge *si haut si bas*' (9499), implying the futility of it. The French phrase clearly adds scorn and a malicious delight in her defeat.

Another notable occurrence of French again concerns a person of whom the author does not approve. It concerns a bishop who became the butt of public indignation during the time of active rebellion against King Henry III's Savoyard favourites in Gloucestershire, about which Robert of Gloucester is well informed. He records how the 'freinss' bishop of Hereford, Peter d'Aigueblanche ('Sir peris de egeblaunche', 11111] is dragged from before the altar and thrown out onto the street, before being imprisoned. The bishop remonstrates with his attackers: '*Par crist* he sede *sir tomas tu es Maveis* / *Meint ben te ay fet*' (11119–20; my italics).[27] The meaning of the last part of the sentence is obliquely explained by the author in the next line: 'vor he adde muche god / þer biuore him ido' (11120–1) (for he had done him much good before that time), especially, the implication is, in a material sense, as another of the king's foreign and grasping favourites. The French put in the bishop's mouth here is not that of a Savoyard speaking continental French, but the French of England in which *ie* has been reduced to the single vowel *e* in 'ben', and 'fait' has become 'fet'.[28] By the time the chronicle was written, the whole event had become a legendary episode within the story of Simon de Montfort and the Baronial Revolt.

In his *Chronicle* Robert of Gloucester shows himself a partisan of Simon de Montfort as the leader of the Baronial Revolt, a position that at the time of writing marks him as defying royal censure and writing for a regional and popular audience.[29] The attack on 7 June 1263 on Peter of Aigueblanche, the Savoyard bishop of Hereford, in his own cathedral had been instigated by Montfort as the first of a series of attacks on Savoyard favourites of Henry III and Queen Eleanor. Aigueblanche, in the popular mind, was held responsible for the rise in taxes and the fear of French invasion following Henry's aspirations in Sicily.[30] It was the first, but not the last of a series of attacks on Henry's royalist, French-speaking supporters

---

[27] Robert of Gloucester states that this 'tomas' was the spy [Thomas] Turberville. Turberville's activities as a spy in 1295 aroused great popular indignation, even giving rise to an Anglo-Norman political song (I. S. T. Aspin, *Anglo-Norman Political Songs* (Oxford, 1953), pp. 49–55). However, at the time of the baronial revolt reported here by Robert of Gloucester, Turberville was still a staunch royalist serving in the retinue of John Giffard (M. Prestwich, 'Turberville, Sir Thomas de (d. 1295), soldier and traitor', *ODNB*).

[28] See E. Einhorn, *Old French. A Concise Handbook* (Cambridge, 1974), p. 137.

[29] Valente, 'Simon de Montfort'.

[30] On the 'Sicilian Business', see M. T. Clanchy, *England and its Rulers 1066–1272* (London, 1983), pp. 235–40.

high places; as Robert of Gloucester states: 'So it ferde oueral. ware me freinsse
nd' (11126) [It was done like this everywhere, where people found Frenchmen/
ench speakers]. The bishop was imprisoned, with his 'alien' canons, in a castle
arby. His castle in Shropshire was sacked, its constable killed.[31] But what was,
erhaps, considered to be his worst crime of all was that, after having lived in
ngland for some twenty-five years, Aigueblanche was reputedly still unable to
eak the English language.[32]

It should be noted that, at the time, the resentment of this stubborn unwilling-
ess to learn the language of the country that fed him was not just a popular senti-
ent or limited to this one person. In one of his biblical commentaries Thomas
ocking, lector of the Oxford Franciscans in the years 1262–5, also fiercely
nsured foreign prelates, who knew 'neither the manners nor the language of
e country'.[33]

These instances of French in an English text hardly allow of assumptions of the
rimary audience's proficiency in French; they are largely self-explanatory, even
ore so in a spoken than in a written context. However, some elementary know-
dge of French was necessary and taken for granted, and its use in high circles
exemplified by the language switch. The use of French in negative portrayals
llies with the general complaints in Robert of Gloucester's *Chronicle* concerning
e use of French, which, according to Robert, handicapped English speakers
cially and forced them to learn a language that he presents as alien, *vnkunde*
537–47). However, it is not so *vnkunde* that he cannot deftly deploy it as a partic-
lar register in his representation of illegitimate or overweening authority.

Taking the three Middle-English chronicles together, it should be noted that
one is motivated by 'antiquarian sentiments' or a desire to underline 'English-
ess' through a preferred, 'English' vocabulary. Words of French origin are used
roughout without authorial comment. Remarkably, in particular in those places
here a perceived sense of oppression of ethnic and linguistic Englishness is
pressed in these works, whether as a result of 'the Normans' or of 'the aliens',
at is, Henry III's Savoyard favourites, the terminology of discontent is decid-
lly francophone. Words typically used in this context are *bondage, taliage* (taxa-
on) and *servage*. These terms are also found, for example, in the Anglo-Norman
emonstrances of 1297, and in the document called *De Tallagio non Concedendo*,
so of *c*.1297, the first a written statement of grievances, among them the maltolt
ax) on wool, the second a repetition of the earlier grievances with protests about
1 attempted extra tax added.[34] Finally, *bondage* is Middle English dressed up as
nglo-Norman; it occurs in a number of Anglo-Norman contexts, again of the

J. R. Maddicott, *Simon de Montfort* (Cambridge 1994), pp. 226–35.
N. Vincent, 'Aigueblanche, Peter d' [Peter de Aqua Blanca] (d. 1268), bishop of Here-
ford and royal councillor', *ODNB*.
Quoted, with references, by Maddicott, *Simon de Montfort*, p. 254 and n. 120.
M. Prestwich, *Edward I* (London, 1988), pp. 420–8; see also Summerfield, *The Matter of
Kings' Lives*, pp. 198–9.

end of the thirteenth century.[35] What has been seen as a polemic of nationalism in these works, based on their expressions of racial and linguistic unity among the oppressed original inhabitants, is thus undermined by the very words used in that polemic. It is Anglo-Norman that provides the terminology for the tool of oppression used by those in power, the 'heie men' who, according to Robert of Gloucester, are the direct descendants of the invading Normans.[36]

What we find, then, is an English language in which French words have been completely assimilated, while snatches or quotations of French, if they are introduced at all, are of the most basic sort. However, they are never used arbitrarily – they are always applied to achieve a particular effect. Some knowledge of French, or at least recognition of French as a negatively marked language, lies at the basis of Robert of Gloucester's exploitation of the French phrases used. For other chroniclers in this period French and French speakers would appear not to be part of their audience's daily experience. Robert Mannyng introduces Latin words and phrases, but always takes great care to explain their meaning fully. These, then, are largely monoglot texts for a largely monoglot, provincial audience (North Yorkshire, the West Country, Lincolnshire), but not necessarily an uneducated audience or one unfamiliar with the other languages in use in England. Their authors, however, are skilled, trilingual author/translators. Indeed, as Rosalind Field has remarked, 'a monolingual author is something of an improbability throughout this period'.[37]

Turning now to the *Bruts* in Anglo-Norman prose, it can be said at once that the two prose texts, the so-called *Oldest Anglo-Norman Prose* Brut *Chronicle* and Rauf de Bohun's *Petit Bruit* yield very few passages in English or Latin, however brief.

Rauf de Bohun's *Petit Bruit* was written for Henry de Lacy, earl of Lincoln, in 1309. In the text, which bears little resemblance to any of the other chronicles discussed here, legends connected with the Danish invasions, Lincolnshire and Edward's claim to Scotland feature prominently. There is as strong a sense of 'us' (or rather: 'nous') versus 'them' in the *Petit Bruit* as there is in the English verse chronicles, the only difference being that, while 'nous' signifies the English, 'they' are Danes, not 'Normans'. A number of English expressions are used in the narrative, such as the word 'Hounhere', an army raised to chase away the Danes: 'grant host qe home apelloit Hounhere' (p. 16/26);[38] Athelstane is referred

---

35 See the *AND* for *bondage*.

36 Robert of Gloucester, 7583, 7540. See also T. Turville-Petre, *England the Nation: Language, Literature, and National Identity, 1290–1340* (Oxford, 1996), pp. 91–8.

37 R. Field, 'Romance in England', in Wallace, *Medieval English Literature*, pp. 152–? (p. 153).

38 D. Tyson, the text's editor, glosses the word as 'a collective name for men and women rebelling against Harthaknut' (*Le Petit Bruit*, p. 2). If *houn-* can be taken to equal Old English *un-*, the meaning would be 'wicked, evil army', as in *uncræft*, evil practice, or *undæde*, wicked deed, crime. It is the only instance of the word in the *AND*, where is marked as Middle English; on the practice of including first or rare occurrences of foreign words in dictionaries, see Trotter in this volume.

to with an English nickname: 'with gilden kroket', a kind of hat or hair-do (p. 14/37), and the word used for 'tribute' is Middle English: 'gersume' ('cinq cent liveris d'argent, qi mult feu hault gersume') (p. 7/40) or, in connection with the Normans, 'certaine gersune' (p. 18/31).

In the *Oldest Version of the Anglo-Norman Brut*, which, according to its recent editor Julia Marvin, was composed in Anglo-Norman around the end of the thirteenth century (p. 1), there is no question of disaster befalling Britain, socially or linguistically, in 1066; the Conquest is the result simply of Harold being stingy, proud and arrogant, while William the Conqueror 'regna noblement' (pp. 240–1). Among the kings listed are two with English nicknames: Edmund Ironside and Harold Harefote. The latter's name is explained by referring to his lightfootedness ('si leger hom a pe [lightfooted] qe hom le appela Harefot', pp. 222–3) but neither epithet is given a literal translation. Changes over time in place-names are recorded in a matter-of-fact way, without emotive anxiety or misgivings. On the other hand, the reign of King John, with the loss of lands, the interdict, the institution of Peter's Pence and Magna Carta, is related in detail and with passion. It is here also that we encounter three words in Latin. They are spoken by Pandulf, a papal legate in the reign of King John: '"Nous vous diroms," fet Pandulf, "in verbo dei, qe vous [...] iames outre cest iour pust estre coronee."'[39] The bias in this *Brut* suggests, as Julia Marvin states, baronial interest or provenance. The text makes a detached, factual impression. The author may not have known English, although he must have known Latin, the language of many of his sources.

If the prose *Brut* largely lacks passion, Langtoft's *Chronicle*, written c.1307–8, has it in abundance. The most widely disseminated of the verse chronicles, it survives in twenty-one extant manuscripts, nine of which, all of Northern origin, are complete, while six of these were written before 1350.[40] One, BL, Royal 20 A XI, containing the complete text from Brutus to the death of Edward I, was given to Robert Mannyng to translate within thirty years of its completion. It is rightly famous for the inclusion of a number of raucous songs in Northern English dialect celebrating the defeat and slaughter of the Scots in the reign of Edward I. The *Chronicle* was not Langtoft's first history in verse: earlier, in 1300, he had versified the correspondence between the Scots, Edward I and Pope Boniface VIII of 1300 on the question of the legality of Edward's claim to Scottish overlordship.[41] Both the English and the Scottish side gave their letters the form of a mini-*Brut*, listing examples of homage or independence from the country's

---

39 '"We tell you," said Pandulf, "*in verbo dei*, that you ... may ever from this day forward be crowned"'; pp. 274–5.
40 For detailed descriptions of the manuscripts, see J.-C. Thiolier, 'Description et Analyse des Manuscrits', in *Le Règne d'Édouard Ier*, pp. 35–148.
41 For the versified correspondence, also known as Langtoft's 'Political Letters', see Thiolier, *Le Règne d'Édouard Ier*, pp. 459–83. See also T. Summerfield, 'The Testimony of Writing: Pierre de Langtoft and the Appeals to History, 1291–1306', in *The Scots and Medieval Arthurian Legend*, ed. R. Purdie and N. Royan, Arthurian Studies 61 (Cambridge, 2005), pp. 25–42.

mythical foundation to the present. Langtoft, in other words, had had some experience of fashioning legendary history for political purposes when he started on his *Chronicle*, which he also wrote with a political aim in mind: to promote a unity of purpose in the struggle against the Scots on a number of levels.[42]

In his *Chronicle* Langtoft makes full use of the eye- and ear-catching effects of changes of rhyme, metre and language: the text itself is written in mono-rhymed *laisses*, an epic style suitable for subjects of national importance and for entertainment, but it also includes semi-documentary material in a variant form: Henry II's will, an example of generosity to the Church, is given in rhymed couplets, while the terms of John Balliol's homage are given in prose. In a performance situation especially, this change in the metrical form of the *laisses* will have given these episodes due emphasis. The work has a great deal of direct speech – which would also enhance performance – and a huge cast: the work's popularity may well be due to the large number of powerful people named in it who could afford to commission a copy of their own.

Even though it is written in Anglo-Norman for a high-status public, Langtoft's *Chronicle*, like the verse chronicles in English, deplores the Norman Conquest and resulting *servage* and *langour*. Langtoft thus strengthens official policies based to a certain extent on scaremongering about possible future invasions, but he does not add the complaints found in the verse chronicles in English, linking a sense of the loss of status and language with the Norman Conquest or with French speakers in general.

English is found, as we have seen, in the conventional places (Brutus' prayer, the arrival of Rowena, Hengist's treachery), but also in the famous words shouted by the decapitated King Edmund's head in English: 'here, here, here!' (ed. Wright, I, 312). This was an iconic *English* king, whose story may have been known to many in the audience; by using the actual words the miracle gains in credibility and wonder, while the king's Englishness is enhanced.[43]

Of the nine so-called political songs two are in Anglo-Norman, three in a difficult, Northern, dialect, and four are mixed: that is, they begin in Anglo-Norman and have stanzas in English added to them. English never precedes Anglo-Norman, and the songs are not macaronic. All of them concern the Scottish wars at the end of the reign of Edward I. The Anglo-Norman songs are not 'popular' songs, even though they have been given that appearance: they are composed of stanzas of three short lines with two heavy stresses, rhyming aab/ccb. The song quoted below provides an example of an Anglo-Norman song, the *b*-rhyme of which is integrated into the *laisse* (on é), while the last line leads on to the next *laisse*:

---

[42] Summerfield, *The Matter of Kings' Lives*, pp. 15–98.

[43] In Longchamps' *Speculum Stultorum*, ed. Mozley and Raymo, the saint's severed head is also recorded as shouting 'her, her', 2136.

Pur le grant honur ke Eduuard le sené
Fist à Jon Bayllof, tel est la bounté
Dount li rays Eduuard / Du ray Jon musard / Est rewerdoné.
De Escoce sait cum pot; / Parfurnyr nus estot / La geste avaunt
parlé.   (ed. and trans. Wright, II, 222; ed. Thiol. 645–52)

(For the great honour which Edward the wise / Did to John Balliol,
such is the goodness / With which king Edward / By king John the
fool / Is rewarded. / Of Scotland be it as it may, / We must continue
/ The history *that we were telling*.)[44]

The English songs are similarly integrated, betraying a certain amount of manip-
ulation, as in the sequence where, following a *laisse* in *–ayt*, we find an Anglo-
Norman song of four stanzas in the pounding rhythm of the popular English
songs, the *b*-rhyme still in *–ayt*, to be followed in its turn by a two-stanza song
in Northern English dialect, with the *b*-rhyme on *–ayt* still intact:

Ore armez vus, si aloums, nul alme se retrayt.
De nos enemys / Kant serount pris / Mercy nul en ait.
[…]
On grene / That kynered kene / Gadered als gayt;
I wene / On summe it es sene / Whar the byt bayt.
                            (ed. Wright II, 244; ed. Thiol. 921–2)

(Now arm yourselves, and let us go, let no soul hold back. / Of our
enemies, / When they shall be taken, / Let no one have mercy. […]
On *the field* / that sharp race / are gathered like goats; / I *think
[that]* / on some it is seen / where *the blade landed*.)

The rhyme on *–ayt* is thus preserved throughout, despite the language change.
Whether Langtoft fashioned his *laisse* around the existing English song, or
changed the words of the English song to suit the Anglo-Norman *laisse*, is a
chicken-and-egg question. That it is a *tour de force* cannot be denied. It is likely
that the section of the *Chronicle* containing these songs was performed at some
festive occasion. The festivities after the knighting of Edward of Caernarvon in
1306, intended to spur newly knighted men on to fight in Scotland, would offer
a plausible venue for such a performance. Unfortunately, however, festivities at
this time are rarely, if ever, reported in anything but the most conventional or
borrowed terms, and so far this must remain speculation.[45]

This survey of the presence or absence of language-switching in the vernacular chronicles in prose or verse, English or Anglo-Norman, written in the half
century between, roughly, 1290 and 1340, has shown that some authors make use

[44] Here, and below, the asterisks denote modifications of Wright's translation.
[45] For further examples and discussion, see my articles 'The Political Songs in the *Chronicles* of Pierre de Langtoft and Robert Mannyng', in *The Court and Cultural Diversity*, ed.
E. Mullally and J. Thompson (Cambridge, 1997), pp. 139–48, and 'The Testimony of
Writing', pp. 25–42.

of the varied linguistic situation in England, enhancing their spiritual message by the addition of Latin, or the political message by the use of French in English and English in French contexts. Such other-language additions may be no more than a few words as well as larger pieces of text that have been cleverly integrated. However, a monolingual history was clearly also an option, depending on the social class targeted; some audiences seem to have preferred their histories entirely in English, others entirely in Anglo-Norman. The authors themselves had linguistic competences in three languages in the case of the English works and at least two (French and Latin) in the case of authors writing in Anglo-Norman. Language-switching was, and always is, a deliberate choice, and as such warrants our attention. Authors might exploit its possibilities to display their linguistic and poetic skills, as Mannyng and Langtoft did, or to give extra force to a political attack aimed at a particular linguistic community. However, even if it concerns nothing more than having an unpopular king swear in French in front of an English audience, it is always done for effect, and always provides information by the way in which it makes the voices of the past and of trilingual England explicit.

6

Uses of French Language in Medieval English Towns

Richard Britnell

The use of French in medieval English towns has no simple explanation. Amongst highly born and better-educated members of English society, French was known as a high-status, international language of conversation, and as a means of access to literature of high quality. In the king's courts it was also an argot of common lawyers, and continued in use as a written language after it had ceased to be spoken in the courts.[1] An explanation of these phenomena in terms of the sociology of social stratification, symbolic representation and social closure would seem to present few problems. But these considerations come nowhere near explaining why French should have been used in the business of urban communities, whose membership was not drawn from the aristocratic or better-educated classes of society, on the whole, and most of whom spoke nothing but English.

Like their counterparts in the shires, urban elites made use of another non-native language, Latin, as the principal language of administration. Their most burdensome task was the management of borough law-courts, and some English boroughs began using written records to keep track of judicial business early in the thirteenth century. The Wallingford rolls date from the 1230s. We have enough surviving evidence to suppose that the keeping of borough court rolls became increasingly widespread during the course of the later thirteenth and early fourteenth centuries.[2] The normal language of all this legal recording was Latin, and this continued well into the early modern period.[3] Most urban financial accounts, like manorial accounts, were similarly compiled in Latin. The best published series, that of the chamberlains of York (1396–1500), shows that throughout the period clerks stuck to Latin as the language of accounting.[4] Both

---

[1] J. H. Baker, *Manual of Law French*, 2nd edn (Aldershot, 1990), pp. 1–6.

[2] G. Martin, 'English Town Records', in R. H. Britnell, ed., *Pragmatic Literacy East and West, 1200–1330* (Woodbridge, 1997), pp. 122–5.

[3] For example, *Leet Jurisdiction in the City of Norwich during the XIIIth and XIVth Centuries*, ed. W. Hudson, Selden Society 5 (London, 1892); *The Making of King's Lynn: A Documentary Survey*, ed. D. Owen, Records of Social and Economic History, n.s. 9 (London, 1984), pp. 409–14, 419–21; *Records of the Borough of Crossgate, Durham, 1312–1531*, ed. R. H. Britnell, Surtees Society 212 (2008); *Selected Rolls of the Chester City Courts, Late Thirteenth and early Fourteenth Century*, ed. A. W. Hopkins, Chetham Society, 3rd series 2 (Manchester 1950).

[4] *York City Chamberlains' Account Rolls, 1396–1500*, ed. R. B. Dobson, Surtees Society 192 (1980). See, too, *Selected Rentals and Accounts of Medieval Hull, 1293–1528*, ed. R. Horrox,

legal recording and accounting were taught skills, with definite formal requirements, and clerks were trained to use Latin for the purpose. The same is true
of routine conveyancing and the writing of other legal instruments. Among the
seven hundred such documents from medieval Coventry there is only one in
French. That is a grant by John de Hastings, lord of Abergavenny, to the prior
and convent of Coventry, authorizing them to acquire property in his fee; in
other words, it is a document that has nothing to do with urban society, and
was destined for a nobleman's archive.[5] On the basis of surviving documentation
we can state, without ambiguity, that Latin was the language of routine formal
recording. This was the language clerks were primarily expert in. There is no
reason to suppose that they found it easier to compose in French; the converse is
more likely to be true.

What languages did town clerks use for preference when they were not
engaged in routine work? There is good evidence that it was usually Latin. A
suitable subject of enquiry for this purpose is the language of the utilitarian notes
and factual memoranda written by clerks into borough registers, often for their
own convenience or edification. Some of these are transcripts of formal instruments and other texts of unknown origin, and the clerk who copied them was
merely preserving the language of the original. But less formal texts created
opportunities for a clerk to choose his language. The index of the Colchester
Oath Book, for example, is in Latin.[6] A lengthy note on recognized allowances
from the borough fee farm due at Westminster is also in Latin, and so are various
antiquarian notes, including a note on the legend of King Cole and the early
history of Colchester, and a rental of properties paying rents to the community
in 1387–8.[7] However, the most persuasive examples of the preference for Latin
in the Colchester registers are the Colchester chronicle composed by the town
clerk in the years 1372–9 and the notes on current affairs written by Michael
Aunger, the town clerk of the period 1380–98. The chronicle – a rare survival
of such literary activity – is written in rather ornate Latin by a town clerk who
evidently fancied his stylistic ability.[8] Michael Aunger's products are briefer and
less pretentious, but are nevertheless in Latin – such as his note on the constitutional dispute of 1394–5, and his note – unfortunately mostly lost – on the Peasants' Revolt of 1381.[9] Even the fifteenth-century Coventry Leet Book, published
by the Early English Text Society because of the large amount of English material

Yorkshire Archaeological Society Record Series 141 (1983), pp. 27, 53–60, 91–109, for
Latin chamberlain's accounts in Hull in 1321–4 and 1464–5.

5 *The Early Records of Medieval Coventry*, ed. P. R. Coss (London, 1986), no. 743, pp. 338–9.
6 So is the index of the Little Red Book of Bristol: *The Little Red Book of Bristol*, ed. F. B.
   Bickley, 2 vols. (Bristol, 1900), I, 2–7.
7 Essex Record Office, Colchester Branch, Colchester Oath Book, fols. 3v–4, 11–18, 20,
   158–69v.
8 Colchester Oath Book, fols. 22v–23v; Essex Record Office, Colchester Branch, Colchester
   Red Paper Book, fols. 5r–1–v.
9 Colchester Oath Book, fols. 20 and 20v, 24, 158–70; Colchester Red Paper Book, fols.
   12, 257v.

contains, has numerous Latin texts, and the clerical memoranda to be found ere are in Latin rather than French.[10] Two of its few French texts are transcripts letters received from Westminster.[11] French, it seems, was not something that erks ordinarily slipped into because it came more naturally. It may even be that oroughs had to employ specialist clerks to compose texts in French for them. ur task is essentially to enquire what those purposes were and, more problem- ically, to explain why French was used at all.

The borough of Colchester has two large medieval registers, one on parchment nd one on paper, both begun in the later fourteenth century.[12] These between em contain only eleven texts in French, comprising less than one per cent of the urteenth- and fifteenth-century material in the registers. Of the eleven texts, six e transcripts of documents that originated outside the borough – two parlia- entary statutes, two royal ordinances, a receipt for the borough fee farm and a adly decayed text that seems to be some newsletter or the like recording Richard 's creation of new nobility in 1397. That leaves only five French texts created in e borough. Two of these are texts (from 1382 and purportedly from 1256) of a roclamation concerning Colchester's rights in the River Colne. The proclama- on was made from time to time 'in Colne Water', so presumably read from a oat. The longest text contains the borough ordinances that established the New onstitutions of 1372, a major document registering new rules concerning the ructure, composition and election of borough government. There is a reworking this text, similarly in French, from about 1410. The only other French document a set of borough ordinances of 1411–12. The Colchester evidence is quite unam- guous that French was used for texts that needed to be publicized – proclama- ons and ordinances. From time to time the burgesses were required to swear uphold the New Constitutions of 1372, together with other borough customs, nd the constitutions were to be read out openly every year before the burgesses efore each election.[13] So far as the record goes, that was the only use of French y the borough administration. It is worth noticing that though the Colchester gisters went on being used long into the Early Modern period there are no rench documents after 1412.

The Coventry Leet Book, ed. M. D. Harris, 4 vols, EETS OS, 134, 135, 138, 146 (London, 1907–13), I, 54–7, 61–71, 73.

The Coventry Leet Book, I, 74–5, 122–5.

The only editions of the Colchester registers are in translation, and so do not serve the purpose of this essay: *The Red Paper Book of Colchester*, ed. W. G. Benham (Colchester, 1902), and idem, *The Oath Book or Red Parchment Book of Colchester* (Colchester, 1907). For these records, see also R. H. Britnell, 'The Oath Book of Colchester and the Borough Constitution, 1372–1404', *Essex Archaeology and History* 14 (1982), 94–101.

'As queux ordeignaunces bien et lealment et perpetuelment tener, ordeine est qe toutz les burgeys reseiauntz soient iures de temps en temps qant il bonement puit estre feat, et toutz les burgeys qe serrount feat en temps auener soient iures de tener et meintener les ordeignaunces desusescriptes sibiein come les vsages et ffraunchises de la ville, et qe cestes ordeignaunces auauntditz soient lus ouertement deuant la comune dan en an au comencement del electioun auantdit.': Colchester Oath Book, fol. 23v.

The Black Book of Winchester, a second small sample, contains ten Frenc texts and, though the variety is rather greater than those from Colchester, th conclusions to be drawn are not greatly different. There are again ordinance in French[14] and the texts of documents from outside the borough.[15] Some of th Winchester texts are letters and documents sent out of the borough – an oath c loyalty to Richard II, a petition to the king and his council, and two petitior to the mayor of London.[16] These are unlike anything in the Colchester sampl but they show that French was an appropriate language for external corresponc ents of high social status. A minor difference from Colchester is that, unlike th recorded oaths taken by borough officers in Colchester, which are recorded i Latin, the oath of the mayor of Winchester is recorded in French.[17] Again, as i Colchester, the register continued to be used for centuries, but there is no Frenc text after one of the petitions to the mayor of London in 1411.

In the Little Red Book of Bristol by far the majority of French texts are boroug ordinances, which dominate the latter part of the register.[18] The many that ai dated show that they concentrate in the period 1346–1419. Most are craft regula tions, but there are also ordinances relating to elections to office, admissions t the freedom, the imprisonment of borough officers and borough liveries.[19] Othe types of document are weakly represented, but they included examples from a the categories we have already observed. There are letters to and from the king, and the oaths of borough officers.[21]

The York Memorandum Book has a richer variety of French texts than th registers we have looked at so far, but does not greatly change the conclusions t be drawn. As elsewhere there are a few texts from outside the borough, includin some of Richard II's statutes.[22] As at Winchester, there is correspondence i French with outsiders of high status.[23] French was also used for oaths; the oat of the escheator of York, of 1398, is recorded in French.[24] However, the princip use of French is again for ordinances, of which there are a great number, partic ularly to regulate the various city crafts. Some are dated, all but one from th period 1375–1416.[25] Most of them, though, are composite productions in whic

14 *The Black Book of Winchester*, ed. W. H. B. Bird (Winchester, 1925), pp. 7–8, 33.
15 *The Black Book*, pp. 19–20, 25–6, 47.
16 *The Black Book*, pp. 5–7, 12–13, 16–17, 28.
17 *The Black Book*, pp. 2–3.
18 *Little Red Book*, I, 110–13; II, 6–22, 26–32, 36–44, 46–9, 51–5, 59–61, 64–7, 71–89, 93–12 135–43.
19 *Little Red Book*, II, 46–9, 55, 64–7.
20 *Little Red Book*, I, 115–26, 134.
21 *Little Red Book*, I, 46–56, 103.
22 *York Memorandum Book*, ed. M. Sellers, 2 vols., Surtees Society 120 and 125 (1912–15 I, 37–9, 214–16; II, 57, 87–8, 113–14, 117.
23 *York Memorandum Book*, I, 36; II, 57–9, 213–14, 236–8.
24 *York Memorandum Book*, I, 252–3.
25 *York Memorandum Book*, I, 16–17 (1375); I, 17–19 (1377); I, 20 (1378); I, 39–40 (1380); I, 4 (1385); I, 41–2 (1388); I, 41 (1389); I, 42 (1389); I, 52–4 (1395); I, 106–8 (1405); I, 211–1 (1416); II, 199 (1455).

ordinances of different dates are strung together. This accounts for some mixed-language texts. Seven clauses of the glovemakers' ordinances are in Latin and three in French. Six clauses of the capmakers' ordinances are in French (undated) but two fifteenth-century clauses are in English. Similarly the earlier clauses of the saddlers' ordinances are in French, the later ones in English.[26] Essentially the conclusion to be drawn is as before: French was a favourite language for ordinances during the fourteenth and early fifteenth centuries, but was otherwise of limited use in the internal administration of the borough. The only substantial body of material in the Memorandum Book of a type not encountered in the smaller boroughs is legal. There is a short treatise on aspects of common law procedure and another on the customs of the city of York.[27] These represent a use of French to codify local custom that is akin to the professional use of French by common lawyers, and instructors in the common law, as a suitable language for legal treatises, like Britton (*c.*1291), 'Fet asaver' (date uncertain), 'La Corone pledee devant justices', 'Novae narrationes', and other legal texts from the thirteenth century onwards.[28] The distinction between ordinances and these codified texts hinges on the presence or absence of words implying a decision; ordinances contain the words 'est ordeigne' ('it is ordained') or something similar, and imply a decision taken by a particular body on a particular day, whereas codified texts list rules in force without any statement of their origin. A comparable use of French for codified local customs is found in a number of towns, such as the Anglo-Norman custumal of Exeter, composed in *c.*1240, or the gild merchant regulations of Reading and Southampton.[29]

On turning from provincial boroughs to London, and in particular the *Liber Albus*, it is immediately apparent that the use of French is more extensive even than in York. Yet the content is largely what might be predicted from our earlier examples. All four types of record known from Winchester occur here; there are texts received from outside the city,[30] letters sent from the community,[31] and the oaths of city officers.[32] In London, though, the influence of French as the professional language for lawyers is even more prominent than in York, and the process of codification here has proceeded further. There are many more texts than elsewhere that record customs without any reference to the process of deciding or

[26] *York Memorandum Book*, I, 48–50 (glovemakers); I, 77–8 (capmakers); I, 88–91 (saddlers).

[27] *York Memorandum Book*, II, 143–5, 251–66.

[28] *Britton: The French Text*, ed. F. M. Nichols, 2 vols. (Oxford, 1865); *Four Thirteenth-Century Law Tracts*, ed. G. E. Woodbine (New Haven CT, 1910), pp. 53–115; *Placita corone or La corone pledee devant justices*, ed. J. M. Kaye, Selden Society, supplementary volume 4 (London, 1966); *Novae narrationes*, ed. E. Shanks, Selden Society 80 (1963).

[29] *The Anglo-Norman Custumal of Exeter*, ed. J. W. Schopp, History of Exeter Research Group 2 (Oxford, 1925); C. Gross, *The Gild Merchant*, 2 vols. (Oxford, 1890), II, 204–7, 214–31.

[30] *Munimenta Gildhallae Londoniensis*, ed. H. T. Riley, 3 vols. in 4 parts, RS 12 (London, 1859–62), I, 367–8, 371–3, 377–85, 387–91, 505–18.

[31] *Munimenta Gildhallae Londoniensis*, I, 408–9, 418–33.

[32] *Munimenta Gildhallae Londoniensis*, I, 306–19, 527–8.

ordaining. Some texts in this category are in part the codification of past ordinances, even though they do not say so, which explains why sometimes a single document switches randomly from French to Latin and back.[33]

So far the discussion has concerned the use of French by urban administrations. The pattern of documentary survival dictates that there is more evidence for this than for other urban linguistic practices, and many forms of private urban record-keeping have left little trace. One use of French by townspeople is so bound up with the formal pattern of social hierarchy that it can only be regarded as dictated by considerations of formal etiquette. French was employed, perhaps normally, as a language in which burgesses petitioned the mayor and council of the city. A series of Bristol craft regulations between 1406 and 1419 were initiated by petitions in French from the craftsmen in question – fullers, dyers, skinners, cordwainers, tanners, weavers, barbers, hoopers – and those petitions were transcribed into the Little Red Book, in some cases directly preceding the texts of ordinances that were also in French. Since there is no reason to suppose that writing in French came easily to the craftsmen themselves, they probably employed a clerk for the purpose. The choice of French rather than Latin or English implies that a vernacular language was appropriate for the purpose of petitioning (and French seems to have been the established language, certainly for parliamentary petitions, from the thirteenth century onwards).[34] In 1418 and 1419 the clerk who copied out petitions and ordinances added a Latin narrative to contextualize the documents in question; the language of the petition and the ordinances is distinguished from the language of clerical professionalism.[35] Some even more striking juxtapositions of different languages come from the following decade. Two petitions in French from the cordwainers, dating from 1425 and 1429, were each recorded with a Latin preamble and followed by a Latin postscript to say that the petition had been accepted by the mayor and council, who agreed to its terms; there are no ordinances as such. The hoopers' petition of 1439, in French, is even more noteworthy. In this case ordinances were drawn up following the petition and their preamble was in French, but the ordinances themselves were compiled in English. They were followed by a concluding narrative in Latin.[36] In the Coventry Leet Book there is a petition of 1384 in French from the master of the Trinity Guild to the mayor and officers of Coventry asking for permission to hold fields in severalty. Here, too, the French petition is sandwiched into a Latin narrative.[37] Individuals, too, used French as a language of petition. The *Liber Albus* has the text of a petition in French presented to the mayor, aldermen and commons of London early in 1376, asking for justice against usurers.[38] This type of record was probably much more common than meets the eye from the number of surviving

---

33 *Munimenta Gildhallae Londoniensis*, I, 358–61, 368–71, 417, 457–67, 470–8, 494–6, 519–27.
34 See the essay by Ormrod in this volume and idem, 'Use of English'.
35 *Little Red Book*, II, 117–22, 135–41.
36 *Little Red Book*, II, 144–50, 159–66.
37 *Coventry Leet Book*, I, 3–4.
38 *Coventry Leet Book*, I, 394–5.

xamples, and the Bristol evidence suggests that French remained a preferred nguage for urban petitioners after it was being abandoned for other purposes.

Another example of the use of French outside city government proper relates the records of the London craft companies, and fits awkwardly with some the conclusions to be derived from formal borough records. The wardens' ccount books and minute books of the Goldsmiths' Company were in French om 1334 to the fifteenth century, when French was gradually replaced by Latin nd English; the Grocers used French as a normal language of routine record ntil 1428, the Drapers till 1436, the Merchant Tailors till 1445 and the Mercers ll 1459.[39] This use of French needs more exploration. It seems out of line with ne normal practices of either manorial or urban recording, and perhaps should ot influence too heavily the conclusions drawn so far. It may be a status matter the context of London society – a claim to be identified with aristocratic and rofessional legal coteries.

In short, then, if we except transcripts of incoming documents, French is used r six principal purposes. Among urban administrations it was used (1) as an ral language suitable for proclamations and ordinances, (2) as an oral language uitable for the taking of oaths, (3) as a language of recognized high status for ommunicating with external authorities such as the king and council, (4) as professional language for legal texts and the codification of custom; among wnspeople more broadly it was used (5) as a polite language in which towns-eople devised written petitions to present to urban authorities, and (6) as an dministrative language of ostentatiously high status outside the principal stitutions of government. Three of the six uses of French (3, 4, 6) involve the nguage as a symbol of status, either of social rank, or of city rank, or of profes-onal rank, and a fourth use, for petitions (5), implies that French was required y borough protocol as a mark of appropriate respect towards mayors and coun-illors. Although the use of French for ordinances and oaths (1 and 2) may have ad a certain symbolic or ritual value, it is seemingly more difficult to account r, given the practicalities of borough administration. Ordinances were charac-eristically directed at ordinary workers and tradesmen, and needed to be under-tood by them if they were to take effect, and oaths had to mean something to the eople who swore them if they were not to be an invitation to perjury.

The widespread preference for French for framing urban ordinances, and for rmulating oaths of allegiance, implies a very particular cultural context that avoured French as a spoken language even though it was not the mother tongue f its writers or hearers. The need for vernacular texts of some kind is not difficult explain. The communal organization of English boroughs in the thirteenth and urteenth centuries made an increasing number of urban authorities answer-ble to some degree to burgesses, and they all needed from time to time (annu-lly in some places) to proclaim publicly formal administrative acts of general

---

* *Wardens' Accounts and Court Minute Books of the Goldsmiths' Mistery of London, 1334– 1446*, ed. L. Jefferson (Woodbridge, 2003), p. xxviii.

concern, such as new bye-laws. Latin, though the language of routine, was
learned language, acquired only through schools. It was spoken in ecclesiastic
and academic contexts, but in few others among the laity, and there is no reaso
to suppose that even grammar school boys were happy speaking it or hearing i
spoken, any more than they would be today. Latin was functionally at home a
a language of record, where it scored over others by the exceptionally standard
ized form of its vocabulary, spelling and grammar, but it foundered as a spoke
language because, essentially, hardly anyone could be expected to understand i
spoken. It was not generally useful for texts that were written to be read in publi

The seemingly obvious language for this purpose was, of course, English, bu
that was not how urban authorities saw the situation. In some contexts Englis
was indeed adopted as townspeople became increasingly inclined to keep writte
records. English was used, for example, in many of the guild statutes returned t
Richard II in 1389.[40] So many sorts of record have been almost wholly lost that i
is impossible to generalize confidently about how much English was written b
English merchants and mercantile bodies for their private purposes; the chance c
records in English surviving was reduced to the extent that they were of privat
or ephemeral status, so the available evidence for written linguistic usage i
heavily skewed. Yet surviving urban records of the fourteenth century leave littl
doubt that English was rejected as an official language even where it would hav
seemed the most rational choice. Many Europeans had become used from at leas
the thirteenth century to employing their own vernacular languages for mor
formal purposes, such as legislation. But in England the long-established use c
French among governing and administrative classes tended to make French th
vernacular of record and of officialdom until late in the medieval period, even i
documents aiming at the general public. The town crier called 'Oyez! oyez!', no
'Hear ye! hear ye!' It is in this context that we can place texts that were writte
in French. French had the advantage over Latin of being a currently spoke
language but, since only a minority of the population read and spoke it, its adop
tion for public use can be explained only in terms of strong cultural habits an
associations.

A sign of the institutionalized preference for French rather than English i
formal documents, well attested throughout the administrative record of medi
eval England, is the use of a French definite article in place of an English on
before place-names and English words for which a clerk knew no Latin equiva
lent, a convention that required the use of three languages in three consecutiv
words. In the Crossgate borough records from Durham in the 1490s, for example
we find such phrases as 'venellum ducens ad le Westorchard', and 'burgagi
jacencia in Sowthstreit in Dunelm super le Estraw'. In 1502 it was alleged that .
housebreaker 'prostravit lez propez et silez ac injuste cepit le bark', and in 1506 .
plaintiff claimed cloth 'pro le jakett inde fiendo'. The French article might be use

---

[40] *English Gilds*, ed. T. Smith, EETS OS 40 (1870).

to substitute for an English word even where no article was required, as in the order given to a burgess in 1503 'quod mundat unum le gutter'.[41]

Maybe the official use of French is sometimes to be interpreted as a Machiavellian device to conceal public business from the general body of burgesses while seeming to address them, but it is difficult to see what borough authorities would have gained by such a ploy if they really wanted to pass on information and put their ordinances into effect. In those circumstances at least, the meaning of the French would surely have to be explained in English, even if the English was not written down. References to any such translation are few, but we have perhaps an example from Colchester in 1373, when the retiring bailiffs 'according to custom' read out and published their ordinances and expounded them to the community 'in the mother tongue' (*in materna lingua*).[42] It is difficult to understand 'mother tongue' as anything other than English, but unfortunately it is not known what language the ordinances in question were translated from.

This use of French was largely abandoned in the fifteenth century, even though the language continued to be used for legal treatises into the early modern period. In Colchester and Winchester, as we have seen, French fell out of use at about the time that Henry V claimed the throne of France, and in Bristol its use had greatly declined by the 1420s. From then on borough authorities were more likely to use English for ordinances, and so avoided the need to have texts glossed after they had been proclaimed. The earliest English ordinances in Colchester are a preamble in the hand of Thomas Rypere, town clerk 1407–14, a gild ordinance of 1418, and ordinances of 1424–5, all more or less coinciding with the abandonment of French.[43] The use of French seems to have peaked around 1350–1415, to be replaced by English quite rapidly after that period. This less inhibited adoption of English was a development for which the earlier use of French was in fact preparatory. A widespread increase in the amount of regulatory activity is a well-observed feature of late medieval urban government. As the need increased for borough officers to publish formal texts accessible to ordinary burgesses, the use of French became increasingly onerous and it rapidly became more customary to write in English in the first place, rather than first write in French and have the text explained. In this way long-standing cultural conventions submitted to the logic of bureaucracy and practical convenience.

---

[41] Durham Cathedral Muniments, Crossgate Courtbook, 1498–1524, fols. 20v, 23v, 42v, 57, 90v. For further discussion of this phenomenon, see D. A. Trotter, 'Bridging the Gap: The Socio(linguistic Evidence of some Medieval Bridge Accounts', and L. Wright, 'On London Mixed Language Business Writing and the Singular Definite Articles *le* and *la*', in Ingham, *Anglo-Norman Language*.

[42] *Colchester Red Paper Book*, fol. 6.

[43] *Colchester Red Paper Book*, fols. 23v–24v, 43, 65v–66v.

7

The French of England in Female Convents: The French Kitcheners' Accounts of Campsey Ash Priory

Marilyn Oliva*

Administrative documents from English medieval female convents are relatively rare. Household accounts – those kept by household officers, or obedientiaries such as treasurers, cellarers and sacrists, for example – which detail their annual income, expenses and supplies that suggest a monastery's internal operations survive for only twenty-seven convents – about twenty per cent – of the 132 female houses in medieval England.[1] Most of these accounts are either fragments, single documents or survive in pairs, date from the late fourteenth to the sixteenth centuries and are in Latin or English. Only about a third have been published.[2] By contrast, significantly more accounts survive – and have been

*   I would like to thank Maryanne Kowaleski and Jocelyn Wogan-Browne for their invaluable input to this essay.

1   To date the convents for which superiors' accounts survive are: Blackborough, Carrow, Marham (Norfolk); Bungay, Campsey Ash, Redlingfield (Suffolk); Catesby, Stamford St Michael (Northampton); Chestnut, St Mary de Pré (Hertford); Grace Dieu (Leicester); Elstow (Bedford); St Helen's Bishopsgate, St Mary Clerkenwell, Syon Abbey (Middlesex); and Swaffham Bulbeck (Cambridge). The obedientiary accounts that survive include treasurers, sacrists and cellarers from: Barking (Essex); Amesbury, Lacock, Wilton (Wiltshire); St Helen's Bishopsgate, Syon (Middlesex); Carrow, Marham (Norfolk); Campsey Ash (Suffolk); Canonsleigh (Devon); Harrold (Bedford); Grace Dieu (Leicester); Marrick (York); Nuneaton (Warwick); Stainfield (Lincoln); St Radegund's (Kent); and Wherwell (Hampshire).

2   Unpublished accounts are known from at least ten houses: Bungay, Campsey Ash, Carrow, Catesby, Elstow, Marham, Redlingfield, Stainfield, Stamford St Michael and Syon. Most published accounts from female houses are calendared or printed in the Victoria County History (hereafter *VCH*) or in *Monasticon Anglicanum*, ed. W. Dugdale, 8 vols. in 6 (London, 1817–40). For fragmentary accounts, see E. Critall, 'Fragment of an Account of the Cellaress of Wilton Abbey, 1299', *Wiltshire Archaeological and Natural History Society* 12 (1956), 142–56: R. B. Pugh, 'Fragment of an Account of Isabel of Lancaster, Nun of Amesbury, 1333–4', in *Festschrift zur Feier des zwei-hundejährigen Bestandes des Haus-, Hof- und Staatsarchivs*, Bd 1, ed. L. Santifaller (Vienna, 1949), pp. 487–98; G. D. Gilmore, 'Two Monastic Account Rolls', *Publications of the Bedfordshire Historical Record Society* 49 (1970), 41–55; D. N. Bell, *What Nuns Read*, *s.v.* Lacock, p. 146. For the fifteenth-century prioress's account from St Mary de Pré, see Dugdale, *Monasticon*, III, 353–61. I refer to other unpublished and published accounts below.

published and mined for all aspects of male monastic society and economy – for medieval England's roughly 7,000 male houses of monks and canons.[3]

The survival of eight household accounts, which run sequentially from 1298 to 1303, from a relatively modest convent of Augustinian canonesses, Campsey Ash Priory, in the county of Suffolk – part of the diocese of Norwich – is thus a great boon.[4] Though the nuns who kept these accounts do not identify themselves with a specific office, the content of their accounts indicates that these nuns were kitcheners, those who supplied the nuns' kitchens with food.[5] While superiors and other obedientiaries – particularly the cellarers – also contributed to a convent's larder that fed, and clothed nuns, and their guests and employees, kitcheners were the obedientiaries who bought food specifically for the nuns' consumption.[6] The information these Campsey Ash accounts can yield, then, is invaluable for our growing knowledge of medieval nuns' lives – especially their diets – and some of their management practices.[7] The accounts are also signifi-

A conservative estimate based on the tables in D. Knowles and R. Neville Hadcock, *Medieval Religious Houses, England and Wales* (Harlow, 1971), pp. 489–92. Not only are there significantly more male houses for which obedientiary accounts survive, but they are also in better shape; tend to cover several years, or even generations of monks and canons; and have more frequently been published. For some examples, see *Extracts from the Account Rolls of the Abbey of Durham, 1303–1541*, ed. J. Fowler, 3 vols., Surtees Society 99, 100, 103 (London, 1898–1901); *Account Rolls of the Obedientiaries of Peterborough*, ed. J. Greatrex, Northamptonshire Record Society Publications 33 (Northampton, 1984); B. Harvey, *The Obedientiaries of Westminster Abbey and their Financial Records, c.1275 to 1540* (Woodbridge, 2002); for the information these documents can offer about monastic life, see B. Harvey, *Living and Dying in England, 1100–1540: The Monastic Experience* (Oxford, 1993).

Four Campsey accounts cover an entire year; another four record income and expenses for periods of ten or six months. They are held in the Suffolk Record Office, Ipswich Branch (hereafter SRO), HD 1538/174 (in this essay further identified, in chronological order, as a–h). They were compiled by Joan de Corpusty (1298–9); Avelina de Ludham (four accounts for ten months from 29 September 1299 to 25 July 1300; 1299–1300; six months from February to August 1300–1; six months from August to March 1300–1); Elizabeth de Melton (three accounts for six months each in 1301; 1301–2; 1302–3).

On obedientiaries in female houses, see E. Power, *Medieval English Nunneries* (Oxford, 1921), pp. 131–4, and for a list of obedientiaries from Romsey Abbey in 1502 including the kitchener's office, ibid, p. 132.

Cellarers, the primary provisioners of monasteries, bought food, but also other goods: see: L. J. Redstone, ed., 'Three Carrow Account Rolls', *Norfolk Archaeology* 29 (1946), 54–91.

For nuns's diets, see D. K. Coldicott, *Hampshire Nunneries* (Chichester, 1989), pp. 75–82, and for editions, Redstone, 'Three Carrow Account Rolls', pp. 41–88; the Syon cellarer's account of 1537 (*Myroure of Oure Ladye*, ed. J. H. Blunt, EETS ES 19 (London, 1873), xxviii–xxxi) and the account of the Barking cellaress's duties printed in *Monasticon*, I, 442–5 (a more accurate edition and commentary is A. Barratt's, 'Keeping Body and Soul Together: The Charge to the Barking Cellaress', unpublished paper, used with kind permission of the author). Accounts and discussions of cellarers not yet used for nuns' diets include the National Archives, Public Record Office [hereafter PRO], PRO, SC6/HVIII/927–9 (Barking, sixteenth century); PRO, SC6/1106/21 (Syon, 1453 and 1455); PRO, SC6/1106/ 12–25 (twelve mid to late fifteenth-century cellarers' accounts).

cant because they are the only kitcheners' accounts from a female house that have come to light, and they are the earliest intact accounts we have from any English female house.[8]

While these accounts are therefore intrinsically significant, they are typical in form and content of those that monks, canons and secular householders produced in Latin and English.[9] The accounts list sources of income, itemize expenses and provide monetary amounts for each. But what distinguishes these kitcheners' records from all other extant nuns' household accounts – and also most comparable monks' and secular householders' – is that they are written in French.[10]

These accounts thus provide us with a unique opportunity to discuss several issues pertinent both to the use of French in England and also to our understanding of female monastic life. The structure and form of the accounts themselves can tell us how language was used by these late thirteenth-century nuns and suggests they may have been at least bilingual. Their use of French, and other languages, moreover, can be supported by the contents of their library. And while scholars have long recognized that nuns and monks could understand French, the issue of class has clouded discussions of its use by nuns. While the form of the accounts can shed light on the use of French in female houses, their contents can yield information about the nuns' social status. What the nuns ate for example, can tell us about their social status in the late thirteenth and early fourteenth centuries. Their social rank and their practical use of French place both the nuns and their household accounts in the context of other contemporary business agents and the records they kept as analyzed by Richard Ingham, William Rothwell and Laura Wright.[11]

The Campsey Ash accounts follow a typical pattern in layout and content. They begin with the obedientiary's name and the dates the accounts cover. 'Sunt les akuntes dame eliz de melton pur le jour seynt michl le apostle del an le rey Edward xxxi deske le jour seynt berthlem procheyn sovant' ('These are the

---

[8] The next earliest account is the Wilton fragment of 1299: see above n. 2.

[9] For male monastic household accounts, see, for example, Flower, 'Obedientiares' Accounts', passim; Harvey, *The Obedientiaries of Westminster Abbey*, passim, and the editions listed above, n. 3. For secular household accounts, see K. Mertes, *The English Noble Household, 1250–1600* (Oxford, 1988), pp. 87–8; and *Household Accounts from Medieval England*, ed. C. M. Woolgar, British Academy Records of Social and Economic History, new series 17–18, 2 vols. (Oxford, 1992–3), passim.

[10] As mentioned above, other extant household accounts from female houses are in either Latin or English. Most male monastic household accounts are in Latin. Mertes and Woolgar note that French is sometimes used in large secular households: Mertes, *The Noble Household*, p. 14; Woolgar, *Household Accounts*, II, 585–8, 588–91 (French), 592–60? (Latin, French, English).

[11] R. Ingham, 'Mixing Languages on the Manor', *Medium Aevum* 78 (2009), 80–97 (seen in typescript with the kind permission of the author); L. Wright, 'Bills, Accounts, Inventories: Everyday Trilingual Activities in the Business World of Later Medieval England' in Trotter, *Multilingualism*, pp. 149–56; and Rothwell, 'Sugar and Spice'.

accounts of Dame Elizabeth de Melton, from the feast of St Michael the Apostle in the thirty-first year of King Edward to the feast of St Bartholomew in the following year'). Elizabeth's income is entered in two sections, one called '*rentes*', the second, '*comune receyite*', communal or common receipts. Rents come from manors, parish churches and tenants, whose names include the articles *de* or *le*: *de* for place-names, *le* for professions. So, for example, Elizabeth collected 2s. 4d. from John de Biskele, and 3s. 4d. from Simon del Roche, and 4s. from '*la femme le barbur*', and 12d. from '*William le taylur*'.[12] Common receipts are payments made to this office by various people – in this case the prioress – and money made from the sale of hides, livestock and agricultural products – here calves and pigs – and in an earlier account, cheese: '*receten de fromage venduag'me*' (received from cheese sold).[13] Elizabeth's rents section concludes with '*la sum x libri xs. ixd.*', and her common receipts section with '*la sum vix libri, vis. id. ob*', and totals of both amounts: '*tote le receyte xxvi libri xvis. xd. ob*'.

The second section includes her expenses. These are divided into two main sections, '*comun depen*' – common or communal expenses – and then those for food: '*char*', '*pesoun*' and '*payn*' (meat, fish and bread), sometimes accompanied by '*offs*' (eggs).[14] In this year, then, Elizabeth purchased, '*xi carcoys de bof, bouet, egeur; 2 M 9 C and 2 mil 9 c de harang*' and various amounts of ling, codling, mackerel, oysters and whelks; '*e en payn, vd., en dim libr de saffron and iii libr de comin iiis. vjd*'.[15] Each section of expenses ends with amounts spent. A debt is noted at the very end of two of the eight accounts; otherwise these kitcheners do not subtract expenses from income as do most other monastic or secular household officers.[16]

Though the structure and layout of the accounts incorporate conventions established in Latin such as the kitcheners' use of Roman numerals for money

12 SRO, HD 1538/174 h (1302–3).

13 SRO, HD1538/174 c (1299–1300).

14 In two of the accounts, '*offs*' is included in the bread section: SRO, HD 1538/174 c (1299–1300), and SRO, HD 1538/174 g (1301–2). In SRO, HD 1538/174 f (1301), the entry heading is bread, saffron, cumin and eggs: '*payn*', '*saffran*', '*comyn*', e '*offs*'.

15 The totals were thus eleven carcasses of beef, bull, heifer; 2,936 herring, 704 redfish, and 72 mackerel and 5d. for bread, half a pound of saffron and 4 pounds of cumin for 3s. 6d. See R. Zupko, *A Dictionary of Weights and Measures for the British Isles: The Middle Ages to the Twentieth Century* (Philadelphia, 1985), pp. 80–3 (for C weight variations), 105–6 (for Mil).

16 The sum still owed or debt is noted at the end and in the lower right-hand corners of both of Melton's accounts: SRO, HD 1538/174 f and h (1301) and (1302–3). For the calculation of income and expenses in other household accounts, see Redstone, 'Three Carrow Accounts', p. 73 (nuns); Flower, 'Obedientiaries' Accounts', p. 51; Harvey, *The Obedientiaries of Westminster Abbey*, p. xl, and *Account Rolls*, ed. Greatrex, pp. 40, 98, 162 (monks); also *Extracts from the Account Rolls*, ed. Fowler, vol. 2, 372, 483. For secular accounts, see Mertes, *The Noble Household*, p. 88; *Household Accounts*, ed. Woolgar, II, 451, 581–2; L. Jefferson and W. Rothwell, 'Society and Lexis: A Study of the Anglo-French Vocabulary in the Fifteenth-Century Accounts of the Merchant Taylors' Company', *ZfSL* 107 (1997), 273–301 (p. 280).

and for quantities of items bought, and of suspensions and abbreviations,[17] the matrix language here is French, with a few examples of code-switching between it and English.[18] Almost all of the vocabulary of the accounts is French, and the use of *del* in a place-name, as in Simon *del* Roche, a common abbreviation in medieval French.[19] Though English words – mutton, whelks, mackerel, oysters, saffron, cumin, and, in other accounts, haddock, congers and rays – crop up without a French definitive article – an indicator of code-switching, especially when preceding a technical term – their appearance in these accounts suggests a couple of possibilities. One is that the kitcheners used English words for items bought locally, as the monks of Durham Abbey did in their contemporary Latin accounts.[20] Most of the fish that the Campsey Ash kitcheners purchased probably came from the nearby ports of Great Yarmouth and Wisbech via local vendors.[21]

Another perhaps more intriguing possibility for the use of English words in these French accounts mirrors what Richard Ingham sees in contemporary manorial accounts: evidence of bilingual professionals who conduct business in French but use English with their employees. Ingham posits that in a manorial context where French was used as a language of business management, 'inter-

---

[17] For Roman numerals in French accounts, see Jefferson and Rothwell, 'Society and Lexis', p. 276.

[18] Or, as Laura Wright would say, French is the prestige language of these accounts: L. Wright, 'Trade between England and the Low Countries: Evidence from Historical Linguistics', in *England and the Low Countries in the Late Middle Ages*, eds. C. Barron and N. Saul (New York, 1995), p. 171. But she might disagree with this assessment of code-switching because she also maintains that the 'enmeshing of medieval Latin or Anglo-Norman by abbreviations and suspensions' should be seen 'as a functional variety in its own right', not necessarily as a sign of code-switching ('Bills, Accounts, and Inventories', p. 151).

[19] Ingham, 'Mixing Languages', pp. 87, 91.

[20] Rothwell found that while French was used by the monks at Durham for imported products, they used English for items locally produced ('Sugar and Spice', p. 654). Though the Durham accounts are in Latin and Rothwell is looking at French and English intrusions into it, it is possible that the Campsey Ash kitcheners used English in this way. While some of these words can also be read as French (*saffron, cumin, congers* and *welkes*, for example), the assimilation of Anglo-Norman content words by the English language made them, as Rothwell notes, cease to seem French, so that what was French to one generation was English to the next: the point being that it is 'virtually impossible to state categorically in many cases whether a word is intended to be French or English', ibid, p. 659 and with reference to L. Wright's 'The Records of the Hanseatic Merchants: Ignorant, Sleepy, or Degenerate?', *Multilingua*, 16 (1997), 335–50 (p. 349). Rothwell's and Wright's insights seem to apply more to fifteenth-century documents, and I would argue here that because of the obvious French of the rest of the accounts, the appearance of English words for fish means they are to be read as English words, despite some shared etymologies between the two languages.

[21] J. C. Bond, 'Monastic Fisheries', in *Medieval Fish, Fisheries and Fishponds in England*, ed. M. Aston (Oxford, 1988), pp. 69–112 (pp. 78, 81); also, A. Saul, 'The Herring Industry at Great Yarmouth, c. 1280–1400', *Norfolk Archaeology* 38 (1981), 33–43. Among Melton's common expenses in her previous account (SRO, HD 1536/174 g, dated 1301–2), is the cost of carting herring but she does not say where from.

ersed with English technical terms', one can see traces of 'the ordinary working
actices of the monolingual English-speaking agricultural workers' and their
ench-speaking bosses.[22] He also sees the appearance of English content words
ithin French manorial accounts as, '... chunks of bilingual discourse' in which
e matrix language was French, with a switch to English for some items of
chnical vocabulary.[23] Though the fishmongers were not agricultural workers,
id the kitcheners not their bosses, a relationship of exchange existed between
e two in that one paid for and recorded the costs of the goods and services of
other, much like the dealings between a manorial agent and a laborer. And
ough names of fish are not strictly speaking technical terms, they are specific
ntent words that local English-speaking vendors would have known and used
hen selling the nuns their fish.[24] It is also possible that the kitcheners might
ve recorded what their vendors said in English because it was easier and faster
write down than the French or Latin equivalents.[25] The linguistic characteris-
s of these accounts thus indicate that the Campsey kitcheners used French as
business language with English words interspersed, suggesting that, like their
anorial, male monastic and merchant contemporaries, the nuns were bilin-
al.[26]

The possibility that at least some of the nuns at this convent were conver-
nt in several languages can be corroborated by their possession of manuscripts
at contained French as well as English and Latin works, two of which had a
ench *ex-libris* inscription.[27] One of these manuscripts is a collection of twelfth-,
irteenth- and early fourteenth-century saints' lives probably put together at

Ingham, 'Mixing Languages', p. 85.

Ibid, p. 84.

L. Wright, 'Some Morphological Features of the Norfolk Guild Certificates of 1388/9: An Exercise in Variation', in *East Anglian English*, ed. J. Fisiak and P. Trudgill (Cambridge, 2001), pp. 79–162. Wright is dealing with Norwich specifically but she mentions (p. 100) that a high density of English-speakers and language contact existed there in part because of the proximity of active ports, including Great Yarmouth (a probable port for the herring the kitcheners at Campsey Ash bought; see above, n. 21).

Wright, 'Trade between England and the Low Countries', pp. 169–79 where she notes that 'the advantages to this mix' [of French and English, or Latin and French] are that it is 'quick to read and write and took up little physical space' (p. 171) and that 'this mix was geographically flexible and recognizable by all parties', i.e., those who heard and wrote the accounts (p. 176).

Ingham, 'Mixing Languages', pp. 88–9; Rothwell, 'Sugar and Spice', passim, though he concludes that the Durham monks, at least later in the Middle Ages, were trilingual; and Wright, 'Trade between England', passim.

These French *ex-libris* inscriptions are from the fourteenth and fifteenth centuries. For other personal inscriptions by Campsey nuns in their manuscripts, see Bell, *What Nuns Read*, pp. 123–6. These details indicate not only a reading population of nuns, but also suggest the presence of a library: see M. Oliva, *The Convent and the Community in Late Medieval England* (Woodbridge, 1998), pp. 67–9. For other documents from Campsey Ash, see n. 60 below.

Campsey Ash for the nuns.[28] It is particularly noteworthy for the fourteent
century French inscription at its close which reads, *'ce livre <est> deviseie a
priorie de Kampsie de lire a mangier'*: 'this book (is) given to or is designed for tl
priory of Campsey for reading at mealtime'.[29] While scholars have debated tl
exact meaning of this inscription, both Wogan-Browne and Russell argue that
suggests communal reading.[30]

The accounts and manuscript holdings of Campsey Ash thus indicate that,
in the case of their male monastic colleagues, French was a language Campsey
nuns were accustomed to using for both practical documents and literary man
scripts in the late thirteenth and early fourteenth centuries.[31] Barbara Harvey, f
example, has looked at the administrative documents of Walter of Wenlock, abb
of Westminster Abbey from 1283 to 1307, and found that while those pertaini
to the relationship between the abbot and his community were written in Latir
as were his contemporary household accounts – his writs and ordinances for tl
abbey were written in French.[32] William Rothwell uses the household accounts
the monks of Durham Abbey to show how French was used in commercial, eccl
siastical, monastic, municipal and legal spheres in medieval England througho
the Middle Ages.[33] He also draws on the Durham household accounts to descril
the trilinguality of commercial and business networks of traders, merchan
clerks and monks that were based on French, Latin and increasingly English
the later Middle Ages.[34]

Scholars have noticed the use of French in female houses, particularly
manuscripts they held, and also in works composed or translated by individu
nuns.[35] David Bell's list of French texts owned by medieval English conven

---

28 London, British Library, MS Additional 70513 (*olim* Welbeck): see further D. Russe
    'The Campsey Collection of Old French Saints' Lives: A Re-Examination of its Stru
    ture and Provenance', *Scriptorium* 57:1 (2003), 51–83; J. Wogan-Browne, 'Powers
    Record, Powers of Example: Historiography and Women's History', in *Gendering t
    Master Narrative: Women and Power in the Middle Ages*, ed. M. Kowaleski and M. Erl
    (Ithaca NY, 2003), pp. 71–93.

29 For this inscription, see Bell, *What Nuns Read*, p. 125 and Wogan-Browne, 'Powers
    Record', p. 88.

30 See Russell, 'The Campsey Collection', pp. 63–4, 64–9: Wogan-Browne, 'Powers
    Record', pp. 75–6.

31 On French literary texts in male houses, see Legge, *Anglo-Norman in the Cloisters*, ar
    the essay by Pouzet in this volume.

32 *Documents Illustrating the Rule of Walter de Wenlock, Abbot of Westminster, 1283–1307*, e
    B. Harvey, Camden 4th series, vol. 2 (London, 1965).

33 Rothwell, 'Sugar and Spice', pp. 647–59.

34 Rothwell, 'Sugar and Spice', passim.

35 Legge, *Anglo-Norman in the Cloisters*, pp. 53, 77, 84–5, 119–20, 122–3 for works writt
    for nuns; pp. 49–51 for individual authors, also Bell, *What Nuns Read*, pp. 69–71;
    Wogan-Browne, ' "Clerc u lai, muine u dame": Women and Anglo-Norman Hagiograp
    in the Twelfth and Thirteenth Centuries', in *Women and Literature in Britain 1150–15(
    2nd edn, ed. C. Meale (Cambridge, 1996), pp. 61–85; F. Riddy, ' "Women talking abo
    the things of God": A Late Medieval Subculture', in *Women and Literature*, pp. 104–2

shows that at least twenty-one had French works in their possession.[36] This information is crucial to our understanding of the role Anglo-Norman played in female monastic life, but discussions of the use of French in medieval English convents have often tended to focus less on how nuns used it or for what purpose, and more on French as a signifier of their social status.[37] Eileen Power, for example, looked at nuns' use of French as a commentary on their lack of Latinity – and thus their lack of higher learning – citing bishops' injunctions to nuns written in French as evidence that they could not understand Latin.[38] Power then equated their apparent language and learning deficits with their aristocratic status, suggesting that because these nuns hailed from society's elite groups, they had no religious vocation and hence were not interested in the pursuit of Latin and other scholarly endeavors, as were their male monastic counterparts. Later scholars, including Dominica Legge and David Bell, echo Power's equation of nuns' use of French with their elite status, and Douglas Kibbee suggests further that French lasted longer in female houses than male ones because nuns could afford to maintain high entry standards, that is, accept women only from wealthy, titled families, despite losses caused by the Black Death.[39] Finally, the equation of a nun's use of French and her social status can also be seen in discussions of Chaucer's Prioress, Madame Eglentine, whose language skills have been

---

[36] Bell, *What Nuns Read*, pp. 231–6. Godstow Abbey also had a rhyming French chronicle (recently discovered and edited by Emilie Amt in *The Register of Godstow Nunnery*, Oxford, forthcoming): on the French of Crabhouse Nunnery, see the essay by June in this volume. For *regulae* in French not included in Bell, see T. Hunt, 'Anglo-Norman Rules for the Priories of St Mary de Pré and Sopwell', in Gregory and Trotter, *De mot en mot*, pp. 93–104; 'An Anglo-Norman Treatise on Female Religious', *Medium Aevum* 64 (1995), 205–31; and 'An Anglo-Norman Treatise on the Religious Life', in *Medieval Codicology, Iconography, Literature, and Translation*, ed. P. Rolfe Monks and D. D. R. Owen (Leiden, 1994), pp. 267–75. Overall at least twenty-four convents owned French manuscripts, roughly the same percentage of the total number of convents as those for which household accounts survive: see p. 90 above.

[37] The exception is Tony Hunt who does not equate nuns' use of French with any social status. Wogan-Browne and Russell assume the nuns at Campsey Ash came from elite groups – which I query below.

[38] Power, *Medieval English Nunneries*, pp. 247–8. For a recent, nuanced discussion of nuns' Latin, see Bell, *What Nuns Read*, pp. 59–66, 77–9.

[39] Legge, *Anglo-Norman in the Cloisters*, pp. 48–9; Bell, *What Nuns Read*, pp. 67–8; Kibbee, *For to Speke*, pp. 59, 68, these without due account of French as an enjoined male monastic language: see e.g. Michael Richter, *Sprache und Gesellschaft im Mittelalter* (Stuttgart, 1979), pp. 148–57 (esp. pp. 149–50), also 78–94. Male Augustinians were forbidden English conversation and enjoined to French and Latin as late as their statutes of 1325 and 1334 (Ralph Hanna, *London Literature 1300–1380* (Cambridge, 2005), pp. 159–60 and 213, n. 13). Bell posits that French endured longer in female convents than in the ports (*What Nuns Read*, p. 68; see also M. D. Legge 'Anglo-Norman as a Spoken Language', *ANS* 2 (1979), 108–17, 188–90 (p. 116), but French was the *lingua franca* of maritime trade for longer than is generally realized: see the essay by Kowaleski in this volume.

variously interpreted as either a sign of her high social status or conversely as a pretense of gentility.[40]

Details from the Campsey Ash kitcheners' accounts allow us to address and even challenge some of these long-held beliefs about the use of French by medieval English nuns. For example, the nuns' social status is visible in part through the food they ate, as revealed in the kitcheners' accounts. As historians of diet have pointed out, diet in times past reflected what particular social groups could afford to eat, since much of the food or drink considered suitable for aristocratic tables was more expensive and harder to procure than food eaten by those lower down the social scale.[41] The food that the Campsey Ash kitcheners bought suggests that the nuns were from middling social ranks rather than from the elite groups historians usually equate with French-speaking nuns.

The accounts reveal that the nuns at Campsey Ash ate a high-protein diet: lots of meat and fish, but not of the most expensive types. The kinds and amounts of meat were fairly consistent over the eight years these accounts cover: the kitcheners bought beef, cow, bull and heifer. Young livestock – calves and lamb – along with pigs, sheep and poultry (chickens, hens, roosters) also appear with regularity though in smaller quantities than beef. The cellarer at Wilton Abbey, a large and wealthy convent of Benedictine nuns, in 1299, purchased a very similar staple of meat products for the nuns and guests there.[42] Though comparisons between what the Campsey Ash nuns bought and what their male monastic counterparts did are not as direct as we might like given their greater wealth and size, it is worth noting that in 1275 and 1278, the cellarers at Battle Abbey bought the same types of meat secured for Campsey Ash, but also other higher-status foods not bought for Campsey, including, for example, wine – lots of it – ale and nuts.[43]

While dietary restrictions officially prohibited nuns and monks from eating flesh meat (the meat of four-legged animals), the nuns ate more beef than any other type of meat, a significant amount of chicken, and not much mutton. This pattern of consumption is typical of those of middling status rather than of wealthy people in medieval England.[44] High-status foods like the veal and lamb

---

40 *The Riverside Chaucer*, ed. L. D. Benson (Boston MA, 1987), pp. 25–6, 209–12; W. Rothwell, 'Chaucer and Stratford Atte Bowe', *BJRL* 74 (1992), 3–28. For a recent survey of scholarship around this issue and the dismissal of the idea that the French of England was a degraded and corrupted version of the French of France, see D. Trotter, 'Not as Eccentric as It Looks: Anglo-French and French French', *FMLS* 39 (2003), 427–38.

41 In addition to types of food, what also differentiated the patterns of food consumption of elite groups from those of lesser standing was the sheer amount aristocratic households and wealthy monks purchased and consumed: C. Dyer, *Standards of Living in the Later Middle Ages* (Cambridge, 1989), p. 58.

42 Critall, 'Fragment of an Account', pp. 142–56.

43 *Accounts of the Cellarers of Battle Abbey, 1275–1513*, ed. E. Searle and B. Ross, Sussex Record Society 65 (Lewes, 1967), pp. 41–6. The monks of Westminster also bought other, fancier foods that the nuns did not buy as a significant percentage of their costs: Harvey, *Living and Dying*, pp. 52, 56–62.

44 Dyer, *Standards of Living*, p. 156.

ese kitcheners bought may have been served on high feast days, especially aster, but the absence of other delicacies – tongue and piglets, for example – d high-status wild and game birds, common to wealthy secular, and wealthy male and male monastic households, places the Campsey Ash nuns' diet more line with the consumer preferences of households of lesser social status.[45]

Although fish was an important component and source of protein in the nuns' iet, their reliance on cured sea fish, compared to the more expensive and desir-le freshwater fish favored by wealthy aristocratic households, also suggests at the nuns' diet was more typical of middling social groups, such as the parish entry.[46] Several types of stockfish were also frequently purchased in large quan-ties, a food characterized by one historian as 'poorman's standard fare'. [47] While red marine fish like this were common in nuns', monks' and gentry families' iets, the Campsey Ash kitcheners also purchased freshwater fish, though in maller amounts than the cured fish and fish from the sea.[48] Since the consump-on of any fresh freshwater fish is a key sign of high status, the small amounts ese kitcheners bought seems to confirm that the nuns' food and diets had more common with what gentry households consumed than what people of higher atus ate.[49] Like many other religious houses, Campsey Ash did have 'exten-

C. Woolgar, 'Diet and Consumption in Gentry and Noble Households: A Case Study from around the Wash', in *Rulers and Ruled in Late Medieval England: Essays Presented to Gerald Harriss*, ed. R. E. Archer and S. Walker (London, 1995), pp. 17–31 (pp. 21–3): the Campsey kitchener did buy doves in 1298/9, Campsey Ash 'a'. For the fancier diet of monks, see Harvey, *Living and Dying*, pp. 34–71. While it might be argued that the nuns' relative poverty and their monastic dietary restrictions dictated the lesser amounts they bought, the latter at least did not seem to be a consideration for the monks.

Dyer, 'The Consumption of Freshwater Fish', p. 33. The Campsey kitcheners bought various freshwater fish and shellfish (whelks and oysters). Since the kitchener some-times describes bass, salmon and trout as 'from the sea', and sometimes simply names them without this description, they are listed in both categories (saltwater and fresh-water). Where she does not say 'from the sea' I take it to mean they are from fresh-water sources, as bass, salmon and trout can be. Shellfish and flounder, herring, plaice and stockfish were the types purchased most frequently. These types are important to note not just because of the difference between the costs and availability of cured as opposed to fresh fish, but also because more expensive and harder-to-procure types, like sturgeon and porpoise, are not found in these accounts. The 1960s excavations at Campsey Ash disclosed oyster shells and the bones of small animals, such as chicken and rabbit: see R. Gilchrist and M. Oliva, *Religious Women in Medieval East Anglia* (Norwich, 1993), p. 90. Note, by contrast, the bones of twenty different types of fish, including sturgeon and porpoise, excavated from the wealthy abbey of St Mary's, Winchester (Coldicott, *Hampshire Nunneries*, p. 78).

Bond, 'Monastic Fisheries', p. 73, thus described because 'it could be almost any variety of cheap dried or salted fish'.

Bond, 'Monastic Fisheries', p. 74; Harvey, *Living and Dying*, p. 47.

See e.g. J. Bond, 'The Fishponds of Eynsham Abbey', *The Eynsham Record: Journal of the Eynsham History Group* 9 (1992), 3–17 (p. 12).

sive fishponds' – as well as a stream that ran through its precincts – and so it i
possible that the nuns ate more freshwater fish than appears in the accounts.[50]

The Campsey Ash accounts' description of the nuns' diet is not the onl
source that suggests that the nuns were more likely to derive from the paris
gentry than from the aristocracy. Other evidence suggesting their middling soci
status is in their names. Though we know the last names of only three of the fou
identifiable nuns for this period – admittedly, a small sample of the probable tot
number of nuns at Campsey Ash at this time[51] – three have surnames of place
within ten miles of the house: two of the kitcheners, Avelina de Ludham, Eliza
beth de Melton and a prioress, Basilia de Wertham. All three places – Ludham
Melton and Wertham – were in fact contiguous neighboring parishes locate
to the south-east of Campsey Ash.[52] Indeed, the kitcheners regularly collecte
rents from the manor of Ludham, and the nuns held the appropriation of th
parish church there also. Corpusty, the surname of the third kitchener, Joan, is
parish farther from Campsey Ash in the county of Norfolk. But the other nuns
surnames suggest a recruitment pattern of local women that typifies this an
other female houses in the county and elsewhere in medieval England in th
fourteenth century and beyond.[53]

A second consideration is that while Campsey Ash was originally founde
in 1195 by members of a local Norman baronial family,[54] and was wealthie
than the other female houses in the county of Suffolk (the 1291 Taxation of Pop
Nicholas gives the value of Campsey Ash as £107 3s. 33/4d.), the assessment c

---

50 Gilchrist and Oliva, *Religious Women*, pp. 90–1. Dyer, 'The Consumption of Freshwate
Fish', p. 27 notes that the standard correlation is between fishponds and aristocrati
households because the ponds were expensive to maintain and because fish farmin
'required specialized labor'. We do not know how the nuns farmed their fishpond
– either directly or by leasing them out – or how well they were maintained, but
sixteenth-century audit of the nuns' possessions showed the annual profits derive
from the nuns' direct farming of them totalled only 3s. 4d.: see *Valor Ecclesiasticus*, ec
J. Caley and J. Hunter (London, 1810–34), III, 416.

51 *VCH, Suffolk*, II, 112 for the suggestion that in 1291 the average population here wa
twenty (information given without a source).

52 W. Skeat, *The Place-Names of Suffolk* (Cambridge, 1913), p. 65 (Ludham and Melton
pp. 103–4 (Wertham). See *VCH, Suffolk*, I, 356 for a Domesday map of Suffolk tha
shows Ludham as adjacent to Campsey Ash and Melton just next to Ludham. Norma
Scarfe notes that Ludham was in Pettistree (*The Suffolk Landscape* (Bury St Edmund:
1987), p. 143). For the contiguous locations of these parishes –Ludham was the ne>
neighboring parish to the south-east of Campsey Ash; Melton was the next paris
to the south-east of Ludham, and Wertham was next to Melton on the south-east
see the map of Suffolk parishes: 'Suffolk: Dates of Commencement of Registers fc
Parishes Formed before 1832', *Genealogical Aids* 32 (Institute of Heraldic and Genec
logical Studies, Northgate, Canterbury, 1983).

53 For the recruiting pattern of the mid-fourteenth century and beyond, see M. Oliv
'All in the Family? Monastic and Clerical Careers among Family Members in the La
Middle Ages', *Medieval Prosopography* 20 (1999), 161–71. For the local origins of nur
elsewhere, see Oliva, *The Convent and the Community*, pp. 58–60.

54 The sisters Joan and Agnes de Valoines, *VCH, Suffolk*, II, 112.

the convent's finances through the fourteenth century was nevertheless 'lean'.[55] This financial state probably would not have attracted the county's aristocratic women, but would have instead appealed to local neighborhood women from the county's population of 'small, relatively prosperous freeholders'.[56] This pattern of recruitment would also be consistent with that of the later period when a prosopographical analysis shows that women from Suffolk's elite families chose not neighborhood county convents, but rather wealthier ones elsewhere to pursue their religious vocations.[57] The same analysis of the nuns of Campsey Ash from 1350 to the convent's dissolution in 1536 also indicates that the majority of nuns at this house came from local manorial and parish gentry families: local landholders whose members often included minor county officials like bailiffs and constables.[58]

The evidence about the nuns' diets contained in the Campsey Ash kitcheners' accounts of the late thirteenth and early fourteenth centuries, along with some suggestive evidence about the nuns' social status in the same period, indicates that these nuns came from a middling group of both parish gentry and substantial freeholders. These nuns are thus comparable to non-elite groups of French users identified by other scholars as people from 'ordinary social backgrounds'.[59]

The accounts of Campsey Ash were, moreover, part of a broader linguistic culture at the convent that included Anglo-Norman, Latin and English literary and documentary material. Among the Campsey nuns' holdings, for example, were a thirteenth-century Latin psalter with a fourteenth-century French inscription of ownership; a fourteenth-century Latin psalter that includes a long prayer in French and a fifteenth-century French inscription of ownership; eleven thirteenth- and fourteenth-century charters, all in Latin except one dated 1358 that

---

[55] *VCH, Suffolk*, II, 112–13. Diocese-wide, Campsey was the second wealthiest house: the 1291 tax shows that Shouldham Priory in Norfolk was wealthier, at £207, with the remaining four houses in this county falling well below these amounts; see *VCH, Norfolk*, II, 412 for Shouldham and pp. 350–1, 369 and 408 for Blackborough, Carrow, Marham Abbey and Crabhouse, respectively.

[56] *The Chorography of Suffolk*, ed. D. N. J. MacCulloch (Ipswich, 1976), p. 68; also M. Bailey, *Medieval Suffolk: An Economic and Social History* (Woodbridge, 2007), pp. 58–61, 64.

[57] With the exception of Bruisyard Abbey (founded in 1366 for the Poor Clares who attracted elite women), this was a diocese-wide pattern: Oliva, *The Convent and the Community*, pp. 54–5. Russell, 'The Campsey Collection', pp. 69–70 identifies specific Campsey nuns as aristocratic but the majority were from parish gentry families. These latter had social and political contact with the county's elite (Bailey, *Medieval Suffolk*, p. 59) and could have acquired shared cultural tastes with the few elite women in the convent.

[58] Oliva, *The Convent and the Community*, pp. 52–61 and n. 57 above.

[59] Ingham, 'Mixing Languages', p. 85. Rothwell, 'Sugar and Spice', p. 657 also finds that the scribes, merchants and accounts' keepers who used French, English and Latin in their accounts were not the socially elite either.

is in Anglo-Norman.[60] A fifteenth-century copy of the *Chastising of God's Children* includes a sixteenth-century inscription in Latin by one of the nuns, Katherine Babyngton, who identifies herself as a sometime prioress who is donating the book to her convent as a gift. [61] Another fifteenth-century manuscript that belonged to Campsey Ash, a collection of English devotional treatises, has a similar inscription, written in English by another nun, Elizabeth Wylby. In this wider context, then, the kitcheners' accounts are not just evidence of a bilingual culture, but perhaps of a multilingual environment of a female monastic population from society's middling ranks who utilized French, Latin and English not only in their record-keeping, but also in the literary manuscripts they compiled, owned and inscribed. The nuns' use of French thus supports recent assessments of the use of the French of England, 'for all manner of cultural and administrative purposes', while at the same time the Campsey Ash kitcheners' accounts themselves provide evidence of the non-elite status of these users of the French of England.[62]

---

[60] Bell, *What Nuns Read*, pp. 123–5 for the psalters; PRO, CP 25/1 212/5 #62 (1211); PRO, CP 25/1 213/15 #36 (1239/40); PRO, CP 25/1 213/15 #43 (1239/40); PRO, CP 25/1 219/74 #12 (1334); London, BL, Cott. Ch. v5 (1321); London, BL, Harl. Ch. 45 C35 (1316); SRO, HD 1538/113/1 includes four Latin quitclaims, three of which are undated; one in this collection, though, is dated 1358 and in French; and SRO, HD 1538/174/1, undated English charter. Other documents known from this house include a prioress's account in Latin dated 1536: PRO, SC6 /Henry VIII/3401; and a sixteenth-century inventory and list of sale items to diverse persons after the convent's dissolution: PRO, SP 5/1/110.

[61] Bell, *What Nuns Read*, pp. 124–5.

[62] W. Rothwell, 'The Role of French in England', *BJRL* 58 (1976), 445–66 (pp. 465–6).

8

The French of England: A Maritime *lingua franca*?

Maryanne Kowaleski*

)ne of the long-standing issues in the study of the French of England revolves round who exactly could speak, write, and read French in medieval England. 1ost scholars accept that few below the level of the aristocracy, upper gentry, nd the clerical elite spoke French regularly, even in the heyday of French terary culture in England which stretched from the late twelfth to the late four-:enth century. We know too that lawyers and judges, most of gentry status but ome from the upper bourgeois or even prosperous yeoman class, could read nd speak French because it was the language of legal treatises and pleading 1 the royal courts. We are, moreover, starting to learn about the use of French 1 other social groups, as the essays in this volume by Marilyn Oliva (on nuns) nd Richard Britnell (on townspeople) attest. My contribution follows on from his work in exploring non-elite, non-literary communities of French in medi-val England by focusing on the use of French among sea-going populations, •articularly mariners and fishermen, but also shipmen/merchants and other •ort-town residents who made their living from the sea. I look at three types f evidence: (1) the Laws (or Rolls) of Oléron, the dominant maritime law code f the medieval Atlantic world; (2) other types of port-town records, such as naritime courts, custumals, and customs accounts that were written in Anglo-'rench; and (3) indications that French may have been spoken or understood by nany English overseas merchants and shipmasters and even a good number of nariners into the fifteenth century.

Maritime disputes in medieval England were settled by recourse to a mari-ime law code called the Laws of Oléron, first extant in recorded form in early ourteenth-century manuscripts but based on customary practices and laws lating from much earlier.[1] The Laws were recorded as judgments in the mari-

I wish to thank Thelma Fenster, Robin Ward, and especially David Trotter for their helpful comments.

The Laws formed the basis of maritime dispute settlement in the British Isles, France, the Low Countries, Germany, Scandinavia, and Spain; see *Monumenta Juridica: The Black Book of the Admiralty*, ed. T. Twiss, 4 vols., RS 55 (London, 1871–6), I, lvi–lxxi, 88–131; II, xlvii–lix, lxxviii–xxi, 210–41, 432–81; III, 4–33; IV, xxvi–lxvi, lxxxvi–ix, 54–129, 303–83, 416–47. See also *The Oak Book of Southampton of c. A.D. 1300*, ed. P. Studer, 3 vols., Southampton Record Society 10, 11, and 12 (Southampton, 1910–11), II, xxix, lxxi, 54–99; K-F. Krieger, *Ursprung und Wurzeln der Rôles de Oléron*, Quellen und Darstel-lungen zur hansischen Geschichte n. F. 15 (Köln, 1970); T. J. Runyan, 'The Rolls of

time courts of Oléron, an island off the coast of France near La Rochelle, which remained largely in English hands from 1154 on. Although scholars have long debated the origins of the Laws, the current consensus is that the original Laws were compiled in southern France in the twelfth century, when the English acquisition of Aquitaine stimulated the growth of the Gascon wine trade and thus quickened maritime traffic between Gascony and its important markets in Britain and Flanders.[2] The Laws were based on past practices, many of which can be traced back to the ancient Rhodian sea law of the Mediterranean, but they survive as judgments in the court of Oléron, which was conveniently located on this important wine route and was a respected venue for the settlement of maritime disputes regarding, for example, what to throw overboard in case of a storm or how to discipline troublesome mariners.[3]

Around 1200 an Anglo-Norman version of the Laws of Oléron was recorded that became, in the early fourteenth century, the basis for the earliest extant copies of the Laws that we have in any language.[4] Some linguistic evidence suggests that the Laws of Oléron were recorded first in Gascon,[5] but the earliest versions are all in Anglo-Norman. It is significant that the earliest copies of the Laws of Oléron are found in English port-town registers, such as the Liber Memorandum of London (believed by Travers Twiss and Paul Studer to be the earliest copy), the Liber Horn of London (believed by Karl-Friedrich Krieger to be the earliest redaction), the Oak Book of Southampton and the Little Red Book of Bristol.[6] All

Oléron and the Admiralty Court in Fourteenth Century England', *American Journal of Legal History* 19 (1975), 95–111. I have been unable to see the most recent edition of the Laws, based on thirty manuscripts, which is cited in *Hale and Fleetwood on Admiralty Jurisdiction*, ed. M. J. Prichard and D. E. C. Yale, Selden Society 108 (London, 1993), pp. xxxv–vi, n. 7.

2   Most scholars, including Runyan, 'Rolls of Oléron', pp. 98–9, as well as D. Burwash *English Merchant Shipping 1460–1540* (Toronto, 1947), pp. 171–6, and F. R. Sanborn *Origins of the Early English Maritime and Commercial Law* (New York, 1930), p. 64, follow Studer (*Oak Book*, II, xxxv–lxxxi) who believes that two families of manuscripts came out of the original (now lost) Gascon version. One family contained the Anglo-Norman and Gascon versions (on which the German and Flemish versions are based), and the second included the Norman and Breton versions, on which the Castilian version is based. See also n. 4, below.

3   Sanborn, *Early English Maritime and Commercial Law*, pp. 37–8. See also *Le Coutumier de l'Ile d'Oléron*, a fourteenth-century manuscript in the Oléronais dialect that includes many chapters relating to the Laws of Oléron but which probably pre-date the Laws; it is reproduced with a translation by Twiss (*Black Book*, II, 254–401) and, more recently in *Le Coutumier d'Oléron*, ed. J. H. Williston (Poitiers, 1992).

4   See above, n. 2 and *Oak Book*, ed. Studer, II. xxxv, lxiii–lxvii; III, 6–14, 1–50.

5   *Oak Book*, ed. Studer, II, lxiv. Studer later backed down from this position (*The Study of Anglo-Norman. Inaugural Lecture delivered before the University of Oxford on 6 February 1920* (Oxford, 1920), p. 9, n. 3) after criticism from C. Bémont on this point in his review of *The Oak Book* in *Revue historique* 109 (1912), pp. 393–5. Krieger (*Ursprung*, pp. 38–40) argues that the Laws were assembled in England sometime before 1286.

6   *Black Book*, ed. Twiss, III, xiii, xv–xvi, 4, n. 1; IV, vii, cxli–cxlii; *Oak Book*, ed. Studer II, xlii; Krieger, *Ursprung*, p. 38, but see also pp. 7–17, 38–71. For transcriptions of and debates on the dating of these and other manuscripts, see Lex Mercatoria and

these copies date from the first quarter of the fourteenth century, though there is abundant evidence to indicate that the Laws were being used to adjudicate maritime disputes at least a century earlier. In the fourteenth and fifteenth century, moreover, additional articles were added to the original twenty-four articles to keep pace with developments in commercial shipping, bringing the total number of articles in fifteenth-century manuscripts (including the Black Book of the Admiralty) up to thirty-five, forty-seven and even eighty-one in some cases.[7]

The fundamental importance of the Anglo-Norman Laws of Oléron to the adjudication of medieval maritime disputes in the Atlantic region should be stressed. Because the articles were based on long-recognized customary practices, from as early as the late twelfth century many of the Laws were being observed in principle by the maritime courts of English port towns, which met 'from tide to tide' to provide the speedy justice needed by men on the move.[8] Cases heard by the admiral, an office that in England dates back to around 1295,[9] were also

---

Legal Pluralism: A Late Thirteenth-Century Treatise and Its Afterlife, ed. M. E. Basile, J. F. Bestor, D. R. Coquillette, and C. Donahue (Cambridge, 1998), pp. 211–12; *Black Book*, ed. Twiss, II, pp. 209–41, III, 4–33. Krieger, *Ursprung*, pp. 123–45; R. M. Ward, *The World of the Medieval Shipmaster: Law, Business and the Sea c.1350–1450* (Woodbridge, 2009), pp. 183–205; T. Kiesselbach, 'Der Ursprung der rôles d'Oléron und des Seerechts von Damme', *Hansische Geschichtsblätter* (1906), pp. 1–60 (pp. 44–60); D. Oschinsky, review of K.-F. Krieger, *Ursprung und Wurzeln der* Rôles d'Oléron', *EHR* 87 (1972), 857.

7 The Liber Horn and Liber Memorandum versions have twenty-four articles, the Oak Book version twenty-seven, and the Bristol version twenty-three (article 15 seems to have been omitted by haplography since articles 15 and 16 both begin with the same phrase; see Lex Mercatoria *and Legal Pluralism*, ed. Basile et al., p. 211, and Ward, *World of the Medieval Shipmaster*, pp. 22–3). The later text of the Laws in the Black Book of the Admiralty (*Black Book*, ed. Twiss, I, 121–31) contains an additional eleven articles, one of which is an ordinance (article 35) purporting to be from the reign of King John that Twiss argues dates from 1201 (*Black Book*, ed. Twiss, I, xlix–li, 129, n. 31), while he claims that another of the extra ordinances dates to the time of Edward I. R. G. Marsden, however, calls the claim for dating article 35 to 1201 'apocryphal'; *Select Pleas in the Court of Admiralty*, ed. R. G. Marsden, 2 vols., Selden Society 6 and 11 (London, 1894–7), I, xi.

8 Most English port towns had maritime courts to hear and determine disputes that occurred at sea: see 'Customs of Newcastle-upon-Tyne', temp. Henry II (*English Historical Documents, 1042–1189*, ed. D. C. Douglas (Oxford, 1953), p. 1040); 'The Domesday of Ipswich', temp. Richard I (*Black Book*, ed. Twiss, II, 22–3); and 'Handlist of the Archives of Great Yarmouth Corporation' (unpublished typescript in the Norfolk Record Office, reproduced by the Historical Manuscripts Commission for the National Register of Archives, 1965), p. 13. See also *Pleas in the Court of Admiralty*, ed. Marsden, I, xiii–xiv. For the use of the Laws of Oléron in local maritime courts during the later Middle Ages, see *Select Cases Concerning the Law Merchant, A.D. 1239–1633*, vol. II: *Central Courts*, ed. H. Hall, Selden Society 46 (London, 1930), pp. xxvii–xxix, xcv–vi, and Burwash, *English Merchant Shipping*, pp. 63–5, 171–2; by this period, many of these courts had become part of admiralty jurisdiction.

9 *Documents Relating to Law and Custom of the Sea*, vol. 1: *A.D. 1205–1648*, ed. R. G. Marsden, Navy Records Society 49 (London, 1915), p. 46; *Pleas in the Court of Admiralty*, ed. Marsden, I, xii–xiii; N. A. M. Rodger, *The Safeguard of the Sea: A Naval History of Britain*, vol. I: *660–1649* (London, 1997), p. 131.

settled using these Laws, which eventually became the basis of admiralty jurisdiction in a court of equity created around the 1350s, which provided justice in
cases of shipwreck, collision, piracy, prize, and other problems arising at sea.[10]
The Anglo-Norman versions of the Laws were also the basis of several translations into Flemish that served as the oldest written maritime laws in Flanders.[11]
The Laws of Wisby, the premier maritime law code in the Baltic, were based in
part on a Flemish translation of the Anglo-Norman Laws of Oléron.[12] The Laws
also served as the basis of maritime law in Brittany, Normandy, and elsewhere in
France, while the king of Castile gave the Laws authority in his Mediterranean
ports.[13] Together these law codes, which shared the same source, were the basis
of all maritime dispute settlement in an enormous region stretching from the
eastern Mediterranean to the Baltic Sea.[14]

Like the Laws, many of the earliest court proceedings conducted before
English admirals and their deputies were documented in French, although the
actual records of cases heard after the formal establishment of the admiralty
court in the late fourteenth century usually survive in Latin.[15] We are not sure,
however, what language was actually spoken in the early maritime courts.
Michael Clanchy considers this question in reference to ecclesiastical and royal
courts, and points out that the language of formal pleadings – at least up to the
reign of Edward I – was probably French and that cross-examinations may well

---

10 Admiralty jurisdiction took time to develop: the first formal records of the court are
     not extant until the 1520s; see *Pleas in the Court of Admiralty*, ed. Marsden, I, xiv–lxxx;
     Law and Custom of the Sea, ed. Marsden, pp. x–xi, xiii–xv.
11 *Oak Book*, ed. Studer, II, xxxi, xxxv, xl, xlvii–ix, liii, lviii; *Black Book*, ed. Twiss, I, lxiii; III,
     xixvii–xix; IV, xxxvii, xliv–l. For the text and a translation of the Purple Book of Bruges
     (containing the Flemish version of the Laws of Oléron, which is based on the older
     Anglo-Norman text), see *Black Book*, ed. Twiss, IV, 302–33; for a text and translation of
     the Sea-Laws in Flanders, see *Black Book*, ed. Twiss, IV, 416–47.
12 *Oak Book*, ed. Studer, II, xxxi, xxxvii, xl–l, xlvii–ix, liii, lviii; *Black Book*, ed. Twiss, III,
     xix–xxiv; IV, xxi–l. For the text and a translation of the Gotland Sea-Laws (which
     contains elements of the Laws of Oléron), see *Black Book*, ed. Twiss, IV, 54–129; for a
     translation of the Laws of Wisby, see *Black Book*, ed. Twiss, IV, 265–84.
13 *Black Book*, ed. Twiss, I, lxvii–lxviii; II, lv, xlvii; *Oak Book*, ed. Studer, II, xxxxvi–ix, xliv–v,
     xlvii, lvii, lx–lxiii.
14 Sanborn, *English Maritime Law*, pp. 74–7.
15 For thirteenth-century inquisitions and proceedings of maritime cases in French, see,
     for example: *Calendar of Inquisitions Miscellaneous: (Chancery) Preserved in the Public
     Record Office* [hereafter *CIM*], 8 vols. (London, 1916–2003), I, 430; *Law and Custom of the
     Sea*, ed. Marsden, pp. 28–9, 46, 50–6; for late fourteenth- and fifteenth-century exam-
     ples, see *Pleas in the Court of Admiralty*, ed. Marsden, I, l, 1–12; II, lx–lxi; the National
     Archives, Public Record Office [hereafter PRO], C47/6/9/2–4, 5 (part of C47/6/9 is
     printed in 'An Early Admiralty Case (A.D. 1361)', ed. C. Johnson, in *Camden Miscellany*
     15, 3rd series 41 (London, 1929), pp. 1–5); PRO, E101/43/1. For the increasing number
     of proceedings in Latin, see *Pleas in the Court of Admiralty*, ed. Marsden, passim; *Black
     Book*, ed. Twiss, I, 246–80, 347–94.

ive been in English, even though the courts' language of record was Latin.[16]
iul Brand goes further in arguing that French was the primary language of the
iyal courts from at least the twelfth century.[17] The same may well have been
iue for the local maritime and admiralty courts. We know, for instance, that the
ith administered to all jurors in admiralty cases was probably in French up until
ie late fourteenth century; the articles that guided jurors' deliberations were
iso recorded in French, a practice that we see in place at the famous Inquisition
i Queensborough in 1375 (which added a further set of articles to the Laws
i Oléron).[18] Since from an early date the jurors in these cases were supposed
i be mariners and merchants familiar with the sea-going life, is it going too
ir to speculate that some – perhaps even most – of these jurors would have
ien able to understand the French oath they took and the articles that guided
ieir presentments, at least into the fourteenth century?[19] The ability of Flemish
ierchants and seamen to serve on a 1317 inquest jury in Yarmouth regarding the
ifamous Flemish pirate, John Crabbe, was possible because such legal proceed-
igs could be conducted in French.[20] Such mixed juries were not uncommon in
ngland, where both maritime and borough custom mandated that half of the
iry members for cases involving a foreign litigant be foreign.[21]

The sea-going merchants on these maritime juries would have been even more
kely to know French. A substantial number of overseas merchants, many of
ihom travelled across the Channel to pursue their trade, especially in the period
efore the Black Death, would have been able to carry on simple conversations
i French in order to negotiate not only purchases and sales, but also arrange-
ients for travel, lodging, and food.[22] French had also become a common written
nguage for business dealings by English merchants by the mid-thirteenth

---

M. T. Clanchy, *From Memory to Written Record: England 1066–1307*, 2nd edn (Oxford, 1993), p. 209.

P. Brand, 'The Languages of the Law in Later Medieval England', in Trotter, *Multilingualism*, pp. 63–76.

See *Black Book*, ed. Twiss, I, xliv–xlvi, 41–87, 168–71, 221, n. 1, 269, 362, 379 for this and evidence of mariners serving on juries in maritime disputes. By the reign of Henry VIII, the admiralty judge alone made decisions: *Pleas in the Court of Admiralty*, ed. Marsden, I, liv.

See, for example, *CIM*, VI, 31; *Hale and Fleetwood*, ed. Prichard and Yale, p. xxxiii; *Black Book*, ed. Twiss, II, xli.

CIM, II, 89. Although the formal pleadings and written records of maritime proceedings were often in French, it is possible that testimony and other discussion in the court were in English; see Clanchy, *From Memory to Written Record*, pp. 207–10.

Pleas of the Court of Admiralty, ed. Marsden, I, xlvii. For this custom in towns, see *Borough Customs*, ed. M. Bateson, Selden Society 18, 21 (London, 1904–6), I, 201. See also M. Constable, *The Law of the Other: The Half-Alien Jury and Changing Conceptions of Citizenship, Law and Knowledge* (Chicago, 1994), pp. 8–24, 96–107, 112–15.

Some idea of what they would have had to say in French can be gleaned from the handbooks written to help English travellers in France; see *Manières de langage*, ed. A. M. Kristol, ANTS 53 (London, 1995).

century.[23] Civic records concerning maritime matters were often in French, suc
as the letters and petitions sent by the Cinque Ports[24] and the correspondenc
between port towns regarding ship service, the recovery of debts, toll exemp
tions, and safe-conducts.[25] The frequent correspondence between English poi
towns and their French and Flemish counterparts on the other side of the Channe
regarding captured boats, mariners, and merchants; business debts owed to thei
merchants; and certificates of good character for travelling merchants and ship
masters, were almost always in French. Particularly interesting is the frequenc
with which lists of tariffs or tolls charged by port towns on incoming and outgoin
ships and cargoes were recorded in Anglo-French, even into the late fourteent
century.[26] The borough custumals of port towns, including all the Cinque Port
Exeter, Sandwich, and Ipswich among others, are all in Anglo-French, althoug
many survive only in later English translations.[27] In the late fourteenth centur

---

23 Rothwell, 'Sugar and Spice'; Clanchy, *From Memory to Written Record*, p. 214; *Oak Boo*
ed. Studer, p. 7.

24 Correspondence between the Cinque Ports was usually in French up until the earl
fifteenth century; see, for example, *Register of Daniel Rough, Common Clerk of Romne
1353–1380*, ed. K. M. E. Murray, Kent Records 16 (Ashford, 1945); so too the extan
summonses and ordinances from the fourteenth-century Brodhull, the court of th
Cinque Ports, see K. M. E. Murray, *The Constitutional History of the Cinque Por*
(Manchester, 1935), p. 157; 'The Manuscripts of the Corporation of Rye', *Appendix*
the Fifth Report of the Historical Manuscripts Commission, Part I (London, 1876), p. 50
Full proceedings are extant from 1432, but only scattered items are in French by th
time, and none appear after 1438; see *A Calendar of the White and Black Books of th
Cinque Ports 1432–1955*, ed. F. Hull (London, 1966), pp. x, 7–8.

25 For correspondence in French by or to English port towns, see *Calendar of Letters from
the Mayor and Corporation of the City of London, A.D. 1350–1370* (London, 1885); J.
Tanquerey, *Recueil de lettres anglo-françaises* (Paris, 1916); H. P. Smith, 'Poole's Ancien
Admiralty Court', *Proceedings of the Dorset Natural History and Archaeological Society* 4
(1928), pp. 126–7; G. F. Chapple, ed., 'Correspondence of the City of London 1298
1370' (unpublished Ph.D. thesis, University of London, 1938); *Anglo-Norman Letters an
Petitions from All Souls MS. 182*, ed. M. D. Legge, ANTS 3 (Oxford, 1941); *William Asshe
bourne's Book*, ed. D. M. Owen, Norfolk Record Society 48 (Norwich, 1981); *Register*
Daniel Rough, ed. Murray.

26 For town tolls on maritime trade recorded in French, see *The Records of the City*
Norwich, ed. W. Hudson and J. C. Tingey, 2 vols. (Norwich, 1906–10), II, 199–20!
234–6; *Oak Book*, ed. Studer, II, 2–17; Hull Record Office, BRE 1 (Bench Book 2, Enrol
ments and Registrations), ff. 149, 170–2; *Anglo-Norman Custumal of Exeter*, ed. J. V
Schopp, History of Exeter Research Group 2 (London, 1925), p. 24; *Black Book*, ed
Twiss, pp. 184–207 (for Ipswich); *Munimenta Gildhallae Londoniensis; Liber Albus, Libe
Custumarum et Liber Horn*, ed. H. T. Riley, 3 vols., RS 12 (London, 1859–62), I, 228–
236–7. See also Rothwell ('Sugar and Spice', pp. 654–6) who notes that French is ofte
used for lists of imported goods in the multilingual account rolls of Durham Priory.

27 For town custumals in French, see *Borough Customs*, ed. Bateson, I, xviii–lvi and mor
recently *Anglo-Norman Custumal of Exeter*, ed. Schopp (dated *c*.1240, and includes
later entry from 1282); *Register of Daniel Rough*, ed. Murray, pp. xvi–vii, 1–27; *Por
smouth Royal Charters 1194–1974*, ed. and trans. G. H. Martin, Portsmouth Record Serie
9 (Portsmouth, 1995), p. 101, n. 11 (for evidence that the original custumal, datin

in New Romney, a fishmonger named Daniel Rough compiled his own register of documents when he served as town clerk, including the town tariffs, election returns, communications with other port towns, and letters of process sent to recover debts owed to New Romney men. Much of Rough's register was in French, some in Latin – particularly entries regarding the king or final concords – and very little in English. When Rough did use Latin, moreover, it was not unusual for him to slip into French.[28] The early fifteenth-century common clerk of the port of King's Lynn, William Asshebourne, also kept a private memoranda book in which he recorded correspondence, petitions and other documents in French.[29] In Southampton, the early fifteenth-century water-bailiff Robert Florys (who had a kinsman in French-speaking Guernsey) kept his port books in Anglo-French, though sprinkled with English and Latin terms.[30] The water-bailiff of Dartmouth in the late fourteenth century also used French in documents he sealed.[31] Ship-building accounts, including some from port towns recording expenses on wages and materials to build barges for the king's service, were sometimes written in French, such as that for London in 1373.[32] The first rutter or sailing directions published in England, moreover, was *Le grant routier* of a

---

from *c.*1270, was in French); *York Memorandum Book*, ed. M. Sellers, 2 vols., Surtees Society 120 and 125 (Durham, 1911–14), II, 251–66 (late fourteenth-century custumal in French); G. Martin, 'The Governance of Ipswich', in *Ipswich Borough Archives 1255–1835: A Catalogue*, comp. D. Allen, Suffolk Record Society 43 (Woodbridge, 2000), pp. xx–xxii (which tentatively suggests that the original custumal of *c.*1200 could have been in Latin, even though the custumal based on the original but recorded in *c.*1291 (printed in *Black Book*, ed. Twiss, II, 2–207) was in French; see also *Ipswich Borough Archives*, comp. Allen, pp. 413–17).

[28] *Register of Daniel Rough*, ed. Murray, pp. xv–vi, lxxi–v. For other French terms in Latin maritime documents, see *Oak Book*, ed. Studer, III, 9; B. Sandahl, *Middle English Sea Terms*, 3 vols. (Uppsala, 1951–82), III, 134,

[29] *William Asshebourne's Book*, ed. Owen. A little over 10 per cent of the 328 items he copied are in French; most are in Latin, a few in English. The fragmentary narrative in French (no. 300) on the origins of trades and the gild merchant in King's Lynn may have been his own composition.

[30] *The Port Books of Southampton or (Anglo-French) Accounts of Robert Florys, Water-Bailiff and Receiver of Petty-Customs, A.D. 1427–1430*, ed. P. Studer, Southampton Record Society 15 (Southampton, 1913), esp. pp. vi–ix; *The Local Port Book of Southampton, 1435–36*, ed. B. Foster, Southampton Records Series 7 (Southampton, 1963), esp. pp. x–xi; note that Studer incorrectly dated the 1426/7 account as 1427/8. Other extant Southampton port customs accounts are in Latin, including that of 1433/4 (Southampton Record Office, S.C. 5/4/2, 6), that of 1439/40 (*The Local Port Book of Southampton for 1439–40*, ed. H. S. Cobb, Southampton Records Series 5 (Southampton, 1961)), and all subsequent accounts.

[31] *Dartmouth*, vol. I: *Pre-Reformation*, ed. H. R. Watkin, Parochial Histories of Devonshire 5 (Exeter, 1935), p. 381.

[32] A. Moore, 'A Barge of Edward III', *Mariner's Mirror* 6 (1920), 229–42, translated in H. T. Riley, *Memorials of London and London Life in the XIIth, XIVth, and XVth Centuries* (London, 1868), pp. 368–9; Sandahl, *Middle English Sea Terms*, III, 144–8, 153.

French pilot, written about 1480 and printed in 1520, with an English translation printed by Robert Copeland in 1528.[33]

Although these instances of maritime record-keeping in French were most common in the port towns of southern and eastern England and occur infrequently after the early fifteenth century, there are enough examples of the everyday use of French in civic administration in northern and western England, even into the fifteenth century, to make us rethink what many have assumed to be the geographic limits of Anglo-French.[34] While the south-eastern port towns show the most frequent signs of French influence, port towns as far north as Hull and York were recording their chamberlain's accounts, ordinances, toll rates, and other documents in Anglo-French well into the late fourteenth and early fifteenth century.[35] The custumal and list of customs rates of the south-western port of Exeter were in Anglo-French, while the duke of Cornwall regularly corresponded with his havener (a resident of Fowey) and other Cornish men in French on such matters as the purchase and transport of wine, the collection of port customs, and the capture of a Norman ship during a fourteenth-century truce.[36] Many

---

[33] D. W. Waters, *The Rutters of the Sea: The Sailing Directions of Pierre Garcie* (New Haven CT, 1967); Burwash, *Merchant Shipping*, p. 32. For two manuscripts of a Middle English rutter, see R. Ward, 'The Earliest Known Sailing Directions in English: Transcription and Analysis', *Deutsche Schiffahrtsarchiv* 27 (2004), 49–92.

[34] Others have noted the spatial focus of Anglo-Norman in the south and east regions of England (for example, W. Rothwell, 'Language and Government in Medieval England', *ZfSL* 93 (1983), 258–70), but have attributed it to proximity to London as the centre of law and administration instead of the influence of mariners and merchants in port towns regularly trading with and visiting France and French-speaking Flanders (and hosting French-speaking mariners and merchants).

[35] For example, Hull Record Office, BRF 2/341–2 (Chamberlain's Account Rolls, 1353/4, 1354/5); BRE 1 (covering 1339–1400), ff. 76–80, 89, 94, 144, 148–52, 161, 170–3, 205–6, 209–10, 232, and so on; BRG 1 (Bench Book 1, covering 1390–1645), ff. 5–9v. *York Memorandum Book*, ed. Sellers. Note also the French petitions sent by other northern ports; *Northern Petitions Illustrative of Life in Berwick, Cumbria and Durham in the Fourteenth Century*, ed. C. M. Fraser, Surtees Society 194 (Gateshead, 1981).

[36] *Anglo-Norman Custumal of Exeter*, ed. Schopp; few examples of French survive at Exeter, though see Devon Record Office, Exeter City Archives, Misc. Roll 90; Exeter Mayor's Court Roll, 1305/6, m. 16d, 1314/15, m. 44d; Book 55, f. 68, Book 51, f. 36; Exeter Bridge Warden's Account, 1349/50 (I thank David Trotter for bringing this account to my attention). See also D. A. Trotter, 'Walter of Stapledon and the Premarital Inspection of Philippa of Hainault', *French Studies Bulletin* 49 (1993), 1–4 for the bishop of Exeter's use of French. One of the very few poll taxes to be written in Anglo-French is that for Dartmouth: M. Kowaleski, 'The 1377 Dartmouth Poll Tax', *Devon and Cornwall Notes and Queries* 35 (1985), 286–95. For French used in the Cornish ports, see *The Havener's Accounts of the Earldom and Duchy of Cornwall 1287–1356*, ed. M. Kowaleski, Devon and Cornwall Record Society n.s. 44 (Exeter, 2001), pp. 199, 214–15, 239, 264–5, 277–8; *Register of Edward the Black Prince preserved in the Public Record Office: Part II (Duchy of Cornwall) A.D. 1351–1365* (London, 1931). The Black Prince also relied mainly on French in his correspondence with local officials in the palatinate of Chester; many of his correspondents were port-town residents who presumably would have been able to read the letters and orders addressed to them; see *Register of Edward the Black*

ristol records are also written in Anglo-French, as are the early custumals of the
ish port towns of Cork, Dublin, and Waterford.[37] Historical linguists seeking
e geographical distribution and origins of the spread of the French of 'England'
ould do well to consider the crucial role of port towns in the early use of insular
rench.[38]

These examples of how French was employed in English coastal communi-
es mainly relate to written records. What, however, is the evidence that illit-
rate English mariners and fishermen may have actually spoken or understood
rench? Mixed crews of different nationalities were not uncommon on medi-
val ships, so English sailors on Flemish or Gascon ships may have employed
rudimentary French to communicate with fellow mariners.[39] Froissart noted
e favourable interaction of English and French fishermen during the Hundred
ears' War:

> They [English fishers] brought news to Sir Simon [governor of Dover Castle]
> as he asked them to, for when they met French fishermen these told them all
> they knew, and sometimes more. Whether France or England are at war or
> not, fishermen at sea would never hurt each other, but are friends themselves
> and helpful when necessary. They buy and sell their fish between them at sea,
> when some have a better catch than others.[40]

Prince preserved in the Public Record Office: Part III (Palatinate of Chester), A.D. 1351–1365
(London, 1932), which also contains fragments of correspondence with North Wales.
[7] The Bristol records in French, which include many gild ordinances (as in *Little Red Book
of Bristol*, ed. F. B. Bickley, 2 vols. (Bristol, 1900)), adhere to the pattern observed in the
essay by Britnell in this volume. For the Irish custumals, see *Historic and Municipal
Documents of Ireland*, ed. J. T. Gilbert (London, 1870), pp. 240–69 (which dates to *c.*1300,
but may contain portions dating to before 1229); *Borough Customs*, ed. Bateson, I, xiv–
xv, xxii, liii–lv.
[8] The civic administration of the south-eastern port towns was in particular influenced
by contact with northern French towns, as evident in their adoption of a similar
municipal office structure and customary law codes (e.g. the similarities between the
Domesday of Ipswich and the *Établissements de Rouen*, a twelfth-century law code
adopted by many French communes). For the text of the *Établissements*, see A. Giry, *Les
Établissements de Rouen*, 2 vols. (Paris, 1883). For the close relationship between London
and Rouen in the twelfth century, when the *Établissements de Rouen* first appeared: J.
H. Round, *The Commune of London* (Westminster, 1899), pp. 246–51. For the similarities
between a clause concerning scolding in the Ipswich Domesday and the custumals of
several northern French towns, see M. Kowaleski, 'Gossip, Gender, and the Economy:
The Origins of Scolding Indictments in Medieval English Towns' (unpublished paper
given at the National Humanities Center, Research Triangle Park, North Carolina,
October 2005).
[9] M. Kowaleski, '"Alien" Encounters in the Maritime World of Medieval England',
Medieval Encounters 13 (2007), 96–121.
[0] Jean Froissart, *Oeuvres de Froissart*, ed. J. M. B. C. Kervyn de Lettenhove and A. Scheler,
25 vols. (Brussels, 1867–77), XII, 8; translation in Froissart, *Chronicles*, G. Brereton, ed.
and trans. (Harmondsworth, 1968), pp. 307–8.

What language were these English fishermen speaking when they exchanged information with their French counterparts at sea? When they chatted with fellow masters about weather conditions, or told tales in harbour-front taverns? When they encountered the customs officials of foreign ports and reported the content of their cargo? That they regularly communicated is without doubt; indeed maritime historians and anthropologists have repeatedly emphasized not only the mobility and foreign contacts of the sea-going life, but also seamen's sense of common purpose and an *esprit de corps* that cut across national boundaries. In the world of medieval England, this *esprit de corps* was frequently expressed in French, as in the *trêves pescheresses* (fishing truces) that proliferated during the fifteenth century, when the English, French, and Flemish governments extended safe-conducts to fishermen of all nationalities, even in the midst of the worst fighting of the Hundred Years War.[41] Agreements about ransoming between individual port towns on both sides of the Channel were also recorded in French; that between New Romney and French mariners living around Harfleur, for instance, survives in a French copy set into an otherwise Latin record of town accounts.[42]

Noteworthy too are the indentures and receipts that witness the payment of wages to shipmasters and their crews for naval service. The formal accounts recording payments to shipmasters and mariners serving the crown were normally in Latin,[43] but the indentures enumerating the terms of employment and receipt of final payments were usually in Anglo-French. These indentures were written in the local port where the ship was arrested for naval duty; both shipmasters and navy paymasters affixed their seals to these Anglo-French indentures and each received a copy. Why choose to record these exchanges in French if shipmasters did not understand what they were sealing? The simplicity and immediacy of the language in these documents, which survive in great numbers in the Public Record Office in London because of the crown's reliance on merchant shipping for naval transport and service, also suggest that even masters of small 22-ton ships from a small port like Wrangle (Figure 8.1) understood basic French.[44]

---

41 These safe-conducts are scattered throughout Thomas Rymer, comp., *Foedera, conventiones, litterae, et cujuscumque generis acta publica inter reges Angliae…*, ed. G. Holmes et al., 3rd edn, 10 vols. (The Hague, 1739–45). See also M. Mollat, 'La pêche à Dieppe' reprinted in his *Études d'histoire maritime (1938–1975)* (Turin, 1977), pp. 38–9. The governments had in mind the crucial provisioning role the fishers played on both sides of the Channel.

42 East Kent Archives Centre, NR/FAC.2, f. 72v of the New Romney Assessment Books for the year 1412. See also Devon Record Office, SM. 1112 (printed in *Dartmouth*, ed. Watkin, pp. 400–1), for a similar agreement made between Dartmouth and St Malo. On this issue, see also Kowaleski, '"Alien" Encounters', pp. 119–20.

43 For some examples of naval accounts in French, see PRO, E101/6/41 (dated 1298), and 14/26, 15/4, 20/29, 20/34, 531/15 (all from the first half of the fourteenth century) and 26/37, 28/23, 29/1, 31/17, 42/8, 42/22 (all late fourteenth century).

44 The indentures were not usually saved because they were summarized on the Exchequer particular or enrolled accounts, but many hundreds survive for the late fourteenth century and may be found in PRO, E101/22/38, 22/30, 29/31, 30/30, 40/1

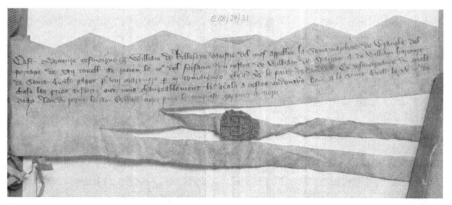

Figure 8.1: An indenture between the Crown and a shipmaster of Wrangle for three weeks of naval service by his 22-ton ship with eight mariners, 15 May 1369. The National Archives, Public Record Office, E101/29/31/23

Shipmasters were the English mariners most likely to be able to converse in French because, in foreign ports from Flanders to Bordeaux, they would have needed to communicate with local customs officials, dock workers, victuallers, and merchants buying or selling their wares. Their range of responsibilities is evident in a type of agreement called a 'charter party': a contract with merchants freighting cargo that set out the obligations of the shipmaster in terms of costs for carriage and advance payments; charges such as pilotage, towage, and port dues; the ship's destination and the route that it would follow; and the time allotted to reach the destination and unload (or load) cargo. Since the bulk of the (very few) charter parties that survive for medieval England are in French, they provide strong evidence that the shipmaster knew enough French to know what he was committing to. These agreements, moreover, were primarily oral contracts; Walter Giffard, shipmaster of the *Saint Mary* of Lyme, hired a Monsieur Mauran in Bordeaux to write his charter party, which he 'signed' with his mark, a kind of cross attached to a fish-like design, not unlike the merchants' marks used to label medieval barrels, sarplers, and other cargo containers.[45]

40/20, 41/2, 41/26, 41/28, 41/29, 41/30, 41/31, 41/32, 41/36, 42/5, 42/6, 42/7. For some early fourteenth-century examples, see PRO, E101/19/14. Very few indentures survive for the fifteenth century, but a group in 1436 are in Latin (PRO, E101/53/12), while in 1450/1 a group of 83 receipts for service and wages was in English; see PRO, E101/54/15. The enrolled accounts also contain more English by the mid-fifteenth century; see PRO, E101/54/14.

45 R. Ward, 'A Surviving Charter-Party of 1323', *Mariner's Mirror* 81 (1995), 387–401. For other charter parties, see *Calendar of Plea and Memoranda Rolls of the City of London*, vol. 3: *1381–1412*, ed. A. H. Thomas (Cambridge, 1932), pp. 193–204; *Documents pour servir à l'histoire du commerce des Pays-Bas avec la France jusqu'à 1585, II, Actes notariés de Bordeaux 1470–1520*, ed. M. A. Drost ('s-Gravenhage, 1989), pp. 3–4; M. K. James, *Studies in the Medieval Wine Trade* (Oxford, 1971), pp. 133–42. By the sixteenth century,

My point here is that communication between English mariners and those from elsewhere may have been eased by the use of French as the *lingua franca* of not only maritime law and some port-town records, but also as the basis of a common argot on the Atlantic littoral.[46] Ship-names recorded in Latin accounts of the thirteenth and fourteenth centuries are frequently in French, which suggests that shipmasters and mariners may have been using French to refer to their ships.[47] We can also see this influence in the large number of English sea terms borrowed from French. For example, the Middle English word for the pilot who guided ships through treacherous waters was 'lodeman' which was borrowed not from the Old English 'ladman' (which meant 'guide') but from the Norman French 'loman' or 'lodman', which had the expanded semantic range of 'skilled navigator through estuaries and ports'.[48] The Anglo-French sense of the word also entered Breton, Spanish, Galician, and Portuguese. Similar borrowings are evident in the medieval Thames vocabulary studied by Laura Wright. Although French influence is not especially prevalent for the names of constructions on the river or for describing the river, it is evident in 75 per cent of the names of inlets (such as 'fleet', and 'sluice'); 60 per cent of fish types ('flounder', 'plaice', 'mackerel', and 'salmon' to name only a few); 50 per cent of objects put into the river, including 'anchor', and 'sounder;' over 40 per cent of the words for types of ships (such as 'barge', 'crayer', 'ketch', and 'galley'); and 31 per cent of the names of people working on the river (including 'mariner').[49]

charter parties were in English; *Pleas in the Court of Admiralty*, ed. Marsden, I, 35–8, 81–3, 112–13.

46 On this point, see also D. Trotter, '*Oceano vox*: You Never know Where a Ship Comes From', in *Aspects of Multilingualism in European Language History*, ed. K. Braunmüller and G. Ferraresi (Amsterdam, 2003), pp. 15–33. For the development of a *lingua franca* (used in particular by merchants and diplomats, but also mariners) in the medieval Mediterranean, see J. E. Wansborough, *Lingua franca in the Mediterranean* (Richmond, Surrey, 1996). Around the Indian Ocean, Arabic became a kind of *lingua franca*, and later 'a sort of nautical Portuguese' achieved the same wider currency; see M. Pearson, 'Coastal Communities and Maritime History', *History in Focus: The Sea* 9 (2005), available online at http://www.history.ac.uk/ihr/Focus/Sea/articles/pearson.html [accessed 11 October 2007]. See also R. Kahane and A. Tietze, *The Lingua Franca in the Levant: Turkish Nautical Terms of Italian and Greek Origin* (Urbana IL, 1958), who discuss the penetration of foreign nautical terms into Turkish via *lingua franca*.

47 M. Kowaleski, ed., *The Local Customs Accounts of the Port of Exeter 1266–1321*, Devon and Cornwall Record Society n.s. 36 (1993); Trotter, '*Oceano vox*', pp. 16, 24–8.

48 See W. Sayers, 'Chaucer's Shipman and the Law Marine', *The Chaucer Review* 37:2 (2002), p. 152, for this and following.

49 L. Wright, *Sources of London English: Medieval Thames Vocabulary* (Oxford, 1996). I counted all words that Wright identified as having a French, Old French or Anglo-Norman etymology. This method is admittedly rough; for the difficulties determining the 'origin' of technical naval terms in a multilingual society, see D. Trotter, '*Oceano vox*', pp. 15–28, and D. Trotter, 'Langue et transmission du savoir artisanal: la construction navale en Angleterre au Moyen Âge', in *La transmission des savoirs au Moyen Âge et à la Renaissance*, vol. 1 : *du XIIᵉ au XVᵉ siècle*, ed. P. Nobel (Besançon, 2005), pp. 319–29. On the widespread adoption of French vocabulary within an urban and commercial context, see also W. Rothwell, 'English and French in England after 1362',

As Bertil Sandahl has pointed out, the common occupational argot of medieval mariners (one of the things that set them apart from landlubbers) led to the adoption of many 'foreign' terms into nautical vocabularies. The French nautical vocabulary includes English and Celtic words describing the operation of a ship, Dutch terms for ship construction, and German words for combat.[50] Old Norse and Low German contributed a particularly large number of sea terms to English, including many that refer to essential parts of the ship, such as 'bow' and 'keel', or to the types of wood and nails used in shipbuilding.[51] In contrast, many of the French terms for parts of ships that found their way into English, such as 'bilge', 'plank', and 'cabin', originally had non-nautical meanings. Another large group of English nautical terms came from Anglo-Norman French that had been influenced by Old Norse, such as 'sail' and 'shroud'. Sandahl has argued that the close correlation between the nautical vocabularies of countries around the North Sea and bordering the English Channel points to the existence of a common core vocabulary among mariners in this region.

This evidence for the adoption of French terms into English maritime vocabulary is suggestive, but obviously not conclusive, if we want to know what languages English seamen were acquainted with during the Middle Ages. English was clearly the primary language of English sailors from at least the thirteenth century on, as evidenced by the Middle English words often used in Anglo-Norman maritime records for technical terms relating to the ship and its gear.[52] By the late fifteenth century, moreover, English had supplanted Anglo-Norman sufficiently that Bordeaux parents included instruction of English as one of the conditions of the apprenticeship contract their son entered into with a Hull mariner.[53] Nonetheless, the regularity with which mariners came into contact with French words in their daily work, the development of a maritime argot to ease communication within mixed crews including non-English sailors, or English sailors on foreign vessels,[54] their frequent travels overseas – particularly to French-speaking lands like Gascony, Picardy, Normandy, and parts of Flanders – and their familiarity and regular contact with the maritime law and

English Studies 6 (2001), 539–59, and J. D. Burnley, 'French and Frenches in Fourteenth-Century London', in *Language Contact in the History of English*, ed. D. Kastovsky and A. Mettinger (Frankfurt am Main, 2001), pp. 17–34. On the assimilation of Anglo-Norman words into English technical registers, see L. Wright, 'Bills, Accounts Inventories: Everyday Trilingual Activities in the Business World of Later Medieval England', in Trotter, *Multilingualism*, pp. 149–56; L. Wright, 'Trade between England and the Low Countries: Evidence from Historical Linguistics', in *England and the Low Countries in the Late Middle Ages*, ed. C. Barron and N. Saul (Stroud, 1998), pp. 169–79.

Michel Mollat, *La vie quotidienne des gens de mer en Atlantique (IXe–XVIe siècle)* (Paris, 1983), pp. 215–16. See A. Jal, *Glossaire nautique : Répertoire polyglotte de termes de marine anciens et modernes*, 2 vols. (Paris, 1848), new edn, 6 vols. (Paris, 1970–2006).

For this and the following, see Sandahl, *Middle English Sea Terms*, I, 21–3; II, 3–6.

Sandahl, *Middle English Sea Terms*, I, 23. See also Trotter, 'Langue et transmission du savoir artisanal'.

J. Bernard, *Navires et gens de mer à Bordeaux (vers 1400–vers 1550)* (Paris, 1968), p. 641.

Kowaleski, '"Alien" Encounters', pp. 107–8.

courts of medieval England, strongly suggest that a large percentage of Englis
sailors (especially those who travelled on overseas routes) from the twelft
into the late fourteenth century (perhaps up to the mid-fifteenth century) coul
understand and speak rudimentary French. English shipmasters were likely t
be capable of understanding and speaking French at a higher level given thei
need to negotiate with continental merchants about freightage and local transac
tions for cargo and victuals, as well as deal with shore-side officials and vendor
in foreign ports.[55] The ability to communicate in French was even more valuabl
for overseas merchants, the same group which was responsible for compiling s
many port-town registers and custumals in French, for serving on mixed jurie
that settled maritime disputes, and for prompting letters and petitions in Frencl
to defend their civic interests.[56] The regular contact between English-speakin;
mariners, shipmasters, and overseas merchants and native French-speakers
moreover, lends further support to those who argue that Anglo-Norman was nc
isolated from continental French.[57]

M. Dominica Legge some time ago speculated that the French of England ma
have survived longer in port towns than elsewhere, given the prevalence of it
use in port-town custumals which, in several instances, included copies of th
Laws of Oléron.[58] The oldest written manuscripts of any medieval sea law are th
early fourteenth-century Anglo-Norman texts of the Laws of Oléron.[59] The Blac
Book of Admiralty, the fundamental text guiding the adjudication of maritim
disputes in England, was also in French. The fact that neither the Laws of Oléroi
nor the Black Book were translated into Latin and English until the sixteentl
century suggests that the French versions were satisfactory to a wide range c
maritime officials and medieval seamen.[60] Portsmen who used French, moreove
were unlike the lawyers, clergy, and aristocracy who employed French in that the

---

[55] On semi-communication as a mode of language contact, see K. Braunmüller, 'Commu
nication Strategies in the Area of the Hanseatic League: The Approach by Semi
Communication', *Multilingua* 16:4 (1997), 365–73; L. Wright, 'Models of Languag
Mixing: Code-Switching versus Semicommunication in Medieval Latin and Medievɛ
English Accounts', in *Language Contact in the History of English*, ed. D. Kastovsky anɪ
A. Mettinger (Frankfurt, 2001), pp. 363–76.

[56] For an example of this latter, see C. D. Liddy, *War, Politics and Finance in Late Medievɛ
English Towns: Bristol, York and the Crown, 1350–1400* (Woodbridge, 2005), pp. 170–5.

[57] For example, D. Trotter, 'Not as Eccentric as it Looks: Anglo-French and French French
FMLS 39 (2003), 427–38; idem, 'L'anglo-normand: variété insulaire, ou variété isolée?
Médiévales 45 (2003), 43–54; R. Ingham, 'Syntactic Change in Anglo-Norman and Cont
nental French Chronicles: Was There a "Middle" Anglo-Norman?', *Journal of Frenc
Language Studies* 16 (2006), 25–49; idem in this volume; idem, 'The Transmission c
Later Anglo-Norman: Some Syntactic Evidence', in Ingham, *Anglo-Norman Language.*

[58] M. D. Legge, 'Anglo-Norman as a Spoken Language', *ANS* 2 (1979), 116.

[59] *Black Book*, ed. Twiss, IV, vii, and above, p. 00.

[60] See *Black Book*, ed. Twiss, I, xxvi–vii, liv, lxxvi, lxxiii.

probably did not know Latin (as Chaucer's shipman bluntly acknowledged),[61] and their knowledge of French was most likely acquired piecemeal under practical circumstances, rather than at school. I do not want to push this point too far,[62] but I believe it is reasonable to argue that a substantial number of English mariners, most of them illiterate, knew enough French for basic communication in foreign ports. In other words, the French of England was for them a practical, living (oral) vernacular, not solely a language of record or status.

---

[61] *The Riverside Chaucer*, ed. L. Benson, 3rd edn (Boston MA, 1987), p. 104, lines 1185–90. See also the Anglo-Norman romance, *Fouke le Fitz Warin*, when a man passing himself off as a foreign merchant speaks good French with the king, but communicates with the mayor of London in a 'latyn corupt' that the mayor easily understands (*Fouke le Fitz Waryn*, ed. E. J. Hathaway, P. T. Ricketts, C. A. Robson, and A. D. Wilshere ANTS 26–28 (Oxford, 1975), p. 56, lines 11–17. Rothwell ('Sugar and Spice', p. 658) suggests that the mayor and fake merchant were speaking in the *lingua franca* French used in business records.

[62] Studer's argument that port records 'show conclusively that French was the language of the sea-faring classes' (*Oak Book*, III, 8) partially endorsed by Foster ('Introduction', *Local Port Book of Southampton 1435–36*, ed. Foster, p. xii) takes insufficient account of other port languages of use and record (English and Latin); see above, n. 30 and (for mid-fourteenth-century Latin local port customs accounts) *The Sign Manuals and the Letters Patent of Southampton to 1422*, vol. 1, ed. H. W. Gidden, Southampton Record Society 12 (Southampton, 1916), pp. 76–87. It is even debatable if medieval Southampton functioned 'in French' (Rothwell, 'Sugar and Spice', p. 650); the port functioned in English, Latin, and French – one of which must have been understood by the hundreds of Italian seamen and merchants who regularly visited Southampton in the later Middle Ages; see Kowaleski, '"Alien" Mariners', pp. 113–15.

9

John Barton, John Gower and Others:
Variation in Late Anglo-French

Brian Merrilees and Heather Pagan

Early in the fifteenth century John Barton, a native of Chester who had studied in Paris, makes the following claim in his *Donait* ('grammar'):

> Pour ceo que les bones gens du roiaume d'Engleterre sont enbrasez a sçavoir lire et escrire, entendre et parler droit françois, a fin qu'ils puissent entrecomuner bonement ove lour voisins, c'est a dire les bones gens du roiaume de France, ... tres necessaire je cuide estre aus Engleis de sçavoir la droite nature de françois ... je, Johan Barton, escolier de Paris, nee et nourie toutez voiez d'Engleterre en la conté de Cestre, j'ey baillé aus avant diz Anglois un Donait françois pour les briefment entreduyr en la droit language du Paris et de païs d'entour.[1]

Barton's own French seems to have a relatively high degree of conformity with standard Middle French but of course with a good sprinkling of insular characteristics such as the absence of weak *e* in spellings, occasional loss of gender distinction and Anglo-French verb forms such as *apperera*, the future of *apparoir*. The suggestion of a model elsewhere is, however, an important feature to note and one that surely did not touch all of the French written in England in the later period.

For centuries insular writers of French had been excusing their ability in the language, from a nun of Barking Abbey in the twelfth century who, in the *Vie de seint Edouard*, deplored her 'faus franceis d'Angletere' to John Gower in the late fourteenth century who explains in the *envoi* to his *Traitié pour essampler les*

---

[1] P. Swiggers, 'Le *Donait françois*: la plus ancienne grammaire du français', *Revue des langues romane* 89 (1985), 235–51; T. Städtler, *Zu den Anfängen der französischen Grammatiksprache* (Tübingen, 1988), pp. 128–37. ('Because the good people of the kingdom of England are keen to learn to read, write, hear and speak good French so that they may communicate easily with their neighbours, that is, the good people of the kingdom of France, ... (and as) I think it very necessary for the English to know the proper nature of French ... I, John Barton, scholar from Paris, born and raised however in England in the county of Chester, have given to the aforesaid English a French grammar to introduce them in a simple manner to the proper language of Paris and the surrounding territory.') For further socio-linguistic comment on this passage, see the essay by Putter in this volume, p. 405, and on Barton's grammar in its context of late medieval manuals, see the essay by Machan.

nantz mariés that his lack of *facunde* or 'fluency' results from his being English.[2]
the early period of Anglo-Norman is distinct from continental varieties, we
n see some uniformity in its expression, though this is mostly in literary texts,
ere being fewer non-literary texts in the twelfth and early thirteenth centu-
es. In the later period there appears to be a greater diversity in the varieties of
sular French, which can in part be attributed to an increasing influence of conti-
ntal French and a perspective that there was a model of which some writers
ere more aware than others.[3] In this essay we shall look at three examples in an
tempt to show some of the differences in a language that still had various func-
ons in fourteenth- and fifteenth-century England.[4]

The first text extract is from the *Anglo-Norman Prose Brut to 1332*,[5] a small
bset of three manuscripts in a larger family of Anglo-Norman prose Bruts
ritten in the late thirteenth and early fourteenth centuries. This particular work
found in three manuscripts and was copied around 1360. There are some chal-
nges in analysing the language of the *Prose Brut*, not the least being that it was
ritten over a period of sixty years. This is true of the *Anglo-Norman Prose Brut*
1332 where the earliest manuscript – Harley 200 – often presents older forms
an the two later copies. The first extract is from the oldest part of the text,
st composed around 1272, and the second from the end of the work and was
mposed after 1332, probably closer to 1350. The final extract is unique to the
ree manuscripts of the *Anglo-Norman Prose Brut to 1332* and was written after
60.

(1) Qaunt Ascanius le roi soun piere le savoit, il fist enquere dez sages mestres
qe savoient grant clergie dez plusours arz lequele ycele damoisele enfaunteroit, filtz ou file. Et qaunt ils avoient bien regardé ceste affeare par lez artz, il
disoient a piere q'ele enfaunteroit une fitz qe primes tueroit sa miere et puis
soun piere. Et issint avint kar la miere morust del enfaunter qaunt l'enfaunt
nasquit et soun piere lui fist apeler Bruyt et lez mestrez disoient a piere qe
cele enfaunt ferroit multz dez maulx en plusors pays et puis vendroit a graunt

This may also be seen as a literary conceit, but we note that the examples are all
insular. See further I. Short, *Manual of Anglo-Norman*, ANTS OPS 7 (London, 2007), pp.
14–15.
This is not to dismiss the continued development of insular French in its various literary
and documentary functions and the influence on this French of English morphology
and syntax. See further the essay by Ingham in this volume.
The features mentioned for the texts that follow can be confirmed in M. K. Pope, *From
Latin to Modern French with especial consideration of Anglo-Norman*, rev. edn (Manchester,
1952), part V, chapters 4, 5; and Short, *Manual of Anglo-Norman*. Variant forms may be
consulted online in *AND*. For the early period, see also B. Merrilees, «La simplification
du système vocalique en anglo-normand», *Revue de linguistique romane* (juillet–déc.
1982), pp. 319–26.
All passages are transcribed from London, British Library, MS Harley 200, also found
in H. J. Pagan, 'The Anglo-Norman Prose Brut to 1332: An Edition' (unpublished Ph.D.
dissertation, University of Toronto, 2006). Two other manuscripts, Oxford, Bodleian
Library, Douce 128 (21702) and Cambridge, Trinity College, R.5.32 (723) are also
known under this name.

honur. Le roy Asqanyus morust qaunt Dieux le voleit et Silveyn resceut la terre et se fist durement amer de sez gentz. Et qaunt Bruyt soun filtz fust de .xv. aunz, il ala une jour a bois pur chacer et sicome cesti Bruyt deveroit trere a une cerf, la seate par mesaventure glasa et occist soun piere.[6]

(2) Le quinte an de son regne le jeofdy aprés la Paske il passa le meer aultre foitz vers le roi de Fraunce pur faire son homage pur la terre de Gascoigne et fust illesqes moult honurablement resceu et puis revint dedeinz les .xv. jours et doncs fist crier solempnes joustes a Dertforde et tost aprés furent criez les joustes en Chepre en la citee de Loundres et grauntz hurdiz faitz a travers le rue pur la roigne et aultres dames pur veer le jeu qe durat .iii. jours.

Avint issint a mesmes les joustes qe le hurdiz où la roigne fust assis et lez aultres dames chai tut droit a la terre a graunt peril de toutz qe leinz fusrent qe fust par mi la defaulte des charpenters dount ascuns fusrent blescez mais nul n'y fust peri. Et pur ceo qe la blame feust en lez charpenters le roi les perdona a la requeste la roigne et fusrent lez hurdiz reparillez tout de nuyt et le jeu l'endemain contenuz bien nobliement.[7]

(3) Ore avetz oy coment Engleterre fust nomé primes Albion et la resoun purquei. Et ore escutez coment ele fust puis nomé Bretayne si en orrez pleinement le bruyt de totes lez batailles et aventures q'ount esté en Engleterre du temps de chescune roy tantqe a temps le roi Edward de Wyndesore le tierce Edward aprés la conqueste et ascune partie de soun temps.[8]

---

6 ('When his father King Ascanius learned of it, he inquired of wise scholars who we greatly learned in many arts as to whether this young woman would bear a son or daughter. And when they had considered this matter well by means of their art, the said to the father that she would bear a son who would first kill his mother and the his father, and so it happened, for the mother died in childbirth when the baby w born. And his father had him called Brut, and the scholars told the father that the chil would do much harm in many lands and then come to great honour. King Ascaniu died when God willed it, and [...] Silvein received the land and made himself dear loved by his people. And when his son Brut was fifteen years old, he went [to th forest] hunting one day with his father. And just as this Brut was about to shoot a stag, his arrow slipped by mischance and killed his father.'): J. Marvin, *The Olde Anglo-Norman Prose 'Brut' Chronicle: An Edition and Translation* (Woodbridge, 2006 p. 75 (see further the essay on the *Brut* by Marvin in this volume). Pagan's additio are noted in brackets. The following two translations are by Pagan.

7 ('The fifth year of his [Edward III] reign, the Thursday after Easter, he crossed the s again in order to pay homage to the King of France for the land of Gascony and l was most honourably received there and returned home within two weeks. Then th important tourney at Dartford was announced and soon after the tourneys at Cheap side in London were announced and great stands were erected across the road in ord for the queen and her ladies to watch the game during the three days. It happene thus at these tourneys that the stand where the queen and her ladies were seate fell to the ground to the great peril of all those who were there. It was the fault the carpenters that people were injured though none were killed. And although th carpenters were blamed, the king pardoned them at the request of the queen and th stands were repaired during the night and the game continued the next day in a mo noble manner.')

8 ('You have now heard how England was first named Albion and the reason for thi And now you will hear how it was then called Britain and you will hear fully the sto

The three *Brut* extracts present a number of typical late Anglo-French developments: the complete disintegration of the declension system and the two-case flexional system (nominative/oblique) is no longer maintained, with the flexional -*s* now only a marker of plurality. For example, the nominative form of the definite article, that is *li* in both the masculine singular and plural, has been completely abandoned in favour of the oblique case, that is *le* and *les*. In fact, there is only one example of an article used in the subject case in the entire work, in what seems to be due to the retention of an older epic form, in the expression, 'li estut, li orguillous Faukes de Breuté' ('the stubborn, the proud Falkes de Breauté').

Similarly, the use of personal pronouns is simplified with the nominative case generally unused. The Anglo-Norman forms: *jeo, nous, vous, lour* are used most frequently. The Harley manuscript exhibits the tendency, which began in the fourteenth century, to use *ils* rather than *il* as the third-person plural subject pronoun. Douce and Trinity use this form even more frequently than Harley, a consequence of being later in date, though there is occasional use of *il* as the third-person plural subject form in the first 3,000 lines of the text, generally in the expression *il y avoient* ('there were').

Also, any notion of grammatical gender seems to have been abandoned. In the first extract we can see such examples as *une fitz* ('a son') or *cele enfaunt* ('this child'), both which would normally be masculine. The gender of nouns fluctuates within the text, with some, such as *la eglise* ('the church') or *le meer* ('the sea') in the second example, appearing to be both masculine and feminine. There is rarely agreement between nouns and their modifying articles and adjectives; expressions such as *la petit Brutaigne* ('little Britain') are not uncommon.

The verbal system has also undergone a number of transformations and the text presents a number of characteristics of later Anglo-French. Examples of this are the variation in infinitive endings such as the form *nurer* found for *nurir* and *accomplier* for *accomplir*. Also, the third-person plural of the present and preterite both end in –*unt*, not unheard of in the twelfth century but certainly more common in the thirteenth and fourteenth.

A number of typical late orthographical changes are also represented in the *Anglo-Norman Prose Brut to 1332*. Certain letters have become interchangeable at this point; *a* and *e* often replace one another in words such as in *aspier* ('to spy') or *erchevesqe* ('archbishop'). There is some hesitation between the use of *o* and *u* in such words such as *tute/tote* or *long/lung* with Douce, the later manuscript, preferring the –*o* or more modern orthography. The digraph *ou* for *u* has been adopted, such as in the word *plusours* or *jour* though *moult* is rare in the text and appears most often as *mult*. The letter *y* has also been introduced as a substitute for *i* as in *nuyt*, perhaps to help avoid confusion with the letters *m, n, u* and *v*. The

of all the battles and adventures that occurred in England during the reign of each king until the time of Edward of Windsor, the third Edward after the conquest, and a portion of his reign.')

consonants *c*, *s* and *z* are interchangeable, for example, one will find *coruza* ('to anger') also spelled *corusa* or *corucea*.

The representation of the diphthongs *ai* and *ei* is variable with *ai* also spelled *ea* as in *meas* or *eai* as in *eaider* and both can also be reduced to *e* in words such as *mestre* and *crestre*. The two diphthongs also seem to be interchangeable in certain contexts; before *l* or *ll* either can be used as in *conseil/consail* or *mervaille/merveille*. Some continental influence is felt as the diphthong *oi* begins to replace *ei* such as in *foi*, and *loi*. The nasal vowels have begun to be spelled *aun* and *oun* as in *resoun* ('reason') or *graunt* ('big, great'), typical of Anglo-French in this period. Despite being used from the beginning of the thirteenth century, there is still some hesitation between these graphies and *an/on* though the former are definitely the preferred spellings. The *an* and *on* digraphs seem to occur slightly more frequently in the initial 2,000 lines of the text, though they are not unknown later.

There are some neologisms in the text; these tend to be nouns or adverbs calqued on known adjectives, such as *admirabilité* ('admiration'), *deblement* ('terribly'), *encurtinez* ('hung with tapestries'), and *reprovance* ('punishment'). There is some influence of English on the vocabulary for directions (*west, north, uppelande*), months (*July*), some adjectives (*huge, hote*) and for measurements (*ferlinge, esterling*) though the French *maille* and *sous* is also used.

The second text comes from British Library, MS Harley 4971, a manuscript which contains a number of texts related to the learning of French. Here the extract we have chosen is devoted to advice on estate management (fol. 7r):[9]

> Si vous desirrez deservier nul seignour ou dame d'estre clerc en leur hostel, al entré de vostre offys, avisez vous bien si vous portez tote le charge de lour hostel a respondre pur chescun offys ou ne mie. Et si vous le frez, donques avisez vous que vous facetz totes lez officers vener devant vous et moustrer escriptz, ou vous mesmez les porrés escrire, totes les choses q'ils ont en lour garde. Et facez donques vous une generale endenture de toux les ditz choses parentre vous et le seignour, dame, ou le seneschall, solonc l'usage de lour court. Et puis facez totes lez officers vener devant vous et facez une remembrance parentre eaux severalment de les chosez q'ils ont en lour offys. Et puis facez chescun de eaux prester lour serement q'ils serveront loialment le seignour et vous rendroit loialment lour acompte de toux les choses a eaux liverer. … Et a noyt facez totes les officers apparier devant vous et moustrer devant vous combien est despenduz de lour offyses le jour chascun par sey : ou primes en chescun offys acomptés primes l'estor et puis l'achat, notant adonques remaynt. Et de ceo la fretz les acomptz desouz le panel. En primes la summe d'estor despenduz, puis la summe d'achat despenduz, et adonques l'un et l'autre summe ensemble encoustes joynant deux filettes. Et adonques pluis en bas encouste remaynt.[10]

---

9   The best-known treatment of this subject is D. Oschinsky's *Walter of Henley and Other Treatises on Estate Management and Accounting* (Oxford, 1971).

10 ('If you wish to serve any gentleman or lady as overseer in their household, when you take up your charge, find out if you are responsible for the total household business

When we examine its language, there is no sense that this is anything but an insular text. Indeed it has most of the features of late Anglo-French.

The orthography, and what can be surmised from it of the phonology, have clear traits of Anglo-French developments in the later period.

Diphthong reduction, a strong feature of earlier AN, is only sparsely reproduced here:

officers, bussel (CF *officiers, boisseau*), but on the whole digraphs are common: *seignour, vous, noyt, rien, bien, loialment, remaint*. However, *pluis* and *eaux* (= *eux*) show digraphs for single vowels.

Weak *e* falls: *frez, offys, acomptz* (CF *ferez, office, acomptes*) but not in *offices*. /z/tz/x are confused: *escriptz, porrés, toux les ditz choses, chosez*.

The morphology too is clearly insular:

Gender and therefore agreement can be variable: *totes les officers, toux les ditz choses*.

There is a single case system with no evidence here of the old *cas sujet*.

Infinitive endings vary: *deservier, vener, apparier* instead of the more usual *deservir, venir, appareir*.

John Gower's French works seem until recently to have fallen between the cracks in both French and Anglo-Norman scholarship. If Dominica Legge in her *Anglo-Norman Literature* of 1963[11] and Ruth Dean in her 1999 *Anglo-Norman Literature: A Guide to Texts and Manuscripts*[12] record his contributions to the French written in England in the Middle Ages, the *Anglo-Norman Dictionary*, in its first edition (hereafter AND1)[13] sets Gower aside as not being part of the Anglo-Norman canon, though the second edition (hereafter AND) promises to right that omission.[14] In their continuation of the Bossuat bibliography of medieval

including each section or not. And if you do, make sure that you have all your staff appear before you and show in writing – or write it yourself – everything for which they are responsible. And prepare a general contract of all matters relating to you and the master, mistress or steward according to the custom of their household. And then have all the staff come before you and make a separate record of everything for which they are responsible. And then have each of them swear that they will serve the master loyally and give you a faithful account of all things handed to them. ... And in the evening have all the staff appear before you and each show you separately how much has been spent in their jurisdiction: and firstly in each section take account of the stock and purchases, noting then what remains. And from this, record the accounts below the panel. First, the total stock spent, then the total amount of purchases, and the two totals side by side making two files. And then, further down, what remains.') See Dean no. 397.

11 M. D. Legge, *Anglo-Norman Literature* (Oxford, 1963).
12 Dean nos. 247.1, 707, 708, 709, 801, 835 (1), 865, 895.
13 L. Stone, W. Rothwell, T. B. W. Reid et al., eds. *Anglo-Norman Dictionary* (London, 1977–92).
14 S. Gregory, W. Rothwell and D. Trotter, eds., *Anglo-Norman Dictionary*, 2nd edn, 2 vols. A–C, D–E (London, 2005). The online version was available after 2003 with restricted access when some of this research was undertaken. A combination of re-edited letters

French literature, Jacques Monfrin and Françoise Vielliard simply omit him alto
gether.[15] Of his language Ruth Dean says: 'Gower's French is not distinctively
Anglo-Norman.' There is some small redemption in the *Dictionnaire des lettre*
françaises where a short article devoted to Gower ends with the following: 'La
critique s'est longtemps montrée injuste pour ce bon ouvrier qui symbolise sous
son triple aspect la culture anglaise du XIVe siècle.'[16]

Gower's use of the French language seems particular. While his phonology and
morphology contain a certain number of traits that are characteristic of Anglo
Norman and of the northern and western dialects from which Anglo-Norman
derives, one intuitively agrees with Ruth Dean's assessment. G. C. Macaulay, in
the introduction to his edition, gives fair coverage of the phonology but much of
the description is based on orthographical rather than rhyming evidence.[17]

Our sample comes from the *Mirour de l'omme*, a long though incomplete alle
gorical poem of over 30,000 lines:

> 'Rende a Cesar ce q'est a luy;
> Ce q'est a dieu, a dieu tout si:
> Mais nous et l'un et l'autre avoir
> Volons, car d'un et d'autre auci
> Portons l'estat en terre yci.
> De dieu avons le plain pooir,
> Par quoy la part de son avoir
> Volons nous mesmes recevoir
> Tout proprement, sique nully
> En partira, si ce n'est voir,
> Qe nous porrons aparcevoir
> Q'au double nous ert remery.
> 'Ensi faisons le dieu proufit,
> Qe riens laissons grant ne petit
> De l'orr que nous porrons attraire;
> Car ly prelat nous sont soubgit,
> Si sont ly moigne ove lour habit,
> Q'ils n'osent dire le contraire
> Du chose que nous volons faire,
> Neis ly curet et ly viscaire:
> Leur falt donner sanz contredit
> Del orr, dont ils nous pourront plaire,
> Ou autrement leur saintuaire
> Du no sentence ert entredit.

and the rest from the first edition is now fully accessible. Gower is to be added to the
second edition.

15 F. Vielliard and J. Monfrin, *Manuel bibliographique de la littérature française du moyen âge*
de Robert Bossuat, 3ᵉ Supplément (1960–80) (Paris, 1986–91).

16 G. Hasenohr and M. Zink, *Dictionnaire des lettres françaises: le moyen âge* (Paris, 1992)
p. 868.

17 *The Complete Works of John Gower*, ed. G. C. Macaulay, 4 vols. (Oxford, 1899–1902), I
The French Works (Oxford, 1899), pp. xvi–xxxiv.

'Mais du Cesar presentement,
Portons le representement
Car nous du Rome la Cité
Ore avons l'enheritement;
Pour ce volons de toute gent
Tribut avoir par dueté.
Voir ly Judieu en son degré,
Neis la puteine acoustummée,
Ne serront quit du paiement:
Ce que Cesar ot oblié
En son temps, ore avons trové,
Les vices qui vont a l'argent.
'Je truis primer qant Costentin
Donnoit du Rome au pape en fin
Possessioun de la terrestre,
Ly Rois du gloire celestin
Amont en l'air de son divin
Par une voix q'estoit celeste
Faisoit crier, si dist que l'estre
Du sainte eglise ove tout le prestre
Ne serront mais si bon cristin,
Comme ainz estoiont leur ancestre,
Pour le venim qui devoit crestre
De ce q'ils ont le bien terrin.'   (*Mirour* 18601–48)[18]

Here we are dealing with a quite different *niveau de langue*, consciously literary, and an Anglo-French that seems closer to continental than insular forms. Few of the rhymes, for example, reflect a local origin (*luy: si, crestres: ancestre*) and

[18] ('Render unto Caesar that which is Caesar's, and unto God that which is God's. But we want to have both, for we bear the estate of both here on earth. From God we have full power, wherefore we will expect quite properly to receive His part without sharing it with anyone unless we can truly see that double will be repaid to us.

'We make God's profit in such a way that we forego nothing – big or small – of the gold that we can attract to us. For the prelates are subject to us, and so are the monks, so they dare not contradict anything we wish done, nor do the priests and vicars. They must give gold to please us; otherwise their sanctuary will be laid under interdict by our ruling.

'But we now represent Caesar also, for we now have the heritage of the city of Rome. Therefore, we want to have due tribute from all peoples. Not even the Jews or ordinary whores shall be exempt from payment. What Caesar had overlooked in his time we have now found: vices that yield money.

'I find that when Constantine gave the pope terrestrial possession of Rome, the celestial King of Glory, high in the air, cried out by means of a heavenly voice that Holy Church with all her priests would never be so really Christian as their ancestors previously had been, because of the poison that would grow out of their possession of worldly goods.'): *Mirour*, ed. Macaulay, *The French Works*, p. 216; trans. as *John Gower, The Mirror of Mankind*, by W. B. Wilson, revised by N. Wilson Van Baak with a foreword by R. F. Yeager (East Lansing MI, 1992).

only the orthography retains some Anglo-Norman features.[19] It is in Gower's vocabulary, however, that we find a mix of both insular and continental terms that points to an increasing consciousness of France as a source and model while not neglecting the Anglo-French he must have learned.

Gower is writing in a century that saw a flourishing of lexical creativity in French, especially through the works of translators such as Jean de Vignay, Pierre Bersuire and Nicole Oresme, but also from its authors.[20] John Fisher, Robert Yeager and others have drawn attention to Gower's knowledge of continental French texts and his own writing reflects, often very directly, his sources. He was also familiar with Anglo-Norman texts such as Thomas of Kent's *Roman de Toute Chevalerie*.[21]

We analyze only a small sample of Gower's vocabulary, the letters A–E which were available in the revision of the AND.[22]

Two categories of words were initially picked out: (1) those that appeared to have an Anglo-Norman flavour or usage, and (2) those that seemed to be continental French. For the latter, if they did not appear in the AND, we assumed they were not part of the regular Anglo-Norman stock. The usual checks were also made of the standard dictionaries of medieval French, such as Godefroy,[23] still a rich source after a hundred years, the Tobler–Lommatzsch *Altfranzösisches Wörterbuch*,[24] as well the *Französisches Etymologisches Wörterbuch*[25] and other sources, including the OED 2 online and a Middle French database in Nancy.[26] After further analysis we established four word-lists rather than two. The groups include:

1. Words that we label 'anglo-normanisants', that is words that appear to be restricted to French as used in England.

---

[19] In a 1910 University of Leipzig dissertation Alfred Tanneberg gives a more detailed account in which we note such features as rhyming of *u* from Latin *u*, which is palatalized in French to *ü* but which in Anglo-Norman remains a back vowel that can rhyme with *u* from Latin long *o*, or the reduction of the diphthong *ui* to *u*. These do not, however, occur frequently. Macaulay suggests that if his use of declension has 'vagaries ... they are by no means so wild in his case as they had been in that of some other writers' (*Complete Works*, I, xvi). Gower seems to pay little attention to gender, though sometimes this appears to be the result of versificational needs rather than a desire for grammatical conformity.

[20] On Oresme's lexis, see further Collette in this volume, pp. 376–9.

[21] See J. H. Fisher, *John Gower: Moral Philosopher and Friend of Chaucer* (New York, 1964), especially ch. 2; R. F. Yeager, *John Gower's Poetic: The Search for a New Arion* (Woodbridge, 1990), passim, but especially ch. 2. See also the essay by Yeager in this volume.

[22] See above, notes 13 and 14.

[23] F. Godefroy, *Dictionnaire de l'ancienne langue française et de tous ses dialectes du IXe au XVe siècle* (Paris, 1881–1902; Kraus reprint 1969).

[24] A. Tobler, rev. E. Lommatzsch, *Tobler–Lommatzsch Altfranzösisches Wörterbuch* (Berlin, 1925–).

[25] W. von Wartburg et al., *Französisches Etymologisches Wörterbuch* (Tübingen, 1948–).

[26] *Dictionnaire du Moyen Français* (DMF). Base de Lexiques de Moyen Français (DMF1), available online at: http://atilf.atilf.fr/dmf.htm.

2. Words that seem to be 'francisants', that is, words from continental French, including use in the northern and western dialects, the principal sources of Anglo-Norman, but not recorded in Anglo-Norman.

3. Words that to date we have not found other than in the works of John Gower, therefore which appear to be neologisms or words where we have not found an earlier attestation – this category alone raises a number of questions about Gower's capacities in French.

4. Words that may be debatable in their form or use but which should be considered in any treatment of Gower's French.

Insular words

he following words were seen as 'anglo-normanisants':

annueler 'annuary' (of a priest)
arbitrement 'decision'
assembleisoun 'meeting'
bountevous 'bounteous'
chericer 'cherish'
chevicer 'make profit'
chymere 'bishop's upper vestment'
concluder 'conclude'
conteckour 'contentious person'
contreplit 'opposition'
coustummer 'customer, buyer'
Delicacie 'name of second daughter of Gluttony'
deliement 'finely'
desallouance 'blame'
desjoyer (se) 'grieve'
dueté 'duty'
enchericer 'favour'
encloser 'enclose'
eneauer 'to wet'
englu 'attachment'
escoleier 'go to school'

This list does not show anything surprising. In some cases there is a different ermination from the expected continental French form (CF):

arbitrement instead of *arbitrage* (CF)
assembleisoun (one citation in AND) instead of *assemblement* (CF)
escoleier – *escoler* exists in CF in an active sense, but this is a neutral verb.

Three words seemed to be back formations, re-entering French from which hey came, slightly emended:

chericer 'cherish'
chevicer 'make profit'
enchericer 'favour'

These have as their radical the base 2 form of inchoative verbs in *-ir*. *Cherir* (*cheris* but *nous cherissons*) is the stem that enters English with the Picard sibilan 'sh'; *cherish* enters English in 1320–30, according to the OED. What may hav happened here is that the second radical with the 'iss' infix has been taken a the main base and the first conjugation terminations are added. It is possible th three examples of *cherice* are subjunctive but the context does not favour such a interpretation. Gower also uses *cherir* and its forms frequently.

– *enchericer* is found in the AND with the sense of 'raise the price of', which is also continental.

Two verbs have forms not found in CF:

– *concluder*, which may be influenced by Latin or again this may be an English form reintroduced into Gower's French. The OED records it in English though not yet with the Gower meanings.

– *encloser* instead of *enclore* (replaced by *inclure* in Mod. Fr.) is made with the second radical or the past participle as base.

The agent noun *conteckour* takes as its base *contec* 'quarrel, argument' most of the examples of which Godefroy locates in AN or Norman.

Delicacie is used by Gower as a proper noun with an implication of strong appetites. The OED notes that the ending 'acy' is entirely of English formation, the corresponding French termination being 'ace'. The adjective *délicat* did not enter French until the fifteenth century.

Godefroy records *desaloer* as a verb but all citations are insular.

The OED notes that forms of *dueté* are not recorded in CF.

Macaulay has some comments on *eneauer*, later used to explain the shrinking of cloth by wetting.[27]

Words used especially in CF

The list of words we have noted as appearing in Gower and used in conti nental rather than insular French is much longer than the insular list. One mus remember that the two share a large common lexis, and we have no doul that the words on this list would be understood by those in England versed i French. However, the first and second editions of the AND do not record thes words being used in other texts composed in England:

abaubir 'confuse'
accusatour 'accuser'
alconomie 'alchemy'
allentis 'sluggish'
amerrir 'diminish, destroy'
angelour 'angelic'
apostazer 'renounce one's faith'
appeticer 'desire'

---

27 Macaulay, *Complete Works*, I, xxxiii.

bilingue 'treacherous'
blasphemus 'blasphemous'
bobancer 'arrogant person'
burgoiserie 'bourgeoisie'
camerette 'bedroom'
ceinturelle 'girdle'
cervoiser 'beer-seller'
chanterole 'song'
charitousement 'charitably'
cohabiter 'live together'
commanderesse 'mistress, manager'
compendiousement 'shortly, in brief'
confessement 'confession'
conjur 'conspiracy'
consailleresse 'counsellor'
constance 'constance'
contendement 'attack'
contrepriser 'counterbalance'
contretencer 'strive against'
contumelie 'offensiveness'
creance 'leash for hawk'
curie 'cookery'
declinement 'ruin'
derisioun 'scorn'
desamiable 'unlovely'
descordement 'discord'
descordour 'out of harmony'
desdetter 'free from debt'
desfouir 'dig up'
deshosteller 'dislodge'
desnaturel 'unnatural'
desreuler 'throw into disorder'
dessaisonner 'put out of harmony'
destabler 'remove (from stable)'
effeminer 'be effeminate'
elat 'proud'
enbastir 'contrive'
enboire 'drink in, up'
encager 'to cage'
enclinement 'inclination, desire'
enfanteresse 'bearer of children'
enhort 'exhortation'
enlarder 'fatten'
ennaturé 'natural'
enpreignant 'pregnant'
enpriendre 'press, imprint'
enquerrement 'enquiry, inquest'
entollir 'take away'
entresemblable 'similar'

errement 'wandering'
esbanoy 'enjoyment'
esbaubis 'confused'
eschangement 'exchange'
s'esclipser 'be eclipsed'
escoupe 'spittle'
esparnie 'sparing'

If the list is largely unexceptional, it is not without interest. For example, there are three words for females functioning in certain roles: *commanderesse, consailleresse, enfanteresse*. All are dealt with by Margarete Lindemann in her book on feminine terminations and the disappearance of *-eresse* in favour of *-euse* and *-trice*.[28]

Historians of French vocabulary traditionally distinguish between those words that form part of the primitive stock and thus show the sound changes that would have taken place as Old French emerged from Gallo-Roman, and those words that are borrowed directly from Latin during the Middle Ages with only a slight francization of their form. In this list from Gower we can therefore note that *accusatour* is closer to Latin than *acuseor* the earlier form, which is thus more an act of 'borrowing' than of 'derivation'.[29] Also close to their Latin roots are words like *apostazer, bilingue, blasphemus, cohabiter* and a number of others. Conversely, there are examples in the list of derivation from French terms that belong to the primitive stock: *abaubir, allentis, amerrir, bobancer, burgoiserie, camerette, ceinturelle, cervoiser* etc. This is a sign that, learned Latinist as he might have been, Gower had a sensitivity for French words deriving from the primitive stock as well as the Latinate.

Another feature of Gower's French usage and further evidence of his familiarity with contemporary French is his adoption of fairly newly minted words. In some cases Gower's use might be the first recorded use of a word that is noted only later for French.

For the following items the standard reference works give these dates:

anguler – 1375 (TLF[30] under *angulaire*; this has a special sense in Gower)
cohabiter – before 1380 (TLF)
contumélie – 1328 (Godefroy 2, 285b cites Oresme, but the TLF gives the *Ovide moralisé* as the first attestation)
elat – (Godefroy 3, 21c records this as first used by Georges Chastellain, but it is also found in Chaucer's 'Monks' Tale' 177, see OED)
entresemblable – (Godefroy 3, 300c cites de Diguilville; we note the AND has *entresembler*).

---

28 M. Lindemann, *Zum Suffixwechsel von «-eresse » zu «-euse » und «-trice » im Französischen* (Tübingen, 1977).
29 Robert Martin uses the terms *dérivation authentique* and *dérivation historique* to distinguish the two processes in his article 'Le préfixe A-/AD- en moyen français', *Romania* 119 (2001), 1–32.
30 TLF = *Trésor de langue française*, available online at http://atilf.atilf.fr/ [accessed 15 October 2008].

For the following we have dates, or approximate dates, that are later than
ower, which could make them first attestations:

apostasier – (TLF under *apostasier* says fifteenth century)
causal – (Godefroy 9, 10c; found as an adjective in Christine de Pizan and not
as a noun)
enpriendre – (Godefroy 9, 446a, Jean Pillot *Gallicae linguae institutio* 1550; we
have found in a copy of the Abavus, Paris BnF 7692, the entry: *Premere* –
empreindre vel appresser, which would place it in the middle of the fourteenth
century, according to Mario Roques).[31]

Neologisms

is not a great leap from these early uses of known words to those that appear
 be creations in French by Gower himself. In no case are we dealing with
►tally new words but rather the adaptation of an existing base with the addition
 suffix or prefix, and possibly with new meanings:

aimal 'pendant'
amontance 'rising' (of balance)
apparantie 'appearance'
bordeller 'fornicate'
brigantaille 'irregular troops'
chincherie 'stinginess'
compescer 'tame'
comploier v.refl. 'be directed'
confederat – p.p. (Gower also has *confederé*)
conivreisoun – 'connivance'
conjoye – subst. – 'joy in common'
conspir – subst. – 'conspiring'
consuëte 'accustomed'
contreplit 'opposition'
cornage 'horn-blowing'
couchour – adj. – 'lazy'
desfuissonner 'decrease'
desparigal 'disparagement'
desprofiter 'be hurtful', (refl.) 'go to ruin'
destager 'disturb', (refl.) 'be disturbed'
destenter (se) 'come forth, (subst.) 'coming forth'
digestier 'digestion'
enbaraigner 'grow barren'
enbreuderie 'embroidery'
engarçonner 'make a servant of'
engouster 'eat'

M. Roques, *Recueil général de lexiques français du moyen âge I : Lexiques alphabétiques*, 2
vols. (Paris, 1936–8).

enhabitable 'dweller'
enperiler 'endanger'
escuieresse 'squiress'
essamplement 'example, teaching'

The example of *apparantie* might have been a misreading of *apparence* were it no
in rhyme with *hypocrisie*. A splendid 'collective pejorative' is created with the
term *brigantaille*, made masculine by Gower in that he uses *du* rather than *de la*
perhaps to allow for a correct syllable count.

> – *conivreisoun* seems to be earlier than any of the citations of *connivance*.
> We have no example of the form *coucheur* before the sixteenth century, and
> this sense of 'lazy' seems particular to Gower. The form *enbreuderie* looks very
> French, but the usual form was *broderie* without the prefix, though the verb
> *embroder* existed. We also note:
> – *enbaraigner* is related to *brehaigner* to 'render infertile' (sometimes 'to
> castrate', but later).
> – *enhabitable* seems a unique creation, close to *inhabitant* and to the adjective
> *habitable*.
> – *escuieresse* is not listed by Margarete Lindemann (see above, p. 130, n.28)
> nor by the AND, nor the various OF dictionaries consulted, though there is a
> close form *escoueresse* for 'female liberator, based on *excutere* 'to shake' (French
> *secouer*). The OED lists *esquiress* as coming into English in the sixteenth century.
> The CF feminine of *écuyer* is *écuyère*.

As we mentioned above, Gower's disclaimer about his abilities in French is t
be taken as a commonplace:

> Et si jeo n'ai de Francois la faconde,
> Pardonetz moi qe jeo de ceo forsvoie.
> Jeo sui Englois, si quier par tiele voie
> Estre excusé ... (*Traitié* xviii, 4)

Certainly Gower's French seems more standard than that of John Barton, and
his overall ability to assimilate contemporary forms, and even to create his own
show a significant comprehension of French.

Other words

In this preliminary study of Gower's French vocabulary, we have added a fourt
group of terms, which might eventually be distributed among the other three
They raise a variety of questions concerning their classification:

alenter, allentir 'to slow'
charuer 'ploughing'
contretenir subst. or verb?
corner – subst. – 'sounding of horn'
enobscurer (var. of *enoscurir* AND1)

132

s'enfievrer 'get fever'

causal – subst. – 'cause'
cloistral – subst. – 'cloisters'
communal – subst. – 'people generally' (AND1 as adj.)

enamourer – p.p. in AND1
atalenter 'desire' (AND1 *entalenter*, also Gower, *entalentir*)
encorager (AND1 *acourager*)
enfiler (AND1 *afiler*)
enlasser (AND1 *alasser* but no en- variant)
esbair (AND1 *abair*)
esluminer (AND1 *aluminer, enluminer*)
esluminous (AND *alumineux*, Godefroy *enlumineur; enlumineus* 16th cent.)

deglouter (AND1 *deglutir*, TL, Godefroy. *degloutir*)

chançonal 'song' (AND *chançonele*)
columbelle 'dove' (AND1 *columbel*)
enfantel 'childish' (AND1 *enfantil*)

assissour 'juror' (AND1, TL judge's assessor)
brocour 'agent, broker' (Godefroy, 'celui qui vend du vin au broc' = 'tapster', etc.)
correctour AND1 'licenced broker' (Godefroy, 'celui qui corrige, supérieur d'un ordre religieux, aussi contrôleur des comptes', TL 'Zurechtweiser')

chitoun 'kitten' (= Northern French form, CF *cheton*)

cirimp 'syrup'
climant = *cliniant* 'winking'
compernage 'dainty food'

In this list there are words where a change of grammatical category has occurred, a feature of Anglo-Norman and of Continental French, as we know from *dinner* and *dîner, supper* and *souper*. This so-called 'dérivation impropre' as Ferdinand Brunot labelled it, can be seen in the substantivized infinitive *corner* and in *causal, cloistral, communal* – all adjectives that are used by Gower as nouns.

Anglo-Norman also commonly interchanged the prefixes *a-, en-* and *es-*, and there are examples of various verbs with those alternations. Continental examples are also frequent. The example of *deglouter* shows a change of conjugation from *degloutir*.

Some words have a slightly different sense, or cultural application, which makes them more Anglo-Norman in use, such as *assissour* and *brocour*.

Macaulay notes that *climant* should probably be read as *cliniant*, 'winking'; our check of the manuscript confirms it is the latter.[32] The 'm' in *cirimp* is difficult to explain and may be an error; *compernage* in the sense of 'dainty food' is a

---

[32] Macaulay, *Complete Works*, I, 417, n. to v. 9591.

variant of *compenage/companage*, but it should be noted that in the manuscript the three examples are written in abbreviated form, that is with a stroke through the descender of 'p'.

Summary

One could of course multiply the examples and the varieties of late Anglo-French texts, signalling their insularity or lack of it. Serge Lusignan has recently shown that English chancery officials, when addressing diplomatic documents in French to continental recipients, seem to have reduced the number of Anglo-Norman features in their language.[33] This is perhaps similar to what Gower is attempting to achieve, recognizing or hoping for a wider audience than merely English. The writer of the *Anglo-Norman Prose Brut* seems to have no such concern. His preoccupation is to tell a straightforward history both as transmitted and perhaps as he saw the last stages. As for the text advising on estate management, this seems to be an example of Anglo-French in a professional and hermetic context, its intended audience no doubt students in a course on practical management.[34]

French will continue to have a variety of uses in the centuries that follow, a language of international commerce, of diplomacy and law, a mark of a cultured and educated person. It will never quite be a foreign language in Britain, and John Barton's French of Paris will continue to be a model for many.

---

[33] Lusignan, *Langue des rois*, ch. V 'La rencontre des français'.
[34] See Oschinsky, *Walter of Henley*.

10

John Gower's French and his Readers

R. F. Yeager

he collected works of the English poet John Gower, who died in 1408, run to
round 30,000 lines, divided into Latin, Middle English and French at roughly
third each. Linguistically speaking, Gower perhaps deserves to be called, as
e often is, a fence-sitter, but there is of course another way to look at Gower's
nree languages. Indeed, he suggests it himself (for I am quite convinced that the
vords are his own) in a Latin poem supposedly penned by 'a certain philoso-
her' and known, from its first two words, as 'Eneidos, Bucolis'.[1] In it, Gower
 found superior to Virgil, whose 'justly famous' three works, the *Aeneid*, the
ucolics and the *Georgics*, are all nonetheless only in Latin, while Gower 'wrote
. three poems in three languages,/ So that broader schooling might be given
 men' ['*Te tua set trinis tria scribere carmina linguis/ Constat, ut inde viris sit scola
ta magis*']. If I am correct in assuming that Gower, '*fingens se auctor esse Philoso-
horem*', wrote that about himself, we have reason to take a greater account than
as been the case of differences in the kinds of work he produced in each of his
nree languages.[2]

Clearly, Gower the writer of French who *ought* to stand outlined visibly before
s had different ambitions for each of the poems he wrote. Because of his evident
rilingual fluency, he could make choices – and must have – about the use to
vhich he wished to put each one.[3] Although he never says so specifically in a
neoretical way, Gower comes close to such a declaration in Prologue *22–*24 of
ne *Confessio amantis* when he states that:

For a full text and translation, see my *John Gower: The Minor Latin Works* (Kalamazoo
MI, 2005), pp. 84–6. See also *The Complete Works of John Gower*, ed. G. C. Macaulay,
4 vols. (Oxford, 1899–1902), IV, 361 (Latin text only). Unless otherwise specified, all
subsequent references to the works of Gower are from Macaulay's edition.

See the Latin commentary Gower wrote for his own *Confessio amantis*, at line 60 of Book
I: 'Hic quasi in persona aliorum, quos amor alligat, fingens se auctor esse Amantem,
varias eorum passiones variis huius libri distinccionibus per singula scribere proponit'
('Here, as if in the guise of others whom love constrains, the author, feigning himself to
be the Lover, proposes to write one by one about their different passions, in the various
sections of this book').

See also J. Gilbert, 'Men Behaving Badly: Linguistic Purity and Sexual Perversity in
Derrida's *Le monolinguisme de l'autre* and Gower's *Traitié pour essampler les amantz
marietz*', *Romance Studies* 24 (2006), 77–89. Gilbert's argument has class and political
implications: see esp. pp. 85, 87.

> ... for that fewe men endite
> In oure englissh, I thenke make
> A bok for Engelondes sake ...

or 'king Richardes sake', depending on the version. And Gower is, I think
making a similar statement, albeit not in so many words, when at the end of hi
life, with the lone exception of the poem 'To King Henry IV/In Praise of Peace
in Middle English (and one other exception discussed later), he seems much t
prefer writing in Latin.

Given that my present concern is the nature of Gower's French and hi
audience, it is not irrelevant to observe that this apparent preference for usin
Latin and English in serious works written after 1399 – along with their relativ
percentages, one poem in English to a dozen in Latin to zero in French – is trans
parently political.[4] Like Richard II, Henry IV also approved of and promote
English in certain contexts.[5] (Henry IV, for example, left the first royal will i
English; his son, whose will is in English too might thus be thought of as merel
following paternal precedent.[6]) Thus when Gower selects English to write point
edly to Henry IV, in an attempt to temper policy, as he does in 'In Praise of Peace
we need to note the politics of its language. We may say the same of the Lati
pieces: Gower also addresses Henry, seemingly directly, in briefer poems, 'Re
celi deus', 'O recolende' and 'H. aquile pullus' in particular, all of which reflec
upon his rulership; and the substantial *Cronica Tripertita*, as the dedicatory epistl
to Archbishop of Canterbury Thomas Arundel that prefaces the All Souls manu
script so obsequiously testifies, was composed to please an intensely partisan
Lancastrian readership as well.[7]

If – following the now fully enshrined theoretical principle that 'absence i

---

4   See D. Pearsall, 'Gower's Latin in the *Confessio amantis*', in *Latin and Vernacular: Studie
in Late-Medieval Texts and Manuscripts*, ed. A. J. Minnis (Cambridge, 1989), pp. 13–2
S. Echard, 'Gower's Books of Latin: Language, Politics and Poetry', *Studies in the Ag
of Chaucer* 25 (2003), 123–56; and my 'Politics and the French Language in Englan
During the Hundred Years' War: The Case of John Gower', in Baker, *Inscribing th
Hundred Years' War*, pp. 127–57.
5   On Richard II's promotion of English, see 'Did Richard Encourage the Englis
Language?', in T. Jones, R. F. Yeager, T. Dolan, A. Fletcher and J. Dor, *Who Murdere
Chaucer? A Medieval Mystery* (London, 2003), pp. 35–9.
6   For the wills of Henry IV and Henry V, see *A Collection of All the Wills, now known t
be extant, of the Kings and Queens of England, Princes and Princesses of Wales, and Ever
Branch of the Royal Blood, from the reign of William the Conqueror to that of Henry th
Seventh, exclusive; with explanatory notes and a glossary*, ed. J. Nichols (London, 1780
pp. 203–6 and 236–42 respectively. English seems to have run in the blood of the dire
Lancastrian line: Henry VI's will is also in English (pp. 291–319); those of Richard
and Edward IV, however, are in Latin (respectively, pp. 191–202, 345–8).
7   For the full text and translation of 'Rex celi deus', 'O recolende' and 'H. aquile pullus
see my own *Minor Latin Works*, pp. 43–5, 46–7. See also *Complete Works*, ed. Macaula
IV, 343–5 (Latin text only). For the epistle to Arundel, see *Complete Works* IV, 1–2 (Lati
only); translated by E. W. Stockton, *The Major Latin Works of John Gower: The Voice o
One Crying and The Tripartite Chronicle* (Seattle, 1962), pp. 47–8. See also L. Stale

presence' – there does not seem to be a scrap of serious writing in French extant that we can attribute indisputably to Gower's latter years (save one, and that a compromised example, as I shall point out shortly), then that dearth must be political too, in one way or another. At the very least, it logically reflects what Gower thought could be done with, and in, French, and for whom – all of which decisions are political in the broad sense. And this leads us directly to identifying Gower's readership – which, for purposes of discussion, we may divide into two: those for whom he probably wrote intentionally, targeting their interests and hopeful of striking the bull's eye, and those who read his work unbeknown to him, picking up a copy from, say, the collection of a friend.

This latter group, although no less interesting than the former – indeed, in several ways quite the *more* interesting – can be addressed here in shorter space. Evidence for who might in the past have borrowed a manuscript or read over a friend's shoulder, or heard that friend reading poetry aloud across a crowded room, is scarce. Nonetheless, one solid case is pertinent here. London, British Library, MS Stowe 951 contains three pieces: an English translation of John of Hildesheim's *Historia Trium Regum* (better known as *The Three Kings of Cologne*); a Middle English poem *Speculum Vitae* (*The Mirror of Life*), thought by many to be the work of William of Nassington; and something called in the manuscript '*Exhortacio contra vicium adulterii*'. This proves to be a Yorkshire-dialect translation of the eighteen French balades that make up Gower's *Traitié pour essampler les amantz marietz*, to which has been added a prefatory stanza, or prologue, and a nineteenth balade, by way of a summing-up. Both are claimed by the translator, who names himself as 'Quixley' in the prologue stanza. Henry Noble MacCracken identified this translator/poet as one John Quixley of Quixley Hall, a minor landholder whose daughter Alice was married in September 1402.[8] MacCracken posited that the careful *pater* John Quixley gave his translation to young Alice as a wedding present.

Well, perhaps. Who knows what the Quixley *père et fille* were like at home? But in general, balade sequences fulminating against adultery are not what most fathers think of as wedding gifts for daughters, and so conceivably we ought to look beyond MacCracken's suggestions for other explanations. Nonetheless, his notion of authorship is important to take up here, because if he was correct about who and what Quixley was, it suggests some important things about Gower's audience. So does the date. Gower was still alive in 1402, and could have been aware of Quixley – perhaps even supplying him with a copy of the *Traitié*. MacCracken, noting that Quixley Hall was only a few miles away from Stittenham, where lived a family of Gowers, supposed that they, as proud relations of the famous London poet, shared their manuscript with their neighbour. But how close John Gower might have been to the Gowers of Stittenham remains

---

'Gower, Richard II, Henry of Derby, and the Business of Making Culture', *Speculum* 75 (2000), 68–96.

[8] H. N. MacCracken, 'Quixley's Ballades Royal (? 1402)', *Yorkshire Archaeological Journal* 20 (1909), 33–50; for his argument regarding authorship, see pp. 37–9.

a cloudy point – and in any case, what is most intriguing about MacCracken's Quixley candidate, apart from the date, is his social class.[9] If someone like John Quixley were reading John Gower's *Traitié* in its original language in 1402, it means that at the beginning of the fifteenth century we might infer the poet's French audience to include literate, regional gentry like the Knevet family of Norfolk, or, in slightly different guise, a Robert Thornton or a Sir John Paston – or even a rural John Carpenter, whose library was old-fashioned enough to have included Gower easily.[10] And in that event, we ought to be pondering potential lines of distribution and dissemination among readers of this class from Southwark to points north, and potentially elsewhere.[11]

But of course, nothing we know of any of these readers' collections indicates they possessed a jot of Gower's in French. And in any case MacCracken quite likely mistook 'Quixley' by a couple of decades and more than that number of leagues. A likelier candidate is one Robert de Quixley, who became prior of Nostell Priory and prebend of Bramham in 1393, maintaining both posts until his death in 1427.[12] Both priory and prebend lie within the honour of Pontefract,

9   J. H. Fisher seems fairly to have settled the question of John Gower's origins in Kent, with small likelihood of any connection with the Gowers of Stittenham, a 'family prominent after the 16th century': see *John Gower, Moral Philosopher and Friend of Chaucer* (New York, 1964), p. 41.

10 On such readers, see, generally, A. I. Doyle, 'English Books In and Out of Court from Edward III to Henry VII', in *English Court Culture in the Later Middle Ages*, ed. V. J. Scattergood and J. W. Sherborne (London, 1983), pp. 163–81. On the Knevets, see *The English Library before 1700: Studies in Its History*, ed. F. Wormald and C. E. Wright (London, 1958), p. 158; on Thornton, see J. J. Thompson, *Robert Thornton and the London Thornton Manuscript: British Library MS Additional 31042* (Cambridge, 1987); on Paston, see *Paston Letters and Papers of the Fifteenth Century*, ed. N. Davis, I (Oxford, 1971), pp. 574–5, 516–18; on Carpenter, see T. Brewer, *Memoir of the Life and Times of John Carpenter* (London, 1856).

11 The idea is important to consider, nevertheless: as Jocelyn Wogan-Browne has reminded me (pers. comm.), 'the first burst of francophone pastoralia is northern', northern links with France were possible via well-placed ports, and 'however un-*anglo-normanisant* and Paris-centered Gower's French might be, that doesn't mean the north couldn't have had connections to and an active reception context for it'.

12 York Archiepis. Reg. Arundel, fol. 43; W. Dugdale, *Monasticon Anglicanum: A History of the Abbies and Other Monasteries, Hospitals, Frieries, and Cathedral and Collegiate Churches, with their dependencies, in England and Wales; also of all such Scotch, Irish, and French Monasteries as were in any manner connected with religious houses in England ...*, new edn J. Caley, H. Ellis and B. Bandinel, 6 vols. [in 9: vol. 6 in 3 parts] (London, 1830), 6.1, p. 91, also prints a chronology of the Nostell priors. A third possibility has been raised obliquely by Ralph Hanna, who notes, 'Quixley is a name derived from a place, modern Whixley, six miles east of Knaresborough. Three later Ripon chaplains share the name and presumably came from there, John, Robert and William'; see R. Hanna, 'Some North Yorkshire Scribes and their Context', in *Medieval Texts in Context*, ed. G. D. Caie and D. Renevey (London, 2008), pp. 167–91 (p. 173). This John Quixley, suggested by Hanna, flourished *c.*1478, his Robert and William *c.*1501. Taking the name of one's place of origin was commonplace for those in orders – and is evident in the form of Prior Robert de Quixley's name. Like the three suggested by Hanna, Prior Robert

ιe great Lancastrian stronghold; Bramham, indeed, being triangularly but about ιurteen miles from there, and from York, and in the ducal gift. Nostell Priory, ι which nothing now remains, stood a bit farther to the south-west. Notably, Jostell was an Austin priory, as was St Mary Overeys in Southwark where Gower ved, doubtless as a corrodian, from the late 1370s until his death in 1408. There ιe several reasons to suspect an Augustinian origin for 'Quixley's' translation, ιnd this Austin connection of Southwark and Nostell thus opens yet another ιossible conduit for the dissemination and transport of Gower's balades north-ιard.[13] From 1215, Augustinian abbots and priors were required to gather every ιree years at Chapter for several days of deliberation, in venues that on occasion ιcluded Nostell and London.[14] Books are known to have passed for copying ιom one Austin house to another; certainly the triennials provide a plausible ιeans, as might too the regular site-by-site visitation of three overseeing canons, ιlected at the triennial Chapters from different houses, in rotation.[15] Finally, ιmong the few facts as yet come to light regarding Robert de Quixley, are one ι two suggestive of his cast of mind, and therefore intriguing. The longest ιnured of its priors, he seems to have laboured successfully to restore not just Jostell's fiscal footing, but its moral balance also – and to have been a believer

had connections with the village of Quixley, near Ripon. On the language of BL, MS Stowe 951, see further *A Linguistic Atlas of Late Medieval English*, ed. A. McIntosh, M. L. Samuels, M. Benskin, with assistance of M. Lang and K. Williams, 4 vols. (Aberdeen, 1986), 3.646 (LP 526), although n.b. the entry analyses only *Speculum Vitae*, locating its origin near Liverpool; *Historia Trium Regum* and 'Quixley's' translation, however, are noted simply as 'not NM'.

William of Nassington, possibly the poet of the *Speculum Vitae*, may have been an Augustinian; John Waldeby, for whom prayers are solicited in two manuscripts of the *Speculum*, was certainly Augustinian. (On Waldeby, see especially M. J. Morrin, *John Waldeby, OSA, c.1315–c.1372: English Augustinian Preacher and Writer: With a Critical Edition of His Tract on the 'Ave Maria'*, Studia Augustiana Historica 2 (Rome, 1972–4).) Potentially more indicative are 'Quixley's' use of Augustine's *Confessions* and *De nuptiis et concupiscentia* in the balade he wrote himself (XIX) as an addendum to the *Traitié*. See my full discussion in the introduction to my edition and translation, *John Gower: Cinkante Balades and* Traitié pour les amantz marietz (forthcoming 2009).

Chapters of the Augustinian Canons, ed. H. E. Salter (London, 1922), pp. ix–x.

Extant Chapter Acts are incomplete, especially for those held in the south, but Acts from Chapters hosted by northern houses have Nostell several times as a gathering-place. While no known record survives of St Mary Overeys as host, the Acts of the Chapter at Newstead in 1371 have the priors of Southwark and Nostell both present; at the Northampton Chapter in 1404, Southwark is unlisted, but Nostell is in attend-ance, alongside the priors of Twynham and Southwick, two closely related houses from the see of Winchester, which also included Southwark. See *Chapters*, ed. Salter, pp. 69, 80. On the passing of manuscripts between Austin houses, see A. Lawrence, 'A Northern English School? Patterns of Production and Collection of Manuscripts in the Augustinian Houses of Yorkshire in the Twelfth and Thirteenth Centuries', in *Yorkshire Monasticism: Archaeology, Art and Architecture, from the 7th to the 16th Centuries*, ed. L. R. Hoey, British Archaeological Association Conference Transactions 16 (Leeds, 1995), pp. 145–53; and see further Pouzet in this volume.

in the power of books to effect the process.[16] Either under his direction or (mor likely) from his own hand, an Act Book of Nostell's priors was written, 'by wa of example for the servants of God' ('ad exemplum servorum dei').[17] Such a ma would have known how to employ Gower's *Traitié*, had it fallen into his hand via one route or another.

But whoever he was, 'Quixley' represents our first category of reader, th serendipitous reader, whose presence one infers but seldom – as apparently i this case – can identify with certainty. For we can be sure that neither John no Robert de Quixley was in Gower's sights when he wrote the *Traitié*. What abou our second audience, then – those for whom Gower thought he was writin in French? Paradoxically enough, Robert de Quixley, prior of Nostell, is in on important sense very likely *just* the reader – or at least, just the *kind* of reader Gower had in mind. What British Library, MS Stowe 951 looks like is a compen dium-in-process for priory use. Certainly it is easier to imagine Yorkshire canon reading Gower's *Traitié* with appreciation than might a Yorkshire bride such a Alice Quixley – or a Flemish immigrant bride, either, for that matter. The long held assumption of Macaulay's (seconded by John Fisher and most others) tha Gower wrote the *Traitié* as a wedding present for his own bride, Agnes Groundol on the occasion of their marriage in 1398 is also dubious.[18] Subject matter aside the formal structure of the eighteen *Traitié* balades, all but the last lacking envoy suggests strongly an earlier moment of composition, *c*.1385–90, that is, betwee the death of Machaut in 1377, champion and model of the envoy-less balade, an the subsequently successful dominance of Deschamps' envoyed balades, a styl he developed, he tells us in his *L'Art de dictier*, deliberately to break free from hi old master.

This formal distinction – balade with or without envoy, Machauldian o Deschampian – lends perspective on Gower's other sequence, the so-calle *Cinkante Balades* – 'so-called' because there are actually fifty-three, two balade having been numbered 'IIII' in the sole manuscript copy we possess (Londo British Library, MS Additional 59495, formerly the Trentham manuscript) an (again, in this sole manuscript) two dedicatory balades to Henry IV appended

---

[16] Not that many Austin priors would have thought otherwise: the Augustinian Rul predicates the availability of books, for liturgy, reading aloud at meals, and individua devotions as well. See, e.g., *The Bridlington Dialogue*: 'Cum autem legimus, nobiscur Deus loquitur' ('For when we pray, we speak to God; and when we read, God speak to us.'). Text from *Robert of Bridlington: The Bridlington Dialogue: An Exposition of the Ru of St. Augustine for the Life of the Clergy*, trans. 'A Religious of C.S.M.V.' (London, 1960 162, 163a. It was a lasting position in the order: 'Codices', stated Robert Richardso (*c*.1530), '*sunt religiosorum armature, contra diaboli tentationem*' ('Books are the armor c the religious against the temptation of the devil'); see *Commentary on the Rule of S Augustine by Robertus Richardinus*, ed. G. G. Coulton (Edinburgh, 1935), p. 146.

[17] *De gestis et actibus priorum monasterii sancti Oswaldi*, from the prologue; West Yorkshir Leeds District Archives, MS NP/c1, fol. 84. On Robert de Quixley's likely authorshir see my discussion in my *John Gower*: Cinkante Balades.

[18] Fisher, *John Gower*, pp. 85–6.

As I have suggested elsewhere, the fact that the *Cinkante Balades* have envoys indicates Gower's probable familiarity with the most famous collection of late fourteenth-century balades, the *Livre de Cent Ballades*, begun by Jean de Saint-Pierre, seneschal d'Eu, c.1386.[19] The *Livre de Cent Ballades* is a love debate, the first fifty being a dialogue between an old knight and a young about the proper ways to wage war and love. An impasse being reached, the opinion of others is solicited, provoking responses by the *crème de la crème* of French chivalric society: Philippe d'Artois, count of Eu, the younger Bouccicaut, Jean de Cresécque, Regnaut de Trie, later the Admiral of France, Jean de Chambrillac, seneschal of Périgord, the dukes of Orléans and Berry, and – quite interestingly for our purposes, Guillaume de Trignonville, friend of Deschamps and Christine de Pizan, and François d'Auberchicourt, whose father Eustace fought with the Black Prince in Spain, and whose relation Jean, a long-time Lancastrian retainer and confidant of John of Gaunt, was probably known to both Chaucer and Gower. Oton de Granson, from whose work Chaucer borrows, composed his own balade responses to *Le Livre* c.1390–1, when the sequence was all the rage in Paris.

So Gower probably had a target as well as a model when he wrote his *Cinkante Balades*. The title is a clue – as are the two dedicatory balades (the second of which is fragmentary, alas!) to Henry IV addressed as 'gentils Rois.' These two dedicatory balades together constitute the anomalous example I mentioned earlier, of Gower's post-usurpation French work. They have misled some of the few readers his balades have attracted over the years into the belief that Gower may have written the entire *Cinkante Balades* sequence for Henry – but this is clearly impossible. There simply were not sufficient hours in the day after 1399 when Gower had so much else in hand, including the *Cronica Tripertita*, revisions to the *Vox Clamantis*, at least three shorter Latin poems, and the Middle English 'In Praise of Peace'. Besides, such stuff had passed its moment. Whether one views the reign of Henry IV as heady times – at least at the beginning – or bloody, the balade sequence concerned with love had no market at the flint-eyed opening of the fifteenth century.

Except, of course, as a propitiatory gift to Henry, who, as a participant in the great tournament held at St Inglevert in 1390, had jousted and feasted with the poets of the *Livre de Cent Ballades* even as that collection circulated for the first time. It must have been a shrewd guess on Gower's part that Henry would have known what he was getting in the *Cinkante Balades,* and appreciated it, as the only effort by one of his countrymen to emulate, if not overtop, his continental friends and poets-in-arms. Oddly enough, Henry's gladness at such a present might have been especially high just after taking power, because we have evidence that at this time the usurper seems to have had it in his head that poets singing a prince's praises and competing with each other around the palace were a necessary (for which read, 'legitimizing') pendant to power – an idea he acquired, one thinks, from spending time in 1398 with Gian Galeazzo Visconti, overlord of Milan,

---

[19] In 'John Gower's Audience: The Ballades', *Chaucer Review* 40 (2005), 81–105.

who had a less pressing, but nonetheless analogous, problem justifying his own right to rule. Not coincidentally, perhaps, both Visconti and Henry attempted to recruit Christine de Pizan to join their retinues as writer-in-residence, in 1401–2.[20] Thus it is important, in thinking about Gower's French audience, to recognize Henry as an example of a reader of the second kind – not, that is, someone like Prior Robert de Quixley, whose essentially serendipitous contact with the *Traitié* Gower undoubtedly never engineered, but rather someone whom Gower knew, and specifically intended to read his French poems.

Yet (paradoxically again) for all their categorical differences, in another, very instructive way, Henry and Robert de Quixley are indeed alike as readers. The two dedicatory balades excepted, Gower did not write any of the *Cinkante Balades* for Henry the man. He clearly did, however, assemble his sequence as an answer of his own to the challenge of French *chevalier* poets of Henry's *type*, his *class*. In the same way, the needs of Quixley the Austin prior of Nostell – not those of the individual Robert de Quixley, the particular Yorkshireman who penned the translation – were likely, as a type or class, to have influenced Gower's design and execution of the *Traitié*. Both of these claims have implications worth considering – but before doing so, it is necessary to say some little about Gower's largest French project, the *Mirour de l'Omme*. Who might Gower have had in mind as his readership for that?

I have left the *Mirour* untouched until now because in many ways it is both Gower's most difficult work to peg as to audience, and also the simplest. The *Mirour*'s sources and formal inspiration are theological and confessional (i.e., the plea to the Virgin at the end), to a degree that Gower never attempts elsewhere. It is also – at least the bulk of it, up to the Marian prayer – the earliest work of his that we have. Moreover, Gower probably shifted his target audience during the *Mirour*'s writing, from a circle of pious *chevaliers* exemplified by Henry of Grosmont, first duke of Lancaster and author of the Anglo-French *Livre de Seyntz Medicines* (d. 1361), to the Austin canons of St Mary Overeys, among whom he took up residence about 1378, and for whose library and use I believe he finally finished the poem, following a hiatus of a number of years.[21] The *Mirour* itself thus reflects, in a single work, something of the two different, but yet similar, audiences I have projected for the *Cinkante Balades* and the *Traitié*: aristocratic Lancastrians and men of the cloth.

What, then, can we learn from such observable confluences in Gower's French poems? Well, first and foremost, perhaps, that there is a remarkable lot more work to do before we fill in lines of understanding currently being laid down. More specifically – and by way of suggesting directions such work might take – let me close with four points.

First, about Gower's French vocabulary. As Brian Merrilees and Heather Pagan

---

20 Christine tells the story herself: see *Christine de Pizan: Le Livre de l'Advision Christine*, ed. C. Reno and L. Dulac (Paris, 2001), pp. 112–13.
21 See further my 'Gower's French Audience: The *Mirour de l'Omme*', *Chaucer Review* 41 (2006), 111–37.

emonstrate in this volume, Gower's French is closer to that of France than to
ie usage of his English predecessors and contemporaries. This clearly reflects
ower's identifiable reading. While true Anglo-Norman works like Thomas
f Kent's *Roman de Toute Chevalerie* are represented in the works from which
e borrows, nonetheless French books written by Frenchmen in France greatly
utnumber them.[22] These latter being Gower's models, and especially given
is centonic poetic proclivities,[23] it is unsurprising that a significant measure of
is lexicon is Central French. What will, I suspect, prove more intriguing with
irther research is the influence of his intended readership on his product. In the
rocess of editing and translating Gower's two balade sequences for publication,
am becoming aware of vocabulary found in the balades but not in the *Mirour*.
uling out such obvious site-specific words as 'benefice' and 'circumcision' (in
ie *Mirour*, not in the balades), or 'Cupide' (the reverse), one finds, alone in the
alades, examples such as 'gai' (*CB* 36.2.10) and 'enmaladis' (*CB* 14.3.19); both are
entral French forms. Intriguing also is a word such as 'chois' – another Central
rench form, which Gower uses three times, one each in the *Mirour*, *Cinkante
alades* and the *Traitié*, but only in a *fin' amour* context; and similarly 'cristal/
ristall,' once in the *Mirour* and three times in *Cinkante Balades*, always conjoined
> ladies' eyes. Gower, it is plain, recognized the dialect – in every sense of that
erm – that his courtly readers employed to converse among themselves, and
'renchified' his own Anglo-Norman (as well as tailoring his poetic forms) to
laim his legitimacy as an equal participant in the discourse. His balades, then,
hould be deemed an ambitious enterprise, in more ways than one.

My second point concerns what the appearance of the *Traitié* in the hands
f the prior of Nostell (assuming my identification of Robert de Quixley as the
orkshire translator is correct), and the use he found for it, has to tell us about
ommunication between Austin canonical houses – and Austin canons, *inter se* –
nder the Lancastrians. Very likely this should prove more revelatory about the
inintended' category of Gower's readers, but perhaps not altogether, since, as I
emarked earlier, Gower must have written the *Traitié* in expectation of readers at
t Mary Overeys. As readers, one Austin canon may have been, for him, as good
s another. But beyond this, the demonstrable presence of a *Traitié* in two Austin
riories many miles, if only a decade or two, apart could be another significant
lue to transmission of French books between confraternal libraries, and hence
f late medieval reading patterns. And so, *ipso facto*, can the 'Quixley' translation
self. Assuming, as I think probable, that Gower's *Traitié* was translated as part
f a programme of Robert de Quixley's to introduce morally redemptive reading
ito his canons' reach, what does it indicate about the state of French fluency in
orkshire in the 1420s that in BL, MS Stowe 951 'Quixley' retains all of Gower's

---

[22] Particularly helpful here are A. Butterfield, '*Confessio amantis* and the French Tradition', in *A Companion to Gower*, ed. S. Echard (Cambridge, 2004), pp. 165–80, and P. Nicholson, *Love and Ethics in Gower's* Confessio amantis (Ann Arbor MI, 2005).

[23] See my 'Did Gower Write Cento?', in *John Gower: Recent Readings*, ed. R. F. Yeager (Kalamazoo MI, 1989), pp. 113–32.

original Latin commentaries to the *Traitié* balades, and even writes one of hi
own (albeit rather clumsily) to accompany balade XIX, even as he turns Gower'
French into English? Again, the testimony of the Chapter Acts may shed som
light here: at the triennial at Northampton in 1325, a statute was passed enjoinin
canons needing to speak during the hours of silence to use only Latin or French
but by 1443, sermons were delivered at the Oseney Chapter only in English an
Latin.[24] Such evidence requires thoughtful investigation.

Third, about the politics – and the aesthetics – of Gower's lexical self
consciousness. Earlier on, I called attention to the political nature of Gower'
election of English, Latin or French for each particular project. Clearly, even th
single-word, lexical decisions of dialect such as those I have just mentioned
although *in parvo*, are precisely the same in political terms as the larger choice o
one tongue or another made with an eye toward swaying an audience. Hence t
say that the *Mirour de l'Omme* was written in French because Henry of Grosmon
(and Edward III) read and wrote French is a complex statement, freighted wit
intelligence no less about Gower's allegiances than about his art. It would b
fruitful, I think, to look for lexical correlations of the vocabulary of Grosmont'
Livre de Seyntz Medicines with the earlier portions of the *Mirour* – and not simpl
by way of establishing a more accurate date for when Gower was writing hi
poem. In this regard, the Lancastrian presence and the proximity and appointiv
power of Pontefract may also be revealing about language in many ways.[25]

And finally, on politics and art again. Dedicatory poem number one to Henr
IV, prefacing the *Cinkante Balades* in the Trentham manuscript, is followed ther
by Latin verses, also addressed to Henry. They contain, I think, two significan
unveilings of Gower's uncommon linguistic self-awareness being applied to hi
readership – of Gower caught in the act, to steal a line from Yeats, of being 'th
Political Man' – both *in macro* (that is, how, for reasons of national politics, as wel
as for personal advancement, he sized up, and appealed to, a *known* reader – i.e
category two) and *in micro* – that is, of the poet pulling the cover off his decision
making process regarding work of what kind to express in what language. I
the third stanza of the dedicatory (French) balade, Gower describes the poem h
writes, in rather lovely fashion, as a locus (rendered literally) 'where the song
flower' ['*u sont les ditz floriz*']. This – very clearly – is intended to contrast wit
the Latin verses following. As he tells us in the following stanza (in what, in
Deschampian balade is technically the envoy, although here in all probability th
appended Latin was intended to serve that function as well): 'Here following i
flawless language,/ Because in Latin I have written my message' ('*Ci ensuant er
de perfit langage,/ Dont en latin ma sentence ai compris*').[26]

---

24 *Chapters*, ed. Salter, pp. 14, xxxi–xxxii.
25 On the *Livre* of Henry of Grosmont and Gower's *Mirour*, see my 'Gower's Frencl
Audience: The *Mirour*'.
26 Gower's fourth stanza is 'O gentils Rois, ce que je vous escris/ Ci ensuant ert de perfi
langage,/ Dont en latin ma sentence ai compris:/ Q'en dieu se fie, il ad bel avan
tage' ('O gentle King, this which I write for you –/ What follows here uses polishe

The Latin following consists of the first eight lines (out of twenty-nine) of Gower's poem 'O recolende', written without a doubt for the occasion of Henry's coronation on 13 October 1399, amalgamated with the four-line prophecy poem 'H. aquile pullus', also composed in 1399, either for the coronation or to celebrate the elevation of the future Henry V to Prince of Wales on the 15th and to duke of Aquitaine on the 23rd, and a two-sentence prayer, in prose, for Henry's prosperity and preservation.[27] Gower is doing something of the greatest interest here in a number of ways. For present purposes, however, let it suffice to note Gower's description, in the French envoy, of the Latin verse immediately following as 'perfit langage', implying, apparently, its superiority over the French of the *Cinkante Balades*. Since this opinion seems of a piece with his practice – his concentration on Latin and English after 1398 (and 'Quixley's' too, for that matter) – we should probably take Gower's expression of preference here seriously, as an indicative frame for future discussions of Gower's French at the end of his life, and perhaps of his later readership, as well.

language,/ Whose message I have written in Latin:/ Whoso trusts in God, he has the best of it.'). Text in Macaulay, *Complete Works*, I, 336; translation my own.

[27] On dating the composition of these poems, see my *Minor Latin Works*, pp. 7, 75, 77–8; and further D. R. Carlson, 'A Rhyme Distribution Chronology of John Gower's Latin Poetry', *Studies in Philology* 104 (2007), 15–55 (pp. 38–40).

Section II
Crossing the Conquest:
New Linguistic and Literary Histories

INTRODUCTION

For all the significance that has been attached to the Norman Conquest, it is becoming increasingly possible to see overlaps and continuities in the multilingual and multicultural England of the eleventh to twelfth centuries.[1] In the opening essay of this section, David Trotter argues that the Conquest was not the defining linguistic event it became in nineteenth- and twentieth-century historiography and shows that French lexis was already functional in some kinds of texts. Elizabeth Tyler further argues that French can help us undo a prevailing narrative of Anglo-Saxon England as lost in the Conquest. Anglo-Saxon culture was already international, multilingual and in part francophone, and provided a context for the explosion of twelfth-century francophone writing in England. (The sole extant manuscript of *Beowulf* itself was of course copied in the latinate, francophone, Danish and English world of the cosmopolitan late Anglo-Saxon eleventh-century court, not too long before the *Chanson de Roland* was copied in the highly latinate, French and English world of Augustinian canons.[2])

There has been a great deal of valuable comparative literary study across the high Middle Ages inclusive of works and figures from England.[3] But study of English literary history as such has sometimes been narrower. The twelfth century at one time for English literary studies consisted principally of *The Owl and the Nightingale* (then dated to Richard I's reign), the fables *Dame Sirith* and *The Fox and the Wolf* and the *Peterborough continuation of the Anglo-Saxon Chronicle* to 1154, plus some Latin writers. One looked at Anglo-Latin writers such as Geoffrey of Monmouth, but went offshore for epic and romance, to the *Chanson de Roland* and Chrétien de Troyes, with perhaps a nod to Marie de France as a writer working in insular culture. Now, not only are insular careers and audiences acknowledged

1   See M. Chibnall, *The Debate on the Norman Conquest*, Issues in Historiography (Manchester, 1999); L. Georgianna, 'Coming to Terms with the Norman Conquest: Nationalism and English Literary History', *Yearbook of Research in English and American Literature* 14, *Literature and the Nation*, ed. B. Thomas (Tübingen, 1998), 33–53.

2   There is no agreement on a specific date for the first extant manuscript of the *Chanson de Roland*, but there is consensus that it is between 1120 and 1170: see Ian Short, 'Literary Culture at the Court of Henry II', in *Henry II: New Interpretations*, ed. C. Harper-Bill and N. Vincent (Woodbridge, 2007), pp. 335–61 (pp. 350–1). On the appropriation of *Roland* to the continental French literary canon, see A. Taylor, 'Was There a *Chanson de Roland*?', *Speculum* 76 (2001), 28–65.

3   For example, R. W. Hanning's pioneering and influential *The Individual in Twelfth Century Romance* (New Haven CT, 1977); Salter, *English and International*, ch. 1; R. M. Stein, *Reality Fictions: Romance, History and Governmental Authority, 1025–1080* (Notre Dame IN, 2006).

for the *Chanson de Roland* and for Chrétien's romances,[4] but in recent work on Anglo-Saxon in twelfth-century manuscripts, we have some hundreds of pieces of anthologized, reused, resituated homiletic and hagiographic works to put alongside French twelfth-century writing in England. All these demand exploration for their relation or lack of relation to each other in the new textual and cultural politics of the twelfth century that is coming into view.[5] It is especially visible on the manuscript page. Among the Anglo-Saxon chronicles, for instance, the *Peterborough Chronicle* used to figure on undergraduate lingustic and literary syllabi as the latest instance of Anglo-Saxon culture.[6] But it is equally a work of Anglo-Norman culture: the 'kyng heanri' who holds his court in the later years of the Chronicle (which terminates at 1154 in the Peterborough account) is Henry I: as if to emphasize this point, towards the end of the *Chronicle* a thirteenth-century Anglo-Norman summary of Brutus' foundation of England is carefully wrapped around the *Chronicle*'s text and a French account of Brutus' founding of London shares the page with the *Chronicle*'s 'Anglo-Saxon' account of King Henry.[7]

Making full use of the multicultural context of early Lincolnshire, Henry Bainton's innovative study detaches the first vernacular post-Conquest history, Gaimar's *Estoire des Engleis* and its patron, Lady Constance Fitzgilbert, from their accepted roles as creators of a nationalizing history. Bainton argues rather that Gaimar's is a regional history from the area of the Danelaw – and one that assigns a very different historiographical role to the Danes than their existence in Bede as agents of the devil punishing the sins of the English. Françoise Le Saux's essay looks at the major Arthurian writer Wace in his multilingual context and explores Wace's awareness and knowledge of English. Geoff Rector's pioneering study explores the feudal lexis of the large, various and multilingual corpus of psalter translations and glosses as a matrix for the overlapping development of lay and monastic reading cultures in the French of England, and offers new ways of integrating the psalter into the broader study of literary culture. Ruth Nisse shows that Anglo-Norman writings are importantly intertextual with Hebrew commentary, not just with English and Latin, while Monica Green's examination of the exceptionally early Anglo-Norman translation of medical works reveals

---

4 On *Roland*, see Short, 'Literary Culture'; on Chrétien de Troyes and England, see B. Schmolke-Hasselmann, *The Evolution of Arthurian Romance from Chrétien to Froissart*, trans. M. and R. Middleton (Cambridge, 1998).

5 *Rewriting English in the Twelfth Century*, ed. M. Swan and E. M. Treharne (Cambridge, 2000); Swan, Treharne and O. Da Rold, 'The Production and Use of English Manuscripts 1060 to 1220' (http://www.le.ac.uk/english/em1060–1220/index.html). For a masterly initial exploration of a particular case, see J. Frankis, 'Languages and Cultures in Contact: Vernacular Lives of St Giles and Anglo-Norman: Annotations in an Anglo-Saxon Manuscript', *LSE* n.s. 38 (2007), 101–33.

6 See e.g. *Early Middle English Texts*, ed. B. Dickins and R. M. Wilson (Cambridge, 1951; 3rd edn, 1956); *Early Middle English Verse and Prose*, ed. J.A.W. Bennett and G. V. Smithers (Oxford, 1966; 2nd rev. edn 1982).

7 *The Peterborough Chronicle (the Bodleian manuscript Laud misc. 638)*, ed. D. Whitelock, with an appendix by C. Clark, Early English Manuscripts in Facsimile 4 (Copenhagen, 1954), fol. 86v.

ultural continuities across the Conquest in technical and scientific writings. Like the Anglo-Latin works commissioned by Tyler's royal Anglo-Saxon women, Green's texts constitute another area where a body of works of little apparent relevance to the production of canonical literary texts in the vernacular can tell us much about the linguistic conditions and assumptions of writing in the high Middle Ages in England.

11

'Stuffed Latin':
Vernacular Evidence in Latin Documents

David Trotter

'Stuffed Latin', or 'latin farci', is a term used for the incorporation of vernacular elements in Latin documents in (especially) southern France during the tenth, eleventh, and early twelfth centuries.[1] A number of the Latin documents from this period contain isolated words, or more importantly, phrases, and also proper names in Occitan. This is in some respects a curiosity: northern France does not exhibit the same pattern, although it has been associated with other Romance-speaking areas, and, in general, it is considered that this is a north–south divide, with the south following the practice and the north eschewing it.[2] Explanations of the phenomenon have not always been entirely charitable: Clovis Brunel comments thus: 'les rédacteurs des actes ont d'abord employé la langue vulgaire au milieu de phrases latines, quand leur ignorance ne leur permettait pas d'exprimer autrement leur pensée'.[3] Nowadays, we would probably see this as a manifestation of perfectly normal language mixing rather than an illustration of linguistic or educational inadequacy.

The ways in which the Romance languages (including, in this case, Occitan) emerged greatly facilitated processes of this type. Occitan, like any other Romance variety, is very largely a direct linear descendant of Latin. Syntactically, to some extent morphosyntactically, and certainly in terms of a shared alphabet and lexis, a process essentially of combination of the two languages into a mixed language text is especially straightforward. Long before the tenth century, Latin coexisted with Romance varieties that were emerging in speech. Thus we have, broadly speaking, a situation where a written language (Latin) is still in use in an area where a vernacular (Romance), itself a derivative of Latin, is being spoken. It is hardly surprising, then, that certain elements of the vernacular should begin to creep into written Latin, as a precursor to the emergence of a fully fledged vernacular writing tradition in Romance.

This is of course something of a simplification of a process that must have been quite complicated, and which will undoubtedly have been quite different

---

[1] C. Brunel, 'Les premiers exemples de l'emploi du provençal dans les chartes', *Romania* 48 (1922), 335–64; J. Belmon and F. Vielliard, 'Latin farci et occitan dans les actes du XIe siècle', *Bibliothèque de l'École des Chartes* 155 (1997), 149–83.

[2] Belmon and Vielliard, 'Latin farci et occitan', p. 149.

[3] Brunel, 'L'emploi du provençal', pp. 337–8.

following local traditions, education and indeed tastes. Nevertheless, my contention is that this pattern is by no means as geographically limited as is often supposed and, at any rate, that the underlying method of analysis that we use when dealing with it in southern France can usefully be transferred to other areas. It is perhaps stretching the definition of 'latin farci' to apply it to medieval England, but it is important nevertheless to recognize just how widespread comparable processes were.

Let me first of all comment briefly on an example of the pattern in Latin and Occitan (its home territory). This is text (A), a tenth-century document concerning the bishop of Rodez and preserved in a fourteenth-century cartulary (it is assumed that the cartulary is a faithful transcription):

(A) Preparatus sit Gardradus, filius <u>Gardradus,</u> si Deusdet episcopus et mater sua <u>Adalaiz</u> mortui fuerint ante illum, quod illo Castello Marino in fidelitate et in opus Sancte Marie de Ruthenis teneat, sine deceptione sancte Marie, suo sciente. Et ille episcopus qui post mortem Deusdet <u>episcopo</u> et <u>Adalaiz</u> matri sue, primus episcopus fuerit, de Sancte Marie de Ruthenis quindecim mansos donet Gardrado, filio <u>Gardrado,</u> de Ruthenis usque ad Biaur in casmansos donet Gardrado, filio Gardrado, de Ruthenis usque ad Biaur in <u>castellania.</u> Et ipse Gardrado, filius Gardrado, talem firmitatem faciat de ipso episcopo de sua vita et de sua membra et de sua terra et de illo Castello Marino et de illa <u>castellania</u> superius scripta per que illum in eum se fidare posceat et debeat: et de illo Castello Marino **no.l decebra** <u>ipso episcopo</u> **nec no lo li vedara, ne no lo li tolra.** Sicut superius scriptum est, **si ho tenra et si ho atendra** ipse Gardradus de sua parte, suo sciente, si ille fuerit, **fors** quantum ipse Deusdet episcopus **l'en absolverat.**[4]

Here there are clearly features that could by no stretch of the most elastic imagination be regarded as Latin. Underlined elements are doubtful (place-names, personal names, a technical term *castellania*) but there can be no doubt about the phrases in bold. They are clearly Romance.

A second text (B) comes from León. Classed by Menéndez Pidal as an example of 'latín vulgar leonés' (a formulation that neatly combines localization and a claim to continued Latinity, even if it is spoken *latín vulgar*), it is analysed by Roger Wright[5] as a Latin graphical representation (i.e. retaining traditional Latin graphies) of an underlying Romance text, and transcribed by him (phonetically) as such, in a rendition which has nonetheless been sharply criticized.[6] The following is an excerpt:

---

4   Aveyron, 961–97, preserved in cartulary of bishop of Rodez [s. XIV]; Belmon and Vielliard, 'Latin farci et occitan', p. 157.
5   R. Wright, *Late Latin and Early Romance in Spain and Carolingian France* (Liverpool, 1982).
6   H. and W. Berschin, 'Mittellatein und Romanisch', *Zeitschrift für romanische Philologie* 102 (1987), 1–19.

(B) In Dei nom*ine*. Ego Splendonius tiui Fredesinde In Do*mi*no salutem. Ideo placuit mici atq*ue* conuenit, nunlliusq*ue* cogentis Inperio neq*ue* suadentis articulo set probria mici acesi uoluntas ut **uinderem tiui** Iam dicte Fredesinde terra In uilla Uiasco **suber** Illa **senrra domniga lloco** predicto Agro **rrodundo**.[7]

[W]right[8] describes this as 'a kind of hybrid between Latin and vernacular' and [n]otes that it 'contains both legal terminology and Romance elements'.[9] I am [f]ortunately perhaps) concerned less with pronunciation (though I agree with [W]right that there is no need to postulate an intermediate spoken *latín vulgar* [l]onés) than with whether individual words are nearer in form to Romance than [to] Latin. Those that are in bold type are phonetically apparently at least some [w]ay to being Romance (*tiui, vinderem, suber*) or frankly already Romance (*senrra, [do]mniga, lloco, rrodundo*). For me, then, this is simply another piece of *latin farci*, [al]beit with a stuffing that follows a Leonese, not an Occitan, recipe. For there [is], as we shall see, more than one way not just to skin a cat, but (in this case) to [st]uff a goose.

Analysis of multilingual material of this type is rarely problem-free. Above [al]l, we lack any real information about contemporary perceptions, and about [m]etalinguistic conceptions of what was meant, for example, by the separated-[n]ess of languages, which we take for granted. Within what one might term the [L]atin–Romance continuum, there are additional complications. In the first place, [si]nce Latin is patently the ancestor of Romance, then, to put it another way, [R]omance is an evolved form of Latin. That means that we are dealing not with [tw]o languages that coexist, or even two varieties of one language that sit side [b]y side, but with one (possibly, but not certainly, distinct) language that is in a [se]nse a continuation (or possibly other variant form) of the other. The written [tr]adition was almost exclusively what we would think of as Latin, and thus there [is] by definition virtually no documented point of comparison for the emergence [o]f Romance and the continuation of Latin. Even the early glossarial evidence, [so]metimes thought of as representing the early forms of spoken Romance, could [b]e interpreted as simply indicating variant or proscribed forms of written Latin. [S]o, in (for example) the *Appendix Probi* of *c*.700,[10] the forms listed could simply be [p]art of an attempt to correct written Latin, and to fend off newfangled Romance-[in]fluenced forms.

In early medieval England, the situation is undoubtedly more complex. Not [o]ne, but two vernaculars are in operation. One of them (Anglo-Saxon) is radi-[ca]lly different from Latin, so that much of what I have just said about the relative

Document from León, from the year 908; Berschin, 'Mittellatein und Romanisch', p. 5, and Wright, *Late Latin and Early Romance*, p. 166.
Wright, *Late Latin and Early Romance*, p. 165.
Wright, *Late Latin and Early Romance*, p. 167.
M. Iliescu and D. Slusanski, *Du latin aux langues romanes. Choix de textes traduits et commentés (du II* siècle avant J.C. jusqu'au X* siècle après J.C.)* (Wilhelmsfeld, 1991), p. 103.

ease of transition between two genetically related languages no longer applies
Against that must be set the fact that, prior to the Norman Conquest, a length
tradition of writing in the vernacular also existed, so that Anglo-Saxon and Latin
had for some time been used to being side-by-side not only in speech, but also a
written languages. The addition of Anglo-Norman to this mixture brings with it
an added dimension: a Romance vernacular, again without, at that time, a tradi
tion of being used in writing in those areas of France from which it came. There
were, it is true, isolated examples of texts in Romance, but they remain just that,
and there is little evidence of a sustained, widespread use of northern Gallo
Romance in literary or non-literary texts anywhere before the Norman Conquest
That, in itself, generates an evidence problem that I shall return to later.

I shall, for the purposes of the insular (British) element of this discussion, be
looking at three separate sources of information. The first of these (C) is not really a
text at all, but the *Dictionary of Medieval Latin from British Sources* (DMLBS). I think
it is worth drawing attention to the DMLBS in this context simply to emphasize
the extent to which any worthwhile dictionary of medieval Latin is by definition
riddled with vernacular evidence. The point, I believe, is important: it is some
times overlooked, just as French specialists are wont to overlook the fact that
the *Middle English Dictionary* (MED) is itself an excellent dictionary of medieval
French. It is hardly surprising that a dictionary of medieval Latin should contain
vernacular elements, since, clearly, it is in part the contact with the vernacular
that caused medieval Latin, and for that matter non-classical Latin across the
Empire, to be modified, expanded, and developed to meet the particular require
ments of local societies and according to differences in the natural world. The
extent to which this was already true during the Empire is brilliantly demon
strated in Jim Adams's far-ranging study of *Bilingualism and the Latin Language.*[12]
With the advent of a second written vernacular after the Norman Conquest, and
the continuation of Anglo-Saxon, it comes as no surprise (or should come as no
surprise) that the DMLBS contains a substantial amount of information about
the history of those languages. Indeed, it is certainly the case that (at least as far
as Anglo-Norman is concerned) the DMLBS often preserves evidence before it
is to hand in written, Anglo-Norman sources. The same, of course, is true of the
MED, notably, but by no means exclusively, in the case of English surnames of
Anglo-Norman provenance. These are often found long before the words that
underlie their frequently Latin manifestations are attested in French document
on either side of the English Channel. In other words, as I have tried to indicat
elsewhere,[13] we need to look at written evidence often in the 'wrong' language

---

[11] M. Pfister, 'Die sprachliche Bedeutung von Paris und der Ile-de-France vor dem 1.
Jh.', *Vox Romanica* 32 (1973), 217–53.

[12] J. N. Adams, *Bilingualism and the Latin Language* (Cambridge, 2003).

[13] D. A. Trotter, 'The Anglo-French Lexis of the *Ancrene Wisse*: A Re-evaluation', in a
Companion to Ancrene Wisse, ed. Y. Wada (Cambridge, 2002), pp. 83–101; idem, ' "No
quite what it says on the tin": Mining the National Archives for Multilingual Docu
ments', World Universities Network video-seminar (University of Bristol, March 2007

in order to unearth the subterranean manifestations of as yet unwritten (or as yet unattested, or lost) vernacular evidence.

The other two documents I want to look at are part of the borough customs of Leicester (D) from 1196, and what is perhaps the most complicated of my three texts, the earliest, the law code known as IV Aethelred (E), from an early twelfth-century manuscript of (perhaps) an early eleventh-century text.

The DMLBS is an exemplary dictionary and it provides an exemplary record of multilingual Britain, filtered through what was always its principal language of record, medieval Latin. Table 11.1 shows (from a couple of pages within the letter 'H') a number of clearly non-Latin lexical items nevertheless preserved in Latin texts and thus recorded in (C), a dictionary of Latin.

Table 11.1: Sample non-Latin lexical items

DMLBS + date	Meaning	MED	OED	DEAF (= OF)
hobelarius a 1124	'light horseman'	a1325	1308	c.1160
hobelus a 1217	'hobby, small hawk'			end 12th c.
hobeus 1306	'hobby, small hawk'	1440	1440	c.1195 hobé
hobinus c.1276	'hobby, small horse'	1298 (in Latin text)	1375	1305
hitha Domesday	'landing place'	1176 (place-name)	c.725	
hogaster 1128 ('pig', earlier than 'sheep')		AL & AF a1400 (earliest is 'sheep')	1420 sense 1, 1175 sense 2 but same cit. as DMLBS	< OE/ME 1270, AN SeneschO
hokum 2 1195; cf. hoga 6 1199	'spit or strip of land (?in bend of river)' (same sense for both hokum 2 and hoga 6	1300 but this sense in place-names only; = hoga (place-names only), c.1125	1600 this sense, OED says < Du. hoek; hoe c.700	hoge c.1140 < ME hough; hoc < Frk. *hôk

The first four words listed in this table are Anglo-Norman, transparently Latinized.

Hitha is a Latinized survival of the long-standing Anglo-Saxon term (hence, for example, *Rotherhithe*).

Hogaster is Anglo-Norman.

Hokum/hoka exemplify the complexities of multilingual etymology. The OED suggests Dutch *hoek* as the source of *hokum*, found in 1195 in Latin; but this sense is found only (in ME) in place-names, and from 1300; *hoga*, also exclusively in toponyms, is found in ME from 1125. The DEAF has a much earlier (c.1140) *hoge*, apparently from ME *hough* (which may be the same word) and *hoc*, from a Frankish *hôk*, which, to the uninitiated, looks as if it is cognate with Dutch *hoek*. Anglo-Norman sources preserve forms that seem to be transmogrifications of *hough*.

Hogaster is similarly entangled: meaning (variously) a boar or a sheep, in

157

its third or second year, as the case may be, and the oldest DMLBS attestation (from 1128) is for a pig; the MED and OED can offer nothing as early, and their first offerings are for sheep not pigs; in Anglo-Norman, the first attestation is in Walter of Henley's *Seneschalcie* (DEAF: SeneschO) of *c*.1270.

The key point regarding *hogaster* is that the Latin evidence, although not quite for the same sense, is conspicuously earlier than the vernacular data, but this is a word that ostensibly originated in the vernacular and then made its way into Latin. The evidence, in short, is back to front. This – like many another – is a muddle that cannot be monolingually resolved because it has not been monolingually generated.

My next example (D), from the borough records of Leicester,[14] is later but (or indeed, perhaps because of that) no less confusing. Here we have a predominantly Latin text (some would say: a Latin text, full stop) from 1196, which has been infiltrated by Romance elements. The Leicester records were discussed by William Rothwell in a paper delivered in Sheffield in 1995; but apart from that, in the main, they have received little attention, and certainly not the attention that from a (socio)linguistic perspective they undoubtedly deserve. Below I reprint a section from the First Merchant Gild Roll, from Wednesday, 9 October 1196, a list of those who entered the guild and of their sponsors (underlining in the text here indicates marking for deletion in the original manuscript). Because the opening section of the record is provided in a facsimile which accompanies the edition, I have been able to provide (for crucial sections) a reproduction, albeit at one or two removes, of the manuscript.

Item Isti intrauerunt in Gildam **Merchatoriam** die festi beati Dionisii primo post aduentum comitis in Angliam post deliberacionem suam de capcione sua in Francia: soluunt de introitu & de tauro & de ansis et tantum debent: […]
S. Galterus de Nicol[ia]: quietus de Introitu et de hansis. <u>Eius plegii: Wilke</u> <u>Waterman, Rob. de Burg[o]</u>. [...]

<u>Galfridus de Eitona</u> **teintor**. Eius plegii: Rob. **halleknaue** Radulfus francus **teintor** [*ed.*: tinctor]: dedit viiis. et debet iis.
S. Rob. **Halleknaue** <u>iiis. iiiid</u>. Eius plegii: Galf. **teintor** de Eitona, Rad. **tinctor** francus: quietus.
Taurus. Rad. teintor francus vi*d*. Eius plegii.

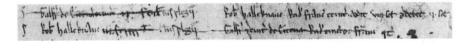

14 M. Bateson, *Records of the Borough of Leicester*, Selden Society 1 (London, 1899), pp. 12–13.

[...]
S. Wchinus filius Willelmi filii Warini vi*d*. Eius plegii: <u>Joh. Warin, Galterus</u>
pikenot: quietus de introitu et ansis per totum.

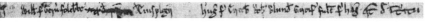

S. Ric. **daunsel** his. iiii*s*. iii*d*. quietus de introitu: <u>eius plegii: Rad. cocus, Joh.</u>
<u>filius **Estephani**</u>.

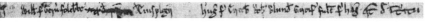

[...] S. Will. filius Geruasii **folebarbe**. Eius plegii: Hugo filius Cireth, Rob.
Blund **Garcifer** fulconis filii Hugonis: quietus de introitu.

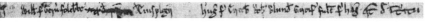

Taurus. Jacobus de **flekeneige** xx*d*. <u>Eius plegii</u>.
S. Will. Longus (deleted payments). Eius plegii: Jacobus de **flekeneie**: quietus
de omnibus Rebus.

A number of words call for comment:

teintor (cf. parallel *tinctor*): the coexistence of the (Romance) form *teintor* and
its Latin cognate (and etymon) *tinctor* is very striking in the relevant two
lines of text, where the only logical conclusion to be drawn is that the two
forms (or the forms in the two languages) are, for the author, interchangeable
(and for that matter, palaeographically hard to distinguish when abbreviated
forms like *teint'* are deployed):

S. Galfridus de Eitona **teintor**. Eius plegii: Rob. **halleknaue** Radulfus francus
teintor [*ed.*: tinctor]: dedit viii*s*. et debet ii*s*.
S. Rob. **Halleknaue** iii*s*. iiii*d*. <u>Eius plegii: Galf. **teintor** de Eitona, Rad. **tinctor**</u>
francus: quietus.

halleknave: 1185 Willelmus Hallecnave MED; *waterman*: (as surname) from
1196 (in this text, cited MED) are two English words (occupational surnames).
pikenot: the meaning of this word is unclear although it does appear to be
English.
daunsel = OF/AN 'young man'.
folebarbe: ME + AF hybrid, 'full beard' [?] The sense is unclear but the word is
obviously vernacular and probably a mixture of Anglo-Norman and Anglo-
Saxon (Middle English).
garcifer: DMLBS, < cf. AN *garçun*, ME *garsoun*, 'servant, groom', an obvious
Latinization of an Anglo-Norman word.

flekeneige, flekeneie = Fleckney (Leics.): chiefly remarkably for the two form
of the toponym.

Finally, there is the case of text (E), the legal text known as IV Aethelred. From
my point of view, this source is problematic principally because of the history
of its transmission, but also because it is (potentially) so early. I say 'potentially'
because the text was apparently originally compiled in the early part of the ele-
enth century (that is, probably a half-century *before* the Norman Conquest), but
it unfortunately survives only in what appears to be the last of five recensions of
a twelfth-century reworking known by the title of *Quadripartitus*, a half-centur
after the Conquest. Critical to any analysis of the multilingual elements[15] in th
text is, therefore, the attempt to determine which elements were in the origin
and which were added by the – naturally, anonymous – author whom Patric
Wormald refers to as 'Q',[16] and who seems every bit as mysterious as his name
sake, the gadget man in the James Bond series. Disentangling the manuscrip
transmission in this regard at least seems to have defeated even the great Liebe
mann who is not, to a philologist, terribly enlightening on the lexis of the text no
the linguistic implications of its chronological evolution. Yet these are crucia
IV Aethelred, of which a portion is reproduced below, is potentially among th
earliest evidence of Anglo-Norman that we have, and certainly constitutes a ver
early example of trilingual language contact. It is not by accident that it shoul
feature (under the siglum *GAS, Gesetze der Angelsachsen*) at the beginning of s
many DMLBS articles.

'IV Aethelred': Customs of Billingsgate, probably 1000–1035, preserved in Quadripar
titus (more than a century later).

> Item rex Lundonie
> **Ealdretesgate** et **Cripelesgate** (id est portas illas) observabant custodes:
> Ad **Billingesgate** si advenisset una navicula, I obolus tolonei dabatur, si maior
> et haberet siglas, I d..
> Si adveniat <u>ceol</u> vel **hulcus** et ibi iaceat, quatuor d. ad teloneum.
> De navi plena lignorum unum lignum ad tol'.
> In ebdomada pañ teloñ III diebus: die Dominica et die Martis et die Iovis.
> Qui ad pontem venisset cum <u>bato</u>, ubi piscis inesset, ipse mango unum obolum
> dabat in telon., et de maiori nave unum d.
> Homines de Rotomaga, qui veniebant cum vino vel craspisce, dabant rectitu-
> dinem sex sol. de magna navi et XX. frustum de ipso craspisce.

---

15 Liebermann observes that 'Das Latein des Werkes [...] wimmelt von unclassische
Wörtern aus des Verfassers Nordgallischer Muttersprache, aus dem Englischen, das
täglich hörte und in seiner Vorlage las, und aus dem Anglonormannischen Recht; n
für Anglonormannen war es überhaupt bestimmt und verständlich' (F. Lieberman
Quadripartitus, ein englisches Rechtsbuch von 1114 (Halle, 1892), p. 33).

16 P. Wormald, *The Making of English Law: King Alfred to the Twelfth Century*, vol. 1: *Legisl*
tion and its Limits (Oxford, 1999), pp. 320–2.

Flandrenses et Ponteienses et Normannia et Francia monstrabant res suas et extolneabant.

Hogge et Leodium et Nivella, qui pertransibant (per terras ibant), **ostensionem** dabant et telon.

Et homines imperatoris, qui veniebant in navibus suis, bonarum legum digni tenebantur, sicut et nos.

Preter **discarcatam** lanam et dissutum unctum et tres porcos vivos licebat eis emere in naves suas.

Et non licebat eis aliquod <u>forceapum</u> facere <u>burhmannis,</u> et dare toll' suum et in sancto natali Domini duos **grisengos** pannos et unum brunum et decem libras piperis et cirotecas quinque hominum et duos caballinos tonellos aceto plenos; et totidem in pascha.

De **dosseris** cum gallinis I gallina telon., et de uno **dossero** cum ovis V ova telonei, si veniant ad mercatum.

<u>Smeremangestre</u> (que mangonant in caseo et butiro): XIIII diebus ante natale Domini unum den. et septem diebus ante natale (Domini) unum alium.

Si <u>portireva</u> vel <u>tungravio</u> compellet aliquem vel alius prepositus, quod toloneum supertenuerit, et homo respondeat, quod nullum tolneum concelaverit, quod iuste dare debuisset, iuret hoc se VII° et sit quietus.

Si **cacepollum** advocet, quod ei toloneum dedit, et ille neget, perneget ad Dei iudicium et in nulla alia lada.

There are a number of troubling problems in this text if it is to be read as Latin. It clearly contains a number of Anglo-Saxon words that may be the result of its production in the early eleventh century. That is not the only explanation since Anglo-Saxon continued to appear in post-Conquest documents. IV Aethelred's Latin displays partial abandonment of core principles of Latin morphosyntax in the form of inflexions – which would in due course be replaced by prepositional constructions and analytical word-order to compensate for the loss of synthetically conveyed grammatical information – but that is not an exclusively pre- or post-Conquest feature. It is endemic from the late Roman Empire across the Latin world. But the most challenging linguistic features here are the Anglo-Norman elements, whose status is the most complex of the three languages concerned, and whose presence in the text is most problematic in terms of the date, construction and transmission of the surviving text. This latter contains place-names that signally fail to comply with Latin morphosyntax: *Flandrenses et Pontejenses et Normannia et Francia; Hogge et Leodium et Nivella*. In terms of lexis, *ceol vel hulcus* demonstrates a contiguity of Anglo-Saxon and Latin (Liebermann thinks this is not a gloss, but cf. DMLBS **cyula**). **Discarcare** is the first DMLBS attestation of this verb (cf. **carcare** from 1166), which is attested in the much earlier *Lex Salica*.[17] There are Anglo-Saxon words: *forceapum* is the only citation sub DMLBS **foreceapum** < AS *foreceap* 'forecheap', 'forestalling (market)'; *burhmannis* is clearly Anglo-Saxon (*burhman*) with Latin inflexion; *portireva, tungravio* likewise.

---

[17] E.g. XXVII: see Iliescu and Slusanski, *Du latin aux langues romanes*, p. 169.

Dosseris, dossero, 'pannier(-load)' is attested in DMLBS **dorsarium**, but the form looks as if it at least could be due to Anglo-Norman *dosser* (DMLBS: cf. AN *dosser* ...); *ostensio* is attested from Classical Latin (cf. DMLBS), but the specific sense here (no. 10 in DMLBS: 'scavage, tax levied on foreign merchants') seems to be a translation of the Anglo-Saxon/Middle English *scauāge* (MED), Anglo-Norman *scawage* (AND) – cf. MED: 'AF **scawage, schawage** (cp. 16th-century NF **escauwage**) & AL **scawagium**; ult. English: cp. OE **scēawian** & ME **sheuen**'.[18] Perhaps most intriguing of all is *grisengos*: DMLBS **grisengus** < Anglo-Norman *grisenc*, cf. DEAF **grisan** G1420,24 (cf. same page of DMLBS: **grisellus, grisillum, grismulettus,** all from Anglo-Norman). If it is Anglo-Norman, how is it in Latin before the Conquest, or what has happened to the documentary record? **Cacepollum** is similarly Anglo-Norman but in disguise: cf. OED2: '[a. med.L. *cacepollus*, ONF. **cachepol* = central OF. *chacepol, chacipol, chassipol,* in med.L. also *cachepolus, chacepollus, chacipollus, chassipullus* (Du Cange), lit. 'chase-fowl', one who hunts or chases fowls. The form of the word appears to indicate that it arose in Provençal, where it would be *cassapol,* or It., where it would be *cacciapollo.* The OF. was apparently adapted from Pr. or med.L.].'

In short, this is a text that eloquently demonstrates the level of language contact in the immediate post-Conquest period, while at the same time highlighting some of the difficulties in analysing documents whose literary and textual ancestry antedates that linguistic watershed. And this, in turn, raises the question of how real, and how marked, that watershed really was. It is perhaps worth stressing the extent of contact, at the highest level, between England and Normandy well before the Norman Conquest: indeed, the Norman Conquest, so-called, is a direct consequence of precisely those contacts, and of the negotiation between Edward the Confessor and Duke William, and even between the Normans and the ill-fated Harold. Those who promulgated a series of laws deriving from the authority of the Anglo-Saxon kings were in contact with Normandy well before 1066.[19] It is thus theoretically possible that any Anglo-Norman element in a twelfth-century recension of a pre-Conquest Latin (or for that matter, Anglo-Saxon) text, could be genuinely pre-Conquest. In the case of IV Aethelred, the case is not proven, but it *could* have happened in that way. At any rate what we have, beyond reasonable doubt, is a Latin text (itself a reworking of an Anglo-Saxon precursor) that preserves, in the early twelfth century, *grisengos,* the first attestation of a Latinized form of an originally Anglo-Norman word, *grisan.* This case, alone, calls into question the viability of (often undernourished) monolingual etymological

---

18 See also N. Middleton, 'Early Medieval Port Customs, Tolls and Controls on Foreign Trade', *EME* 13 (2005), 313–58.

19 See the essay by Tyler in this volume for some literary and cultural arguments against the definitiveness of the Conquest, also her 'Talking about History in Eleventh-Century England: The *Encomium Emmae Reginae* and the Court of Harthacnut', *EME* 13 (2005), 359–83.

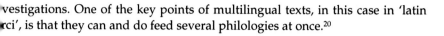

vestigations. One of the key points of multilingual texts, in this case in 'latin
rci', is that they can and do feed several philologies at once.[20]

A further element in the linguistic jigsaw derives from those relatively few Anglo-
Saxon words that have been transmitted into French. But this, too, is problematic, for
the simple reason that the Anglo-Saxon words cannot be proven to have made their
way into any form of French before the Norman Conquest, simply because there is
almost no textual evidence in Old French of any sort (or from any area) at so early a
date (cf. Pfister,'Die sprachliche Bedeutung'; Berschin 'Mittellatein und Romanisch',
p. 8 and n.14). Indeed, the consensus for the most obvious among the Anglo-Saxon
borrowings (the cardinal points of the compass: north, south, east, and west) is that
they were transferred from Anglo-Saxon into Anglo-Norman, and thence made their
way into continental French. While this is a pattern of transmission that seems in some
respects to go against that which is normally presumed for the process of the evolution of continental French and the development of its offshore dialect cousin, Anglo-
Norman, it is the only hypothesis that the current state of documentary evidence
permits.

12

From Old English to Old French

Elizabeth M. Tyler*

Coming to the French of England from the standpoint of the literature of Angl
Saxon England provides a space in which to step away from the narrative
loss that so powerfully shapes the Anglo-Saxonist's view of the literary cultur
of England across the eleventh and twelfth centuries. According to this narr
tive, somewhere in the eleventh century, the world of *Beowulf*, the Exeter Boc
and Ælfric disappeared. Although the Norman Conquest is seen as the dea
knell of Anglo-Saxon literature in this narrative, scholars generally lose intere
well before 1066. In many ways, 1023 and the death of the famous homilist ar
legal-writer Wulfstan, archbishop of York, marks the end of what has traditio
ally been seen as Anglo-Saxon literature. This narrative of loss has left a blar
space between the early eleventh century and the explosion of Latin and Fren
writing in the twelfth-century Anglo-Norman realm.[1]

This blank space impacts on the understanding of the emergence of writte
French in post-Conquest England because it masks the remarkable overla
between late Anglo-Saxon and early Anglo-Norman literary cultures. If *Beow*
and Ælfric are taken as characteristic of Anglo-Saxon literature, there seen
little link between Old English and Anglo-Norman, as well as Old French mo
broadly. However, when we begin to see how open Anglo-Saxon England w.
to new learning from the end of the tenth century onwards and how the rel
tionship between English and Latin began to shift well before 1066, England
participation in the 'making of Europe' comes into focus.[2] This participation

---

* I am grateful to Bruce O'Brien and Jocelyn Wogan-Browne for comments on earli
drafts of this essay and to those who made comments on the version read at the 20
York French of England conference.

1 For recent, authoritative accounts of English literary culture that convey a sense of lo
across the events of the eleventh century or offer a narrative that largely ceases in t
1020s, see: S. Lerer, 'Old English and its Afterlife', in Wallace, *Medieval English Liter*
ture, pp. 7–34; R. D. Fulk and C. M. Cain, *A History of Old English Literature* (Oxfor
2003), esp. pp. 26, 226; and D. Donoghue, *Old English Literature: A Short Introducti*
(Oxford, 2004). *A Companion to Anglo-Saxon Literature*, ed. P. Pulsiano and E. Treharr
(Oxford, 2001) stands apart because of its inclusion of Treharne's essay, 'English in t
Post-Conquest Period' (pp. 403–14) persuasively arguing for the vitality of Engli
from 1060 into the thirteenth century. However, the period from Wulfstan to t
Conquest is still largely unrepresented.

2 The phrase is borrowed from the title of Robert Bartlett's book: his view of the eme
gence of Latin Christendom has shaped my understanding of the place of litera

evident in Æthelred's marriage to Norman Emma in 1002 and in Cnut's fascination with the Holy Roman Empire, which we must set alongside his patronage of skalds if we are to see the European scope of his ambition.[3] In this essay, I will argue that the remapping of late Anglo-Saxon literary culture has much to offer for understanding the context in which Anglo-Norman emerged as a written language and, at the same time, that there is much to be learned about eleventh- and even tenth-century Anglo-Saxon literary culture from looking at cross-Conquest connections.

I

Ian Short's article 'Patrons and Polyglots: French Literature in Twelfth-Century England' is of tremendous importance for the study of late Anglo-Saxon literary culture. Three main points made by Short are particularly relevant. The first is his identification of the centrality of trilingualism to the vibrancy of the literary culture of Norman England. The second is his insistence that the 'vernacularization of culture' was 'one of the most important, and one of the least widely recognised, aspects of the new intellectual vitality of the twelfth century'. The third is his recognition that the long-established use of English as a written language encouraged the flourishing of French as a written language.[4] All three propositions have radical implications for how we might rethink English literary culture in the century before the Conquest in order to recognize its intellectual vitality, its deeply European character and the important consequences it had for literary culture from the twelfth century onwards. Anglo-Saxonists preoccupied with mourning the passing of *Beowulf* have missed these dimensions of Old English and Latin literature in the tenth and eleventh centuries.

Short's article identifies England as the location of the first French scientific text, *chanson de geste*, historiography, legal text and so forth.[5] The time is ripe, especially given increased scholarly interest in Anglo-Saxon scientific learning and increased literary study of historiography, to look at all these categories afresh for late Anglo-Saxon England. Getting back behind Short's list, chronologically, opens up points of contact between the written culture of England before and after the Conquest. Simply comparing the twelfth-century texts listed in Dean's catalogue of Anglo-Norman manuscripts with the eleventh-century manuscripts in Ker's *Catalogue of Manuscripts Containing Anglo-Saxon* and Gneuss's *Handlist*

---

culture across the Conquest: *The Making of Europe: Conquest, Colonization and Cultural Change, 950–1350* (Harmondsworth, 1994).

3   T. Bolton, *The Empire of Cnut the Great: Conquest and Consolidation of Power in Northern Europe in the Early Eleventh Century* (Leiden, 2009); M. Townend, 'Norse Poets and English Kings: Skaldic Performance in Anglo-Saxon England', *Offa* 58 (2001), 269–75.

4   Short, 'Patrons and Polyglots', pp. 229–49 (pp. 230–2).

5   Short, 'Patrons and Polyglots', p. 229.

of Anglo-Saxon Manuscripts reveals quite startling connections.[6] Perhaps surprisingly this exercise has as much to tell us about Anglo-Saxon literature as it does about Anglo-Norman literature. Links emerge between saints lives, legal texts, medical texts and lapidaries, as well as texts of other kinds.

There is much scope for work in the area of the overlap between eleventh- and twelfth-century vernacular texts in English and Anglo-Norman. Here, I give only a few examples from across several genres in order to substantiate this point. In the field of law, links between Old English and Anglo-Norman are evident in the English context of the production of the first written law code in French, the *Leis Willelme*. From the time of Æthelbert of Kent's conversion in the early sixth century, Anglo-Saxon written legal culture was almost exclusively carried out in the vernacular, and the *Leis Willelme* situate themselves within this tradition. The incipit reads: 'Cez sunt les leis e les custumes que li reis Will' grantad al pople de Engleterre apres le cunquest de la terre. Iceles meimes que li reis Edward sun cusin tint devant lui.'[7] Both English and Anglo-Norman were used to transmit new medical learning from the Mediterranean. Although there is a gap of over a century between late Anglo-Saxon texts and the first appearance of medical learning in Anglo-Norman, Green sees Anglo-Saxon translation practice as paving the way for later Anglo-Norman developments. Cross-Conquest interest in scientific learning is further evident in the innovative Old English lapidary found in the mid-eleventh-century manuscript London, British Library, MS Cotton Tiberius A.III and in the flourishing, from the early twelfth century onwards, of Anglo-Norman lapidaries that drew on Marbod's twelfth-century Latin poem *De lapidibus*.

Lives of Mary of Egypt in Latin, English and then French testify to the interconnections between Latin and these vernaculars in both England and Northern France. The life of Mary of Egypt was popular in Northern France in Latin versions across the tenth to twelfth centuries, as the poetic accounts by Flodoard of Rheims (d. 966) and Hildebert of Lavardin (d. 1133) testify. Hildebert's poem, which participates fully in his deep engagement with classical Latin poetry, especially Ovid, was known in England from at least the mid-twelfth century, when it might have been copied by or for the nuns of Barking Abbey (as well as at other religious foundations). Among the early French accounts of Mary of Egypt is one included in the Anglo-Norman *Gracial*, a collection of miracles of the Virgin by Adgar, who wrote between 1150 and 1170. The poem was dedicated to Maud, who is most likely identified as the abbess of Barking (*c*.1175–95) and illegitimate

---

6   Dean; N. R. Ker, *Catalogue of Manuscripts Containing Anglo-Saxon* (Oxford, 1957); and
     H. Gneuss, *Handlist of Anglo-Saxon Manuscripts: A List of Manuscripts and Manuscript
     Fragments Written or Owned in England up to 1100* (Tempe AZ, 2001).
7   ('These are the laws and customs which King William granted to the people of England
     after the conquest of the land. Those same which King Edward, his cousin, held before
     him'): see Dean no. 32; F. Liebermann, *Die Gesetze der Angelsachsen* (Halle, 1903), I,
     492–520 (prologue). For discussion, see B. O'Brien, 'Translating Technical Terms in
     Law-Codes from Alfred to the Angevins', in Tyler, *Conceptualizing Multilingualism*,
     forthcoming.

aughter of Henry II. Although the English translation of the Mary of Egypt life ccurs in a very early eleventh-century manuscript alongside works by Ælfric, s representation of female sexuality is distinct from the familiar approach of ɪe Benedictine Reformer who transforms female saints into models of male ɪonastic piety.[8] The attitude towards sexuality evinced in the Old English Mary ϵ Egypt points towards possibilities for different kinds of Anglo-Saxon audi- nces, perhaps, if post-Conquest Barking interest in the saint is any indication, ɪcluding women.

What I am emphatically not suggesting, by trying to open up the overlap etween vernacular literary cultures of eleventh- and twelfth-century England ⁄ith a small selection of examples, is that we look for a simple one-to-one rela- onship between texts in English and texts in Anglo-Norman in order to develop reductive paradigm in which French written culture is derived from the English. he picture is far more complex, involving some movement of texts from English ɔ Anglo-Norman, but also, and just as importantly, the ways in which both ɪrnaculars work to make accessible new kinds of Latin scientific, literary and ɹligious learning. The Anglo-Saxon legacy to the twelfth century is not solely bout the vitality of English (though this is critical, as Elaine Treharne and Mary ̄wan's English Manuscripts project is making increasingly clear) but about ɪnglish, Latin and French coming into a shared European literary culture, which ⁄as, in turn, deeply shaped by the precocity of English as a written vernacu- ̄r.[9] It is within this larger framework of the relationship between English, Latin ɪd French that I want to focus, in the remainder of this essay, on the continuity ϵ history-writing and poetry in England across the tenth, eleventh and twelfth ɪnturies. Texts in these genres reveal the increasing importance of the court as a ɔcation of innovative literary culture, where the laity, and especially lay women, ɪaimed classical learning as a means of negotiating dynastic ambition amidst ̄e politics of conquest. These preoccupations can also be followed in the royal ɪnneries where many of these lay women were educated. This use of the clas- ɪcal past has come to be seen as a central dimension in twelfth-century French ɔmance; here I will argue that it is just as characteristic of eleventh-century, and ɪrlier, English literary culture.[10]

C. Cubitt, 'Virginity and Misogyny in Tenth- and Eleventh-Century England', *Gender and History* 12 (2000), 1–32.

'The Production and Use of English Manuscripts 1060–1220' (www.le.ac.uk/ee/em1060to1220).

Among studies of the classical past in twelfth-century French literature, see espe- cially: L. Patterson, *Negotiating the Past: The Historical Understanding of Medieval Litera- ture* (Madison WI, 1987); F. Mora-Lebrun, *L'Enéide médiévale et la naissance du roman* (Paris, 1994); and C. Baswell, *Virgil in Medieval England: Figuring the Aeneid from the Twelfth Century to Chaucer* (Cambridge, 1995). For the classical past in late Anglo-Saxon England, see my forthcoming *Crossing Conquests: Women and the Politics of Literature in Eleventh Century England* (Toronto, forthcoming).

II

While it might seem that all there is to be said about shift from English to French as a language of history-writing in the twelfth century is that Gaimar used a version of the Anglo-Saxon Chronicle as a basis for his *Estoire des Engleis*, Gaimar' move was made possible by a number of developments in history-writing in late Anglo-Saxon England.[11] These developments began long before French came into its own as a language of history, and they relate to the strange relationship of Latin and English in the pre-Conquest period. As Lapidge writes: 'The Latin written by Anglo-Saxons is notable for its contorted, uncontrolled (often incomprehensible) syntax and its ostentatious parade of obscure vocabulary.'[1] Considering this hermeneutic style as a social phenomenon brings into focus it role as a hyper-learned form of Latin, meant to mark out its users as member of an elite clerical circle; it was not intended to facilitate communication. Such a style could only become dominant in a context, like Anglo-Saxon England in which written communication was carried out in the vernacular: in other words, written English enables the practice of hermeneutic Latin in England because English did so much of what Latin did on the Continent – law, poetry government, history-writing, science and so forth. Paradoxically, hermeneutic Latin encouraged lay access to the 'story-world' of Rome.[13] The Old English translations of Orosius, *Apollonius of Tyre*, *The Letter of Alexander* and Boethius are part of a world in which Latin had retreated from communication.[14]

The Anglo-Saxon Chronicle, surprisingly, fits into this picture of lay access to the Roman story-world. These vernacular chronicles, while being monastic productions, were not unconnected to the royal court and, although they have little to say about Roman history and legend, they do allow us to see the powerful place of the classical past in late Anglo-Saxon England. When known readers of

11 Geffrei Gaimar, *L'Estoire des Engleis*, ed. A. Bell, ANTS 14–16 (Oxford, 1960). Bell writes that Gaimar used a Chronicle 'akin to, but not identical with, the Peterborough version' (p. liv), which is edited most recently in *The Anglo-Saxon Chronicle: A Collabora tive Edition, 7, MS E*, ed. S. Irvine (Cambridge, 2004). See further the essay by Bainton in this volume.

12 M. Lapidge, 'The Hermeneutic Style of Tenth-Century Anglo-Latin Literature', *Anglo Saxon England* 4 (1975), 67–111. The quotation can be found in *The Anglo-Saxon Chron icle: A Collaborative Edition 17, The Annals of St Neots with Vita Prima Sancti Neoti*, ed. D Dumville and M. Lapidge (Cambridge, 1983), p. xcvii.

13 This productive phrase and concept, which refers to Roman myth and history and their long reception in the post-classical world, is T. P. Wiseman's in his *The Myths of Rome* (Exeter, 2004), esp. pp. 10–12.

14 *The Old English Orosius*, ed. J. Bately, EETS SS 6 (London, 1980); *The Old English Apol lonius of Tyre*, ed. P. Goolden (London, 1958); *The Letter of Alexander to Aristotle* in Old English can be found in A. Orchard, *Pride and Prodigies: Studies in the Monsters of the Beowulf-Manuscript* (Cambridge, 1995), pp. 224–53; and *The Old English Boethius*, ed M. Godden and S. Irvine (Oxford, 2009). For another social view of hermeneutic Latin see R. Stephenson, 'Byrhtferth's *Enchiridion*: The Effectiveness of Hermeneutic Latin in Tyler, *Conceptualizing Multilingualism*, forthcoming.

the Chronicle are considered, there are strong connections with court and elite aristocratic circles. For example, the nobleman Æthelweard (Ælfric's patron) translated or caused the Chronicle to be translated from English into Latin in the late tenth century so that it could be sent to his kinswoman, the Ottonian Abbess Matilda of Essen.[15] Wulfstan may himself have read and added to the Chronicle. As advisor to both Æthelred and Cnut, Wulfstan was well known in the early eleventh-century court. We should not imagine, especially given that one of his interventions in the Chronicle is critical of King Edgar's court, that Wulfstan's reading of history did not inform the advice he offered to kings. Later in the mid-eleventh century, manuscript D of the Chronicle, probably compiled within the entourage of Ealdred, bishop of Worcester and then archbishop of York, is courtly in its outlook. Ealdred, who was sent by Edward the Confessor to bring back the latter's nephew, Edward the Exile, from Hungary and who crowned both Harold Godwineson and William the Conqueror, was at the heart of the English court across the reign of three kings.[16]

There are, moreover, connections between the vernacular Chronicle and classical frameworks for understanding history. When Æthelweard translates the Chronicle into Latin, for example, he uses allusion to parallel the arrival of Hengest and Horsa on British shores to the arrival of Aeneas in Actium, an event that, in the *Aeneid*, foreshadows Octavian's victory and his assumption of sole rule of the Empire.[17] In the eleventh century, a copy of the Old English *Orosius* was bound together with the Chronicle (London, British Library, MS Cotton Tiberius B.I), and back in the early tenth century, the scribe who made the earliest extant copy of the Old English *Orosius* (London, British Library, MS Additional 47967) also copied the Winchester version of the Chronicle (Cambridge, Corpus Christi College, MS 173).[18] This association of *Orosius* and the Chronicle attests to

---

[15] *The Chronicle of Æthelweard*, ed. A. Campbell (London, 1962). For recent discussion, see: E. van Houts, 'Women and the Writing of History in the Early Middle Ages: The Case of Abbess Matilda of Essen and Aethelweard', *EME* 1 (1992), 53–68.

[16] *Anglo-Saxon Chronicle ... MS E*, ed. Irvine, s.a. 959 (p. 56). P. Wormald, 'Archbishop Wulfstan and the Holiness of Society', rpt in his *Legal Culture in the Early Medieval West* (London, 1999), pp. 225–51; T. Bredehoft, *Textual Histories: Readings in the Anglo-Saxon Chronicle* (Toronto, 2001), pp. 106–10; and S. Baxter, 'MS C of the Anglo-Saxon Chronicle and the Politics of Mid-Eleventh Century England', *EHR* 122 (2007), 1189–1227.

[17] *The Chronicle of Æthelweard*, p. 7 and *Aeneid* iii, 277 (and see Campbell's introduction to the *Chronicle*, p. xlix).

[18] Katherine O'Brien O'Keeffe argues that the C manuscript of the Chronicle was 'designed to complement the already existing *Orosius*' (*The Anglo-Saxon Chronicle: A Collaborative Edition, 5, MS C* (Cambridge, 2001), p. xxiii) and 'Reading the C-Text: The After-Lives of London, British Library, Cotton Tiberius B. I', in *Anglo-Saxon Manuscripts and Their Heritage*, ed. P. Pulsiano and E. M. Treharne (Aldershot, 1998), pp. 137–60 (pp. 138–40)). On the scribe of the A manuscript of the Chronicle and the earliest surviving copy of Orosius, see: M. B. Parkes, 'The Palaeography of the Parker Manuscript of the *Chronicle*, Laws and Sedulius, and Historiography at Winchester in the Late Ninth and Tenth Centuries', *Anglo-Saxon England* 5 (1976), 149–71 (for a dissenting view, see: D. Dumville, *Wessex and England from Alfred to Edgar: Six Essays on Political, Cultural and Ecclesiastical Revival* (Woodbridge, 1992), pp. 55–139).

a notable willingness to juxtapose the Roman past with Anglo-Saxon history in a manner that may have encouraged a comparative approach to understanding history and politics, and which entailed using the Romans to think about the present.[19]

The Old English *Apollonius* allows us to see the use of the Roman past in pre- and post-Conquest English literary culture within a European framework. The Latin *Historia Apollonii* was extremely popular throughout Europe, and the story very early makes its way into French; twelfth-century troubadours and romance writers knew it. Its English version appears to be of the late tenth century and is preserved in a mid-eleventh-century manuscript of largely penitential material that has connections to York and Winchester and to Wulfstan. The Wulfstan connection again brings us close to, if not into, the courts of Æthelred and Cnut. Many have wondered what the Old English *Apollonius* – often termed (without much thought) the first Western European vernacular romance – is doing amid this penitential material. An eleventh-century Northern Italian chronicle suggests an answer. There Apollonius is referred to in an admonitory and court context – to rebuke a king who has slept with his daughter-in-law.[20] *Apollonius* also reveals specific genealogical links between the textual cultures of Normandy and England. These are not about direct movement of a text from one realm to another (though it is tempting to speculate about that possibility), but about participation in a common European literary tradition. The Latin *Apollonius* was known to the Norman court in the early eleventh century. The text appeared together with poems which, according to Elisabeth Van Houts, satirize the marriage of Emma and Cnut and with poems closely associated with the patronage of Emma's mother Gunnor. The use of *Apollonius*, in an admonitory context, would perhaps have been familiar to Emma on both sides of the Channel.[21]

Emma brings us to her *Encomium Emmae Reginae* – an account of the Danish Conquest of England written for Emma by a Flemish monk to protect her amid the bitter factionalism of the court of her son Harthacnut (r. 1040–2).[22] The *Enco-*

---

[19] On the importance of Orosius' comparative approach to empires, see: M. S. Kempshall, *Rhetoric and the Writing of History, 400–1500* (Manchester, forthcoming).

[20] E. Archibald, *Apollonius of Tyre: Medieval and Renaissance Themes and Variations* (Cambridge, 1991); this volume includes a text and translation of the *Historia* (pp. 112–81) and an excerpt and translation from the *Chronicon Novaliciense*, ed. L. C. Bethmann, MGH SS 7 (Hanover, 1846), p. 64. For discussion of the place of the Old English version in Cambridge, Corpus Christi College, MS 201, see P. Wormald, *The Making of English Law: King Alfred to the Twelfth Century*, vol. 1: *Legislation and Its Limits* (Oxford, 1999), pp. 205–10.

[21] For *Historia Apollonii* in Paris, Bibliothèque nationale, MS lat. 8121A, see: *Jezebel: A Norman Latin Poem of the Early Eleventh Century*, ed. J. Ziolkowski (New York, 1989), p. 29. On the two poems and the marriage of Cnut and Emma, see: E. van Houts, 'A Note on *Jezebel* and *Semiramis*, Two Latin Norman Poems from the Early Eleventh Century', *Journal of Medieval Latin* 2 (1992), 18–24.

[22] *Encomium Emmae Reginae*, ed. and trans. Alistair Campbell (London, 1949), reprinted with supplementary introduction by Simon Keynes (Cambridge, 1998). My discussion of Emma and her *Encomium* draws on my articles: 'Fictions of Family: The *Enco-*

ium was written to have an impact in Harthacnut's quadrilingual court – its
audience was the Anglo-Danish and Anglo-Saxon aristocracies, including the
francophone Edward the Confessor and his retinue. Multilingualism, then, is the
context for the *Encomium*'s deliberate and explicit invocation of a classical framework – Cnut is Aeneas, Emma is Octavian and the Encomiast is Virgil. Emma, the
text's patron and informant, took a hand in its deployment of a classical framework – although she herself appears not to have been Latinate. It is worth pausing
to take note that a lay person need not be Latinate to have an engagement in and
control over the classical past. Emma's influence is evident in the text's way of
combining the classical and Scandinavian story-worlds and in its sensitivity to
Anglo-Saxon rejection of Trojan origins.[23] Moreover, for the *Encomium* to succeed
in its attempt to use the classical past to create a new myth of English and Danish
unity, such stories had to have circulated amid the linguistically and culturally
competing communities of Harthacnut's court (or at the very least to have been
explained to them).

In the context of Harthacnut's court, language choice was crucial, and one
of the most striking features of the *Encomium*, especially given its lay audience,
is that it was written in Latin; up until this point, English was the language of
history-writing, as the Chronicle and the dominance of the Old English *Orosius*
over the Latin text among Anglo-Saxon manuscripts underscore. The *Encomium*
is evidence that the Danish conquest of England along with Emma's marriage to
Æthelred had changed the status of English at court. The production of the *Encomium* in Latin situated it away from the factionalism of Harthacnut's court stemming from the Danish conquest – Latin was no one's mother tongue and thus
very useful. But for Latin to be a language of consensus-building at court, it had
to break from the hermeneutic style.[24] The relatively straightforward prose and
episodic organization of the *Encomium* underscores how suited the text was to
extemporaneous exposition in the vernacular, be that English, Danish or French.
The language, style and form of the *Encomium* need to be seen not as an accident
of its Flemish authorship but as the deliberate choice of Emma, and one related
to her francophone background. This becomes more obvious when observed
through the lens of romance-speaking expectations of the role of history-writing.
In her work on historiography in the courts of Louis the Pious and Charles the

mium Emmae Reginae and Virgil's *Aeneid*', *Viator* 36 (2005), 149–79 and 'Talking about
History in Eleventh-Century England: The *Encomium Emmae Reginae* and the Court
of Harthacnut', *EME* 13 (2005), 359–83. With the exception of P. Stafford's essential
Queen Emma and Queen Edith: Queenship and Women's Power in Eleventh-Century England
(Oxford, 1997), pp. 28–40, works cited in my earlier articles are not referenced here.
See my 'Trojans in Anglo-Saxon England: Precedent without Descent', in *Troy and the
European Imagination*, ed. E. Archibald and J. Clarke (Cambridge, forthcoming).
E. van Houts discusses the attractiveness of the writings of Flemish monks who wrote
non-hermeneutic Latin: 'The Flemish Contribution to Biographical Writing in England
in the Eleventh Century', in *Writing Medieval Biography: Essays in Honour of Professor
Frank Barlow*, ed. D. Bates, J. Crick and S. Hamilton (Woodbridge, 2007), pp. 122–4 (I
am grateful to the author for kindly sending me this article in typescript).

Bald, Janet Nelson argues that history-writing was a courtly form of couns⬚ facilitated by the linguistic proximity of Latin and French.[25] If we attribute som⬚ agency over the language of her text to Emma, we can see that, as English cou⬚ culture became more international, a different kind of Latin was needed tha⬚ would allow it to take on a communicative role that had previously belonged t⬚ English. At the same time, we can also see how the circulation of stories abou⬚ Rome in English enabled this shift.

A generation later, Edith, daughter of Earl Godwine, sister of the warrin⬚ brothers Harold and Tostig, and wife and widow of Edward the Confesso⬚ followed in her mother-in-law's footsteps as the patron of Latin historiograph⬚ The *Vita Ædwardi* was written for her by a Flemish monk or cleric as her husban⬚ approached the end of his life without an heir; it was not finished until after th⬚ Norman Conquest. These were trying times by any reckoning and the anony⬚ mous author is explicit that he is writing to support her.[26] Again, the questio⬚ needs to be posed: how could a Latin work, in verse and prose, do this, especiall⬚ one which, in its use of classical allusion, is highly sophisticated? In his cla⬚ sicizing verse, the Anonymous interweaves the story-worlds of Virgil, Statiu⬚ Lucan and notably Ovid as he attempts to make some sense of recent events.[27]

The question of why Edith bothered to patronize a poet amid the chao⬚ of 1065–7 has much to tell us about English literary culture on the eve of th⬚ Conquest. Her choice reveals the close ties between English and Northern Frenc⬚ literatures, while making it clear that the impetus for lay ownership of classica⬚ legend lay not in Northern France but in England. Attention to the *Vita*'s patro⬚ Edith, and to the women around her can open up the relationship of England an⬚ France before the Conquest. Like other elite women in late Anglo-Saxon Englan⬚ Edith was the highly educated product of the royal nunnery of Wilton. Over th⬚ course of the tenth and eleventh centuries, Anglo-Saxon royal nunneries becam⬚ important places for the education of elite women – some to high standards ⬚ Latinity. Thus, there was a group of royal and aristocratic women who we⬚ players in Edith's story and educated enough to form the audience for the *Vi⬚ Ædwardi* and its verse. These learned and politically active women, moreove⬚ were not confined to the nunnery; many were educated there to become wiv⬚ rather then nuns. During their lifetimes, they moved both between court an⬚ cloister and across the Conquest. Edith herself moved not only between Wilt⬚ and Edward's court but also between Wilton and William's court. She was n⬚

---

25 J. Nelson, 'Public Histories and Private History in the Work of Nithard', *Speculu⬚ 60 (1985), 251–93 and 'History-writing at the Courts of Louis the Pious and Charl⬚ the Bald', in *Historiographie im frühen Mittelalter*, ed. A. Scharer and G. Scheibelreit (Vienna, 1994), pp. 435–42.

26 *The Life of King Edward Who Rests at Westminster*, ed. by F. Barlow, 2nd edn (Oxfor⬚ 1992). Stafford, *Queen Emma and Queen Edith*, pp. 28–52. My discussion of the *Vi⬚ Ædwardi* is indebted to Stafford's work on Edith.

27 Detailed discussion of the poetry of the *Vita Ædwardi* will be included in my *Crossi⬚ Conquests* (forthcoming); for preliminary discussion, see my 'The *Vita Ædwardi*: Th⬚ Politics of Poetry at Wilton Abbey', *ANS* 31 (2009), 135–56.

alone. The flight of Harold's daughter Gunnhild from the nunnery to elope with Count Alan the Red presents a visible example of how the world of educated Anglo-Saxon elite women fed into the new Norman aristocracy of England. The mobility of these educated women is important to see if we are interested in the ways in which Anglo-Saxon literary culture contributed to that of the twelfth century.[28]

It is Ovid who can help us to see how the *Vita Ædwardi* connects to continental literary culture. Among the most exciting and innovative dimensions of Latin poetry in the late eleventh and early twelfth century was its turn to Ovid, where poets, increasingly engaged with secular matters, including the representation of female voices and perspectives, found nourishment. Ovidian poetics in turn became a defining feature of the beginnings of French vernacular poetry; the importance of this movement from Latin to the vernacular has been well studied and rightly emphasized. The key figures in this revolution are the group of poets often called the 'Loire School' – Marbod of Rennes (1035–1123), Baudri de Bourgueil (1045/6–1130), and Hildebert of Lavardin (1056–1133).[29] The date of the *Vita Ædwardi*, begun before the Norman Conquest, is critical here: both in his style and in his choice of patron, the anonymous author was on the cutting edge of this new poetic movement. (Baudri's famous historical poem for Countess Adela of Blois, William the Conqueror's daughter, on the other hand, is unlikely to have been written before 1085 at the earliest.[30]) The linguistic texture of the *Vita* and its thematic concerns, which include self-conscious metapoetic reflection on the nature of fiction and the value of the classical pagan story-world that is reminiscent of the poetry of the Loire School, situate this poem, written for an English queen, as the centre of a poetic revolution that would come to transform European literary culture in the twelfth century.[31] (That I had cause to mention the Loire writers Marbod, for his lapidary, and Hildebert, for his life of Mary of Egypt, earlier in this essay in connection with the types of text that occur in Latin, English and French across the eleventh and twelfth centuries, should here underscore the way the *Vita Ædwardi* is fully integrated within a cross-Conquest literary culture on both sides of the Channel.[32])

---

[28] The material in this paragraph is presented in fuller detail, with bibliographic references, in my 'Crossing Conquests: Polyglot Royal Women and Literary Culture in Eleventh-Century England', in Tyler, *Conceptualizing Multilingualism*, forthcoming; S. Hollis, *Writing the Wilton Women: Goscelin's* Legend of Edith *and* Liber Confortatorius (Turnhout, 2004) is essential for understanding Wilton.

[29] For some of their poems, see: Marbod, *Carmina varia*, PL 171, cols. 1647–86 (1st series) and 1717–36 (2nd series); Baudri of Bourgueil, *Poèmes*, ed. J.-Y. Tilliette, 2 vols. (Paris, 1998 and 2002); and Hildebert, *Hildebertus: Carmina Minora. Editio altera*, ed. A. B. Scott (Munich, 2001). G. A. Bond, *The Loving Subject: Desire, Eloquence, and Power in Romanesque France* (Philadelphia, 1995), pp. 42–69; and J.-Y. Tilliette, '*Troiae ab oris*: Aspects de la révolution poétique de la seconde moitié du XIe siècle', *Latomus* 58 (1999), 405–31.

[30] Baudri, *Poèmes*, II, pp. 1–43. K. LoPrete, *Adela of Blois: Countess and Lord (c.1067–1137)* (Dublin, 2007), pp. 482–3.

[31] See above, note 28.

[32] See pp. 166–7.

The composition of Loire school poetry at or for Wilton was no isolated event. The prolific Flemish hagiographer Goscelin wrote his only prosimetrical work for Wilton, which the poet Serlo of Bayeux described as a *fæcunda versibus urbs* (a city eloquent in poetry).[33] Poetry appears to have been central to the education of Anglo-Saxon royal women and this continued into the Anglo-Norman period. The ties between Wilton and the Loire are, moreover, social as well as textual. When Goscelin's beloved and highly learned Eve, who became a child oblate before the Conquest, left Wilton about 1080, she did not seek out just any continental hermitage, but a cell attached to the Angevin nunnery of Le Ronceray whose nuns were the poetic correspondents of Baudri and Hildebert.[34] In the early twelfth century, the poet Muriel (praised by Baudri, Hildebert and Serlo of Bayeux) appears to have come from Le Ronceray to Wilton.[35] Muriel's journey to Wilton moreover alerts us to the way that Francophone women came to share in the nunnery culture of the Anglo-Saxons, ensuring that it fed into developments in twelfth-century literary culture. The Anonymous' claim that Queen Edith knew French makes perfect sense in the context of her husband Edward's court but it may also have made sense within Wilton before as well as after 1066.

Despite its Flemish author and its links with Loire poetry and post-Conquest literary cultures, the *Vita Ædwardi* was not a continental text that just happened to be written for an Anglo-Saxon queen. The work participates in the Latin literary culture of England – the Anonymous had read poetry by Wulfstan Cantor and Frithegod as well as Emma's *Encomium*. In the *Vita*'s mocking of Welsh claims to Trojan origins, we find a distinctively Anglo-Saxon response to the widespread European desire to share ancestors with the founders of Rome. Like the *Encomium*, this text is powerfully drawn to Troy and yet it remains acutely conscious that Anglo-Saxon kings traced their lineage elsewhere, back to the Germanic god Woden and biblical figures.[36] The *Vita Ædwardi* cannot be detached from Anglo-Saxon literature as simply an instance of pre-Conquest Normanization. It is

---

33 Goscelin, *Vita Edithae*, edited by A. Wilmart, 'La légende de Ste Édith en prose et vers par le moine Goscelin', *Analecta Bollandiana* 56 (1938), 5–101, 265–307. For Wilton as the audience of Goscelin's *Vita Edithæ*, see Hollis, *Wilton Women*, pp. 245–80. Serlo of Bayeux's poem to Muriel is edited in *The Anglo-Latin Satirical Poets and Epigrammatists of the Twelfth Century*, ed. T. Wright, 2 vols., RS 59 (London, 1872), II, 233 (l. 3).

34 Goscelin, *Liber Confortatorius*, ed. C. H. Talbot, *Analecta Monastica* series 3, 37 (1955), 1–117. P. Dronke, *Women Writers of the Middle Ages* (Cambridge, 1984), pp. 84–91; G. Signori, 'Muriel and the Others ... or Poems as Pledges of Friendship', in *Friendship in Medieval Europe*, ed. J. Haseldine (Stroud, 1999), pp. 199–212; and Hollis, *Wilton Women*, p. 229.

35 J. Stevenson, 'Anglo-Latin Women Poets', in *Latin Learning and English Lore: Studies in Anglo-Saxon Literature for Michael Lapidge*, ed. K. O'Brien O'Keeffe and A. Orchard, 2 vols. (Toronto, 2005), II, 86–107 (pp. 95–100); Signori, 'Muriel and Others', dissents.

36 D. Dumville, 'Kingship, Genealogies and Regnal Lists', in *Early Medieval Kingship*, ed. P. H. Sawyer and I. N. Woods (Leeds, 1977), pp. 72–104, esp. 77–96; F. Ingledew, 'The Book of Troy and the Genealogical Construction of History: The Case of Geoffrey of Monmouth's *Historia regum Britanniae*', *Speculum* 69 (1994), 665–704 (p. 685); M. Innes, 'Teutons or Trojans? The Carolingians and the Germanic Past', in *The Uses of the Past*

multaneously an English and a European text, whose poetry enables us to see ow English literary culture before the Conquest would participate in, and influ- nce the future direction of, European literary culture in Latin and the vernac- lar. It is not fanciful to see a genealogical link between the *romans d'antiquité* nd the *Vita*. The *Roman d'Eneas'* Ovidian reading of the *Aeneid* and the *Roman de hebès'* concern for Oedipus' warring sons (read Harold and Tostig) would not ave been foreign to Edith.[37]

Although scholarship has yet to bring it fully into the light, the afterlife of he *Vita* adumbrates cross-Conquest continuities that found expression in both rench and Latin, in royal nunnery culture. The nun of Barking's Anglo-Norman fe of Edward the Confessor, which goes back, via Aelred of Rievaulx and Osbert f Clare's versions, to Edith's *Vita Ædwardi*, may have been written with the inten- on of influencing Henry II to look favourably on her royal nunnery.[38] Earlier I iscussed the possible interest of the nuns of Barking in Hildebert's life of St lary of Egypt. A copy of this text is added, in the mid-twelfth century, into an rlier twelfth-century manuscript containing the Wilton version of Goscelin's fe of the Anglo-Saxon princess St Edith, alongside an account of the passion of er brother, the tenth-century Anglo-Saxon king, Edward the Martyr.[39] Edward as buried at the royal nunnery of Shaftesbury and his *passio*, written in the late leventh or early twelfth century, in part rewrote an earlier text that Christine Fell as argued was written for this nunnery.[40] Tantalizingly elusive cross-Conquest nks between nunneries lie here (suggesting areas for future research). Less peculatively, the make-up of the Cardiff manuscript shows that the franco- hone nuns of post-Conquest Barking were strongly invested in perpetuating he memory of Anglo-Saxon royal saints.

In his book, *The Loving Subject*, Gerald Bond has identified Adela as the first oman to see that the patronage of poetry could be used to enhance her polit- al status. He argues that she thus 'mediated' between the learning of medieval atin poetry and the court (i.e. a lay audience): a seminal moment in literary istory – both for Latin and for French.[41] This innovation was actually initiated y Edith when she commissioned the classicizing poetry of the *Vita* as a way to

in the Early Middle Ages, ed. Y. Hen and M. Innes (Cambridge, 2000), pp. 227–49 (pp. 248–9) and my 'Trojans in Anglo-Saxon England'.

Enéas: Roman du XIIe siècle, ed. J.-J. Salverda de Grave, 2 vols. (Paris, 1925), and *Roman de Thèbes*, ed. G. Raynaud de Lage, 2 vols. (Paris, 1966–7). Orderic Vitalis has Robert Courthose refer to himself as a Polynices figure in an angry address to his father William the Conqueror. M. Chibnall interprets this as evidence that 'stories based on the Theban legend were told in lay circles at least when Orderic was writing (*c*.1127), nearly thirty years before the appearance of the vernacular *Roman de Thèbes*': *The Eccle- siastical History of Orderic Vitalis*, ed. M. Chibnall, 6 vols. (Oxford, 1968–80), III, 100.

Dean no. 523. *La vie d'Edouard le Confesseur: Poème anglo-normand du XIIe siècle*, ed. Ö. Södergård (Uppsala, 1948). J. Wogan-Browne, *Saints Lives*, pp. 249–51.

See above, pp. 166–7 and on the Cardiff manuscript, see Bell, *What Nuns Read s.v.* Barking; Ker, *MMBL* II, 348–9.

Edward, King and Martyr, ed. C. Fell (Leeds, 1971), pp. xvii–xx.

Bond, *Loving Subject*, p. 156.

explain herself amid the cataclysmic events of 1065–7. While this move flow
ered in the Latin and French poetry of the twelfth century, its roots were dee
in Anglo-Saxon England, and I would argue that the habit of using the Roma
story-world to think with – something that was, early on, possible for lay aud
ences because of the vernacular translation of texts like *Apollonius*, Orosius an
Letter of Alexander – is part of the genealogy of this text, which has, furthermor
identifiable post-Conquest descendants.

If any further proof of the impact of Anglo-Saxon nunnery education o
Anglo-Norman literary culture is needed, there is one last Wilton girl to conside
Edith/Matilda, patron of poetry and history-writing, whose marriage to Henr
I united the Anglo-Saxon and Norman dynasties.[42] Her education, parentag
and marriage equipped her to bridge the literary culture of Anglo-Saxon an
Anglo-Norman England, a point made by William of Malmesbury. After high
lighting her illustrious ancestry, he records his patron's Wilton education, he
withdrawal from the court, and her love of poetry.[43] The terms in which h
remembers Edith/Matilda illustrate how much she had in common with Edith
the queen whose English name, rich in associations with the West Saxon dynast
she shared until she took the illustrious Norman name of the Conqueror's wif
Matilda on her marriage. Poets of the Loire School, Marbod, Hildebert and Serl
of Bayeux, wrote poetry for and about her, just as the unknown poet of the *Vit*
had composed for Queen Edith several decades earlier: family and educationa
ties connect the two women, whereas ties of literary affiliation connect the poet
who wrote for them.[44] If Edith/Matilda was the patron of the Anglo-Norma
Voyage of St. Brendan, then the royal women of Anglo-Saxon England took a ver
direct role in encouraging the beginning of French written literary culture.[4]
Regardless of this identification, in the line that extends from Emma to Edith
Matilda and from Wilton to Barking, we can see how what Anglo-Saxon roya
women did with texts not only fed into the literary culture of the twelfth centur
but were among its stimuli.

---

[42] As Margaret of Scotland's daughter, Edith/Matilda was the great-granddaughter c
the Anglo-Saxon king Edmund Ironside, who was the half-brother of Edward th
Confessor and the son of Æthelred. For a detailed study of Edith/Matilda's life
including a chapter on her patronage of the arts, see L. Huneycutt, *Matilda of Scotlan
A Study in Medieval Queenship* (Woodbridge, 2003).

[43] William of Malmesbury, *Gesta Regum Anglorum*, ed. R. A. B. Mynors, R. M. Thomso
and M. Winterbottom, 2 vols. (Oxford, 1998–9), I, 754–8.

[44] A. Boutemy, 'Deux poèmes inconnus de Serlon de Bayeux et une copie nouvelle de so
poème contre les moines de Caen', *Le Moyen Age* 48 (1938), 241–69 (p. 242), and E. va
Houts, 'Latin Poetry and the Anglo-Norman Court 1066–1135: The *Carmen de Hastinga
Proelio*', *JMH* 15 (1989), 39–62 (pp. 50–1).

[45] *The Anglo-Norman Voyage of St Brendan by Benedeit*, ed. E. G. R. Waters (Oxford, 1928
Huneycutt, *Matilda of Scotland*, pp. 139–43.

III

Edith/Matilda brings us, if not back to Gaimar, at least close to the world for which he wrote. Although Gaimar was not writing for the royal court, he was certainly watching developments there. He claimed that he could have written a better poem about Henry I than the one which Adeliza, Edith/Matilda's successor as the king's wife, commissioned from the poet David and also that his own patron, Constance, knew this David's work.[46] Female patronage evidently extended beyond the court (perhaps with the old Anglo-Saxon royal nunneries contributing to this trend in their provision of examples and royal role models).

It is not only in his translation of the Anglo-Saxon Chronicle into Anglo-Norman verse that Gaimar reveals himself to be the heir of Anglo-Saxon. To see this, we need to reach back to *Beowulf*, which, in the final analysis, does not come out of another world, unconnected to the beginnings of Anglo-Norman literature. As Henry Bainton argues elsewhere in this volume, Gaimar uses the romance of Havelock and Argentille to reinstate the Danes in English history. Lincolnshire-based Gaimar and his patron turned to fiction to remedy the Anglo-Saxon Chronicle's unsatisfactory and polemical portrayal of the Danes as little more than savage Vikings. Just as we might wonder what Gaimar was doing starting with Havelock and claiming that the Danes arrived in Britain before the English, the Danes and Geats of *Beowulf* have caused much consternation.[47] This 'national' epic is not about the English – an untidiness that recalls discomfort that the earliest manuscript of the *Chanson de Roland* was produced in England, not France.[48] From this perspective, Scandinavians emerge as a cross-Conquest preoccupation. Moreover, these Scandinavians do not take us very far away from a focus on the Roman story-world. On the contrary, Gaimar's claim that he wrote an earlier poem that began with Troy recalls the juxtaposition of the Anglo-Saxon Chronicle with the Old English *Orosius*. Even more, Gaimar's claim recalls the way *Beowulf* follows the *Letter of Alexander* in its manuscript.[49] Alexander and his letter are, of course, the stuff of early romance; epic *Beowulf* is thus not as far as we might think from the currents of twelfth-century literary culture.[50] The

---

[46] Gaimar, *Estoire*, lines 6477–520 (pp. 205–6).

[47] Gaimar, *Estoire*, lines 1–816 (pp. 1–25). On the Danish problem in the nineteenth-century scholarship, see: T. A. Shippey and A. Haarder, eds., *'Beowulf': The Critical Heritage* (London, 1998), pp. 44–7, and, from among many recent discussions, the papers by A. C. Murray, R. I. Page and R. Frank in *The Dating of Beowulf*, ed. C. Chase (Toronto, 1981), and J. D. Niles, 'Locating *Beowulf* in Literary History' in his *Old English Heroic Poems and the Social Life of Texts* (Turnhout, 2007), pp. 13–63.

[48] A. Taylor, 'Was There a Song of Roland?', *Speculum* 76 (2001), 28–65 (pp. 33–6, 52–3), and S. Kinoshita, *Medieval Boundaries: Rethinking Difference in Old French Literature* (Philadelphia, 2006), pp. 1–45.

[49] London, British Library, MS Cotton Vitellius A.xv. The make-up of the manuscript is discussed by Orchard in *Pride and Prodigies*.

[50] R. Stoneman, 'The Medieval Alexander', in *Latin Fiction: The Latin Novel in Context*, ed. H. Hofmann (London, 1999), pp. 238–52, and L. Harf-Lancer, 'Les romans d'Alexandre

juxtaposition of Scandinavians and Trojans, which *Beowulf* and Gaimar share, points to the way in which the Anglo-Saxon lineage of Gaimar extends beyond his translation of the Chronicle to his participation in the vernacularization of the Roman story-world, which allowed the Anglo-Saxon, and then the Anglo-Norman, lay aristocracy a head start in developing that very European habit of using the Roman past to understand the present. This habit, which would flower in the early *romans d'antiquité*, marked both Gaimar's *Estoire* and *Beowulf*.

Using the Romans to think with, of course, has a long European pedigree: Merovingians, Carolingians and Normans all traced their ruling dynasties back to Troy, and Carolingians and Ottonians explicitly saw the Roman emperors as their predecessors. But the Anglo-Saxons handled the Roman story-world distinctively: as a model but not as an origin legend.[51] What is so striking in the peculiar Anglo-Saxon negotiation of Rome is that we can catch glimpses of secular figures (Æthelweard, Emma and Edith) taking direct control of the interpretative framework that Rome provided. This control stands in sharp contrast to Dudo's granting of Trojan origins to the Danish ancestors of the Normans in a text intended not for the ducal court but for clerical audiences outside Normandy.[52] In this regard, what might seem an odd omission in Gaimar – the absence of claims that the Danes who settled Britain before the Anglo-Saxons descended from Trojan refugees – looks more like a typically English spin on the Trojans.

To conclude, I want very briefly to suggest what Gaimar can show us about *Beowulf* (rather than *vice versa*). This move surrenders, somewhat, to that old Anglo-Saxonist desire to redeem *Beowulf* – even though it finds support in Sarah Kay's approach to the simultaneity of *chanson de geste* and romance.[53] But Gaimar, with his Danes and Romans, can indeed help us to rescue *Beowulf* from the Germanic mists and to secure this poem a place in European literary history. Reading *Beowulf* through historiography and romance makes the point that it was not the Conquest that brought England into Europe. Anglo-Saxon literary culture, including (rather than in spite of) *Beowulf*, played a key role in shaping European literary culture in the twelfth century: a role the Conquest accelerated rather than pre-empted.

---

et le brouillage des formes', in *Conter de Troie et d'Alexandre*, ed. L. Harf-Lancner, L. Mathey-Maille and M. Szkilnik (Paris, 2006), pp. 19–27.

51 See above, pp. 171, 174.

52 Dudo, *De moribus et actis primorum Normanniæ ducum*, ed. J. Lair (Caen, 1865–72). L. B. Mortensen, 'Stylistic Choice in a Reborn Genre: The National Histories of Widukind of Corvey and Dudo of Saint-Quentin', in *Dudone di San Quintino*, ed. P. Gatti and A. Degl'Innocenti (Trent, 1995), pp. 77–102 (pp. 88–92, 100–1); Tyler, 'Trojans in Anglo-Saxon England'.

53 S. Kay, *The Chansons de Geste in the Age of Romance* (Oxford, 1995).

13

Translating the 'English' Past: Cultural Identity in the *Estoire des Engleis*

Henry Bainton*

he title of the only identifiable work by Geffrei Gaimar, *L'Estoire des Engleis*, has ▪ng and unfairly coloured its reception, and has cast dark shadows over the ▪uances of its contents.[1] The *Estoire* is frequently perceived as an unproblemati- ▪lly national history,[2] a product of a time when the homogenous 'Normans' and ▪e monolithic 'English' vied for control over the territory of an unproblematic ▪ngland and its singular, English, past.[3] It is seen above all as a straightforward ▪eans by which the Normans who commissioned it could attach themselves to, ▪d root themselves in, England and its past and so 'become' 'English'.[4]

And perhaps such perceptions are not surprising. Firstly, the *Estoire* is the ▪rliest known historiographical work in Anglo-Norman, which leads to the ▪npression that it is evidence of the Anglo-Norman language – and those who ▪sed it – asserting themselves by claiming the right to write history. Secondly, the

This essay began life as a dissertation written under the supervision of Dr Elizabeth Tyler, for whose generous help and encouragement I am most grateful; sincere thanks are also due to the University of York's Department of History and the Richard III Society, who provided financial support that made the research for this essay possible.

Geffrei Gaimar, *L'Estoire des Engleis by Geffrei Gaimar*, ed. A. Bell (Oxford, 1960). Trans- lations will be those of the Rolls Series edition of the *Estoire*, modified where necessary: *Lestoire des Engles Solum la Translacion Maistre Geffrei Gaimar*, ed. T. D. Hardy and C. T. Martin, 2 vols., RS 91 (London, 1888); see now *Geffrei Gaimar, Estoire des Engleis/History of the English*, ed. and trans. Ian Short (Oxford, 2009).

Thus, for example, Ian Short's pioneering study, 'Gaimar et les débuts de l'historiographie en langue française', appears in a collection entitled *Chroniques Nationales et Universelles* (Göppingen, 1990), pp. 155–62 (emphasis mine); John Gill- ingham's 'Gaimar, the Prose *Brut* and the Making of English History', in *The English in the Twelfth Century*, ed. J. Gillingham (Woodbridge, 1995), pp. 113–22, appears in the 'national identity' section of the collection.

K. S. B. Keats-Rohan, 'The Bretons and Normans of England 1066–1154: The Family, the Fief, and the Feudal Monarchy', *Nottingham Medieval Studies* 36 (1992), 42–78, prob- lematizes the 'Normans' as a homogenous group.

See, for example, John Gillingham's view that 'It looks as though Gaimar was writing for women and men who thought of themselves as English, French-speaking, but English enough to think of the Anglo-Saxon past as their past' (J. Gillingham, 'Henry of Huntingdon and the Twelfth-Century Revival of the English Past', in *Concepts of National Identity in the Middle Ages*, ed. L. Johnson and A. Murray (Leeds, 1995), pp. 140–1).

Estoire is heavily reliant on the *Anglo-Saxon Chronicle* and is often considered t
be a mere verse translation of it.[5] So in turn it is hard not to see it as a Norma
claim to the right of writing the history of *England* in particular. And thirdly i
was produced in the second quarter of the twelfth century, precisely when histo
rians consider the distinctions between Englishness and Norman-ness to hav
been breaking down. It was a time when, in R. H. C. Davis's formulation, 'th
Normans belonged to England as much as England belonged to them'.[6]

In his seminal work *The Normans and their Myth*, Davis suggests that 'th
general idea of reconciling the Normans and the English was undoubtedly i
the air', and 'formed the essential background to ... Gaimar's work'.[7] Many hav
followed him in seeing 'reconciliation' between the English and the Norman
as *the* defining context of the *Estoire*, with Hugh Thomas, Ian Short and Jea
Blacker mentioning either reconciliation, integration or assimilation of Englis
and Norman identities (or ethnicities in Thomas's case) in their discussions o
the text.[8] And together with Rhys Davies, these scholars have all seen the *Estoir*
as being actively involved in the promotion of a new Anglo-Norman identit
that rested on an adoption by the Anglo-Norman settlers of the English past a
somehow their own.[9]

But all of these ideas rest on the assumption that the 'English past' – either a
an abstract concept or as the subject of a narrative – was a pre-existing, static an
unitary object just waiting to be absorbed by the new settlers, as if it were som

---

5   James Campbell describes the *Estoire*'s use of the Anglo-Saxon Chronicle as 'inde
    fatigable rendering' (J. Campbell, 'Some Twelfth-Century Views of the Anglo-Saxo
    Past', in *Essays in Anglo-Saxon History*, ed. J. Campbell (London, 1986), p. 215). Joh
    Gillingham describes the *Estoire* as a 'tour de force ... turning the archaic prose o
    Old English annals into a national history written in fashionable French verse' (Gil
    ingham, 'Gaimar, the Prose *Brut* and the Making of English History', p. 114). Fo
    the version(s) of the *Chronicle* used by Gaimar, see I. Short, 'Gaimar's Epilogue an
    Geoffrey of Monmouth's *Liber vetustissimus*', *Speculum* 69 (1994), 323–43 (p. 331), an
    English Historical Documents c.500–1042, ed. D. Whitelock, 2nd edn (London, 1979
    p. 113. D. Roffe, 'Lady Godiva, the Book, and Washingborough', *Lincolnshire Past an
    Present* 12 (1993), 9–10, discusses where Gaimar may have seen a copy of the *ASC*.
6   R. H. C. Davis, *The Normans and their Myth* (London, 1976), p. 131.
7   Davis, *Normans and their Myth*, p. 130.
8   H. M. Thomas, *The English and the Normans* (Oxford, 2003), p. 359, considers that Gaima
    used his history 'to promote reconciliation' between these two 'ethnic' groups; Jea
    Blacker sees Gaimar 'bringing English history to the Norman courtly class in an effor
    to help them integrate the new culture into their sense of identity and to assimilate i
    a limited fashion' (J. Blacker, *The Faces of Time: Portrayal of the Past in Old French an
    Latin Historical Narrative of the Anglo-Norman* Regnum (Austin, 1994), p. 171; Ian Shor
    studies how Gaimar was 'able to point, through the medium of literature, to som
    common ground between the Normans and native British ... [to promote] nationa
    self-legitimation [and] cultural assimilation' (Short, '*Tam Angli quam Franci*', p. 169).
9   R. R. Davies, 'The Peoples of Britain and Ireland, 1110–1400: IV Language and Histor
    ical Identity', *TRHS* 6th series, 7 (1997), 1–24 (p. 19): 'These historians [Gaimar an
    Henry of Huntingdon] were quite clear what they were about; they were constructin
    an image, a historical mythology, of the past of the English people.'

sort of *thing* over which possession was simple, and the possession of which could be fought for, lost or won. I shall argue in this essay that, far from creating such a unitary narrative that could easily be assimilated into a new national historical mythology, the translation from the standardized literary language of the Anglo-Saxon Chronicle (late West Saxon) to a *non*-standardized French vernacular opened a textual space in which heterogeneous and competing narratives of belonging could be inscribed, where allegiances could be multiple and identities could slide. And far from being a simple translation, I shall argue that the *Estoire* is both aware of and cautious about the specifically West-Saxon ideology of the *Chronicle* and makes correspondingly canny use of it. I shall show this by examining the startling agency given to the Danes in the *Estoire* – a group neither English nor Norman and so largely overlooked by Anglo-Normanists – and tentatively suggesting that the post-Conquest severing of the literary language and historical mythology of pre-Conquest England from its West Saxon guardians encouraged the regional diversity of post-Conquest England to be articulated and explored.

It is hard to continue to think of the history narrated in the *Estoire* as belonging solely to the *Engleis* when we consider that, rather than being populated by the English alone, Gaimar's historical *Engleterre* is inhabited from the very beginning by Britons, Saxons and Danes. The inclusion of the Danes enables the *Estoire* to resist making the 'passage of dominion' from the declining Britons to the rising English the smooth and unproblematic process related in the Anglo-Saxon Chronicle (henceforth ASC) and in histories of England written by Gaimar's contemporaries.[10] The *Estoire* is vague about the Danes' origins, making the priority and legitimacy of the claims of these groups to the land difficult to establish. All that is revealed of the Danes' past, indeed, is their historical enmity towards the Britons 'Pur lur parenz ki mort esteient/ Es batailles que Arthur fist' (vv. 36–8).[11]

The effect of including the Danes as historical agents in the Arthurian, pre-English past means that the Saxons are figured as not only an *estreine gent*, but as a *gent* doubly *estreine*: they are alienated both from the land of *Bretaine* and from a significant – and, in literary terms, very fashionable – period in its history. And while the *Bretun* ultimately fade into historical oblivion after their defeat at Saxon hands, the Danish presence persists in the *Estoire*. Indeed, Gaimar does not let the *Engleis* of the *Estoire* forget that the Danes were settled in *Bretaine* long before they were: seventh-century Danish raiders and the eleventh-century king Cnut both justify their invasions by pointing out that their ancestor king Dane

---

10 The 'periodization' of British history in twelfth-century historical writing is explored by R. W. Leckie Jr, in *The Passage of Dominion. Geoffrey of Monmouth and the Periodization of Insular History* (Toronto, 1983). See especially ch. 3 for Gaimar's unique treatment of the process.

11 'Because of their kindred, who had died/ In the battles which Arthur fought' (RS, lines 37–8).

had been granted the land in fief from God a thousand years before Cerdic even turned up.[12]

The closer one looks indeed, the more one notices that, when Gaimar either narrates episodes not covered in the *Chronicle* or elaborates on those that are (so for well over half the work), Danes – and their relationship with either the English or the Britons – are almost always involved. The standard pattern seems to be that of reconciliation followed by enmity brought on by an act of treachery. In the Haveloc episode which, as a whole, is an elaboration of the enmity between Briton and Dane, the Briton king of Norfolk, Edelsi, and the Danish king of Lincolnshire, Adelbrit, were so close that 'il furent cumpaignun par fei' ('they were sworn companions', vv. 53–7). Their friendship is exposed as rather shallow, however, when after Adelbrit's death Edelsi disinherits his daughter Argentille by marrying her to the supposedly base-born Haveloc. Similarly the Danish king Cnut and the English Edmund Ironside are described as 'freres en lei' (brothers-in-law) who reigned more equally 'que ne funt frere ne parent' ('than brothers or kinsmen do', vv. 4389–92) – before this unity is shattered by the 'mal felun' and 'traïtur', Eadric Streona (v. 4429). Another set-piece narrative is dedicated to describing the reconciliation between Edward the Confessor and the Danish earl Godwine who murdered the West Saxon aetheling Alfred. It looked worryingly as if the murder of Edmund Ironside had been repeated, and

---

12 'Bien sachiez', Cnut reminds the English king Edmund, that 'luinteinement/ L'orent [la terre] Daneis nostre parent;/ Pres de mil anz l'ot Dane enceis/ Que unc i entrast Certiz li reis' (vv. 4311–14) ('You should know well that long ago/ The Danes my forefathers had [the land]/ Nearly a thousand years ago Dane had it/ Before ever king Cerdic came there' (RS, lines 4315–18)). For the view that this claim is 'no mere afterthought, but an integral part, indeed the climax, of the narrative', and that the first reference to a king Dan (who is unmentioned by Gaimar's contemporaries) was probably made in the lost first part of the *Estoire* but 'must derive ultimately from a Danish source', see A. Bell, 'Gaimar's Early "Danish" Kings', *Proceedings of the Modern Languages Association* 65 (1950), 601–40, esp. pp. 629–30. This ancient Danish right to the rulership of England is also attested later in the twelfth century: in William of Newburgh's *Historia rerum anglicarum* (composed 1196–8), Philip Augustus's legates demand the 'Antiquum ... jus regis Dacorum in regno Anglorum' from Cnut IV of Denmark as part of his daughter Bothild's dowry (*Chronicles of the Reigns of Stephen, Henry II and Richard I*, ed. R. Howlett, 4 vols., RS 82 (London, 1884–9), I, 368). Richard FitzNigel, explaining the origin of Danegeld in the *Dialogus de scaccario* (composed in the 1170s), mentions that 'bellicosa illa et populosa gens Dacorum ... sibi de antiquo iure in eiusdem regni dominatione uendicabant, sicut Britonum plenius narrat historia' ('the warlike and numerous Danes ... claimed some right to the kingdom by ancient law, as *The History of the Britons* more fully relates') (*Dialogus de scaccario: The Dialogue of the Exchequer and Constitutio domus regis: The Establishment of the Royal Household*, ed. and trans. E. Amt and S. D. Church (Oxford, 2007), pp. 84–5). The possibility that the *historia Britonum* to which the reader is referred by FitzNigel is Gaimar's (lost) *Estoire des Bretuns*, or a common source, is tantalizing.

odwine's followers are concerned that 'se Godwine est pris,/ Nel pot garir rien
·rrïene/ Mes pis murrat que Edriz Estriene' (vv. 4840–2).[13]

Although there is clear tension between the Danish and the English in
ιe *Estoire*, there is no sense in which the Danes are figured as the agents of
·od's anger as they are in the ASC or contemporary Latin histories. Henry of
luntingdon, for example, figures the Danish defeat of the Northumbrians in 857
ϸ a divine punishment for their treachery in electing an ignoble king.[14] Gaimar,
·y contrast, figures it as purely a local seigneurial dispute in which the Danes
·ere merely allies of the wronged party. Anton Scharer suggests that Henry's –
nd the ASC's – insistence on the ignobility of Ælla arose from a desire to stress
he exalted nature of Cerdic's dynasty' and to imply that 'Cerdic's was the only
ingly family left'.[15] The idea of the Danes as a plague on the English for their
ns, meanwhile, was a distinctly Bedan perspective that was wholeheartedly
ϸ-opted by Alfred's court, not least in the writing of the ASC itself.[16] But by
ιaking the Danes allies of the Northumbrians rather than simply the enemies
f the English, Gaimar gives both the Danes and the Northumbrian aristocracy
 distinct role in the history of a region quite apart from the more familiar story
ι which the invasion of the Danes was merely a prelude to the West Saxons
ϸhting them off for all of Christian England.

It is the Haveloc episode as a whole, however, that best shows the complica-
ons caused by the Danish presence in the *Estoire*. Although its position imme-
iately following the prologue makes it appear that the East Anglian territory
ϸon which Haveloc's story centres is very much part of *Bretaine*, by the end
f the episode Lincolnshire and Norfolk seem firmly rooted in the sphere of
ιfluence of Denmark. Adelbrit is described in the prologue as one of the kings
f *Bretaine* but, after reclaiming with Argentille both his own inheritance and
ers, Haveloc becomes simultaneously king of Norfolk, Lincolnshire and of
ιenmark (a mirror image, incidentally, of Cnut's eleventh-century empire). The
ϸsult of this manoeuvre is to undermine certainty as to which kingdom, *Bretaine*
ϸ Denmark, the East Anglian provinces are affiliated, with the effect that the
istinction between the two kingdoms becomes less sharp.

The East Anglian kingdoms' dual affiliations are epitomized by making
 specific place – Grimsby in Lincolnshire – the point at which the two king-
ϸoms (*Bretaine* and Denmark) converge. Grimsby, which is mentioned as many

---

'If Godwine is taken,/ No earthly thing can save him;/ And he will die a worse death
than Eadric Streona' (RS, lines 4846–8, modified).

'Among the people of that country there was great discord due to their habitual
treachery [prodicione], since they had expelled their king, Osbert, and taken another,
an ignoble man [degenerem] called Ælle' (Henry of Huntingdon, *Historia Anglorum*,
ed. D. A. Greenway (Oxford, 1997), p. 282).

A. Scharer, 'The Writing of History at King Alfred's Court', *EME* 5 (1996), 177–206 (pp.
177–85, 179).

Cf. S. Foot, 'The Making of *Angelcynn*: English Identity before the Norman Conquest',
TRHS 6th series, 6 (1996), 25–49 (p. 37).

times throughout the *Estoire* as *Bretaine* itself,[17] is a place of un-belonging and exile, the hinge-point between two realms. It is to Grimsby that Argentille and Haveloc flee from the *Bretun* Adelsi's court, in voluntary exile because of the *huntage* of their marriage (vv. 301–3); it had been to Grimsby that Haveloc was carried as a child by Grim, in exile from Denmark, after his father king Gunter had been killed by Arthur. Grimsby's exiled founders came from the sea, driven ashore by another group of drifters, the outlaws (*uthlages*, v. 425), who, like the exiles, belong nowhere but no-man's land. The exiles turn their boat into a house (v. 439), and, making their living with a boat (v. 440), they take to the sea that lies between Denmark and England for their livelihood as fishermen and salters (vv. 441, 450). Their makeshift house-boat suggests transience; it lacks foundations and is out of place on the land. And so belonging fully neither to the land of Denmark nor to *Bretaine*, it is towards the unclaimed sea that the gaze of the founders of Grimsby is turned.

The presence in the work of such a wasteland, where affiliation to a nation or kingdom is so ambiguous, undermines the fixity of the notion of a subject's national or regnal allegiance, and so puts into question the allegiance of the *Estoire* to the *Engleis* alone. Grimsby's inhabitants are 'inbetween subjects', 'always split between here and there and self and other'.[18] While 'border zones' such as Grimsby have been seen as the place where identities are most hotly contested,[19] in the *Estoire* Grimsby functions as a place where identities can slide and be refigured. It is through reference to Grimsby that the doubleness of Haveloc's own belonging and allegiance is revealed. While still in Norfolk, Argentille asks him 'Amis, u est li tuen lignage?'; he replies 'Dame ... a Grimesbi' (vv. 304–5).[20] But when Haveloc and Argentille arrive in Grimsby, Haveloc's foster-sister Kelloc reveals to him that '*Danemarche* out par heritage,/ Si out son pere e son linage' (vv. 399–400, emphasis mine).[21] From the moment in Grimsby that Kelloc relating the story of an exiled heir to the Danish throne, tells Haveloc 'Ço este vus, si cum jo crei/ Danz Avelocs le fiz le rei' (vv. 419–20),[22] Haveloc is never again referred to by the '*Bretun*' name Cutheran by which Gaimar has referred to him up until this point. It is only in a place of un-belonging that Haveloc receive a new name, a new *lignage* and a new *eritage* – not in *Bretaine*, but in Denmark. It is only by going to Grimsby that Argentille and Haveloc can be told of Haveloc's

---

[17] Which may have prompted James Campbell to suggest that the main purpose of the episode (lacking, as it does, any historical weight) was to provide 'an interesting history, otherwise lacking, for Grimsby' (Campbell, 'Some Twelfth-Century Views' p. 222).

[18] M. R. Warren, *History on the Edge: Excalibur and the Borders of Britain* (Minneapolis 2000), p. 10.

[19] Warren, *History on the Edge*, pp. 8–11.

[20] 'My love, where is your family?'; '"Lady", he said, "at Grimsby"' (RS, lines 306–7).

[21] 'He had Denmark for his inheritance,/ So had his father and his ancestry' (RS, line 401–2).

[22] 'You are he, as I believe/ Dan [i.e. 'lord', 'sir'] Haveloc, the king's son' (RS, line 421–2).

rightful inheritance, before they can reverse their exile, reclaim their respective lands and ultimately unite them so that Haveloc would rule both Denmark as well as the land 'Des Hoiland tresqu'en Colecestre' (v. 803).[23]

The Lincolnshire marshes where the patroness of the *Estoire* – Constance FitzGilbert – held her lands may indeed have seemed an ambiguous space, as Grimsby is in the *Estoire*.[24] The area has been described as 'cut off from the rest of the country to the west by the great swell of the Wolds rising up ... the coastal settlements thus being obliged to look either across the Humber or seawards'.[25] Above all, writes Phythian-Adams, 'it is a world that looks across the North Sea to its Danish roots ... a cultural outlier of the Scandinavian world'.[26] Place-name studies and dialectology, meanwhile, suggest that twelfth-century Lincolnshire was deeply penetrated by the 'hugely significant influence of a Norse-speaking community' that had settled in Lincolnshire from the ninth century, but which disappears from the historical and archaeological record at some time before the twelfth.[27] Although the extent and longevity of this settlement are very uncertain, for the purposes of this essay, this much is clear: Lincolnshire would have been far more deeply penetrated by Scandinavian cultural influences than Hampshire where Constance FitzGilbert was raised.[28] It is hard to imagine that Constance would *not* have noticed the cultural and linguistic differences between West Saxon Hampshire and Anglo-Danish Lincolnshire. Gillian Fellows-Jensen has noted that 'the Scandinavianization of English place-names [in Lincolnshire], by local people who used them, can be shown to have been quite common in the Twelfth Century', and that 'the local dialect was strongly influenced by

---

23 'From Holland up to Colchester' (RS, line 805) – i.e. from south-east Lincolnshire to the Essex coast, effectively all of East Anglia.

24 For the patronage of the work, see J. Blacker, ' "Dame Cunstance la Gentil": Gaimar's Portrait of a Lady and her Books', in E. Mulallay and J. Thompson, eds., *The Court and Cultural Diversity: Selected Papers from the Eighth Triennial Congress of the International Courtly Literature Society* (Cambridge, 1997), pp. 109–19, and A. Bell, 'Gaimar's Patron, Raul le Fiz Gilebert', *Notes and Queries* 12th series 8 (1921), 104–5. For the Fitz-Gilbert family more generally, see D. M. Williamson, 'Ralf son of Gilbert and Ralf son of Ralf', *Lincolnshire Architectural and Archaeological Society Reports and Papers* 5 (1953), 19–26. For a speculative reconstruction of the *Estoire*'s audience and its situation in the Lincolnshire landscape, see H. Bainton, 'History between the Province and the Nation: Localising Gaimar's *Estoire des Engleis*' (MA dissertation, University of York, 2005).

25 C. Phythian-Adams, 'Environments and Identities: Landscape as Cultural Projection in the English Provincial Past', in *Environments and Historical Change. The Linacre Lectures 1998*, ed. P. Slack (Oxford, 1999), pp. 118–46 (p. 125).

26 Phythian-Adams, 'Environments and Identities', p. 130.

27 D. Parsons, 'How Long Did the Scandinavian Language Survive in England? Again', in *Vikings and the Danelaw*, ed. J. Graham-Campbell et al. (Oxford, 2001), pp. 299–312 (p. 299). See also A. Vince, 'Lincoln in the Viking Age', in *Vikings and the Danelaw*, pp. 157–79, and P. H Sawyer, *Anglo-Saxon Lincolnshire* (Lincoln, 1998), esp. pp. 104–12.

28 Gillian Fellows-Jensen considers north-east Lincolnshire to have been one of the heaviest areas of Scandinavian settlement in England (G. Fellows-Jensen, *Scandinavian Personal Names in Lincolnshire and Yorkshire* (Copenhagen, 1968), pp. xxii–xxvi).

Scandinavian'.[29] On more than one occasion, indeed, Gaimar himself uses words of demonstrably Scandinavian origin.[30] Although dialectology provides no firm answers as to how long Scandinavian language was spoken in the area, Thomas Hahn suggests that the 'post-conquest subjects of the Danelaw must have spoken a dialect that was neither standard English nor the Danish of Copenhagen, but that participated in some mutually intelligible "interlanguages" ... with other speech groups in England'.[31]

Here is not the place to enter the heated debate about the language of the Danelaw, but Hahn's further suggestions that there was an 'abrupt severing of English from an official standard' following the Norman Conquest, leading to an 'intensification of the influence of pre-literate languages' such as Scandinavian on spoken English, and 'an astonishing assimilation of Norse words and syntax'[32] has rich implications for our interpretation of the *Estoire*. In its translation of the ASC the *Estoire* moved from a literary language to a non-standardized, mainly spoken dialect, analogous to the breakdown of standardized English that followed the Conquest. The very vernacularity of the *Estoire* may well have had the crucial effect of opening a discursive space where the oral narratives of (probably) localized provenance, such as that of Haveloc, could be rendered into written form.

The *Estoire* figures the ASC as a text imbued with West Saxon royal authority. Gaimar's description of the ASC is placed between the reigns of two kings within a West Saxon regnal list, as if the Chronicle were a West Saxon ruler itself (vv. 2311–37). It is a book, moreover, that belongs to Wessex. Unlike the other sources that Gaimar enumerates, which travel from reader to reader with remarkable ease, he describes 'l'estoire de Wincestre' as being chained up in the powerhouse of the Anglo-Saxon church, Winchester Cathedral. And Winchester Cathedral, if

---

29 G. Fellows-Jensen, 'Conquests and the Place-names of England, with Special Reference to the Viking Settlements', in T. Andersson et al., *Ortnamn och Språkkontakt* (Uppsala, 1980), pp. 192–209 (p. 197).

30 There are two incidences of the word *uthlage* ('outlaw', v. 425, v. 2610), which is of Old Norse origin (cf. Old Icelandic *útlagi*, Old Swedish *utlagha*: AND records Gaimar's as the earliest use of this word). William Sayers has noticed that Gaimar used conventional Gallo-Romance nautical terminology when he wrote about Norman seafaring, but when Scandinavian vessels are mentioned, he uses words of an Old Norse provenance (W. Sayers, 'Ships and Sailors in Geffrei Gaimar's *Estoire des Engleis*', *Modern Languages Review* 98 (2003), 299–310). Alexander Bell's two glossarial studies, 'Glossarial and Textual Notes on Gaimar's *Estoire des Engleis*', MLR 43 (1948), 39–46, and 'Further Glossarial and Textual Notes on Gaimar's *Estoire des Engleis*', MLR 49 (1954), 309–21, make no mention of Scandinavian influences.

31 T. Hahn, 'Early Middle English', in Wallace, *Medieval English Literature*, pp. 61–91 (p. 64); cf. D. Bardney, 'Lexis and Semantics', in *The Cambridge History of the English Language*, ed. N. Blake (Cambridge, 1992), vol. 2, pp. 409–99 (pp. 418–19). The literature on the nature of Scandinavian in England is huge and controversial, but M. Barnes, 'Norse in the British Isles', in *Viking Revaluations*, ed. A. Faulkes (London, 1993), pp. 65–84, provides a succinct overview.

32 Hahn, 'Early Middle English', p. 66.

e agree with Helmut Gneuss, was not just the powerhouse of the Anglo-Saxon church, but the birthplace and sustainer of standardized literary Old English self.[33]

Standardized Old English died a death when institutions such as the Winchester scriptorium stopped being able to support it. The effect of the decline of standardization may well have been that the differences that that manoeuvre had effaced could begin to re-emerge. The presence of a written French vernacular in England may have had the effect of enabling the textualization of previously oral narratives of Scandinavian origin, such as the Haveloc tale, which had been noticeably excluded from West Saxon texts such as the ASC. And even if the origin of those narratives was not Scandinavian, the fact that they at least gave a greater role to the Scandinavians as protagonists may well have only been enabled by the breaking of the link between the language of a politically hegemonic group – the West Saxons – and the dominant role previously afforded them in their written histories. It has been said that through the writing of the ASC the separate beginnings of Alfred's subject peoples are brought to one end: that of unitary rule from Wessex', and that in uniting the 'multiple early histories' of the Anglo-Saxon kingdoms, the ASC suggested that the *Angelcynn* 'will have one future, together'.[34] The crucial effect of translating the ASC into French was that, by dissolving the association between West Saxon political and linguistic hegemony, the unity of the future for the English envisioned by the ASC could return to the multiplicity of its origins.

---

[33] H. Gneuss, 'The Origin of Standard Old English and Æthelwold's School at Winchester', *Anglo-Saxon England* 1 (1972), 63–84.

[34] Foot, 'The Making of *Angelcynn*', p. 35.

14

The Languages of England:
Multilingualism in the Work of Wace

Françoise H. M. Le Saux

The Prologue of Lawman's *Brut* famously refers to Wace as 'a Frenchis clerc'
who presented his *Roman de Brut* to 'Ælienor þe wes Henries quene',[1] thus
projecting an image both of social success and of foreignness: Wace is French
(as opposed to the English Lawman), and his patron (real or hoped-for) is the
no-less-foreign Eleanor of Aquitaine. And indeed, there is no disputing Wace's
significance within French cultural history: he was the first writer to have
written about King Arthur in the French vernacular, and his style influenced
that of the great Chrétien de Troyes. However, Wace is equally significant in
the development of Anglo-Norman, and hence, of English literature. His *Roman
de Brut*, Lawman's source, gave rise to a thriving literary genre in both Anglo-
Norman French and English, and was arguably more popular in England than
in France, particularly in the thirteenth century,[2] while his earlier *Vie de saint
Nicolas* is found not only in two professionally copied manuscripts, but also
in a thirteenth-century commonplace book alongside poetry, prose, recipes and
accounts in both English and Anglo-Norman French.[3] The text it preserves bears
the marks of having been copied many times beforehand and written down
by someone whose command of French was far from perfect. In other words,
Wace's *Vie de saint Nicolas* was part of the general culture of thirteenth-century
England, just like the *Roman de Brut*. This popularity of a French-speaking writer
in medieval England is not in itself especially noteworthy; after all, French was a
dominant language in the cultural melting-pot that was twelfth- and thirteenth-
century England. However, the stance implicit in a few scattered passages of
Wace's works suggests that the poet himself had an altogether more complex
cultural identity than that assumed by Lawman.

---

1 *Laȝamon: Brut. Edited from British Museum MS Cotton Caligula A ix and British Museum
 MS Cotton Otho C xiii*, ed. G. L. Brook and R. F. Leslie, 2 vols. (London, 1963–78); the
 text quoted here is from the Caligula text, lines 19–20. This passage has been used
 as evidence to date the *Brut*; see F. Le Saux, *Laȝamon's Brut: The Poem and its Sources*
 (Cambridge, 1989), pp. 2–4.
2 Some sixteen manuscripts and fragments of Anglo-Norman manuscripts of the work
 are still extant, amounting to over half of the surviving copies of the text.
3 Oxford, Bodleian Library, MS Digby 86; usually dated 1272–82, and probably from
 Worcestershire.

Just about everything we know about Wace is derived from what he tells us of himself in his poems, in particular in his *Roman de Rou*, composed between 1160 and 1175, which is widely thought to have been roughly the time of his death. In this dynastic history of the dukes of Normandy, the poet repeatedly opposes Normandy and France, politically, morally and culturally: an opposition that extends to his perception of his own day. In an autobiographical aside, Wace tells the reader that, born on Jersey and sent to school as a small child to Caen, he went to France for higher education: 'pois fui longues en France apris'('I was then educated for a long time in France').[4] This statement is notoriously vague, but one thing is clear: 'France' is distinct from the poet's Norman homeland. Moreover, throughout the *Roman de Rou*, France – whether in its restricted meaning of 'Ile de France' or more widely as 'the regions under the authority of the king based in Ile de France' – is a foreign, hostile power. This is true also in Wace's sources, in particular in Dudo of St Quentin, where the French and their kings are regularly vilified as being treacherous, grasping and always on the lookout to harm the Normans; but no effort is made by the poet to attenuate his sources' antagonism towards 'France'. On the contrary, his French kings constitute a striking rogues' gallery, the perfect foil to his gallant dukes of Normandy.

Wace's implicit repudiation of the 'French' from the privileged inner circle of intended readers of his *Roman de Rou* is arguably foreshadowed in the *Roman de Brut*, where a distinction appears to be made between the Normans and the French. This occurs in one of Wace's learned asides on onomastics, in this case the changes in the name of the city of London:

> Puis sunt estrange home venud
> Ki le language ne saveient,
> Mais Lodoïn pur Lud diseient;
> Puis vindrent Engleis e Saisson
> Ki recorumpurent le nun,
> Lodoïn Lundene nomerent
> E Londene longes useerent.
> Norman vindrent puis e Franceis,
> Ki ne sourent parler Engleis,
> Ne Londene nomer ne purent
> Ainz distrent si com dire pourent,
> Londene unt Londres nomee.
> Si unt lur parole guardee.
> Par remuemenz e par changes
> Des languages as genz estranges,
> Ki la terre unt suvent conquise,

---

[4] *Le Roman de Rou* de Wace, ed. A. J. Holden (Paris, 1970); 'Troisième Partie', line 5308. Unless specified otherwise, translations are from G. S. Burgess with E. M. C. van Houts, *The History of the Norman People: Wace's* Roman de Rou (Woodbridge, 2004).

Sovent perdue, sovent prise,
Sunt li nun des viles changied.   (*Roman de Brut*, 3762–78) [5]

('Then foreigners arrived who did not know the language but
said "Lodoin" for "Lud". Then the Angles and Saxons arrived, who
corrupted the name in turn, calling "Lodoin" "Lundene", and for a
long time "Londene" was used. Next the Normans and the French
came, who did not know how to speak English nor how to say
"Londene", but spoke it as best they could. They called "Londene"
"Londres", thus keeping it in their language. Through alterations and
changes in the languages of foreigners, who have often conquered,
lost and seized the land, the names of towns have changed.')

At a cursory glance, 'Norman' and 'Franceis' may seem to be close synonyms,
echoing the near-synonyms 'Engleis e Saisson' for the English; but this is
undermined by the emphasis on the concept of sequence expressed by 'puis
et' – 'and then'. The Normans are presented as having preceded the French: in
other words, Wace appears be making a distinction between the Normans who
conquered England under Duke William in 1066, and the Angevin–Aquitanian
rulers of the land a century later. This stance might appear to be counter-intu-
itive – after all, Henry II was Norman through his mother – but his father was
the duke of Anjou, Normandy's hereditary enemy, and if one bears in mind the
fact that he had to wage war in Normandy for about a decade in order for his
son's claim to the duchy to be recognized by the Norman barons, the scope for
resentment on the part of Wace (and indeed his Norman contemporaries) should
not be underestimated.

The syntax of lines 3769–70 hints at another level of cultural divide: it would
not be impossible to construe the passage as suggesting that the inability to cope
with the English language was characteristic of the French – but not necessarily of
the Normans. Such an interpretation would appear to be at odds with the wider
context: both the Normans and the French are instances of 'genz estranges' who
are the agents of language change, and both belong to the same readerly community targeted by the *Roman de Brut*. An earlier passage, also dealing with the
names of London, thus explicitly opposes the English and the speakers of French
(1237–8): 'Londene en engleis dist l'un / E nus or Lundres l'appelum' ('People
call "Lodoin", "Londene", in English, and we now call it "Lundres"'). Through

5   All quotations from Wace, *Le Roman de Brut*, ed. I. Arnold, 2 vols. (Paris, 1938, 1940);
unless specified otherwise, translations are from *Wace's Roman de Brut: A History of
the British. Text and Translation*, ed. and trans. J. Weiss (Exeter, 1999). The significance
of these onomastic passages for our understanding of the political and ideological
assumptions underlying Wace's work has been discussed most recently by G. Paradisi,
'"Par muement de langages": Il tempo, la memoria e il volgare in Wace', *Francofonia*
45 (2003), 27–45, and L. Mathey-Maille, 'L'Etymologie dans le *Roman de Rou* de Wace',
in *De sens rassis: Essays in Honor of Rupert T. Pickens*, ed. K. Busby, B. Guidot and L. E.
Whalen (Amsterdam, 2005), pp. 403–14, esp. pp. 404–9; also, more recently, L. Mathey-
Maille, *Écritures du passé: Histoires des ducs de Normandie* (Paris, 2007), esp. pp. 214–17.

ᴉe use of the first-person plural, Wace is aligning himself with the people who call ᴉondon 'Londres'. Yet at the same time, he is making it clear that even if his chosen ᴉudience does not know English, he himself has no problem with the English ᴉame of the town, which is still used (as evidenced by the present tense of the ᴉerb 'dist', 1237). It is therefore not inconceivable that lines 3769–74 of the *Roman ᴉ Brut* are deliberately ambiguous, worded in such a way as not to alienate the ᴉrench reader, yet subtly flattering two specific in-groups: the (Anglo-)Norman ᴉcholars, of whom Wace is a condign representative, and those (Anglo)-Normans ᴉhose ties with English speakers gave them some familiarity with the English ᴉnguage (exemplified in an earlier generation by Orderic Vitalis).

The idea that Wace might have known English has recently been gaining ᴉround among scholars, though to my knowledge Laurence Mathey-Maille ᴉas the first to suggest in print that the poet 'semble pratiquer l'anglais avec ᴉisance'.[6] There are three features in Wace's works that appear to support ᴉis view. First, his open acceptance of English sources as learned authorities; ᴉecond, his knowledge of English vocabulary and culture; and finally, his stance ᴉ a passage of the *Roman de Rou* where he appears to be positing close kinship ᴉetween the Norman and the English languages.

Wace's regard for English sources is evident even in his earlier hagiographical ᴉoems. His *Conception Nostre Dame*, probably composed in the second quarter of ᴉe twelfth century, echoes an English version of the legend of the establishment ᴉf the feast of the Conception of Our Lady. Interestingly, Wace also preserves his ᴉurce's ambivalence towards Duke William's conquest of England – the feast, ᴉccording to the *Conception*, was established by angelic decree in atonement for ᴉe bloodshed caused by William. The death of Harold in particular is presented ᴉs a sin weighing on William's conscience, and the new feast is the king's attempt ᴉ assuage his guilt; this is a version of events that goes against what is known ᴉdependently of Wace's work, since the feast of the Conception of Our Lady was ᴉctually abolished by William, together with other Anglo-Saxon observances, ᴉllowing his reform of the liturgical calendar.[7] A muted ambivalence towards ᴉe Norman Conquest of England, one may note, is also found in Wace's *Roman ᴉ Rou*, which similarly draws upon English sources as well as Norman ones. ᴉ this respect, Wace may be seen as precursor of the post-colonial revisionist ᴉindset evidenced in the thirteenth-century *Vita Haroldi* and recently discussed ᴉy Robert M. Stein.[8] These 'English' sources would typically have been written ᴉ Latin and would therefore not necessarily have required first-hand knowledge ᴉf the language and culture; however, Wace's acceptance of English tradition was

---

'L'Etymologie ...' p. 405. This view is repeated in her *Écritures du passé*, p. 216.
This reform was imposed by William and implemented by Archbishop Lanfranc. For a chronology of the gradual reinstatement of the feast in post-Conquest England, see G. Paradisi, *Le passioni della storia: scrittura e memoria nell'opera di Wace* (Roma, 2002), p. 44.
R. M. Stein, *Reality Fictions: Romance, History and Governmental Authority, 1025–1180* (Notre Dame IN, 2006), esp. ch. 2, pp. 65–90.

not limited to learned Latin authorities. The *Roman de Brut* betrays a marked bia. in favour of the English population and a corresponding contempt for the Welsh of Wace's day. The poem gives short shrift to the British remnant:

> Tuit sunt mué e tuit changié,
> Tuit sunt divers e forslignié
> De noblesce, d'onur, de murs
> E de la vie as anceisurs. (*Roman de Brut*, 14851–4)

('They [the Welsh] have quite altered and quite changed, they are quite different and have quite degenerated from the nobility, the honour, the customs and the life of their ancestors.')

By contrast, stories transmitted by unlettered English farmers are presentec as authoritative evidence regarding the history of Cirencester, validating anc completing the written, Latin sources:

> Pur ço que par muissuns fud prise
> E par muissuns issi cunquise
> La soleient jadis alquant
> E funt encor li païsant
> La cité as meissuns nomer
> Pur la merveille recorder   (*Roman de Brut*, 13617–22)

('Because it was taken through sparrows and conquered by sparrows, some people formerly used to call it – and the peasants still do – 'the Sparrow City', to remember the extraordinary event.')

This passage is regularly quoted as suggesting first-hand knowledge of part of England in the *Roman de Brut*; the legend is so localized that it is difficul to explain how the poet might have come across it, other than by his havin travelled through the area. There is no insuperable difficulty in accepting tha this might have been the case; if Wace was, as is likely, a clerk in the servic of the Norman ducal administration, there would doubtless have been ampl opportunities to cross the Channel, if only to report to the royal treasury i Winchester. Direct contact with English people in the south-west of the countr could also have contributed to Wace's contemptuous view of their unruly Welsh neighbours.

On the whole, however, Wace's affinity with the English is tenuous in hi earlier works; we have to wait for his final and possibly most personal work, th *Roman de Rou*, for this aspect to become at all prominent. Not only, as noted b Laurence Mathey-Maille, does he make a point of translating the English battle cries at Hastings, thereby laying some claim to knowledge of the language;[9] h also appropriates his sources' anti-French bias to blur the distinction betwee Norman and English. Normandy and England are depicted as being linke to one another from the outset. Rou, the founder of the House of Normand

---

[9] 'L'étymologie ...', p. 405, n. 10; *Écritures du passé*, p. 216, n. 65.

subdues England for the beleaguered King Athelstan, and out of sheer generosity of spirit declines his offer of half the realm as reward. A bond of mutual respect is thus established between the Norman ducal line and the English crown. The close connection with England continues under Rou's son, William Longsword: at the request of King Athelstan of England, he ensures that Louis, son of King Charles of France and nephew of Athelstan, is made heir to the French throne. The entanglement with England becomes more complex under Duke Richard II. King Aethelred, married to Richard's sister Emma, does indeed try to invade Normandy, but matrimonial policy also makes the Norman dukes and the English kings natural allies. When King Svein conquers London, Aethelred seeks refuge with his wife and sons (and the royal treasure) at Richard's court in Rouen.[10] Edward and Alfred, the heirs to the English throne, are thus brought up by their Norman kinsman; Richard's son and successor, Robert, will in turn be the advocate of the English princes, actually delivering an (unsuccessful) ultimatum to King Canute/Cnut to restore the kingdom to Edward – the future Confessor – and Alfred (2731–44), and planning an invasion of England to impose their claim to the crown. These ties underpin William the Conqueror's claim to the English throne, but also allow Wace to view the Conquest as virtually a form of civil war between two sister nations.

These two sister nations are depicted as being culturally as well as politically close, with the Norse and English languages mentioned in the same breath and in such a way as to suggest common origins. Indeed, the very name of the Normans proclaims their non-French identity. Wace introduces his discussion of the meaning of the name 'Norman' by quoting what appears to be the translation of a garbled English proverb:

> Engleiz dient en leur langage
> A la guise de lor usage:
> 'En nort alon, de nort venon,
> nort fumes touz, en nort manon.'
>
> (*Roman de Rou*, II, 312, lines 103–6)

('The English say in their language, according to their usage: "We are going to the north, we come from the north, we were born in the north, we live in the north." ')

The point actually made is unclear, and the only word that could be English – 'nort' – could equally be French; more so than a proverb, these lines call to mind the textbook phrases one finds in foreign-language primers throughout the ages, their usefulness residing more in the grammatical structures they illustrate than their immediate meaning. The function of the passage appears simply to be that of proving to the reader that Wace has a greater knowledge of English than just

---

[10] The Anglo-Saxon Chronicle gives a slightly different version of these events, which William of Jumièges is clearly recounting from a Norman perspective. See *The Gesta Normanorum ducum of William of Jumièges, Orderic Vitalis and Robert of Torigni*, ed. and trans. E. M. C. van Houts (Oxford, 1992–5), notes to V, 7–8.

that derived from learned sources, thus enhancing his personal authority on the subject. This explanation of the 'nort' component in 'Norman' is then followed by that of the 'man' element: 'Mant en engleiz et en norroiz / senefie homme en franchois': 'man' in English and Norse means 'homme' in French (*Rou*, II, 312, lines 109–10). In a passage that brings to mind the (admittedly debatable) under-current of contempt for the inability of the French to cope with English names in the *Roman de Brut*, the erudition and linguistic skill of Wace the Norman are contrasted with the ignorant French:

> Franceis dient que Normendie
> Ceo est la gent de north mendie;
> Normant, ceo dient en gabant,
> Sunt venu del north mendiant.
> (*Roman de Rou*, Troisième partie, I: 164, lines 75–8)

('The French say that Normandy is the land of beggars from the north. The Normans, people say in jest, came begging from the north.')

The French pseudo-etymology for the name of Normandy, 'north mendie', with its implications that the Normans are a nation of beggars, is exposed as unschol-arly and malicious; it also makes it quite clear that we are dealing with two very distinct ethnic and cultural groups. On the other hand, Wace's explanation of the etymology of the names of the Normans and Normandy posits not just kinship between English and Norse, but near-identity – a piece of cultural revisionism no less radical than the rewriting of the past found in the *Vita Haroldi*, that on ostensibly impeccable scholarly grounds firmly places the French-speaking Normans on the side of the English, rather than on that of the French-speaking French of the Isle de France or, indeed, of Anjou.[11]

Wace's stance is thus, arguably, not so much that of a Norman as of an Anglo-Norman. This is not surprising. By the time the poet completed the *Rou*, he was an old man, one of the last representatives of a generation who had known first-hand witnesses of the events of 1066 – Wace mentions the testimony of his father regarding the number of ships that left for England on that occasion. The poet's memories of the aftermath of the Conquest would have been vivid, in particular the recurrent political unrest it caused in Normandy well into his maturity. Young people of Wace's generation were also educated at a time when knowledge of English might have been a real advantage, and when it was probably relatively easy to find English-speakers in Normandy: religious houses and secular lords with cross-Channel estates, including the king of England himself, will have required personnel with good language skills. Moreover, if Wace's family had a tradition of service in the ducal household, it might have gone hand in hand with

---

11 Mathey-Maille (*Écritures du passé*, pp. 110–11) sees this as a good example of a pheno-menon of 'contamination' of historical time by the 'temps de l'actualité': 'Lorsque Wace ou Benoît dénoncent la perfidie des Français, présentés systématiquement hostiles aux Normands, ce sont les Français de la seconde moitié du XIIe siècle [...] que vise leur critique acerbe et cinglante.'

e fostering of specialized linguistic skills including English, and possibly even
)tions of Norse – though it must be admitted that the likelihood of Wace having
1y sort of fluency in his people's original tongue is slim, as the language had
1 but died out in Normandy by the twelfth century. The (admittedly garbled)
)mment in the *Rou* that Duke Robert the Magnificent's chamberlain Turstin was
1ace's maternal grandfather would lend some likelihood to the poet's claims to
1ow these vernaculars.

However, likelihood is not proof. The passage expounding the etymology
the name of Normandy and the Normans could have been borrowed from
rderic Vitalis, who of course was born in England: in itself, it cannot be consid-
ed significant evidence of linguistic abilities on Wace's part beyond mastery
Latin and French. The mention of the English name for Cirencester and the
)ries told by the English peasants about the town could have been relayed by
1 informant, who could equally have been at the origin of Wace's knowledge
' English battle-cries and traditions. Of greater significance is the poet's readi-
!ss to appropriate this knowledge and give it personal validation. This is not
)mething he does lightly; Wace was first and foremost a scholar, who attached
eat importance to the reliability of his sources, while maintaining a healthy
epticism towards them. The confidence with which Wace handles snippets of
1glish, and his reliance throughout the *Roman de Rou* on English sources, shows
early that for him, this is not an alien culture.

While most of the evidence present in Wace's works is compatible with indi-
ct transmission rather than personal knowledge of the English language, there
one passage that may be construed as pointing in the direction of the latter. It
:curs in the section on Edward the Confessor, in a learned aside explaining the
eaning of the name of the island of Zornee (Thorney), on which Westminster
bbey was built:

> Zornee out nom, joste Tamise.
> Zornee por ço l'apelon
> que d'espines i out foison,
> e que l'eve alout environ.
> Ee en engleis isle apelon,
> ee est isle, zorn est espine,
> seit raim, seit arbre, seit racine;
> Zornee ço est en engleis
> isle d'espines en franceis.   (*Rou*, II, 91, lines 5510–18)[12]

his passage is difficult to translate, partly owing to the subject matter (like all
xts dealing with translation issues), but mainly because of the syntactic flex-
'ility of verse, which allows more than one interpretation of these lines. In any

Burgess translates these lines as follows: 'It was called Zornee [Thorney], near the
Thames. We call it Zornee because there was an abundance of thorns there and because
it was surrounded by water. *Ee* in English we call *isle; ee* is *isle, zorn* is *espine,* either
branch or tree or root. Zornee in English is the *isle d'espines* in French.'

case, to make sense of the passage, it is necessary to forgo the elegance expecte
of a published translation. Literally, it could be rendered in the following wa
'It had the name "Zornee", by the Thames. We call it "Zornee" because the
were plenty of thorns there and water flowed around it.' The following line
particularly ambiguous: '"Ee" in English we call island', meaning either: '
English, we call "isle", "ee" '; or (the more usual understanding of the passage
'[What] in English [is called] "ee", we call "isle" '). "ee" means island, "zorr
means thorn, whether branch, bush or root. "Zornee", in English, is "island
thorns" in French.'

The salient feature here is that the narrator is unambiguously aligning himse
with the English (or more correctly, the Anglo-Normans). The use of the fir
person plural stresses that the narrator is someone who belongs: *we who kno
this place* call the island Thorney; *we locals* call the island by its English nam
– and what's more, we know what the name means. And our reference is th
English word, not the French one: 'In English, we call an island *ee*' (or, to tur
the sentence around, '*ee* is the word for 'island' in English'). The implicatio
inescapably, is that Wace is defining his target audience as being at home wi
English names, and for whom the English language is a familiar linguistic bac
drop. As ever with a medieval text, there is a possibility that the passage mig
be an interpolation, or was modified by a later scribe. This, however, is not likel
The passage figures in all four extant manuscripts of the *Rou*, and variants
this point are minor, with only one telling exception. Manuscript D – a moder
transcription by abbé Duchesne – reads for line 5514: 'Et ie en Engleiz ille l'ape
l'on'; a clumsy and clearly inferior reading to that of the other manuscripts (th
excessive alliteration of 'l' turns the line into something of a tongue-twister), b
which shows that one scribe at least felt uneasy at the 'anglocentric' attitud
betrayed by these lines. The narrator is projecting himself as someone for who
the English language is part and parcel of his cultural identity. Such knowledge
not assumed on the part of the non-Anglo-Norman part of his audience – amor
whom one assumes he counted Henry II himself, a snub that would certainly n
have endeared the poet to him.

The full significance of the Thorney passage comes to light when one compar
these lines with other onomastic asides in both the *Rou* and the *Brut*. The co
principle repeatedly expounded by Wace is that of the transitoriness associate
with a post-lapsarian world: place-names, like kingdoms, change. Foreign popu
lations displace older ones, causing the decay and collapse of civilizations. The
is no stability, and the only way to ensure enduring memory is through the work
of historians like himself – a theme formulated at some length in the prologue
of the *Rou* in particular. Yet this principle of change appears to be negated wi
regard to the Normans and the English. Whereas the name of London mutate
and corrupts to become Londene, then Londres, the name of Thorney remai
stable. The people to whom Norman, Jersey-born Wace belongs are agents
continuity rather than rupture: they preserve names. Objectively, the reaso
Thorney island did not see its name changed is probably its relative unimpo
tance; but within the value system outlined in Wace's works, it is an indicatio

of the compatibility of the Normans and the English. Such a stance suggests a degree of emotional commitment that goes well beyond bits of bookish information gathered from written authorities.

So did Wace know English? According to his own standards, definitely. He knew his English historians (albeit in Latin), he appears to have travelled in England and mixed with the local populations, and he is proud to claim knowledge of English traditions, English sayings and English vocabulary. Did he know the language well? That of course is a different matter. Even if he had English-speaking relations in his family (which is not impossible), English would have been at best a second language.[13] Moreover, present-day experience in Brittany shows that it is not uncommon to have strong feelings of cultural affinity without actually being very proficient in a language. Wace seems to have undergone something of an identity crisis during the rule of Henry II, which could account for the apparent realignment of his cultural and personal loyalties at some time prior to the composition of the *Roman de Rou*. On the other hand, it could be that these loyalties were always there, but not allowed to be expressed in too overt a manner. Or simply, Wace could be representative of a more general trend towards a greater acceptance and knowledge of English among the speakers of French in England (and Normandy?) during the second half of the twelfth century.[14] One thing, though, is certain: if Wace had known that a generation after the composition of the *Roman de Brut*, an English poet was going to qualify him as a 'Frenchis clerc', he would not have been best pleased.

---

[13] Or indeed, third language, if one counts Latin.

[14] On multilingualism and the evolution of attitudes towards English in Anglo-Norman England, see Short, '*Tam Angli quam Franci*'; also D. Bates, 'La Normandie et l'Angleterre de 900 à 1204', in *La Normandie et l'Angleterre au Moyen-Âge. Colloque de Cerisy-la-Salle (4–7 octobre 2001)*, Actes publiés sous la direction de Pierre Boutet et Véronique Gazeau (Caen, 2003), pp. 9–20.

15

An Illustrious Vernacular:
The Psalter *en romanz* in Twelfth-Century England

Geoff Rector

Two distinct cultural impulses govern the vernacularization of literary reading and taste in twelfth-century England: one, familiar from the 'mettre en romanz' claims of so many romances, that seems to draw outwards or downwards *from* Latin towards the vernacular; and another that understands translation into *romanz* as a movement *upwards* towards refinement from the demotic, the local and the unpolished. To account for both impulses is to balance the sociolinguistic and literary dynamics of post-Conquest English life against the broader cultural phenomena of the twelfth-century renaissance. In this environment, *romanz* is both ennobled and ennobling, an instance of the 'illustrious, cardinal, royal and courtly vernacular' by which all the 'municipal vernaculars ... are measured ... and compared' that Dante dreamed of in the *De vulgari eloquentia*.[1]

Dante's account has two fundamental virtues as a descriptive model for twelfth-century insular literary and sociolinguistic life. First is its awareness of the dynamic co-existence of multiple vernaculars. Unlike the two-term, Latin and vernacular 'mettre en romanz' model, post-Conquest England is diglossic, a condition in which Latin operates in a hierarchical relationship with a number of vernaculars. As Tim William Machan has argued, the 'force of diglossia lies not simply in the coexistence of several languages ... but in the dynamics between these languages and the [distinct] social' and aesthetic 'tasks' they are seen as capable of performing.[2] In Dante's terms, the 'illustrious vernacular' is defined, not only by its interaction with Latin and a 'municipal vernacular', but also by its operation within a socially, aesthetically elevated environment.

This essay will argue that, in Anglo-Norman literary culture's formative period (1100–70), the francophone vernacular (*romanz*) functions similarly to Dante's 'illustrious ... and courtly vernacular'. 'Measured' against an English perceived as a demotic vernacular, *romanz* is conceived of as socially, rhetorically and aesthetically high. And as Dante's 'illustrious vernacular' would do, *romanz* acquires these capacities in being perceived, at one and the same time, as both 'below' and 'beside' Latin, as both its handmaiden and its metonymic sibling. After considering a series of anecdotes offered retrospectively from the

---

1 Dante Alighieri, *De vulgari eloquentia*, in W. Welliver, *Dante in Hell: The* De vulgari eloquentia: *Introduction, Text, Translation, Commentary* (Ravenna, 1981), p. 81.
2 T. W. Machan, *English in the Middle Ages* (Oxford, 2003), p. 77.

ter twelfth century that confirm this picture of an illustrious *romanz*, I will turn
to an often overlooked but remarkable group of Psalter translations, glosses and
commentaries produced in England and northern France, which together represent what is arguably the single most comprehensive body of *romanz* literature
produced prior to the explosion of narrative romance in the last quarter of the
twelfth century. The vernacular Psalms illustrate both *romanz*'s capacity to bear
Latin's illustrious functions and its relative position above English.

Romanz as an illustrious vernacular

Gervase of Tilbury's *Otia imperialia* (*c.*1210), a work somewhere between twelfth-
century English historiography and Walter Map's *De nugis curialium*, recounts
English history for the leisurely study of Otto IV, a grandson of the Emperor
Henry II brought up in the English court. Within his beguilingly distorted
history of the Norman Conquest (II.21), Gervase invents a pre-Conquest Norman
upbringing for Harold Godwinson; Gervase writes:

> During his boyhood, at the command of his uncle the king, he [Harold] was
> educated in the household of the duke of Neustria (commonly known as
> Normandy); for it was the custom among the English nobility to have their
> sons brought up among the French [apud Gallos], so that they could learn
> how to handle weapons, and remove the barbarism of their native speech [et
> ad lingue natiue barbariem tollendam].[3]

Looking back over a century, Gervase casts the sociolinguistic dynamics of post-
Conquest English life back into pre-Conquest Anglo-Saxon England. English is
conceived as the rough, demotic language of a localized aristocratic childhood.
The courtly enculturation of the English male elite requires formation *apud Gallos*,
so that native, childhood habits of conduct and speech can be, as Gervase's
verb *tollo*, with its predominating ideas of upward movement, suggests, 'refined,
raised up, exalted'. *Romanz* is not just a language, but a process of formation
cultivated by an English aristocracy as a marker and an engine of upward social
movement.[4]

In this function, *romanz* maintains a metonymic or fraternal, as much as ancillary, relationship with Latin – but everywhere also in relationship with a lower
demotic vernacular. This is evident from well-known anecdotes about pastoral
eloquence in the twelfth century. Samson, abbot of Bury St Edmunds, and
Odo, abbot of Battle Abbey, were praised for their 'eloquen[ce] in both French
and Latin', languages linked together above a demotic 'mother tongue' that is
often regionally localized – not just English, but, in Samson's case, 'the speech

Gervase of Tilbury, *Otia imperialia: Recreation for an Emperor*, ed. S. E. Banks and J. W.
Binns (Oxford, 2002), II.21, pp. 474–5.
H. M. Thomas, *The English and the Normans: Ethnic Hostility, Assimilation and Identity,
1066–1220* (Oxford, 2003).

of Norfolk'. This dynamic among the three languages, moreover, imagines bot.
Latin and *romanz* as elevating languages. In his *Speculum duorum*, Gerald of Wale
chastises his nephew who, in neglecting his education, has left himself ignorar
of 'all languages, and chiefly two, Latin and French, which are most importan
among us.'[5] Like Gervase's *tollo*, Gerald's verb *praesto* – to distinguish one's sel
to excel or surpass – indicates refinement and distinction.[6] Neither Latin no
French is here cast as a 'foreign' language; they are rather, in equal measures, th
learned *koiné* 'among us'.

As the praise of Samson and Odo suggests, *romanz* is a language of spiritua
distinction as well as of aristocratic refinement – and, indeed, the two hav
deep ties. Godric of Finchale's miraculous acquisition of Latin and then French
familiar from Ian Short's essay, 'On Bilingualism in Anglo-Norman England', i
significant in this respect. Godric, revered for his sanctity and spiritual insight, i
nonetheless isolated from the local monastic and clerical community because o
his (English) monolingualism; in two separate anecdotes, he is granted first Lati
and later French, thus overcoming the divisions within the social and spiritua
communities marked by language difference.[7] The significance is not only in th
similarity of these two stories, but in their repetition. The second story place
the gift of French in a narrative position held previously, in this narrative an
in hagiographical tradition, by Latin. *Romanz*, like Latin, offers Godric both
'unified language that could circumvent the problems caused by mutually unin
telligible dialects' and a medium of spiritual eloquence and instruction.[8]

The initial conclusion from these anecdotes confirms the findings of othe
scholars. However, our understanding of *romanz*'s status as *medially* 'illustriou
and courtly' needs to be refined to understand its emergence in England as
literary language. In this dynamic (not hierarchy) among languages, *romanz*'
simultaneously ancillary and fraternal relation to Latin metonymically repeat
Latin's qualities and functions. Yet, *romanz*'s second dynamic, the refining move
ment up from a more demotic and regional vernacular, throws into relief on
of the hallmarks of the twelfth-century renaissance: the vernacularization of th
texts and resources of literary education. It is in the context of this dynamic tha
we can best locate the history of the *romanz* Psalter, vernacular translations of th
pre-eminent text of Christian spiritual, ethical and even discursive formation.

---

5   Gerald of Wales, *Speculum duorum: or, A Mirror of Two Men*, ed. Y. Lefèvre and R. B. C
    Huygen; English trans. B. Dawson (Cardiff, 1974), p. 132. See Thomas, *The English an
    the Normans*, p. 382.
6   Thomas, *The English and the Normans*, p. 382.
7   I. Short, 'On Bilingualism in Anglo-Norman England', *Romanische Philologie* 33 (1979
    80), 467–79 (p. 475).
8   Thomas, *The English and the Normans*, p. 385.

The Anglo-Norman psalters

Between 1120 and 1170, an unprecedented amount of cultural labour was devoted to translating the Psalter and its accompanying texts – prayers, canticles, glosses, and commentary – into *romanz*. The focus of this labour is unsurprising, since the Psalter was the foundational book of Christian spiritual formation and liturgical practice, a primer for grammar and spiritual eloquence, and just as significantly, the lodestone of vernacular devotion in Anglo-Saxon literary culture.[9] Because the culture of the *romanz* Psalter shares its sociolinguistic dynamics and its reading practices with other *romanz* works of the period – Philippe de Thaon's *Comput* (*c*.1113–19) and *Bestiary* (*c*.1121–35); the *Vie de saint Alexis* (*c*.1115–25); Benedeit's *Voyage of St Brendan* (*c*.1120–5); the *Jeu d'Adam* (*c*.1135–50); Gaimar's *Estoire des Engleis* (*c*.1138–9) – its coherence offers a unique opportunity to consider the broader emergence of *romanz* literary culture in England.

The central document in the culture of the *romanz* Psalter is the Montebourg Psalter (Oxford, Bodleian, MS Douce 320b), a modest manuscript containing the oldest extant text of the Oxford Psalter, which is a complete prose translation of all 150 Psalms of the Gallican Psalter made in England (possibly Canterbury) in the very early twelfth century (*c*.1115), and which has sometimes been described as the oldest extant work of Anglo-Norman literature.[10] As Ruth Dean shows, there are no fewer than twelve complete extant copies of the Oxford Psalter predating 1300; seven of them from the twelfth century, all of English provenance, and among which we find the luxurious Winchester Psalter (London, BL, MS Cotton Nero C.IV, *c*.1150).[11] The number of complete extant copies of the Oxford Psalter (to which we must add dozens more partial or fragmentary texts) is a witness to the scale of the public taste for, and the literary labour dedicated to, the Psalter *en romanz*.[12]

Yet the Oxford Psalter represents a fraction of the twelfth-century literary work on the *romanz* Psalter. Prior to 1170, three, possibly four, other distinct translations of the Gallican Psalter were made in England. There is the Arundel Psalter (London, British Library, MS Arundel 230), a largely word-by-word translation of the Psalms presented inter-lineally with a Latin text.[13] A second distinct translation is found in the fragmentary Orne Psalter (Paris, Archives Nationales,

---

[9] P. Riché, *Les écoles et l'enseignement dans l"Occident chrétien de la fin du Ve siècle au milieu du XIe siècle* (Paris, 1979), p. 223; N. Van Deusen, ed., *The Place of the Psalms in the Intellectual Culture of the Middle Ages* (Albany NY, 1999); Dean nos. 445–8, 451–2.

[10] See J. Bonnard, *Les traductions de la Bible en vers français au Moyen Âge* (Geneva, 1967), pp. 130–49; S. Berger, *La Bible française au moyen âge: étude sur les plus anciennes versions de la Bible écrites en prose de langue d'oïl* (Paris, 1884), pp. 3–4, 16–17; Dean no. 445, p. 240.

[11] Dean no. 445, p. 240.

[12] B. Woledge and H. P. Clive, *Répertoire des plus anciens textes en prose française depuis 842 jusqu'aux premières années du XIIIe siècle* (Geneva, 1964), p. 97.

[13] Arundel Psalter: Dean no. 446. Woledge and Clive no. 39.

AB xix, 1734), which, although laid out interlinearly, is actually a freer and much more literary rendering of the Gallican Psalter.[14] A third version of the Gallican Psalter, 'unrelated to the [other] French translations of the twelfth century', is extant within the body of a complete *romanz* Psalter commentary produced *c*.1165 for Laurette d'Alsace.[15] This vernacular Psalms commentary, based largely on Gilbert de la Porrée's *Media Glossatura*, offers a complete interlinear translation up to Psalm 50, and then a 'loose translation' of the remaining Psalms 'incorporated within the commentary as part of the exposition'.[16] Leena Löfstedt has argued that the extensive quotation of the Psalms in the Old French translation of Gratian's *Decretals* (Brussels, Bibliothèque Royale 9084), which dates from the period 1164–70, is dependent, in turn, on a prior translation of the Vulgate Psalter independent of any of these three versions.[17] Neither was the Gallican Psalter the only version of the Psalter translated in *romanz* in England in this period. There is also a complete Anglo-Norman translation of the Hebrew Psalter – the only translation of the Hebrew Psalter made in any medieval French dialect – extant in, but certainly pre-dating, the deluxe Psalterium triplex known as the Eadwine Psalter (1155–60).[18] As Ruth Dean's bibliography shows, the catalogue of translations of the Psalms in their many forms goes on and on: *romanz* translations of the Penitential Psalms, of the Psalms of St Hilary, of occasional Psalms, an abbreviated *romanz* Psalter of St Jerome, and so on.[19]

Three of the earliest of these manuscripts confirm the illustrious and courtly nature of their vernacular medium. The most deluxe and best known of these manuscripts, the Eadwine Psalter (Cambridge, Trinity College, MS R.17.1, *c*.1155–60), is a luxurious triple Psalter, whose complex scriptorial engineering is matched only by the splendour of its pictorial programme.[20] The text of the Eadwine Psalter presents the Latin version of the Gallican Psalter, centrally, with interlinear and marginal Latin glosses; in smaller lateral columns, we find the corresponding text of both the Romanum Psalter with an interlinear Anglo-Saxon translation; and the Hebrew Psalter with an interlinear Anglo-Norman translation.[21]

---

14 Dean no. 447; Woledge and Clive no. 41 and p. 14; Y. Le Hir, 'Sur les traductions en prose française du psautier', *Revue de Linguistique Romane* 25 (1961), 324–8.
15 Durham, Cathedral Library, A.II.11–13. *The Twelfth-Century Psalter Commentary in French for Laurette d'Alsace: an Edition of Psalms I–L*, ed. S. Gregory (London, 1990), pp. 6–7.
16 Gregory, *The Twelfth-Century Psalter Commentary in French*, p. 6.
17 L. Löfstedt, 'Le Psautier en ancien français', *Neuphilologische Mitteilungen* 100:4 (1999), 421–32.
18 See D. Markey, 'The Anglo-Norman Version', in *The Eadwine Psalter: Text, Image and Monastic Culture in Twelfth-Century Canterbury*, ed. M. Gibson, T. A. Heslop and R. W. Pfaff, Publications of the Modern Humanities Research Association, vol. 14 (London, 1992), pp. 139–56.
19 See Dean nos. 445–57.
20 T. A. Heslop, 'Decoration and Illustration', in *The Eadwine Psalter*, p. 25.
21 P. P. O'Neill, 'The English Version', in *The Eadwine Psalter*, p. 124.

On first inspection, the *mise-en-page* suggests that the two vernaculars are subordinate to the Latin text in equal measure. They are both written in 'small informal hands' in lateral columns between the gutter and the larger, formally written Latin text.[22] As Patrick O'Neill notes, 'the English and the French gloss are so similar in their interlinear form and glossarial function that to explain the presence of one should cast light on the presence of the other'.[23] However, 'even here there is evidence that the French gloss was regarded as the more important of the two'.[24] As O'Neill shows, the Old English text is unevenly corrected, and, perhaps most importantly, wherever 'the English and the French vie for space', the Old English gloss is 'sacrificed by being omitted' to maintain the integrity of the French text.[25] And although there is significant evidence for the recopying and reading of Old English at Christ Church Canterbury in this period, the Old English glosses here are a 'linguistic gallimaufry' of forms from 'several periods and dialects' and seem to be offered either as a sign of cultural continuity with Canterbury's Anglo-Saxon past or, in O'Neill's assessment, 'more as a formal parallel to the French than as a text to be read and studied in its own right'.[26] Whatever the possible different functions of the vernacular translations, the Old English text is presented in a relatively subordinated way, while care is taken to present the French text in a discursively coherent form that can serve the studious reading of the Hebrew Psalter.

The 'royal and courtly' characteristics of *romanz* are evident in another Psalter from the period: the Winchester (or Henry of Blois) Psalter, produced at St Swithun's Winchester under the patronage of its bishop Henry of Blois sometime between 1129 and 1161. The Psalter begins with thirty-eight full-page miniatures (fols. 2–39) depicting Christian history, a deluxe iconographic programme that continues in its historiation of the Psalms initials.[27] Like the Eadwine Psalter, the Winchester Psalter is rich in vernacularity, although, in this case, only in *romanz*. All of the full-page images are accompanied by Anglo-Norman *tituli*, the Canticles and Prayers following the Psalms are all found in *romanz*, and most importantly, the Latin text of the Gallican Psalter is laid out in parallel columns with a version of the Oxford Psalms translation.

Where *romanz* operates between Latin and English in the Eadwine Psalter, the *romanz* of the Winchester Psalter operates alongside Latin. We can see this first and foremost in the *mise-en-page* of the parallel Latin and *romanz* columns. The two texts are laid out in exactly the same stichic verse form, with each *littera notabilior* initial in the *romanz* text presented in the same colour and at an exactly

---

[22] T. Webber, 'The Script', in *The Eadwine Psalter*, pp. 13–24.

[23] O'Neill, 'The English Version', p. 136.

[24] O'Neill, 'The English Version', p. 137.

[25] O'Neill, 'The English Version', p. 137.

[26] O'Neill, 'The English Version', p. 137, quoting H. Kuhn, 'The Vespasian Psalter Gloss: Original or Copy', *PMLA* 74:3 (1959), 161–77 (p. 168).

[27] F. Wormald, *The Winchester Psalter* (London, 1973), p. 125.

parallel position on the page as its corresponding Latin initial.[28] This pattern of arrangement represents the two texts as reiterative and analogous. Like the textual *mise-en-page*, the decorative programme asserts a parallel or horizontal rather than a hierarchical relationship between the French and Latin texts. The 'B' initials of 'Beatus Vir' in Latin and 'Beonuret Barun' in *romanz*, for example, are of equal size and similar design; the only distinction – and it is indeed significant – is found in the change from the leaf-scroll decoration of the vernacular 'B' to the image of David as Psalmist in the bows of the Latin 'B' (fol. 46r).

The *romanz* text of the Winchester Psalter is not presented as an interlinear *ancilla* to a superordinate Latin text. The vernacular text does not directly aid the reading of the Latin Psalms. Rather, the two texts are equally available – and as the *mise-en-page* insists, available as equals – to the reading eye. The *romanz* text is illustrious in this respect because it offers a distinct act of continuous literary reading, and thus a distinct instance of spiritual and ethical formation. But the vernacular text of the Winchester Psalter can also be understood as 'royal and courtly', not least because of its material connections to Henry of Blois. We also see these 'royal' and 'courtly' characteristics in the language of the Winchester Psalter's text of the Oxford Psalter, which bears striking lexical and ideological similarities to the language of courtly romance. This courtly style is signalled from the first words of the first Psalm: where the earliest Oxford Psalter text of Psalm 1 begins 'Beneurez li huem chi ne alat el conseil des feluns', the text in the Winchester Psalter begins 'Beonuret Barun qui ne alat el cunseil des felun' ('Blessed is the baron who does not take counsel with the wicked', fol. 46r). By locating the problems of good counsel and felony in the lives of the 'Baruns', the Winchester text frames the *romanz* Psalms in both the stylistic registers and the ethical problems of the courtly aristocracy.[29] This courtly reframing invites us to see the feudal dimensions of the first Psalm's preoccupation with 'la lei de notre seignor', the 'conseil des dreituriers' and 'l'eire des feluns'.[30]

Unlike the Eadwine or Winchester Psalters, the Oxford Psalter text found in Bodleian Douce 320 (the oldest extant text of the *romanz* Psalter) is both decoratively and materially humble: there is, for example, no colophon, no prologue or epilogue, no marginal notation, glossing or commentary; no illumination nor any historiation.[31] In relation to the decorative luxury and social elevation of the Eadwine and Winchester Psalters, the Montebourg Psalter is not, on first inspection, particularly 'illustrious' or 'courtly'. Yet, in its *mise-en-page*, the text of the Oxford Psalter reveals, in a rather more humble way, a similarly illustrious elevating and formative vernacular.

---

28 For an image of this page, see Wormald, *Winchester Psalter*, p. 92, fig. 95.
29 London, British Library, MS Cotton Nero C.IV, fol. 46r.
30 Ibid. ('the law of our Lord'; 'the counsel of the righteous'; 'the paths of the unrighteous').
31 See further R. J. Dean and M. D. Legge, eds., *The Rule of St. Benedict: A Norman Prose Version*, Medium Aevum Monographs VII (Oxford, 1964).

The system of enlargement and rubrication of the *litterae notabiliores* in Psalters offers one standard way of determining their uses. Through various means, mostly planned in the initial lining of the text but also, in one case, added later by the rubricator, the Montebourg Psalter enlarges the initials to Psalms 1, 26, 51, 80, 101, 109 and 118.[32] This corresponds to the traditional divisions of neither the Biblical not the liturgical Psalter, but is a mix of the two systems that nonetheless organizes the Psalms into seven groups (nos. 1–25, 26–50, 51–79, 80–101, 101–108, 109–117, 118–150) of approximately the same length (generally 20–25 psalms).[33] This organization, then, cannot serve liturgical performance, as is suggested by the lack of antiphons and other such apparatus, but it can serve the needs of devotional and meditative reading practices, which demanded the division of the Psalms into manageable units of daily reading.

The meditative use of the Oxford Psalms is supported as well by their *mise-en-page*. The text of the Oxford Psalms is written on the page as prose, and the individual verses, although marked off with coloured *litterae notabiliores*, are continuous within the paragraph of each Psalm. This arrangement conforms neither to the older *per cola et commata* arrangement of the Psalms, where each element of a period is given a new line, nor to the later stichic verse arrangement, where each verse begins on a new line with a *littera notabilior*, both of which, as Malcolm Parkes shows, aid liturgical psalmody.[34]

The Montebourg Psalms are also given a remarkably consistent system of punctuation derived from the punctuation marks, or positurae, that were designed to aid in the production of meaning and, in particular, rhythm in the liturgical performance of the Psalms.[35] However, as Parkes has shown, over the course of the eleventh and twelfth centuries, these positurae 'were inserted methodically into copies of all kinds of texts' in monastic libraries, including those books

---

[32] The space left for the rubrication of initials is normally two lines. This provides a standard against which to measure the enlargement of other *litterae notabiliores*. First, the 'B' (fol. 37r) of the first Psalm is afforded six lines, while the initials of Psalms 51 (fol. 48r) and 101 (fol. 61v) are given each four lines. Three lines are given for the initials of Psalms 80 (fol. 56r) and 109 (fol. 64v), which are divisions within the liturgical system, but also to the initial of Psalm 118 (fol. 66v), which is not. The only other Psalm to receive a decorative attention drawing it out from the standard two-line enlargement is Psalm 26 (fol. 41r). Even though the original ruling provided only the standard two lines, the scribe wrote the first two words entirely in red capitals, as 'LI SIRE', an arrangement that is not repeated in any other Psalm.

[33] There were two general systems for the division of the Psalms into distinct groups, using enlarged initials. There are the 'Biblical Psalters' that divide the Psalms into either three (1, 51, 101) or more rarely five (1, 41, 72, 89, 106) groups, making them available as discrete units of study. Much more common is the liturgical division of the Psalms into eight nocturns (1, 26, 38, 52, 68, 80, 97, 109), the discrete groups to be performed at the morning and evening office of each day: V. Leroquais, *Les psautiers manuscrits latins des bibliothèques publiques de France*, 3 vols. (Paris, 1940), I, xliv–lvii.

[34] M. Parkes, *Pause and Effect: An Introduction to the History of Punctuation in the West* (Berkeley, 1993), pp. 35–8.

[35] Parkes, *Pause and Effect*, pp. 35–6.

employed for the studious reading of the *lectio divina* and the devotional reading of the *otium* or *vacantes libros*.[36] All of these features point to the same conclusion: that the Oxford Psalter was designed to furnish a practice of devotional or meditational reading. Such practices, whether conducted in cloister or court, demanded brief, self-contained texts of the Psalms, organized into an 'economy of the daily readings', that would carry the Psalter's poetic or rhythmical *ductus* so as to achieve its end of refinement.[37]

The very vernacularity of the Oxford Psalms speaks, in the end, to the role of *romanz* in the sociolinguistic dynamic that gave us Anglo-Norman literature, particularly in light of the one thing the Montebourg Psalter most notably lacks: Latin. Here the *romanz* Psalter is presented without any accompanying Latin text of any kind – it is available, *by itself*, as a self-sufficient literary instrument of studious reading and spiritual distinction. The widespread culture of the vernacular Psalms shows that *romanz* was, at once, both subordinate to Latin, in not being suited for liturgical performance, and parallel to it in its capacity to bear the practices of spiritual and discursive distinction attributed to the devotional reading of the Psalms. In manuscripts like the Winchester Psalter, we see that these forms of spiritual distinction are inseparable from the aristocratic social distinction with which *romanz* is more commonly associated. The Oxford Psalms might also be said to have, however obscured and subordinated, a relationship with English. The larger culture of the vernacular Psalms, being so widespread in England in the period, might be seen as employing *romanz* as a devotional *lingua franca* operating above the regional variation and localization of English. We could thus see the Oxford Psalms as an accommodation of the vibrant culture of the Anglo-Saxon Psalter to the new sociolinguistic dynamics of post-Conquest life. In its small size, its humble presentation of the vernacular Psalms, its vernacular Canticles, and devotional rather than liturgical organization, the Montebourg Psalter seems in every respect to follow the template of a series of Anglo-Saxon Psalters designed for private devotions, which Jane Toswell sees as a direct antecedent of the Book of Hours.[38] That is, although in its oldest extant text the *romanz* Psalter appears without the accompaniment of either Latin or English, it is elevated to its illustrious condition by metonymically reproducing them both.

---

[36] Parkes, *Pause and Effect*, pp. 35, 38.

[37] On the literary and social implications of overlapping lay and religious reading cultures here, see G. Rector, 'En sa chambre sovent le lit: Otium and the Pedagogical Sociabilities of Early *Romanz* Literature (*c.*1100–1150)' (forthcoming).

[38] M. J. Toswell, 'The Late Anglo-Saxon Psalter: Ancestor of the Book of Hours?', *Florilegium* 14 (1995–6), 1–24.

16

Serpent's Head/ Jew's Hand:
Le Jeu d'Adam and Christian–Jewish Debate in Norman England

Ruth Nisse*

he *Ordo Representacionis Ade*, or *Jeu d'Adam*, has long been understood as a
lay about language. With the two distinct registers of its first section, the Latin
turgy of Septuagesima and the lively Anglo-French dialogue between God
called *Figura* – and his subjects, Adam, Eve and the serpent (*Diabolus*), the
lay dramatizes not only the Fall but the nature of representation itself. In an
ifluential reading by Eugene Vance, Latin is 'the universal timeless medium
f *grammatica* itself and therefore closest to truth; Romance was a mere histor-
al accident, a degraded image of its Latin prototype ... the artistic vehicle
f man's worldly desires'.[1] The playwright makes full use of this bilingualism
the Devil's temptations; in the form of the serpent, he cannily deploys the
ontemporary French idiom of feudal relations in an attempt to incite Adam to
bellion and that of the courtly love lyric to seduce Eve.[2]

In this essay, I will argue that the *Jeu d'Adam*'s engagement with contempo-
ary ideas about language and representation actually involves a *trilingualism*:
eyond its concern with Latin as opposed to its temporal, vernacular 'double', it
ontends with the originary and suppressed language of its own biblical sources,
lebrew. It is not surprising, of course, that a play about the Fall and Redemption
f mankind and the intelligibility of biblical prophecy should replicate Chris-
an concerns with the Hebrew language that go back to the patristic era. Augus-
ne in *De civitate Dei* gives great weight to Hebrew as the only language before
e flood, the language that preserves not only the writing but the *speech* of the
atriarchs and prophets and, possibly, even the language spoken by Adam and
ve.[3] Jerome, above all, initiates the Church's ambivalent approach to Hebrew by

I would like to thank Sahar Amer, Robert L. A. Clark, Thelma Fenster and David
Trotter for their many helpful suggestions about this essay.

E. Vance, *Marvelous Signals: Poetics and Sign Theory in the Middle Ages* (Lincoln NE,
1986), p. 194.

R. L. A. Clark, 'Eve and her Audience in the Anglo-Norman *Adam*', in *Crossing Boundaries: Issues of Cultural and Individual Identity in the Middle Ages and the Renaissance*, ed.
S. McKee (Turnhout, 1999), pp. 27–39.

Augustine, *De civitate Dei* xvi.11, ed. B. Dombart and A. Kalb, 2 vols. (Stuttgart, 1981),
II, pp. 142–5. For a discussion of Hebrew and Augustine's hermeneutic theory in the

translating the Bible directly from Hebrew rather than the Greek Septuagint. I
his theory of translation, Jerome emphasizes the importance of a 'Hebrew Truth
(*Hebraica Veritas*) to be found in the original source; simultaneously, he frequentl
alters the meanings of words and passages to suit Christian doctrine and dispute
with contemporary Jews on numerous points of interpretation.[4]

With regard to these issues, I have discovered a Hebrew word in the *Je
d'Adam* – just one word, ראש/ *rosh* (head) – but located at a crucial theologica
moment in the narrative: God, having returned to paradise after Eve and Adar
have eaten the fruit, curses the serpent, translating and amplifying Genesis 3: 1!

> Femme te portera haïne
> Oncore te iert male veisine;
> Tu son talon aguaiteras,
> **Cele te sachera le *ras***
> Ta teste ferra de itel mail
> Qui te ferra mult grant travail. (479–84)

> ('Woman will detest you;
> Forever she will be an evil neighbour to you.
> You will lie in wait for her heel,
> She will pluck you by the head.
> She will strike your head such a blow
> That it will cause you great hardship.')[5]

This is meant to express the Vulgate's: 'Inimicitias ponam inter te et mulierem
et semen tuum et semen illius. **Ipsa conteret caput tuum** /et tu insidiaberi
calcaneo eius.' The Hebrew text is:

> ואיבה אשית
> בינך ובין האשה
> ובין זרעך ובין זרעה
> **הוא ישופך ראש**
> ואתה תשופנו עקב

A literal English translation of the Hebrew original reads: 'I will put enmity
Between you and the woman,/ And between your offspring (lit. seed) and hers;
They (it=the seed) shall strike at your head/ And you shall strike at their heel.

   story of the Fall, see E. Jager, *The Tempter's Voice: Language and the Fall in Mediev*
   Literature (Ithaca NY, 1993), pp. 33–5.

4 Jerome, 'Prologue to the Pentateuch', *Biblia Sacra Iuxta Vulgatam Versionem*, ed. R. Webe
   (Stuttgart, 1983), pp. 3–4. See also H. F. D. Sparks, 'Jerome as Biblical Scholar', in *Tl*
   Cambridge History of the Bible, ed. P. R. Ackroyd and C. F. Evans, 3 vols. (Cambridge
   1970), I, pp. 510–41.

5 *Le Jeu d'Adam (Ordo Representacionis Ade)*, ed. W. Noomen (Paris, 1971). All translation
   of *Le Jeu d'Adam* are from D. Bevington, *Medieval Drama* (Boston MA, 1975), pp. 80–12
   with occasional minor modifications.

6 *JPS Hebrew-English Tanakh*, Jewish Publication Society of America 2nd ed (Philade
   phia, 1999), p. 6.

In these difficult lines from the *Jeu d'Adam*, the word 'ras' has proved especially mysterious, baffling Romance philologists and the play's editors alike, all
of whom recognize that it must mean 'head' in conjunction with the 'teste' that
follows.[7] The Anglo-Norman Dictionary concurs with the Tobler–Lommatzsch
Altfranzösisches Wörterbuch, giving the definition as 'head (?)'. *Ra's* is the Arabic
word for 'head', a cognate of the Hebrew, and as such could very well have been
known in twelfth-century England. Most recently, Sahar Amer has demonstrated
that otherwise unknown words in Anglo-Norman texts can be traced to Arabic
roots.[8] A much more likely explanation of the 'ras' in the *Jeu d'Adam*, however,
is that it is a mis-transliteration of the Hebrew 'rosh' that appears in the original
text of Genesis.[9] An author who did not himself know Hebrew, like the playwright of the *Jeu d'Adam*, could have easily thought that the three letters *resh,
aleph, shin* (or *sin* depending on the diacritical mark) were pronounced 'ras',
especially if he only saw them in a Torah scroll or another Hebrew manuscript
written without vocalization marks.[10] Furthermore, the transliteration of *shin* as

7 Noomen explains the solution he finds most likely as 'Les vers 481–2 doivent corres-
   pondre, quoiqu'on en ait dit, à *Ipse conteret caput tuum, et tu insidiaberis calcaneo eius*
   (Gen. 3: 15). Les deux vers suivants sont à considérer comme une amplification. ...
   Sacheras doit sans doute être lu, ainsi que l'a proposé Foerster, comme *cacheras*, pour
   francien *chalcheras* ... de *chalchier*: « fouler aux pieds »; *le ras* doit par conséquent être
   considéré comme un hapax signifiant « tête »' (*Jeu d'Adam*, pp. 88–9). Most recently,
   David Trotter has read the line as 'Cele t'es[ç]lachera [=esquasser] le ras', meaning 'she
   will break (crush) your head' (pers. comm.).
8 S. Amer, 'Lesbian Sex and the Military: From the Medieval Arabic Tradition to French
   Literature', in *Same Sex Love and Desire among Women in the Middle Ages*, ed. F. C.
   Sautman and P. Sheingorn (New York, 2001), pp. 179–98. Amer specifically discusses
   the transmission of Arabic sexual vocabulary in Étienne de Fougères' *Livre des Manières*,
   dedicated to Cecily, countess of Hereford. This line of interpretation complements the
   groundbreaking work of Charles Burnett on the study of Arabic by Adelard of Bath
   and his circle. The word *ra's* in fact appears in Adelard's Latin translation of the ninth-
   century astronomical tables of al-Khwarizmi in a reference to the star 'race elhamel'
   (*ra's al-hamal*), the 'head of Aries'. See *Die Astronomischen Tafeln des Muhammed ibn Musa
   Al-Kwarizmi in der Bearbeitung des Maslama ibn Ahmed al-Madjriti und der Lateinischer
   Übersetzung des Athelhard von Bath*, ed. H. Suter, A. Bjørnbo and R. Besthorn (Copenhagen, 1914), pp. 20, 245. On Adelard's later importance in the courts of Henry II, see
   C. Burnett, *The Introduction of Arabic Learning into England* (London, 1997), pp. 31–60.
9 Another, earlier, possible use of 'ras' meaning 'head' appears in Wace's *Roman de
   Brut* (1155). King Leir, addressing Fortune, laments 'Tost as un vilain halt levé/ E
   tost le ras desuz buté.' The large number of scribal variations of this line suggests the
   word 'ras' was not well understood by subsequent readers; the *Roman de Brut*'s most
   recent editor, Judith Weiss, translates 'ras' here as the second-person singular of *ravoir*:
   'Quickly you raise a peasant up, and quickly push him down again.' See *Wace's Roman
   de Brut: A History of the British*, ed. J. Weiss (Exeter, rev. edn, 2002), pp. 50–1.
10 The author of the *Jeu d'Adam* may also have been familiar with Jerome's translitera-
   tions in his *Liber interpretationis Hebraicorum nominum*: Jerome provides the meaning
   'caput' for three Hebrew names: *rus* (for Rosh the son of Benjamin in Genesis 46:
   21), *res* (for the letter 'resh' at the heading of Psalm 119: 153) and *ros* (for Resa, Jesus'
   ancestor in Luke 3: 27). See the edition by P. de Lagarde in Jerome, *Opera*, Pars I, 1,
   Corpus Christianorum Series Latina 72 (Turnhout, 1959), pp. 57–161.

's' is a very frequent error among Christian Hebraists from Jerome on: a twelfth-century example is found in the *Ysagoge* of Odo the Englishman (*c*.1135), where the author transliterates the relative pronoun 'asher' (אשר, the same three letters in the word 'rosh' – *aleph, shin, resh*) as 'asser' in the phrase *asser eloheha adonai anohi* (I am the Lord your God who …).[11] Even a hundred years later, a Hebrew grammar attributed to Roger Bacon in Cambridge University Library, MS Ff.6.13, refers to the letter ש solely as 'sin' and explains the diacritical mark on the left or right as a distinction between 'stronger' and 'weaker' pronunciation rather than different sounds.[12]

In order to consider why the playwright would insert the Hebrew word for 'head' into his vernacular dialogue, it is important to look ahead to the play's final section, an expanded version of the *Ordo Prophetarum*, a text commonly associated with Christmas liturgy, but also, as M. F. Vaughan has shown, the Annunciation.[13] Beginning with 'I call upon you, O Jews', this was the most popular medieval text among those who took the Jews to task for not believing the Hebrew bible's prophecies of Christ. In the *Jeu d'Adam*, Isaiah appears on stage second to last in the procession of prophets to deliver the first of two prophecies, 'And there shall come forth a rod out of the root of Jesse' (Isaiah 11: 1), when 'someone from the synagogue' (*quidem de synagoga*) jumps up to dispute with him by demanding:

> Est ço fable, ou prophecie?
> Que est iço que tu as dit?
> Truvas le tu ou est escrit? (884–6)

> ('Is this a fable or prophecy?
> What is this you've said?
> Did you invent it or is it written?')

After insulting the prophet for a few more lines, the Jew enigmatically asks:

> Tu ses bien garder al miroir?
> Or me gardez en ceste main
> *Tunc ostendet ei manum suum*
> Si j'ai le cor malade ou sain. (898–900)

> ('You know well enough how to look in a mirror?
> Now look at this hand for me and tell
> *Then he will show him his hand*
> if my heart is sick or healthy.')

---

11 Odo, *Ysagoge in Theologiam*, in *Écrits théologiques de l'école d'Abélard*, ed. A. Landgraf (Louvain, 1934), pp. 63–289. For the passage in question see pp. 132–3. D. E. Luscombe constructs an outline of Odo's intellectual milieu in 'The Authorship of the *Ysagoge in Theologiam*', *Archives d'histoire doctrinale et littéraire du Moyen Age* 43 (1969), 7–16.

12 'Sin vero punctatur aliquando in dextera parte supra vel intra, sic ש tunc sonat fortiter. Set quando punctatur a sinistra parte supra vel intra tunc sonat debiliter ש.' *The Greek Grammar of Roger Bacon and a Fragment of his Hebrew Grammar*, ed. E. Nolan and S. A. Hirsch (Cambridge, 1902), p. 207.

13 M. F. Vaughan, 'The Prophets of the Anglo-Norman *Adam*', *Traditio* 39 (1983), 81–114.

Isaiah finally tells the Jew that he is 'sick with error' (*mal de felonie*, 901), wherepon he converts to Christianity just in time to hear Isaiah's second prophecy, ne ultimate contested proof-text: 'Behold a virgin shall conceive in her womb nd bear a son, and his name shall be Emmanuel (Isaiah 7.4).' In this dialogue, vhich turns a static apologetic text into a parody of Jewish–Christian debate, the nedieval Jew assumes that his hand will be like a mirror to the Jewish Isaiah but nstead finds himself utterly alien, lost in Christianity's unbridgeable temporal istance between the Hebrew Bible and the contemporary rabbinic 'synagogue'. n a recent article on the role of the Jew – '*Quidem de Sinagoga*' – and Judaism, ennifer Goodman has argued that the *Jeu d'Adam* was intended as a kind of pros-lytizing dramatic sermon, heard or 'overheard' by French-speaking English Jews n the steps of a London or Norwich church located near a synagogue.[14] While it s possible that local Jews could have seen the play, its treatment of prophecy has nore to do with internal Christian hermeneutic debates and anxieties over the roper use of the Hebrew language and Jewish exegesis: it is directed, in other vords, at so-called 'Judaizers' rather than actual Jews.

It is also in the *Jeu d'Adam*'s view of prophecy that Genesis 3: 15, sometimes alled the Protoevangelion – the first prophecy of redemption – assumes crucial ignificance. In his exegesis of the text in the *Hebrew Questions on Genesis*, Jerome xplains, quoting Paul: 'It shall watch your head and you shall watch its heel. More correctly, it has in the Hebrew it will crush your head and you shall crush s heel. For our footsteps are indeed shackled by the serpent, and *the Lord shall rush Satan under our feet swiftly* (Romans 16.20).'[15] In the late eleventh and twelfth enturies, theologians, following the Vulgate's mistranslation of the Hebrew nasculine pronoun *hu* (referring to the noun 'seed') as the feminine *ipsa*, began o favour a Mariological reading of Genesis 3: 15. In these accounts, Eve's sin is edeemed in the Virgin Mary, who conquers the devil. As Bernard of Clairvaux xplains: 'To whom is this victory given except for Mary? She (*ipsa*) without a oubt crushed the poisonous head, and wholly reduced to nothing all the devil's uggestions of both carnal allurement and mental pride.'[16]

Erich Auerbach famously noted in *Mimesis* that the *Jeu d'Adam* consider-bly alters its biblical source by having the newly fallen Adam prophesy his

---

J. Goodman, '*Quidem de Sinagoga*: The Jew of the *Jeu d'Adam*', in *Medieval Cultures in Contact*, ed. R. F. Gyug (New York, 2003), pp. 161–87.

Jerome's Hebrew Questions on Genesis, ed. and trans. C. T. R. Hayward (Oxford, 1995), p. 33; see also Hayward's commentary, pp. 115–16. This was a standard medieval exegesis of the Protoevangelion, quoted in the *Glossa Ordinaria* to Genesis 3: 15.

Bernard of Clairvaux, *In Laudibus Virginis Matris*, Homilia II. 4. *Opera*, ed. J. Leclercq, C. H. Talbot and H. Rochais, 8 vols. (Rome, 1966), IV, pp. 23–4. Ut pauca loquar de pluribus, quam tibi aliam Deus praedixisse videtur, quando ad serpentem ait: Inimicitias ponam inter te et mulierem? Et si adhuc dubitas an de Maria non dixerit, audi quod sequitur: Ipsa conteret caput tuum. Cui haec servata victoria est, nisi Mariae? Ipsa procul dubio caput contrivit venenatum, quae omnimodam maligni suggestionem tam de carnis illecebra quam de mentis superbia deduxit ad nihilum. See Vaughan, 'The Prophets', pp. 96–7.

own redemption even before God returns to paradise; in his diatribe against hi 'foolish wife *(femme desvee)*', Adam declares that 'Ne me ferat ja nul aïe, / Fo le Filz que istra de Marie (719–20) [None will ever aid me/except the Son wh will come forth from Mary]'. Nevertheless, Figura's curse on the serpent, the las words he says before throwing all of them out of paradise, still emphasizes tha the saviour will ultimately come from Eve's body:

> Mal acointas tu sun traïn
> Ele te fra le chief enclin
> Oncore raiz de lui istra
> Qui toz tes vertuz confundra. (487–90)

> ('You meddled evilly in her company
> She will bow your head.
> A root will spring from her
> Who will confound all your powers.')

The playwright's inscription of the Hebrew *rosh* into his version of the Proto evangelion is a curious theological move, at once calling attention to the Vulgat as a translation of another, prior language in the midst of his own 'fallen' Anglo Norman vernacular and associating Hebrew with the devil's head, the sourc of all evil. The *Jeu d'Adam* here gives voice to the same ambivalent work on th Hebrew language that was being carried out in the contemporary French an English schools.

One twelfth-century English scholar who made unusually prominent use o written Hebrew is the previously mentioned Odo the Englishman; nothing i known of him beyond his work, which includes commentaries on the *Aeneid* an Martianus Capella's *De Nuptiis Philologiae et Mercurii* as well as the *Ysagoge i Theologiam* dedicated to Gilbert Foliot, later bishop of Hereford and London. Odo was evidently influenced, however, by Hugh of St Victor's call to study th Hebrew Bible in its original language in order to correct the errors of the Vulgate and by the Victorines' engagement with the contemporary literal-linguisti Hebrew exegesis produced by Rabbi Yitzhak ben Solomon (Rashi), Joseph Qar and their Northern French school.[18] The *Ysagoge* is divided into three books the first is on the creation and fall of mankind, the second on redemption, an the third on angels. In the second book, by far the longest, Odo emphasizes th importance of using the Hebrew Bible as evidence when debating with Jews i order to convince them of the truth of Christian exegesis; while he character izes the Jews as an enemy to be defeated, he quotes Paul's dictum 'To the Jew

---

17 M. Evans identifies the commentaries on Virgil and Martianus (and a lost *Timeu* commentary) with Odo, based on affinities of thought and style with his *Ysagoge*, i 'The *Ysagoge in Theologiam* and the Commentaries attributed to Bernard Silvestris' *JWCI* 54 (1991), 1–42.

18 B. Smalley, *The Study of the Bible in the Middle Ages* (1952; repr. Notre Dame IN, 1964) pp. 83–111; A. Abulafia, *Christians and Jews in the Twelfth-Century Renaissance* (London 1995), pp. 95–7.

I became as a Jew in order to convert Jews'.[19] To this end, Odo begins by setting out some aspects of the Hebrew alphabet and script and differences between Hebrew and Latin grammar. He opens his discussion of the Old and New Law with juxtaposed Hebrew and Latin versions of the Ten Commandments, at first both transliterating the Hebrew and providing the simplified system of vocalization marks that Judith Olszowy-Schlanger has identified in various manuscripts produced by twelfth- and thirteenth-century English Christian Hebraists.[20]

Odo then moves on to a discussion of Hebrew prophecies of the advent of Christ, beginning with the Protoevangelion, Genesis 3:15, up to 'rosh', which he says clearly extols the merit of the Virgin – all the more clearly, since he provides a Latin translation different from the Vulgate that corrects Jerome's 'ipsa' but translates 'isha' (woman) as 'virago' (heroine): *Odium ponam inter te et viraginem, et intra semen tuum et semen eius; conteret caput tuum*.[21] Odo, moreover, often changes not just the Vulgate but also, as Avrom Saltman has described in detail, the Masoretic Hebrew text.[22] For example, the very next example on this page, supposedly from Deuteronomy 18:15 – 'The Lord your God will raise up for you a prophet from among your own people, like myself; him you shall heed' – is really the passage as quoted in Acts 3:22 and 7:37 retranslated back into imperfect Hebrew.[23] Odo continues his section on prophecy with a long series of biblical proof-texts, many of them taken, as Saltman has shown, from Gilbert Crispin's widely circulated *Disputatio Judei et Christiani* (1092/3) and many of which also interestingly appear in the *Ordo Prophetarum* of the *Jeu d'Adam*. He next cites Isaiah 7: 14, strikingly translating the Hebrew term *'alma* as *abscondita* rather than *virgo*, in a kind of minor concession to Jewish glossators.[24] That he was aware of contemporary Jewish exegesis is clear from a remark he makes on the Hebrew word *sheol* (which he includes in Hebrew script – שאול – and mis-transliterates as *sool*) in Psalm 48:16, '*Deus redimet animam meam de manu inferi, cum acciperet me* ('This citation convinces us, O Jews, *sheol* does not always mean a pit as you say, but also means the inferno').[25] Rashi, for example, literally explains *sheol* as the grave (*kever*) in his commentary on Genesis 37: 35.[26] For Odo, both the standard

---

[19] Odo, *Ysagoge*, p. 126: '*Factus sum*, inquit Paulus, *tanquam Iudeus Iudeis, ut Iudeos lucrifacerem*' (1 Corinthians 9: 20).

[20] Odo, *Ysagoge*, pp. 132–4. J. Olszowy-Schlanger, 'A Christian Tradition of Hebrew Vocalisation in Medieval England', in *Semitic Studies in Honour of Edward Ullendorff*, ed. G. Khan (Leiden, 2005), pp. 126–45.

[21] Odo, *Ysagoge*, p. 140. It is worth noting that Odo's citation of Genesis 3:15 is not taken from his main source, Gilbert Crispin's *Disputatio Judei et Christiani*.

[22] A. Saltman, 'Gilbert Crispin as a Source of the Anti-Jewish Polemic of the Ysagoge in Theologiam', in *Confrontation and Coexistence*, ed. P. Artzi (Ramat Gan, 1984), pp. 89–99.

[23] Odo, *Ysagoge*, p. 140; Saltman, 'Gilbert Crispin as a Source', p. 95.

[24] Odo, *Ysagoge*, pp. 141–2.

[25] Odo, *Ysagoge*, pp. 160–1: 'Hoc loco convicimus, o Iudee … sool non semper pro fovea, ut dicis, sed et pro inferno sumi' (Saltman, 'Gilbert Crispin as a Source', pp. 97–8).

[26] *Mikra'ot Gedolot 'Haketer': Genesis* II, ed. M. Cohen (Ramat Gan, 1999), p. 102. See also Saltman's discussion of Jewish anti-Christian polemics on *sheol* in Joseph Kimhi's *Book of the Covenant* (Toronto, 1972), p. 98, n. 63.

Latin and Hebrew biblical texts are secondary to his construction of a convincing theological polemic, and he clearly believes that with his knowledge of Hebrew, he could in a sense create his own *Hebraica veritas*.

A vituperative debate on the proper use of Hebrew within Christian hermeneutics and the understanding of prophetic discourse had emerged in the midtwelfth century between Hugh of St Victor's two Anglo-Norman disciples Andrew and Richard. The Hebraist Andrew of St Victor developed a methodology whereby he accepted the biblical glosses of Rashi and his followers – which he learned from local Jewish scholars – as a literal-historical level of meaning, upon which he then based the allegorical Christian truth. In his Isaiah commentary, he applies this approach even to the verse on the birth of Emmanuel, incorporating Rashi's gloss that the passage refers to the birth of Isaiah's own son by his young wife, the 'prophetess' of the subsequent chapter.[27] While Andrew refers to the Jews in his commentary on Isaiah 7:14 as 'enemies of the truth', he accepts the Jewish reading as a historical level of the text that comes from a time before the advent of Christ; and this is how he responds to those who call him a Jew and a perverter of scripture. One such critic is Richard of St Victor, whose scathing polemic *De Emmanuele* is entirely devoted to attacking Andrew's commentary.

For Richard, Andrew and his pupils are precisely 'judaizers' for suggesting that the Jewish gloss could have any validity, even for a past era superseded by Christian truth. For both exegetes, the central issue at stake is that contemporary Jews continue to interpret the Bible in their own way; they were well aware that the glosses on *Isaiah* in particular contained some of the most powerful Jewish anti-Christian polemics. Rashi, for instance, in his discussion of Isaiah's wife (the *'alma*) interprets the 'sign' of the verse to be that 'the divine spirit will rest upon her and she will name him Emmanuel'; he then rather cryptically refutes certain unnamed *poterim*, interpreters who say that the sign is that she was an *'alma* and therefore not capable of giving birth. Abraham Ibn Ezra, whose linguistic glosses were known to Northern French and English Jews, provides a more explicit anti-Christological reading, emphasizing that the word *'alma* simply means *na'ara* (young woman), either a virgin or married, and that the masculine form is *'alem* (young man).[28]

In Richard's view, set out in *De Emmanuele*, there are no multiple senses of Isaiah 7:14; the passage can mean only one thing – that the Virgin Mary will give birth to Christ. Throughout the text, he defines Jewish error, and by extension Andrew's judaizing exegesis, as diabolic: 'Through these words of the prophet whereby the Christian is illuminated, the Jew is blinded, and the devil is humiliated. … Whereas Christian simplicity takes the plain path and runs without stumbling, Jewish perfidy is drowned, and the devil is choked.'[29] Moreover, he

---

27 Smalley, *Study of the Bible*, p. 163.

28 *Mikra'ot Gedolot 'Haketer': Isaiah*, ed. M. Cohen (Ramat Gan, 1996), pp. 56–7.

29 Richard of Saint Victor, *De Emmanuele Libri Duo*, in *Richardi Canonici Operum Pars Prima Exegetica*, PL 196.605D: 'Ecce in eiusdem ipsis verbis prophetiae unde Christianus illuminatur, inde Judaeus excaecatur, diabolus infatuatur. … Ecce ubi Christiana simplic-

eclares the Hebrew *'alma'* simply to mean 'virgin', accusing Andrew of falling
rey to Jewish *'ambages'*, verbal circumlocutions or evasions. In a further example
f Richard's immoderate tone in this text, he insists: 'You see clearly how the
rofits that our seducer won with fraudulence by means of the woman will be
st again through her seed. If only the Jews would at last wake up! If only they
ould at last come to their senses and realize that this [Mary] is the woman and
ese her offspring, about whom the Lord said to the serpent: *I will put enmity
tween you and the woman, between your seed and her seed!*'[30] Richard's point is that
rophecy always works the same way, from Genesis 3: 15 on; it is only because of
eir corruption and malice, and not historical change, that the Jews interpret the
me words differently from Christians.

The *Jeu d'Adam* represents, I would argue, a reaction against 'judaizing' in line
ith Richard of St Victor's. After the nameless Jew is rebuked by Isaiah in the
rdo Prophetarum section of the play, he concedes:

> Nos te tendrom puis por maistre
> E ceste generacion
> Escuterai puis ta leçon. (910–12)

> ('We will take you for our master,
> And this generation
> Will hearken to your teaching.')

he prophet seamlessly proceeds to tell the Jew to listen to 'the great wonder'
a grant merveille, 913); he then delivers the Vulgate of the Emmanuel prophecy,
llowed by a longer vernacular account:

> *Ecce virgo concipiet in utero et pariet filium et vocabitur nomen eius
> Emanuhel.*
> Pres est li tens, n'est pas lointens
> Ne tarzera, ja est sor mains,
> Que une virge concevera
> E virge un filz emfantera
> Il avra non Emanuhel
> Message en iert Saint Gabrïel.
> La pucele iert virge Marie
> Si portera le fruit de vie,
> Jhesu, le nostre salvator
> Qui Adam trarra de grant dolor.   (917–30)

---

itas planam viam invenit, currit, nec offendit, Judaica perfidia submergitur, diabolus
suffocatur.'
• Richard of Saint Victor, *De Emmanuele*, PL 196.627D: 'Vides certe quomodo seductor
noster fraudulentiae suae lucra quae per mulierem aquisivit, iterum per semen muli-
eris amisit. Utinam tandem aliquando Judaei evigilent! Utinam tandem aliquando
sapiant, et intellegant hanc esse mulierem, hanc eius esse prolem de quibus a Domino
dictum est ad serpentem: Inimicitias ponam inter te et mulierem, inter semen tuum et
semen illius!'

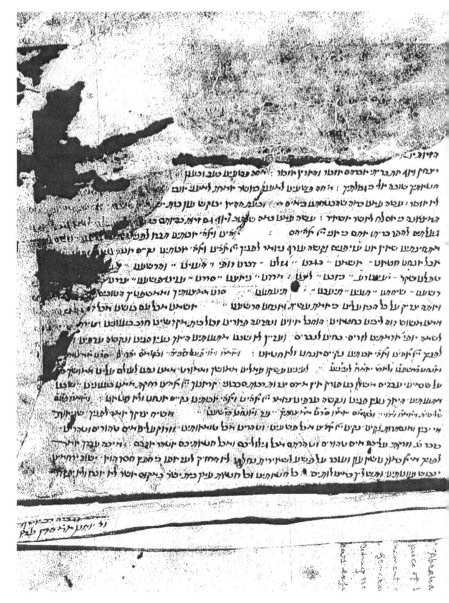

Figure 16.1: Cambridge, Pembroke College MS 59, front binding

('*Behold a virgin shall conceive in her womb and bear a son, and his name shall be called Emmanuel.*
That time is near, it is not far,
It will not delay, it is at hand,
That a virgin will conceive
And a virgin will bear a son
He will have the name Emmanuel.
Saint Gabriel will be the messenger.
The maid will be the Virgin Mary;
She will carry the fruit of life
Jesus our saviour
Who will recover Adam from his great sorrow.')

As Vance points out in his reading of the *Jeu d'Adam*, the dramatic dialogue ends when the Jew acquiesces, and all that remains is prophetic utterance.[31] The translation of the prophecies from Latin into Anglo-Norman French is, he says, 'a partial redemption and revalorization of the language itself', a way to make the vernacular sacred after the Fall.[32]

For these prophecies to remain intelligible, however, the Latin text must be fixed in its meaning, entirely removed from any possible new Hebrew interpretations of its original source. Hence the *Jeu*'s inscription of the one word 'rosh', in a context that identifies this holy tongue with the devil's crushed head, attempts to secure Hebrew's role as a subservient language rather than as a continuing source of meaning from the beginning of prophecy itself. Just as French becomes a potentially holy language in the course of the *Jeu*, Hebrew becomes the superseded vehicle of biblical truth.

I will conclude my argument with an artefact that I think has deep resonance with the *Jeu d'Adam*'s use – or abuse, as the case may be – of Hebrew; it originates from the same time as the play and is perhaps from the same geographical area. Figure 16.1 shows a folio of a twelfth-century Hebrew manuscript that had been pasted onto the front board of a late twelfth-century glossed Isaiah from the Abbey of Bury St Edmunds, now Cambridge, Pembroke College, MS 59.[33] The Hebrew text, supposedly pasted into the binding in order to reinforce the cover, is taken from a prayer book; it is a series of four *selihot*, liturgical poems recited during the period between Rosh Hashana and Yom Kippur. The *Viduy*, or communal confession of sins (seven full lines from the top) appears much as it remains today in Ashkenazi prayerbooks, beginning in alphabetical order

---

[31] Vance, *Mervelous Signals*, p. 207.

[32] Vance, *Mervelous Signals*, p. 205.

[33] Colette Sirat transcribes the Hebrew text, identifies the individual selihot, and discusses how they appear in other twelfth-century liturgical texts. She also provides an exhaustively thorough description of the Hebrew manuscript and the binding of the Latin manuscript: C. Sirat, 'Paléographie Hebraïque Médiaévale', *Rapports sur les Conférences de l'École Pratique des Hautes Études*, IVe section (Paris, 1975), pp. 559–74. See also J. Olszowy-Schlanger, *Les manuscrits hébreux dans l'Angleterre médiévale: Étude historique et paléographique* (Louvain, 2003), pp. 262–4.

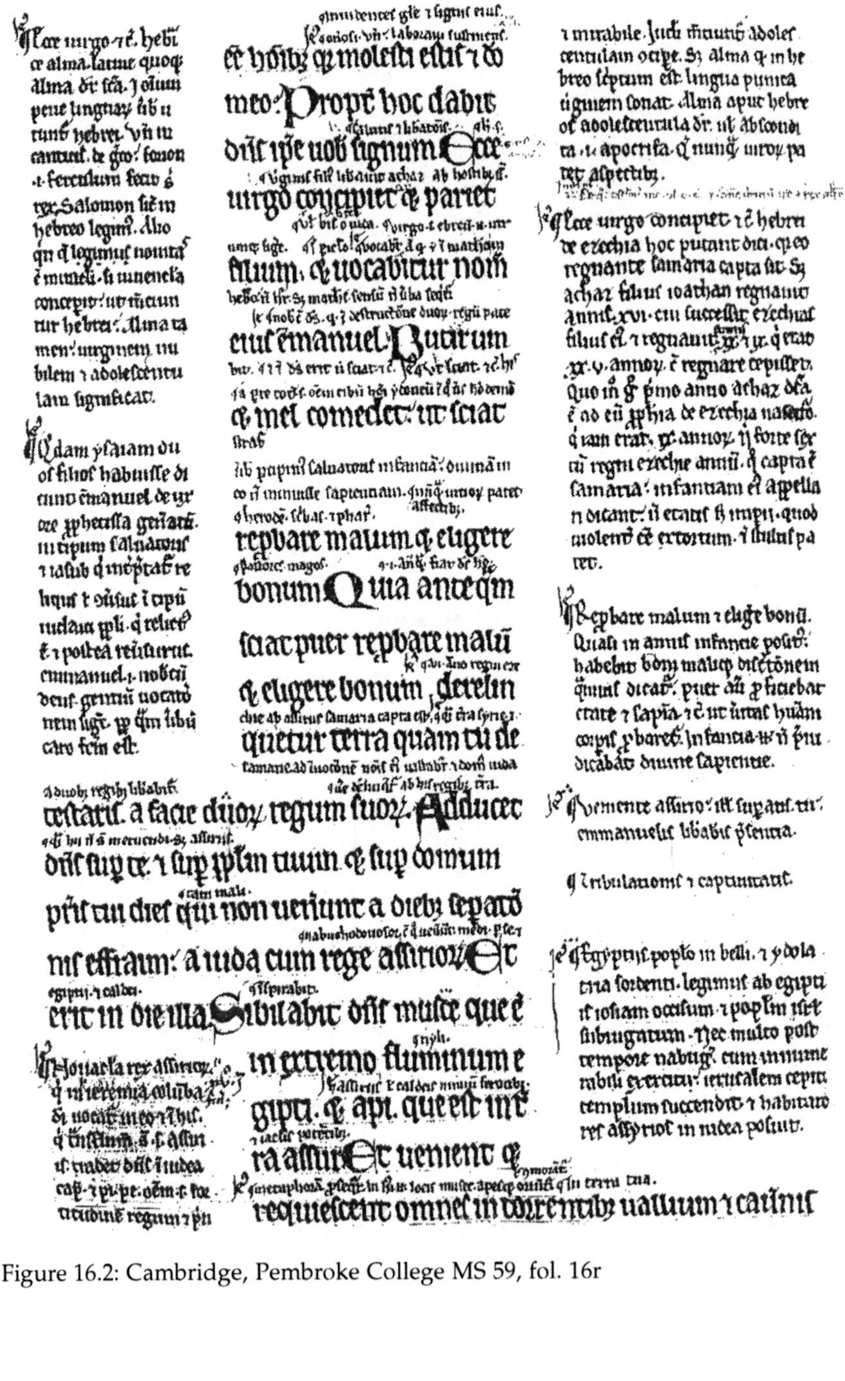

Figure 16.2: Cambridge, Pembroke College MS 59, fol. 16r

ith the words: אשמנו, בגדנו, גזלנו, דברנו דופי ('we sin, we betray, we steal, we speak
ander'). The Latin manuscript itself is the book of Isaiah glossed largely with
rome's *Commentariorum in Esaiam*, directed at the Jews and 'Judaizers' of his
ay. In Jerome's prologue to this work, which he wrote to the 'virgin of Christ'
ustochium, he explains that Isaiah is not just a prophet, but also an evangelist
nd an apostle, as demonstrated by his passage on the birth of Emmanuel to the
irgin. Figure 16.2 shows the Emmanuel prophecy itself as it appears on fol. 16r
f the Bury glossed Isaiah, framed by Jerome's commentary directed to Jews,
efending his translation of *'alma* as 'virgin'. The Hebrew binding is intended
s a concrete illustration of Jerome's ideas: Hebrew is the husk containing the
uit of Latin Christian Truth. The Bury monks who put the manuscript together
erhaps even understood the nature of the Hebrew atonement liturgy as a Jewish
dmission of sin within the Christian narrative, related to the admonitions of the
vangelist' prophet Isaiah.

The Isaiah manuscript has traditionally been assigned to after 1190, when the
ews were expelled from Bury under Abbot Samson, presumably leaving some
ooks behind; yet it could just as likely date from earlier in the century, when Jews
ill lived near the abbey. As Rodney Thomson has argued, the books acquired
r the library of Bury from the time of Abbot Hugh I (1156–80) on represent a
onscious program' of interest in the learning of the Paris schools, including not
ıst the entire glossed Bible, but works by Hugh of St Victor, Peter Comestor,
ilbert de la Porrée and Stephen Langton.[34] Part of the abbey's programme, even
 it assumed these authors' interest in the Hebrew Bible, emphatically strove to
eep the Hebrew language in the same place as it is in *Le Jeu d'Adam:* under
raps and under foot.

R. M. Thomson, 'The Library of Bury St. Edmunds Abbey in the Eleventh and Twelfth
Centuries', *Speculum* 47 (1972), 617–45.

17

Salerno on the Thames:
The Genesis of Anglo–Norman Medical Literature

Monica H. Green

Over the past two decades, Tony Hunt has edited nearly half the corpus of the
Anglo-Norman medical texts and recipe collections surveyed by Ruth Dean in
1999.[1] Although the recipes – whose sources are inherently difficult to trace
no matter what language they are written in – represent a diverse array of
learned and 'popular' origins, Hunt's detailed researches make clear that all of
the major texts he edited were direct translations of Latin works. As a medical
historian specializing in Latin medical literature, I can confirm from the broader
Western European perspective the now common view that Anglo-Norman was
'precocious'. Aside from a collection of Hebrew medical translations (all, apparently, the work of a single translator working in southern France between 1197
and 1199) and an apparently isolated translation of Roger Frugardi's *Chirurgia*
(*Surgery*) into Occitan in 1209, the Anglo-Norman works appear to be the earliest
vernacular medical writings since the translations into Anglo-Saxon in the tenth
and eleventh centuries, themselves a unique phenomenon.[2] Although the Old
French medical corpus has yet to be adequately surveyed, at the moment no

---

1   Dean nos. 406–41 (items 439 and 440 are generic headings of recipes and charms; item
    441 is not medical, despite its title, *De Generaus Medecines*), which includes references
    to Hunt's many publications: see also: T. Hunt, 'Old French Translations of Medical
    Texts', *FMLS* 35 (1999), 350–7; T. Hunt, 'Code-Switching in Medical Texts', in Trotter
    Multilingualism, pp. 131–47; T. Hunt, *Three Receptaria from Medieval England*, Medium
    Aevum Monographs, n.s. 21 (Oxford, 2001); and T. Hunt, 'Les Pronostics en anglo-
    normand: Méthodes et documents', in *Moult obscures paroles: Etudes sur la prophétie
    médiévale*, ed. R. Trachsler, J. Abed and D. Expert, Cultures et Civilisations Médiévales
    39 (Paris, 2007), pp. 29–50. I have not been able to consult E. Valentine, 'An Edition
    of the Anglo-Norman Content of Five Medical Manuscripts of the Fourteenth and
    Fifteenth centuries' (unpublished Ph.D. thesis, University of Exeter, 1990).
2   On the anonymous Jewish translator, see R. Barkaï, *A History of Jewish Gynaecological
    Texts in the Middle Ages* (Leiden, 1998), pp. 24–8. On the Anglo-Saxon corpus, see most
    recently M. A. D'Aronco, 'How "English" is Anglo-Saxon Medicine? The Latin Sources
    for Anglo-Saxon Medical Texts', in *Britannia Latina: Latin in the Culture of Great Britain
    from the Middle Ages to the Twentieth Century*, ed. C. Burnett and N. Mann, Warburg
    Institute Colloquia 8 (London, 2005), 27–41; and D. Banham, 'A Millennium in Medi-
    cine? New Medical Texts and Ideas in England in the Eleventh Century', in *Anglo-
    Saxons: Studies Presented to Cyril Roy Hart*, ed. S. Keynes, A. P. Smyth and C. R. Hart
    (Dublin, 2006), pp. 230–42.

other vernacular tradition would seem to match the amount of material avail-able in Anglo-Norman until the fourteenth century. Both the Anglo-Saxon and the Anglo-Norman corpora, moreover, share a central characteristic: they make a fundamentally Mediterranean system of medicine accessible to readers (and auditors) in the north.

The Anglo-Saxon and Anglo-Norman translators were able to accomplish this in part because outside southern Italy itself (whence much of the Latin litera-ture derived) few other places in Western Europe had, at least in the twelfth century, so large a presence of Latin medical literature in their monastic houses, cathedrals and (perhaps) courts as did England. In fact, viewed from the wider European perspective of Latin literature, England is distinctive in the breadth of the materials from which translators could have drawn but apparently did not. Again, comparing the known Anglo-Norman corpus to the output of that lone Jewish translator in southern France, all the texts that were rendered into Hebrew are known to have been available in England and Normandy at the same time: Constantine's *Pantegni*, the *Articella* texts, the so-called *Macer floridus* (*De viribus herbarum*), etc. There are in Anglo-Norman none of the major works of theory or medical encyclopedias. We will never know, of course, how many Anglo-Norman medical texts once existed but now have left no trace. The interests reflected in the Anglo-Norman texts we have nevertheless suggest less concern to make a 'foreign' body of medical texts available in their totality than to make certain kinds of material accessible to particular audiences.

The Latin medical corpus of the 'long twelfth century'

I am currently engaged on a general history of the so-called medical school of Salerno in the twelfth century. Salerno – among other places in southern Italy – was a hub from which a large body of new medical writings emerged over the course of the 'long twelfth century', that is, from *c.*1075 to *c.*1225. At Salerno it is clear that, for the first time since late Antiquity, regularized theoretical training was being offered, with a core curriculum of texts and scholastic habits of exegesis and glossing. In order to assess what is uniquely Salernitan (or at least southern Italian) about the twelfth-century Renaissance as it pertains to medi-cine, I have been compiling a handlist of all Latin manuscripts from anywhere in Western Europe that date from this 'long' twelfth century and contain medical writings (375 codices to date, and at least 145 distinct texts). The central role that England and the northern Norman realms played in twelfth-century medicine can be gauged by the fact that at least 25 per cent of these codices seem to have been produced in England or northern France. Of the 145 distinct texts, at least ninety – well over half – are represented in insular or northern French copies.

In one respect England and Normandy may have been even more richly endowed with medical literature than southern Italy itself. In a recent essay, I noted a peculiarity in the circulation of the new twelfth-century Salernitan texts of praxis. For Salernitan works of theory – primarily the so-called *Articella* texts and their commentaries, but also works such as anatomical treatises – a fairly broad circulation pattern can be found, both chronologically and geographically. Thus it is that copies of the *Articella* texts (the *Isagoge* of Hunayn ibn Ishaq, the Hippocratic *Aphorisms* and *Prognostics*, the *De pulsibus* of Philaretus, the *De urinis* of Theophilus, and later the *Megategni* of Galen) that date from every quarter of the twelfth century are to be found in central France, Germany, northern Italy and England. Nearly all the Salernitan works of praxis, however, which constitute the bulk of Salernitan production in the twelfth century, are found only in late twelfth-century copies (no matter their date of composition). And they are primarily copies of northern origin, from England or northern France.[3] Indeed, for many of these texts, we have no southern Italian exemplars at all, and were it not for certain key elements suggesting southern Italian origin (e.g. unique elements of *materia medica* with Arabic names and preparations such as syrups), it would be nearly impossible to tell, on the basis of the manuscript evidence, that 'Salerno' was not on the Thames! One need only look at the 1202 catalogue of Rochester Cathedral with its twenty-nine different medical texts – including many of the major early medieval, Constantinian, and Salernitan texts, as well as a 'Medicinale anglice' – to get a sense of how deeply southern Italian medicine had saturated the English landscape.[4]

The rapidity with which works were moving from southern Italy to England can be seen with the *Chirurgia* (*Surgery*) of Roger Frugardi. This is an unusual Salernitan text in that it is precisely dated: *anno ab incarnatione domini mclxx regnante gloriosissimo rege Guillermo feliciter*, i.e., the Sicilian king William II (r. 1166–89).[5] The *Chirurgia* differs from many other Salernitan texts of praxis in that it *is* found in southern Italian copies – and early ones at that. But its quick circulation to England is also clear: a *Cyrurgia magistri Rogeri* shows up in the catalogue of the Premonstratensian Abbey of St James at Welbeck in Nottinghamshire in the 1190s, and another copy (here called *Liber cirurgiae magistri Rogeri Salernitani*) is found at Durham Cathedral by the end of the century. To be sure, the first known translation of Roger's *Chirurgia* comes from the south of France, a verse translation into Occitan made by Raimon d'Avignon in 1209.[6] But while the Old

3   M. H. Green, 'Rethinking the Manuscript Basis of Salvatore De Renzi's *Collectio Salernitana*: The Corpus of Medical Writings in the "Long" Twelfth Century', in *La 'Collectio Salernitana' di Salvatore De Renzi*, ed. D. Jacquart and A. Paravicini Bagliani, Edizione Nazionale 'La Scuola medica Salernitana' III (Florence, 2008), pp. 15–60.

4   R. Sharpe, et al., *English Benedictine Libraries: The Shorter Catalogues*, CBMLC 4 (London, 1996), pp. 523–5.

5   H. Valls, 'Studies on Roger Frugardi's *Chirurgia*' (unpublished Ph.D. dissertation, University of Toronto, 1995), p. 5.

6   For more on Roger, see Green, 'Rethinking the Manuscript Basis'. On the Occitan translation, see L. Paterson, 'La médecine en Occitanie avant 1250', in *Actes du Premier Congrès International de l'Association Internationale d'Etudes Occitanes*, ed. P. T. Ricketts (London, 1987), pp. 383–99; and *eadem*, 'Military Surgery: Knights, Sergeants, and Raimon of Avignon's Version of the *Chirurgia* of Roger of Salerno (1180–1209)', in *The Ideals and Practice of Medieval Knighthood II*, Papers from the 3rd Strawberry Hill Conference, ed. C. Harper-Bill and R. Harvey (Woodbridge, 1988), pp. 117–46.

rench and Anglo-Norman translations are not precisely datable, they were defi-
itely made by the middle of the thirteenth century when they both appear in the
ingle manuscript that now documents their existence.[7]

Finding that there were ties between England and southern Italy is hardly
urprising given the common Norman domination of the Regno, Normandy,
nd England. An often-cited litany of literary evidence shows awareness of
outhern Italian (and particularly Salernitan) medicine by Norman and Anglo-
lorman writers: Orderic Vitalis' story of Ralph 'the Ill-Tonsured', a member of
 powerful Norman family who was 'so skilled in medicine that in the city of
alerno, which is the ancient seat of the best medical schools, no one could equal
im except one very learned woman'; Marie de France's *Les Deuz Amanz*, where
ne protagonist refers to a female relative she has in Salerno, 'who has been there
or more than thirty years and who has practised the art of physic so much that
he is well-versed in medicines'; Chrétien de Troyes's *Cligès* with its depiction of
nree ineffectual Salernitan physicians who are unable to rouse the 'dead' Fenice;
nd, in the thirteenth century, the Parisian poet Rutebeuf's wicked parody of the
alernitan healer Trota. Knowledge of the medical activities at Salerno is amply
ocumented from Adelard of Bath (d. *c.*1150) to John of Salisbury (d. 1180) to
iervase of Tilbury (d. *c.*1222), whether or not they actually travelled there them-
elves. A variety of other English bureaucrats and scholars were employed at, or
ssociated with, the Norman Sicilian court: Robert of Selby (fl. 1137–51), chan-
ellor under Roger II; Thomas Brown (d. 1180), possibly Roger's *capellanus regis*;
ichard Palmer (d. 1195), archbishop of Messina, and so on.[8] Diplomatic ties
etween southern Italy and Normandy and England continued right through
ne end of the twelfth century: both Eleanor of Aquitaine and her son Richard the
ion-hearted are said to have stopped there on their journeys to the Holy Land,
nd in 1177, after some back-and-forth negotiations, Eleanor's daughter (and
ichard's sister) Joanna married William II of Sicily. Just who was responsible
or ferrying all this medical literature up to the North is not yet clear, though for
ne moment the answer is immaterial. Clearly, Normandy and England benefited
ichly from these southern Italian ties.

Generating Anglo-Norman medicine: for whom and why?

lunt has characterized the Anglo-Norman medical corpus as falling into two
ategories: either 'popular' works (by which he means recipe collections largely
evoid of any theoretical elements that explained the causes of disease) or

Both are edited in T. Hunt, *Anglo-Norman Medicine*, 2 vols. (Cambridge, 1994–7), I,
45–136, 137–45.
C. H. Haskins, 'England and Sicily in the Twelfth Century', *EHR* 26 (1911), 433–47,
641–65, esp. pp. 435–8; and entries for all these individuals in *ODNB*. See also G. A.
Loud, 'Il regno normanno-svevo visto dal regno d'Inghilterra', in *Il Mezzogiorno
normanno-svevo visto dall'Europa e dal mondo mediterraneo: Atti delle tredicesime giornate
normanno-sveve, Bari, 21–24 ottobre 1997*, ed. G. Musca (Bari, 1999), pp. 175–95.

'learned' (those that not simply describe therapy but also discuss causes and symptoms).[9] We can well imagine two different kinds of readers, for each of whom the attractions of the vernacular may have been somewhat different. On the one hand, when it came time to prepare medicines to treat the sick, one needed to know exactly what herb or plant was called for, in what amounts, and how to prepare it. For anyone with less than full command of Latin technical medical vocabulary, only the vernacular would have been truly intelligible. If used as 'self-help' resources, we can perhaps imagine that lay people formed the principal audiences of recipe collections (and we should surely include many clerics under the heading 'lay' with respect to medicine). On the other hand, the vernacular may have been attractive to medical practitioners who are increasingly documented taking on specialist identities in England in the twelfth and thirteenth centuries, with books both informing them and adding to their social prestige.[10] In at least one case, there was a particular audience that straddled this boundary between 'self-help' and those practitioners desirous of a more theoretical engagement with medicine: laywomen who were concerned to take care of their own medical needs.

It is not at all unusual for multiple renditions of the same text to be known for medieval medical translations. There are, for example, at least nineteen different translations of Roger Frugardi's twelfth-century *Chirurgia* into a total of seven different languages; six translations are into Hebrew alone. Such duplication of effort probably arose from the fact that translations were often made for personal use only, or for a particular recipient, and so did not circulate far beyond the circle in which they were produced. It may be simply a factor of poor survival but Anglo-Norman is unusual in that, save for a portion of Johannes Platearius' *Practica brevis*, which is found in two versions,[11] only one Latin text was translated multiple times: the *Liber de sinthomatibus mulierum* (Book on the Conditions of Women), a work that circulated on its own in Latin before being used as the opening piece of the so-called *Trotula* ensemble. This is documented in four Anglo-Norman versions.[12] That means that of the seven distinct translations of

---

9   Hunt, *Anglo-Norman Medicine*, I, v.

10 On the increasing adoption of *medicus* as a self-identifier in the twelfth century, see E. J. Kealey, *Medieval Medicus: A Social History of Anglo-Norman Medicine* (Baltimore, 1981); on the role of literacy and book-ownership in the processes of professionalization, see M. H. Green, *Making Women's Medicine Masculine: The Rise of Male Authority in Pre-Modern Gynaecology* (Oxford, 2008), Introduction.

11 See Hunt, *Anglo-Norman Medicine*, I, 147–315; and T. Hunt, 'An Anglo-Norman Medical Treatise: The *Gardein du Cors*', in *The Editor and the Text*, ed. P. E. Bennett and G. A. Runnalls (Edinburgh, 1990), pp. 145–64.

12 To the three Anglo-Norman translations of the *Liber de sinthomatibus mulierum* identified in M. H. Green, 'A Handlist of the Latin and Vernacular Manuscripts of the So-Called *Trotula* Texts. Part II: The Vernacular Texts and Latin Re-Writings', *Scriptorium* 51 (1997), 80–104 (pp. 89–90, 92–3), add to the copies of *Quant Dex nostre Seignor* ('Handlist', pp. 90–2), formerly known only from Continental copies, the following Anglo-Norman copy: London, Public Record Office, MS E 163/22/2/1, s. xiii (England?), fol. 1r–v. *inc* 'Devs nostre sire quant ont le siecle estore des autres creatures.' A one-leaf fragment

the *Trotula* into medieval French, more than half were either made directly into Anglo-Norman or circulated in Norman England. (The other three French translations are of fourteenth- or fifteenth-century origin and are documented only on the Continent.) Also part of the Salernitan *Trotula* tradition was material on cosmetics, and we find in Anglo-Norman two texts on cosmetics, both of which clearly derive from southern Italian materials.

What is most intriguing about these six Anglo-Norman texts on women's medicine is not simply that they are topically about women, but that they are (at least nominally) *addressed* to women. This is in contrast to all but one of the half-dozen Latin texts on women's medicine (including cosmetics) that came into circulation in the eleventh and twelfth centuries and the three Hebrew gynaecological and cosmetic texts translated from Latin at the end of the twelfth century in southern France.[13] One Anglo-Norman translation of the *Liber de sinthomatibus mulierum*, called *Secrés de femmes*, is couched as a sermon directed at both a male and a female listening audience. It takes the sections of the *Liber de sinthomatibus mulierum* (or its Urtext, the *Tractatus de egritudinibus mulierum*) specifically devoted to generation and moulds them into instructions for married couples on how to conduct themselves sexually so as to ensure good coupling and healthy offspring. Beginning with a fulmination against the fertility-inhibiting effects of male homosexuality, the text later addresses passages directly to women: 'Lay the wool [dipped] in the milk of a she-ass ... upon your navel tightly. Afterwards

presenting the opening of the text (equals Latin edition, ¶¶1–9), it is bound within a volume of Exchequer records (King's Remembrancer: Miscellanea of the Exchequer). It was edited by A. E. R. Davis (unpublished M.Phil. thesis, Lincoln College, Oxford, 2002), which I have not yet been able to examine. My thanks to Theresa Tyers for providing me with a copy of the text, and to Jocelyn Wogan-Browne for confirming its Anglo-Norman character. A sixth copy of the text, likewise identified since I published my handlist in 1997, may have also been Anglo-Norman: London, formerly in the Thomas Phillipps collection, MS 1109, s. xiv ex. (England), fols. 8r (–11v?). See *Catalogue of Thirty-Nine Manuscripts of the 9th to the 16th Century from the celebrated collection formed by Sir Thomas Phillipps (1792–1872), the Property of the Trustees of the Robinson Trust, which will be sold by auction by Messrs Sotheby & Co. ... Tuesday, 30 November 1965* (London, 1965), pp. 62–3. The Sotheby's catalogue gave the title as *Liber Galieni de sinchomatibus mulierum, inc.*: Dieux nostre sire quant out le munde estoree. ... Other contents, in French: *Liber Ypocratis de aquis; Ars flebotomandi per venas.* In Latin: text on urines; *Practica maior, media, et minor* of Roger de Barone; *Circa instans*; Platearius, *Summa; Antidotarium Nicholai*; a quid pro quo and various remedies. The first documented owner is Richard Nix, bishop of Norwich (1501–35), in 1512. This manuscript was sold at Sotheby's in London, 30 November 1965; its current whereabouts are unknown.

13 On the Jewish gynaecological treatises – all translated by the same southern French Jew mentioned above in n.2 – see Barkaï, *History of Jewish Gynaecological Texts*; and particularly on the Hebrew *Trotula*, see Carmen Caballero Navas, 'Algunos "secretos de mujeres" revelados: El Šeʾar yašub y la recepción y transmisión del *Trotula* en hebreo [Some "secrets of women" revealed. The *Sheʾar yašub* and the reception and transmission of the *Trotula* in Hebrew]', *Miscelánea de estudios Árabes y Hebraicos, sección Hebreo* 55 (2006), 381–425.

lie down with your lord in bed, [and] you and he perform your will together.'[14] The treatise *Quant Dex nostre Seignor*, probably also translated in the first half of the thirteenth century, is addressed in its entirety to women. Beginning with the summary of God's creation of male and female that had opened the Latin text, this translation then turns the original Latin's claim that women are reluctant to reveal their diseases to male physicians into an explicit call for a text women can use themselves: 'And because women are more ashamed to discuss their *cuvinie*[15] with men than with women, I have made this little book in a language they know well.'[16] This prose text was rendered into Anglo-Norman verse by the mid thirteenth century at the latest. This latter work (which I refer to by its incipit, *Bien sachiés femmes*) reorients the text toward a masculine audience. It begins with what seems an unambiguous address to women, but then immediately switches its perspective:

> Women, you may be certain that here is truly written [women's] knowledge about having children and giving birth. Everything is here divulged about their [*lur*] secrets. ... Here they [*eles*] will certainly find out / What causes these diseases and how they are healed.[17]

There is some dissonance here. That initial direct address ('Bien sachiés, femmes') is in fact a feint, for from the moment it refers to '[women's] knowledge' and 'their secrets', women become the object of discussion, not participants in a dialogue. They are 'they', not 'you'. Rather, it is clear that the text has become a vehicle by which male *mires*, *escolers* and *clers* can take instruction

---

14 *Secrés dé femmes* (Dean no. 424, 'Obstetrics'), Cambridge, Trinity College, MS O.1.20, fol. 22va: 'En lait d'<e> anesse laine o tot les somellons / Sor vostre nomblil estreit tresbien le liez. / Apré[s] a vostre baron en .i. lit coucherez, / Vous et il ensemble vos volentés facez.' The phrase 'o tot les somellons' ('with all the tips [presumably of some kind of plant]') makes no sense here. Perhaps it was transposed from another place in the text.

15 Perhaps a form of *cuvine* (AND online, accessed 8 July 2008, s.v.), here possibly in the sense of 'sexual matters'.

16 *Quant Dex nostre Seignor*, London, Public Record Office, MS E 163/22/2/1, s. xiii (England), fol. 1r: 'E de co que femmes sunt plus huntuses de dire lur cuuinie a hummes que a femmes. Si faz cest livret el language quels mieuz sevent. e si autres en cest livrer eo que io sai plus besuignable dez diz ypocras. & Galien. & Cleopatre. & Costentin. dunt les maus viennent & cument & ose ___ hom. & coment enguarist.' This passage reads somewhat differently in the contemporary copy made in or near Paris, London, British Library, MS Sloane 3525, fols. 246v–247r: 'Et pour ce ke femes sunt plus huntuses de dire lor enfermetez as homes ke as femes, si lor fax icest liure en language ke eles lentendent, que les unes sachent les autres aidier. Bien sachent que ie i met del mielz ke lor besoigne a lor enfermetez, que ie ai troue des diz Ypocras et Galien et Costentin et Cleopatras, et ici troueront dont li mal uienent et comant porront guarir.' For the original Latin text, see Green, *Making Women's Medicine Masculine*, pp. 50–1.

17 *Bien sachiés femmes* (Dean no. 422, 'Gynecology'), Cambridge, Trinity College, MS O.1.20 (1044), s. xiii² (England), fols. 216r–235v, edited in Hunt, *Anglo-Norman Medicine*, II, 76–107, lines 1–4, 11–12.

reflecting a process of masculinization of women's medicine that was being
plicated elsewhere in Europe.[18] The fourth Anglo-Norman version of the *Liber*
sinthomatibus mulierum (which I refer to by its incipit *Si com Aristotele nous dit*)
ems to claim a female audience and, simultaneously, tries to warn away a male
1e; this, too, would replicate a common rhetorical trope in later medieval texts
women's medicine.[19] The composition date of the *Si com Aristotele* is unclear;
is known only from a single fourteenth-century copy, though it is unlikely that
placement here amid mostly Latin scientific texts reflects its original context
circulation.

The idea that some element of Anglo-Norman medical literature started off in
e early or mid thirteenth century as a feminized phenomenon is indicated by
e cosmetic texts as well, both of which clearly date from the thirteenth century.
he genre of the prescriptive cosmetic treatise seems to have been initiated in
atin by the author of the Salernitan *De ornatu mulierum*, a work of perhaps the
id-twelfth century, which covered various aspects of female cosmetics from
re of the hair and face to the genitalia. The anonymous Salernitan author saw
s immediate audience as other male practitioners, like himself, who wished
earn 'either glory or a delightful multitude of friends' not by giving knowl-
dge of beauty treatments directly to women, but by having them come *to him*
r diagnosis and instruction.[20] While his text was never translated in its inde-
endent form, it or similar collections of Salernitan cosmetic instructions seem
directly to have spawned the two Anglo-Norman cosmetic texts. One is a
quence of more or less random beauty treatments in 172 octosyllabic verses,
ymed in couplets. Composed in the early or mid-thirteenth century, the poem
addressed to 'any woman, be she lady or maid, who wishes to have a beau-
ful face' ('La quele, que soit dame ou pucele, / Ki desire avoir la face bele').[21]
milarly the *Ornatus mulierum*, a treatise with a versified prologue in twenty-
ree couplets followed by a prose text, examines various facets of cosmetic treat-
ents. It was composed sometime in or before the second half of the thirteenth
ntury, and is addressed to 'women of nowadays' so that 'you yourselves can

See further Green, *Making Women's Medicine Masculine*, pp. 170–2.
Si com Aristotele nous dit (Dean no. 423, 'Menstruation'), Cambridge, Trinity College, MS O.2.5 (1109), s. xiv¹ (England), fols. 123rb–124va. See Green, *Making Women's Medicine Masculine*, pp. 173–4.
For a general description of the *De ornatu mulierum*, see M. H. Green, 'The Development of the *Trotula*', *Revue d'Histoire des Textes* 26 (1996), 119–203 (pp. 139–43). On authorship and audience claims, see Green, *Making Women's Medicine Masculine*, pp. 45–8.
The treatise beginning 'La quele, que soit dame ou pucele' (which Dean refers to as 'Cosmetics', no. 425) has elements in common with the Salernitan *De ornatu mulierum*, but it is not a direct translation. See J. R. Gilleland, 'Eight Anglo-Norman Cosmetic Recipes: MS. Cambridge, Trinity College 1044', *Romania* 109 (1988), 50–67. Most of these are also found within the *Physique rimee* in Cambridge, St John's College, MS D.4 (James 79), fols. 83rb–99rb. Both versions are edited in T. Hunt, *Popular Medicine in Thirteenth-Century England: Introduction and Texts* (Cambridge, 1990), pp. 204–7, 215–16.

preserve your beauty and even increase it'.[22] A creative reworking of miscella
neous southern Italian lore, this text cites as its sources Dame Trote (ten times
a 'Saracen' woman of Messina (eight times), the 'ladies of Salerno' (twice), and
lady of Pontremoli, a *vetula*, the ladies of Apulia, the countess of Gurney, and on
unnamed woman (once each). Although the author claims offhandedly to hav
drawn on the works of Galen, Constantine and Hippocrates, he asserts forcefull
that most of what he knows he has learned directly from the 'Saracen' woman i
Messina and from Trota in Salerno. This author, therefore, has not simply relie
on southern Italian informants (whether textual or personal or even imaginar
does not really matter here), but wishes to claim the southern Italian authen
ticity of his work as its chief marketing point. As he says, 'whatever lady doesn
believe [that the Saracen woman and Trota have been his teachers] is a fool'.[23]

What scenario could have given rise to these six texts addressed to womer
Given what we are beginning to learn about women's culture in the courts c
the twelfth and thirteenth centuries, we can well imagine female patronesses c
vernacular literature who had the authority and the wish to commission work
like these for their own use.[24] In her final index, Ruth Dean lists known commis
sioners or dedicatees of Anglo-Norman texts. Nearly half (twenty-six) of th
sixty names are female. The way in which the *Ornatus mulierum* in particula
sets up certain fictions about transmitting women's knowledge of cosmetics ma
reflect an only slightly embellished image of real lines of communication amon
aristocratic women in Northern and Southern Europe. Indeed, as I have argue
elsewhere, it may have been such interest *coming from England* that inspired a
unknown scribe to sit down in Salerno and transcribe the teachings of the fame
practitioner Trota into her work on women's medicine, the *De curis mulierun*
True, that Latin text, which incorporated three Anglo-Saxon words as glosse
and which is only documented, in its original form, in insular manuscripts, is nc
known in any Anglo-Norman redaction.[25] But if we are looking for evidence c
particular *feminine* interests in medicine, the Latin *De curis mulierum*, which wa
clearly composed to instruct a female audience, shows that such interests coul
be found in England already in the first half of the twelfth century.

---

[22] *L'Ornement des Dames (Ornatus mulierum): Texte anglo-normande du XIIIe siècle. Le pl*
ancien recueil en français de recettes médicales pour les soins du visage, publié avec une intr
duction, une traduction, des notes et un glossaire, ed. P. Ruelle (Bruxelles, 1967), p. 23. Th
text is known only from Oxford, Bodleian Library, MS Ashmole 1470 (SC 7005), s. xiii
fols. 276ra–279vb.

[23] *L'Ornement*, ed. Ruelle, p. 34. The other contents of the manuscript (Oxford, Bodleia
Library, MS Ashmole 1470 (SC 7005), s. xiii²) are Latin Salernitan medical texts.

[24] Short, 'Patrons and Polyglots'; and the essay by Tyler in this volume.

[25] On the genesis of the *De curis mulierum* and its Anglo-Saxon terms – *chinke, digg*
and *gladene* – see Green, 'Development of the *Trotula*', pp. 135–8; and Green, *Makin*
Women's Medicine Masculine, pp. 53–8, 62–3, 66. For the genesis of Trota's writing
and her 'international' reputation, see also M. H. Green, 'Reconstructing the *Oeuvre* c
Trota of Salerno', in *La Scuola medica Salernitana: Gli autori e i testi*, ed. D. Jacquart an
A. Paravicini Bagliani, Edizione Nazionale 'La Scuola medica Salernitana' I (Florenc
2007), pp. 183–233.

Thinking trilingually (and quadrilingually)

From the perspective of the Anglo-Normanist, the medical corpus is far from impressive. We do not know the name of a single translator, and aside from the verse adaptation of the earlier prose *Quant Dex nostre seignor* discussed above, there are few connections (stylistic or otherwise) that link any one Anglo-Norman medical text to any others. If there was a coherent 'translating plan' behind any of these works – such as may have motivated the Old English translations associated with King Alfred, or the programmes of works translated from Arabic to Latin in Spain or from Latin to Hebrew in southern France in the twelfth century – none seems to be apparent now. None of the texts is dated or even roughly datable beyond inferences that can be made paleographically from the manuscripts. Several texts are incomplete and few seem to be particularly noteworthy in terms of their literary style. Nevertheless, this corpus of writings merits study.

In her fascinating essay in this volume, Elizabeth Tyler makes the point that the Anglo-Norman corpus of historical writings takes on a new dimension when seen from the perspective of the Anglo-Saxonist. In the field of medicine, a glance at the Anglo-Saxon tradition is enlightening, too, though as much for its contrasts as for its similarities. The Anglo-Saxon medical corpus reflects a ninth- and tenth-century revival of Latin medical texts that had been circulating since late Antiquity. The Anglo-Norman corpus, in contrast, which begins unceremoniously with a group of recipes from the end of the twelfth century,[26] jumps immediately to the twelfth-century Salernitan corpus as its basis and, as I have indicated above, eschews the large quantity of theoretical works (a genre of medical writing that the Anglo-Saxon corpus had tentatively embraced) in favour of empirical remedies stripped of theory that could be used for self-help by laypersons, and works of praxis that could aid the general practitioner or surgeon. These differences raise the question whether there is any meaningful connection between Anglo-Saxon and Anglo-Norman medicine at all. Tony Hunt, who has worked most extensively on the Anglo-Norman medical texts, has several times expressed his opinion that many of the earliest works derive from continental exemplars, in which case it would seem futile to look for any connections with earlier Anglo-Saxon precedents.[27] Nevertheless, Hunt feels comfortable assigning the translation of Roger Frugardi's *Chirurgia* to England, and his arguments against insular origin for several other texts hinge on employment of a single word of Germanic origin.

My present concern is not to press the debate between insular and continental origins, but rather to raise a different question: 'What happened to Anglo-Saxon medical terminology?' In any culture, the names of plants, diseases and body parts reflect generations of investment in making meaning of the natural world, and I know of no medieval medical translation project where the intel-

[26] T. Hunt, 'The Medical Recipes in MS. Royal 5 E. vi', *Notes and Queries* 231 (1986), 6–9.
[27] E.g. Hunt, *Anglo-Norman Medicine*, I, v, 21, 160–1; II, 12–14.

lectual investment in finding or creating equivalent terms was not huge. Was Anglo-Norman already so rich in medical terminology that translators as well as medical practitioners could blithely toss away the investments made by the earlier Anglo-Saxons? This seems a great and pressing question, and Tony Hunt has once again laid a path by editing many of the synonymies that performed the crucial work of this cultural 'translation' and by noting the importance of code-switching and various glossing techniques that continued to make texts in one language intelligible to readers who, for one reason or another, still wanted to know what the terms referred to in another.[28] Notably, Anglo-Saxon medical terminology survives in the twelfth century in the form of glosses added to Latin texts as well as an extended Latin/Anglo-Saxon glossary that synthesized several earlier texts in the same genre. Although the latter includes no new terminology coming from Arabic medicine (sugar, for example, does not appear here) and very few French words, it is found in a manuscript from the first half of the twelfth century that brought important elements of the 'new' southern Italian medicine (including gynaecology) to England.[29]

To return, then, to the question with which I opened this essay: why, if so much medical material was available in England from the twelfth century on, was so little of it rendered into Anglo-Norman? The simple answer, I think, is that Latin remained the *lingua franca* of medical theory because it had been the language in which the 'new medicine' of the late eleventh and twelfth centuries arrived. After all, linguistic investments had already been made in Latin medical terminology by Constantine the African and other southern Italian translators and editors of the eleventh century, and by the many twelfth-century glossators and commentators who continued to attempt to render this new medicine intelligible. On this view, the great works of theory and analysis – Gariopontus' *Passionarius*, Ibn al-Jazzar's *Viaticum*, al-Majusi's *Pantegni*, even Hunayn ibn Ishaq's introductory book of medical theory, the *Isagoge* – would never have been seen as candidates for translation because there was no other language in which to render so many abstract concepts.

Why, then, make vernacular translations of the equally new Salernitan treatises of praxis: Roger Frugardi's *Chirurgia*, Johannes Platearius' *Practica brevis*, and the guidelines of professional deportment in Archimattheus' *De instructione medici*? Here we might see the impetus as more sociological than intellectual. Along with texts from the south also came notions of medicine as a profession. It is surely no coincidence that in writers like Chrétien de Troyes and Rutebeuf

---

28 T. Hunt, *Plant Names of Medieval England* (Cambridge, 1989); and Hunt, 'Code-switching in Medical Texts'.

29 Oxford, Bodleian Library, MS Laud misc. 567, s. xii[1] (England), fols. 67r–73r; the glossary is edited in J. R. Stracke, *The Laud Herbal Glossary* (Amsterdam, 1974). For a similar negotiation between Anglo-Saxon and Latin from this period, see the handsomely illustrated copy of the Latin pseudo-Apuleius and pseudo-Dioscorides *Ex herbis feminis* with 57 vernacular glosses, owned by St Augustine's, Canterbury (Oxford, Bodleian, MS Ashmole 1431, s. xi/xii).

e have satirical mocking of the pretensions of these new itinerant physicians. rather doubt that we should assume that complete lack of facility with Latin as the motive either for translating or for owning texts such as these, though it ould be good to have more evidence of how such vernacular texts were used.

The great puzzle remains how to explain the many recipe collections, most of hich are dizzyingly macaronic. This is the least studied field of medical writing nearly all vernaculars, and I do not pretend to be able to explain this amazing iversity of texts. But I wonder if the English tolerance for willy-nilly mixtures ' languages in recipe collections (something I have encountered to this degree no other vernacular tradition) might not stem from attempts to find work- le compromises between the still vital terminology of Anglo-Saxon with the ew language(s), new *materia medica*, and new therapeutic practices flooding into ngland at the same time that so many political changes were happening in the te eleventh and twelfth centuries.

Explaining the texts on women's medicine thus turns out to be the easiest art of this analysis. If (as I suspect) female patronage was behind the particular vestment in the gynaecological and cosmetic texts – a phenomenon of Anglo- orman that would not be duplicated in any other vernacular tradition until e fourteenth century – that may well be because women in Normandy or ngland, having become aware that texts on these subjects were being produced southern Italy, commissioned works 'in a language they know well'. The uant Dex nostre Seignor was still being directed at a female audience when it was ndered into Middle English in the late fourteenth century. Whether women's gagements with medical writing continued unabated in England for over three undred years cannot yet be determined. But the long-term effects of England's es with southern Italy and the role of multilingualism in those cultural transfers nnot be denied.[30]

For the Middle English text that employs *Quant Dex nostre Seignor*, see *The Knowing of Woman's Kind in Childing: A Middle English Version of Material Derived from the 'Trotula' and Other Sources*, ed. A. Barratt, Medieval Women: Texts and Contexts 4 (Turnhout, 2001). Only a third of the twenty-one vernacular translations of the *Trotula* were directed toward female audiences. On all of them, see Green, 'Handlist'; and Green, *Making Women's Medicine Masculine*, ch. 4.

Section III
After Lateran IV:
Francophone Devotions and Histories

INTRODUCTION

The richness of thirteenth-century French literary culture in England has been partly acknowledged in various ways, notably by scholars of Middle English romance, some of whom have long studied the interrelations between their texts and the francophone romances that precede and continue alongside them.[1] The field continues to be vigorous, but there is still much fascinating work to be done.[2] Beyond romance, still more work remains in integrating the large corpus of French devotional and doctrinal writing that both precedes the Fourth Lateran Council and intensifies after it. What was once supposed to be a period in which there was a gap in the production of vernacular pastoralia while English was 'underground' is in fact full of francophone texts. Jocelyn Wogan-Browne argues here for continuities in this reading culture from the thirteenth to the fifteenth centuries: there is no need to wait until the English texts of the late fourteenth century to investigate lay and clerical relations in the devotional and doctrinal vernacular texts produced in order to form the confessionally articulated self. Helen Deeming and Jean-Pascal Pouzet, working with the different broad corpora they have studied in depth (respectively, manuscripts with musical notation and manuscripts associated with the Augustinians), show how important the Frenchness of Latin clerical culture is in the religious writings of thirteenth-century England. Laurie Postlewate gives an account of the fascinating socio-political aspects of the writings of Nicolas Bozon, one of the most varied and prolific Franciscan friars writing in England, whose wide range of devotional, doctrinal and satirical works was composed in the late thirteenth

---

S. Crane (Dannenbaum), *Insular Romance: Politics, Faith and Culture in Anglo-Norman and Middle English Literature* (Berkeley, 1986); R. Field, 'Romance' in *The Oxford History of Literary Translation in English*, vol. 1, ed. Roger Ellis (Oxford, 2007), pp. 296–331; eadem, 'Romance in England, 1066–1400', in Wallace, *Medieval English Literature*, pp. 152–78; J. Weiss, *The Birth of Romance* (London, 1996), rev. and republ. as *The Birth of Romance in England*, FRETS 3 (Arizona, 2009). See, more recently, L. Ashe, ' "Exile-and-return" and English Law: The Anglo-Saxon Inheritance of Insular Romance', Literature *Compass* April 2006, http://www.blackwell-compass.com.

A recent paper by Thea Summerfield, for instance, argues that, in the Auchinleck Manuscript (often assumed to be a prototypically English and 'post' Anglo-Norman manuscript), Guinevere's 'franglais' response to a wooing Arthur signifies the French of *cortoisie* and constitutes a special *koiné within* English romance (itself aware of French – i.e. Anglo-Norman romance – as its intertext) rather than a citation of French as foreign. In the same manuscript, Inga of 'Espayne', the putative foundress of 'Ingland', announces herself in England in what is claimed as Spanish but is in fact Anglo-Norman. See Summerfield, 'Kings and Gentlemen, Saints and Saracens: Language Variety in Medieval English Romances', to be published in Putter and Jefferson, *Medieval Multilingualism*.

and early fourteenth centuries. Delbert Russell's study of Marie de St Pol, a la
patron operating on both sides of the Channel, and her early fourteenth-centur
version of the late twelfth-century life of Edward the Confessor produced by
nun of Barking links court and monastery, Capetian and Plantagenet inherit
ances and further demonstrates the diachronic continuity and internationalism
of England's francophone culture.

In the fourteenth century there is continuing circulation and composition i
French both insular and continental in varying genres, including romance an
epic, travel writing, lyric, pastoral and doctrinal, devotional, historiographic an
hagiographic texts.[3] Historians have contributed much to the study of Englis
courts and their francophone cultures, and valuable attention (continued i
Michael Bennett's essay on Anglo-French court culture in this volume) has bee
given to the cross-fertilization between England, France and the Low Countrie
that so largely uses French as its medium.[4] So too, some reassignation of textua
provenances has become possible: Bennett argues strongly for Mandeville'
travels as initially an insular text. But outside the prestigious circles of French
born and French speaking royal families in England and the elite among thei
immediate relatives and courtiers, the picture is less clear. Were such court
closed or open 'reading communities'? How far did wider literate social groups
less elite nobility and gentry, clerics, bureaucrats, professionals – see themselve
as allied with francophone elite culture, how far did they also sustain French
Julia Marvin's study of the vitality and longevity of the prose *Brut* compose
in Anglo-Norman around 1300 opens up some avenues to these wider readin
circles. The fourteenth century is the great century of the *Brut*, a hugely influen
tial shaping of most people's sense of origins and cultural geography in medi
eval England. Versions are extant in at least four languages (Anglo-Norman
Latin, English, Welsh with, additionally, continental French copies of the Anglo
Norman versions) and some 250 manuscripts (including insular fifteenth-centur
French manuscripts).[5] Through close attention to differing manuscript copies
Marvin shows how wide the class-range and the purposes of *Brut* readers coul
be. Twentieth-century work on the canonical texts of English literature has ofter
tended to set aside this important legendary history and its continuing multi
lingual career, but it is an inescapable feature of the cultural landscape. So to

[3] See e.g. M. Corrie 'Harley 2253, Digby 86, and the Circulation of Literature in Pre
Chaucerian England', in Fein, *Studies in the Harley Manuscript*, pp. 427–44.
[4] See also M. Vale, *The Princely Court: Medieval Courts and Culture in North-West Europe
1270–1380* (Oxford, 2001); A. Butterfield, *The Familiar Enemy*.
[5] On the *Brut* manuscripts, see L. M. Matheson, *The Prose 'Brut': The Development of
Middle English Chronicle* (Tempe AZ, 1998); for recent work on Middle English Bru
manuscripts, see W. Marx with R. Radulescu, *Readers and Writers of the Prose* Bru
Trivium 36 (Lampeter, 2006). On Anglo-Norman *Brut* manuscripts, see further Marvi
in this volume. For a valuable survey of Anglo-Norman prose historiography i
general, see John Spence, 'Anglo-Norman Prose Chronicles and Their Audiences', i
English Manuscript Studies, 1100–1700: XIV, Regional Manuscripts, ed. A. S. G. Edward
(London, 2008), pp. 27–59.

according to Nicholas Watson's argument here, fourteenth-century bible translation in Anglo-Norman remained alive but has been hidden from our current perspective as an effect of a fourteenth-century linguistic politics in which all but English vernacular bible translation was occluded, thus helping us to leave unchallenged our own assumptions about the bible and French in later medieval England.

Finally, Rebecca June's study of the register of Crabhouse nunnery in the fourteenth and fifteenth centuries forms a capstone for the themes of history, memory and forgetting important to this section: the forgettings and occlusions of our stereotypical narratives tend to posit the loss of an entire language in the adoption of another, while the evidence, as shown here, continues to suggest partial, varying and highly specific contexts for linguistic shifts and a rich cultural and literary scene.

18

'Cest livre liseez ... chescun jour': Women and Reading c.1230–c.1430

Jocelyn Wogan-Browne*

ιe changing emphases of vernacular pastoralia as they imagine and support
ϱ confessor's or the penitent's role are increasingly acknowledged as part of
:ulturally and politically charged reading history of great importance in late
ɹrteenth- and fifteenth-century Middle English studies.[1] A kind of reading
ɑt may be loosely characterized as penitential – reading conceived as a disci-
ɪned, interior scrutiny of the self in relation to the particular ontology of
ɪristian salvation history – remains a leading model of self-knowledge and
lf-fashioning in medieval culture from Lateran IV to Chaucer's *Parson's Tale*
d beyond. This essay argues that, like a number of other reading histories,
nitential reading cannot be adequately considered without due attention to
ϱ feminized francophone literary culture of the twelfth to thirteenth centuries
d its continuations and bequests in the later period. The resources represented
this literary culture, which, in England, preceded, contributed to and devel-
ᵉd the concerns of Lateran IV, have been largely overlooked.[2] The vernacular
sults of Lateran IV have been unproblematically accepted as arriving in the
ᵉ fourteenth century in the form of an 'efflorescence' of late medieval devo-
nal and doctrinal texts in Middle English, even though for the century and a
lf before that efflorescence it is French that is the dominant language of pasto-
ɪia and the formation of the self in England. A great deal of research remains
be done on the francophone devotional and doctrinal texts of women's (and
ᵣmen's) reading from the twelfth to the fifteenth centuries.[3]

I thank Christopher Baswell, Carolyn Collette and Elizabeth Tyler for generously
helpful readings of this material, initially given in a different form as the University
of York Riddy Lecture, 2006.

See e.g. K. C. Little, *Confession and Resistance: Defining the Self in Later Medieval England*
(Notre Dame IN, 2006).

For fourteenth-century occlusions of Anglo-Norman, see the essay by Watson in this
volume.

But see the essay by Postlewate in this volume; *'Cher alme': Religious Practice and Devotion in Anglo-Norman Piety*, ed. and trans. T. Hunt, J. Bliss and H. Leyser (FRETS OPS
1, forthcoming); M. B. M. Boulton, trans., *Piety and Persecution in the French of England*
(FRETS, forthcoming); C. Batt, trans., *Henry of Lancaster, The Book of Holy Medicines*
(FRETS, forthcoming).

Many women patrons and readers could be adduced here,[4] but I have chose
to represent this reading culture by close consideration of two iconic images
the thirteenth-century female penitent, from the Lambeth Apocalypse and fro
the guide for anchoresses known after one of its Middle English versions
Ancrene Wisse. It is here, on the thirteenth-century page, which is often a franc
phone page and a page produced for women, that we can see and feel somethir
of the impact of Lateran IV, what both church and laypeople did with it, ar
how the image of the female reader models the idea and modes of vernacul
penitential reading.

A striking image of a woman patron and reader is found in the *Lambe*
Apocalypse made either 1265–7 or 1271–4 for Lady Elena de Quincy (d. 127*
second wife of Roger de Quincy, earl of Winchester (d. 1264), or 1265–81 f
Lady Margaret de Ferrers (d. 1281), wife of William Ferrers, earl of Derl
(d. 1254).[5] Illustrated apocalypses, which began as part of monastic ruminatic
on the Bible, became a new genre of lay patronage in thirteenth-century Englan
customized and formatted for both clerical and lay users. As with psalters ar
books of hours, women were notable patrons and readers of these books.[6]
the end of *Lambeth's* lavishly illustrated Latin apocalypse text and commentar

---

4 On patronage, see the essays by Tyler and Russell in this volume; Short, 'Patrons ar
   Polyglots'; Gee, *Women, Art and Patronage*. For twelfth- and thirteenth-century exam
   ples, see Dean no. 79 (Alice de Curcy: *chanson de geste* /historiography); for doctrin
   and devotional texts, 458 (Alice de Condet), 451–2 (Laurette d'Alsace), 558 (Dan
   Mahaut), 589 (Lady Aline [de Zouche?]), 626 (Eleanor of Provence), 631 (Eleanor
   Castile); for a bestiary and for voyage literature, 347, 504 (Adeliza of Louvain, Edith
   Matilda queens of Henry I); for historiography 1 (Constance Fitzgilbert) and perha,
   54 (Isabella Marshal); for hagiography 505 (Christina of Markyate), 508 (Mary, abbe
   of Barking), 536 ('une ancele saint Laurent'), 521, 545 (Isabella, countess of Arunde
   522 (Eleanor of Provence). Female patrons are of course but one (important) eleme
   of a francophone literary culture of women audiences, writers, and book-owne.
   see J. Wogan-Browne, *Saints' Lives and Women's Literary Culture, c.1150–1300* (Oxfor
   2001); eadem, 'Women's Formal and Informal Traditions of Biblical Knowledge
   Anglo-Norman England', in *Saints, Scholars, and Politicians: Gender as a Tool in Mediei
   Studies: Festschrift in Honour of Anneke Mulder-Bakker on the Occasion of Her Sixty-fif*
   Birthday, ed. M. van Dijk and R. Nip. (Turnhout, 2005), pp. 85–109.
5 London, Lambeth Palace, MS 209. See N. Morgan with M. Brown, *The Lambe*
   Apocalypse [facsimile and commentary] (London, 1990), fols. 40r–53v. On fol. 48r, tl
   patroness wears de Ferrers arms on her dress and de Quincy on her cloak, and ma
   be either Margaret, as a wealthy widow, giving prominence to her father's arms ov
   her late husband's, as argued by Gee, *Women, Art and Patronage*, pp. 46–7, or Elean
   de Quincy giving prominence to her husband's arms, as argued by Morgan, *Lambe*
   Apocalypse, p. 79. Eleanor de Quincy was the daughter of William de Ferrers ar
   Margaret de Ferrers was the daughter of Roger de Quincy. Each woman is the other
   stepdaughter and stepmother (perhaps unsurprisingly, given the endogamous clima
   of baronial marriage strategies: see S. L. Waugh, 'Marriage, Class and Royal Lordsh
   in England under Henry III', *Viator* 16 (1985), 181–207, esp. pp. 189–91).
6 For apocalypses, see further Morgan, *Lambeth*, pp. 17–37, 92; individual examples
   Morgan, *EGM*, including Lambeth (Morgan, *EGM [II]*, no. 126, pp. 101–6); Dean nc
   473–8.

thirteen folios of customized illustrations and diagrams are added – images of saints, of the Virgin's interventions, of Christ's passion, of the Veronica icon (fols. 46v–53v).[7] Much quieter than the preceding Apocalypse illustrations – colour-washed but unilluminated – these pages could be said to be visually 'vernacular'. So too, their accompanying verses and labels are largely Anglo-Norman.[8] Though apparently marginal to the main Latin text and commentary, these additional leaves continue and apply the work of apprehending the Apocalypse in visual and textual penitential discourses. They offer a summative and exemplary response to the eschatological urgency of the Apocalypse tailored to the viewpoint of the female patron of the book. She herself is represented in them in several iconic appearances.

The image on which I will focus here is fol. 53r's diagram of a lady holding a shield under a tree (Figure 18.1), extensively labelled in Anglo-Norman (Table 18.1).[9] *Par la dame est signifie repentant*, says the lady's label: that is, the lady signifies repenting, with penance as a process: doing penance is to be a lady – a soul – in a penitential configuration, and also to be the reader of that allegory of penance. As Nigel Morgan points out, this diagram has connections both to other additions in *Lambeth* and to the book as a whole in the resemblances between the lady as penitent, the manuscript's image of its patron (fol. 48r) and Mary Magdalen in the *noli me tangere* illustration of this customized sequence (fol. 49r).[10] The correspondences here identify the book's owner as both individual and generic. She is its inscribed reader and its exemplary penitent and subject.

As the Anglo-Norman labels explain, the figure of the lady sits under the tree of this world, assailed by the arrows of devilish suggestion, but with the flies of vain worldly thoughts brushed away by the *flabellum* of a guardian angel. She holds the shield of Trinitarian faith to ward off the arrows of the devil. She is also directly under the angelic sword of anguish in the Last Judgment, with the dove of the Holy Spirit as expressed in scripture perched on her chair, the serpent of the devil's disturbance crushed under her foot, and the river of scripture as expounded by the preacher available to her gaze. Tension arises from the less expected figure of the peasant-churl whose axe threatens the trunk of the lady's sheltering tree. But, like the churl with the club who represents the pitilessness of the lady in the *Roman de la rose*, this figure has to be read counter-intuitively, for he is as much a part of God's plan as the lady herself: his axe is the sentence of Judgment and the preaching of the Gospel, and the tree he threatens represents the world.

---

7   For detailed discussion, see Morgan, *Lambeth*, pp. 51–71.
8   A diagram widely used in preparation for confession labels its cherubim's wings in Latin (fol. 48v): a Latin prayer appears beneath the final Veronica image of Christ's face (fol. 53v). Anglo-Norman verses accompany the Theophilus illustrations (fols. 46r–47r: Dean no. 565).
9   I have made a fresh transcription without modern capitalization and accent marks, but have gratefully referred to Nigel Morgan's elegant transcription of this diagram (Morgan, *Lambeth*, pp. 258–9).
10 Morgan, *Lambeth*, pp. 59–60.

Figure 18.1: Diagram for a noblewoman: The Lambeth Apocalypse, Lambeth Palace Library, MS 209, fol. 53r

Table 18.1: Labels for the penitence allegory, Lambeth Apocalypse, fol. 53r.

par le coc en larbre est signifie le precheur
qui defule e le preie a despire.
by the cock in the tree is signified
the preacher who tramples on it [the tree]
and urges contempt for it.

 larbre
st munde.
the tree
s world.

par langle remuant les musches od
le muscher le aide del
angle qui est gardain
de chescun home.
by the angel moving the flies with
the fly-swatter the help of the
angel who is the guardian
of each human.

 les musches
 ueines pensees qui des
 bant le repentant
ant.
the flies the empty thoughts which
der the penitent at prayer

 langle od lespee
i est pres del ha
el: la destresce del
uin iugement.
the angel with the sword
ich is close to the head:
 anguish [legally 'distress, distraint']
the divine judgment.

par le diable se
tant: les sug
gestions del diable.
By the devil shooting
the suggestions [legally 'submissions']
of the devil.

 la Dame est signifie
pentant.
the Lady is signified
itence [lit. repenting].

par lescu: lel
fei.
by the shield: true
faith.

 le columb:
saint espi
 qui espunt
sainte escriture.
the dove the
y spirit which
ounds holy scripture.

hield: detail

ere	le pere ne est		saint
	le saint espirit		espirit
eu est pere			est saint espirit
		deu	
fiz ne est le pere	le saint espirit ne est le fiz		
		est	
		fiz	

par la coigne: la senten
ce del iugement ou le pre
chement del euungele
by the axe: the sentence of the
Judgment or the preaching
of the Gospel

par le coluere agaitant
al talon: le desturbement
que le diable se aforce a faire
as leals al issue del alme.
by the snake watching
at the heel: the hindrance
that the devil strives to exert
on the faithful at the
departure of the soul.

 leuue: deuine escriture la quele le precheur demustre.
the water: divine scripture which the preacher explains.

The churl's impact is suggested by the fact that only his foot, the angels' wing and the preacher-cock pierce the frame of the image. Where the preacher-cock treads the world underfoot, the churl threatens to topple it. Since the churl's labour associates him with the Judgment and the Gospel, we can perhaps understand his social class as expressive of the rhetorical *stilus humilis* of the latter. Perhaps he also signals the intuitive access of the simple to Gospel meaning – the access of those who, in Langland's *Piers Plowman*, can 'percen with a Paternoster the paleys of heuene / And passen Purgatorie penaunceless' (B-text, X, lines 462–3) – while their superiors in learning and in socio-economic status may enter with difficulty. In fact, like Langland's brilliant Tree of Charity allegory, the Lambeth diagram achieves a number of tensions and unexpected nuancings partly because it can refer to commonly held, but here particularly deployed, mnemonic schemata. Not least of these effects is the condensing of the old triad of world, flesh and devil to two, with the world as that intuitively likable tree, not – like the devil – an attacker. The discomfort of abandoning such an instinctive affiliation is as disruptive as a peasant hacking down your forest.

In some ways we are offered here an image of an aristocratic thirteenth-century landholder with the concerns appropriate to her class. She is surrounded by male subordinates and agents, not omitting the churl (on whose agrarian labour land-based wealth depended), and she herself (as was often the case) is charged with the defence of her territory: it is the lady who holds the shield. And yet, the lady figure is not really in a landscape, but in a space that is at once cosmic and interior, defined as such by the relations between the components of the page and their meanings. The shelter of the world, the imminence of judgment, the continuous exposure to attack and distraction, the refreshment of scripture, the necessity of the shield – this page is simultaneously meditative and urgent in its account of how humans should read their position and what to do about it. The *Lambeth* lady is a feminized and generalizable icon for the human soul, a version of the existential position of all humans.

The penitence diagram models a new kind of individual reading, but in practice the book includes collective and oral modes as well. The public, formal Latinity of *Lambeth*'s text and commentary may have been explicated for the patron and her ladies by her clerics, and the *memoriae* and diagrams of the concluding sequence invite both collective and individual reading.[11] The book is not large (212 × 196 mm in its Apocalypse pages) and the labels on the penitential diagram page require either turning it in one's hands to read what would otherwise be upside-down, or the presence of at least one other person if all the labels are to be read. (Hence the upside-down label for the churl's axe is not only an enactment of the challenge implicit in this figure, but an assumption about how the diagram will be used.) The sideways and upside-down labels insist on an appro-

---

[11] See further N. Morgan, 'Books for the Liturgy and Private Prayer', in *The Cambridge History of the Book in Britain*, vol. II: *1100–1400*, ed. N. J. Morgan and R. Thomson (Cambridge, 2008), pp. 291–316 (pp. 314–15). For some later devotional trees see Boffey, pp. 387–93 below.

priately meditative reading. They offer access by their vernacularity, and then turn that access into a process by forcing the turning of the book. Whether or not the patroness depended on her clerks for exposition of her Latin apocalypse text and commentary, the heart of her reading is articulated in this vernacular process of response. Moreover, the diagram of the lady penitent gives access as well as a body-posture to the reader as part of the reading process. It creates a somatically enforced reading space and time so that a woman who has necessarily lived much in the world as an earl's wife can inhabit a time and space for meditative reading. It models for her the *otium* of serious, disciplined lay and clerical penitential reading.[12]

The *Lambeth Apocalypse*'s vernacular diagram bears comparison with the best-known text of thirteenth-century women's reading, *Ancrene Wisse*, a guide for anchoresses of *c.*1225–30, composed in the West Midlands for three women recluses.[13] Originally written in rich and supple English (an English from an Anglo-French linguistic environment, variously multilingual in the sources of its lexis, and drawing on Latin traditions for its rhetoric), *Ancrene Wisse* has been largely read as a Middle English text, although it has also long been noted as a work translated *from* English *into* French and Latin across the thirteenth to the sixteenth centuries.[14] Two separate thirteenth-century translations into insular French, one of perhaps the 1230s–1240s and the other of *c.*1254–64, are extant, and a third French version was the source of a fifteenth-century retranslation into English.[15] The manuscripts of the thirteenth-century translations witness to continuing fourteenth- and fifteenth-century use respectively: the third translation implies some interchanges of continental and insular adaptation and borrowing in and out of French.[16] The earlier

---

[12] See further G. Rector, '*En sa chambre sovent le lit: Otium* and the Pedagogical Sociabilities of Early *Romanz* Literature (*c.*1100–1150)' (forthcoming), and the essay by Rector in this volume.

[13] *Ancrene Wisse: A Corrected Edition of the Text in Cambridge, Corpus Christi College, MS 402*, ed. B. Millett with R. Dance, 2 vols, EETS OS 325, 326 (Oxford, 2005, 2006), II, pp. xi–xiii.

[14] But see D. Trotter, 'The Anglo-French Lexis of *Ancrene Wisse*: A Re-Evaluation', in *A Companion to Ancrene Wisse*, ed. Y. Wada (Cambridge, 2003), pp. 83–101. For scholarship on the *Guide*, see B. Millett, with the assistance of G. B. Jack and Y. Wada, *Ancrene Wisse, the Katherine Group, and the Wooing Group*, Annotated Bibliographies of Old and Middle English Literature, II (Cambridge, 1996), pp. 34–45 (henceforth cited as *Bibliography*).

[15] For the earlier translation, extant in London, British Library, MS Cotton Vitellius F VII, see the diplomatic edition by J. A. Herbert, *The French Text of the Ancrene Riwle*, EETS OS 219 (London, 1944): for the later translation, *The French Text of the Ancrene Riwle*, ed. W. H. Trethewey, EETS OS 240 (London, 1958); on the third translation, see J. H. Fisher, *The Tretyse of Love*, EETS OS 223 (London, 1951), pp. ix, xiv–xviii.

[16] For pioneering recognition of the French versions, see H. E. Allen, 'Wynkyn de Worde and a Second French Compilation from the "Ancrene Riwle" with a Description of the First (Trinity Coll. Camb. Ms. 883)', in *Essays and Studies in Honor of Carleton Brown* (New York, 1940), pp. 182–219. C. Innes-Parker explores the implications of the manuscript evidence in 'The Legacy of *Ancrene Wisse*: Translations, Influences and Readers', in Wada, *Companion*, pp. 149–55. For the Middle English *Ancrene Wisse* text in Cambridge, MS Pepys 2498 as a translation in a manuscript mostly composed of

thirteenth-century French translation, which I will call *La Reule*, is a close translation of an early version of *Ancrene Wisse*.[17] Whether or not, as Dobson suggested, this version was made for Lady Annora de Braose, a member by birth and by marriage of two important Welsh Marcher families and subsequently an anchoress at Iffley in Oxfordshire,[18] *La Reule* must have been translated for a female readership of similar or higher class-status to *Ancrene Wisse*'s original audience of three 'gentile wummen' recluses.[19] *La Reule*'s penitential reading is, I shall argue, profoundly similar to that of the *Lambeth Apocalypse* in more than their shared thirteenth-century French.

La Reule presents its reader with an image of herself in the iconography of the lady of romance:

> Une dame fut de ses enimis assise tout environ, sa terre t[ou]te destruite, et ele tout povre dedenz un chastel de terre. L'amour nepurquant d'un poestif roi fust vers lui si tres a demesure donee q'il pur dauneure lui envea ses messages un apres altre, sovent plusours ensemble: lui envea beaubelez beaz et plusours, soucours de vitaille, aide de ses genz pur tenir son chastel. Et ele receust tout aussi come rien ne lui fust, et issi fust dure de queor qe de s'amour ne poeit il estre ja le plus pres. Qe volez vous plus? Il vint meismes a la fin: lui moustra sa bele face sicome cil qe fut de touz homes le plus beel a regarder; parla si tresdoucement et paroles si deliciouses q'eles porreient morz resusciter; ovra mult des merveilles et fist grant mestrie devant ses oilz; lui mostra son poer; li cunta de son reigne; li offri de faire reine de tout ceo qil avoit.[20]

A wooer's messages and behaviour submitted to female scrutiny is a common feature of romance, medieval and modern, and the nuptial discourses of medieval

---

translations from the Anglo-Norman, see R. Hanna, 'Pepys 2498: Anglo-Norman Audiences and London Biblical Texts', ch. 4 of his *London Literature 1300–1380* (Cambridge, 2005), pp. 148–221 (esp. pp. 154–7).

17 Millett, ed. *Ancrene Wisse*, I, EETS OS 325 (Oxford 2005), p. xv, who also notes that the hand of this translation's extant manuscript is similar to that of the late thirteenth-century Douce Apocalypse (Dean no. 475; Morgan, *EGM [III]*, no. 143), i.e. a royal example of the same kind of book as *Lambeth*, but with Anglo-Norman text and commentary.

18 E. J. Dobson, *The Origins of* Ancrene Wisse (Oxford, 1976), pp. 299–31.

19 *The English Text of the* Ancrene Riwle *Edited from Cotton MS Nero A. xiv*, ed. M. Day, EETS OS 225 (London, 1957), p. 85/24.

20 ('A lady was surrounded by her enemies, her land all brought to ruin in a castle of clay. But a powerful king had fallen in love with her so inordinately that to win her love he sent her his messengers, one after another, often many at once: he sent her many splendid presents of jewellery, provisions to support her, help from his noble army to hold her castle. She accepted everything as if it meant nothing to her, and was so hard-hearted that he could never gain her love. What more do you want? At last he came himself, showed her his handsome face as he who was of all men the most handsome to see, spoke so tenderly and with words so beguiling that they could resurrect the dead, did great feats before her eyes; told her about his kingdom; offered to make her queen of all he owned'): *The French Text of the Ancrene Riwle*, ed. Herbert, pp. 283/27–284/17 (u/v and i/j normalized, modern punctuation and capitalization), henceforth referenced by page and line number in the text. For the reading instructions quoted in this essay's title, see p. 317/1213.

pirituality.[21] Here, of course, Christ the lover-knight is the wooer and the lady who looks cold-heartedly at the Word of God in its embodied form is both the enclosed woman reader and the soul, dwelling in the earthen castle of the body.[22] Like the *Lambeth* lady, the female reader in and of the text here models an existential stance generalizable for all humans. The scene powerfully combines romance with meditative and penitential attention to Christian redemption. Both secular and sacred romance can be exegetical and enumerative in their modes ('how shall I love thee? let me count the ways…'), and as the lover-knight dies for the unrepentant lady, *La Reule* glosses his shield, by enumerating correspondences, as the human body of Christ incarnate, stretched out on the cross (*La Reule*, pp. 285/29–33). Just as a brave dead knight's arms are hung high in the church in his memory, adds *La Reule*, so this shield – that is, the crucifix – is placed where it can be most easily seen – in church – as a memorial and reminder. The shield becomes a mnemonic device for all of redemptive history.[23]

Like the *Lambeth* image, *La Reule* considers and shapes the body and its reading. As has often been noted, this text is so thoroughly designed for its anchoritic female readers that its eight parts are structured as an enclosure. *La Reule* prescribes a daily *horarium* and liturgical observances in Part One, and in Part Eight an 'Outer Rule' of life, or, in its own metaphor, a 'handmaiden rule' ('come ancele', p. 2/18–19) regarding diet, deportment etc. In between, the Inner or 'Lady Rule' ('come dame', p. 2/17–18), moves from the custody of the senses and the feelings to temptation, confession and penance, culminating in Part Seven, which is devoted to love defined as purity of heart ('amour qe fet le queor pur et cler', pp. 279/33–4).[24] The soul-lady is both deep within this culminating section of her lady rule (in Part Seven), and textually close to the resumption of her outer handmaiden rule (in Part Eight). Part Seven's reading anchoress – the would-be pure heart within the body within the cell drawn simultaneously outward and yet deeper within itself in the contemplation of the lover-knight's sacrifice – is a powerful image of meditative penitential reading and the work of conforming the troublesome heart. In this 'essample' (*La Reule*, p. 283/25), any reader can be the soul-lady, as well as a reader of her, and reading – the scrutiny of God's Word – becomes the soul's work.

C. Cannon, 'The Form of the Self: *Ancrene Wisse* and Romance', *Medium Aevum* 70.1 (2001), 47–65; J. Wogan-Browne, 'Virginity Always Comes Twice: Virginity and Romance, Virginity and Profession', in *Maistresse of My Wit: Medieval Women and Modern Scholars*, ed. L. d'Arcens and J. Ruys (Turnhout, 2004), pp. 335–69 (pp. 351–7).

On reading the person of the Christ lover-knight as an extension of reading as the perusal of codices, see V. Gillespie, '*Lukynge in haly bukes*: *Lectio* in some Late Medieval Spiritual Miscellanies', *Analecta Cartusiana* 106 (1984), 1–27 (repr. in his *Looking in Holy Books: Essays on Late Medieval Religious Writing in England* (Cardiff, 2005).

For the complexity of thought and rhetorical effect of this passage, see G. Shepherd, ed. *Ancrene Wisse* (Exeter, rev. edn, 1991), pp. lxx–xxx; for the rich network of associations and texts around the lady and the shield, see M. Evans, 'An Illustrated Fragment of Peraldus's *Summa* of Vice: Harleian MS 3244', *JWCI* 45 (1982), 14–68.

For a diagrammatic representation, see Cannon, 'Form of the Self', p. 51.

No wonder that this scene (at least in its English version) has attracted s
much comment: its implications for a feminized ideology and practice of readin
are legion, and its combination of discourses could hardly be more powerful an
eloquent.[25] *Ancrene Wisse*'s medieval (and modern) success partly derives fro
the complexity and fullness with which it images the human reader as constantl
seeking solitude with the soul's beloved amid a storm of memories, desires, rel
tionships and obligations, even as it also makes her disciplined and consumin
reading of the Word a feminized and valued mode of life, a legitimated withdraw
into anchoritism. The very conformity of inner and outer between the text an
its *destinataires* persuasively presents the image of feminized reading and make
it exportable and generalizable. Even before *Ancrene Wisse*'s spectacular trilingu
career among various reading communities was fully launched, its handling of si
and confession seems to have envisaged a wider range of penitents than the origin
three anchoresses living their entire life, as *Ancrene Wisse* and *La Reule* tell them, a
one of disciplined penitential awareness (al is penitence ant strong penitence, þet
eauer dreheð, 132/1; tout est penance quantqe vous soffrez, mes chieres soeres, *L
Reule*, p. 249/9–12).[26]

As an elite woman reader and (in viewing her diagram under the shadow c
the Apocalypse) a practitioner of penitential discourse, Lady Eleanor is in fac
extremely close kin to the readers inscribed in *La Reule* – laywomen practisin
a religious life of voluntary penitential asceticism and enclosure as the matri
of their relation with Christ. In its very form, *La Reule* shapes the reading bod
as a series of imaginative enclosures, so that the reading of the text informs an
maintains both external and interior *habitus* for its audience. So too, as we hav
seen, the *Lambeth* Apocalypse addresses the somatics of reading.

In both *Apocalypse* and *Reule*, some autonomy is necessarily encoded in th
iconography of female penitential reading: the work of such reading cannot b
effected without constituting audiences producers of their own selves. The ques
tion of the reader's time and space and the paradoxical notion of leisure for th
work of reading is necessarily articulated for women in lay or semi-religiou
lives (for professionally latinate monks and clerks it is institutionally alway
already licensed). Such reading time is controlled by the reader's own *horariu*
or timetable, whether that is a matter of the lay anchoress's private devotions, c
the female householder's use of her psalter, book of hours or apocalypse: as *L
Reule* says of itself in the title quotation to this essay, 'read some of this book, *mo*

---

25 The classic study of *Ancrene Wisse*'s readers is B. Millett, 'Women in No Man's Lanc
English Recluses and the Development of Vernacular Literature in the Twelfth an
Thirteenth Centuries', in *Women and Literature*, pp. 86–103; for pastoral and penitenti
reading, see also S. Uselmann, 'Women Reading and Reading Women: Early Scrib
Notions of Literacy in the *Ancrene Wisse*', *Exemplaria* 16.2 (2004), 369–404. For rece
comment on this scene, see e.g. Cannon, 'Form of the Self', and C. Batt, D. Reneve
and C. Whitehead, 'Domesticity and Medieval Devotional Literature', *LSE* 36 (2005
195–250 (pp. 198–214).

26 See Millett and Dance, *Ancrene Wisse*, II, pp. xxiv, xxxiv–xxxv; B. Millett, '*Ancrene Wiss
and the Conditions of Confession', *English Studies* 80 (1999), 193–215.

or less, each day *when you have free time* ('cest livre liseez quant vous estes en eise chescun jour, *meins ou plus*', *La Reule*, p. 317/13–15, italics mine).

It is also important that in the reading of the *Lambeth* patroness and the anchor-esses, images are valued equally, whether they are those prompted in the mind of a reader as they read text, or whether the image is actually the text of the reading. Medieval theories of the art of memory define it as inclusive not just of the psycho-physiological memory function but of everything believed to be present to the soul. The art of memory is not only a matter of specific mnemonic techniques for learning information, but necessarily a re-membering of what, who, and where one is. Thus, images need not simply illustrate the narratives or discourses alongside which they appear. They themselves contain active powers of recall and reimprinting: they are intrinsic to understanding one's position in a divinely created world of sense-data.[27] The image of the lady in the earthen castle defended by the lover-knight is for these purposes exactly the same kind of thing as the lady under the tree holding her shield.

Though both images powerfully represent the solitary reader, both are gener-alizable. Memorial reading can be done in solitude and silence but, in the thir-teenth century's various kinds of reading, can equally be the object of communal reading.[28] As with *Lambeth*, *La Reule* envisages several reading modes. The recluses are adjured to read some part of *La Reule* each day as they find time, but they are also instructed to read aloud to their maids what *La Reule* says about servants (pp. 315/36–316/3), and they are also addressed collectively at various times as the community of solitaries so paradoxically typical of the anchoritic life ('et vous, mes chieres soeres', *La Reule*, p. 1/18; 'vous mes trescheres soeres', p. 307/11–12; 'od honestes countes solacez vous ensemble', 'refresh yourselves by telling suitable stories together', p. 311/5–7). Both *Reule* and *Apocalypse* are also designed for reading and rereadings, in which a number of different subject positions might be selected by the reader. In this imagistically rich vernacular, the site of activity, whether in the Lambeth lady-penitent's visual *memoriae* or the textually created images of *La Reule* and other treatises, lies importantly *in the reader* rather than the text and illustrations. Much of the work we associate in modern literary canons with the development of subjectivity and self-fashioning is here carried out less in the text than in the interactions of users, text and book.

Women are important here both as consumers and as agents. The informal and occasional character of vernacular writing tends towards the explicit and innovative as clerics respond to the demands, and imagine the needs, of specific

---

[27] M. Carruthers, *The Book of Memory: A Study of Memory in Medieval Culture*, 2nd edn (Cambridge, 2008), pp. 275–8, 324–32. N. Morgan, 'Patrons and Their Devotions in the Thirteenth-Century English Psalters', in *The Illustrated Psalter*, ed. F. O. Büttner (Turn-hout, 2005), pp. 309–22 (pp. 317–18). See also Hanna, *London Literature*, pp. 167–72 for a subtle account, though one ascribing less agency to women patrons and readers.

[28] As Millett points out, *Ancrene Wisse* is innovative as 'vernacular literature composed with readers rather than hearers in mind' while continuing to cater for a diversity of audiences and modes: 'Women in No Man's Land', pp. 93, 99.

patrons. Female *destinataires* and the development of a text across a range of reading communities are linked phenomena: the texts of women's reading are exportable, pervasive, mediating and enabling for groups of every kind, both lay and clerical (especially given the franco-latinate character of insular monasticism and secular clerisy).[29] As Felicity Riddy influentially showed for the study of fourteenth-century reading, overlaps between female lay and religious reading and the orality of female literary culture are resources, not an absence of 'proper' literacy.[30] This makes for a wider, richer, shared reading culture than has yet been fully noticed for the (largely francophone) thirteenth century, and one with important conti-nuities with later centuries. Though most readily observable among elite readers (who tend also to have more traceable textual communities and networks), such reading may go further down the social scale than we think, both because of the class mixes of later medieval nunneries and of the households of noblewomen. (Should we imagine the anchoresses of *La Reule* as expounding the portions concerned with servants *ex tempore* in English to their maids? Were such servants wholly without French?[31])

Even more importantly, women are not just the *destinataires* but the agents of texts and they share interests with clerics in vernacular text production. The figure of the queen or noblewoman as a prestigious icon of literary patronage was well established in insular culture (certainly from the eleventh century onwards).[32] In the many texts of devotion and doctrine produced for women by their household clerics and chaplains, the social authority of the patron's vernacular language becomes interwoven with the Latinate authority of the cleric in the production of texts.[33] Established twelfth- and early thirteenth-century traditions of this alli-ance between women patrons and clerical writers and their overlapping social and institutional networks may indeed have contributed, *inter alia*, to the dissem-ination of pastoralia after Lateran IV.[34]

---

[29] Legge, *Anglo-Norman in the Cloisters*: see also the essay by Pouzet in this volume.

[30] F. Riddy, ' "Women talking about the things of God": A Late Medieval Sub-Culture', in Meale, *Women and Literature*, pp. 104–27.

[31] For the surprising class-range of aspirations to Anglo-Norman in the twelfth century, see I. Short 'On Bilingualism in Anglo-Norman England', *Romance Philology* 33 (1979–80), 469–79 (pp. 474–8). See the essay by Oliva in this volume for an argument that later medieval francophone nuns are not all elite, but include middling local and urban gentry; and on the reach of devotional and doctrinal French see further the essay by Deeming in this volume.

[32] See the essay by Tyler in this volume and n. 4 above.

[33] J. Wogan-Browne, ' "Our Steward, St Jerome": Theology and the Anglo-Norman Household', in *Household, Women, and Christianities in Late Antiquity and the Middle Ages*, ed. A. Mulder-Bakker and J. Wogan-Browne (Turnhout, 2005), pp. 133–65 (pp. 133–4).

[34] For Lady Joan de Tatershul's ownership of a customized penitential manual and her association with Grosseteste, bishop of Lincoln, see A. Bennett, 'A Book Designed for a Noblewoman: An Illustrated *Manuel des Pechés*', in L. L. Brownrigg, ed., *Medieval Book Production: Assessing the Evidence* (Los Altos Hills CA, 1990), pp. 163–81 (pp. 167, 173 and fig. 5, colour plate E).

The strong thirteenth-century tradition of women's cultural patronage
tends to the martial and the chivalric. The anchoress of *La Reule* is to gaze at
the shield of Christ the lover-knight in the register of spiritual eroticism, but also
focus her own sense of self and her tools for reading the self through it. The
Lambeth Apocalypse diagram, similarly, offers no passive representation of penitence as female: this lady holds the Trinitarian shield of faith with both hands in
sustained and concentrated effort as the devil's arrows rattle down on it. So
too, a thirteenth-century treatise of erotic spirituality and religious regulation is
addressed to a 'bele soer' and tells its reader to joust for her heritage by using her
memory as a lance and by deploying the image of the crucifixion as her shield –
'demeine tei cum humme' – 'act like a man' she is told – 'do wel and aue wel'.[35]
Images of women in battle against the enemy are not rare: rather, they have
special valence in the thirteenth century's many forms of holy violence – crusade,
invasion, apocalypse, conversion, expulsion. Vengeance against Jews or Saracens
frequently overseen by the Virgin Mary herself. *Lambeth*'s closing customized
sequence illustrates the Virgin arming St Mercurius so that he can defeat Julian
the Apostate in holy war (fol. 45v): so too, the socio-economic contribution and
support of women to crusade was indispensable.[36] Nicole Bozon's beautiful
poem *Comment le fiz Deu fu armé* shows the Virgin entering Christ's chamber to
arm him in thigh plates and leg armour – cuissons and greaves of flesh, nerves,
sinews.[37] We could also think forwards to the famous image in the fourteenth-
century *Luttrell Psalter* where Sir Geoffrey Luttrell is shown on his caparisoned
war horse (fol. 202v). Here, Michael Camille has argued, Sir Geoffrey is handed
his shield by his daughter-in-law Beatrice Scrope, who thus arms him with a
future genealogy.[38] Women, that is to say, have an important presence as biolog-
ical, cultural, social and political patronesses in thirteenth-century textual and
manuscript culture as in other places.

La Reule can here typify the longevity of the cultural bequests of thirteenth-
century women to posterity. Its extant late thirteenth- or early fourteenth-century
manuscript (London, British Library, MS Cotton Vitellius F vii) is a collection of
Anglo-Norman penitential and didactic texts. As has been often remarked, the
manuscript was given by Joan of Kent, widow of Thomas Holland, the eighth
Earl, to Eleanor Cobham, duchess of Gloucester, probably between 1433 and
1441, before the latter's trial for sorcery.[39] At this date, *La Reule*'s French must

B. Hill, 'British Library MS. Egerton 613– II', *Notes and Queries* 223 (December 1978),
492–501 (p. 499, paragraphs 20–2). On this text, see further Wogan-Browne in Putter
and Jefferson, *Medieval Multilingualism*.
See e.g. N. R. Hodgson, *Women, Crusading and the Holy Land in Historical Narrative*
(Woodbridge, 2007).
The Anglo-Norman Lyric: An Anthology, ed. and trans. B. J. Levy and D. L. Jeffrey
(Toronto, 1990), pp. 186–91.
M. Camille, *Mirror in Parchment: The Luttrell Psalter and the Making of Medieval England*
(London, 1988), pp. 53–4.
Joan of Kent was the direct descendant of Maud, countess of Clare (d. 1288), who
presented an early *Ancrene Wisse* text (in BL, MS Cotton Cleopatra C. vi) to her

have been much easier to read or hear for some audiences than early Middl
English versions of *Ancrene Wisse*. The extant fourteenth- and fifteenth-centur
English texts of *Ancrene Wisse* are themselves adapted and updated from earl
Middle English: the French text of *La Reule* will have performed a comparabl
function in the fifteenth century, that of mediating a complex early thirteenth
century West Midlands *koiné*. As a gift, the manuscript will not have been a reli
or a curio, but a book participating in an active reading culture. In the previou
generation, Eleanor de Bohun (d. 1399) left to her daughter Isabella, abbess ti
1421 of the Minories (the Franciscan house at Aldgate, London), a small librar
of French books, including 'Les Pasturelx Seint Gregoire', a text also included i
MS Cotton Vitellius F.vii.[40] (In the early fifteenth century, the Minories were als
bequeathed a copy of *Ancrene Wisse/La Reule* by John Clifford.[41]) *Ordinalia*, Bible:
regulae and text-collections in both insular and continental French were still i
use in English nunneries in the late fourteenth and fifteenth centuries, som•
times given by laywomen, as in the reading culture discussed by Felicity Riddy.
Certainly, women at the social level of the two known owners of *La Reule*, lik
their husbands and brothers, used both French and English across their docu
mentary and literary range well into the fifteenth century. One member of th
royal Lancastrian circle around Eleanor Cobham and Joan of Kent, as Ale×
andra Barratt has shown, was Eleanor Hull, among whose translations is th
neo-Anselmian *oreysons e meditaciouns* of which a copy is included in the extar
manuscript of *La Reule*.[43]

The richness of the oral and textual reading culture of women patrons, aud•
ences and book-owners has been usefully explored following Riddy's concept•
alization of it as a subculture. Considering the francophone tradition of femal

refounded house of Mynchenlegh (formerly Canonsleigh): H. E. Allen, *Times Litera•
Supplement*, 22 March 1934, p. 212. The Cleopatra manuscript includes Anglo-Norma•
poems (Dean nos. 913, 984).

[40] N. H. Nicolas, *Testamenta vetusta*, vol. 1 (London, 1826), pp. 146–9 (p. 149). *The Ni•
Words of Charity* by Alberic of Cologne (printed by de Worde together with the *Tretyse •
Love*, Fisher, pp. xiii–xv, 126–30, 141–3) also appears in the thirteenth- and fourteenth
century BL, MS Arundel 288 (Dean no. 617) together with the 'Peines de Purgatori•
associated with the second French translation of *Ancrene Wisse* (Dean no. 645) and th
oreysons e meditacions found in Cotton Vitellius F. VII (Dean no. 942).

[41] It is not known whether the text was in French or English or whether this correspond
to any of the extant manuscripts: Millett, *Bibliography*, p. 59. Henry IV granted the alie
priory of Appuldurcombe, Isle of Wight, to the Minories in 1399 (A. F. C. Bourdillo•
The Order of Minoresses in England (Manchester, 1926), p. 46): for a French copy of par•
of the second French translation coming from Appuldurcombe (in MS Bodley 90), se
Millett, *Bibliography*, p. 57.

[42] Riddy, 'Women talking …'. For a minimal list of securely provenanced French text
see D. N. Bell, *What Nuns Read*, Index II, pp. 231–6. For *ordinalia* in French, see e.g. Be•
s.v. Lacock, p. 147; for registers and accounts, see the essays by June and Oliva in th
volume; for nunnery acquisitions of French collections from laywomen, see e.g. Be•
pp. 112–16 (Barking, nos. 13 and 15).

[43] A. Barratt, 'Dame Eleanor Hull: The Translator at Work', *Medium Aevum* 72 (2003•
277–96.

patronage and readership highlights the ways in which this female subculture is permeable with, and contributes to, other more dominant cultural groups. Women readers are important for the ways in which they and their texts are so often the model adapted for *everyone's* texts: feminized reading is not a cultural analogy but a source. *Ancrene Wisse*, for example, is dramatically developed in its second thirteenth-century French translation by being made the spur to, and distributed amid the parts of, a large Anglo-Norman *Compileison* on penitence composed between *c.*1254 and 1274. This text is a good example of a work of women's reading being adapted for still wider audiences. Where *La Reule* instructs specific women readers to 'read some of this book each day' (*cest livre liseez … chescun jour*, p. 317/12–13), *La Compileison* offers itself to the composer's 'sweet dear brothers and sisters in God, men and women of religious life, and to all those, male and female, who will read this writing or will hear it read by others' (*duz chers freres e suers en deu, hommes e femmes de religion, e a tuz icels e celes [ke] cest escrit lirront ou de autre lire le orrunt*).[44] Such a textual career is paradigmatic for a number of significant thirteenth-century texts and manuscripts. The very reasons that once seemed to cut off women's francophone literary culture from the mainstream history of literature in medieval England – its Frenchness, its association with high class status – are in fact the vectors of an important contribution to, and matrix for, English literary culture.

---

[44] *The French Text of the Ancrene Riwle*, ed. W. H. Trethewey, EETS OS 240 (London, 1958), p. 159/5–7; see also N. Watson and J. Wogan-Browne, 'The French of England: the *Compileison, Ancrene Wisse*, and the Idea of Anglo-Norman', in *Journal of Romance Studies* 4.3, Special Issue *Cultural Traffic in the Medieval Romance World*, ed. S. Gaunt and J. Weis (Winter, 2004), 35–59.

19

French Devotional Texts in Thirteenth-Century Preachers' Anthologies

Helen Deeming

Informally produced miscellanies originating in late twelfth- and thirteenth-century Britain constitute an under-exploited resource for the study of medieval literate society. Often written by a number of scribes over a period of time, these books can be particularly difficult to date or localize, although it seems that – in the main – they were produced within religious communities and most often small houses or dependent cells. Their script, layout and production are all of fairly modest standards, and they seem to have been practical books, for those whose access to more extensive textual resources may have been limited. What the manuscripts lack in elegance of presentation, though, they more than make up for in their rich variety of devotional and doctrinal contents, which point to a wide range of practical uses including, but not limited to, preaching.[1] Within this group, the two manuscripts to be considered here, London, British Library, MS Harley 524 and Maidstone Museum, MS A.13, are relatively unusual in including material in French among their primarily Latin contents. This essay endeavours to show that the multilingual contents of these anthologies shed new light on the transmission of pastoral literature in the vibrant devotional culture of the thirteenth century.

British Library, MS Harley 524 is a collection of hundreds of short texts on devotional, moral and liturgical topics. It was written in England by a number of mid-thirteenth century scribes, whose *textura* hands are – while not poor – at least informal in execution. Indeed, the whole design of the book suggests an informality in production: the parchment leaves are of uneven size, thickness and quality, and frequently leaves or parts of leaves are left blank. In some (but not all) cases, these blanks fall at the ends of gatherings, suggesting that the quires were copied separately without a high degree of coordination to ensure that one ran on neatly from another. The contents include sermons, short tracts, verses, prayers, lists and diagrams, with different items on the same topic often copied together in small groups. But the overall book shows no coherent organization or planning: there is no apparatus of reference, and the topics follow no readily discernible order. In some places, leaves have been left blank mid-gathering,

---

[1] This larger group of miscellany manuscripts forms the subject of my forthcoming book, *Miscellany Manuscripts and the Collecting of Texts: Scribes and Readers in Twelfth- and Thirteenth-Century Britain*.

ossibly so that materials relating to the topic of the adjacent texts might be
added later. In other places, leaves or parts of leaves have been tipped in, so that
ems could be inserted at relevant places where space had not been left for them.

Both the physical design of the book and the nature of its contents suggest that
was compiled in a scrapbook-like assembly, one that was brought together over
me and perhaps deliberately left open-ended so that any of the small group of
ribes involved in its production could add in new items when they became
available. Although the layout is not elegant – texts tend to spill into the lower
margin and decoration is minimal – some aspects of it are clearly practical: at
eir start, texts tend to be preceded by a rubric identifying their topic, and in
ome places the main ideas of a text are written as a short list at the beginning,
ith lines or brackets in the margin to direct the eye towards them. So though
would be hard to locate a particular item within the book unless one knew its
ontents thoroughly, at the level of the page, the layout gives the reader easy
cess to the divisions and sub-divisions within the contents.

There is a conspicuous lack of attributions among the texts and their rubrics, a
ature that makes it unlikely that MS Harley 524 was the notebook of a univer-
ty scholar. Furthermore, the general tenor of the contents suggests practical
inistry rather than scholastic theology: there are texts on prayer and confes-
on, on the significance of the vestments worn at mass, and lists of miracles and
f mortal sins. Interspersed between the prose texts are large numbers of short
erses, often couplets, encapsulating a particular theme in a brief and memorable
ay.

Almost all of MS Harley 524's contents are in Latin: the only exception is a
mall amount of Anglo-Norman French, contained within a single gathering.[2]
ike many of the gatherings, this one is codicologically separable from its neigh-
ours: its beginning coincides with the start of a new text and a change of hand,
nd its final verso is blank.[3] The hands represented in this gathering are also
resent elsewhere in the manuscript, but both the use of French and some differ-
nces in the kinds and arrangement of its contents set the gathering apart, and
ake it suitable for examination as a separate entity.

The collation of the gathering is difficult to make out because of the tight
odern binding of the book and several tipped-in leaves or partial leaves. Fol.
2 is the start of the gathering proper, following a tipped-in stub, and a section
f Latin texts copied by a single scribe begins here and continues until fol. 62v.
ol. 63r contains a piece of notated music: a Latin sacred song in two parts whose

---

The French items have apparently gone unnoticed in previous literature and are not
listed in Dean. I am currently preparing an edition of these texts for publication in
article form.
Although written by the same group of scribes, it is possible that the quires could have
been intended to be carried separately on different journeys, before they were bound
together. On the other hand, the external leaves of the quires show no particular signs
of wear, as do those of another miscellany, London, British Library, Royal 5 F. vii; see
H. Deeming, 'The Songs of St Godric: A Neglected Context', *Music & Letters* 86 (2005),
169–85 (p. 176).

musical notation, comparable to the manuscript's text-hands, is legible and accu
rate, but hardly elegant.[4] It is the only piece of music in the manuscript, an
the only leaf on which the two-column format used elsewhere is abandonec
evidently the scribe knew enough about the presentation of music to realize tha
a layout using the full width of the page was likely to be more successful tha
one in columns.[5] Fol. 63v begins a series of prayers, with antiphons and hymn
drawn from the liturgy: like the texts presented elsewhere in the manuscrip
these are grouped according to topic. Almost every item is preceded by a rubri
identifying it as 'oracio', 'antiphona' and so on, and sometimes also signallin
its topic. As can be seen from Table 19.1, the topics covered include a number c
saints, the Trinity and the Holy Spirit, but the majority of the items focus on th
Blessed Virgin and the Cross. There is no liturgical or calendar ordering to thi
devotional collection, and its concentration on Mary and the Cross align it wit
books intended for meditative, personal devotions. Neither is there an obviou
pattern linking the saints included here, while the texts themselves are from
variety of sources: some liturgical, some in verse, some well-known and other
less so. But the overall impression of the collection is not one of randomnes
it seems rather to be quite deliberately structured, with items labelled 'oracic
tending to frame the other items within each group. In contrast to the longe
more discursive prose texts elsewhere in the manuscript, this little collection c
very short prayers and related items seems to have more to do with the actua
practice of devotion than the study of doctrine. I wonder if a reader of this book
or someone to whom they passed on this material, could have used it as a kind c
self-assembled personal 'liturgy'. As in the reciting of a rosary, this series focuse
the mind intensely on specific devotions in turn, and thus could have been use
to give structure to a private devotional act.

The French texts occur on fols. 65v and 66r during the final group of this devo
tional series, the second of the two devoted to the Cross. There is no differenc
of hand or layout between the French texts and the Latin ones that precede an
follow them: as can be seen, they are rubricated in Latin in the same way a
the surrounding texts, and there is nothing to suggest that the scribe conceive
of these as requiring any different treatment. Within the first French prayer i
further evidence for the use of these items in devotional practice: whereas th
two Latin texts that close this group are punctuated with crosses, directing th
reader to make the sign of the cross at appropriate moments, part-way throug
the French prayer, the text itself is interrupted while the reader is directed to 'sa
here three Our Fathers':

4 A facsimile and transcription of the musical piece, 'Veri floris sub figura', may b
   found in *Early English Harmony: from the 10th to the 15th Centuries*, ed. H. E. Wooldridg
   and H. V. Hughes, 2 vols. (London, 1897–1913), vol. 1, plate 31, and vol. 2, pp. 61–2.
5 For further discussion of the successes and shortcomings of music scribes, particularl
   in books not primarily designed for the inclusion of music, see H. Deeming, 'Observa
   tions on the Habits of Twelfth- and Thirteenth-Century Music Scribes', *Scriptorium* 6
   (2006), 38–59.

Table 19.1: The devotional series in British Library, MS Harley 524

fol.	Rubric	Incipit	Thematic group
63r	–	Veri floris sub figura (with musical notation in two parts)	Mary
63v	commemoratio de trinitate antiphona	Libera nos salva nos iustifica nos	Trinity
	Oracio	Omnipotens sempiterne deus qui deduisti famulis tuis	
	Orac[i]o ad crucem		Cross
	Antiphona	Salva nos christe salvator per virtutem	
	Item ad crucem	Perpetua nos domine pace custodi	
	Ad sanctam mariam oracio	Porrige nobis domine sancte pater	Mary
	Ad sanctam Iohannem ewangelistam. Oracio	Beati iohannis apostoli tui et evangeliste	John ev.
	Ad sanctum blasium	Deus qui beatum blasium ita in petra fidei solidasti	Blaise
	ad sanctum eustachium oracio	Deus qui tuos athletas gloria celesti remunera	Eustace
	De sancta cristina oracio	Indulgentiam nobis domine beata cristina virgo et martyr	Christina
	Sequencia De sancta maria	Ave maria gracia plena dominus tecum virgo serena (verse)	Mary
64r	Imnus	Magnificat anima mea dominum.	
	Sequencia De sancta maria	Salve regina misericordie. vita dulcedo. et spes nostra salve	
	Oracio	Omnipotens sempiterne deus qui gloriose semper virginis	
	Oracio de virgine	Deus qui beatam virginem mariam semper	
64v	Ym[n]us	Veni creator spiritus mentes tuorum visita (verse)	Holy Spirit
	Oracio	Per te accessum habeamus ad filium tuum o benedicta	Mary
65r	–	Regina clemencie maria vocata (verse, lineated)	
	antiphona	Gaude dei genitrix virgo immaculata	
	Antiphona	Missus est gabriel angelus ad mariam virginem	
65v	oratio	Te domina mea clementissima virgo dei genitrix	
	oracio	Domina mea sancta maria	
	oracio ad crucem	En la honourance de la sainte veraie croiz	Cross
	Oracio ad coronam	Beals sire deux por lamor de la sainte coroune	
	Ad manus	Beals Sire deux. por lamor des sainz clouz. que en vos beles mains furent fichiez	
66r	Ad pedes	Beals Sire deux pour lamor des sainz clous qui en vos beals piez furent fichiez	
	Ad lanceam	Beals sire deux por lamour de la sainte lance	
	antiphona de cruce	Salve crux sancta que in corpore christi	
	antiphona de cruce	Crucem tuam adoramus domine	

or*acio* ad crucem
En la honourance de la sainte veraie croiz beals sire dex. que vos soustenistes
en passiu*n* por touz pecheours raiendre. di. ici. treis pa*ter* no*ster*. que vos hui
en icest ior pour lamor de la sainte veraie croiz me defendez de hounte. e de
vergoigne. e mal. E de mesave*n*ture. E de e*n*conbrier de me*n* cors. E me doin-
siez pardurable vie. e repos p*ar*durable. e espace de penitance. e amendement
de vie. (British Library, MS Harley 524, fol. 65v)

[Prayer to the Cross
In honour of the holy true Cross, good Lord God, which sustained you in your
Passion, ransom for all sinners. Say here three Our Fathers. Now in this day,
for the love of the holy true Cross, defend me from disgrace, and from shame,
and evil, and from misadventure, and from burdens to my body, and grant
me eternal life and everlasting rest and time for repentance and amendment
of life.]

The text as written here seems to be functioning as a 'script' for live performance rather than an abstracted written record of materials that might be used
in that way: a little like the rubrics of liturgical books or the *didascalia* of play-
texts, these directions interact with the texts themselves to suggest a performa-
tive envisaging of them.[6] The French prayers are directed to different members
of the crucified body and emblems of the Crucifixion, thus using a visual stimulus to focus the mind on the mysteries of the Passion. Prefiguring a trend that
would become increasingly significant in pastoral literature in the following two
centuries, the prayers invite the reader to engage their inner senses to empathize
directly with Christ's suffering, as did a fifteenth-century text that exhorted the
reader to 'ymaginne in þin herte as þou seiʒe þi lorde' through a visual meditation on the Passion.[7]

One explanation for the choice of devotions in the whole collection could be a
visual or spatial inspiration, with each group of devotions corresponding to the
paintings or altars in a chapel or church, or even the images in a Book of Hours,
or other illustrated manuscript. I have not found a corresponding visual series to
match the topics of the MS Harley 524 series, but evidence of meditative reading
in front of visual images can be found elsewhere: one early fourteenth-century
set of Anglo-Norman prayers and meditations includes a section to be read

---

6   Such indications of performance are given an admirably nuanced interpretation in
    C. Symes, 'Prescription, Proscription, Transcription, Improvisation: Re-Assessing the
    Written and Unwritten Evidence for Pre-Modern Performance Practice', in *Scripted
    Orality*, ed. D. Pietropaolo (Toronto, forthcoming). For further discussion of perform-
    ance indications in MS Harley 524, see below.
7   J. C. Hirsch, 'Prayer and Meditation in Late Medieval England: MS Bodley 789',
    Medium Aevum 48 (1979), 55–66. There are also similarities with the fourteenth-century
    Middle English 'Arma Christi' poem, often transmitted in manuscripts decorated with
    actual depictions of the instruments of the Passion; see R. Hope Robbins, 'The "Arma
    Christi" Rolls', *MLR* 34 (1939), 415–20.

hen you see the crucifix before you, whether in the minster, or in your book'.[8]
s personal, private devotions, these series were not bound by the linguistic norms
the standard liturgy, and were able to explore the possibilities of French as a
nguage of prayer and worship for their readers. As comparison with my next
ample will show, these books certainly emanated from clerical circles: while the
xts within them may have been passed on, through preaching and other forms of
storal care, both to other religious and to laypeople, they provide further secure
idence of the cultivation and interest in Francophone pastoralia among the thir-
enth-century clergy.[9]

Before discussing more fully the significance of the French texts in MS Harley
?4 I wish to make a comparison to another manuscript with a number of simi-
rities, Maidstone Museum, MS A.13.[10] Like the former manuscript, the texts
Maidstone are loosely grouped, and spaces have been left blank for later
lditions to each group: further items have been added, and also marginal
otes relating to the first layer of texts and a certain amount of cross-referencing
etween pages. Almost all of the manuscript's texts are in Latin, although three
e in French,[11] and a slightly higher number in Middle English.[12] Maidstone also
ontains a devotional series rather like the one in MS Harley 524, except that
is entirely in Latin, and nearly all its prayers and devotions relate to a single
ibject, that of the Virgin.

The two most substantial French texts in Maidstone occur in a gathering also
ontaining the majority of the English texts as well as some Latin. On fol. 93v
ere is a five-stanza French poem on the subject of Mary,[13] and later in the gath-
ing there is a set of eleven stanzas on the inevitability of death, extracted from
much longer poem called 'Les Vers de la Mort', composed in the 1190s.[14] The
athering opens with three English verse texts, the first of which is an abbrevi-

---

'Quant vus veez le crucifix devant vus ou a muster ou en vostre livre', Dean no. 942.
I am grateful to Jocelyn Wogan-Browne for this reference.

As Nicholas Watson and Jocelyn Wogan-Browne have put it, 'the French of England
was a significant language of pastoralia'; 'The French of England: the *Compileison*,
Ancrene Wisse, and the Idea of Anglo-Norman', *Journal of Romance Studies* 4.3: Special
issue: *Cultural Traffic in the Medieval Romance World*, ed. S. Gaunt and J. Weiss (Winter
2004), 35–59 (p. 41).

For full description, see Ker, *MMBL*, III, 317–21. See also C. Brown, 'A Thirteenth-
Century Manuscript at Maidstone', *MLR* 21 (1926), 1–12; C. Brown, 'The Maidstone
Text of the "Proverbs of Alfred"', *MLR* 21 (1926), 249–60. Ker rejected Brown's attri-
butions of the manuscript to the Cluniac Priory of Northampton in one article, and
Revesby Abbey in the other: see Ker's *Medieval Libraries of Great Britain: A List of
Surviving Books* (London, 1964), pp. 135, 158.

For the Anglo-Norman texts, see Dean nos. 609, 804.

On these, see Brown, 'A Thirteenth-Century Manuscript', and idem, 'Proverbs'.

Dean no. 804.

Les Vers de la Mort par Hélinant, moine de Froidmont, ed. F. Wulff and E. Walberg, SATF
(Paris, 1905). The specific stanzas excerpted are listed in Ker, *MMBL*, III, p. 318, and
the item is listed as 'a sermon or meditation composed of eleven scattered stanzas from
Les Vers de la Mort' in Dean no. 609. See also Brown, 'Proverbs', pp. 259–60, where he
retracts his earlier suggestion that the manuscript originated at Revesby Abbey.

ated version of the 'Proverbs of Alfred' and the last of which, a song warning (
the perils of dying unconfessed, is provided with musical notation.[15] Betwee
the two French poems and on the final two leaves of the gathering are Lati
texts, consisting of moralizing tales and miracles of the Virgin: the twin theme
of the gathering, then, are devotion to the Virgin and lessons in good condu(
and preparing for death. Like the topics in the MS Harley 524 devotional serie
these are themes of practical, everyday religion, and not of academic theology: a
discussed further below, it may be no coincidence that in both manuscripts, th
French texts coincide with such topics.

Also like MS Harley 524, the Maidstone manuscript is liberally peppere
throughout with short verses, including the other French item, a couplet o
fol. 49v. This occurs within the longest section of the manuscript, some eight
folios with over three hundred topic headings, each of which is followed by
list of references relating to that topic. Most of the references are to Biblical an
patristic authorities, but a considerable number of short verses summarizin
the theme (including the French couplet and several others in English) are als
included. This section of the manuscript seems to have been designed as a pra(
tical work of reference for someone involved in preaching or other ministr
and was again left open-ended and added to over time by one or more scribe
Although, like MS Harley 524, a coherent scheme of organization is not apparen
here across the entire book, some of Maidstone's sub-sections show internal plan
ning, and the book's contents could certainly have been used efficiently by
reader familiar with them. For example, one list of definitions is ordered alph.
betically, and elsewhere, several sections of sermons are arranged in order of th
liturgical calendar.[16]

Despite their similarities, there are also important differences between thes
two manuscripts. In Maidstone, both the complete texts and the references ten
to be attributed to their authors, and the authorities quoted are – in the main
of serious scholarly repute (Seneca, Aristotle, Jerome, Augustine, Bede, Gregor
to mention a few). In making these attributions, the scribes have imbued th
manuscript with a somewhat more scholarly tone than MS Harley 524: a reade
preparing a sermon or composing a didactic text of his own with the aid of th
manuscript would have had immediately to hand both the words and the name
of the *auctoritates*, with which to sprinkle his text. Yet despite their different att

---

[15] The notated lyric, 'Man mei longe' is reproduced in facsimile in C. Page, 'A Catalogu
and Bibliography of English Song from Its Beginnings to *c.*1300', *Royal Musical Associ*
tion Research Chronicle 13 (1976), 82; an edition may be found in E. J. Dobson and F. L
Harrison, *Medieval English Songs* (London, 1979), no. 6a; but the edition raises man
problems, examined – with specific reference to 'Man mei longe' – in John Stevens
review of the volume in *Music & Letters* 62 (1981), 461–6 (pp. 462–4). The scribe respon
sible for the musical notation was evidently less experienced than the notator at wor
in MS Harley 524: for a discussion of his difficulties, see Deeming, 'Observations o
Music Scribes', p. 46 and plate 7.

[16] Ker, *MMBL*, III, p. 319.

tudes towards authorship, both books represent a single-volume compendium that could be consulted, without reference to other books, for a selection of texts of various kinds relating to particular topics. By implication, both books could have been particularly beneficial to those whose access to more substantial textual resources in the form of libraries was limited: such groups could include the mendicant orders, particularly during their travels, and the monks and canons of small, poorly endowed houses or dependent cells.

Neither book falls squarely within the purview of sermon studies,[17] because complete sermons form a relatively small part of their total contents, but both fit the description of what Siegfried Wenzel calls 'random sermon collections': 'their sermons appear interspersed with short passages that must have been felt to be useful for preachers: theological commonplaces, distinctions, mnemonic verses, exempla with or without moralizations, and the like'.[18] Whether or not they contain sermons, miscellanies preserving selections of this kind of material may likewise represent a kaleidoscope of materials that could be used as sources for those engaged in religious instruction. To the friar preparing a sermon, or the monk charged with reading aloud in the monastic refectory, and to any reader looking for material for private devotional reading, such books provided valuable – and compact – resources.[19]

There are few precise clues to the origins or early functions of Maidstone MS A.13 and MS Harley 524. MS Harley 524 may have circulated unbound to begin with: Maidstone certainly did, since it has a pronounced crease down the length of all the pages increasing in depth towards the back of the book, suggesting that it was folded lengthways.[20] Maidstone's folding in half and Harley's separable quires may be indicators that the books travelled around, as their compilers added new contents and made use of the existing ones. Both books ended up in religious houses later in the Middle Ages: Maidstone contains some accounts of the hospital of St John in Northampton, added in the fourteenth century,[21] and MS Harley 524 has had fifteenth-century letters from an abbot of Osney added to its final leaf. But there is no evidence that these later homes were also the places of origin of the manuscripts, although the North Midland dialect of the scribe

---

[17] S. Wenzel, *Preachers, Poets and the Early English Lyric* (Princeton, 1986), pp. 4–8; S. Wenzel, 'Sermon Collections and their Taxonomy', in *The Whole Book: Cultural Perspectives on the Medieval Miscellany*, ed. S. G. Nichols and S. Wenzel (Ann Arbor, 1997), pp. 7–21.

[18] 'Sermon Collections', p. 15.

[19] V. Gillespie, '*Doctrina* and *Predicacio*: The Design and Function of Some Pastoral Manuals', *LSE*, n.s. 11 (1980), 36–50; B. M. Kienzle, 'The Twelfth-Century Monastic Sermon', in *The Sermon*, ed. B. M. Kienzle, Typologie des sources du Moyen Âge occidental 81–3 (Turnhout, 2000), pp. 298–9.

[20] A leaf from the manuscript, clearly showing this vertical crease, is reproduced in Deeming, 'Observations on Music Scribes', plate 7.

[21] Ker, *MMBL*, p. 320.

of Maidstone's English texts suggests an origin not far away,[22] and – from their content – both books are likely to have been produced by and for clerics.

What is striking about these two anthologies – and others like them – is the diversity of their materials: whether they were intended for private reading, for instruction, or for preaching, their compilers seem to have selected their materials from well beyond the usual scope of devotional and religious texts. This creative attitude towards choosing material for devotional and didactic purposes goes hand-in-hand with the books' haphazard organization: both suggest that their compilers gathered together anything that might feasibly serve their purpose, and added it to their books whenever and wherever they happened to find it. For longer texts, this might be when a new exemplar became available to the scribe, but for the very short texts, particularly the memorable couplets, the scribe might simply have heard them and written them down from memory.

Most interesting, in terms of this variety of materials, are the prevalence of poetry and the inclusion of French (and – in the case of Maidstone – English too). The former is in keeping with what may be termed a general fashion for versified religious texts in this period, both in Latin and in the vernaculars. This trend emerges from a recognition that verse could serve an important function in religious instructions, perhaps making texts more engaging to read, and certainly easier to memorize.[23] It is for this reason that fourteenth- and fifteenth-century preachers are known to have quoted from verses and songs in their sermons,[24] and it is the same impulse that lay behind the creation, in the twelfth and thirteenth centuries, of versified Biblical and devotional texts, and the collection in books like Maidstone and MS Harley 524 of verse texts on religious topics.

The use of French also fits with a wider trend, from at least the early thirteenth century, of translating devotional and pastoral texts into French and of composing new ones in that language.[25] Best known are the many translations and new compositions in French during the thirteenth century that can be connected to royal and noble families, particularly women: Edward II's queen, Isabella, had a French translation of the Old Testament, and John of Howden translated his

---

22 Dobson and Harrison, *Medieval English Songs*, p. 122.

23 The various functions of verse in religious instruction are outlined by Wenzel, *Preachers, Poets and the Early English Lyric*, pp. 80–1.

24 D. B. Jeffrey, *The Early English Lyric and Franciscan Spirituality* (Lincoln NE, 1975); S. Wenzel, *Verses in Sermons* (Cambridge MA, 1978); Wenzel, *Preachers, Poets and the Early English Lyric*; A. J. Fletcher, *Preaching, Politics and Poetry in Late Medieval England* (Dublin, 1998), all concentrate on the use of English verses in sermons, but Latin songs were also sometimes used in this way: C. Page, 'Angelus ad Virginem: A New Work by Philip the Chancellor?', *Early Music* 11 (1983), 69–70; T. B. Payne, 'Aurelianis civitas: Student Unrest in Medieval France and a Conductus by Philip the Chancellor', *Speculum* 75 (2000), 589–614. A very early example of this practice occurs in an eleventh-century Anglo-Saxon sermon: J. Moore, 'Rex Omnipotens: A Sequence Used in an Old English Ascension Day Homily', *Anglia* 106 (1988), 138–44.

25 Short, 'Patrons and Polyglots'.

ɔem on the Passion, *Philomena*, into French for Eleanor of Provence.[26] Yet even
.ore abundant are French religious texts owned and used in less elevated circles:
ɔth male and female religious houses acquired translations of monastic Rules,
iints' Lives and other devotional literature around this time.[27] Recent research
ıs increasingly drawn attention to the importance of the French of England as
language of devotion and religious instruction, alongside its roles in courtly,
lministrative and mercantile situations.[28] Far from being the sole preserve of the
ity, both written and spoken French continued to be pervasive among English
erics throughout the thirteenth century and beyond, and indeed may often have
ıabled the transmission of religious literature between religious orders, and from
erics to laity.[29]

The rise of the French vernacular for written religious texts during the thir-
enth century is linked to ecclesiastical reforms that addressed the need for
ıprovement in clerical education, as well as in the instruction of the laity. These
forms, surrounding the papacy of Innocent III and the decrees of the Fourth
ateran Council in 1215, encouraged priests and confessors to find new ways
' conveying the teachings of the Church.[30] The effect was an atmosphere of

---

C. Baswell, 'Latinitas', in Wallace, *Medieval English Literature*, pp. 122–51 (p. 148).

Legge, *Anglo-Norman in the Cloisters*. For monastic *regulae* in French, see Dean nos.
710–14. A particularly interesting hagiographical manuscript is the Campsey collection
(London, BL, Add. 70513): for which, see D. Russell, 'The Campsey Collection of Old
French Saints' Lives: A Re-examination of its Structure and Provenance', *Scriptorium*
57 (2003), 51–83; and J. Wogan-Browne, 'Powers of Record, Powers of Example: Hagiography and Women's History', in *Gendering the Master Narrative: Women and Power in
the Middle Ages*, ed. M. Erler and M. Kowaleski (Ithaca NY, 2003), pp. 37–56.

See especially Watson and Wogan-Browne, 'The French of England', passim; J.-P.
Pouzet, 'Quelques aspects de l'influence des chanoins augustins sur la production
et la transmission littéraire vernaculaire en Angleterre (XIIIᵉ–XVᵉ siècles)', *Académie
des Inscriptions et Belles-lettres, Comptes rendues* (2004), pp. 169–213 and the essay by
Pouzet in this volume; C. Cannon, 'Monastic Production' in Wallace, *Medieval English
Literature*, pp. 316–48.

An excellent example of this is the *Compileison* discussed by Watson and Wogan-
Browne: 'Geoffrey of Wroxham could have used, or at least envisaged the use of his
text in the multifarious contexts of medieval Norwich – refectory reading, confessional
duties within or outside the priory, in the Norwich hospitals, or even in solitary study.
… In the *Compileison*, *Ancrene Wisse* is also an East Anglian French text for use by men
and women, lay and religious, in one of the busiest and most diverse urban contexts
of the medieval English eastern coastlands. The idea of Anglo-Norman here becomes
much more demotic, much less exclusive. At the very least it is a language of dissemination and training in Geoffrey of Wroxham's Benedictine context. At the most it is
understood and used among a wide range of religious and semi-religious (their social
estates in this period by no means confined to upper gentry and nobility …) – one
aspect of the multifarious cultural traffic of late medieval Norwich'; 'The French of
England', p. 52.

J. Sayers, *Innocent III: Leader of Europe 1198–1216* (London, 1994), ch. 4; A. Bennett, 'A
Book Designed for a Noblewoman: An Illustrated *Manuel des Péchés* of the Thirteenth
Century', in *Medieval Book Production: Assessing the Evidence*, ed. L. Brownrigg (Los
Altos Hills CA, 1990), p. 163.

creativity and enthusiasm towards pastoral duties, leading those involved i
preaching and ministry to explore new texts and new kinds of texts to serve the
purpose, whomever they were instructing. Seeking out new materials, wheth
in Latin, French or English, and focusing on themes of individual salvatic
(through prayer, confession and penance),[31] the ecclesiastics of the post-Latera
era strove to stem the tide of heresy and to restore the authority of the Church.

It is this impulse that led to the compilation of anthologies such as the tw
considered here. In their choice of assorted texts in three languages, in pros
verse and even songs with musical settings, and drawn from new sources as we
as conventional authorities, Maidstone and MS Harley 524 are models of th
new attitude to religious instruction. The precise identity of their first owne
is unrecoverable, but such books could have been used to compile sermon
either to be preached by friars or secular canons to the laity or by members
the enclosed orders within their religious communities. They could also hav
been used by almost any literate person for private reading or personal study, c
by someone with a didactic calling, for instructing others in leading a Christia
life. Such books could have had more than one use, and their refreshing – albe
jumbled – range of texts shows them to be a product of the spirit of creativit
abounding in religious contexts during this period of reformation.

Though they are not beautiful artefacts, and their physical features suggest the
were put to pragmatic uses rather than being aesthetically prized, these misce
lanies have a charm that results from their individuality. As windows onto th
hidden world of the private performance of devotion they are immensely valuab
not least because they place the French language so centrally within that new
revitalized devotional tradition. Moreover, they exhibit enormous practical valu
covering the gamut of religious experience. One final text from MS Harley 5.
epitomizes these concerns: beginning 'pro dolore dentium' (or 'for tooth-ache')
is a prayer in French with extensive performance instructions in Latin, offering
devotional solution to an everyday problem:

¶ Pro dolore denti*um* dicat*ur* cotidie du*m* legit*ur* evangeli*um* post gloria tibi
domine. + la croiz el no*m* deu *et* seint lorenz seit entremei *et* la dolor des dent.
por les almes Ioachim *et* anne. pat*er* noster. *et* faciat signu*m* crucis in fauci*bus*
(British Library, MS Harley 524, fol. 66r)

[¶ To be said for tooth-ache every day when the gospel is read, after the Gloria
tibi domine, + In the name of God and St Laurence, may the Cross be between
me and the pain in my teeth, for the souls of Joachim and Anna. Our Father.
And make the sign of the cross on the throat.]

---

[31] These themes came to dominate vernacular religious literature during the centur
Watson and Wogan-Browne write of 'a widespread mid-thirteenth-century elevatic
of confession and penance to a place where they can virtually correspond to the life
the soul'; 'The French of England', p. 45.

The Latin instructions specify the occasion and frequency of the prayer's reciting, and the additional prayer and ritual gesture that should follow it, while the shift from the rubric to the prayer itself is articulated by the move from Latin to French. Such an item seems destined to be enacted, not simply studied, and for those who used this book, and those to whom they passed on the practical wisdom contained within it, such texts must have been of great comfort indeed.

20

Augustinian Canons and their Insular French Books in Medieval England: Towards An Assessment

This essay presents elements from a book in preparation provisionally entitled, 'Augustinian Canons and the Making of English Culture, c.1150–c.1540', which naturally includes a consideration of manuscripts in the French language in Augustinian hands. In the larger study, the aim is to cover French books imported from the Continent to England, and, most particularly, books produced in England in Insular French. The first category will include books acquired directly from France, but for English Augustinians this is not likely to yield very much, as the English Augustinian houses are among those with fewest institutional links, or links severed at an early date, with the Continent.[1] Indirect acquisition from France, through particular gifts of books presented to an Augustinian house, is more promising, but its channels and circumstances are very difficult to assess, though they can be guided by memorial inscriptions.[2]

It is with materials principally inherent in the second category, and over a fraction of the whole period, that this essay is concerned.[3] Further to a famous first approach to the topic by M. Dominica Legge nearly sixty years ago,[4] in what follows I consider manuscripts containing Insular French with clear signs of Augustinian association, bearing in mind that a distinction between manuscripts

---

* For generous response, I thank Hugo Azérad, Caroline Boucher, André Crépin, Ralph Hanna, Tony Hunt, Linne Mooney, Nigel Morgan, Jean-Claude Thiolier, Rod Thomson, Jocelyn Wogan-Browne, Bob Yeager – and particularly Nigel Ramsey, James Willoughby and my parents and sister.

1 See J. C. Dickinson, *The Origins of the Austin Canons and Their Introduction into England* (London, 1950); D. Knowles and R. N. Hadcock, *Medieval Religious Houses, England and Wales*, 2nd rev. edn (London, 1971); D. M. Robinson, *The Geography of Augustinian Settlement in Medieval England and Wales*, 2 vols. (Oxford, 1980); K. Stöber, *Late Medieval Monasteries and their Patrons: England and Wales, c.1300–1450* (Woodbridge, 2007).

2 One Latin example is Cambridge, King's College, MS 2, on which see M. Gullick and T. Webber, 'Summary Catalogue of Surviving Manuscripts from Leicester Abbey', in *Leicester Abbey: Medieval History, Archaeology, and Manuscript Studies*, ed. J. Story, J. Bourne and R. Buckley (Leicester, 2006), pp. 173–92 (pp. 173–4).

3 Space precludes my treatment of the books of the canonesses, but see e.g., Cambridge, Trinity College, MS B.1.45 and, for another canonesses' manuscript online, see D. W. Russell, *The Electronic Campsey Project* at http://margot.uwaterloo.ca/campsey/.

4 Legge, *Anglo-Norman in the Cloisters*, especially ch. VI, 'Canons and a Canoness', pp. 57–76.

roduced with the scribal and intellectual resources of Augustinian houses, and
anuscripts otherwise acquired and held in their libraries is far from easy – such
the case, for instance, for two manuscripts from East Yorkshire displaying
arious formats of French text: Oxford, Bodleian Library, MS Digby 53, a gram-
atical and religious Latin miscellany, including substantial glosses in French
nd English, from Bridlington Priory; and, more flamboyantly perhaps, London,
ritish Library, MS Harley 1770, one of the trilingual 'Surtees' Psalters, with an
-libris from Kirkham Priory; the former may well have been a 'house' product,
hereas it is less clear whether the latter also was.[5] Also examined in the larger
udy (and *in parvo* here) are works of Augustinian authorship, especially in
anuscripts once located in Augustinian libraries, or disseminated through
ugustinian channels, either within the order, or from Augustinian houses
 those of other orders (of Cistercian and Premonstratensian communities in
articular), or outside regular communities. The presence of works originally by
ugustinian writers in the library records of other orders presumably betrays
gns of inter-order dissemination at some stage, and this may be instrumental in
acing the fortunes of some books containing Insular French.[6]

Taken cumulatively, the evidence of Augustinian agency in the authorship,
wnership, production and dissemination of Insular French material is consider-
ɔle, even amid the wealth of Latin material, and the limited, though significant
ray of material in English. Moreover, in spite of the bibliographical achieve-
ents of the later twentieth century, inadequately covered areas of research
main. As A. I. Doyle points out, following N. R. Ker himself, *Medieval Libraries*
 Great Britain excludes 'most of the business volumes which survive from the
istitutions listed' – a limitation in scope not remedied in Ker's *Medieval Manu-
ripts in British Libraries* or, as Doyle notes, in Davis's *Medieval Cartularies of
reat Britain*.[7] Archival documents, in particular administrative and business
aterials (cartularies, account-books, rentals, and miscellaneous registers) need
ore consideration, as they include documents written in French. The evidence
f the medieval conspectus of some Augustinian libraries promises a more
ystematic survey, but is indicative rather than complete. Firstly, both the mid

---

Ker, *MLGB*, pp. 12 (Digby 53), 106 (Harley 1770).
For book circulation between Augustinians and Cistercians in Yorkshire, see
A. Lawrence-Mathers, 'The Augustinians and their Libraries', in her *Manuscripts in
Northumbria in the Eleventh and Twelfth Centuries* (Cambridge, 2003), pp. 177–93.
Ker, MLGB, p. viii; A. I. Doyle, 'Book Production by the Monastic Orders in England
(c.1375–1530): Assessing the Evidence', in *Medieval Book Production*, pp. 1–19 (p. 2);
G. R. C. Davis, *Medieval Cartularies of Great Britain* (London, 1958), with additions and
amendments notably by P. Hoskin, N. Vincent et al., and R. Hayes, in *Monastic Research
Bulletin*, respectively 2 (1996), 3 (1997), 4 (1998); see also the extended coverage of religious houses in the indexes of the National Register of Archives, at http://www.hmc.
gov.uk/nra/searches/, and the web resource initiated by N. Ramsay, at http://www.
ucl.ac.uk/history/englishmonasticarchives.

to late thirteenth-century *Registrum* prepared by the Oxford Franciscans,[8] an
the extant catalogues and book-lists edited by A. G. Watson and T. Webber, onl
present evidence for a fraction of Augustinian houses: out of a total of (only
thirty-four, there are extensive records only for three of the largest establishment
in England: Bridlington (East Yorkshire), Llanthony (Secunda) (Gloucestershire
and Leicester (Leicestershire).[9] Secondly, these records create only a still-lif
account – and often a deferred, indeed distorted one – of necessarily changin;
library resources within those institutions, with books borrowed, lent or unde
some form of private use generally not reported – with few exceptions, such as a
Anglesey Priory (Cambridgeshire) – nor even all books for common use alway
included systematically in domestic census at a given period – except, perhaps
in such meticulous book-lists as those compiled by William Charyte at Leiceste
in the last years of the fifteenth century.[10] Significantly, Leland's famously versa
tile accounts complement or corroborate earlier available evidence for only si
houses, while constituting the sole source of survey known to survive for eightee
– more than half of them.[11] Just as for the other orders, the Protean nature c
pre-Dissolution Augustinian libraries is further reflected in the very substantie
portion of extant Augustinian manuscripts (together with some printed books,
which cannot be matched against any items recorded in the known book-list
or catalogues – a somewhat daunting lack of symmetry, yet one suggesting tha
discoveries are not geared only to such bibliographical matching.

In that patchy picture, the recording of French books must labour under th
vicissitudes of cataloguers' persuasions: thus reliable evidence from the circuit
of visitations reported in the Franciscan *Registrum* is corroborated by othe
sources, but does not seem to signal any French material – plausibly reflectin;

---

8   *Registrum Anglie de libris doctorum et auctorum veterum*, ed. R. A. B. Mynors, R. F
    Rouse and M. A. Rouse CBMLC 2 (London, 1991), pp. i–iv and cxxix–cxxxiv. On th
    Registrum's dating see J. Higgett with J. Durkan, *Scottish Libraries* CBMLC 12 (Londor
    2006), p. xxxvi.

9   *The Libraries of the Augustinian Canons*, ed. A. G. Watson and T. Webber CBMLC
    (London, 1998). In his revised description of London, BL, MS Cotton Tiberius A
    IX (dated July 2004; available at http://www.bl.uk/catalogues/manuscripts.html
    J. Harrison notes that fol. 101r contains a 'Memorandum of liturgical vestments, uter
    sils & books' of Osney Abbey, with revisions (*saec.* xiii/xiv)', not recorded by Watso
    and Webber.

10 On Charyte, see recently R. Sharpe, 'Library Catalogues and Indexes', in *The Cambridg*
    History of the Book in Britain, vol. II: *1100–1400*, ed. N. Morgan and R. M. Thomso
    (Cambridge, 2008), 197–218 (pp. 212–13).

11 D. N. Bell, 'Monastic Libraries: 1400–1557', in *The Cambridge History of the Book i*
    Britain, vol. III: *1400–1557*, ed. L. Hellinga and J. B. Trapp (Cambridge, 1999), 229–5
    idem, 'The Libraries of Religious Houses in the Late Middle Ages', in *The Cambridg*
    History of Libraries in Britain and Ireland, ed. E. S. Leedham-Green and T. Webber, 3 vol
    (Cambridge, 2006), I, 126–51 – with an emphasis on the medieval library as 'a shiftir
    accumulation of changing materials' in the latter essay (p. 126); see also R. Sharpe, 'Th
    Medieval Librarian', in *Cambridge History of Libraries*, I, 218–41.

the visitors' principal focus of interest on Latin patristic texts.[12] The various extant Augustinian lists edited by Watson and Webber, on the other hand, even though they cannot be taken as absolute representatives, seem to have given the French texts in them a more proportionate share of attention than the fraternal visitors to Augustinian houses. Moreover, the amount of Insular French in these lists compares favourably with that found in the extant records of the other major habitual monastic consumers of French, the Benedictines, Cistercians and Premonstratensians.[13] Though there is, for instance, only one short section of the book-list for Augustinian Leicester that could compare in number or nature with the famous Beauchamp bequest of manuscripts of French romances to the Cistercian house at Bordesley (Worcestershire) in 1306 – this being probably a temporary addition of French books sooner or later destined for dispersal[14] –the Charyte lists nevertheless contain significant records of French texts that would be of interest to Augustinian houses – religious, didactic, grammatical and legal.[15] The grouped Leicester French books – presumably all Insular French, judging by their summary description – are entries 1425–35 (1435 being probably a repeat of 1434): items 1425, 1428, 1431 are Biblical; items 1426, 1427, 1429, 1432 romances; 1430 looks legal; 1433 is a *Mandeville* – which may compare with London, British Library, MS Harley 212 from the Augustinian Priory at Bolton in West Yorkshire (discussed below)[16] – and 1434 (1435) appears to be Walter of Bibbesworth's *Treatise*.[17] Although this grouping does not eclipse the appearance of scattered Insular French materials elsewhere in the catalogue records (item 1298, *Decretals* 'in gallico', being a good case in point), nor does it preclude the possibility of 'unobtrusive' French within Latin manuscripts, not signposted in the summary entries or second-folio indications,[18] it is – rather unsurprisingly – in the realms of 'Romances', 'Historica' and the variously subdivided field of

---

[12] As noted by T. Webber, 'Monastic and Cathedral Book Collections in the Late Eleventh and Twelfth Centuries', in *Cambridge History of Libraries*, I, 109–25 (p. 118).

[13] *English Benedictine Libraries. The Shorter Catalogues*, ed. R. Sharpe, J. P. Carley, R. H. Thomson and A. G. Watson, CBMLC 4 (London, 1995); *The Libraries of the Cistercians, Gilbertines and Premonstratensians*, ed. D. N. Bell, CBMLC 3 (London, 1992). This favourable proportion corroborates Hanna's remark that 'one striking feature of surviving Augustinian books is the heady percentage in the vernacular, including Anglo-Norman': R. Hanna, 'Augustinian Canons and Middle English Literature', in *The English Medieval Book: Studies in Memory of Jeremy Griffiths*, ed. A. S. G. Edwards, V. A. Gillespie and R. Hanna (London, 2000), pp. 27–42 (p. 36).

[14] M. Blaess, 'L'abbaye de Bordesley et les livres de Guy de Beauchamp', *Romania* 78 (1957), 511–18; eadem, 'Les manuscrits français dans les monastères anglais au Moyen Age', *Romania* 94 (1973), 321–58; *Libraries of Cistercians, Gilbertines and Premonstratensians*, ed. Bell, pp. 4–10; Bell, 'Libraries of Religious Houses', p. 143.

[15] *Libraries of Augustinian Canons*, ed. Watson and Webber, A.20, A.21 (pp. 104–400).

[16] On *Mandeville* manuscripts and contexts, see M. J. Bennett, '*Mandeville's Travels* and the Anglo-French moment', *Medium Aevum* 75 (2006), 273–92.

[17] *Libraries of Augustinian Canons*, ed. Watson and Webber, pp. 358–9.

[18] An Augustinian example of 'unobtrusive French' is London, British Library, MS Cotton Tiberius A. IX, in the possession of St Frideswide Priory at Oxford (discussed below).

'religious' activities, that the majority of French books are to be found in this and some of the other Augustinian lists. It may be for these categories of books in particular that Ralph Hanna's insightful observation that 'reliance on local French texts, especially after 1350' may betray Augustinian agency takes its full measure.[19] Consider, for instance, an early fourteenth century surviving Insular French book from Llanthony (Secunda). Item 12 in the Llanthony list is now Oxford, Corpus Christi College, MS 36; its booklets contain an Insular French version of several *Sermons* of Maurice de Sully (followed by some Latin sermons), a copy of the *Merure de Seinte Eglise* (translated from the *Speculum Ecclesie*), another of the so-called *Poème anglo-normand sur l'Ancien Testament*, and fragments of further French Biblical rewriting.[20] Although it is difficult to assign it to Llanthony workmanship, the decorative features of some initial letters suggest some continuity from the 'house style' of some Western houses developed between the late eleventh and late twelfth centuries and exemplified, *inter alia*, in surviving books from Cirencester and Llanthony.[21]

From an examination of extant records, the necessity of further systematic gathering and analysis of the scattered evidence for all houses is clear, especially for those known to have been well-endowed and culturally active establishments, but for which little apparently survives. With their long-standing traditions of intellectual pursuits at Oxford or in its immediate vicinity, Osney Abbey and St Frideswide's Priory are good cases in point, with, for Osney, a meagre report in the *Registrum* and no catalogue of books known to survive, except for the six entries reported by Leland (with not one French book among them), and nothing at all, it seems, for the Oxonian priory.[22] There is, however, the direct evidence of at least two manuscripts containing Insular French having been in the medieval library at Osney, and one at St Frideswide's. The Osney books are Oxford, Bodleian Library, MS Digby 23, less famous for its first booklet

---

19 Hanna, 'Augustinian Canons and Middle English Literature', p. 36.
20 *Libraries of Augustinian Canons*, ed. Watson and Webber, A.16.12 (p. 39); *Poème anglo-normand sur l'Ancien Testament. Edition et commentaire*, ed. P. Nobel, 2 vols. (Paris, 1996). Another manuscript of the text, London, British Library, MS Egerton 2710, was associated (through an inscription, fol. 83v) with the Benedictine nuns at Derby, where there was also an Augustinian house – might inter-order contact be presumed? For the first century of Derby's existence (from *c*.1160 until 1257), the Benedictine nuns were in the care of the Augustinian abbot and canons of Darley Abbey (also in Derby); see Knowles and Hadcock, *Medieval Religious Houses*, pp. 140, 156, 252, 258.
21 J. J. G. Alexander, 'Scribes as Artists: The Arabesque Initial in Twelfth-Century English Manuscripts', in *Medieval Scribes, Manuscripts and Libraries: Essays Presented to N. R. Ker*, ed. M. B. Parkes and A. G. Watson (London, 1978), pp. 87–116; R. M. Thomson, 'Minor Manuscript Decoration from the West of England in the Twelfth Century', in *Reading Texts and Images: Essays on Medieval and Renaissance Art and Patronage in Honour of Margaret M. Manion*, ed. B. J. Muir (Exeter, 2002), pp. 19–34, revised in his *Books and Learning: Twelfth-Century England: the Ending of 'Alter Orbis'* (Walkern, Herts., 2006), pp. 73–84.
22 On Osney Abbey, see D. Postles, 'The Learning of Austin Canons: The Case of Oseney Abbey', *Nottingham Medieval Studies* 29 (1985), 32–43.

ntaining a glossed copy of Calcidius' translation of Plato's *Timaeus*, than for
second one with the *Chanson de Roland*, both booklets having been bound
gether possibly, but not necessarily, before the manuscript was presented to
sney;[23] and the first part of London, British Library, MS Cotton Tiberius A. ix
ols. 2r–106v), a historical miscellany damaged in the fire at Ashburnham House,
cluding (fols. 52r–98r) the late thirteenth-century *Chronicle* of Thomas Wykes,
Wycke (1222–*c.*1290), a canon of the house (and a prolific member of an inter-
ting group of thirteenth-century Augustinian historians), containing a short
rtion in Insular French (fols. 77vb–78ra) – both manuscripts were reported by
er, the latter, of course, with no reference to its small French constituents.[24] One
sular French book known to have been at St Frideswide's (though possibly not
e only extant one) is now Paris, Bibl. nat. MS f. fr. 24766, containing the works
another resident canon, Angier's *Dialogues de saint Gregoire* (fols. 2–151) and
e de saint Gregoire (fols. 153–74), the completion of both works exactly dated
om two colophons, respectively 29 November 1212 and 30 April 1214.[25]

A comprehensive list of book attestations in all sources, even beyond those
nstituted by documents from religious houses, together with direct evidence
book survival, is therefore needed to supplement presently available records
print. Such a need is probably well illustrated by some Augustinian houses
Yorkshire for which no catalogue or book-list is extant. Evidence of scribal
tivity at Bolton Priory is scanty, but the *Compotus* covering the years 1286–
325 yields significant clues in matters of book-making and book-holding in a
iddle-sized house in the west of Yorkshire bordering on Lancashire.[26] Whereas
e community was in business with York for some of the charters of appro-
riation of churches (in accounts for 1302–3), and at least for one of its books

M. B. Parkes, 'The Date of the Oxford Manuscript of *La Chanson de Roland* (Oxford, Bodleian Library, MS Digby 23)', *Medioevo Romanzo* 10/2 (1985), 161–75; A. Taylor, *Textual Situations: Three Medieval Manuscripts and Their Readers* (Philadelphia, 2002), pp. 26–70 (pp. 36–64); I. Short in *La Chanson de Roland – The Song of Roland: The French Corpus*, ed. J. J. Duggan (Turnhout, 2005); and K. S.-J. Murray, 'La mise en recueil comme glose? Le thème de la *translatio studii* dans le ms. Digby 23 de la Bibliothèque Bodléienne à Oxford', *Babel* 16 (2007), 345–55.

Ker, *MLGB*, p. 140, where only the first booklet of Digby 23 is ascribed to Osney. The revised description of Cotton Tiberius A. IX by J. Harrison (mentioned n. 9) like-wise ignores the 'unobtrusive' Insular French constituent incorporated in Wykes's *Chronicle*, but mentions the other French item from Osney, *Prophecies of Merlin* (dated 'saec. xiv[2/4]'). On Wykes, see A. Gransden, *Historical Writing in England c.550 to c.1307* (London, 1974), principally pp. 463–70; R. Sharpe, *A Handlist of the Latin Writers of Great Britain and Ireland Before 1540* (Turnhout, 2001), entry 1863.

Ker, *MLGB*, p. 141. For Angier and Insular French books at St Frideswide's, see most recently J. Wogan-Browne, 'Time to Read: Pastoral Care, Vernacular Access and the Case of Angier of St Frideswide', in *The Literature of Pastoral Care and Devotion in Medieval England: Essays in Honour of Bella Millett*, ed. C. Gunn and C. Innes Parker (York, forthcoming). I thank Jocelyn Wogan-Browne for pre-publication communication of this article.

The Bolton Priory Compotus 1286–1325, together with a priory account roll for 1377–1378, ed. I. Kershaw and D. M. Smith (with T. N. Cooper) (York, 2000).

(unspecified 'chronicles' in the accounts for 1312–13), and whereas it bought 'book of sentences' (presumably Peter Lombard's commentary) from an unspec fied source in 1304–5, the accounts for the years 1297–8 record money paid f gold, colours, and the illumination and binding of a missal, and those for 1309–: attest expenses 'pro uno libro qui vocatur *Veritates Theologie*' – presumably th famous *compendium* by Hugh of Ripelin, OP – and the buying of parchment.[27] is unclear whether mere acquisition or also copying is meant, but expenses f arranging parchment preparation often coincide with the specification of bool or charters copied. If 'house' scribal work is to be understood by those simult neous records, or by other records of the cost of parchment bought, or prepare at different times (in the accounts for 1298–9, 1302–3 notably), then provisic for other such scribal endeavours might well have been made in other now lo records of the priory.

Two proven extant Bolton books are in Insular French. Although it is impo sible to assign London, British Library, MS Harley 212, a version of Mandeville *Travels* in Insular French with a Bolton *ex-libris*, to Bolton 'house' work with an certainty, its plain layout and competent, though undistinguished, Anglicana a not impossible in such an establishment. Oxford, Bodleian Library, MS Fairfa 24, an almost all-French manuscript made up of two booklets, might likewis be associated with domestic book-making, but most probably not at Bolton.[28] I first defective booklet, containing as its first text (fols. 1r–20v) a now acephalot copy of the first redaction of Pierre de Langtoft's *Chronicle*, has been shown b Jean-Claude Thiolier to offer a text closest to the original, but not from Yorkshir – which might tie in with his recent compelling arguments in favour of Lincoln shire origins for the Bridlington canon, and Langtoft's leaving Yorkshire for goc after 1293 (perhaps with some drafts of his *Chronicle*).[29] Whereas the presenc of (defective) material pertaining to estate management attributed to Robe Grosseteste at the very end of the second booklet (excerpts from *Les Reulles Sei Robert*, fol. 63rv)[30] cannot be conclusive about provenance without further wor (given the rather wide dissemination of that text, originally from Lincolnshire the last item in the first booklet, a *tenso* on the crusade of 1270, apparently writte

27 *Bolton Priory* Compotus, ed. Kershaw and Smith, respectively pp. 148, 152, 347, 18 81–2, 274.

28 The enigmatic presence of MS Fairfax 24 at Bolton is an inference from its pos medieval *ex-libris*, supported by the fact that Colonel Fairfax drew substantially fron Yorkshire dispersed collections, some specifically Augustinian – he owned at least on Bridlington book, MS (*olim*) Fairfax 15 (now MS Auct. D. Inf. 2. 7), and the cartularie of Kirkham Priory (MS Fairfax 7) and Wartre Priory (MS Fairfax 9).

29 J.-C. Thiolier, 'Pierre de Langtoft: historiographe d'Edouard Ier Plantagenêt', in *Angle Norman Anniversary Essays*, ed. I. Short, ANTS OPS 2 (London, 1993), pp. 379–94 (p 389–90 and n. 57); idem, 'L'itinéraire de Pierre de Langtoft', in *Miscellanea Mediaevali Mélanges offerts à Philippe Ménard*, ed. J.-C. Faucon, A. Labbé and D. Quéruel (Pari 1998), II, 1329–53 (pp. 1340–2).

30 D. Oschinsky, ed., *Walter of Henley and Other Treatises on Estate Management an Accounting* (Oxford, 1971), pp. 388–415 (MS Fairfax 24 not collated, p. 196).

in collaboration between Henry de Lacy, earl of Lincoln (*c*.1249–1311) and Walter of Bibbesworth, unique to the manuscript (fols. 19r–20v), would once more suggest a Lincolnshire origin. Immediately after this text, 'Henricus dei gracia Rex Quod Brownfeld' and '[Amen] Nicholes brounfeld amen' appear at the end of this first booklet (fol. 20v); the mode of inscription would seem to be referring to a scribe, but this and the dating are problematic here. It is likely, but not entirely clear, that these scribal inscriptions predate a Bolton association, and it is at present impossible to assess whether there is any link with the (presumably) earlier Robert de Brounfeld recorded as rector of Melmerby (Cumberland) 1346×1354.[31] The Langtoft text in MS Fairfax 24, and the history of the manuscript (its first booklet in particular), are thus different from the coordinates of two early, textually close and distinctly Yorkshire productions of the first redaction of the *Chronicle*, London, British Library, MSS Cotton Julius A. v. and Harley 114, possibly issued from the same *scriptorium*. MS Harley 114 is an Augustinian manuscript, bearing a versified *ex-libris* from the priory of North Ferriby (also West Yorkshire), which suggests the name of 'John Styrton' as that of the donor to that institution. It is likely that Yorkshire Augustinian houses were instrumental in the early dissemination of what might have been regarded as production by a fellow canon – with, in this case, a route of circulation possibly running east (from Bridlington Priory, home to Langtoft 1271×1293) to west – and such collaborative dissemination within the order is conceivable for other works as well, in Yorkshire and elsewhere. Concerning the whereabouts of Langtoft, Thiolier has also tellingly pointed out the proximity between the Arrouaisian Abbey at Bourne (Lincolnshire) and a Bridlington dependency since as early as 1128×1132, the parish church at Edenham (about two miles north-west from Bourne). Not inconceivably, it is perhaps partly through a channel of internal dissemination, from dependent church to mother house, that MS Fairfax 24 – its first booklet at least – moved from a Lincolnshire origin out to a Yorkshire one, and subsequently reached Bolton.

It is likewise convenient to adduce piecemeal evidence for Drax Priory, a moderately endowed foundation. As noted by J. Moran, the community of Drax was the recipient of a Bible before 1450 – which cannot now be traced in any obvious way (nor can its language be known).[32] As its cartulary from the mid-fourteenth century (Oxford, Bodleian Library, MS Top. Yorkshire c. 63) attests, Drax Priory held endowments in Yorkshire and also as far south as in Leicestershire and Lincolnshire – which may leave possibilities for cultural contacts beyond economy, just as for Bridlington. One such enigmatic hint is preserved in

---

[31] Nothing seems to be known of this Nicholas 'Brownfeld / Brounfeld'; Thiolier, *Edition critique et commentée de Pierre de Langtoft, Le règne d'Edouard Ier* (Créteil, 1989), I, 69–70, thinks there might be two individuals here. On Robert de Brounfeld, see S. H. Cavanaugh, *A Study of Books Privately Owned in England: 1300–1450*, 2 vols. (Ann Arbor, 1980), I, 144 (Brounfeld's will is dated 17 November 1353).

[32] J. A. H. Moran, *The Growth of English Schooling 1340–1548: Learning, Literacy, and Laicization in Pre-Reformation York Diocese* (Princeton, 1985), p. 188 (and n. 8).

Oxford, Bodleian Library, MS Douce 132, in the form of a list of books or booklets in an early fourteenth-century hand on fol. 82v (at the end of the second booklet of the manuscript, which contains a copy of Guillaume le Clerc's *Bestiary*).[33] This list presumably gathers the contents of the lending library of an individual whose hand also wrote hitherto unnoticed annotations on the *Fables* of Marie de France copied in the first booklet (fols. 35r–61v). Douce 132 shares medieval physical history with Douce 137 (though they are now two separately bound volumes), both together having been once the collection of texts, according to P. Robinson, first of (probably) two successive Berkshire or Oxfordshire lawyers, and thereafter of William Rede, bishop of Chichester. Textual evidence in the latter manuscript points to legal activity in Berkshire and Oxfordshire late in the first half and early in the second half of the thirteenth century, and Robinson considers, on the strength of palaeographical features, that the first three booklets of Douce 137 and the first one of Douce 132 were produced at Oxford. For Douce 137 one should also mention the identification by T. Hunt of a hitherto unknown version of the Insular French *La Terre des Sarrasins* (fols. 2v–4r) – another being famously found in London, British Library, MS Harley 2253, which has strong connections in the West Midlands (perhaps with the Ludlow Stokesays in particular), and some of whose textual exemplars might have been indirectly inherited from Augustinian channels.[34] Further to these associations, in the lending list now in Douce 132 both the reference to the unidentified 'prior de Drax' and that to 'Willelmus Ermyn' link the volume with Yorkshire; I have noted elsewhere that William (de) Ayrminne also appears in the Bolton *Compotus*, at least once on a par with the Cliffords, the founding family of the house.[35]

Among the many promising purposes which looking at Insular French Augustinian books might serve, one is to offer tangible evidence of resources in French

33 Oxford, Bodleian Library, MS Douce 132, fol. 82v. I have transcribed and briefly commented on this list in 'Quelques aspects de l'influence des chanoines augustins sur la production et la transmission littéraire vernaculaire en Angleterre (XIIIe –XVe siècles)', *Comptes Rendus de l'Académie des Inscriptions & Belles-Lettres* 2006 (for 2004), pp. 169–213 (pp. 187–9). The list had been transcribed for the first time by R. W. Hunt on 9 March 1959: see 'Bodley References, Letters about Manuscripts', Box II, Duke Humphrey's Library. For a third transcription, see P. R. Robinson, 'A Study of Some Aspects of the Transmission of English Verse Texts in Late Medieval Manuscripts' (unpublished B.Litt. dissertation, Oxford, 1972), p. 208, and eadem, 'The "Booklet": A Self-Contained Unit in Composite Manuscripts', *Codicologica* 3 (1980), 46–69 (pp. 56–7, 64–7). I differ in some details from Robinson's transcription and interpretation.

34 For *La Terre des Sarrasins*, see Dean no. 332, and (edited from Douce 137) T. Hunt, 'Haymarus's *Relatio Tripartita* in Anglo-Norman', *Medieval Encounters: Jewish, Christian and Muslim Culture in Confluence and Dialogue* 4/2 (1998), 119–29. On Harley 2253's associations and possible indirect Augustinian links, one could start from C. Revard, 'The Papelard's Priest and the Black Prince's Men: Audiences of an Alliterative Poem, c.1350–1370', *Studies in the Age of Chaucer* 23 (2001), 359–406 (pp. 395–6 and n. 79).

35 J. L. Grassi, 'Royal Clerks from the Archdiocese of York in the Fourteenth Century', *Northern History* 5 (1970), 12–33 (pp. 13–15, 18–20, 27); *Bolton Priory* Compotus, ed. Kershaw and Smith, pp. 332 (and n. 204), 459, 461–2, 488, 498, 544; Pouzet, 'Quelques aspects de l'influence des chanoines augustins', pp. 189–90.

ailable in a given house, such as may consolidate the writing and dissemina-
on of works in other languages as antecedent or adjacent material (whether
not textual sources), again possibly within retrievable Augustinian agencies.
this respect – but not exclusively – religious literature is once more a fruitful
ea.[36] Some French texts entertain intricate discursive relationships with Latin
aterials. Thus, both 'best copies' of Edmund of Abingdon's original *Speculum
eligiosorum* and the derivative *Speculum Ecclesie* have been remarked by their
litor to have been in Augustinian hands: in this capacity, the former Latin trea-
se is Oxford, Bodleian Library, MS Hatton 26 (fols. 183v–204v) associated with
e Priory of St Thomas the Martyr at Baswich, near Stafford, the latter one being
ondon, British Library, MS Royal 7. A. i (fols.12r–22v), which was owned by
Mary Overy Priory in Southwark.[37] (The situation is further enriched if we
onsider – in the light of John Gower's association with the Augustinian priory
Southwark – that the whole of the first booklet of London, British Library,
IS Harley 3490, the 'Rede / Boarstall' manuscript of the *Confessio Amantis*, is a
teenth-century copy of Edmund of Abingdon's *Speculum Religiosorum*, written
the same scribe as the subsequent Gower article.[38]) The *Speculum Ecclesie* is
Latin retranslation, made in the second half of the thirteenth century, of the
sular French *Merure de Seinte Eglise*, itself originally stemming from an exem-
lar of the *Speculum Religiosorum*. Further to the significant role played by Augus-
nian communities in the preservation of both theological *libelli* in Latin, it may
e added that one of the best copies of the intermediary *Merure* is to be found
a manuscript also associated with Augustinian ownership, Oxford, Corpus
hristi College, MS 36, a Llanthony Secunda book (as seen above).[39] According
the Charyte catalogue, the house at Leicester likewise seems to have acquired
ree booklets of the *Speculum Religiosorum* in theological anthologies (A. 20. 306i;
. 20. 907a), or bound with provincial constitutions and councils (A. 20. 1389b),
d possibly one of the *Speculum ecclesie* (A. 20. 469aq), as part of a compendious
ook of theology and devotion headed by articles written by Alexander Nequam
a fellow Augustinian (from Cirencester) and a rather well-circulated authority
rough internal channels of this order, some of whose works initiated a substan-
al body of glosses in English or French.[40] Through such cumulative evidence,

See the case for evidence of the early dissemination of the *Vie de Saint Gilles* (thought
to be originally from Barnwell Priory, Cambridgeshire) in Cambridge, UL, MS Ii.1.33
(fol. 120r) studied comprehensively by Frankis, 'Languages and Cultures in Contact:
Vernacular Lives of St Giles and Anglo-Norman Annotations'.
Edmund of Abingdon, Speculum Religiosorum *and* Speculum Ecclesie, ed. H. P. Forshaw,
Auctores Britannici Medii Aevi 3 (London, 1973), pp. 1–2, 7.
D. Pearsall, 'The Rede (Boarstall) Gower: British Library, MS Harley 3490', in *The
English Medieval Book*, ed. Edwards, Gillespie and Hanna, pp. 87–99; see further my
'Southwark Gower – Augustinian Agencies in Gower's Manuscripts and Texts' (forth-
coming in the proceedings of the first John Gower Society Conference).
Mirour de Seinte Eglise (St Edmund of Abingdon's Speculum Ecclesiae*), ed. A. D. Wilshere,
ANTS 40 (London, 1982); Dean no. 629.
Libraries of Augustinian Canons, ed. Watson and Webber, pp. 179, 279, 355, 208–10.

what remains palpable in the pattern of dissemination and transformations c
Edmund's original work could be presumed to reveal a strand of distinctiv
Augustinian interest, agency – and meddling.

Other Insular French works in turn may stand as sources before English tex
with clear Augustinian associations. Among the French sources lying behind th
alliterative *Siege of Jerusalem* associable with Bolton Priory, MS Fairfax 24 (if
reached the priory early enough) may conveniently materialize a discursive lin
through its transmission, in the second booklet, of a substantial portion of te
of the (so far) unique Insular version of the *Bible en françois*, attributed to Rog
d'Argenteuil on the Continent.[41] At an early stage, this version coalesced wit
didactic material of the type of 'Dialogue / Enseignement' from father to so
itself a spin-off from Insular French *Lucidaire* matter – this would appear to be
branch distinct, therefore, from that represented by the *Lumiere as lais* originally b
the Augustinian canon Peter de Peckham (*al.* Fetcham).[42] Thanks to Tony Hunt
forthcoming edition of the *Dialogue of Father and Son* contained in Cambridg
Emmanuel College, MS 106, fols. 119r–142r, I have been able to recognize tha
fols. 47r–61v of Fairfax 24 constitute another version of the same redaction, wit
significant variations.[43] Interestingly, the Emmanuel manuscript also contains
copy of the *Merure de Seinte Eglise* (fols. 62r–105r), among its extensive collectio
of Insular French texts in different scribal hands.

This brief survey hopes to have communicated the extent to which Insula
French books await more systematic investigation, if one attempts to sketc
a literary geography of Augustinian agencies. Such a geography involves
consideration of retrievable patterns of authorship, production or dissemina
tion for a significant number of manuscripts and their texts and contexts. On
field of research concerns the global connections and particular transits of book
between English Augustinian mother houses and their appropriated churche
as well as their various Insular dependencies – whether this meant priories c
cells.[44] One other particularly fascinating aspect of this 'reconstructive poetics' c
Insular French Augustinian books is that it verifies once more, in varying degree
of complexity, the living connections between works produced and circulate

Beside Cirencester and Leicester, the Augustinian circulation of Nequam's works i
attested at Barnwell (Cambridgeshire), Bridlington, Llanthony (Secunda) and Waltha
(Essex). On the glosses, see T. Hunt, *Teaching and Learning Latin in Thirteenth-Centur
England*, 3 vols. (Cambridge, 1991).

[41] This was recognized by R. Hanna, in a letter dated 2 October 1990: see 'Letters abo
Bodleian Manuscripts X', Duke Humphrey's Library. On the continental versions
the *Bible en françois*, see *Grundriss der Romanischen Literaturen des Mittelalters* VI (Heide
berg, 1968–70), VI/1, 31, and VI/2, 65 (item 1492).

[42] Dean nos. 630 and 632–4.

[43] M. R. James, *The Western Manuscripts in the Library of Emmanuel College: A Descripti
Catalogue* (Cambridge, 1904), pp. 90–4; Dean no. 633. I thank T. Hunt for pre-public
tion communication of his edition of the *Dialogue* in *Anglo-Norman Piety* (T. Hunt,
Bliss and H. Leyser, FRETS OPS 1 forthcoming).

[44] On the latter categories, see M. Heale, *The Dependent Priories of Medieval English Mona
teries*, Studies in the History of Medieval Religion 22 (Woodbridge, 2004).

in this language and in Latin and English – among areas where such fruitful Augustinian interplay occurred, sermon literature has more to offer, and so do manuscripts containing music, for instance.[45] The recognition of such intricate features may help to discover a little more about books in Augustinian institutions and their forms of circulation. The larger historical and socio-literary dimensions behind such endeavours may enhance our understanding of forms of cultural continuity and change in the fortunes and channels of Augustinian *otium* in medieval England.

---

[45] H. L. Deeming, 'Music in English Miscellanies of the Twelfth and Thirteenth Centuries' (unpublished Ph.D. dissertation, 2 vols., Cambridge, 2005). Thus Oxford, Bodleian Library, MS Ashmole 1285, from Southwark, contains (fol. 235v) the Insular French piece 'De ma dame' (Deeming's no. 23); see further K. D. Hartzell, *Catalogue of Manuscripts Written or Owned in England up to 1200 Containing Music* (Woodbridge, 2006), pp. 387–8 (no. 240).

21

Eschuer peché, embracer bountee: Social Thought and Pastoral Instruction in Nicole Bozon

Laurie Postlewate

As we reflect on the social contexts of the French language in medieval England, it is important to consider the strong tradition of homiletic texts providing cate-chetical instruction, and moral and spiritual guidance.[1] Produced in an environ-ment of increased awareness of the catechetical needs of both the clergy and the laity, and in response to the mandates of Lateran IV in 1215 and the 1281 Council of Lambeth, these works are among the most imaginative in the Anglo-Norman corpus.[2] In explaining sin, how and why one should confess, and what it is to be a good Christian, texts of pastoral instruction deploy a lively cast of characters and images that seek to inspire contrition and piety. They also provide a way of understanding the habits, concerns, preoccupations and social behaviour of the authors who composed the works and the public(s) to whom they were addressed.

One important source of homiletic literature in Anglo-Norman is the *œuvre* of Nicole Bozon, a Franciscan poet and preacher whose works from the late thirteenth century include a collection of prose exempla, a compilation of verse proverbs, saints' lives, satirical and allegorical poems, songs to the Virgin and verse sermons. In the prologue to his exempla collection, Bozon states that his purpose is to help his public *eschuer peché, embracer bountee* – eschew sin and embrace goodness. Bozon's depiction of *peché* and *bonté* provides one more piece in the larger puzzle of the 'who and why' of the French of England. We will focus here on the *Contes moralisés* and the 'Char d'Orgueil', two works that reveal particularly well the concern for social sins that permeates Bozon's *œuvre*. The prose exempla collection, the *Contes moralisés*, presents a variety of types of mate-rial often employed in preaching: facts from natural history, fables, short narra-tives, recipes and local lore.[3] The collection consists of 145 rubrics developed into short chapters, the majority of which begin with a similitude, that is, an analogy between a fact from natural history and some trait of human behaviour; these are

---

1 Dean, 'Homiletic', pp. 323–91.
2 For thirteenth-century pastoral legislation in England, see E. A. Jones, 'Literature of Religious Instruction', in *A Companion to Medieval English Literature and Culture c.1350–1500*, ed. P. Brown (Malden MA, 2007), pp. 407–22.
3 *Les contes moralisés de Nicole Bozon*, ed. P. Meyer and L. T. Smith (Paris, 1889), hence-forth quoted by page number in the text.

llowed by moral lessons and related Scripture quotations. The 'Char d'Orgueil'
a satirical poem of 560 lines of alexandrine couplets in the form of an allegor-
al picture of the parts of Lady Pride's carriage. To each element in the picture
the carriage and the entourage that attends Lady Pride the author attributes a
n, an example of sinful behaviour or a sinful person.[4] These two texts demon-
rate how catechetical teaching of the post-Lateran period was communicated
lay audiences through storytelling, allegory and poetry. The present essay will
amine the content and form of Bozon's works, and discuss the conclusions we
ight draw from his use of the French language in pastoral instruction.

Bozon's *œuvre* is marked by strident satire that targets corruption of the
itural order of society; people neglect and abuse their station in life and try to
pear higher and more powerful than their God-given estate. In his exempla,
e author repeatedly reminds his public that the proper functioning of society
pends on the willingness of each member to do their – and only their – job. In
e same way that the beasts of the earth are given by God to help man, each one
a different way, so each order or estate in society is ordained to fulfil a certain
nction:

> Lui bon clerke Basilius nous dit en un livere qe Exameron est apellé qe les
> uns bestez en terre par Deux meismes soñt ordeinez pur travailler, e rien ne
> valent a manger, sicum chivale e asne, les autres soñt donez pur sustenañce de
> manger, si ne valent rien a travailler, com berbitz, porcs, gelinez, owes; e soñt
> les altres qe ne valent ne pur manger, ne pur travailler, mès soñt ordeinez pur
> la meisoun garder e purger, cum chiens e chatez. Les chiens gardent, les chatez
> purgent. Auxint est en religioñ e en chescun hostel de prodhome: les uns gentz
> valent pur un mestier, les autres pur autres e si ne deit nul autre reprover, cum
> dist seint Pool Cor.13: 'En un cors soñt plusours members, e chescun vault pur
> soñ office.' (*Contes moralisés*, p. 24)

> ('The good clerk Basilius tells us in a book entitled the Hexameron that there
> are some beasts of the earth that are ordained by God himself to work, and are
> not to be eaten, such as the horse and the ass; others are to be eaten and are
> worthless for work, such as sheep, pigs, hens, geese; others are neither to be
> eaten or to be worked, but they are given for guarding and purging the house,
> such as dogs and cats. The dogs guard and the cats purge the house. So it is
> in religion and in the home of every good man: some people are good for one
> job, and others for other jobs, and so they should not insult each other, just as
> Saint Paul says in Cor. 13: "In a body there are several members, and each one
> is suited for its function."')[5]

In another exemplum, Bozon provides a comparison of the functioning of
ciety to the compiling of Biblical concordances. Each brother participating in
e compilation of a concordance was assigned a letter with which he worked

---

Deux poèmes de Nicholas Bozon, ed. J. Vising (Göteborg, 1919). Quotations referenced in
the text by 'Char d'Orgueil' and page number in this edition.
All translations are my own.

279

exclusively so that the concordance could be completed. In the same way, eac
person in society should stick to the work of his or her station in life:

> Pur ceo vodereie qe chescun feseit com fierent jadis les freres qe compilerent les
> concordañces. Chescun prist gard a la lettre qe a lui fust mandee. Cil qe aveit
> A ne avoit qe fere de B, e cil qe out gard de B, rien se entirmettout de C: et si
> qe chescun lettre del abicee a divers estoit liveree, et chescun se prist a sa lettre,
> e nul ne vousist de autri fet se entremetter. Par tant vindrent al noble livere
> dount seint Esglise est mout solacee. Issy voderey qe chescun, clerke e lay, hors
> de religioñ e en religion, preïst gard a la lettre qe lui est deliverée, ensynt qe
> Adam e Aliz ne se entremeïssent de Batholomé, ne Beatriz, ne Colyn ne Colette
> de autres, fors chescun de la sue. (*Contes moralisés*, pp. 160–1, also p. 115)

('For this reason, I would have everyone do as did the brothers who used to
compile concordances. Each one took charge of the letter that had been given
to him. The one who had A did not bother with B, and he who had B did not
concern himself with C; thus each letter of the alphabet was given over to a
different man, and each one took his letter, and no one tried to interfere with
those of the others. And in this way they managed to make a noble book that
is of great help to Holy Church. Likewise I would have each one, both clergy
and lay, from outside and from within the Church, take charge of the letter that
is given to him, with the result that Adam and Alice would not interfere with
Bartholomew, nor would Beatrice, or Colin or Colette meddle with others, and
each one would remain with the letter that is his.')

But, Bozon warns, people are seldom satisfied with their place in life. The
want to move up, to appear to be what they are not and to have more than the
do. The similitude of the estates quoted above is followed by the fable of th
peacock who complains to Destiny that he cannot sing like the nightingal
Destiny responds with a sharp upbraiding that summarizes Bozon's view c
those who would complain of their lot in life: 'Soyez paé de ceo qe avez' (B
content with what you have).

In the 'Char d'Orgueil', the estates conceit furnishes both the subjects of satir
and a formal structure for the poem. As Bozon creates a picture of the carriage c
Lady Pride he also constructs a cross-section of society and the specific sins assc
ciated with each group; the diagrammatic scheme, a common approach to th
exposition of sins in penitential literature of the period, reflects the post-Latera
concern with the circumstances of sin. Not surprisingly, there is criticism of th
wealthy and privileged – those who have in this life. But even more attentio
is given to those who serve and administer to the wealthy and groups that ar
subject to social ambition.

Bozon begins with the horses that draw Lady Pride's carriage. The *limoun*
the centre shafts to which the horses are attached, represent the cruelty of bai
iffs who harass the poor: the latter have nowhere to turn, they just pay thei
money and cry for mercy.[6] This description initiates a series of eighteen estate

---

6 *Deux poèmes*, ed. Vising, p. 8.

which are described as parts of the horses pulling Pride's carriage, *Denaturesce* and *Deleauté*. The names of these horses signal that the sins they represent are of a particularly social nature: *denaturesce* is the hard-heartedness and ingratitude that spoils many a friendship and family bond; *deleauté* denotes the breaking of social connections. The horse *Denaturesce* is depicted over three quatrains: his head is the *grans seigneurs* who are hard-hearted to their poor friends, his feet are the bad children who disrespect their parents, his tail is the executors who dishonour the wishes and memory of their dead friends. The sins of the executors are of special significance for Bozon; he gives a more detailed description of this group than for any of the other social types in the 'Char d'Orgueil'. The unworthy executor forgets his dead friend whose soul lies in pain at the bottom of his tomb because no one will say prayers on his behalf. Then, to make matters worse, the executor marries his friend's widow and, instead of singing pious songs for the dead man's soul, he drinks and dances. Bozon concludes with a warning that we should take care of our own souls in this life, because friends and family cannot be trusted to assist us after our death.

> Donk vient un bel amy e espouse sa bele
> E beyt de la toune e trype la sautele
> E chaunte pur ly alme va la ry durele,
> Autre eyde ne avera de cely ne de cele.
> Pur Deu, seinours, pernet garde taunt cum estes en vie,
> Ffetes ben pur voz almes, ne vous afyet mye
> En amy ne en parent après la departye.
> Ceo qe lerret après vous destrut ert e seysie.   ('Char d'Orgueil', p. 10)

> ('Along comes his fine friend and marries his beloved
> And he drinks to the music and dances a jig
> And sings a 'tralala' for his friend's soul
> Who will get nothing more from him or her.
> Good men, for God's sake, be on guard in this life
> Take care of your souls, and do not rely
> On friend or family after your goods have been divided.
> What you leave behind will be seized and destroyed.')

Bozon's description of *Deleauté* includes fourteen different parts evoking a total of thirteen types in society, as outlined in Table 21.1.[7]

Two of these are *clercs*: prelates and religious. Six are civil and commercial professions: sergeants, minstrels, bailiffs, merchants, lawyers and provosts. Another five are types of people found in society: bad neighbours, meddlers, *bon garçons* (boys who *seem* good), bad company and *recevours* (receiving agents). The professional estates presented here each abuse the station and power of their profession. For example, the prelates and religious seek a life of material comfort instead of tending to the needs of the faithful; the peace officers are overly severe in finding fault in people; the merchants deceive their customers. The remaining

---

7   *Deux poèmes*, ed. Vising, pp. 10–13.

Table 21.1: *Bozon's allegory of Deleauté*

Part of the horse	Estate
spotted gray colour	lay, clergy, Holy Orders
head	prelates
eyes	peace officers
nostrils	singing minstrel
teeth	bad neighbours
tongue	meddlers
ears	bailiffs
feet	'nice' boys
spine	religious
stomach	provosts
tail	bad household
hide	receivers
gait	merchants
neighing	lawyers

social types mentioned are accused simply of bad behaviour in society. The *bons garcons*, who are compared to the clopping feet of the horse, prance about primping themselves and worrying about their appearance; they rarely go to church and do not bother to fast. The bad neighbours and meddlers are accused of sins of the tongue, an important type of transgression addressed in both the 'Char d'Orgueil' and the *Contes moralisés*. The horse's tail, *male meynee*, is a bad household, which abases a gentleman's reputation and takes away his honour.

The second estates series in the 'Char d'Orgueil' is structured around the noble household of Lady Pride and includes twenty-two types of domestic servants and administrators. This series begins with Pride's personal entourage and proceeds to the servants, as shown in Table 21.2.

Table 21.2: *Servants and administrators in the household of Bozon's Lady Pride*

Function in Lady Pride's service
Driver; driver's helper;
Three ladies-in-waiting; Seven maidens-in-waiting
Three knights; Squires
Three chaplains; Three clerics
Justice and Seneschal; Seneschal; Treasurer;
Marshal; Pantry-man; Cup-bearer; Bookkeeper
Laundress; Matron and chambermaid
Worker with horse and cart
Poulterer; Meat chef; Kitchen boy

Each member of Pride's household displays a clear deformation of their job. The justice and *seneschal* work against the people; the cup-bearer makes everyone drink too much; the meat chef orders too much meat; the kitchen boy neglects to wash the dishes. The sins of some of this riotous crowd are limited to the specific abuse they commit, like the *mareschal* who is uncharitable:

Plus ly greve un soper despendu en charité
Ke troiz repaz ou quatre en veyne glorie wastee.

('Char d'Orgueil', p. 27)

('It upsets him more to give one dinner in charity
Than to waste three or four meals in vainglory.')

he sins of others in the group are allegorized. For example, the kitchen boy's
egligence in his washing-up duties is compared to the way many 'fine' boys
rget to go to confession:

Le garson de qysine trop est enbrowé,
E si lest par negligense sa vessele deslavee;
Ceus sunt les pygaceours qe memes se unt oblyé
De laver par confession lor almes de pecché.   ('Char d'Orgueil', p. 29)

('The kitchen boy is himself dirty,
And through neglect he leaves the dishes unwashed;
These are the fine boys who themselves have forgotten
To wash their souls of sin in confession.')

While Bozon's invective is at times directed against those who have status in
ociety, he is also concerned with those who are in the presence of the rich and
ho consequently desire wealth for themselves – social climbers at all levels,
ho are compared in the *Contes moralisés* to the glow-worm who sprouts wings
d flies only briefly before falling back to earth.[8] We also find the fable of the
wl who was raised in a hawk's nest and yet remained an owl and acted as one;
the English proverb that Bozon quotes puts it: 'Strouke oul and schrape oule
d evere is oule oule'.[9] This fable leads Bozon to comment on those of low birth
ho, temporarily, rise to a higher status:

Auxint est de plousurs gents que soñt nez de bas lignage. Mès ke il soyent en
haut mountez, sovent apris e enformés en religioñ ou en siecle ou en dignetee,
touz jours retornent a lur estat e a la nature doñt il soñt neez.

(*Contes moralisés*, p. 23)

('So it is with many people of low birth. Even if they have risen in rank, often
from having received an education in religion, in the world or in a position
of dignity, they consistently return to the rank and nature in which they were
born.')

Turning to the specific sins of these groups, we see a wide range of misbehav-
ur, including gluttony and vanity, disrespect for elders, and pernicious gossip.
everal broad categories or types of sin emerge: of these materialism, and abuse
f one's power and station in life, are the most significant. For Bozon, the root
f much of the sin in the world is *vile purchace de terrien aver* – wealth and the

---

Contes moralisés, ed. Meyer and Smith, pp. 94–5.
Contes moralisés, ed. Meyer and Smith, p. 23.

desire for more of it. This leads servants to imitate their masters, and masters t
persecute and cheat their servants; it is the cause of children turning against the
parents, noblewomen dressing in ridiculous attire, widows wanting to remarr
and neighbours speaking ill of each other. Bozon compares *coveteise* – covetou
ness – to a strong onion that makes a person thirst for more and more wealt
makes them swell, gives them a headache from thinking about how they can g
more, causes their eyes to tear because they must stay up all night guarding the
possessions – and for all that gives little nourishment![10]

The rich must also put great effort into hiding their wealth, and Bozon liker
them to the stag who hides from the hunter as soon as he begins to put on weigh

> Sicom le cierf en tens de gresse se doute de chescun noyse, qe l'em lui voille
> toler la peel, e pur ceo se tient en covert, auxint les richez se musse[n]t del
> clamour des poverez pur saver lur bienz. (*Contes moralisés*, p. 138)

> ('Just as the stag, who when he is fat remains in hiding because he fears at the
> slightest noise that his skin is about to be taken from him, so the rich, in order
> to keep their wealth, hide themselves when they hear the poor complaining.')

For Bozon, excessive wealth actually shortens one's life: he compares thos
who get rich and live it up to pigs who do nothing but eat and sleep. These cre
tures profit no one until their death when they become pork chops for others! Th
poor workers, on the other hand, are like the ass who serves others all his life, bu
whose death benefits no one.[11] The man who accumulates wealth can also expe
to lose it all as soon as he dies, for friends and family will be lining up for the
share as soon as he passes on. This is shown by the ants who live on a mountai
in India, guarding selfishly a rich treasure of gold and gems; when the heat of th
burning sun eventually drives them underground, others come along and ste
the treasure.[12]

The evils of materialism are evoked in an even more concrete way in th
'Char d'Orgueil' where the carriage provides literal and figurative evidence
the abuse of wealth. Fully one-half of the poem's lines are devoted to a detaile
description of the *char de mult grant custage* that Pride has fashioned for herse
The vehicle is heavily ornamented and covered in a scarlet drape; on the insid
of the carriage we find a pretty rug and fancy cushions. The carriage is pulle
by four *chasseurs* (expensive horses normally reserved for hunting) who wea
jewelled collars. These collars lead to a commentary by Bozon on the moral
dangerous obsession that many women have with their dress and appearance –
preoccupation that distracts them from the harsh reality of their own mortality.

Women's dress and their behaviour in social gatherings are the focus of
divergence from the allegorical picture of Pride's carriage that appears like

---

[10] *Contes moralisés*, ed. Meyer and Smith, p. 109.
[11] *Contes moralisés*, ed. Meyer and Smith, pp. 41–2.
[12] *Contes moralisés*, ed. Meyer and Smith, p. 122.

self-contained *dit* in the centre of the 'Char d'Orgueil'.[13] This digression on the vanity of women follows the description of the fourth of Pride's horses, *Envye*, an impetuous animal who, desiring to make himself noticed, spends his annual income in only two or three days. From this point, Bozon evokes the problem of women who go to celebrations in fancy headdresses. When they arrive, looking like horned beasts, the women examine the heads of the others, they talk loudly and make a spectacle of themselves. They gobble their food and guzzle their drink, while table attendants rush about to serve them. Bozon stresses the connection here between two kinds of sin of the tongue often associated in penitential manuals, gluttony and indiscreet conversation.

These women pretend to love one another, but each one is trying to outdo the others, both in dress and in gossip. With considerable humour, Bozon describes how these ladies, not satisfied that only the front of their gowns be seen, intentionally fall down so that the embroidery on the back of the dresses will also be exposed. As soon as they get home the ladies begin redoing their outfits for the next party. But these *précieuses ridicules* are not really as well-off as their clothes make them appear, and Bozon furnishes this display of fashion as an example of how the poor wretch plays at being rich.[14]

The abuse of power is a problem of equal seriousness and urgency for Bozon, who adopts the position that the rich bear the responsibility of caring for the less fortunate. The *grans seigneurs* who are cruel to their tenants are like vultures who peck at their chicks to prevent them from getting too fat. The lords are directed by Bozon to think of their power and will as two wings to be used to protect their wards.[15] But the rich do not hesitate to prey on the poor who, dependent and defenceless, are easy targets. This is demonstrated by the lion's desire to devour the helpless ass:

Le philosophre Plynie nous dit en son livere qe le leon par graunt nature a haigne vers le asne, ne mye par deserte, mès par desir que ad de sa char manger. Auxint est des richez homes: ilz trovent encheson vers les poveres, ne mye pur ceo que ils eyent mal deservi, mès pur ceo que ils vodrent de lour aver. (*Contes moralisés*, p. 37)

('The philosopher Pliny tells us in his book that the lion naturally hates the ass, not because he deserves it, but because the lion wishes to eat his flesh. So it is with rich men: they find reasons to accuse the poor, not because the poor have deserved it, but because the rich wish to take their goods.')

Bozon directs particularly harsh criticism against administrative officials who, he says, should protect the weak peasants against the powerful lords. The

---

13 *Deux poèmes*, ed. Vising, pp. 15–20. This section of the poem is transmitted as a self-contained *dit* in London, British Library, MS Royal 8 E XVII, fols. 108v–109r.

14 L. Postlewate, 'Preaching the Sins of the Ladies: Nicole Bozon's "Char d'Orgueil"', in *Cultural Performances in Medieval France*, ed. E. Doss-Quinby, R. Krueger and E. J. Burns (Cambridge, 2007), pp. 195–202.

15 *Contes moralisés*, ed. Meyer and Smith, p. 13.

seneschal or steward should behave like the wild boar that defends her young against predators.[16] Bailiffs and prelates, in a social category between the lords and the people, are also criticized as especially inclined to persecute the poor and ignore the faults of the rich and powerful. Bozon warns of the danger of entering into any position of delegated power – *en bailli*. These are professions with only superficial honour, as evidenced by the bailiff whose status is like the antlers of the stag. Just as the antlers are shed in due season, so the bailiff must eventually end his term and lose his prestige and pride.[17]

While they are with their subjects, the delegates of power act and speak boldly, promising to advocate for them to the master; but as soon as the latter approaches they withdraw meekly. These are like the snail who acts like the *gran seigneur* when with his own kind, but who retreats to his shell at the slightest resistance – or sign of rain.[18]

The prologue of the *Contes moralisés* announces the author's intention to provide examples to help the faithful '*eschuer peché, embracer bountee*'. We have seen ample evidence in this work and in the 'Char d'Orgueil' of *peché*; one might well ask where is the *bonté*? There is scant evidence of virtue in the *Contes moralisés* and none at all in the 'Char d'Orgueil'. But even if he places greater emphasis on the identification and description of sin, goodness is not entirely neglected by our Franciscan. In works such as the *Proverbes de bon enseignement* and, especially, in his verse lives of female saints, Bozon encourages the cultivation of personal goodness through frugality, humility and modesty; Christian *bonté* that is accessible to a lay public.[19] Bozon also demonstrates a typically Franciscan concern with social virtue: the practice of poverty and charity, and the power of preaching as a means of counteracting evil in society. The picture of goodness that emerges from Bozon is distinctively public and concerned with virtue in society. The subjects of Bozon's hagiography, for example, distinguish themselves through active piety and evangelization, and they set examples which, Bozon says, any devout person could imitate. Martyrdom and eremitism are de-emphasized in the saints' lives to render a more practical and sociable image of holiness.

An essential link between *peché* and *bonté* in Bozon is the importance of penance and confession: the recognition of sin and the turning from vice to virtue. Several entries in the *Contes moralisés* are devoted to confession, which Bozon compares to a remedy to counteract snake or dog bite. In a clever play on *confection* and *confession*, Bozon compares this remedy to one that promises to cure the affliction of mortal sin.[20] He also describes confession as a means of cleansing the soul: in

---

16 *Contes moralisés*, ed. Meyer and Smith, pp. 11–12.
17 *Contes moralisés*, ed. Meyer and Smith, pp. 123–4.
18 *Contes moralisés*, ed. Meyer and Smith, pp. 143–4.
19 *Les proverbes de bon enseignement de Nicole Bozon*, ed. A. C. Thorn (Lund, 1920); *Three Saints' Lives by Nicholas Bozon*, ed. M. A. Klenke (St Bonaventure NY, 1947); *Seven More Poems by Nicholas Bozon*, ed. M. A. Klenke (St Bonaventure NY, 1951); *Saint's Lives in the French of England: St George, St Faith and St Mary Magdalen, and the Legendary of Nicholas Bozon*, trans. L. Postlewate and D. Russell (Tempe AZ, forthcoming).
20 *Contes moralisés*, ed. Meyer and Smith, pp. 107–8.

ιe same way that hyssop powder mixed with water cleanses the face, the tiny
articles of confession when mixed with heartfelt repentance purify the soul.[21]
ιnd one should confess regularly. Just as the elephant goes to the river to wash
imself twice a year, so man should cleanse his soul two – or even three – times
year.[22]

In the final verses of the *Char d'Orgueil*, we hear the voice of the preacher
ιlling his public to recognize their sins and hasten to confession:

> Pur ceo, seynours, haston nos, haston a confession
> Taunt cum tens nous est graunté, de trover remission;
> Kar si nous seyouns tyeus ke taunt atendoun
> Ke les chivals seyent ferrez de fers de obstinacioun,
> E les fers seyent tachez des clous de desperacion,
> Ja ne estoyt penser de trover donk pardoun.   ('Char d'Orgueil', p. 29)

> (For this reason, seigneurs, let us hasten to confession
> While we still have ample time to find forgiveness;
> For if we are among those who wait
> For the horses to be fitted with shoes of obstinacy,
> And the shoes attached by nails of despair,
> We must not expect to find pardon there ...)

This brings us to the reception of Bozon's works and what it may tell us about
ιe use of French in England. There are three points we would like to make
ɔncerning Bozon's intended audience. First, Bozon's choice of French as the
ιedium of pastoral instruction was for reasons other than linguistic necessity.
he linguistic features of Bozon's works, as well as internal references in them,
lace his literary production in the late thirteenth and early fourteenth century, at
time when many nobles, gentry and wealthy bourgeois understood and some-
mes spoke French, but generally as a second language that they learned for
dministrative and professional purposes, and as a vehicle of cultural transmis-
ιon and social distinction.[23] Perhaps significantly, the *Tretiz de Langage* of Walter
ιbbesworth, one of a number of linguistic aids attesting to the special status of
ɾench as a language of social advantage, is transmitted in British Library, MS
ιdditional 46919, a Franciscan multilingual commonplace book that contains
ɔth the *Contes moralisés* and the 'Char d'Orgueil.'[24]

- *Contes moralisés*, ed. Meyer and Smith, p. 81.
' *Contes moralisés*, ed. Meyer and Smith, p. 125.
ᵇ In the *Contes moralisés*, terms, place-names and aphoristic sayings in English are
  inserted into the French text. While these are not of a frequency deserving the term
  macaronic, they support the idea that Bozon's public was English-speaking. These
  insertions, as well as the Biblical source quotations in Latin, were a normal part of the
  preacher's practice of compiling and reworking narrative and descriptive material.
ᵏ For this manuscript and other friar miscellanies, see A. Kehnel, 'Poets, Preachers and
  Friars Revisited: Fourteenth-Century Multilingual Franciscan Manuscripts', in *The
  Beginnings of Standardization*, ed. U. Schaefer (Frankfurt, 2006), pp. 91–114.

A second point concerns the social estate of Bozon's audience: religious o lay? Bozon, like many other writers working with renewed commitment to th pastoral mission, may well have been composing for fellow preachers and clerg who used exempla and diagrammatic allegories in preparing sermons and cat chetical instruction. Overall, the manuscripts transmitting Bozon's *œuvre* suppo the hypothesis of primary reception by preachers and confessors. However, th content of the works points to a lay audience as the eventual recipients of Bozon teaching. While many homiletic texts in the French of England were compose for the purpose of instructing religious and/or clergy in their own lives, this not the case for Bozon, who focuses instead on strictly secular sins and secul estates.[25] The specificity of detail with which he describes the circumstances o sin allows us to seek an even more precise idea of his audience than is permitte with the lay/clergy distinction. If we compare Bozon with other penitenti works of the thirteenth century such as the *Manuel dé Pechez*, he is distinctive i the intensity with which he targets sins of consumption and social ambition i the middle to lower ranks of society. Bozon does not mention, for example, th problem of aristocrats who force their children into marriages without mutu consent or with the wealthy who interfere in elections to holy orders, or th granting of benefices, as we see in the *Manuel dé Pechez*.[26] Of greater danger t society in Bozon's view are women who dress to appear of higher social ran than they are, and household administrators, servants and even peasants wh act like their masters. Here we find demonstrations of materialism in virtually a classes of society and proof of the perilous looseness of social categories:

> Ore bestorne le siecle tant qe saphir tourne en moustard e gravel tourne en rubie, qar les gentilez devinrent failliz e les pesauntz devienent gentilez. Doñt la reisoñ si est tiel qe poverez gentz de basse lignage pernent ensample de la Ruge mier qe de sa nature ne est pas colurée, eynz prent colur de un roche ou ele se abate, e la soñt trovez les rubiez. Auxint foñt les poverez: les uns se mettent al court, les autres al escole. E ceo qe ne ont pas par nature, par graunt travaillie se purchacent sen e curtesie.   (*Contes moralisés*, p. 22)

> ('At present the world is turned upside down, and the sapphire is turned to mustard and pebbles are turned to rubies, for the noble are failing and the peasants are becoming noble. For this reason, the poor of low birth are like the Red Sea which is not naturally coloured, but rather takes on the colour of the rocks on which it breaks and where rubies are found. It is so with the poor: some put themselves at court, others in school. And the wisdom and courtesy which they have not by nature, they acquire for themselves through hard work.')

[25] L. Postlewate, 'From Preaching to Storytelling: The Metaphors of Nicole Bozon', i *Framing the Text: Reading Tradition and Image in Medieval Europe*, ed. K. L. Boardma C. Emerson and A. Tudor, *Medievalia* 20 (Binghamton NY, May 2001), 73–91.

[26] See E. J. Arnould, *Le Manuel des Péchés: Etude de littérature religieuse anglo-norman* (Paris, 1940), pp. 76, 82.

While the inclusion of a broader spectrum of sinners does not necessarily mean that Bozon was addressing those groups directly, we should not exclude the possibility that as a Franciscan homilist, he was doing just that. The Brothers Minor were, after all, known to preach and teach to a wide range of the faithful, and many of the social types mentioned in Bozon's works would have been employed in the noble or bourgeois household and therefore likely to hear the same sermons and receive the same teaching as their superiors. What is perhaps more significant is that Bozon features them prominently in the picture of sin and considers them just as susceptible to pride, greed and social ambition as any *dame* or *seigneur de haut parage*. This leads us to reflect on the possible association of Bozon's social commentary and the choice of French as the language of pastoral teaching. His was an audience for whom French was, like clothing, a powerful social marker. Franciscans are known for exploiting the literary and cultural preferences of their audiences in order to transmit their message with vigour and impact, and the Franciscan talent for utilizing the images, forms – and language – that had the greatest appeal for their audience is well attested. Bozon quite deftly manipulated his public's predilection for French while warning them against the pursuit of social distinction that was, at least in part, behind their use of the language.

The literary legacy of preachers and poets who, like Bozon, were working in a period of invigorated pastoral instruction to the laity, is rich and important. The French homiletic works of the late thirteenth and fourteenth centuries seem to have nourished the slightly later production of such works in Middle English, some of which are translations or adaptations from the French, such as Robert Mannyng of Brune's *Handlyng Synne* or the English versions of Robert Grosseteste's *Chasteau d'Amour* and *Peines de Purgatoire*, and others that were in form and content inspired by French sources.[27] Further discussion of how Middle English authors of moral and penitential literature used their French models is beyond the scope of the present essay. In conclusion, we can say that a number of these, such as *Handlyng Synne*, reveal a tendency that we have detected here in Bozon to adapt their pastoral instruction to the needs of a more inclusive, and often humbler, audience. In this way we see that works of pastoral instruction in the French of England hold a transitional role in the history of insular religious literature, and that they anticipate later expressions of sin and goodness in English.

---

[27] For discussion of a similar connection between Anglo-Norman and Middle English lyrics, and of the role of the mendicants in that tradition, see S. Wenzel, *Preachers, Poets, and the Early English Lyric* (Princeton, 1986). See also more generally Watson in this volume.

22

The Cultural Context of the French Prose *remaniement* of the Life of Edward the Confessor by a Nun of Barking Abbey

Delbert W. Russell

The *Vita Edwardi* by Aelred of Rievaulx, dedicated to Henry II and written about 1161–3, is a politically engaged work, designed to bolster the claims of legitimacy of Henry II as descendant of both Norman and English royal families.[1] The *Vita Edwardi* was twice translated into French verse, first by a nun of Barking shortly after 1163, and almost a century later, by Matthew Paris, in a translation for the court of Henry III, dedicated to Queen Eleanor of Provence.

But it is the twelfth-century life from Barking, of almost 7,000 lines, not the thirteenth-century life by Matthew Paris, that later makes the Channel crossing. The verse life by the nun of Barking is extant in three incomplete manuscripts, all dating from the late thirteenth century. Two are of English origin: the Campsey manuscript copy ends abruptly at line 4240, while the Vatican manuscript lacks a quire containing about 1,500 lines at the beginning of the text. The third verse copy is in a Picard manuscript datable to 1292, where roughly the first 4,500 lines were incorporated into the text of Wace's *Brut*, inserted seamlessly into the historical chronicle.[2]

In the first quarter of the fourteenth century the life from Barking was rewritten in prose in the French manuscript, now London, BL Egerton 745, created for the de Châtillon family, counts of St Pol, near Amiens. This is the only extant copy that contains the complete narrative, although reworked in prose and slightly shortened, of the life from Barking. In what follows I propose to look more closely at the manuscript context of this reworking.

---

[1]   Edward was canonized on 7 February 1161, and the translation to the new shrine in Westminster Abbey was delayed until 13 October 1163 when Henry II could be present. On the development of the cult and the translation of the body, see *The Life of King Edward who Rests at Westminster: attributed to a monk of St Bertin*, ed. and trans. F. Barlow (London, 1962), Appendix D, pp. 112–33 (p. 132). Barlow shows that Aelred's rewriting of the prophecy of the Green Tree was key in establishing the legitimacy of Henry II as continuator of the Anglo-Saxon dynasty (pp. 88–90).

[2]   The Campsey copy is British Library, Add. 70513, fols. 55v–85v; the Vatican manuscript is Rome, Biblioteca Apostolica Vaticana, MS Reg. Lat. 489, fols. 1r–35r; the Picard copy is Paris, BnF, f. fr. 1416, fols. 157r–181r. All three versions are available on *The Electronic Campsey*, http://margot.uwaterloo.ca.

MS Egerton 745 was first described in detail by Paul Meyer in 1910. He characrized it as 'un très beau livre français, écrit de deux mains vers le milieu du XIVe ècle et illustré, en certaines parties, de riches miniatures'.[3] The patronage of the manuscript is indicated by a miniature on fol. 33, showing a knight wearing the eraldic arms of the counts of Châtillon St Pol (Figure 22.1). Meyer proposed Jean e Châtillon (d. 1344), or more likely his son Guy de Châtillon (d. 1360, while a ostage in England), as patron, since in his view the manuscript dated from the mid-fourteenth century.

Since Meyer's article, little attention has been paid to the manuscript. In 1997, a survey of illuminated manuscripts in the British Library, Janet Backhouse ated of Egerton 745 that 'the style of the best miniatures in this volume bears a mily resemblance to the work of Honoré', a well-known Parisian illuminator orking in the last decades of the thirteenth century.[4] In 1998 Alison Stones also mmented briefly on Egerton 745, noting that its extensive illustrations had argely been ignored. Two of the works in the manuscript stand out because of the number and quality of illuminations: the *Vie de s. Eustache* has nine full-page luminations, while the *Vie de s. Denis* has forty-six miniatures, some of which re two columns wide. The remaining texts have a single opening illumination, sually one column wide. Professor Stones identified the major artist, responble for the *S. Denis* and *S. Eustache* illuminations (along with the single Edward lumination, according to Golden, cited below), as a Parisian illuminator ctive in the early fourteenth century, associated with the bookseller Thomas Maubeuge, for whom the more distinguished painter Jean Pucelle also worked. tones suggested the likely patron was Marie de Bretagne, grand-daughter of Henry III of England, daughter of the duke of Brittany, and wife of the Norman magnate Guy de Châtillon, based on the choice of five saints lives included in the manuscript: two Breton saints (St Martin de Vertou and St Gildas), Edward the onfessor of England, along with St Denis and St Eustache, culted intensively at the Abbey of Saint Denis by the Capetians.[5]

In a 2001 doctoral thesis Judith Golden expanded on this analysis.[6] She argues that the iconography of the *Vie de s. Denis* in Egerton 745 is similar to that of the opy of *S. Denis* made for Philippe le Bel in 1314–17. She confirms the similarities the style of painting in Egerton 745 with that of the so-called Papeleu master,

---

See P. Meyer, 'Notice du Ms. Egerton 745 du Musée Britannique', *Romania* 39 (1910), [pt 1] 532–69 (p. 532); *Romania* 40 (1911), [pt 2] 41–69.

J. Backhouse, *The Illuminated Page: Ten Centuries of Manuscript Painting in the British Library* (London, 1997), no. 76, pp. 96–7.

A. Stones, 'The Stylistic Context of the *Roman de Fauvel*, with a Note on *Fauvain*. Appendix B: The Stylistic Subgroups surrounding the Fauvel Master', in *Fauvel Studies: Allegory, Chronicle, Music, and Image in Paris, Bibliothèque National de France, MS français 146*, ed. M. Bent and A. Wathey (Oxford, 1998), pp. 529–67 (pp. 545–8).

J. K. Golden, 'Patronage and the Saints in the Devotional Miscellany British Library MS Egerton 745' (unpublished Ph.D. thesis, University of Pittsburgh, 2001).

Figure 22.1: Knight, wearing the arms of the counts of Châtillon St Pol, kneeling before Our Lady (BL, MS Egerton 745, fol. 33 rb)

active into the 1320s, now plausibly identified as Richard de Verdun, son-in-law of the Parisian illuminator Honoré.[7]

In an article based on her thesis, Golden proposes that the unique series of nine full-page illuminations that are placed at the beginning of the life of *S. Eustache* constitutes a separate narrative of Eustache, planned by Marie de Bretagne for the education of her son, offering 'guidance for a good Christian life as husband, father, and civil servant'.[8]

Golden's argument for proposing Marie de Bretagne as patron is a slight expansion of that of Alison Stones, based on the choice of saints' lives and the narrative sequence of the illuminations. But the significance of the inclusion of these saints, and their specific treatment in this manuscript, extends beyond suggesting a probable patron.

Inherent in this choice of lives is a claim to cultural identity in not just two, but three, separate cultural spheres: Norman (and/or French), Anglo-French (or Anglo-Norman) and Breton. The order of importance of these identities is suggested by the level of illumination used, and only two lives have an extensive number of miniatures. As Golden notes, the Egerton *S. Denis* is one of six extant copies of this prose life that are intensively illuminated. It is the only one commissioned by an aristocratic family, as opposed to copies made for royalty, or for the Abbey of St Denis itself. The commissioning of a lavishly illuminated life of *S. Denis* for a family manuscript lays an obvious and strong claim to the patronage of the saint. But was this claim to be seen as a reminder to the French royal family that they do not enjoy a monopoly on the patronage of St Denis, or was it to serve as a reminder of the patron's own family claims to the French crown?

Earlier studies have shown that the monks at St Denis were very active in their role as propagandists for their saint as protector of the royal family, and of their abbey.[9] French literary texts of the twelfth century had earlier associated St Denis with the Capetians, who are often represented as carrying the banner of the saint into battle. In these texts Denis is the patron protector of both the king's person and of France.[10] This remarkably successful propagation of the cult of St Denis as a national saint by the Capetians and the Abbey of St Denis stands in

---

[7] Golden, 'Patronage', pp. 140–1, citing R. and M. Rouse, Illiterati et uxorati: *Manuscripts and their Makers: Commercial Book Producers in Medieval Paris, 1200–1500* (London, 2000), I, 140–3; F. Avril, *Les fastes du gothique: le siècle de Charles V* (Paris, 1981), p. 280; F. Avril, *L'art du temps des rois maudits: Philippe le Bel et ses fils* (Paris, 1998), p. 187.

[8] J. Golden, 'Images of Instruction, Marie de Bretagne, and the Life of St. Eustace as Illustrated in the British Library Ms. Egerton 745', in *Insights and Interpretations*, ed. C. Hourihane (Princeton, 2002), pp. 60–84 (p. 74).

[9] See, for example, C. J. Liebman, *Etude sur la vie en prose de saint Denis* (New York, 1942); R. Bossuat, 'Traditions populaires relatives au martyre et à la sépulture de saint Denis', *Le Moyen Âge* 62 (1959), 479–509; G. M. Spiegel, 'The Cult of Saint Denis and Capetian Kingship', *JMH* 1 (1975), 43–69.

[10] Spiegel, 'The Cult of Saint Denis', pp. 59–65 (p. 62), analyzes how the cult embraced both the king's person and the people of France, and was an effective tool in creating this identity.

sharp contrast, as Paul Binski has noted, to the efforts of Westminster Abbey and the Plantagenets in England, where 'St Edward remained an institutional saint, a saint more of Westminster and its political elite than of the nation.'[11]

It was to respond to the opposition directed at the regent during the minority of Louis IX that the monks of St Denis created the new *vita* of St Denis and Dagobert in 1233, to emphasize the protective role of the saint both towards his Abbey, and the French crown.[12] In this respect they were doing exactly what had been done for the life of Edward the Confessor by Aelred of Rievaulx in the twelfth century.

Conscious appropriation of the cult of St Denis continued to be used as a defence of their legitimacy by the reigning family, as witness the new life of St Denis commissioned by Philippe le Bel in 1314, and later, the public homage of Philippe de Valois before the relics of the saint at the Abbey of St Denis, following his coronation in 1328.[13]

The cult of St Denis was also operative as a national defence in the epic *Florent et Octavien*, composed shortly after the French defeat at Poitiers in 1356, to rally public support for the defeated and captive French king and to re-establish belief in the divine support offered by St Denis to the kings of France throughout history.[14]

I evoke these details relative to the life of *S. Denis* to suggest that the reception of these texts in Egerton 745 was likely to be very complex in the fourteenth century. The commissioning of a lavishly illustrated life of *S. Denis*, similar to that commissioned by Philippe le Bel in 1314, completed and presented to his son Philippe V in 1317, is an act with multiple resonances.

The prominence given in Egerton 745 to the lives of saints Denis and Eustache (the cult of Eustache in France was also centred at the Abbey of St Denis) suggests that the patron who commissioned the manuscript identified strongly with the Capetian family. The marriage in 1308 of Mahaut, daughter of Marie de Bretagne and Guy de Châtillon, to Charles de Valois, brother of the king, and father of the future Philippe VI, would provide one such close link.

The inclusion of the life of Edward the Confessor in this manuscript, on the other hand, lays claim to a Plantagenet heritage, and can perhaps be seen as ongoing support for the Plantagenet response to the Capetian cult of St Denis. Aelred's *Vita Edwardi* not only depicts Henry II as the fulfilment of Edward's prophecy, in which the dynastic tree again bears fruit, it also suggests that a new unity existed between the Norman invaders and the English. In the words of Ian Short, Aelred's biblical imagery expresses 'the perception, that at least some contemporaries had, of the relationship between the English and Norman elements that made up Anglo-Norman society – that the stage was now set for real and rapid advance in the

---

11 P. Binski, *Westminster Abbey and the Plantagenets: Kingship and the Representation of Power, 1200–1400* (New Haven CT, 1995), p. 53.
12 Spiegel, 'The Cult of Saint Denis', pp. 53–4; Bossuat, 'Traditions', pp. 481–2.
13 Bossuat, 'Traditions', pp. 481–5.
14 Bossuat, 'Traditions', pp. 487–99 (p. 487).

rocesses of social assimilation and integration'.[15] The nun of Barking's verse
anslation of Aelred's *Vita Edwardi* maintains this ideological thrust, by empha-
zing what Jocelyn Wogan-Browne has called the 'sacralizing mystique' of a
ecifically English kingship, and expanding on the theological discussion of the
ture of charity and chastity found in her source text.[16]

The prose reworking of the life from Barking included in Egerton 745 often
mains remarkably close to its source text, although it omits many of the personal
flections of the nun narrator, including some of the theological subtlety, and
ferences to Henry II as being alive. The French prose version also adds a unique
cond miracle effected at Barking Abbey, at the end of the narrative, for which
ere is no known source.

While the scope of the current study does not allow a detailed discussion of
e nature of these reductions in authorial comment in the prose reworking, the
eatment of one key passage in the text should be noted. As Jocelyn Wogan-
rowne has pointed out, in the central scene following the wedding celebra-
ons in which Edward calls his wife to his private chamber and exhorts her to
nounce carnal marriage and join him in living in perfect chastity, the Barking
'e of Edward is 'the only version to give Edith a point of view and to add a
eech for her (lines 1371–86) on the wedding night', thereby dramatizing and
aking more emotionally intimate both the male and female wish for chastity.[17]

In the prose *remaniement* the exhortation by Edward to his wife, lines 1345–68,
significantly shortened (dropping lines 1353–64, which develop the reference to
e love of God for his bride, Chastity, as *fin' amur*: 'Desque a sa presence la meine,
La lui rent tute la duçur / Del delit de sa fin' amur.' He [God] brings her into his
esence, where he gives her all the sweetness of the joy of his perfect love.)

The prose version of Edith's response, however, preserves all the details of the
erse text:

Quant la royne ot oy tes paroles touz ses cuers s'en esjoi. Ele respondi moult
liément au roy: 'Biaus douz chiers sires, biau douz amis, je vous rent pour
ceste requeste graces et mercis de tout mon povoir, quar ce avoie je touz temps
desirré et moult avoie Dieu prié que il gardast ma chaasté. Et aussi que vous
avez dit a moi, vous pri je, et requier pour Dieu que ma priere puist valoir
que dendroit de nous vous voilliez garder chaasté. Quar a ce qu'il me samble,
vous avez mon desirrer. Je ferai ce qu'il vous plaira et vous honorerai et amerai
comme mon chier seigneur. Et Diex nous doinst le povoir de garder chaasté
aussi que il nous en a douné la volenté.'[18]

Short, *'Tam Angli quam Franci'*, p. 172.
J. Wogan-Browne, *Saints' Lives and Women's Literary Culture, c.1150–1300: Virginity and its Authorizations* (Oxford, 2001), pp. 245–56 (p. 249), and passim.
J. Wogan-Browne, ' "Clerc u lai, muïne u dame": Women and Anglo-Norman Hagio-
graphy in the Twelfth and Thirteenth Centuries', in *Women and Literature in Britain, 1150–1500* (Cambridge, 1993), pp. 69–70. Edith's speech is not in the Latin sources.
See http://margot/uwaterloo.ca (*EgE_w523–38*) for an electronic edition of these
texts; extracts from the prose version are printed by Meyer, 'Notice du Ms. Egerton
745', [pt 2] 41–69, but this passage is not included.

(When the queen heard these words her heart rejoiced, and she replied with great joy to the king: 'My dear kind lord, dear sweet friend, I thank you with all my might for this request, for I have always desired, and often prayed to God that he preserve my chastity. And just as you have asked me, I now ask you, and request, in the name of God's love, that my prayer may have the power to give you the will to preserve our joint chastity. For it seems to me that your desire is also my own. I will do everything as you wish and will honour you and love you as my dear lord. And God grant us the strength to remain chaste just as he has given us the desire for chastity.')

The prose version of Edith's speech follows the verse text almost word fc word, except for the last sentence, which subtly makes the final prayer a wish fc their joint strength (*vous* is changed to *nous*), as opposed to that of Edward alon Although the prose version has omitted the precocious courtly expression c male desire for chastity, couched in terms of *fin' amur*, the preservation of Edith voiced desire, as well as the addition of a new miracle sited at Barking Abbe suggests the influence of a female patron who was familiar with the sophist cated (female) spiritual tradition of Barking Abbey, which may lie behind th patron's preference for the Barking version of the life of Edward as opposed t the more contemporary (male) version by Matthew Paris.

The choice of the Barking version of the text can perhaps also be read a extending the claim on the patronage of Edward beyond that of the English cour through its re-emphasis on Barking Abbey as the source of this life. Yet, despi having been chosen for inclusion in the manuscript, the Barking text is not give the same prestigious presentation as the lives culted at St Denis. In contrast t the lavish cycle of miniatures used for both *S. Denis* and *S. Eustache*, the life c Edward the Confessor has only one miniature at the beginning of the text. shows Edward carrying a crippled beggar on his back to the altar of St Pete at Westminster Abbey, in a humble and literal embrace of charity (Figure 22.2 Against advice from his household that he should not debase himself in this wa Edward persists in carrying the beggar, ignoring the public gibes and mocker from bystanders. This scene also emphasizes the curative powers vested i Edward's body, powers that were more routinely claimed by the Capetians.

The two short Breton saints' lives in prose, extant only in this manuscrip which signal the Breton heritage of Marie de Bretagne, each also have only on introductory miniature. The miniature for Martin de Vertou depicts the strang dynastic marriage of his parents. The mother of Martin was born without a rigt hand. When her parents arrange her marriage, they are obliged to settle for royal husband of lower social status because of this deformity. When St Martin c Tours performs the marriage ceremony, however, he insists the bride extend he right arm to her betrothed, and miraculously her deformed arm has been mad whole. After the ceremony, the parents, seeing that their daughter is now mot marriageable than in the past, annul the betrothal, and seek a husband of highe dynastic standing. But during the performance of the second wedding, thei daughter is returned to her congenital deformity. St Martin instructs the parent to return their daughter to her first husband, and her hand will be restorec

Figure 22.2: King Edward carrying a crippled beggar to the altar of St Peter, Westminster (BL, MS Egerton 745, fol. 91ra)

Figure 22.3: Marie, countess of St Pol and Mary Magdalen (CUL, MS Dd.5.5, fol. 236r)

Whatever lesson is to be drawn from this text, it does seem to speak directly to magnates, both male and female, who were constantly involved in the politics of dynastic marriages.

The miniature chosen for the life of Gildas, which shows a monk teaching a young male pupil, might be seen as a standard image, since Gildas was renowned as a scholar, teacher and historian. The only episode in the narrative that refers to Gildas as a teacher, however, can also be read as a comment on dynastic marriages. A young woman is given in marriage by her father to a powerful magnate, but only on the condition that she is placed under the protection of Gildas. As her

ther feared, his daughter is murdered by her tyrant husband, a serial killer
his earlier wives, having despatched each one as soon as he learned she was
regnant. Summoned by the distraught father, Gildas miraculously casts the
rant and his household into the abyss, and resuscitates the murdered woman
the name of Christ. She is sent to her father's household to await the birth of
er child, who is then educated in the liberal arts by St Gildas, while the mother
placed in an abbey. Although the miniature chosen for this life emphasizes the
le of the saint as a teacher of the liberal arts, the student is the product of an
usive dynastic marriage. Is this miracle, which has much in common with folk
les of ogres, here used as a comment on the vulnerability of noble women as
jects in the dynastic economy?

Although cultural identity expressed by the choice of saints must be one
ncern of the patron, there are broader moral and social issues that are common
all of these cultural identities, and these serve as a reminder that Egerton 745
primarily a collection of devotional pieces. This is clearly shown by the prayer
the Madonna for intercession on his behalf, which is placed in the mouth of the
ight wearing the arms of Châtillon St Pol. (See Figure 22.1 above.)

The identity of the figure represented may be, as Stones and Golden argue,
ther the son of Marie de Bretagne, or her husband Guy, as a memorial for him
ter his death in 1317. But this devotional collection must also have served as a
ltural model for the female members of the Châtillon family, in their lives both
magnates and as patrons of books. It may even have been commissioned by
e of them as a tribute to both her parents.

Two of the five daughters of Marie de Bretagne and Guy de Châtillon are
own to have been patrons of books, having commissioned illuminated brevi-
ies in which they are represented in poses very similar to that of their male
lative in Egerton 745, and both played important roles in the dynastic politics
the time (Figure 22.3 and Table 22.1).[19]

The marriage of Mahaut in 1308 to Charles de Valois was mentioned above.
1321 the marriage of her sister, Marie de St Pol, to Aymer de Valence, earl of
mbroke, was negotiated directly by Edward II and Philippe V, a sign of its
tional importance to both England and France. Aymer de Valence was one of

---

N. J. Morgan, '49. Breviary', in *The Cambridge Illuminations: Ten Centuries of Book
Production in the Medieval West*, ed. P. Binski and S. Panayotova (London, 2005), pp.
132–4. Morgan also refers to a breviary commissioned by Mahaud (Cividale, Museo
Archeologico Nazionale, MS CXL) in which both women are shown with the arms of
Châtillon-St Pol-Valence and Châtillon-St Pol-Valois, respectively (see F. Avril, *Un chef-
d'œuvre de l'enluminure sous le règne de Jean le Bon: la* Bible moralisée *manuscrit français
167 de la Bibliothèque Nationale* (Paris, 1972), p. 108; and G. Bergamini, 'Un brevario
francescano del XIV secolo nel Museo di Cividale del Friuli', *Le Venezie francescane :
rivista semestrale di storia, arte e cultura*, n.s. 3 (1986), 29–42). J. Ward, 'St Pol, Mary
de, countess of Pembroke (*c*.1304–77)', in *ODNB* (http://www.oxforddnb.com/view/
article/53073 [accessed 5 April 2006] prints a second image of Marie from CUL, MS
Dd. 5.5, fol. 91r.

Table 22.1: Family connections of Marie de St Pol

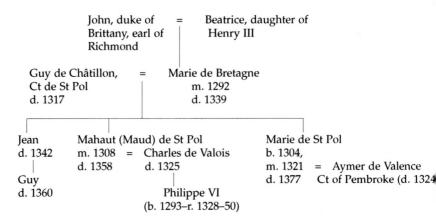

the most powerful barons of England, closely associated with Edward II, and he held extensive lands in England as well as holdings in France.

Of the two sisters, Marie de St Pol had a long widowhood of fifty-three years (1324–77), during which she successfully negotiated her dual cultural identities both as a French-born countess, and as a major English magnate, managing her estates on both sides of the Channel, and at times involved in diplomacy between the English and French royal families.[20] Although she maintained social relations with other wealthy dowager patrons, such as Elizabeth de Burgh, Isabelle of France (mother of Edward II) and Joan of Bar, countess of Warren, very little direct evidence remains of how Marie de St Pol constructed her cultural identity through the reading or patronage of books.[21]

From circumstantial evidence we can speculate that she may have been present at Campsey during a mealtime reading from their collection of French verse saints' lives.[22] Or she might have known texts such as the Tretiz of Walter

[20] M. J. Bennett, 'Isabelle of France, Anglo-French Diplomacy and Cultural Exchange in the Late 1350s', in Age of Edward III, ed. J. S. Bothwell (Rochester NY, 2001), pp. 215–2 (pp. 219–21); H. Jenkinson, 'Mary de Sancto Paulo, Foundress of Pembroke College Cambridge', Archaeologia 66 (1915), 401–46 (pp. 409–12). Mary was in France in 1329 1331–4 and 1352–7, and joined Isabelle of France in entertaining French royalty in England, 1357–8.

[21] See F. A. Underhill, For Her Good Estate: The Life of Elizabeth de Burgh (New York, 1999 pp. 3–4, 102–22, and passim; Jenkinson, 'Mary de Sancto Paulo', pp. 427–8; Bennett 'Isabelle of France', pp. 219–21: for a summary of Marie de St Pol's patronage in all media, see Gee, Women, Art and Patronage, Appendix A, pp. 165–6.

[22] Underhill notes that Elizabeth de Burgh often visited Marie's religious foundation at Waterbeach and Denny (For Her Good Estate, p. 105). Elizabeth's daughter-in-law Maud of Lancaster (sister of Henry of Lancaster), countess of Ulster, entered Campsey convent in 1347, leaving in 1364 to enter Bruisyard, newly founded by Lionel of Clarence for her benefit. The founding nuns at Bruisyard came from Denny. Elizabeth

of Bibbesworth, written for Denise de Munchensi (from whom Marie inherited, through her husband, the patronage of the first house of Minoresses in England, at Waterbeach, which she later moved to Denny Abbey).[23] The *Livre de seyntz medicines* by Henry of Lancaster must have been known to her through their mutual friend Elizabeth de Burgh, and their joint interest in lay piety. She would have known as well the courtly literature favoured by Isabelle of France, whose will lists a number of well-known secular texts. Michael Bennett speculates that Marie may have had a more impressive library than Queen Isabelle, although only one secular book, the courtly *Godefroy de Bouillon* (recorded in Jean le Bon's library as a gift from the countess of Pembroke),[24] is connected with her name, and the will of Marie de St Pol only mentions her devotional books and breviaries.[25]

Although Marie de St Pol lived principally in England, in a manner that shows a high level of cultural assimilation in Anglo-Norman society, she followed French cultural models in her foundations created in mid-century. Minor details of her two major charities (such as the fact that her house of Minoresses followed the modified, French royal rule,[26] or the stipulation that preference in admission to the Cambridge college she founded in 1347 be given to French scholars, who should speak Latin, or failing that, French, while in college[27]), suggest that her sense of cultural identity was still dual and cross-Channel, similar to the multiple cultural identities claimed in Egerton 745. This would not have been out of place

---

entertained both Lionel and Marie de St Pol at the same time in 1350 (Jenkinson, 'Mary de Sancto Paulo', p. 422, n. 4). Although there is no record of Marie de St Pol visiting Campsey, given these close social relationships such a visit would have been likely. On the foundation of Bruisyard (which involved conflict at Campsey), see A. F. C. Bourdillon, *The Order of Minoresses in England* (Manchester, 1926), pp. 23–4, 47–9.

23 Bourdillon, *The Order of Minoresses*, pp. 14–19; T. Hunt, 'Bibbesworth, Walter de (b. in or before 1219, d. in or after 1270)', *ODNB* (http://www.oxforddnb.com/view/article/2340 [accessed 29 March 2005].

24 M. J. Bennett, 'Mandeville's *Travels* and the Anglo-French Moment', *Medium Aevum* 75 (2006), 273–92 (p. 281).

25 For Marie's will, see Jenkinson, 'Mary de Sancto Paulo', pp. 432–5. On the breviaries, see note 19, above. Marie presumably also owned a copy of the *Miroir de l'âme*, extant in a later, fifteenth-century, manuscript, London, BL Royal 16.E.V, in which the text is dedicated to Marie de St Pol. The *Miroir* is an early vernacular religious treatise created at the Capetian court before 1252. See S. Field, 'From *Speculum anime* to *Miroir de l'âme*: The Origins of Vernacular Advice Literature at the Capetian Court', forthcoming in *Medieval Studies*; and 'Reflecting the Royal Soul: The *Speculum anime* Composed for Blanche of Castile', *Medieval Studies* 68 (2006), 1–42.

26 See Bourdillon, *The Order of Minoresses*, pp. 3, 51; Morgan, '49. Breviary', p. 133; and J. Ringrose, 'The Foundress and Her College: Marie de St Pol', in *Pembroke College Cambridge: A Celebration*, ed. A. V. Grimstone (Cambridge, 1999), p. 5. The rule allowed each nun to have one servant.

27 Ringrose, 'The Foundress and Her College', p. 9. It was standard university practice in Paris and England to ban the use of the vernacular in favour of Latin. We note, however, that three Oxford colleges also accepted the use of French as well as Latin (Lusignan, *Langue des rois*, p. 195).

in Anglo-Norman England of the time, where, after the victory at Poitiers, the francophone English court of Edward III, awash with French nobility as hostages, could claim at the Feast of the Garter at Windsor in 1358 to be 'the cultural capital of the francophone world'.[28]

By the end of her life in 1377, however, Marie de St Pol was increasingly involved in supporting the Franciscan movement, and her ties with France may have been weakening. She had been dispossessed of most of her French lands by Charles V in 1372, and in her will she refers to the constant support she has received from the king of England, to whom she makes several bequests. To the queen of France also she leaves important relics, and a book of hours given to her by the queen of Scotland, while to the king of France she bequeaths a sword with a broken blade: 'item: je devise a mon tresredoubté seigneur le roi de ffrance une espee que j'ai qui est sanz pointe et que mon bien amé Willecok de ma chambre la lui porte ou autre qui lui sache dire de quele maniere elle est'.[29] Point taken – and still made, it will be noted, in the French vernacular.

The language used in her will brings us to one final, intriguing question. What was the nature of the romance vernacular used by Marie de St Pol? Her St Pol family was from Picardie, and she lived mainly in England, yet neither Egerton 745 nor the testament of Marie de St Pol show marked Picard or Anglo-Norman features.[30] Jenkinson reports that none of the surviving documents seems to have been written by Marie herself; in the active administration of her property she depended on a number of professional men; a typical example of one of these attorneys is 'John of St Pol (presumably an early protégé from France), who became first an Exchequer clerk and ultimately archbishop of Dublin.'[31] A man such as this, and others of the *familia* of Marie de St Pol, were no doubt capable of writing the vernacular in either the Continental or the Insular style, whichever was appropriate for the situation, in keeping with the multiple cultural identities of the countess of Pembroke.

[28] Bennett, 'Isabelle of France', p. 224: see also the essay by Bennett in this volume.
[29] (Item: I bequeath to my very honoured lord the King of France a sword which I have which has lost its point, and which my well beloved servant of the chamber Willecok is to carry to him, or some other person who will know how to tell him what kind of sword it is.)
[30] See Lusignan, *Langue des rois*, who studies the deliberate use of dialects of French in administrative documents. My thanks also to Prof. Lusignan for comments on this essay.
[31] Jenkinson, 'Mary de Sancto Paulo', p. 416.

23

The Vitality of Anglo-Norman in Late Medieval England: The Case of the Prose *Brut* Chronicle

Julia Marvin

'ith over fifty manuscripts in three basic versions, the prose *Brut* chronicle ippears to survive in more copies than any other long Anglo-Norman work. ve manuscripts exist of its Oldest Version, which was written around the 'ginning of the fourteenth century in the north of England and which offers complete history of Britain from the fall of Troy to the death of Henry III in :72.[1] Based on (among other things) the *Historia regum Britannie* of Geoffrey Monmouth, Wace's *Roman de Brut*, Gaimar's *Estoire des Engleis*, a version of e Latin chronicle of the Premonstratensian house of Barlings, hagiographic aterials and romance matter such as that of Havelok, the Oldest Version is ndamentally secular in focus and interest, with a constant emphasis on the aties of kings to their people, the importance of smooth royal succession id the desirability of peace and order. It goes out of its way, and rewrites its iurces, to create an engaging narrative of British history as one of fundamental intinuity – rather than one of recurrent decadence, invasion and displacement, in the Galfridian paradigm.[2]

Composed for stakeholders in society, but not for the highest clerical or court ites, the work proved extremely appealing, and the Oldest Version of the nglo-Norman *Brut* became the core of a text expanded with Anglo-Norman rologues and continuations into the 1330s: the so-called Short Version survives thirty-one to thirty-three manuscripts, and the Long Version in fourteen to xteen, depending on one's methods of classification and counting.[3] The Long 'rsion served as the basis for the two Middle English translations of the prose 'ut, which gave rise to still more revisions and continuations running into the teenth century. According to Lister Matheson, over 180 Middle English *Brut* anuscripts (comprised of elements of some 215 manuscripts in all) survive.[4]

The Oldest Version runs to about 110 printed pages in its modern edition: *The Oldest Anglo-Norman Prose 'Brut' Chronicle: An Edition and Translation*, ed. and trans. J. Marvin (Woodbridge, 2006).

For an overview, see *Oldest*, ed. Marvin, pp. 1–67.

See *Oldest*, ed. Marvin, pp. 47–51; Dean, nos. 36, 42–6. For a manuscript of the Short Version where the *Brut* is paired with an Anglo-Norman copy of Froissart, see the essay by Croenen in this volume, pp. 414–15.

L. M. Matheson, *The Prose 'Brut': The Development of a Middle English Chronicle* (Tempe AZ, 1998), p. 6. This is the major single study to date of the Middle English manuscripts:

Subsequent Latin translations of the prose *Brut* were made, from both Anglo
Norman and Middle English, surviving in perhaps nineteen manuscripts, but as
yet almost entirely unstudied.[5]

Possibly the oldest surviving manuscript, Paris, Bibliothèque Nationale de
France, MS nouv. acq. fr. 4267, was in existence in 1338, and the latest manu
scripts date from the late fifteenth century, overlapping with, and in some case
based on, printed editions of the Middle English *Brut*, which was first published
by Caxton in 1480 as *The Chronicles of England* and went through thirteen printed
editions by 1528.[6] The Middle English *Brut* by no means supplanted the Anglo
Norman versions of the text: by the count in Ruth Dean's catalogue, around
quarter of the manuscripts in French date from the fifteenth century.[7] The prose
Brut tradition, then, represents the phenomenon of a work circulating simulta
neously in different versions in the three main literary languages of England
serving an array of audiences.

Little evidence survives of the early provenance of prose *Brut* manuscripts
Book-lists and wills bespeak fourteenth- and fifteenth-century ownership by
the secular gentry, as well as religious houses, but owners' inscriptions tend to
begin with the late fifteenth or sixteenth century. Although the manuscripts do
not tell the names of their earliest owners, they take many forms across time
and place, running from the cheap to the lavish, with a variety of presentation
apparatus and later annotation, all of which provide opportunity to see the way
in which the chronicle was presented, read, and reconceived by its scribes and
readers.[8] In this essay, I will confine myself to a scattering of examples from the
Anglo-Norman *Brut* tradition, which I hope will suggest the vitality in late medi
eval culture not only of the *Brut* in particular, but of Anglo-Norman literature in
general.

One might reasonably expect the appearance as well as the content of the
prose *Brut* to vary more widely over time, as different branches of the tradition
diverged, but the surviving manuscripts of the Oldest Version manifest mark
edly different designs for, understandings of, and uses of even this earliest state
of the text.

for recent work on the prose '*Brut*', see Marx with Radulescu, *Readers and Writers*
the Prose 'Brut', and for a partial database of Middle English *Brut* manuscripts, see the
Imagining History project, directed by John Thompson at Queen's University, Belfast
http://www.qub.ac.uk/imagining-history/resources/short/index.php. The project
publications are listed at http://www.qub.ac.uk/imagining-history/outputs/index.
htm.

5   Matheson, *Prose 'Brut'*, pp. xx–xxi, 39–47.
6   Matheson, *Prose 'Brut'*, pp. xxxii–xxxvi.
7   Dean pp. 24–7, 30–4. She lists six manuscripts as 'XIV/XV' and eleven, four of which
    are continental, as fifteenth century.
8   More formal and thoroughly planned revisions of, and additions to, the content of the
    chronicle, the selection of works to accompany the *Brut* in a given codex and linguistic
    evidence as such are of course also enormously informative, but they will not be the
    focus of this discussion.

I will begin with the example of London, British Library, MS Additional 35092, a very well prepared and extremely portable manuscript from the third quarter of the fourteenth century, containing only the prose *Brut*, its single-column pages (which have been trimmed) now just around 118 × 77 millimetres. With its highly legible anglicana formata hand, rubric section headings (organized mostly by kings' reigns), large initials dividing sections, and proper names touched with red, the text is easy to navigate. Although small enough to be designed for private reading, the book is also clear enough to be read aloud. In the basic layout of rubrication and initials, it resembles two larger and far less meticulously produced manuscripts of the Oldest Version, Paris, Bibl. Nat., MSS f. fr. 14640 and nouv. acq. fr. 4267.[9] But it is distinctive not only in its size, but in the quality of its text – despite being the latest of the manuscripts of the Oldest Version, it also appears to contain the best surviving text of it.[10] No annotations aside from later marks of ownership appear in the manuscript, so it offers no additional information as to how it was used. This of course does not mean that the manuscript was not read, or read carefully: the comprehensiveness of the existing apparatus and the smallness of the margins may have made annotations unnecessary or impractical.

The other two surviving manuscripts of the Oldest Version offer more hints about their making and use, and each takes the chronicle in a somewhat different direction.

Oxford, Bodleian Library, MS Douce 120 dates from the mid-fourteenth century and appears to be the work of a single scribe likely to have been making a copy for himself, in some haste. Compared to the professionally produced, handsome Additional 35092, it is a humble book. Its pages are box-ruled in a single column, its text in a current anglicana hand with sporadic, awkward efforts at a more formal script and proper names often touched with red. Instead of section headings, the text has running heads consisting of proper names found on the pages below (Figure 23.1). This approach clearly saved time and effort in design; it may also suggest a maker who already knew the basic narrative of British history and needed only names to find what he wanted. His exemplar was apparently missing a leaf at one point, and he left an appropriate amount of space blank in (evidently vain) hopes of finding another copy to fill in the material.[11] Towards the end of the *Brut* text, he begins to supplement the text with material from Pierre de Langtoft's *Chronicle*, first integrating it up to the *Brut*'s conclusion, then putting Langtoft into prose, and finally copying Langtoft outright, as if the effort

---

9 F. fr. 14640 (early to mid-fourteenth century) has leaves measuring approximately 192 × 138 mm; nouv. acq. fr. 4267 (with an inscription dated 1338) has leaves measuring approximately 204 × 139 mm. See *Oldest*, ed. Marvin, pp. 59–61.

10 See *Oldest*, ed. Marvin, pp. 58–9, 65–7. Richard Ingham notes, however, that on preliminary examination Additional 35092 appears to be less linguistically conservative than f. fr. 14640 (pers. comm., 10 August 2007).

11 Fol. 41r–v.

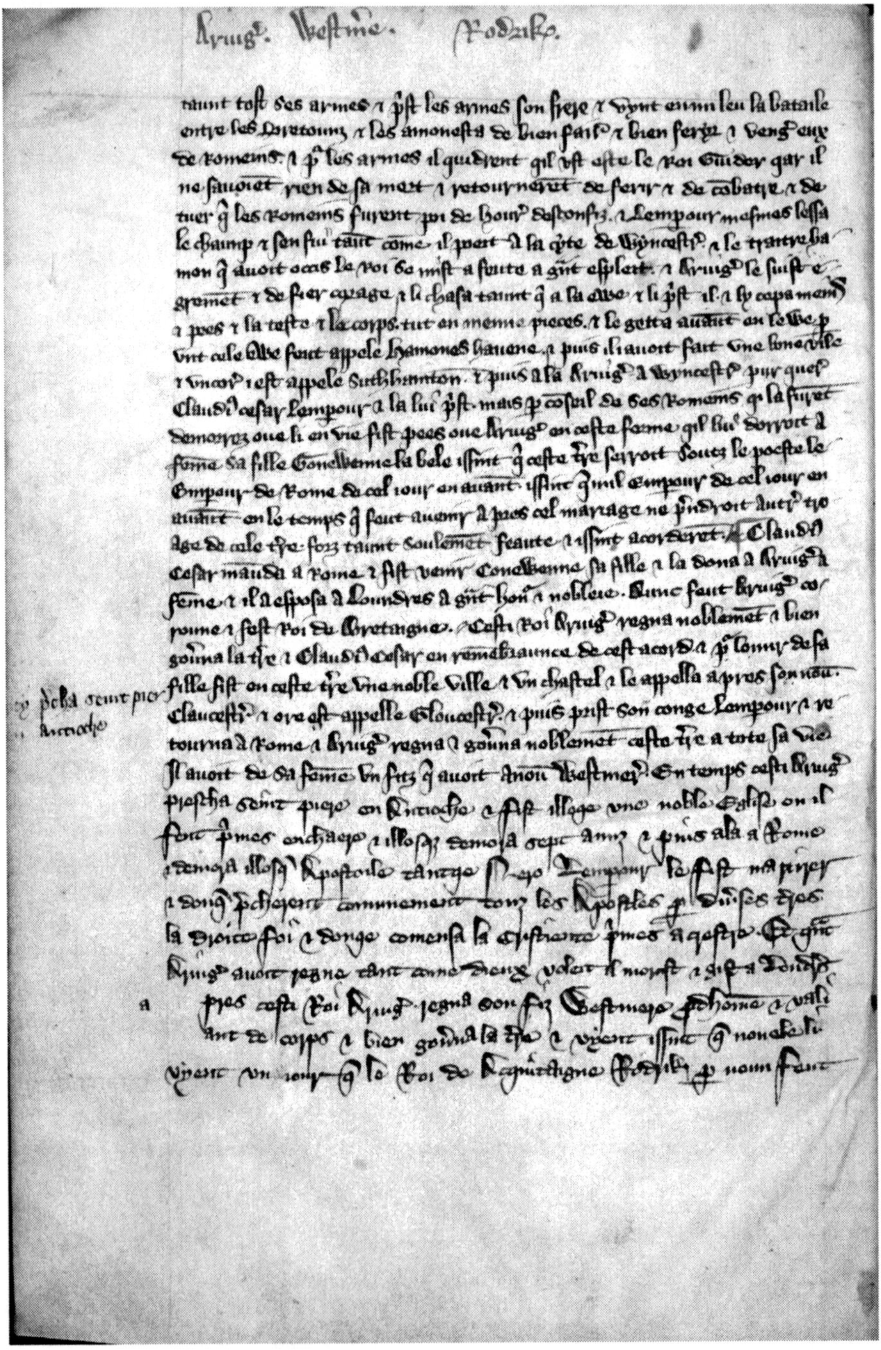

Figure 23.1: The Bodleian Library, University of Oxford, MS Douce 120, fols. 4v–5r (Anglo-Norman prose *Brut*, Oldest Version), showing the text's layout, the variability of the scribal hand and a later annotation on St Peter's preaching in Antioch

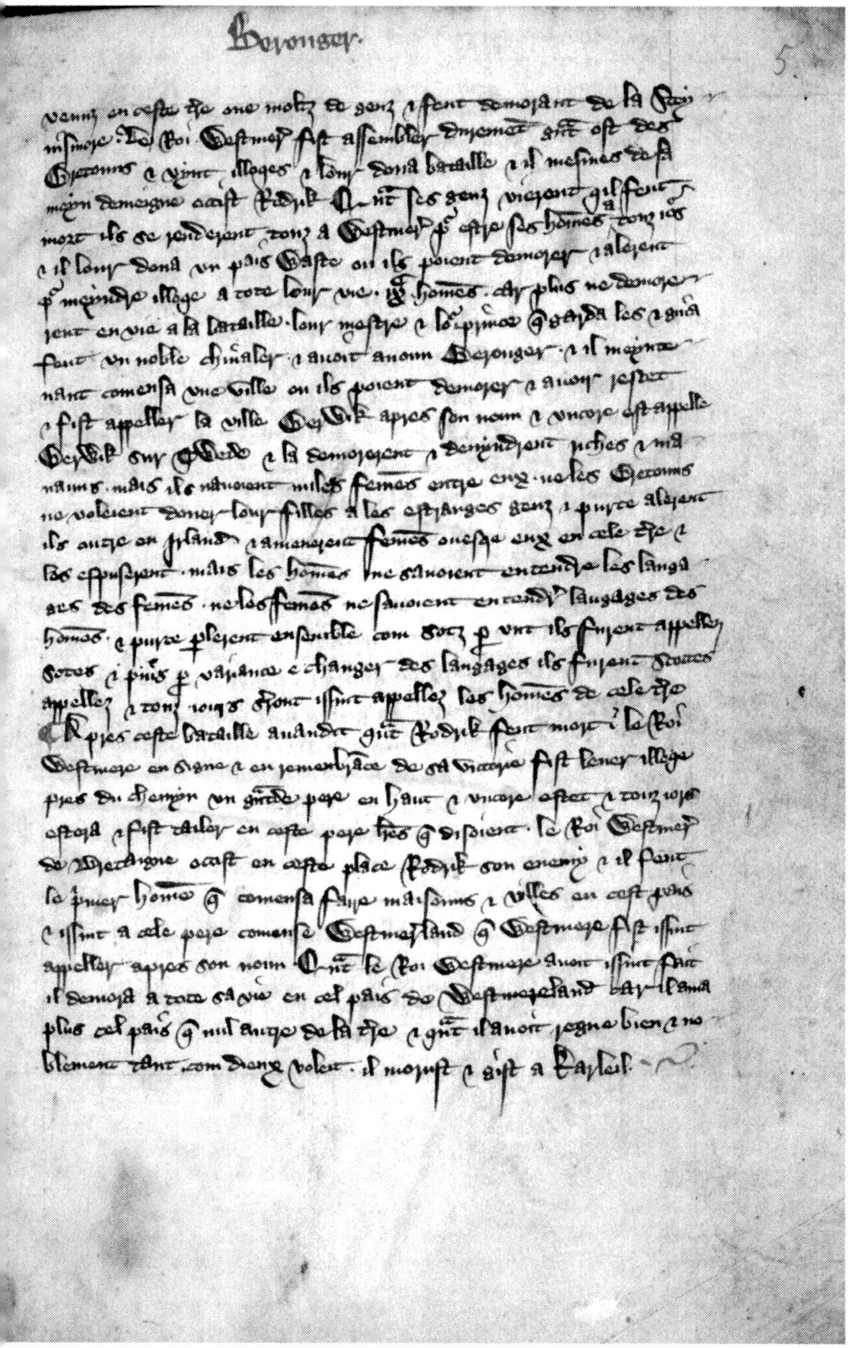
Beronger.

venuz en ceste terre one moltz de genz e sont demorant de la Rei
nmore. Le Roi Westmer fist assembler durement grant ost des
Bretons e vint illoqes e lour dona bataille e il mesmes de sa
mein demeigne occist Rodrik. Quant ses genz virent qil fust
mort ils se rendirent touz a Westmer pur estre ses homes touz iours
e il lour dona un pais Waste ou ils purroient demorer e aleient
pur meindre illoqe a tote lour vie. Ses homes qe plus ne demore-
rent en vie a la bataille. lour mestre e lour primer qe garda les e gouerna
fust un noble chivaler e avoit a noun Beronger. e il maine-
nant comensa une ville ou ils purroient demorer e a lour reseit
e fist appeller la ville Berwik apres son noun e unqore est appelle
Berwik sur Twede e la demoreient e demeindrent peches e mal-
veistés. mes ils navoient nules femmes entre eux. ne les Bretons
ne voleient doner lour filles a les estranges genz e pur ce alerent
ils outre en Irland e amenerent femmes ovesqe eux en cele terre e
les espouserent. mes les homes ne savoient entendre les langages des femmes. ne les femmes ne savoient entendre langages des
homes e pur ce parlerent ensemble com gotz pur quoi ils furent appellez
gotes e puis par variance e chaunger des langages ils furent Scotes
appellez e touz iours serront issint appellez les homes de cele terre
Apres ceste bataille avandit quant Rodrik fust mort le Roi
Westmere en signe e en remembraunce de sa victorie fist lever illoqe
pres du chemin une grande pere en haut e unqore ester e touz iours
estera e fist tailler en ceste pere lettres qe disoient. le Roi Westmer
de Bretaigne occist en ceste place Rodrik son enemy e il fust
le primer home qe comensa faire maisons e villes en cest pais
e issint a cele pere comense Westmarland qe Westmere fist issint
appeller apres son noun. Quant le Roi Westmere avoit issint fait
il demora a tote sa vie en cel pais de Westmareland ben e leaument
plus cel pais qe nul autre de la terre e quant il avoit regne bien e noblement tant com Dieux voleit. il morust e gist a Karlel.

of recasting the verse had become too onerous.[12] (The manuscript begins and ends incomplete, so there is no telling how far he got.) All this suggests a maker with a serious interest in British history, and far more interest in the content of his book than in its appearance.[13]

The French annotations of a later reader, writing in a secretary-influenced hand, demonstrate interest in the history of Christianity (e.g. the birth of Christ, St Peter's preaching in Antioch, the coming of Christianity to England and St Alban) and fiscal affairs (e.g. the ransom of Richard Lionheart and taxes taken for the confirmation of the charters).[14] They show the uses to which the chronicle could be put as a mine of information.

It would be easy enough to characterize the workaday Douce 120 as the kind of manuscript that would have been owned by a person of relatively modest means, as Francis Douce was when he bought it at the age of nineteen in 1776, at the very start of his career as a collector. But an inscription at the book's beginning suggests just how little the origins of a manuscript may predict the course of its later life. On 31 October 1519, George Neville, third baron of Bergavenny, knight of the Garter and at the time counsellor and friend to Henry VIII, wrote in it, 'thys book is myn G. Bergavenny which J leve yn my chamber att London'. His note shows that he valued the book enough to have it with him in London and to want to make sure it did not stray in his absence – all of which suggests that it may have been a book he read and did not merely possess.

MS Douce 120 was not the only prose *Brut* in the powerful Neville family: the same George Neville or his father also owned the mid- to later fifteenth-century Middle English prose *Brut* Oxford, Bodleian, MS Laud misc. 733, a substantial, fully decorated and illuminated text paired with a treatise on heraldry – far more beautiful, far more expensive, and far less portable than Douce 120.[16] The one could serve better as a status object, the other as a book to be carried and consulted: books at the opposite ends of the material spectrum of prose *Brut*s have their role to play within a single family. Though a deluxe manuscript might not travel far down the social ladder, a modest or even cheap one might well travel far up it. And though Anglo-Norman is generally characterized as the language of higher status in England, in this particular instance, the Middle English manuscript is the object of far higher prestige.

---

12 On Langtoft, see Dean no. 66.

13 See *Oldest*, ed. Marvin, pp. 63–5, 413–16: it now contains iii+64+i leaves measuring approximately 222 × 155 mm.

14 Fols. 4r, 4v, 5v, 8v, 51r and 60r.

15 As transcribed in F. Madan, H. H. E. Craster et al., *A Summary Catalogue of Western Manuscripts in the Bodleian Library at Oxford*, 7 vols. in 8 (Oxford, 1895–1953), IV, 52; see A. Hawkyard, 'Neville, George, third Baron Bergavenny (c.1469–1535)', *ODNB* (Oxford, 2004; online edn, Jan. 2008) http://www.oxforddnb.com/view/article/1993 [accessed 5 March 2008].

16 It has iii+181 leaves measuring approximately 302 × 209 mm, with the *Brut* beginning on fol. 18r. See Matheson, *Prose 'Brut'*, pp. 266–7, on this manuscript's version of the *Brut*.

The last of the five surviving manuscripts of the Oldest Version, Oxford, Bodleian, MS Wood empt. 8, suggests yet another set of aspirations and uses for a *Brut* manuscript. Dating from the second quarter of the fourteenth century, elaborately ruled in a single column and beautifully written in an anglicana legal hand, it was designed with a substantial apparatus in mind: each section has a very brief rubric heading, amounting to little more than the names of the pertinent kings, worked into the right side of the text column, and space for a two-line initial (never added) on the left.[17] Between sections, several lines of space have been left blank, perhaps for illustration or for a more elaborate synopsis of the content (Figure 23.2). In the absence of whatever guidance was meant to have been added, a later user of the book has provided an apparatus of his own.

The reader now finds careful Latin annotations throughout, composed in shield-shaped blocks, added by a single writer working in blackish ink, using a clear secretary-influenced hand. Names of kings and places, notable events and incidents with exemplary value are all pointed out, sometimes with apt moral observations. So comprehensive are these annotations that additions by still later readers are almost entirely limited to various nota markings. This comprehensiveness, along with the formality of the annotations' layout and the pen-flourishes and elaborate capital letters to be found in them, all show that they were designed to become part of the book's apparatus – they are not casual notes nor the kind of memoranda, such as those found in MS Douce 120, by a reader marking a few pet issues. The Latinity of the annotations only makes their ambition clearer: they essentially elevate the *Brut* from a simple, popularizing vernacular narrative to the sort of work that a reader of Latin might consult for information or edification.

MS Wood empt. 8 thus represents a far more authoritative-looking chronicle than the pocketbook Additional 35092 or the hasty, untidy Douce 120: from the beginning of the tradition, different manuscripts of the *Brut* evinced different understandings and evoked different responses from later readers. The book was to continue to prove an adaptable one.

The Anglo-Norman Short Version constitutes a broad and under-studied group, into which most Anglo-Norman prose *Brut* manuscripts fall. It has so far been classified in only the roughest way: its manuscripts include a continuation related to the *Anonimalle Chronicle*, reaching into the 1330s, and generally also a prologue consisting of a version of the poem *Des Grantz Geanz*, the story of the foundation of Britain as Albion by Albine and her sisters before the arrival of Brutus.[18] Some Short Version manuscripts contain rubric headings similar

---

[17] Its leaves measure approximately 262 × 180 mm; like MS Douce 120, it ends incomplete, with the beginning of a continuation present. See *Oldest*, ed. Marvin, pp. 61–3, 411–12.

[18] For the *Anonimalle Chronicle*, see Dean no. 47; for Albina texts, Dean nos. 37–41; J. Marvin, 'Albine and Isabelle: Regicidal Queens and the Historical Imagination of the Anglo-Norman Prose *Brut* Chronicles', *Arthurian Literature* 18 (2001), 143–91.

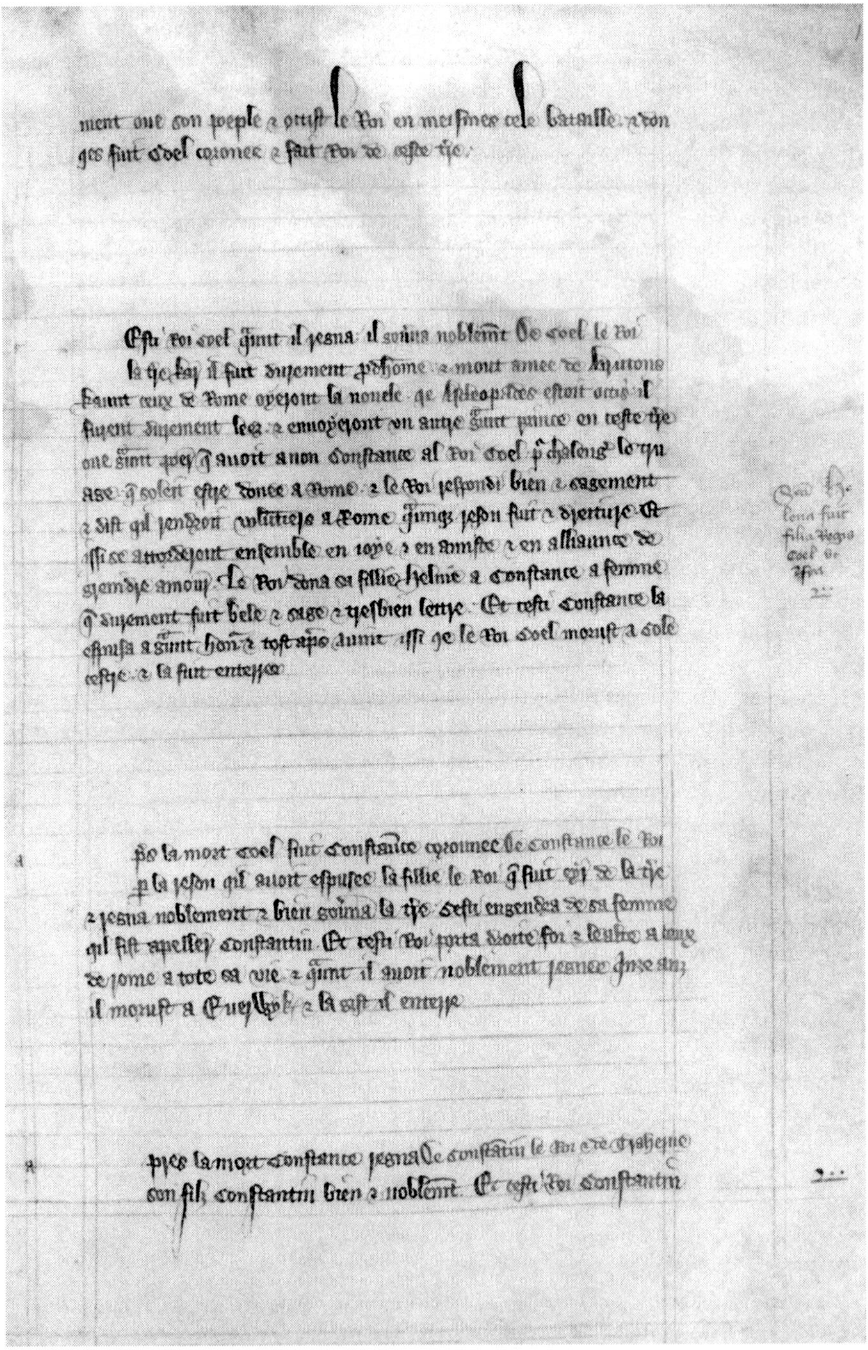

Figure 23.2: The Bodleian Library, University of Oxford, MS Wood empt. 8, fol. 12r (Anglo-Norman prose *Brut* chronicle, Oldest Version), showing the text's layout, later Latin annotation on St Helen and nota markings

ɔ those of the Oldest Version.[19] If, as seems likely, the rubricated manuscripts represent the earlier stages of the Short Version, then the headings dropped out at ome point in transmission, the result being a running narrative marked only by arge initials (or spaces for them) at the beginning of sections, far more difficult to avigate than texts with even the simplest of apparatus. For some readers, as for he scribe who reworked Wood empt. 8, the response was to provide relatively eavy annotation.

Oxford, Bodleian, MS Rawlinson D 329 provides a good example of the way ɔ which such annotations might accumulate over time (Figure 23.3). This four-ɔenth-century manuscript, written in anglicana script in a single column, begins vith genealogical medallions and Latin material in verse on the kings of England rom William the Conqueror to Edward II, followed by the Anglo-Norman *Brut* ɔntinued to 1333/4, and concluding with a brief chronicle in French focused on ɔcotland.[20] The *Brut* text has initials at the beginnings of sections, but no other ɔuilt-in apparatus. An annotator writing in French, in an anglicana hand, has ɔrovided names of kings and other important figures in the margin – essentially he same kind of basic apparatus as in the original state of MS Wood empt. 8. hese additions make the chronicle far more navigable. Much, much later, an ɔntiquarian interested in the origins of place-names has supplemented the 'rench additions with some annotations in English. Again, as with Wood empt. , these notes are written tidily and often placed at the beginning of the sections ɔ question, rather than right alongside the material noted. They constitute an laboration of the apparatus of the chronicle for purposes of reference rather than he occasional casual marking (as with pointing hands or simple nota marks) of tems of interest.

Both sets of the manuscript's readers, then, take the *Brut* seriously as a work vorth consulting and making more readily consultable. Whether the later anno-ator would have made the effort to add the kings' names had they not already een provided for him, and whether the presence of the earlier annotations ncouraged him to add his own, are, of course, among the innumerable unknow-ble things about the book's history and use: each new set of modifications to an xisting manuscript creates a different book for subsequent readers, who may or nay not envision the book in the same way as a previous reader, but are at least quipped, and possibly even induced, to do so.

The coexistence of French, Latin and English within these manuscripts, with heir multilingual texts and layers of annotation, is a further reminder of the ɔolyglot nature of late medieval (and later) reading. In the cases just described, he alterations of the manuscripts broaden their possible uses. It could be argued hat the Latin annotations of Wood empt. 8 might narrow the audience for the

---

ɔ For example, Oxford, Bodleian, MS Douce 128; London, BL, MS Harley 200; and Cambridge, Trinity College, MS R 5 32.

ɔ Its leaves measure approximately 228 × 150 mm. It contains the name of Thomas Fabian, bookseller, perhaps the one active in the 1670s to 1690s at the sign of the Bible in St Paul's Churchyard. On the Scottish material, see Dean no. 28.

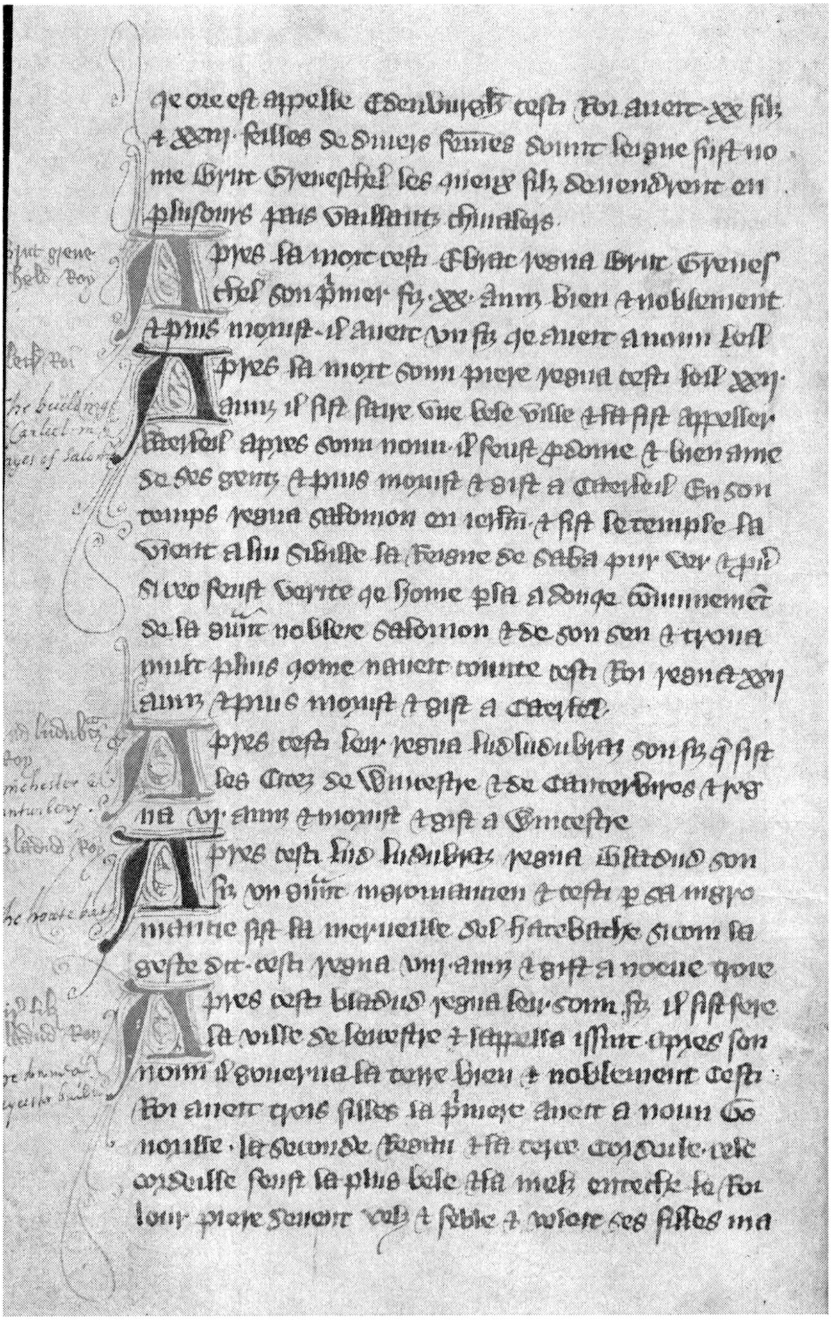

Figure 23.3: The Bodleian Library, University of Oxford, MS Rawlinson D 329, fol. 18v (Anglo-Norman prose *Brut* chronicle, Short Version), showing the text's layout, later French annotation giving kings' names and English annotation on Carlisle, King Solomon, Winchester, Canterbury, Bath and Leicester

book, with their overlay of material off-putting to strictly vernacular readers – but it could also be argued that the Latin annotations, simple and name-laden as they are, might be usable to a reader literate in French and only enhance the prestige of the volume. Readers then as now might well be in the habit of unself-consciously navigating several languages at once or selecting within a codex the works they found most accessible. An Anglo-Norman text could be, and evidently was, approachable and worthwhile for readers inclined to make or read notes in French, Latin or English. Linguistic divides were not, in practice, as sharp as current disciplinary divides might make them seem – and again, quick and broad conclusions about what kind of reader might take interest in a prose *Brut* are likely to be unwarranted, especially conclusions suggesting that the chronicle would only have appealed to those without access to more 'respectable' works.

This is not to say that the language of a given *Brut* text was never an issue, or never of conscious significance to its readers. Oxford, Bodleian, MS e Mus. 108, a well-prepared fifteenth-century single-column manuscript of the Short Version, provides a case in point.[21] One later reader, writing in a hasty scrawl, may or may not have been interested in the content as such, but was practising French while reading, for about twenty French words from the text have been added in the margins, along with their English equivalents. The vocabulary is not obscure (e.g. 'voluntiers', translated as 'gladly').[22] One may surmise that this reader's French was not advanced. And it may come as no surprise that the vocabulary annotations die out about a quarter of the way through: the challenge may have been too great, or the reader's energy may have flagged. Readers of the prose *Brut* often seem to have begun their work with unsustainable ambition. In general, *Bruts* tend to be most heavily marked at the beginning, towards the end (with recent events of more immediate consequence), and in the reign of King Arthur, in an indication as to which parts of the book got the most attention.

The Long Version of the Anglo-Norman prose *Brut* seems likely to have been a revision of the Short Version.[23] In addition to replacing the prologue, providing a different continuation from 1307 to 1333, adding prophecies of Merlin, recasting the language of the text slightly, and making a few revisions to the content, the Long Version reworks the *ordinatio* of the text in a way that may represent a systematic response to the Short Version's lack of apparatus, analogous to but more thorough than the ad hoc efforts of the Short Version's readers. The great majority of Long Version manuscripts were given substantial apparatus at the time of their making, in the form of chapter numbers and chapter headings.[24] Although scribes inserting rubrics in spaces left during the writing of the main text would naturally shorten or expand them for purposes of copy-fitting, the

---

[21] It is written in a secretary hand, and its leaves measure approximately 254 × 180 mm.

[22] Fol. 13r.

[23] See Marvin, 'Albine and Isabelle', pp.153–4; *Oldest*, ed. Marvin, pp. 49–51.

[24] It should be noted, however, that at least one Long Version manuscript, London, BL, MS Royal 20 A 3, lacks headings, and more study of the development of the Long Version is needed.

headings become more or less standardized and tend to be quite detailed, verging on synopsis. For example, 'Del Roi Madhan coment il regna en pees toute sa vie. Et de Mempriz; & de Maulyn ses filz; & coment Mempriz occist Maulyn son frere & coment lups luy sakerent en pieces. Capitulo vii°' (About King Madhan, how he reigned in peace his whole life. And about his sons Mempriz and Maulyn, and how Mempriz killed Maulyn his brother and how wolves tore him to pieces. Chapter 7).[25]

Many Long Version manuscripts are also fairly large and presented in a two-column format, which, along with the apparatus, make the prose *Brut* resemble Latin histories like Ranulph Higden's *Polychronicon* or the works of Matthew Paris. Chapter numbers are a feature of works to which one might wish to make reference, and a few late manuscripts do possess tables of capitula as finding tools.[26] Over time, and over the course of revision and elaboration, the Anglo-Norman *Brut* became literally and figuratively a weightier book. The main translation of the prose *Brut* into Middle English was based on an Anglo-Norman Long Version text of the same grouping as the Ashmole manuscript quoted above, and many manuscripts of the Middle English *Brut* follow this same model and have similar apparatus.

With the advent of the Middle English prose *Brut*, the Anglo-Norman *Brut* did not fade into obsolescence. Rather, Anglo-Norman *Brut* manuscripts continued to be read (and annotated) and written through the fifteenth century, when, as noted above, about a quarter of surviving Anglo-Norman *Brut* manuscripts were copied. Although fourteenth-century Anglo-Norman *Bruts* run the gamut from the scrappy to the well-made and decorated, the surviving later manuscripts tend for the most part to be nicely produced. Perhaps the market for cheap *Bruts* moved to the Middle English versions.

The most luxurious prose *Bruts* in French are not insular at all, but three late continental texts of the Long Version.[27] Of these, Paris, Bibliothèque Sainte-Geneviève, MS 935 provides the most striking example of the recasting of the *Brut* for another time, place and audience. The book was produced in the late fifteenth century and follows the typical Long Version format in an impressively large size, with two columns and elaborate rubric chapter headings and numbers, as well as a table of capitula added in a separate signature.[28] It also features eight miniatures, with work attributed by François Avril to the Maître du Froissart de Philippe de Commynes.[29] The miniatures are idiosyncratic: they illustrate episodes from the chronicle that might not be considered the most

---

25 Oxford, Bodleian, MS Ashmole 1804, fol. 51r.
26 For example, London, BL, MS Royal 19 C 9; Paris, Bibl. nat. MS f. fr. 12155; and Paris, Bibliothèque Sainte-Geneviève, MS 935, all deluxe fifteenth-century continental manuscripts of the Anglo-Norman Long Version.
27 See n. 26.
28 Its leaves measure approximately 380 × 270 mm.
29 Also known as the Master of the Harley Froissart, http://liberfloridus.cines.fr/textes/biblio_fr.html [accessed 6 March 2008].

Cr commance lextrauct
Des cromques Danscle
terre qui par auāt estoit
nōmec par deux autres
nome. Le premier nom
dont elle fut nommec
fut albion pour albine
fille Du roy Diodicine
de cire. Sf lautre nom
fut bretaigne pour bru
tine le premier conquef
teur dicelle. Sr Dernere

ment fut elle nommec
anrtleterre pour antlist
le saxon lequel nom liu
est Depute touf ioures De
moure. Premier chape

[initial] ula noble ter
re De sire ef
toit vnef no
ble roy puis
sant et De tresvrant
renom qui eut nom
Diodicine qui se noble ent

Figure 23.4: Paris, Bibliothèque Sainte-Geneviève, MS 935, fol. 9r (Anglo-Norman Prose *Brut*, Long Version), showing the exile of the regicidal princess, Albine, and her sisters

obvious choices. Although some are scenes easily represented with standar iconography (a battle, a marriage, a baptism), others, like the murder of Edwar the Martyr by a henchman while his stepmother looks on, are clearly based o careful reading of the text.[30] Considerations of space here allow for only two brie examples, the manuscript's first and last illustrations.

The chronicle opens with an illumination of the moment from the Lon Version's prologue at which the princess Albine and her many sisters, wh have killed their husbands in a bid for autonomy, are set adrift in punishmer (Figure 23.4).[31] They will arrive on a deserted island, mate with incubi and giv birth to the giants whom Brutus will exterminate when he takes possession o the land he will then call Britain. Other illustrated *Brut* manuscripts that depi Albine also depict elements of the Brutus story, but this one does not.[32] It make British history begin with exclusive attention to female crime and exile rathe than heroic male conquest and foundation. Women appear in fully half of th manuscript's miniatures, in contexts that emphasize their criminality and/c their influence over the men in their lives.

The last illumination of the text shows the reconciliation of Louis VI of Franc and Henry I of England in 1120 (Figure 23.5).[33] Accompanied by a cleric and a armoured knight, Louis stands at the centre of the composition, his height an uprightness emphasized by the mountain behind him, his staff held straight. S off to one side, Henry stands shorter than not only Louis but even than the hat c the attendant next to him; Henry's knee is bent to Louis, on a line continued b his angled staff and the tree in the immediate background, while the horizont line of the city in the background presses him down. All of the pictorial elemen that aggrandize Louis diminish Henry. But the text itself has something else t say about who is on top:

> Le Roy de France fut desconfitz et eschappa a grant paine, et tous les pluiseurs de ses gens furent prins, et le Roy Dangleterre fist de eulx sa voulente. Les vns mist il en prison, et les autres mist il a mort, et les aucuns fist il francement aler quitez et deliures. Mais depuis furent les deux rois accordez.

> (The king of France was defeated and escaped with great difficulty, and the greater part of his men were captured, and the king of England did with them as he pleased. Some he put into prison, others he put to death, and some he freely set at liberty. But afterwards the two kings were reconciled.)

Here the illustration has been designed not only to redirect the reader's atter tion but to undermine the explicit content of the chronicle itself: the page tel of a high point of English success on the Continent, but the English submissio that it *shows* appeals much more to a continental eye, and indeed, correspond

---

[30] Fols. 56r, 66v, 80v and 94v.
[31] Fol. 9r.
[32] For example, Royal 19 C 9, fol. 8r; Laud misc. 733, fols. 18r and 22v.
[33] Fol. 113r.

Figure 23.5: Paris, Bibliothèque Sainte-Geneviève, MS 935, fol. 113r (Anglo-Norman prose *Brut*, Long Version), showing the reconciliation of Louis VI of France and Henry I of England in 1120

much better to later history.[34] The miniature makes Louis and Henry's reconciliation prefigure more recent, and different, events. These and the other miniatures make for a jaundiced reading of British history, with an emphasis on crime, loss and female dominance quite at odds with the vision of the Oldest Version's text.

By sheer number, geographical and temporal scope and evidence of use, the corpus of *Brut* manuscripts testifies to the enduring liveliness and value of Anglo-Norman narrative. It also testifies to the many ways in which the same

---

[34] Initial spot-checking of the manuscript does not reveal substantive revisions to its text of the Long Version, but further examination is needed.

book could serve audiences with different tastes, wealth, loyalties and interests. Although almost all *Brut* continuations after the 1330s were in English,[35] the Anglo-Norman versions did not fall into disuse. For some two hundred years the Anglo-Norman *Brut* continued to be remade for audiences ranging from the person copying and supplementing the text for himself to the wealthy commissioner of a deluxe text. These audiences found the *Brut* chronicle a source of geographical and historical information, moral exempla, linguistic instruction and political and legal precedent. For them, Anglo-Norman narrative was far from moribund, or the jargon of a small professional class, but instead available, accessible and of continuing significance.

The corpus is sobering as well as rich, for it complicates rather than simplifies the picture of who read the chronicle, when and for what. If only any two or three of the manuscripts surveyed above had survived, one might form quite a different and far more limited impression – exaggeratedly plebeian, intellectual or aristocratic – of the prose *Brut*'s contemporary identity. But that is of course just the situation confronted by students of most medieval works, Anglo-Norman or otherwise. Whatever is to be learned must be learned from what is in all likelihood a tiny remnant of manuscripts, and we have little way of knowing how representative the extant sample may be, particularly given the probable greater survival rate of deluxe manuscripts, or at least the most decorative parts of them. Surviving manuscripts provide only partial evidence for generalizations about what 'kind' of work a medieval text was, or what the boundaries of its readership were – especially when the text is a vernacular one composed in straightforward language. The *Brut* manuscripts offer a firm reminder that surviving evidence of who *did* read a given work, and how, cannot be extrapolated into evidence of who *did not*.

A simple inscription of ownership tells us no more than that – ownership – not whether the owner read, liked or understood a book. Annotation provides an invaluable record of actual readers' thought, but activities that leave physical traces behind are the merest fraction of the whole life of a book, which may be read or heard hundreds of times for every person who makes a new mark in the text. The best-loved, most used, most heavily marked books – those that historians of reading would be most eager to see – are those most likely to have been loved right out of existence long ago.

The surviving *Brut* manuscripts give us far more to go on than we are accustomed to where medieval vernacular books are concerned.[36] The Anglo-Norman texts in particular hint at a broader, more active Anglo-Norman literary culture in late medieval England than other works might suggest, and they open a window on reading and book-production as practised beyond the most privileged levels

---

35 An exception is the Anglo-Norman continuation from 1307 to 1398 in Oxford, Corpus Christi College, MS 78.

36 The very amplitude of the evidence poses its own challenges, from identification, classification and cataloguing forward, particularly in the case of the Middle English versions of the chronicle.

f society. Even so, what we can know serves as an index of how much immeasurably more we cannot know, how much has vanished and how circumscribed ur scholarly claims must be if they are to be responsible. In their variety and umber, the *Brut* manuscripts tell us a great deal about themselves and their aders: they also bring to mind a world of readers, manuscripts and works not mply overlooked, as those in the *Brut* tradition have often been, but entirely st.

24

France in England: Anglo-French Culture in the Reign of Edward III

Michael Bennett

The fourteenth century sees a major shift in secular literary culture in England. In the reign of Edward I (1272–1307) French was the accepted medium of high literary expression. By the beginning of the fifteenth century English had largely displaced French as the language of composition in most literary genres. While the 'rise of English' has been examined from a number of perspectives, until recently less attention has been paid to exploring French culture in fourteenth-century England.[1] This essay reviews a range of evidence relating to the availability, circulation and production of French texts in the middle decades of the fourteenth century. Focusing on the English royal court and the aristocracy in the age of Edward III, and on cultural relations between England and France in the first period of the Hundred Years' War, it complicates linear accounts of the decline of French by examining the flowering of French literary culture in England during this time.[2] It uses the terms 'Anglo-Norman' and 'Anglo-French' to distinguish, loosely, between texts derived mainly from older insular traditions and texts that reveal an engagement with recent continental works. Focusing on the changing terms of political and cultural relations between England and France, it seeks to enrich an understanding of French literary culture in England between the 1340s and 1360s.

The English royal court, broadly conceived to embrace wider sections of the aristocracy and aspirants to high society, obviously played a crucial role in the maintenance of French culture. The Plantagenets were French by descent and married French or francophone queens. Edward I's first wife, Eleanor of Castile, was the daughter of the countess of Ponthieu. The marriage of the future Edward II to Isabelle, daughter of Philip IV of France, was merely the most notable of many matches between the English and French royal and noble

---

1   In general see W. Calin, *The French Tradition and the Literature of Medieval England* (Toronto, 1994); W. Rothwell, 'The "faus franceis d'Angleterre", Later Anglo-Norman', in *Anglo-Norman Anniversary Essays*, ed. I. Short, ANTS OPS 2 (London, 1993), pp. 309–26. On the diverging status of insular and continental Frenches in the linguistic repertoire of the late Middle Ages, see the essay by Machan in this volume.
2   See J. I. Wimsatt, *Chaucer and his French Contemporaries: Natural Music in the Fourteenth Century* (Toronto, 1991), and J. M. Bowers, 'Chaucer after Retters: The Wartime Origins of English Literature', in Baker, *Inscribing the Hundred Years War*, pp. 91–125, esp. pp. 99–102.

families.[3] Among the English magnates around 1300, the earls of Norfolk, Surrey, Pembroke and Hereford were married, respectively, to the daughters of the duke of Hainault, the count of Bar and the count of St Pol, and the widow of the count of Holland. The English Channel was no cultural barrier. The Plantagenets had a considerable profile in the Francophone world. Edward I loomed large in the romantic imagination in northern France and the French-speaking Netherlands.[4] Eleanor of Castile, his queen, brought Ponthieu as her dowry. Amiens, a major centre for manuscript illumination, produced many books for the English market. Girard d'Amiens wrote *Escanor* for Queen Eleanor around the time of her visit to Amiens in 1279.[5] The queen herself commissioned a French translation of Vegetius' *De re militari* for Edward I.[6]

If Edward II and Isabelle of France had anything in common, it was a passion for reading French romances. Edward shared the interest with his male friends as well: the chamber accounts reveal a loan of *Tristan and Iseult* to Hugh Despenser.[7] The accounts of the privy wardrobe in the mid-1320s suggest that the royal collection supported a community of readers.[8] The book borrowers included great ladies like the countess of Cornwall, noblemen like the earl of Hereford, and several household knights. The fact that the books were delivered to clerks acting on behalf of lords and ladies may indicate that the books were read aloud to groups.[9] There was serious reading as well as light entertainment. At her death in 1317 the countess of Norfolk owned a French translation of the *Authenticum* of Justinian.[10] In the 1320s Queen Isabelle borrowed French translations of the Old Testament and Vegetius as well as romances like Raoul de Houdenc's *Le Roman de Méraugis de Portlesguez*. After her fall from power in 1330, Isabelle had even more time for literature. The inventory of her goods reveals her ownership of a range of French books, including Brunetto Latini's *Trésor* and copies of romances of *King Arthur*, *Tristram and Iseult*, *Sir Perceval* and *Sir Gawain*.[11] The accounts

---

3   Edward I married three of his daughters to Henri, count of Bar; John, duke of Brabant; and John, count of Holland.

4   For example, in the chronicle of Lodewijk van Velthem of Brabant: Salter, *English and International*, p. 97.

5   R. S. Loomis, 'Edward I, Arthurian enthusiast', *Speculum* 28 (1953), 114–27 (p. 116); Girard d'Amiens, *Escanor: Roman arthurien de vers de la fin du XIIIe siècle*, ed. R. Trachsler, 2 vols., Textes littéraires français 449 (Geneva, 1994).

6   Morgan, *EGM [II]*, no. 150; Gee, *Women, Art and Patronage*, p. 9.

7   Society of Antiquaries, MS 122; N. Fryde, *The Tyranny and Fall of Edward II 1321–1326* (Cambridge, 1979), p. 15.

8   London, British Library, Additional MS 60854.

9   J. Vale, *Edward III and Chivalry: Chivalric Society and its Context 1270–1350* (Woodbridge, 1982); C. Revard, 'Courtly Romances in the Privy Wardrobe', in *The Court and Cultural Diversity: Selected Papers from the Eighth Triennial Congress of the International Courtly Literature Society*, ed. E. Mullally and J. Thompson (Cambridge, 1997), pp. 297–308.

10 British Library [hereafter BL], Royal MS 20.D.ix.

11 The National Archives [hereafter TNA], Public Record Office [hereafter PRO], E 101/393/4 (Inventory of Isabelle of France's goods), fol. 8r; BL, Cotton MS Galba E XIV, fol. 50 r.

of her household in the year before her death in 1358 reveal a great deal about her tastes.[12] They document, for example, her ownership of two more French romances, *Holy Grail* and *Sir Lancelot*, and her friendship with two French-born dowagers, Jeanne, Countess Warenne and Marie, countess of Pembroke, the daughters, respectively, of the count of Bar and the count of St Pol.[13]

Edward III grew up in a bookish milieu. At his accession Walter de Milmete presented him with two Latin works of princely instruction.[14] Philippa of Hainault gave him a handsome copy of Latini's *Trésor*, possibly as a wedding present.[15] In 1332 Roger de Stavegni presented him with a copy of his crusading treatise *Du Conquest de la Terre Sainte*.[16] Early on in his reign Edward paid 100 marks for what must have been a very handsome book of romances from his cousin, a nun of Amesbury.[17] His passion for chivalry and his emulation of Arthur had literary underpinnings.[18] His marriage strengthened the links between England and the French-speaking Low Countries. Edward and Philippa spent a great deal of time on the Continent in the late 1330s, and their third and fourth sons were born in Antwerp and Ghent. Especially significant in respect of French cultural influence in England was the movement across the Channel of poets and musicians from this region. Jean de le Mote, who crossed to England around 1340, was a well-known poet.[19] Jean Froissart, who was in Queen Philippa's service from 1362 until 1367, may have first visited England in the 1350s.

---

12 BL, MS Cotton Galba E XIV. For discussion, see M. J. Bennett, 'Isabelle of France, Anglo-French Diplomacy and Cultural Exchange in the late 1350s', in *The Age of Edward III*, ed. J. S. Bothwell (York, 2001), pp. 215–25.

13 The founder of Pembroke College, Marie was a patron of letters and learning: H. Jenkinson, 'Mary de Sancto Paulo, Foundress of Pembroke College, Cambridge', *Archæologia* 2nd series 16 (1915), 401–46, esp. pp. 432–5, 443–6. Her copy of *Godefroy de Bouillon* found its way into the French royal library in the Louvre: J. W. Bennett, *The Rediscovery of Sir John Mandeville* (New York, 1954). p. 172, n. 8. For her manuscript of the Barking life of Edward the Confessor, see further the essay by Russell in this volume.

14 J. J. G. Alexander, 'Painting and Manuscript Illumination for Royal Patrons in the Later Middle Ages', in *English Court Culture in the Later Middle Ages*, ed. V. J. Scattergood and J. W. Sherborne (London, 1983), pp. 141–62. The texts were Latin, but were probably expounded to him in French.

15 Gee, *Women, Art and Patronage*, pp. 9–10.

16 Vale, *Edward III and Chivalry*, p. 51.

17 F. Devon, *Issues of the Exchequer, being a Collection of Payments made out of His Majesty's Revenue, from King Henry III to King Henry VI* (London, 1837), p. 143.

18 For a discussion of the influence of romance, most especially the romance of *Perceforest*, on Edward III's conception of a house for the Round Table, see J. Munby, R. Barber and R. Brown, *Edward III's Round Table and the Windsor Festival of 1344* (Woodbridge, 2007), ch. 8.

19 Wimsatt, *Chaucer and his French Contemporaries*, ch. 2. He performed as a musician before the king at Eltham in 1343: N. Wilkins, 'Music and Poetry at Court: England and France in the Late Middle Ages', in *English Court Culture in the Later Middle Ages*, ed. Scattergood and Sherborne, pp. 183–204 (pp. 190–2).

Outside this courtly world, French was widely read and used.[20] It was less equently the language of vernacular composition. Romance was one of the lories of the Anglo-Norman tradition, and examples of the genre were still read nd copied in the fourteenth century. Yet most of the romances had been written enerations earlier, and reworking increasingly took the form of translation.[21] nglo-Norman survived best in prose rather than poetry and in contexts – chiv-lric, legal and historical – where French vocabulary and forms of expression had reatest currency. In respect of religious literature, linguistic conservatism was kewise a strong force.[22] Nonetheless across the board the trend was towards anslation from Anglo-Norman and composition in English. Two of the most mbitious Anglo-Norman works of the late thirteenth century – Pierre de Lang-ft's chronicle and William Waddington's *Manuel des pechiez* – were translated y Robert Manning of Bourne in the first decades of the fourteenth century.[23] One f the last major Anglo-Norman chronicles, the *Scalacronica*, was written in the 350s by a northern knight, Sir Thomas Gray of Heaton. The *Brut* was translated ato English in the 1360s. Although the Norman French text was read and copied a the fifteenth century, *Brut* continuations were composed in English from the 380s.[24]

There is some evidence of new work in French in early fourteenth-century ngland. In addition to chronicles and treatises, there were new literary endeav-urs. Nicholas Bozon, a Franciscan friar, was a prolific poet active in the first ecades of the fourteenth century.[25] In the early 1340s a handsome anthology, ondon, British Library, MS Harley 2253, including English as well as French erse, was compiled for a noble household in the Welsh marches.[26] It contains bliaux and lyrics in French that seem fresh and contemporary.[27] In the 1350s ad 1360s there were further developments, but much more obviously associ-ted with the court and cross-Channel exchange. In 1354 Henry of Grosmont, uke of Lancaster, wrote *Le Livre des seyntz medicines*, a devotional treatise of ame literary ambition. Though an intensely private work, it had some circula-

See for examples the essays by Britnell, Ingham, Kowaleski, Oliva in Section I of this volume.
Humphrey Bohun, sixth earl of Hereford (d. 1361), for example, lent his name to a translation of *William of Palerne* into the English of the south-west midlands. *William of Palerne*, ed. W. W. Skeat, EETS ES 1 (1867), lines 164–8, 5529–33: T. Turville-Petre, 'Humphrey de Bohun and *William of Palerne*', *Neuphilologische Mitteilungen* 75 (1974), 250–2; T. Turville-Petre, *The Alliterative Revival* (Cambridge, 1977), pp. 40–1.
On, for example, the question of continuing fourteenth-century Anglo-Norman Bible translation, see the essay by Watson in this volume.
T. Turville-Petre, *England the Nation: Language, Literature and National Identity, 1290–1340* (Oxford, 1996), pp. 14–17.
On the Anglo-Norman *Brut* and its circulation, see the essay by Marvin in this volume.
M. A. Klenke, 'Nicholas Bozon', *Modern Language Notes* 69 (1954), 256–60; and see further the essay by Postlewate in this volume.
Studies in the Harley Manuscript: The Scribes, Contents, and Social Contexts of British Library MS Harley 2253, ed. S. Fein (Kalamazoo MI, 2000).
Studies in the Harley Manuscript, ed. Fein.

tion. It is represented in three English manuscripts, one incomplete.[28] Aroun‹ 1357 a writer identifying himself as John Mandeville, English knight and pilgrim produced one of the most widely disseminated works of the late Middle Age‹ The insular French version survives in twenty-four manuscripts, most of then dating after 1400, and ten of them continental manuscripts.[29] Finally, Geoffre‹ Chaucer and John Gower were in all likelihood writing French verse in the 1360‹ R. H. Robbins argued long ago that Chaucer began his literary career writing i‹ French.[30] It has likewise been argued that John Gower, whose *Miroir de l'Omme* ‹ usually dated around 1376, began his writing career in the 1360s.[31]

Mandeville's Travels has an uncertain place in English literary history, but on of particular relevance to this essay's argument. This major text is generall‹ ignored in accounts of French culture in fourteenth-century England. Thoug‹ the author proclaimed himself to be English, and was accepted as English b‹ contemporaries, scholars have had some reason to be sceptical. Over recen‹ decades the prevailing opinion in the Anglophone world has been that *Mandev ille's Travels* was first written in northern France.[32] This view derives in part fror‹ an understandable reluctance to accept the author's credentials as a travel-write‹ and from a number of historical anomalies. It garners support from the fact tha‹ the earliest dated text was produced in Paris in 1371, but more generally fror‹ doubts about the English context. Michael Seymour, the main protagonist o‹ this view, has pointed out that the author drew on a range of sources undocu‹ mented in English libraries, most particularly a French anthology of travel litera‹ ture compiled by Jean le Long, canon of St Omer, in the early 1350s. Even if th‹ reasoning is allowed, *Mandeville's Travels* remains important in an assessment o‹ French culture in England. Indeed its career in England would in some respect‹ be even more extraordinary if it is continental in origin. The Anglo-Frencl‹

---

28 Henry of Lancaster, *Le Livre de Seyntz Medicines*, ed. E. J. Arnould, ANTS 2 (Oxfor‹ 1940); Dean no. 696; J. Krochalis and R. J. Dean, 'Henry of Lancaster's *Livre de Seyn‹ Medicines*: New Fragments of an Anglo-Norman Work', *The National Library of Wale‹ Journal* 18 (1973), 87–94.

29 Dean no. 341.

30 R. H. Robbins, 'The Vintner's Son: French Wine in English Bottles', in *Eleanor ‹ Aquitaine: Patron and Politician*, ed. W. W. Kibler (Austin TX, 1976), pp. 147–72; R. ‹ Robbins, 'Geoffrey Chaucier, poète français, Father of English Poetry', *Chaucer Revie‹* 13 (1978), 93–115.

31 R. F. Yeager, 'Gower's French Audience: the *Mirour de l'Omme*', *Chaucer Review* 4‹ (2006), 111–37, and see further the essays by Yeager and by Merrilees and Pagan i‹ this volume.

32 Josephine Bennett presented cogent arguments for the priority of the Anglo-Norma‹ text, and a number of contemporary scholars including C. Deluz and C. W. R. ‹ Moseley have favoured English authorship: Bennett, *Rediscovery of Sir John Mandevill‹ Jean de Mandeville: Le Livre des Merveilles du Monde*, ed. C. Deluz (Paris, 2000); *The Trave‹ of Sir John Mandeville*, ed. C. W. R. D. Moseley (Harmondsworth, 2005). Nonetheles‹ M. C. Seymour has proved an influential advocate of a French original: M. C. Seymou‹ *Sir John Mandeville* (Aldershot, 1993); *The Defective Version of Mandeville's Travels*, e‹ M. C. Seymour, EETS OS 319 (Oxford, 2002), p. xi. R. Dean accepted Seymour's arg‹ ments: Dean, p. 187.

version is a distinct and arguably superior work. There is no precedent for such a reworking of a continental French text after the thirteenth century. Such an enterprise would seem distinctly odd in the 1350s, let alone in the 1360s. The more obvious need was for an English translation. Indeed the first of a number of English translations was probably made by the 1370s. If the insular French version were not the original version, its career in France, where it achieved some circulation, including in fine manuscripts, would likewise be wholly remarkable.

There are good reasons to reverse the assumptions of recent scholarship.[33] It now appears that the earliest witness to *Mandeville's Travels* is an insular rather than a continental text. An incomplete manuscript, now in private hands, can be dated on palaeographical grounds to the 1360s.[34] The assumption of an insular Anglo-French original allows for more economical and plausible reconstructions of the work's textual history. The earliest dated copy, produced in Paris in 1371, exhibits a high degree of textual corruption and padding. Its association with John of Burgundy's plague treatise, an English text that otherwise had no circulation on the Continent, is perhaps telling with respect to its ultimate provenance.[35] Above all, the assumption that the text was first written in Anglo-French accords with what the author says about himself and with what the first generations of readers, on the Continent as well as in England, believed. Needless to say, this reassignment of *Mandeville's Travels* has implications for any assessment of French literary culture in England in the middle of the fourteenth century. It attests an author and an audience for an ambitious literary enterprise in Anglo-French. It implies, too, that the author had access to a French anthology of travel literature, not otherwise evidenced in England. The difficulty of assigning Mandeville to a literary culture conceived as *either* insular *or* continental testifies to the internationalism of francophone culture in England at this period.

England's capacity to participate in French literary culture was augmented in the middle decades of the fourteenth century by the circumstances of war and diplomacy. As Elizabeth Salter observed, 'the transmission of high-class French materials to this country must have been easy and continuous'.[36] In the campaigns of the mid-1340s and mid-1350s English nobles spent a great deal

---

[33] For a more detailed discussion, see M. J. Bennett, '*Mandeville's Travels* and the Anglo-French Moment', *Medium Aevum* 75 (2006), 273–92.

[34] The manuscript formerly belonged to the duke of Manchester, was auctioned by Sothebys, and sold by Quarich to Sir John Galvin of Vancouver, BC, Canada. It is described, with a photograph, in Sotheby's catalogue, *Western Manuscripts and Miniatures: London, 23 June 1987* (London, 1987), lot 84, pp. 104–5. It can be consulted on microfilm in the British Library. An inspection of the microfilm, RP3761, indicates that a good deal of the text is missing. It begins in chapter 11 and ends in chapter 31, with other bifolia missing. I thank Professor Ralph Hanna for alerting me to the existence of this manuscript, and Professor A. S. G. Edwards for contacting me with information on recent ownership.

[35] L. M. Matheson, 'Médecin sans Frontières? The European Dissemination of John of Burgundy's Plague Treatise,' *American Notes and Queries* 18, no. 3 (2005), 17–28.

[36] Salter, *English and International*, p. 242.

of time in France. English *chevauchées* were not wholly conducive to productive cultural encounters, but they did rake in booty, including some valuable French manuscripts.[37] Access to a text like Jean le Long's anthology, produced in St Omer, a short ride from Calais, was as easy for Englishmen as for most Frenchmen. The English military occupation of parts of France obviously provided opportunities for cultural appropriation. English soldiers in Poitou took an interest, by no means wholly literary, in the Lusignan legend of Mélusine.[38] In composing *Mélusine ou la noble histoire de Lusignan* in the early 1390s, Jean d'Arras sought out William Montagu, earl of Salisbury, who had returned to England with some earlier version of the story.[39] Diplomacy provided the most favourable circumstances for cultural exchange. Henry of Grosmont, for example, spent a great deal of time in France in peace as well as war. In 1352 he visited Paris as the guest of the king of France, and in 1354, when he wrote the *Seyntz medicines*, he was involved in diplomacy at Calais and Avignon.

The role of French prisoners in cultural exchange needs also to be considered. From the 1340s there was a steady stream of French nobles taken prisoner in battle and brought to England to be held for ransom. Their captivity was the occasion for further movement back and forth across the Channel as ransoms were negotiated and needs supplied. Geoffroi de Charny, for example, came to England twice as a prisoner, firstly in 1342 and then in 1350–1.[40] On the first occasion he was the prisoner of Sir Richard Talbot at Goodrich castle not far from Ludlow, raising the intriguing possibility of a connection with the French works in MS. Harley 2253, compiled by a scribe in the neighbourhood around 1340.[41] Charny apparently wrote his *Livre de chivalrie* during his second captivity, when he was based in London.[42] Raoul de Brienne, count of Eu, another prominent prisoner, jousted at Windsor in 1348 and brought to England a troupe of minstrels.[43] The scale and potential significance of this French presence in England dramatically increased in the aftermath of the Battle of Poitiers. In 1356 King Jean of France and a large company of French noblemen were taken prisoner and brought to England. Jean was allowed to return in 1360, but only on condition of his place

---

37 BL, Royal MS 19 D. II is a French Bible acquired at Poitiers and sold by the Black Prince to William Montagu, earl of Salisbury.

38 John Creswell, the English captain at Lusignan in the 1370s, claimed to have witnessed an apparition of Melusine the serpent: Jean d'Arras, *Mélusine ou la noble histoire de Lusignan: Roman du XIVe siècle*, ed. J.-J. Vincensini (Paris, 2003), pp. 810–12.

39 D'Arras, *Mélusine*, pp. 111–13.

40 R. W. Kaeuper and E. Kennedy, eds., *The Book of Chivalry of Geoffroi de Charny: Text, Context and Translation* (Philadelphia, 1996), pp. 5–6 and 11–13.

41 According to Carter Revard, the scribe was active in and around Ludlow, and was possibly a chaplain or clerk in the service of the Talbots or Sir Lawrence Ludlow of Stokesay castle: C. Revard, 'Four Fabliaux from London, British Library MS Harley 2253, Translated into English Verse', *The Chaucer Review* 40 (2005), 111–40 (p. 114).

42 *The Book of Chivalry of Geoffroi de Charny*, ed. Kaeuper and Kennedy, p. 22.

43 He was in England from 1346 to 1350. Fine instruments made for the minstrels sent by him from France were given to the Black Prince's minstrels in 1352. Wilkins, 'Music and Poetry at Court', pp. 194–5.

ing taken by his three younger sons. In conditions of honourable captivity
ıd enforced idleness the French prisoners found solace in literature. Jean's
counts record the acquisition of books in London and later, when in captivity
 Somerton, in Lincoln.[44] While at Hertford castle he set his chaplain, Gace de
ı Buigne, to work on *Le Roman des deduis*, a hunting treatise that drew on his
:periences in England.[45]

The presence of King Jean in England acted as a special stimulus to pageantry
ıd cultural display. In May 1357 the Black Prince led him into London, where
? was lodged in the duke of Lancaster's splendid Savoy palace.[46] Edward III
:ld a great banquet at Westminster 'to honour the great splendour of royalty
?ver seen before in England'.[47] Over summer there was a concourse of foreign
ignitaries, including two cardinals on a peace mission, who prostrated them-
·lves before the English king.[48] In autumn there was a tournament at Smithfield
 the presence of the three kings, and over the Christmas there were jousts at
Iarlborough and a torch-lit tournament in Bristol.[49] They proved merely dress
·hearsals for the grand tournament and feast at Windsor on St George's Day
$58. King Jean, the guest of honour, wryly observed how his kingdom had paid
·r the renovated castle and the spectacular display. As one chronicler enthused,
ıere had not been such a display of chivalry since the time of King Arthur.[50]

In the late 1350s the court of Edward III could claim to be the centre of the
·ench-speaking world. While Edward found piquancy in the use of English
ıottoes,[51] and his martial success prompted celebratory verse in English for
)pular consumption, there can be little doubt that the events of this time would
ıve given new stimulus to French culture in England. Needless to say, much
: this culture was ephemeral, and has not left any textual record. Nonetheless
ıere is some evidence that this activity had a literary dimension. The household
:counts of the king's mother, Queen Isabelle, in 1357–8 record her participation
ı the festivities of the time and her interaction with other members of the royal
mily, her aristocratic friends and prominent French nobles. They document
ıe comings and goings of minstrels, and the holding of a 'school' of minstrelsy

---

He purchased a psalter, a *Roman de Renard*, a *Garin le Loherain* and a *Tournament of Antichrist*: L. Delisle, *Recherches sur la librairie de Charles V*, 2 vols. (Paris, 1907), I, p. 331. Delisle, *Librairie de Charles V*, p. 331; Wilkins, 'Music and Poetry at Court', pp. 194–5. Jean Froissart, *Oeuvres*, ed. J. M. B. C. Kervyn de Lettenhove, 24 vols. (Brussels, 1867–77), vi, pp. 13–14; Henry Knighton, *Knighton's Chronicle 1337–1396*, ed. and trans. G. H. Martin (Oxford, 1995), pp. 150–1; R. Delachenal, *Histoire de Charles V*, 5 vols. (Paris, 1909–31), ii, pp. 54–9 (p. 54 n). *The Anonimalle Chronicle, 1333–81*, ed. V. H. Galbraith (Manchester, 1927), p. 41.

Edward sat between two royal captives, Jean of France and David II of Scotland: *The Kirkstall Abbey Chronicles*, ed. J. Taylor, Thoresby Society 42 (1952), p. 62.

Knighton's Chronicle, pp. 150–3.

For the Bristol tournament, see *Eulogium (historiarum sive temporis)*, ed. F. S. Haydon, 3 vols., RS 9 (London, 1858–63), III, p. 227.

Eulogium historiarum, III, p. 227. Henry Knighton simply stated that the splendour of the occasion was beyond his powers to relate: *Knighton's Chronicle*, pp. 158–9.

Vale, *Edward III and Chivalry*, pp. 65, 81.

in London that presumably drew minstrels from the Continent as well as from across Britain. In addition to meeting King Jean on a number of occasions, Queen Isabelle sent him copies of French romances. Her friend the countess of Warenne lent him a French bible. King Jean's accounts reveal his devotions and almsgiving, his interest in church music, his passion for the hunt, and his purchase of psalter and some romances. This makes a plausible milieu for the composition and early circulation of *Mandeville's Travels*. The text is variously dated as 1357 in the insular version and 1358 in the continental. One of the Anglo-French versions includes a Latin letter dedicating the work to Edward III. Routinely dismissed as 'spurious', this letter was clearly regarded as authentic by early chroniclers and copyists.[52] One English man moving in interesting circles at this time is John Mandeville, parker of Enfield Chase and retainer of Humphrey Bohun, earl of Hereford. He took venison to Queen Isabelle at Christmas 1357, and probably hosted hunting events for the French king and other noble captives. Another was Geoffrey Chaucer who, as page of the countess of Ulster, presumably accompanied his mistress when she visited Queen Isabelle in 1358 and attended events at court.[53]

Accounts, wills and inventories reveal a French literary culture that was better established than surviving manuscripts would suggest. While a few of the French romances documented in such sources can be identified with extant texts, most cannot. In such cases it would be inadvisable to do more than assume some generic correspondence between a recorded title and a known text. It cannot be assumed that the romances lent by Queen Isabelle to the French king were old works. It would be especially interesting to know, not least in view of her liaison with Roger Mortimer, whether the *Sir Lancelot* was a special commission. Surviving English manuscripts do not adequately reflect the range and quality of the French romances that provided sources and inspiration for Middle English romances like *Sir Gawain and the Green Knight*.[54] The records certainly attest owner-ship and circulation of influential texts that have not survived in English manu-scripts. The *Roman de Renart* is a case in point. For some time literary scholars have contended, on the basis of its absence from English manuscripts, that it was not known in fourteenth-century England, and have attributed evidence of English familiarity with the legend, including Chaucer's *Nun's Priest's Tale*, to

---

52 *The Buke of Iohn Maunduill*, ed. Sir G. Warner (Westminster, 1889), p. xxix; *Mandeville's Travels, translated from the French of Jean d'Outremeuse*, ed. P. Hamelius, 2 vols., EETS OS 153 and 154 (London, 1919, 1923), II, p. 14. The dedication is a feature of Seymour's insular manuscripts, sub-group A: M. C. Seymour, 'The Scribal Tradition of Mandeville's *Travels*: the Insular Version', *Scriptorium* 18 (1964), 34–48 (pp. 36–7).

53 The countess of Ulster attended the festivities at Marlborough at Christmas 1357. *Chaucer Life Records*, Part III, ed. E. A. Bond and W. D. Selby (London, 1886).

54 For the depth and breadth of the *Gawain*-poet's engagement with French romance see E. Brewer, 'The Sources of Sir Gawain and the Green Knight', in *A Companion to the Gawain-Poet*, ed. D. Brewer and J. Gibson (Cambridge, 1997), pp. 243–55.

intermediary sources.[55] Yet a copy of this text was in the royal collection in the 1320s, and King Jean of France obtained a copy from a bookseller in Lincoln in 1359.[56] Guillaume de Deguileville's trilogy – the *Pèlerinage de la vie humaine* (1330–2, and 1355), the *Pèlerinage de l'âme* (1355–8) and the *Pèlerinage Jhesu Crist* (1358) – was likewise influential in England long before English translations in the 1420s.

From the late thirteenth century there were a number of new works composed in France that circulated widely throughout the French-speaking world. They point to the need to acknowledge, in the history of French in England, the importance of successive waves of continental influence and reception. The *Somme le roi*, written for Philip III of France in 1279–80, doubtless soon came to the attention of the English royal family. The existence of copies in England, however, has to be inferred from the legion of English adaptations and borrowings beginning in the mid fourteenth century. As a work of the imagination, Guillaume de Lorris and Jean de Meun's *Roman de la rose* was to prove highly influential. It would be surprising indeed if there were not copies in England by the beginning of Edward III's reign. In his survey of the three hundred manuscripts containing the *Roman de la rose*, Langlois only found two that were in England in the late fourteenth century. One passed through the hands of an English friar, John Lincoln, and is now in Florence.[57] The other belonged to Sir Richard Stury, chamber knight of Edward III and Richard II, and after him, Thomas of Woodstock, duke of Gloucester, Edward III's youngest son.[58] The existence of other copies of the *Roman de la rose* in England, however, can be inferred from a study of its translation. It appears that around the 1370s at least two translations were made, using at least three different French texts. Geoffrey Chaucer represented himself as writing the *Legend of Good Women* to make amends to ladies for having translated the *Roman de la rose*. If he had no hand in the surviving text, a composite work, there must have been at least three translations.[59]

In respect to more recent French poetry, the lack of manuscript evidence in England is even more striking. The poems of living writers were presumably recited from notes, and early manuscripts presumably circulated privately. The lack of documentation, however, cannot mean that texts were unknown. Jean de le Mote dedicated his elegy of William, count of Hainault, *Li Regret de Guillaume*, to Queen Philippa, but no presentation copy is extant or recorded.[60] The

55 N. F. Blake, 'Reynard the Fox in England,' in *Aspects of the Medieval Animal Epic*, ed. E. Rombauts and A. Welkenhuysen (Leuven, 1975), pp. 53–65.

56 *Comptes de l'argenterie des Rois de France au XIVème siècle*, ed. L. Douet d'Arcq (Paris, 1851), p. 224.

57 E. Langlois, *Les manuscrits du Roman de la Rose. Description et classement* (Lille, 1910, repr. Geneva, 1974), p. 187 (Florence, Biblioteca Riccardiana, MS 2775).

58 Langlois, *Les manuscrits du Roman de la Rose*, pp. 141–2 (BL, Royal 19.B.XIII).

59 R. Sutherland, ed., *'The Romaunt of the Rose' and 'Le Roman de la Rose': A Parallel-Text Edition* (Oxford, 1967), p. xxxiv.

60 It survives in a single manuscript in the Bibliothèque Nationale in Brussels. Wilkins, 'Music and Poetry at Court', pp. 190–4.

Roman de Perceforest, written in Hainault around the same time, was almost certainly known in English court circles, but does not appear in any English manuscript.[61] After moving to England Le Mote continued to write verse, none of which survives except his interchange with the celebrated Philippe de Vitry.[62] Jean Froissart, who joined Queen Philippa's household in the 1360s, wrote a great deal of verse in England, but nothing survives, except perhaps the book of love poems he presented to Richard II in 1395.[63] His *Meliador* (c.1370), like Girard d'Amiens' *Escanor* (c.1280), was written with an English audience in mind, but is not extant in English manuscripts. The clearest witness to the literary activity of Le Mote and Froissart and the availability of their work in England is their influence on Chaucer. Le Mote's *Regret* was a likely source for Chaucer's *Book of the Duchess*.[64] Chaucer and Froissart were colleagues at the English court in the 1360s, and over the years drew on each other's work.[65] The reception in England of Guillaume de Machaut, the most influential French poet in the mid fourteenth century, is especially hard to document. His first patron was the future King Jean, and it is pleasing to imagine that Jean brought copies of his work, including the highly influential love poem *Remède de Fortune*, to England in 1356.[66] Machaut subsequently found patronage with the king of Navarre, an ally of Edward III, and then with King Jean's son Jean, duke of Berry. When the latter prince took his father's place as a prisoner in England, Machaut wrote, on the occasion of his departure, the *Dit de la fontaine amoureuse* that presumably crossed the Channel with him. Even if some other French poets looked to Edward III for patronage, Machaut did not. Nonetheless there is ample reason to believe that his verse had some profile at the English court in the 1350s. He was a formative and continuing influence on Chaucer.[67]

Geoffrey Chaucer is a natural focus in any discussion of French literature in fourteenth-century England.[68] The son of a vintner of London, he first appears as a page in the household of the countess of Ulster, the wife of Lionel of Antwerp,

61 Munby, Barber and Brown, *Edward III's Round Table*, p. 100.
62 F. N. M. Diekstra, 'The Poetic Exchange between Philippe de Vitry and Jean de la Mote: A New Edition', *Neophilologus* 70 (1986), 504–19.
63 Salter, *English and International*, p. 244. On the circulation of Froissart's manuscripts, see further the essay by Croenen in this volume.
64 C. L. Rosenthal, 'A Possible Source of Chaucer's *Booke of the Duchesse – Li Regrete de Guillaume* by Jehan de la Motte', *Modern Language Notes* 48 (1933), 511–14.
65 Wimsatt, *Chaucer and his French Contemporaries*, ch. 6.
66 *'Le jugement du roy de Behaigne' and 'Remède de Fortune' by Guillaume de Machaut*, ed. J. I. Wimsatt et al., Chaucer Library (Athens GA, 1988).
67 J. I. Wimsatt. 'Guillaume de Machaut and Chaucer's Love Lyrics', *Medium Aevum* 47 (1978), 66–87. For Chaucer's extensive use of a single Machaut poem, see J. I. Wimsatt, 'Chaucer, Fortune, and Machaut's *Il m'est avis*,' in *Chaucer Problems and Perspectives: Essays Presented to Paul E. Beichner*, ed. E. Vasta and Z. P. Thundy (Notre Dame IN, 1979), pp. 119–31.
68 For much of what follows, see D. Pearsall, *The Life of Geoffrey Chaucer: A Critical Biography* (Oxford, 1992), chs. 1–2.

dward III's second surviving son. He was probably in the countess's company
·hen she visited Queen Isabelle at Hertford castle in 1357, and again when she
:tended the Garter celebrations at Windsor castle. He was able to use his facility
·ith the language and conventions of polite society to advance himself rapidly at
·urt. His appointment to the household of Edward III with a handsome annuity
f twenty marks suggests that the king placed a high premium on his services
; a courtier and diplomat, both requiring mastery of French. His marriage to
·hilippa Roet – the daughter of Sir Payn Roet, a Hainaulter in the service of Queen
·hilippa, and indeed the damsel and probably the god-daughter of the queen –
·nsolidated his position as an intermediary between the English court and the
·roader French culture of the day. Needless to say, the likelihood is that he began
·is literary career by writing poetry in the French of England. On this point, as
·n others, extant manuscripts prove a poor guide. Little or nothing survives to
·ocument the French period of Chaucer's career, whether in terms of his own
·ork or the sources of his inspiration. This is the special interest of the Univer-
·ty of Pennsylvania MS French 15. Though it is not an English manuscript, and
·ates from the end of the fourteenth century, it includes the sort of French verse
·iat probably circulated in English courtly circles in the 1360s. It may have been
··mpiled by Otto de Granson, a Savoyard knight and pupil of Machaut, who
··rved in the household of Edward III. It has the additional interest of containing
· series of French lyrics attributed to 'Ch' that may be Chaucer's juvenilia.[69]
·iven Chaucer's own profile among contemporary French poets, and indeed his
·iendship with Otto de Granson, the appearance of his work in a continental
·ollection would not be especially surprising.[70]

In any account of shifts between French and English in the literary culture of
·te medieval England, it is obviously necessary to eschew linearity and embrace
··mplexity. This is not merely a matter of recognizing the richness and resilience
·f the Anglo-Norman linguistic and literary heritage. It is necessary to acknowl-
·lge the impact of cultural developments in other parts of the French-speaking
·orld. From the late thirteenth century onwards, French served as the medium
··r the transmission across the Channel of translations from Latin, including the
·ible, classical texts and encyclopaedic works; new works of the imagination,
··ost especially the *Roman de la Rose*; and the new poetics of Machaut and his
··llowers. The impact on the French of England of the reception of these works –
··e foundational texts of the new lay, vernacular culture of the later Middle Ages
·was considerable. But fourteenth-century England was no passive recipient of
·ew continental influences. Henry of Grosmont probably had an expectation of
··ntinental readership; *Mandeville's Travels* had a major impact on the imagina-

J. I. Wimsatt, *Chaucer and the Poems of 'Ch' in University of Pennsylvania MS French 15*,
Chaucer Studies 9 (Cambridge, 1982).
Wimsatt, *Chaucer and the Poems of 'Ch'*.

tion of the French-speaking world; Chaucer won the respect of his French peer for his verse. This cultural milieu is more appropriately termed Anglo-French.[71]

Dynastic and political factors certainly shaped the terms of engagement between England and France. In the first two-thirds of the fourteenth century the English royal family was almost entirely French. From his mother, Edward inherited a plausible claim to the French throne, and from his wife, he gained important allies in the French-speaking Low Countries, where two of his sons were born. The successful prosecution of war in France provided opportunities for a number of noble families to augment their French interests and connections. In the wake of the English king's triumphs in the 1340s and 1350s poets and artists from other parts of the French-speaking world were increasingly drawn into England's orbit. Nonetheless there seems to have been a change of mood at the English royal court by the 1360s. Following the disastrous campaign of 1359–60, in which he failed to secure coronation at Reims, Edward III lost some of his appetite for war. Chaucer himself was captured during this campaign and held to ransom.[72] After the Treaty of Bretigny in 1360 Edward ceased to use, for a time, the title of king of France, and in 1362 the chancellor opened parliament in English and a statute was passed specifying the use of English in pleading in the royal courts of law.[73] There was something of a generational change at the English court. The death of Queen Isabelle in 1358 was followed a decade later by the death of Queen Philippa in 1369. It was during this time that Chaucer presumably encouraged by his courtly patrons, seemingly made a decisive commitment to English.

The conditions that sustained and invigorated French literary culture in mid fourteenth-century England did not wholly disappear. Facility in various kinds of French remained a prized or necessary accomplishment in elite and other circles into the fifteenth century, and French culture retained its prestige and allure. War and diplomacy with France, though increasingly sharpening national antagonisms, continued to provide some stimulus to francophone culture in England not least during Richard II's peace process in the 1390s and in the wake of Henry V's victories in France.[74] Still, it can be claimed that the 1360s represent a watershed, especially in regard to literary composition in Anglo-French. The demographic crisis associated with the Black Death of 1348–9, compounded by the return of the plague in the 1360s, reduced England's capacity for cultural production and encouraged consolidation. John Trevisa, writing in the 1380s, attributed

---

71 William Rothwell uses the term 'Anglo-French' in this sort of context: Rothwell, 'Henry of Lancaster and Geoffrey Chaucer: Anglo-French and Middle English in Fourteenth Century England', *MLR* 99 (2004), 313–27.

72 The ransom demanded – in excess of the standard ransom for a young man of his station – would seem to reflect French recognition of his status at court: C. J. Rogers *War Cruel and Sharp: English Strategy under Edward III, 1327–1360* (Woodbridge, 2000).

73 For more detailed discussion, and for the continuing use of French in administration see Ormrod, 'Use of English', esp. pp. 772–81.

74 For Anglo-French literary culture in England in the fifteenth century, see Section I below.

declining competence in French to the shift to English as the medium of instruction by a new generation of grammarians after the Black Death. The small size of the Francophone community in England necessarily set limits on its capacity to participate fully – as writers as well as readers – in the literary culture of the French-speaking world. At the royal court and in aristocratic circles the balance between the vernaculars certainly tilted decisively towards English in the 1360s. Ironically, the main legacy of the Anglo-French achievement of the 1340s and 1350s is to be found in the enrichment and elevation of English literature.

25

Lollardy: The Anglo-Norman Heresy?

Nicholas Watson

Anglo-Norman and the 'Common Tongue'

My title, a play on the title of a famous article by Anne Hudson, is supposed to produce a frisson of donnish surprise, ideally accompanied by other affects, ranging from a shocked 'What in heaven?' to the curious 'My goodness, how interesting', all the way to the weary 'Here we go again'.[1] On the one hand, the title may seem opportunistic in its attempt to link Anglo-Norman to a heresy that, particularly over the last decade, has represented the *dernier cri* in late medieval scholarly fashion. On the other, the title's insistence on positing a link between a movement whose demotic radicalism is implied by the word 'lollard' itself and a language that, until recently, was widely associated with social and religious conservatism may make the title seem merely unbelievable.[2] Admittedly, as the evidence this volume amasses for the vigour of Anglo-Norman into the fourteenth century and beyond attests, it is becoming steadily less workable to speak of the late fourteenth century (the period in which Lollardy, with its forceful ideas about the use of the English vernacular, came to the fore in England) using the well-worn language of 'the triumph of English', a phrase that still smacks of the old topos of the 'Norman Yoke'.[3] But our deepest scholarly narratives – and 'the triumph of English' is a deep narrative indeed – do

---

1   A. Hudson, 'Lollardy: The English Heresy?', in *Religion and National Identity*, ed. S. Mews, Studies in Church History 18 (Oxford, 1982), pp. 261–83.

2   On the word 'lollard' (perhaps from Middle Dutch *lollaert*), see A. Cole, 'William Langland and the Invention of Lollardy', in *Lollards and Their Influence in Late Medieval England*, ed. F. Somerset, J. C. Havens and D. Pitard (Woodbridge, 2003), pp. 37–58. For a survey of topoi stereotyping Anglo-Norman, see N. Watson and J. Wogan-Browne, 'The French of England: The *Compileison*, *Ancrene Wisse*, and the Idea of Anglo-Norman', *Journal of Romance Studies* 4.3, Special Issue, ed. Gaunt and Weiss (2004), 35–59.

3   For 'Norman yoke', which derives from the era of the English Civil War, see M. Chibnall, *The Debate on the Norman Conquest* (Manchester, 1999), ch. 2. 'The triumph of English', the title of a book by B. Cottle (London, 1969), is in long-standing use in histories of English and has acquired general currency. On 20 December 2001, for example, the *Economist* ran an article called 'The Triumph of English: A World Empire by Other Means'. The phrase's implied allusion to Petrarch's *Trionfi*, and thus to Renaissance neo-classicism, gives it further evocative power, to the obvious disadvantage of Anglo-Norman.

ot live by evidence alone. Core national, religious and literary historical beliefs
re bound up in their survival. If they die at all, they die slow and die hard.

All the same, from a historical point of view, we should by now be surprised
hat the possibility of a connection between Anglo-Norman religious thought
nd England's famous movement of dissent should itself occasion surprise.
part from its theological stances on transubstantiation, predestination, image
eneration and suchlike, and its ecclesiological ones on monasticism, clerical
orruption and the role of the first estate in policing the Church's temporal inter-
sts, early Wycliffism is best known for its commitment to a specific biblicism.[4]
his classified the whole of Scripture as 'Goddis lawe', and during the 1380/90s
d, *inter alia*, to the production of the *Wycliffite Bible*, the first full prose Bible in
nglish, accompanied by a campaign in support of propositions like this one,
rom a series of tracts in a fifteenth-century London manuscript:

> Siþen þat þe trouþe of God stondiþ not in oo langage more þan in anoþir,
> but whoso lyueþ best and techiþ best plesiþ moost God, of what langage þat
> euere it be, þerfore þe lawe of God, writen and tauȝt in Englisch, may edifie
> þe commen pepel as it doiþ clerkis in Latyn – siþen it is the sustynance to
> soulis þat schulden be saued, and Crist comandid þe gospel to be prechid for
> þe pepel schulde lerne it, kunne it, and worche þerafter.
> (Cambridge University Library, MS Dd.vi.26, fos. 41v–42r)

Hence, indeed, the argument of Anne Hudson's article, 'Lollardy: The English
Ieresy?', which explores the link between Wycliffism and advocacy of the written
ernacular as a 'common' medium of instruction, and is still one of the best intro-
uctions to the theological reverberations that accrued around the vernacular as
 language of access at the end of the fourteenth century.[5]

The vernacular in question here is, of course, English, just heading out on its
ng, chippy career as God's other language: the language of 'The Bible and Shake-
peare'. As we shall see, Anglo-Norman is not mentioned in Lollard accounts of
e vernacular and has hardly featured in scholarship on the Lollards, the history
f English Bible translation, or the vernacular as a 'common tongue'. Yet consider
e following three sets of facts:

. English's claim to be the language of access or mass religious communication
as, in the late fourteenth century, indeed relatively new. Despite the persist-
nce of Old English through the twelfth century in some monastic contexts,
etween the late twelfth century and the production of the *South English Legen-
ry* in the late thirteenth century, the 'common tongue' of written vernacular
eligious instruction was not English but French. Not only does this become

---

The classic study is A. Hudson, *The Premature Reformation: Lollard Texts and Wycliffite History* (Oxford, 1988).
For the vernacular as a 'common tongue', see the preface to F. Somerset and N. Watson, eds., *The Vulgar Tongue: Medieval and Postmedieval Vernacularity* (University Park PA, 2004).

crudely clear if we compare, say, the lists of religious works in Ruth Dean's *Anglo-Norman Literature* with the twelfth- and thirteenth-century religious works referred to in Hartung's *Manual of Middle English* and James M. Morey's *Book and Verse*: an exercise which, despite Dean's omission of many works such as the *Somme le roi*, known in England but written on the Continent, shows an overwhelming preponderance of religious works in Anglo-Norman over works in Middle English for the period 1150–1300.[6] It can also be shown by looking at the role French plays in the production and circulation of major English religious works throughout the thirteenth and much of the fourteenth centuries. A significant majority of these works draw on Anglo-Norman sources rather than or in addition to, Latin ones as a matter of preference, either because translation from French was easier or, perhaps, because a work's existence in the French vernacular legitimated its rendering into the English. This is true of early fourteenth-century works from the Middle English *Apocalypse* to the *Northern Homily Cycle* and the Middle English *Mirror*, both based at least partially on Robert of Gretham's *Miroir*; to Robert Mannyng's *Handlyng Synne*, based on William of Waddington's *Manuel dez pechiez*; all the way to *The Prick of Conscience*, with its extensive use of *Les peines de purgatorie* and characteristic adoption of the Anglo-Norman 'octosyllabic' couplet.[7]

Moreover, French, not English, is the vernacular medium in which religious works travel from one part of England to another. The *Somme le roi* and *Miroir de seinte eglise* are both translated into different dialects of English repeatedly by translators who again preferred to work with French, not Latin, and were either unaware of one another's efforts or preferred interlingual translation (from French to English) to intralingual (from one dialect of English to another).[8] Even

---

6 Middle English religious writings *c*.1150–*c*.1300 include the late twelfth-century *Ormulum* and *Vices and Virtues*; the dozen works in the early thirteenth-century *Ancrene Wisse* group; the late thirteenth-century *Surtees Psalter* and other biblical poems; the *South English Legendary* (*c*.1275); *Cursor Mundi* (*c*.1300). Dates and definitions are tricky but by most definitions the corpus does not much exceed 50 substantial works. See A. Hartung, *A Manual of Writings in Middle English, 1050–1500* (New Haven CT, 1967); J. M. Morey, *Book and Verse: A Guide to Middle English Biblical Literature* (Urbana IL 2000). Dean lists 544 religious works, of which some 200 are brief prayers or might be considered variants of one another. For a database of late Old English works, see *The Production and Use of English Manuscripts 1060 to 1220* at http://www.le.ac.uk/ee em1060to1220/index.html.

7 For these works, see Morey, *Book and Verse*, items *AJC* and *NHC* (the sources of which are multiple and not yet fully clarified); *The Middle English Mirror: Sermons from Advent to Sexagesima*, ed. T. G. Duncan and M. Connolly, Middle English Texts (Heidelberg 2003), from which subsequent quotations from the Anglo-Norman and Middle English versions are taken; *Handlyng Synne*, ed. I. Sullens (Binghamton NY, 1983); R. E. Lewis and A. McIntosh, *A Descriptive Guide to the Manuscripts of The Prick of Conscience* (Oxford, 1982). Anglo-Norman prosody permits variation between heptasyllabic and octosyllabic lines (and on occasion still longer and shorter lines) in rhyming couplets.

8 For Middle English versions of *Somme le roi*, including the Kentish *Ayenbite of Inwyt* the south-east Midlands *Book of Vices and Virtues* and the Yorkshire *Speculum vitae*, see Hartung, *Manual*, 7, pp. 2258–1, 2263–4 (by R. R. Raymo). For Middle English versions

the most famous English work of the period, *Ancrene Wisse*, was for a century dependent on Anglo-Norman and Latin in reaching outside its original dialect area in the West Midlands, arriving in (probably) Oxford in one Anglo-Norman translation and in Norwich and other urban centres in a second, as part of the *Compileisun*, generations before its earliest non-Western English manifestation, as the London *Pepys Rule*.[9] In helping to develop what in the fifteenth century became a relatively standardized written English, Wycliffism was not only contributing to a process that the dominance of Anglo-Norman had held back for two centuries; it was building on a conception of the role of the vernacular in creating a broadly based, mixed lay and religious, reading community directly derived from Anglo-Norman.

2. The most important antecedents to the *Wycliffite Bible* – what Geoffrey Shepherd called 'English Bible Versions Before Wycliffe' – are thus not English but French.[10] The *Wycliffite Bible* is the culmination of a century-long process of accretive prose translation, comprising works such as *The Life of Soul*, *Book to a Mother*, and the *Fourteenth-Century English Biblical Version*, all of which draw extensively on the gospels and epistles.[11] These works bear comparison with French projects such as the *Epîtres et Evangiles de Jean de Vignay* (1330s), just as they and the *Wycliffite Bible* bear comparison with the *Anglo-Norman Bible*, England's first full prose vernacular Bible, compiled at about the same time as these English works.[12] Moreover, several of these English Bible versions – the *Mirror*, the *Apocalypse*, the Pepysian *Gospel Harmony*, and others – are translated, not from Latin, but from Anglo-Norman.[13]

---

of the *Mirour de seinte eglise*, most of which are from the Anglo-Norman and not from any of the Latin versions of Edmund's *Speculum religiosorum*, see Hartung, *Manual*, 9.32.3116–17 (by V. Lagorio and M. Sargent).

9   For what is known about the circulation of *Ancrene Wisse* manuscripts, see the extensive materials gathered and discussed in B. Millett, *Ancrene Wisse, the Katherine Group, and the Wooing Group*, Old and Middle English Annotated Bibliographies (Cambridge, 1996).

10   G. Shepherd, 'English Bible Versions Before Wycliffe', in *The West from the Fathers to the Reformation*, vol. 2 of *The Cambridge History of the Bible*, ed. G. W. H. Lampe (Cambridge, 1963), pp. 362–87.

11   *The Lyfe of Soule: An Edition with Commentary*, ed. H. M. Moon (Salzburg, 1978); *Book to a Mother*, ed. A. J. McCarthy (Salzburg, 1981); *A Fourteenth Century English Biblical Version*, ed. A. C. Paues (Cambridge, 1902). No work has been done on possible French sources. For a new study, which makes some allusion to the Anglo-Norman and Middle English background to the Wycliffite Bible, see M. Dove, *The First English Bible: The Text and Context of the Wycliffite Bible* (Cambridge, 2008).

12   For Jean de Vignay, see S. Berger, *La bible française au moyen âge* (Paris, 1884), pp. 221–9. Dean no. 469 gives a brief bibliography on the Anglo-Norman Bible.

13   See *Middle English Mirror*, ed. Duncan and Connolly; Morey, *Book and Verse*, *AJC* and *PGH*. For discussions, see Ralph Hanna III, *London Literature 1300–1380* (Cambridge, 2005), pp. 148–221; J. Wogan-Browne, '"Our Steward, St Jerome": Theology and the Anglo-Norman Household', in *Household, Women, and Christianity*, ed. Mulder-Bakker and Wogan-Browne, pp. 133–65, especially pp. 134–9.

Behind all these works, moreover, is a long tradition of Anglo-Norman and English poetic Bible versions, some derived from the Vulgate, others (as Morey has noted) indebted to Peter Comestor's *Historia scholastica*.[14] Wycliffites insisted on prose, not verse, which they associated with *fable*, and took their Bible straight up, understanding it as law, not as narrative or chronicle – thus as requiring precise verbal rendition, not the individualized acts of shaping and amplification associated with poetry and historiography.[15] But these are choices aware of the alternative models for providing lay access to the Scriptures they reject, and not necessarily in opposition to those models. Comestor's *Historia*, for example, makes an appearance in a Middle English translation closely associated with the *Wycliffite Bible*, John Trevisa's prose translation of the *Historia*'s descendant, Ralph Higden's *Polychronicon*; parts of the *General Prologue* to the *Wycliffite Bible* narrate the Bible as history in much the Comestorian tradition.[16] Outside the scholarly context of the *Wycliffite Bible* itself, reformist English prose Bible translation can be as partial and artistically shaped as any Anglo-Norman verse rendition. *The Lanterne of Light* renders passages of the Bible into hypnotic English semi-verse, while *Book to a Mother* weaves fluent prose Bible, narrative paraphrase and hortatory exegesis into one, seamless exposition.[17] Apart from its refusal of verse, even the cross-section of Middle English Bible translation we can characterize as inflected by Wycliffism provides a variety of translation methodologies and attitudes that stands comparison with, and has learned from, Anglo-Norman.

3. There are clear continuities between aspects of Anglo-Norman lay piety and that of the English works associated with the early history of Lollardy, not least because the two bodies of writing were written for the same kinds of people: aristocrats, gentryfolk, parish priests, and the urban laity. For example, Wycliffite pastoral theology could not dispense with the domestic lessons found in the Book of Tobit, despite acknowledging that the work is apocryphal; the two Tobits, Raphael, Sarah of the seven husbands, Asmodeus the jealous demon, and

---

[14] J. Morey, 'Peter Comestor, Biblical Paraphrase, and the Medieval Popular Bible', *Speculum* 68 (1993), 6–35.

[15] On 'fable' as a term of contempt within Wycliffite discourse, see A. Hudson, 'A Lollard Sect Vocabulary?', in Hudson, *Lollards and Their Books* (London, 1985), pp. 164–80.

[16] For Trevisa, see *The Idea of the Vernacular: An Anthology of Middle English Literary Theory 1280–1520*, ed. J. Wogan-Browne, N. Watson, A. Taylor and R. Evans (University Park PA, 1999), 2.2. Where possible, citations of Middle English prologues are from this book, cited as *Idea* in the body of the text, followed by part, excerpt, and line number. For the *General Prologue*, see *The Holy Bible ... by John Wycliffe*, ed. J. Forshall and F. Madden, 4 vols. (Oxford, 1850), from which subsequent quotations from this work are taken.

[17] See N. Watson, 'Fashioning the Puritan Gentry-woman: Devotion and Dissent in *A Book to a Mother*', in *Medieval Women: Texts and Contexts in Late Medieval Britain: Essays for Felicity Riddy*, ed. J. Wogan-Browne et al. (Turnhout, 2000), pp. 169–84; N. Watson, 'Vernacular Apocalyptic: On *The Lanterne of Light*', *Revista Canaria de estudios Ingleses* 47 (2003), 115–28.

e homeopathic burning fish are as ubiquitous in reformist English religiosity
they are in other vernacular contexts. This suggests we can trace a line of
ɔmiletic lay instruction from Guillaume le Clerc's *Vie de Tobie* in the thirteenth
ntury, through *Book to a Mother*, which makes much use of Tobit around 1370,
 to the Wycliffite *General Prologue*.[18]

In *London Literature 1300–1380*, Ralph Hanna brilliantly demonstrates the
istence, as early as the 1320s, of urban lay communities formed around works
ːe the *Mirror* and the *Pepys Rule*, whose ethical puritanism long caused them to
 understood as later, Lollard productions, but which also exhibit strong conti-
ɪities with Anglo-Norman sources, especially the *Miroir* (see n. 13). The *Miroir*
ɪdeed anticipates later Lollard calls for open access to the Scriptures:

> Ore pri io de quor parfunt
> Tuz cels ki cest escrit auerunt
> Qu'il le present a deliuere
> A tuz cels k'il voldrunt escriure.
> Kar custume est del Deu sermun:
> Plus est cher cum plus est commun.
> Qui Deu sermun en celant mie
> Semble ki il ait de Deu enuie,
> E as almes fait guere grande
> Qui lur tout lur iurnel uiande.   (*Miroir* 635–44)

Now ich beseche wiþ gode hert to alle þat þis writ han, þat hii lene it wiþ
gode wille to al þat it wil writen. For þe custome is of Goddes word, þe more
þat it spredeþ obrode, þe better it is, & þe more hii quemen [*please*] God þat
it owen. For he þat heleþ [*conceals*] Goddes word, it semeþ þat he haþ enuie
to God, & to soules he doþ gret harme, for he benimmeþ [*deprives*] hem her
fode. (*Mirror* 21)

ne of the tracts in Cambridge University Library, MS Dd.vi.26 is still using the
ɪiroir a century later, adapting its image of the Scriptures as an apple tree whose
ɪuit remains hidden until shaken by the clergy to form yet another argument in
ɪvour of full English Bible translation.[19]

For the *Vie de Tobie*, see Dean no. 468. For a study, see J. Wogan-Browne, 'How to Marry
Your Wife with Honour and Fin' Amour: Forming Men for Marriage in Anglo-Norman
England', in *Thirteenth-Century England*, ed. R. Britnell, M. Prestwich and R. Frame (Woodbridge, 2003), pp. 131–50. Wycliffite interest in the apocryphal Book of Tobit is explored
in an unpublished paper by Laura Kuruvilla, who notes that the General Prologue to
the *Wycliffite Bible* cites Tobit as 'profitable to the symple puple' even though it is 'not
of bileeue' (Ch. 11, p. 35). The story of Tobit also dominates several central chapters of
Book to a Mother.
'Holy writ haþ þe lyknesse of a tree þat beriþ fruyt. ... Whanne it is þikke l[e]ued,
litil or nouȝt is seen of his fruȝt. But whanne men schaken þe tree þe fruyt falliþ
doun faste and þike. And þan swetenesse is knowe þat was hidde aforn, and whanne
men eten it, it plesiþ hem wel. So it fareþ bi holy writ ...' (fol. 51v). Thanks to Fiona
Somerset for drawing my attention to this passage. Compare *Miroir* 197–214, on which
see M. Connolly, 'Shaking the Language Tree: Translating the Word into the Vernacular

Middle English scholars assume that translation of a religious work int English shifts its ideology as a matter of course – so that, for example, the 'C translation of *The Mirror of Holy Church*, which universalizes the work's appeal t *gent de religiun* to address it to 'eueri cristene man and wommen þat wol be saued is striking a pose intimately linked with the work's Englishing.[20] But when Trev sa's *Dialogue* presents his patron, Thomas, Lord Berkeley, as championing acces to knowledge by commissioning an English *Polychronicon* (*Idea* 2.2), the continu ties with Gretham's *Miroir*, commissioned by his 'trechere dame, Aline', or wit Pierre d'Abernon de Fetcham's production of the popular *Lumere as lais*, are a notable as the discontinuities.[21] By about the 1350s, literary Anglo-Norman ma gradually have come to be perceived as suitable for relatively private projec such as Henry of Lancaster's *Livre de seyntz medicines*, even if the 1350s and 136(do see an efflorescence of Anglo-Norman didactic and historical works in pros from the *Anglo-Norman Prose Brut* and *The Travels of Sir John Mandeville* to Thoma Gray's *Scalacronica*.[22] But in the thirteenth century, *Miroir, Compileisun, Lumere lais, Mirour de seinte eglise, Apocalypse, Chasteau d'Amour* and similar works a fully as ambitious in their breadth of appeal and theological agendas as the English offspring.

In short, preliminary though these observations are, in its relationships to th vernacular, its mixed lay and religious readerships, and even its biblicism, th English heresy that is Lollardy has a clear, intricate and important connectio to the Anglo-Norman texts out of which late Middle English religious writin largely emerges. More particularly, it has a connection with a series of thirteentl century works that clearly position Anglo-Norman as a 'common tongue', written language long better suited to crossing dialect boundaries than English

The forgetting of Anglo-Norman

Clear, intricate, important – yet surprising; indeed, almost unresearche Margaret Deanesly's great book of 1920 on *The Lollard Bible* restricts its intere in the French Bible to the Continent.[23] Scholars from Shepherd to David Danie largely ignore Anglo-Norman, preferring to trace a thin, brave line of texts, fro the *Ormulum* to Rolle's *English Psalter*, said to link the Anglo-Saxon Golden Ag of translation to the glories of the fourteenth century, as the Norman Conques

---

in the Anglo-Norman *Miroir* and Middle English *Mirror'*, in *The Medieval Translator* ed. R. Voaden, R. Tixier, T. S. Roura and J. R. Rytting (Turnhout, 2003), pp. 17–27.

[20] Oxford, MS Bodley 416, fol. 111r; I am indebted to Natalie Huffels and R. Blair Morr for making a transcription of this text.

[21] See Wogan-Browne, '"Our Steward, St. Jerome"'; Pierre d'Abernon de Fetcham, *Lume as lais*, ed. G. Hesketh, ANTS 54–57 (London, 1996–9).

[22] On the *Brut* and Mandeville, see further the essays by Marvin and Bennett in th volume. On *Scalacronica*, see Dean no. 74: a recent edition of the latter part of the wor is Andy King, *Scalacronica*, Surtees Society 209 (Woodbridge, 2005).

[23] M. Deanesly, *The Lollard Bible and Other Medieval Biblical Versions* (Cambridge, 1920).

in Daniell's plangent words, 'set the religious life of England back into the night'.[24] Not that the fault lies only with Bible historians and Middle English scholars, for work on Anglo-Norman Bible versions is almost non-existent. Still relying on Bonnard's and Berger's studies from the 1880s, Anglo-Normanists have not yet made any concerted attempt to insist on the subject's relevance to the history of English Bible translation.[25]

Anglo-Normanists are used to having their huge field ignored, and it may seem naive to criticize them for not having tilled any specific corner of that field or to assert astonishment that yet another part of the ragged boundary between it and Middle English studies fails to match. But there is a long history to this failure, the roots of which, indeed, go back to the period itself: to the initial acts of assimilation of the place of literary Anglo-Norman by Middle English early in the 1300s and the strategic forgetting of Anglo-Norman later in the century. The canonical form of this history is attained in the sixteenth century, which turned the Age of Wycliffe and Chaucer into a revolutionary precursor of the Reformation and further obscured the close ties between fourteenth-century and thirteenth-century Anglo-Norman and Middle English religiosity, while insisting (in a manner that still affects our own thinking) that the only true Bible translation is as literal as possible and in prose. Still undergirding the institutional structures that separate English and Anglo-Norman studies, this periodization also, I suggest, still shapes our scholarly habits.

In *England the Nation*, Thorlac Turville-Petre draws attention to a form of fourteenth-century English prologue that goes like this (from the *Northern Homily Cycle*, c.1315):[26]

> Forthi will I of my povert
> Schau sum thing that Ik haf in hert,
> On Ingelis tong that alle may
> Understand quat I wil say.
> For laued men havis mar mister,
> Godes word for to her,
> Than klerkes that thair mirour lokes,
> And sees hou thai sal lif on bokes.
> And bathe klerk and laued man
> English understand kan
> That was born in Ingeland,
> And lang haves ben tharin wonand.

---

[24] Shepherd, 'English Bible Versions Before Wycliffe'; D. Daniell, *The Bible in English: Its History and Influence* (New Haven CT, 2003), p. 56.

[25] Berger, *La Bible française*; J. Bonnard, *Les Traductions de la Bible en vers français au moyen âge* (Paris, 1884). There are, of course, more recent editions of certain Anglo-Norman biblical works: see, e.g., *Poème anglo-normand sur l'Ancien Testament*, ed. P. Nobel, 2 vols. (Paris, 1996); *Li Romanz de Dieu et de sa mere d'Herman de Valenciennes*, ed. I. Spiele (Leiden, 1975).

[26] T. Turville-Petre, *England the Nation: Language, Literature, and National Identity, 1290–1340* (Oxford, 1996).

> Bot al men can noht, i-wis,
> Understand Latin and Frankis.
> Forthi me think almous it isse
> To wirke sum god thing on Inglisse. (*Idea*, 2.1.61–77)

This early version of an interestingly varied topos shares the association of 'English' and 'Ingeland' with the better-known and more assertive *Cursor Mundi* prologue, but differs from it by aligning French, not with a territory, France, but with the learned language, Latin. Thus the 'mirour' in which 'klerkes' can examine themselves but from which the 'laued' are cut off here is likely to be not the Latin Bible but one of the work's source texts, the *Miroir*, the work from which the *Northern Homily Cycle*'s use of the 'choice of English' topos may conceivably derive:

> Point de latin mettre n'i uoil,
> Kar co resemblereit orgoil;
> Orgoil resemble ueraiement
> Co dire a altre qu'il n'entent.
> E si est co mult grant folie
> A lai parler latinerie;
> Cil s'entremet de fol mester
> Ki uers lai uolt latin parler.
> Chescun deit estre a raisun mis
> Par la langue dunt il est apris. (*Miroir* 79–88)

Latin ne wil Y sette non þerine, for it semeþ as it wer a pride for to telle anoþer þat he vnderstondeþ nouȝt. And so it is ful gret foli to spek Latyn to lewed folke, & he entermetteþ him of a fole mester þat telleþ to hem Latin. For ich man schal ben vndernomen & aresoned eftter þe langage þat he haþ lerd.
(*Mirror* 5.7–11)

The later *Speculum vitae* may also borrow from the *Miroir* for its own version of this topos: 'Na Latyn I wylle speke na waste/ Bot Inglysche that men uses maste' (*Idea*, p. 336).

Turville-Petre suggests that a motive behind the 'choice of English' topos in these texts is nationalist. But in the *Northern Homily Cycle* and *Speculum vitae* it may, rather, be regional and utilitarian: the probably York-based authors are responding to the written vernacular's potential as a 'common tongue', demonstrated by verse Bibles such as the *Miroir*, by adapting it to the linguistic conditions of the north where there was, it has been claimed, a relative paucity of French readers, at least outside urban centres such as York. The potential for alienation from French exists within this topos, and is realized by the *Cursor Mundi* prologue: 'French rimes here I rede/ Communely in iche a stede/ That mast ys worth for Frenche man' – although even here we should note that French is a 'commune' language, said to be read everywhere (*Idea* 3.10.79–81). Yet the fact that French is treated inconsistently by the topos and assigned any role other than its real one of literary 'common tongue' suggests that its displacement is less important to these prologues than the legitimation of English Bible instruction, through claims for an association between English and the 'leued' and the close imitation of authorizing Anglo-Norman models. Middle English religious verse here asserting its *equivalence* to works like the *Miroir*, not its difference.

One of the latest examples of the 'choice of English' topos is Thomas Usk's comment in *The Testament of Love* from around 1386 that 'certes, there ben some that speken their poysye-mater in Frenche, of whiche speche the Frenchemen have as good a fantasye as we have in heryng of Frenchemennes Englysshe': a discordantly negative reference to a language still capable of so innovative a project as John Gower's *Mirour de l'Omme* (*Idea* 1.4.19–21). Standard late fourteenth-century secular practice, however, is to borrow from French silently, as Chaucer does for much of *The Book of the Duchess*. So too does Gower in *Confessio Amantis*, which confines itself to a sideways glance at the literary Anglo-Norman in which its poetic practice is rooted by anachronistically claiming its use of English as innovative: 'for that fewe men endite/ In oure Englissh, I thenke make/ A bok for Engelondes sake' (*Idea*, 2.11.29–31). In these secular texts, the silence that hangs over an omnipresent French makes its own claim to equality, not least because it demands an appreciation of its own, suave internationalism from its readers.

Religious texts of this period, particularly those generated by the controversy on Bible translation that erupted in the 1380s, efface Anglo-Norman for different reasons, this time in the interests of constructing a dichotomy between Latin and vernacular, learned and 'lewed', around which arguments about Bible translation can rage. In the process they also do something more drastic for future relations between Middle English and Anglo-Norman studies, more drastic, indeed, for how scholarship has reconstructed the entire history of medieval England's vernaculars. Creating a pioneering account of a continuous English literary history going back five centuries to the Anglo-Saxons – one that comprises the earliest history of English-language writing that we have – they rewrite the history of Bible translation as though it can be told wholly through a canon of Middle English texts, referring to French only as the vernacular of France:

> If worldli clerkis loken wel here croniclis and bokis, thei shulden fynde that Bede translatide the Bible and expounide myche in Saxon (that was English, either comoun language of this lond, in his tyme); and not oneli Bede but also king Alured, that foundide Oxenford, translatide in hise laste daies the bigynning of the Sauter into Saxon – and wolde more, if he hadde lyued lengere. Also Frenshemen, Beemers, and Britons han the Bible and othere bokis of deuocioun and of exposicioun translatid in here modir langage. Whi shulden not English men haue the same in here modir langage?
>
> (*General Prologue to Wycliffite Bible*, Ch. 15, p. 71)

Other versions of this canon, which frequently recurs in controversial contexts in Latin and English, mention two fourteenth-century texts, Rolle's *English Psalter* and John Gaytryge's *Lay Folks's Catechism*, alluded to in Richard Ullerston's Oxford *Determinatio* of 1401 and its abbreviated English translation, while the lists of non-English languages into which the Bible has been translated always include French – usually in the company of two or three of Spanish, German,

Czech, Flemish, Italian, Armenian, and Greek – but seldom acknowledge tha French is an insular tongue, and never mention any translation written in vers (*Idea* 2.4). Two exceptions are Trevisa's *Dialogue* of 1387, which in a famou passage cites the Anglo-Norman *Apocalypse* as a precedent for Bible translatior besides interestingly implying that English Bibles are translated from French, no Latin (*Idea*, 2.2.97–112),[27] and another of the MS CUL Dd.vi.26 translation trea tises, which has a clear reference to legal uses of Anglo-Norman:

> ʒif þe kynge of Englond sente to cuntrees and citees his patente on Latyn or Frensche and [h]ot[e] to do crie his lawes, his statutes, and his wille to þe people, and it were cried oonly on Latyn or Frensche and not on Englisch, it were no worschip to þe kynge ne warnynge to þe people, but a greet desseyt. Ryʒt so þe kynge of heuene wolde þat his lawe and his welle were cried and tauʒt openly to þe pepel. And but it were tauʒt hem opunly on Englische þat þei mowen knowen it, ellis it is aʒens þe worschip of God and gret henndrynge.
>
> (CUL, Dd.vi.26, fols. 5v–6r; emendation mine)

This passage implies as good an explanation as we are likely to get for the efface ment of Anglo-Norman in the translation controversy, despite this controversy' status as the most extensive body of theoretical reflection on language in Middl English. Here, Anglo-Norman has come to signify a language of legal record, semi-vernacular no longer susceptible of being understood as a common tongue while English is not only the language everyone understands but the languag of proclamation: the language which, by making it public, *instantiates* the law. For neither side in the translation debate does Anglo-Norman thus provide helpful precedent.

By acknowledging that English's superior claim to signify universal acces rests on its use in public and oral contexts, the passage also opens out on t a question with which defenders of Bible translation had serious difficulty: th question of why an English Bible must be written, not expounded aloud b clerics, as Arundel was to argue was proper in his *Constitutions* of 1409, whic allowed translation of the Bible in preaching as well as protecting pre-*Wycliffi Bible* vernacular versions.[29] Since Anglo-Norman and Middle English vers Bibles were no doubt still being used for oral instruction – and since the verse c the *Miroir* or the *Northern Homily Cycle* indeed signifies clerically mediated ora instruction – defenders of the *Wycliffite Bible* were obliged to stress its *writte* quality, signified by its use of the legal medium of prose, not verse. To groun their view of the English Bible as 'Goddes lawe', they thus required a version c English that appropriated both Anglo-Norman's specialized relationship wit

---

27 D. Trotter, 'The Anglo-Norman Inscriptions at Berkeley Castle', *Medium Aevum* 5 (1990), 114–20.

28 Ormrod, 'Use of English'. For the use of French proclamations in late medieval town see the essay by Britnell in this volume.

29 N. Watson, 'Censorship and Cultural Change: Vernacular Theology, the Oxford Trans lation Debate and Arundel's *Constitutions* of 1409', *Speculum* 70 (1995), 822–64.

344

written law and English's with the universal, combining the symbolic associations of both languages. A potential blunder in this controversial context, the proclamation metaphor, with its admission that Anglo-Norman, not English, is the language of legal record, and its deployment of a still active understanding of English as an oral medium, thus raises as many issues as it settles.

A history of the English Bible told around an Old and Middle English prose canon by Wycliffites and moderates such as Ullerston was an important part of the legacy the late fourteenth century bequeathed to sixteenth-century Protestant historiography and nineteenth-century biblical scholarship. For sixteenth-century historians deeply read in the medieval period but also committed to a negative view of the 'Roman' church, such as John Foxe in the *Acts and Monuments*, the history had only to be twitched to make sound polemical sense. In Foxe's rewriting, the Anglo-Saxon church is naturally a biblicist church after its own lights, since it partakes of the virtue Protestantism attributed to the Early Church in general, and can thus ground the controversial claim that the English Church was always national as well as Catholic and so never legitimately subject to the pope. The medieval record's silence about the twelfth and thirteenth centuries betokens, not the ascendancy of Anglo-Norman vernacular theology, but the disappearance of true religion under the weight of papalism, indulgences, purgatory, the friars and the ascendency of 'private religion': perversions of the gospel that lead to the unleashing of Satan from his chains and the onset of the Last Days, which Foxe dates, unfortunately for Anglo-Normanists, to 1324–60. Presenting the history of the orthodox counter-attack against Wycliffe largely through lists of condemned articles, trial records and other public sources, Foxe also generalizes what, after Arundel's *Constitutions*, became orthodox opposition to the *Wycliffite Bible* in order to align it with the grand claim that the Church of Rome eternally opposed the gospel – revising the Wycliffite picture of their Bible as the heroic proclamation of a gospel *newly* under threat from the church of the Antichrist. In Foxe's account, Wycliffe's heroism, closely associated with that of the resurgent literary English of Chaucer, anticipates both the overthrow of Romanism and its vile censoring of God's word and the reestablishment of English and the gospel under the Tudors. Despite more than cameo appearances by Thomas à Beckett (as villain) and Robert Grosseteste (as hero), Anglo-Norman is not even vilified in this account; it might as well not have existed.[30]

A scholarly version of much the same account, which draws heavily on the *General Prologue* to the *Wycliffite Bible*, is given in Forshall and Madden's intro-

---

[30] John Foxe, *Acts and Monuments*, at http://www.hrionline.ac.uk/johnfoxe/transcript. html, which edits four editions published in Foxe's lifetime. See the opening of Book V in the 1570 edn, pp. 493–4, which dates the unloosing of Satan, gives a list of 'faythfull learned men' who withstood the pope during the previous 300 years, and makes 1360 into the pivotal year after which the last great persecution of the Church, and the heroic resistance of the elect, commences. Book IV gives sections to Beckett and Grosseteste, among others. Book V deals with Wycliffe and his followers, down to John Hus.

duction to their great edition of the *Wycliffite Bible* in 1850, produced at a time of rising interest in national languages, when the truth of a broadly Protestant account of the history of Bible translation held sway even among Roman Catholics, constantly reinforced by, among other things, the publication of annotated editions of Foxe. From there a line of influence can readily be traced through Deanesly and Shepherd to (among others) Daniell, who still finds something 'mysterious' about the advent of the *Wycliffite Bible*, preserving the tradition in which it marks a crucial moment in Protestant eschatological historiography, an epochal break with an anti-vernacular past.[31] Even more than the topos of the 'Norman Yoke', which has a parallel genealogy in egalitarian theologies of the seventeenth century – but which at least gives Anglo-Norman a role in the plot, even if it is the antagonist's role – the association of late fourteenth-century English with a religious reformation as well as a cultural renaissance has thus contributed to the separation of Middle English and Anglo-Norman studies down almost to the present, and thus done its part in the silencing of Anglo-Norman in general accounts of English literary history. A casual victim of the triumph of mythical history and its epoch-making tendencies over the complexities of the past, the contribution of Anglo-Norman religiosity to late medieval reformist religious thought in English still remains hard to see or to assimilate.

This is why, in conclusion, nobody can yet answer the question posed in my title. Perhaps the *Wycliffite Bible* owes a direct debt to one or another Anglo-Norman Bible; very likely this is the case for more of its Middle English prose predecessors than the few whose sources have already been traced; and there can be small doubt that Middle English reformist theological thought in general will prove to owe a debt to texts and ideas first presented in Anglo-Norman, and to its complex and changing relation to how literary, legal and other varieties of Anglo-Norman *signified* through the thirteenth and fourteenth centuries. What that debt may be is impossible to say as yet because nobody has done the work; nobody has done the work because, thanks to the remarkable staying-power of theological models of history and of literary topoi, the question itself has not been easily visible. Making questions visible is the project of a volume like this one and, in a wider sense, a major project of contemporary Anglo-Norman studies, as it pushes its way at last into the literary historical limelight. This is at least as important a process for Middle English scholars as for Anglo-Normanists themselves, to the real extent that the distinction will continue to exist. For only once Anglo-Norman's curious occlusion as the 'other' English vernacular is fully exposed and rectified can we hope to integrate our still fractured picture of late medieval English literary history.[32]

---

31 Daniell, *The Bible in English*, p. 66: 'Something new, with a mysterious element to it', a clause clearly redolent of the old Protestant narrative of Wycliffite heroism acting under direct divine inspiration.

32 This essay presents in summary form arguments developed at greater length in my forthcoming book, *Balaam's Ass: Vernacular Theology and the Secularization of England, 1050–1550*.

26

The Languages of Memory:
The Crabhouse Nunnery Manuscript

Rebecca June

he Crabhouse nunnery manuscript, with its entries from the late thirteenth
› the late fifteenth century, has been called many things:[1] quaint, picturesque,
ɔnfusing, or just plain jumbled. Although some scholars refer to it as a cartu-
ıry, the British Library labels the manuscript a 'register', as does Mary Bateson,
ₛ sole editor to date.[2] Davis includes the manuscript in his *Short Catalogue*
ᶠ *Cartularies*, but lists it in the category 'Other Registers, etc.' because it was
ıt some point wrongly described as a cartulary'.[3] For lack of a better term, I
'ill refer to the manuscript as simply that – the Crabhouse manuscript, for
 is, in fact, a jumble, its fifty-four folios containing a verse prologue in Latin
ınd French; a prose foundation legend and cartulary in French; three separate
ₑntals – two in Latin, one in French; a terrier in Latin and another in French;
vo fairly long records commemorating a generous donation that are almost
ₑrmon-like in tone and address – written in French but with introductions in
ₑrse; and finally, two entries in English: a brief memorandum of a wedding and
n annal-like entry commemorating the works of three prioresses but devoting
ıough attention to one of them to verge on hagiography. The table appended
 this essay describes the contents of the Crabhouse manuscript in their order
f appearance, with more detail than can be found in published guides to the
ₑxt, including Bateson's edition. The table also assigns a range of entry dates to
ıe various contents of the manuscript, those dates differing in several instances
ɔm those given in other printed sources.

Given the Crabhouse manuscript's mixed nature, it is no surprise that
ıost scholarship on the manuscript to date has focused on trying to unravel
ıe nunnery's convoluted history. The following discussion, however, will
ɔcus primarily on the literary aspects of the Crabhouse manuscript – its form,

London, British Library, MS Additional 4733.

M. Bateson, 'The Register of Crabhouse Nunnery', *Norfolk Archaeology* 11 (1892), 1–71
(with some omissions of the manuscript material). My edition and translation of the
Crabhouse manuscript's prologue and legend, including a discussion of the appropri-
ateness of the terms 'register' or 'cartulary' in relation to the manuscript, will appear
in *The French of England: Vernacular Literary Theory and Practice, c.1130–c.1500*, ed.
J. Wogan-Browne, T. Fenster and D. Russell (forthcoming).

G. R. C. Davis, *Medieval Cartularies of Great Britain, A Short Catalogue* (London, 1958),
p. xiv.

language, tone and narrative objectives. While it may seem strange to speak c
narrative objectives in relation to a text like this one whose contents are prima
rily concerned with various property transactions, scholars have recently begu
to look at monastic records, more specifically at cartularies, as deliberatel
constructed documents, produced not only to record and organize a commun
ty's archives, but to tell a story, to create a history and an identity for a particula
group. As Constance Bouchard writes,

> The familiarity these cartularies now have may obscure a crucial aspect of
> their composition: they were novel, even revolutionary when they were first
> put together in the eleventh through thirteenth centuries, and represented a
> new way of organizing and thinking about both a monastery's past and its
> possessions. [...] [M]onastic scribes used them to create and to meditate upon
> a useful past for their houses.[4]

Bouchard and others stress the function of cartularies as arranging rather tha
simply ordering the past, with scribes choosing to include some archival record
and exclude others, to give emphasis to some records – spatially, linguisticall
or temporally – while downplaying others, to give meaning, in other word.
through the selection and presentation of a community's documents, to tha
community's history. Many of the recent studies of cartularies as narrativ
constructs have focused on continental or Anglo-Saxon documents, so the Crak
house manuscript presents an opportunity to examine a later 'English' exampl
and discuss the ways in which the Crabhouse nuns utilized their documentar
resources to construct an identity for themselves, asking – among other ques
tions – what purpose does French serve in the nuns' story of themselves?

Crabhouse nunnery was located in the marshy fens of the county of Norfolk o
the western banks of the River Ouse. Crabhouse was never a very large nunner
Its records refer to a gift made to provide clothing for ten nuns at one time,[5] an
upon dissolution four nuns were in residence. But despite the nunnery's isola
tion and diminutive size, it has received a good deal of attention including topc
graphical and antiquarian studies of Norfolk in the early and mid-nineteent
century,[6] Bateson's edition and an historical narrative by Augustus Jessopp i
the late nineteenth century,[7] and more recently, studies of nunneries that loo

4   C. B. Bouchard, 'Monastic Cartularies: Organizing Eternity', in *Charters, Cartularies, an
     Archives: The Preservation and Transmission of Documents in the Medieval West*, ed. A.
     Kosto and A. Winroth (Toronto, 2002), pp. 22–32 (p. 22). For another helpful collectio
     of essays on this topic, see *Les cartulaires méridionaux*, ed. D. Le Blévec (Paris, 2006).
5   MS Addit. 4733, fol. 19r.
6   See, for example, G. H. Dashwood, 'Notes of Deeds and Survey of Crabhous
     Nunnery, Norfolk', in *Norfolk Archaeology* (Norwich, 1859), pp. 257–62; F. Blomefiel
     and C. Parkin, *An Essay Towards a Topographical History of the County of Norfolk* (Londor
     1808), pp. 173–6; W. White, 'Norfolk: Wiggenhall St. Mary Magdalen', in *Willia*
     White's History, Gazetteer, and Directory of Norfolk (Sheffield, 1845).
7   A. Jessopp, 'Ups and Downs of an Old Nunnery', *Frivola* (London, 1896), pp. 28–82.

to learn more about the lives of medieval women.[8] In all of these two centuries of scholarship, however, there are not two studies of Crabhouse that agree as to the details of its history. Who founded the house, when it was founded and how it negotiated its existence with its monastic and secular neighbours are questions that have yet to be answered definitively. This essay will suggest some answers to those questions, but more importantly, it will argue that the form of the Crabhouse manuscript itself deliberately resists answers to such questions.

The Crabhouse history formally begins on the manuscript's second folio, but on the first folio (designated by the Roman numeral *i* in the table below), there is a memorandum written in English, dated 1476, making this the latest entry in the manuscript and one of only five or so to include specific or approximate dates. The memorandum describes the marriage of Thomas Hunston and Margaret Kervyle, performed in the Crabhouse monastery. Margaret's sister was a nun at Crabhouse, and the couple had to obtain a special license to be married there as well as pay a fee to the vicar of St Mary Magdalen to perform the marriage. The memorandum is concerned with the marriage at hand, but more so with preventing any future claims by the vicar for performing services in the nuns' church. The memorandum notes the authorities involved in the transaction and the monies exchanged, as well as oral testimony of the vicar's statements in the case. In contrast to this rather prosaic entry, the manuscript's formal opening – thirty-three lines of neatly written French rhyming verse in loose octosyllables – invokes the aid of Mary and Jesus and calls upon men and women of all secular social positions to listen to the story of the founding and holdings of Crabhouse. The verse goes on to assert that greed and inequality lead people to take from holy church her due, so assurance must be made to protect and increase her franchise. The verse prologue ends by stating that it would be difficult to write the entire business in rhyme, so the author will continue otherwise, that is, in prose.

Following the author's statement of intent, the manuscript's foundation legend begins:[9]

---

8   See especially T. Coletti, *Mary Magdalene and the Drama of Saints: Theater, Gender, and Religion in Late Medieval England* (Philadelphia, 2004); R. Gilchrist and M. Oliva, *Religious Women in Medieval East Anglia: History and Archaeology c.1100–1540* (Norwich, 1993); R. Gilchrist, *Contemplation and Action: The Other Monasticism* (New York, 1995); M. Oliva, *The Convent and the Community in Late Medieval England: Female Monasteries in the Diocese of Norwich, 1350–1540* (Woodbridge, 1998); S. Thompson, *Women Religious: The Founding of English Nunneries after the Norman Conquest* (Oxford, 1991). Crabhouse also appears as a symbol of moral decay in an early twentieth-century biography: T. Hake and A. Compton-Rickett, *The Life and Letters of Theodore Watts Dunton*, 2 vols. (London, 1916), II, 93–4.

9   Jadis esteyt une pucele, le quer de ki li Seynt Espirit mova de quere lu de deserte ou ele poeyt servir Deu saunz desturbaunce de terriene choce; si trova cest lu ke ore est apelé Crabhus tut savagine, et de graunt partie envirun de totes pars n'esteyt habitaciun de home, et unkore en les jours ke ore sunt si sunt acune gent ne mie de sessaunte anz, ke diunt ke lur peres lur desoyunt ke il poeyunt penser ke la ne fut nul mesun estaunt ne terre sayne ne habité de cest part Bustardesdole. Cele pucele avaunt dite trova cel lu a sun pleyser, si assembla oweske li altres puceles et se firunt aparalier une chapele

Once there was a maiden whose heart the Holy Spirit moved to seek a desert place where she could serve God without disturbance from any worldly thing; and she found this place, which is now called Crabhouse, all wild, and for a large part of the region in every direction there was no human habitation, and even in the present day there are some not even sixty years of age who say that their fathers told them they could remember when there was no house standing nor any reclaimed or inhabited land on this side of Bustard's Dole. The aforesaid maiden found that place to her liking, so she gathered with her other maidens, and they built a chapel [...]: in that place they served God many days. But the devil who never ceases to bring low all good works put in the hearts of those who were his ministers to despoil the maidens, who did so to the extent that they abandoned the place [...]; so they made their dwelling place that still exists beside the river, and to be more certain of possessing their place and their dwelling in peace, they appointed themselves an immediate lord upon whom they could depend, for an annual rent [...]. Many years later a wave of water came that flooded their dwellings for which reason they left and never again returned, and how and where they lived afterward I have not learned, except only of one who became a recluse in the cemetery of Mary Magdalen at Wiggenhall, who kept the muniments of the aforesaid place of Crabhouse, which either in her lifetime or after her death were taken to the house at Castle Acre where they are still. After the aforesaid flood waters had subsided, the lord whom they chose had the property of Crabhouse recorded as if in his acquisition, and he held it for himself for a long time, until he gave it in marriage, together with his sister, to one who was called Elmer Cook, the chaplain of Crabhouse. [...] his sister who was thus gifted was called Agnes, and there is a charter for this gift [...]. The aforesaid Elmer and Agnes gave half of the hermitage of the aforesaid place of Crabhouse, with half the land nearest the chapel, to Roger the canon and to all who served God in the same place as canons for twelve deniers per year in rent to him and to his heirs, and concerning this there is a charter.

[...]: en quel lu meynt jour Deu servirunt. Mes li diable ki ne fine de abesser touz bons overaynes mist en le quers de ceus ke esteyunt ces ministres les avaunt dites puceles rober, ke issi feseyunt par quey le lu dekerpirunt [...]; si firunt lur habitacion juste la rive ke uncore est, et pur estre le plus certeyn de aver lur lu et lur habitacion en pays, si lur firunt un chef seniur de ki ille poeyunt tener pur annual rente [...]. Meynt an aprés si vinc une crestine de ewe ke surmunta lur habitacion par quoy il se departirunt et n'ent plus repeyrerunt et coment ne ou enaprés vesquirunt n'ay entendu, fors soulement de l'une ke se fit recluse en le cymeterie de la Marie Magdaleyne de Wigenhale la quele out les monumenz de le avaunt dite lu de Crabhus, les queus, ou en sa vie ou enaprés sun morir, furunt enporté a la mesun de Chastelacre ou uncore sunt. Aprés ke le avaunt dite crestine de euwe esteyt chayue, li seniur ke il visent fet del tenement del avaunt dit lu de Crabhus si entra cum en sun achete, et li tint ben lung tens, si ke ataunt ke il le dona cum en mariage owoc sa sorur a un ke esteyt apelé Aylmer Kok le chapeleyn de Crabhus. [...] sa sorur ke issi esteyt doué fut apelé Agneys, et de cest doun illia une chartre [...]. Cil avaunt dit Aylmer et Agneys donerunt demi le armitorie del avaunt dit lu de Crabhus owoc tote la demi terre plus pres la chapele a Roger le chanun et a touz ke serverunt Deu en meyme le lu en habit de chanoyne, pur duze deners par an de rendre a li et a ces heyrs, et de ceo il i a une chartre.

From these three passages – the marriage memorandum, verse prologue and prose legend – representing the earliest and latest entries in the Crabhouse manuscript, a pattern of concerns emerges, concerns that continue throughout the entire manuscript. First, each of the passages calls attention to oral testimony as a part of communal memory. Whether in the form of statements overheard by another vicar, or of understanding gained by hearing a written text read aloud, or of recollections passed from one generation to the next, oral testimony is claimed here as carrying legitimate legal authority. This pattern persists throughout the remainder of the manuscript, as well; for instance, a number of cartulary entries include the formulaic phrase, 'il ny a nul home ke unkes oyt dire' ('no man ever heard it said'). However, each of these references to oral testimony is carefully noted in writing, indicating that the Crabhouse nuns were only too aware that oral testimony could be challenged and that written records could serve as more permanent guarantees. On the other hand, we should not be fooled by these first passages' references to written records into believing that the nuns considered legal documents more authoritative than other forms of social memory. In 1931 Otto Meyer argued that foundation narratives occur in 'privileges which are not foundation charters in the proper sense of the word'.[10] According to Meyer, foundation legends locate a founding in mythical time and include miraculous events in an attempt to legitimize an institution lacking more immediate foundational documents. But as the Crabhouse legend itself presents it, such is not the case in this instance. The women's records were preserved by the lone recluse who remained behind after the flood and were transferred to Castle Acre priory at some point. Those records could presumably have been copied into the Crabhouse cartulary. This same pattern is evident in the cartulary of Godstow nunnery.[11] Like the Crabhouse manuscript, the Godstow cartulary's Latin version contains a French foundation legend, but the legend is immediately followed by three separate foundation charters, one listing King Stephen and Queen Matilda as witnesses and another confirmed by Henry II.

For both the Godstow and Crabhouse women, then, the existence of foundation charters – even royal charters – did not preclude the choice of recording the nuns' history in legendary form, legends that place women front and centre in their community's formation. K. J. P. Lowe noted this same tendency in nuns' chronicles written in Italy during the fifteenth and sixteenth centuries, observing that the women's legends complicate the idea of foundation by raising the following questions: When does a foundation take place – upon endowment, when the site is occupied, when nuns are first present, or when there is an offi-

---

Translation and paraphrase by H. Wolfram, 'Political Theory and Narrative in Charters', *Viator* 26 (1995), 39–51 (p. 49).
London, Public Record Office, E 164/20, and Emilie Amt, paper on 'The Anglo-Norman Foundation Legend of the Godstow Nuns' delivered at the Fordham University French of England conference, New York, Spring 2007. See *The Cartulary of Godstow Abbey*, ed. E. Amt (Oxford, forthcoming). On the role of anchoresses in the foundation and development of communities, see Thompson, *Women Religious*, pp. 16–37.

cial ceremony? Also, who is the founder of a religious house – the person with the initial idea, the person who financed the foundation, the builder, or the first nun?[12] The choice of including *both* charters and a legend in the Godstow cartulary, as well as the choice of telling the legend of a nameless *pucelle* rather than copying existing foundation charters with named donors and recipients into the Crabhouse manuscript, indicates that in composing their cartularies these women were not simply interested in compiling legal evidence of their holdings and privileges. Instead, the nuns chose to reframe their histories as narrative, making the women themselves the primary agents in establishing their respective houses – rather than the secular men who granted them lands, or the religious men who exercised the inevitable ecclesiastical oversight.

Tension between the Crabhouse nuns and their male neighbours, particularly their monastic neighbours, is the next pattern apparent in the three passages that open the Crabhouse manuscript: the English memorandum attempts to forestall any potential claims to perform services in their church by the neighbouring church's vicar; the verse prologue outlines one of the manuscript's objectives as creating a defence against plunderers of holy church, and the legend describes those plunderers in the nunnery's history as men holding religious office. Even before their own chaplain gives half their property to Roger and the canons of Reinham, or before the man they hired to look after their affairs records their property as if his own and gives it to his sister upon marriage, the legend characterizes those who would despoil the nuns' good works as the devil's 'ministres'. 'Minister', which appears only this one time in the manuscript, is an interesting choice of word. In Latin, 'minister' had taken on an ecclesiastical meaning by the second century. In French, 'ministre' carried primarily secular connotations in the first half of the twelfth century but, by the end of that same century, the word often referred to ecclesiastical positions, as it would a century later when 'minister' first entered English.[13] To characterize the Crabhouse nuns' earliest opposition as the devil's 'ministers' rather than say, the devil's 'seneschals' (a word that appears elsewhere in the manuscript to describe secular administrative positions) thus sets the tone for the nuns' history of dealings with their ecclesiastical counterparts.[14] The Crabhouse nuns do, in fact, have a rocky relationship with their monastic neighbours for a great deal of their history. Marilyn Oliva refers to the nuns as 'pawns' in ongoing political struggles among the monastic houses in the area,[15] and the manuscript makes mention of disagree-

---

12 K. J. P. Lowe, *Nuns' Chronicles and Convent Culture in Renaissance and Counter Reformation Italy* (Cambridge, 2003), p. 98.

13 AND *s.v.* ministre, also Tobler–Lommatsch, *s.v* menistre, ministre; MED *s.v.* ministr 2a. OED *s.v.* minister, 2nd edn, 1989.

14 See e.g. fol. 34r. Similarly, the Anglo-Norman *Espurgatoire seint Patriz* attributed to Marie de France employs the terms 'serganz' and 'privez' for the devil's followers, reserving ecclesiastical terms for clerics – even those who give in to temptation: see *Saint Patrick's Purgatory: A Poem by Marie de France*, trans. M. J. Curley (Tempe AZ, 1997), vv. 2202, 2291.

15 Oliva, *Convent and Community*, p. 25.

ments between the nuns and the religious men, once referring angrily to their own chaplain as a 'traytur'.[16] It was not until 1328 that the relationship with local clergy changed, for in that year a wealthy man named Robert de Welle restored the nuns' property by buying back the portion lost to Roger and the Reinham canons after the flood. Even then, however, the entry that follows the commemoration of Robert de Welle's gift advises the nuns to be wise with their property in preparation for future trouble. Finally, in 1420 the nuns' relationship with the clergy hits a peak of goodwill when Joan of Wiggenhall serves as prioress and, with the help of two clerical cousins, sets about rebuilding the nunnery, the manuscript referring to these men repeatedly as 'frendes' rather than aligning them with the devil's ministers of the legend.

The Crabhouse nuns' negotiations with their secular and religious neighbours go far, I believe, in explaining the choice of languages in their manuscript. When Augustus Jessopp described the use of French in the Crabhouse text, he explained the choice as evidence that the nuns were putting on airs.[17] The fenlands surrounding Wiggenhall parish where Crabhouse was located are not known for a high presence of Norman aristocracy; however, Castle Acre Priory, holder of the Crabhouse muniments mentioned in the legend, was founded by the earl of Warenne, so the use of French *could* be seen as a kind of social ladder-climbing – a way for the nuns to elevate themselves in the eyes of their community. On the other hand, French could just as easily alienate the nuns from the English neighbours on whom they depended for their livelihood. For example, one fourteenth-century entry refers to land held for the nuns by the king as 'Minchynggedole' – *minchin* (Old English *mynecenu*) meaning 'nun', a reminder that the Crabhouse nuns' neighbours had long Anglo-Saxon memories.[18] So for the nuns, French appears to have been chosen in good part because it is *not* Latin. As the language of civic discourse, French could offer the nuns a measure of public formality for their documents, while also constructing distance between the women and their Latin-loving brethren.[19] As part of the rationale for the translation of the Godstow cartulary into English, its translator points out that harm comes from not being able to read one's own muniments and that women cannot depend on men to be available to protect them.[20] Significantly, it is only after the Crabhouse nuns have recovered their holdings from the canons that their manuscript begins to include records in Latin.

The shift from French to Latin in the Crabhouse manuscript brings us to the third pattern in this document's construction of identity – that pattern being anonymity, or what the manuscript does not say. In the manuscript's opening passages described earlier, the author or narrator never identifies him or herself.

---

16 Fol. 7v.
17 Jessopp, *Ups and Downs*, pp. 45–6.
18 Fol. 34r.
19 On the French of civic discourse, see the essay by Britnell in this volume.
20 *The English Register of Godstow Nunnery*, ed. A. Clark, 3 vols., EETS OS 129, 130 and 142 (London, 1905–11), I, 25.

Neither does the author identify any of the Crabhouse nuns by name. In fact, despite existing records that identify Leva, daughter of Godric of Lynn as the *pucelle*, the founding mother of the nunnery, and Joanna as the lone recluse who preserves the Crabhouse muniments when flooding forces the nuns to leave, the Crabhouse manuscript itself refrains from naming all but a few of the nuns' leaders.[21] The first two prioresses named, the only two mentioned for half of the manuscript, are Katherine and Christina, referred to only once as prioresses 'par la comun assentement de tuz les sorurs' ('by the common consent of all the sisters').[22] Table 26.1 below notes the language used throughout the manuscript to describe the nuns; notably, until the time of Agnes of Methelwolde (on fol. 22), the nuns are typically referred to as a collective: 'la mesun de Crabhus', 'la curt de Crabhus', 'la eglise de Crabhus'. It is only under the strong leadership of Agnes and Joan that the nunnery's dealings begin to be described in terms of 'la priuressa' – sometimes as 'la priuressa et convent', but increasingly as 'la priuressa' alone. During Prioress Agnes's term of office, the land records also take on a regnal tone, with repeated references to Britain and the Rey or Rege, and by the time of Joan of Wiggenhall's term as prioress, she appears single-handedly to rebuild Crabhouse from decay and even fire, with the only mention of her fellow nuns appearing when Joan takes down the dortur 'dredyinge perisschyng of her sistres whiche lay there-inn', Joan's sisters thus reduced to inert bodies in contrast to her strong leadership.[23]

The manuscript begins, then, by describing the Crabhouse nunnery's identity as an anonymous and collective body of women defending themselves from a hostile world of floods and immoral men, a body of women who are primarily defined by what they are not: not English, not Latin, not intimately connected to, nor completely independent from, either their secular or religious communities – these women are exiles, *pucelles* seeking peace in a desert place. By the end of the fourteenth century, however, that exilic identity has transformed from one of vulnerability to one of strength. Crabhouse is now both English and Latin, a participating member of its larger communities. Yet to the end (which is really the beginning, going back to the 1476 memorandum on the first folio of the manuscript), the Crabhouse women are still defending themselves from potential threats, and even Joan can be seen as re-enacting the nameless *pucelle*'s role as

---

[21] Charters for Castle Acre Priory identify a Leva, daughter of Godric of Lynn, granted a hermitage south of Wiggenhall by William of Lesewis (see W. Dugdale, *Monasticon Anglicanum ...*, ed. J. Caley, H. Ellis and B. Bandinel, new edn, 6 vols. (London, 1830), 5, p. 69, item iv and p. 70, item v; (*Leva* is incorrectly transcribed as *Lena*). For discussion of the identification, see Thompson, *Women Religious*, p. 25; Oliva, *Convent and Community*, p. 25, and Gilchrist and Oliva, *Religious Women in East Anglia*, p. 77. The recluse Joanna, named in Castle Acre's charters as Johannes (Dugdale V, p. 69, item i), is the first of a number of anchorites associated with Crabhouse from the twelfth through to the fifteenth centuries (Gilchrist and Oliva, *Religious Women in East Anglia*, pp. 77, 99).

[22] Fol. 3v.

[23] Fol. 52v.

ounder and builder of her community of sisters. It is the nuns' narrative of foun-
lation that allows for this flexibility in the Crabhouse manuscript. Because they
ramed their beginning as a 'semi-fabulous story' of romantic exile,[24] the women
re able to claim varying degrees of difference or identity with the world they
rofessed to escape – whether that world manifests itself in language, natural
henomena or property holdings; meanwhile, their community maintains a
ense of integrity throughout its transformations by way of its founder's claim to
gency – that agency taken up and re-enacted either by the nuns as a collective or
y their individual prioresses, both named and unnamed.

Consequently, rather than thinking of this manuscript as chaotic, a jumble of
lisconnected languages, forms and events, a more productive perspective might
e to think of it as circuitous and accretive, an alternative model of communal
nemory. When Augustus Jessopp wrote his version of the Crabhouse history in
886, he followed a particular model of history that might be called the 'dead
ody' model, a history in which the past is conceived of as a succession of dead
odies laid end to end: Harold of England's dead body followed by William's
lead body, followed by William the Second and so forth. In the first pages of
essopp's history of Crabhouse, Jessopp describes the deaths of the Crabhouse
uns ten times. In a corresponding period of time (that covered in the foundation
egend), the manuscript mentions death only once, noting the uncertain fate of
he unnamed *reclus* while stressing the survival of the nunnery's muniments that
he preserved. Moreover, death in relation to the nuns is only directly mentioned
ne other time in the entire Crabhouse manuscript. In the same way that the
nanuscript declines to comment on changes of language and form, moving
rom poetry to prose, from legend to land record, from English to Latin to French
vithout anxiety and only the barest of mentions in the case of the shift from verse
o prose at the manuscript's beginning, the manuscript also declines comment
n the passing of its prioresses.[25] Languages run into each other over the course
f three centuries just as one prioress after another steps into the shoes of the
unnery's nameless founder, creating an identity for Crabhouse as one timeless,
iving body.

Jessopp wrote his history in 1886, and while critiqueing nineteenth-century
istorians may be a popular and convenient pastime, I suggest that both the dead
ody and living body models of memory have always been with us. In fact in
885, just one year before Jessopp wrote his history of Crabhouse with its atten-
ion to chronology and succession, another author offered a different model of
enerational identity. In an under-studied sonnet sequence by the poet Augusta
Vebster titled *Mother and Daughter*, sonnet seventeen describes the relationship

---

4 Bateson, *Register*, p. 5.
5 Although it may be objected that kalendar *obits* and mortuary rolls (not extant for
Crabhouse) rather than registers and cartularies are the particular genres for such
comment, the Crabhouse history nonetheless remains strikingly unconcerned with the
proprietorship of relics and dead bodies.

between parent and child as symbiotic.[26] Rather than the violent Freudian model in which parent spawns child who then grows up to crowd out and replace the parent, Webster offers a model of history in which the parent is perceived as the roots of an organism and the child as that organism's seasonal growth. The roots give life to the new growth, but that new growth, in turn, keeps the roots alive – a model of history that allows for continuity and transformation simultaneously. This model is very obviously apparent in the Middle Ages in the iconography of family trees, as well as less obviously so in the cyclical nunnery calendars that Jocelyn Wogan-Browne describes as 'more important than the linear chronology of historical time' for creating communal identities in which dead and living co-existed in mutually beneficial ways.[27] The Crabhouse manuscript, I believe, asks us to think about languages in the Middle Ages in a symbiotic rather than sequential or hierarchical sense as well: Latin was kept alive by the languages it gave birth to, and as Nicholas Watson notes in his essay for *The Idea of the Vernacular*, it was native English speakers who preserved the prestige of French in medieval England.[28] Parents do not always banish their children. Children do not always turn on their parents. Sometimes the family simply adds on to the existing house.

[26] A. Webster, *Mother and Daughter, an Uncompleted Sonnet-Sequence* (London, 1895), p. 31.
[27] J. Wogan-Browne, 'Dead to the World? Death and the Maiden Revisited in Medieval Women's Convent Culture', in *Guidance for Women in Twelfth-Century Convents*, trans V. P. Morton (Cambridge, 2003), pp. 157–80 (p. 169).
[28] N. Watson, 'The Politics of Middle English Writing', in *The Idea of the Vernacular*, ed. Wogan-Browne et al., pp. 331–52 (p. 332).

Table 26.1: The Crabhouse Manuscript contents and description

Folio #	Language	Description	Date
i	English	Fee paid to vicar of M. Mag. for marriage in St Mary, Crabhouse.	1476
1r	Latin inc/ French	Verse preface to legend/cartulary. 'Here you will learn how Crabhouse began'. Addressed to all social classes.	1271–1328
1v–2v	French	Foundation legend. No specific names given of women – only *pucelles* and a *reclus*. Charters not in possession of Crabhouse, but frequent mention of their existence. Women lose their property 3 times: once to devil's *ministres*, once to flood and once to their chaplain and his wife who divide the property between the women and the canons of Reinham.	1271–1328
3r–15v	French	Descriptions of charters in Crabhouse possession begin (post-flood). 2 prioresses mentioned – Katerine (3v) and Cristiene (13r). Both described as elected by the women of the house. Crabhouse described as *curt* and *mesun*.	1271–1328
16r–17r	French	Rental	1271–1328
Two leaves cut after f. 17			
17r–18v	French	Space filled with various transactions in 5 different hands, at least one is identifiably later, so space has been filled in when history discontinued. Later hands refer to *priuresse* in records, earlier to *mesun*.	various
19r	French	Unique hand (Agnes de Methelwolde?). Record of gift made by 'our most important founder', Robert de Welle. Begins with 4 octosyllabic lines of verse in different hand. Addressed to *cheres sorurs* in 1st person plural.	1328
19v	French	1st person plural passage advising *cheres sorurs* to be wise with possessions in preparation for difficult times. Lists improvements made to their property under Agnes but does not mention her name. Begins with 2 lines of verse.	1328
20r	French and Latin	Space filled in with 3 items in 3 different hands. One in Latin which refers to *Priorissa de Crabbehous*, one refers to *cheres sorurs*.	various
20v–21v	French	Rental – no prioress named	1328–44
One leaf cut			
22r–28r	French	Rental of properties in time Agnes de Methelwolde was prioress (1315–44) during reign of Edward III. Various terms for Crabhouse: *curt, priuresse et covent, mesun, eglise, priuresse et les dames*.	1344–1420
29v	French	*la priuresse* (confused transcription in Bateson)	1344–1420
One or more leaves missing			
30r–31v	French	Land records stress regnal, nationalistic language, e.g. *Bretanye, Rey*.	1344–1420

32r–33v	Latin	Records in Latin (same hand as French in 22r+). Stress on regnal language in juxtaposition with *prioresa de Crabhus: comite Brittanie & ipse de Rege*.	1344–1420

One or more leaves missing

34r–35v	French	Back to *priuresse*. No mention of *convent*, *mesun*, *curt*, etc.	1344–1420

3 leaves cut after f. 34

36r–41r	Latin	Terrier for time that Joan of Wiggenhall was prioress. References to *prioress and convent*, *domus* predominate.	1420–70
42v–49r	Latin	Rental under Joan of Wiggenhall. References to *prioress and convent*, *Crabhouse*, some regnal language, but more often simply *prioress*.	1420–70
49v–50r		blank (possibly meant for decoration? Joan's works begin on verso with rubrication but no decoration).	
50v–53r	English	Account of the works performed during Prioress Joan of Wiggenhall's term *aftir the Resynacyon of Dame Mawde Talbot, Prioresse beforne hire*. All works are performed by *sche*, listed by year of *ocupacion*. Other women only mentioned as rescued from danger when Joan rebuilt their dortur and when one woman's negligence resulted in a fire that burnt down the hall. The work is all accomplished by Joan and her *frendes* – clerics named in the text (2 were her cousins). Her work responds to *mischeef* of buildings.	1444+
53v	English	Different hand. Tallies total costs of Joan's building projects. Joan described as *the queche regnyd xxiiii years & more*.	1444+
53v	English	Continues in previous hand (from 50v) with account of work performed by Stevyn Boole in 1469 *ix yere before the decees of dame Margery Daubeney, than prioresse of Crabhouse. Also in the time of Dame Awdre Wulmere the next prioresse* ...	1470+

3 leaves cut

Section IV
England and French in the late Fourteenth
and Fifteenth Centuries

INTRODUCTION

In the late fourteenth and fifteenth centuries, insular French texts become rarer in comparison with the continental French texts circulating in England, but copies of historiographical and other texts continue to be produced, and new prayers, hymns, psalters, letters, accounts, wills, petitions, and other documents and records continue to be composed. The Frenches of England remain as working languages in the different registers of various occupational communities and for particular social rituals. Beyond the fifteenth century, French is a much less substantial presence in England, though the idea of French continues to play a role in English understanding of insular cultural and linguistic history.[1]

Although this final section looks at areas and subjects in some cases familiar from Anglo-French literary studies, the co-presence of Section I above provides a context in which such areas can be seen among many Frenches of England, rather than as *the* French or the English tradition. The opening essay of Section IV, Tim Machan's study of late medieval linguistic repertoires, takes this linguistic perspective further, up to the early modern period. Machan analyses the diverging roles of insular and northern French in English's (largely unreciprocated) engagement with French in the late medieval period and England's developing involvement with the languages of its early modern colonies. His essay also serves to reminds us once again that the subsequent separations of French and English should not retrospectively shape our perception of the status of late medieval languages and their uses.

In this section the topics treated include the teaching of language in the medieval period and the multilingualism of lexis and composition in a range of text-types and literary traditions, and of patronage and manuscript artistry in late medieval English culture. These are aspects of a late fourteenth- and fifteenth-century society of diplomacy and war where cultural traffic and mutual awareness at both elite and other levels is intense, but they are also the consequence of the preceding and contemporary multilingualism of insular culture. Carolyn Collette looks at a shared political and ethical language developed around the same terms in both English and French in the late fourteenth and fifteenth centuries. Julia Boffey persuasively traces the presence of French in the background of a late medieval English text, offering an exemplary demonstration of multilingual thinking about texts. Ad Putter studies the multilingualism, especially the French and 'Frenchness', of late medieval love-letter poems in the records of the

---

[1] See the essay by Machan in this section, and D. Williams, *The French Fetish from Chaucer to Shakespeare* (Cambridge, 2004).

gentry Armburgh family and of a Norfolk abbot, and relates them both to literary tradition and to the sociolinguistics of late medieval letter-writing in England.

The final four essays of the volume exemplify the intricacies of manuscript creation and circulation in a period of high mobility and cultural interchange and the way in which full accounts of provenance and circulation tend to defy nationalizing categories.[2] Godfried Croenen's essay on the manuscript traditions of Froissart's *Chroniques* and of his poetry from the late fourteenth to the seventeenth century concludes that on the Continent Froissart was largely perceived as an English poet, although only his *Chroniques* (extant *inter alia* in at least one Anglo-Norman copy alongside a *Brut*) were successful there, his poetry being restricted to royal and elite circles. Martha Driver examines the *œuvre* of a scribe, Ricardus Francisus, and an illuminator, the Fastolf Master, and supplies an updated list of the large number of manuscripts on which they worked. Both men were probably French, but, in the light of their English patrons in France and their francophone patrons in England to say nothing of their own travels there themselves, their work has to be seen as extremely mobile and fluid in its localization. Andrew Taylor places one such similarly 'mobile' manuscript within the cross-cultural strategies of its patron, John Talbot, to offer new readings of the uses and significance of French in Talbot's career and of the luxurious book he presented to Margaret of Anjou, wife of Henry VI. Finally, Stephanie Downes reminds us of the circulation in French of Christine de Pizan in England by studying two major manuscripts and their uses there.

It will be evident that there are many more micro-histories and linguistic and cultural affiliations that could be considered, not only in this late medieval phase, but throughout the history of French in England, or better, of the Frenches of England. The indicative force of the studies gathered in this book and the cumulative tale they tell should, however, at least demonstrate that the main outlines of our linguistic and cultural accounts of medieval England require revision, and that there is much profitable and fascinating investigation to be done before we have multilingual histories of English culture and still more before we have them for medieval Britain.

---

2   The historiography of the Hundred Years' War is too large an area to enter into here, but it is worth noting that the role of the Hundred Years' War in various stories of nation is as contentious as that of the Conquest. While most contributors here see the War as tending to sustain a multilingual and multicultural state of affairs in England, it has been taken in some earlier historiography as a 'distraction from the proper process of defining and enhancing the insular nation state, so that, for instance, the loss of Gascony in 1453 takes on a curious role as a form of cultural-linguistic-nationalistic liberation for the English (we lost the war, but won our identity)' (M. Ormrod, pers comm.). See further e.g. M. Vale, *The Ancient Enemy: England, France and Europe from the Angevins to the Tudors 1154–1558* (London, 2007); Baker, *Inscribing the Hundred Years War*; A. Butterfield, 'Guerre et paix: l'anglais, le français et « l'anglo-français »', *Séance publique annuelle du 20 juin 2008, Comptes Rendus de l'Académie des Inscriptions et Belles-lettres*, 9 (2009) forthcoming.

27

French, English, and the Late Medieval Linguistic Repertoire

Tim William Machan

ʼe linguistic repertoire of late medieval England was complex, unstable, and
ʼcially charged. If the languages an individual used – Latin, French, English,
ʼ any of the indigenous Celtic languages – were in part functions of birth and
ʼbringing, their use in particular domains helped sustain the dynamics of
ʼciety. Like individual speech acts, moreover, languages had meaning in rela-
ʼn to one another. The meaning of French within England's repertoire, for
ʼample, evolved from not only its uses but also its status in relation to the
ʼher languages of the repertoire, individually as well as collectively. And like
ʼguistic history, language dynamics can raise some challenging questions.
ʼhat did French mean to Anglophones? What did English mean to Francoph-
ʼes? How did these meanings change over time? These are the kinds of ques-
ʼns I want to address here. Specifically, I want to examine how the meaning
ʼ French within the English linguistic repertoire changed from the end of the
ʼiddle Ages to the beginning of the early modern period. And to do so, in view
ʼ the fact that such issues are systemic, I want to consider not just the relations
ʼ French and English to one another but also each language's relations to other
ʼguages and traditions.

Sociolinguistic accounts of late medieval English have often focused on French
ʼd Latin and on the way English, in an old metaphor, 'triumphed' over them.
ʼell-established as this metaphor may be, it seems odd from at least the perspec-
ʼe of French, whose late medieval and early modern sociolinguistic history does
ʼt point to anything like an agonistic struggle with English. The events of this
ʼstory in fact concentrated more on continental linguistic and cultural concerns.
ʼie such concern is the role Latin in particular served as both a model and a
ʼeans for self-identification, for French as well as English. To modern histor-
ʼal linguists as well as early medieval speakers, for example, the 813 Council of
ʼurs in effect created French by identifying it as the spoken language and distin-
ʼishing it from Latin, the written language that was to be codified and whose
ʼonunciation was to remain constant and literal.[1] Translations of Latin classics,
ʼcluding Latin versions of Aristotle's works, were hallmarks of Charles V's
ʼmed fourteenth-century French translation program, while two centuries later,

---

G. Rohlfs, *From Vulgar Latin to Old French: An Introduction to the Study of the Old French
Language*, trans. V. Almazan and L. McCarthy (Detroit MI, 1970), p. 68.

in Joachim du Bellay's seminal statement on the excellence of French, Latin still served as a touchstone for his argument about the value of the French language. An apologia for French directed especially at Francophones who undervalued their native tongue, du Bellay's 1549 *Defence and Illustration of the French Language* begins with the supposition that all languages descend from a single, common source and proceeds to the assertion that when languages do differ from one another in quality and expressiveness – as Latin and Greek apparently do from French – the difference is due not to any intrinsic linguistic disparity between the languages but rather to the degree to which their speakers have cultivated them. If French has any faults, then, they are due to the failure of Francophones to promote and appreciate their own language.[2]

A second concern that helped shaped French sociolinguistic identity at the end of the Middle Ages was the functioning of France as a political entity in Western Europe. France may in fact have been particularly advanced in this regard, since already in the fourteenth century, in his *Politiques*, Nicholas Oresme associated a form of national identity with language.[3] More significantly for my purpose here, during this period French political concerns, like their linguistic counterparts, focused on the Continent. In the sixteenth century, conflicts between France and Italy in particular prevailed in discussions of both politics and language, with several commentators like the printer Henri Estienne, author of *La precellence du langage françois*, expressing concern over the 'corruption' of French by Italian, especially under the influence of Catherine de Medici at the French court. In this way Latin, and Italian in particular, offered a triangulation for French sociolinguistic identity,[4] though other nations could also provide a kind of awful warning of what France – and French – needed to avoid. Eustache Deschamps, for instance, may have praised Chaucer as a 'grant translateur', as wise as Socrates and poetically gifted as Ovid, but in advancing an almost jingoistic sense of the excellence of France and French, he could also disparage other languages and cultures with élan. Hungary, he says, is 'a hell on earth', while the essence of the Bohemian soul is 'lice, fleas, pigs, mold'.[5] Internally, such sentiments sustained the political unification of the region, most forcefully expressed, perhaps, in the thirteenth-century Albigensian crusade, which resulted in the incorporation of Toulouse into the French kingdom and the disruption and curtailment of Occitan culture. Linguistic and cultural consolidation were thus of a piece.

The third continental issue in late medieval French sociolinguistic identity that I want to consider is the gradual identification of French with northern

---

2   J. du Bellay, *The Defence and Illustration of the French Language*, trans. G. M. Turquet (London, 1939), p. 22.

3   S. Lusignan, *Parler vulgairement: les intellectuels et la langue française aux XIIIe et XIV siècles*, 2nd edn (Paris, 1987), pp. 108–10. On Oresme, see also the essay by Collette in this volume.

4   M. Huchon, *Le français de la Renaissance* (Paris, 1988), pp. 26–8; J. Chaurand, *Nouvelle histoire de la langue française* (Paris, 1999), p. 158.

5   E. Deschamps, *Selected Poems*, ed. I. S. Laurie and D. M. Sinnreich-Levi, trans. D. Curzon and J. Fiskin (New York, 2003), balades 1309 (pp. 188–9) and 1326 (pp. 194–5).

specifically Parisian, French. Comments on French regional variation persist throughout the Middle Ages and point to the kind of metalinguistic awareness that can produce just such an identification. Already in the late twelfth century, the Picard poet Conon de Béthune, in response to complaints about his non-Parisian accent, proudly declared that if his are the 'mos d'Artois', his language is nonetheless comprehensible; and just a few years later Aimon de Varennes, in his romance *Florimont*, uses 'langue de fransois' in a way that effectively equates French with the northern, Parisian variety. A century later another romance specified 'le françoise de Paris' as the variety used by the king and queen, and in 1325 the so-called Anonymous de Meung asked that his rough language be excused, as he was not born in Paris and this was the variety he had learned from his mother.[6]

Certainly, the late Middle Ages was a crucial moment in the movement towards a standardized variety of French, but, within the context of the solidification of political power in northern France,[7] comments like these and the political actions they underwrote point as much if not more towards legal, rather than simply linguistic, unification as the primary objective. This would seem true of historic attempts to suppress, contain, and even replace Occitan, and of several early modern documents that explicitly advance the centrality of Parisian France. And it would also seem true of edicts like that of Charles VIII, in 1490, that the 'dits et dépositions de témoins dans les cours de justice du Languedoc seront mis ou rédigés en langage françois ou maternel'.[8] Similar ordinances by Louis XII in 1510 and François I in 1535 use language to further these legislative concerns, culminating in François's 1539 Ordinance of Viller-Cotterêts, which expansively dictates that henceforth all legal and administrative actions should be rendered not in Latin but in northern French.[9]

From the thirteenth through to the sixteenth century, French sociolinguistic identity thus changed in two crucial ways. First, French in general came to replace Latin in many of the prestigious domains, though Latin certainly remained important in diplomacy and as the focus of much scholarly discussion. And second, northern French emerged as the pre-eminent variety of French, producing a new kind of diglossia in the spoken language, with Parisian French as the High variety and the various rural dialects as the Low ones. By the sixteenth century this urban/rural divide increased and became more socially loaded to the advantage of Parisian speakers, when grammarians took to identifying and stigmatizing pronunciations and forms like the use of plural verbs with singular subjects as low-class as well as rural.[10]

What is absent from my discussion so far, of course, is England and English.

---

6 R. A. Lodge, *French: From Dialect to Standard* (London, 1993), pp. 100–1.
7 Lusignan, *Parler vulgairement*, pp. 91–127.
8 Quoted in A. Judge, 'French: A Planned Language?', in *French Today: Language in Its Social Context*, ed. C. Sanders (Cambridge, 1993), p. 9.
9 Quoted in Lodge, *French: From Dialect to Standard*, p. 126.
10 Lodge, *French: From Dialect to Standard*, pp. 146–50.

Not only did Francophones not in fact scheme to replace English, as English chroniclers and politicians would claim; they seem to have given very little thought to English at all, beyond using the incompetence of Anglophones speaking French as the matter for insults and narrative twists in various fabliaux and romances.[11] Even so, as I noted at the outset, discussions of late medieval England's linguistic repertoire by literary and linguistic scholars alike often offer a narrative of contest and struggle. On the one side stand Latin and French and the various powerful domains they occupied and defined. On the other stands the humble and ambitious vernacular, English, whose speakers, whether through independent if coordinated action or as a manifestation of some kind of sociolinguistic drift, specifically targeted the roles of Latin and French within England's repertoire and thereby sought to replace these languages with English as an act of linguistic and social appropriation. In this way, the linguistic shifts of the early modern period become political as well as teleological, shifts in which a triumphant English or a vernacular that constructs resistance and identity serves as an active, purposeful agent almost irrespective of the institutions it mediates and constructs.

It is true enough that the history of English in this period mirrors the history of French in prominent and important ways. Just as in the French linguistic repertoire French came to subsume many of what had been Latin's domains, so did English in the English repertoire. Just as Parisian French, further, came to serve as, in effect, the High language in France, so did a southern variety of English centred in London eventually play that role in England, and in both cases an initial urban/rural distinction became infused with undertones of moral discrimination as well as correct usage. And just as the political emergence of France corresponded with the proliferation of grammars and testimonies to the excellence of French, so England's identity as a European and global power, with colonies, eventually, in North America, Africa and Asia, accompanied the cultivation of English grammars and rhetorics, which, like their French counterparts, could represent a standard language as a matter of national security and identity. According to the first sentence of Alexander Gill's Preface to his 1621 *Logonomia Anglica*, 'Gentis Anglicæ, & linguæ origo vna est: ea a Saxones, & Anglos, Germaniæ populos refertur'.[12] And it is also true that a discursive tradition focused on French and the aspirations of its speakers figured significantly in England's political self-representation at the end of the medieval period. Already in 1295, in a royal letter to the archbishop of Canterbury, Edward I stated in Latin that Philip IV of France 'proposes, if his power should prove equal to the horrid purpose of his wicked plan, to destroy completely the English tongue from the

---

11 See A. Butterfield, 'English, French and Anglo-French: Language and Nation in the Fabliau', Special Issue of *Zeitschrift für deutsche Philologie: Mittelalterliche Novellistik im europäischen Kontext*, ed. M. Chinca, T. Reuvekamp-Felber and C. Young (Berlin, 2006), pp. 238–59.

12 A. Gill, *Logonomia Anglica* (London, 1621; rpt Menston, 1968), no sig.

and'.[13] In the decades to come, as France came through the Hundred Years' War to play an even more significant role in English politics and self-definition, this claim that a French victory would lead to the demise of English became a kind of political rallying cry, repeated in Parliamentary addresses of 1340, 1344, 1346, and 1376.[14] Such warnings seem to smack of jingoism and opportunism more than any genuine anxiety, for even as some Anglophones used the putative death of English to motivate political action, Froissart suggests that others continued to cultivate French in the hope, perhaps, of achieving victory in France and legitimating their and their king's continental ambitions.[15] It was a bit of jingoism echoed even in popular forums, however. Robert Holcot voiced a common claim when he said that William the Conqueror had hoped to unify the Normans and Anglo-Saxons with the French language, while in Robert of Gloucester's well-known assessment of England's fourteenth-century linguistic repertoire, French and English co-exist as essentially sociolects, the former spoken by the 'heieman of þis lond' and the latter by 'lowe men'.[16]

But if such concerns encourage the perception of language shift in late medieval England as a kind of purposeful, agonistic struggle between English and French or Latin, additional local evidence – as well as the general context of untargeted change – suggests otherwise. Here, I want to concentrate on what the study of the French language in England suggests about the status of that language and its meaning in England's sociolinguistic history. Following on the increased immigration and influence of Francophones in English politics from the reign of Henry III, a work like Walter of Bibbesworth's *Traitié*, with its emphasis on the functional vocabulary of aristocratic life, provides clear testimony of the fact that though French was diminishing as a birth language, it retained its social desirability. An active fourteenth-century tradition of French grammars testifies to this same effect,[17] as does the increasing recognition, by both medieval speakers and modern scholars, that late medieval Anglo-French had developed its own grammatical and discursive rules that defined it less as simply a corruption of continental French, as was once frequently argued, and more as a distinctive variety.[18]

[13] Quoted in W. Stubbs, ed., *Select Charters and Other Illustrations of English Constitutional History from the Earliest Times to the Reign of Edward the First*, 9th edn, ed. H. W. C. Davis (Oxford, 1913), p. 480.

[14] J. Fisher, *The Emergence of Standard English* (Lexington KY, 1996), pp. 45 and 160–1.

[15] J. Chaurand, *Nouvelle histoire de la langue Française* (Paris, 1999), p. 114.

[16] M. Richter, *Sprache und Gesellschaft im Mittelalter: Untersuchungen zur Mündlichen Kommunikation in England von der Mitte des Elften bis zum Beginn des Vierzehnten Jahrhunderts* (Stuttgart, 1979), pp. 36–8; Robert of Gloucester, *The Metrical Chronicle*, ed. W. A. Wright, RS 86 (London, 1887), lines 7538–47.

[17] K. Lambley, *The Teaching and Cultivation of the French Language in England during Tudor and Stuart Times* (Manchester, 1920), pp. 3–25.

[18] William Rothwell has been perhaps the most forceful advocate for the integrity of Anglo-French. See, for example, his 'A quelle époque a-t-on cessé de parler français en Angleterre?', in *Mélanges de philologie romane offerts à Charles Camproux*, ed. R. Lafont

The point I wish to emphasize is that as Anglo-French diverged from northern French, the two varieties assumed different roles in England's linguistic reper toire. The native variety may have been what people spoke, but the continenta variety was the one to which they aspired. Perhaps in this one area more preco cious than France itself, English grammars of the fourteenth and fifteenth centu ries consistently describe northern French, and sometimes 'la droite langage de Paris', as the sweet variety that they taught. The explicit focus of the 1396 *Manière de langage* is thus 'douce francés, qu'est la plus beale et la plus gracious langage et la plus noble parlere aprés latyn de scole que soit en monde et de toutz gentz melx preysé et amee que nulle autre'.[19]

Perhaps a decade later, John Barton prefaces his French grammar by noting that he was an 'escolier de Paris, nee et nourie toutez voiez d'Engleterre en la conté de Cestre, j'ey baillé aus avant diz Anglis un Donait françois pur les brief ment entreduyr en la droit language du Paris et de païs la d'entour, la quelle langage en Engleterre on appelle "doulce France"'.[20] Further, a work like the *Manière*, which appeared in three versions by 1415, initiated a new kind of French textbook. Rather than a detailed grammar or a list of words useful for domestic aristocratic life, like Bibbesworth's *Traitié*, the *Manière* offered model puta tive conversations for travellers and merchants working in France. Much like a modern Berlitz book, such models were meant to provide Anglophones with shortcuts to the kinds of experiences they might encounter, though the dialogues can seem as much cultivated whimsy as ordinary conversation, and in any case 'ordinary' (as always) is open to definition. The 1399 *Manière* includes a list of useful insults, while one of its models illustrates a conversation about the deposi tion of Richard II and crowning of Henry IV – which would seem to be a conver sation with a limited life-cycle.[21]

This conversational model became increasingly popular during the later Middle Ages; always a measure of market tastes, Caxton's publications include another such volume, the 1483 *Dialogues in French and English*. This same prag matic emphasis on model conversations appears again in grammars prepared for the kind of aristocratic audience for whom in earlier generations French might well have been regarded as a native, or at least nearly native, language. Thus

---

et al., 2 vols. (Montpellier, 1978), 2, pp. 1075–89. See also the essays by Ingham and Kunstmann in this volume.

[19] ('sweet French, which in all the world is the most beautiful and most graceful language, and the most noble speech after school Latin, and more than any other language valued and loved by all people'): *Manières de langage*, ed. A. M. Kristol, ANTS 53 (London, 1995), p. 3.

[20] ('Scholar of Paris, born and bred in all English manners in the county of Chester; I have presented to the foresaid English a French Donat as a brief introduction to the correct language of Paris and its environs, the which language is called sweet French in England'): T. Städtler, ed., *Zu den Anfängen der französischen Grammatiksprache: Textausgaben und Wortschatzsdudien* (Tübingen, 1988), p. 128. On Barton, see also the essays by Merrilees and Pagan and by Putter in this volume.

[21] *Manières de Langage*, ed. Kristol, pp. 54–5, 65–6.

Giles Duwes's *An Introductory for to Learn to Read, To Pronounce, and to Speak French*, which appeared in four editions before 1550 and which is dedicated to Henry VIII's daughter Mary, begins with a brief grammar after which follows a series of dialogues illustrating the reception of a messenger, discussions of food, love, war, and peace, and philosophical consideration of the human soul. Duwes's *Introductory* has additional relevance to the status of French in sixteenth-century England. A tutor at the Court of Henry VIII, Duwes was also a native of France, and in justifying his grammar he makes much of nationality as a grammarian's primary qualification: 'shulde it nat seme a thynge selde and strange / to se a frenchman endeuoir and inforce himself to teche vnto the Germayns the langage of Almaine ... for touchyng my self to whom the sayd tonge is maternall or naturelle'.[22] In this justification, he was responding to his fellow court tutor John Palsgrave, a London native who in 1530 had published a massive *Lesclarcissement de la langue Francoyse*, which devotes its thousand-plus pages to French grammar, especially pronunciation. At least in part, the exchange between Duwes and Palsgrave reflects a conflict between native speakers, who regard the language as perforce their own, and self-acknowledged second-language learners, who assert their ability to acquire native fluency but whose very existence affirms the non-native status of French. Yet it was a smaller, simpler kind of grammar book – in comparison to those of Duwes and Palsgrave – that came to define the genre in the early modern period. These volumes were aimed not at the court but at a wider audience of merchants and travellers, with their own pragmatic needs. And the genre reflected a thriving business: altogether the fifteenth century witnessed fifty-two printed manuals for teaching French to Anglophones and the sixteenth 139 – a total of 191 printed manuals in a two hundred-year period.[23]

Dynamics like this, alongside the emphasis of much late medieval English grammatical discussion of French, have implications for the changed status of French within England's linguistic repertoire. They do indeed suggest that speakers recognized a distinction between what they heard in England and what they identified as French, the focus of instruction. It was not Anglo-French but northern French, the language of 'doulce France' and a distinct non-indigenous language, that these speakers sought to learn. Already in the *Manière de langage*, this identification of French with France is made clear in the claim that the work will teach its readers to 'bien adroit parler et escrire doulz franceoys selon l'usage et la coustume de France'. As Serge Lusignan has noted, there is a striking contrast here with Bibbesworth's *Traitié*, for French is by definition

---

[22] G. Duwes, *An Introductory for to Learn to Read, to Pronounce, and to Speake French Trewely* (London, *c*.1532; rpt Menston, 1972), sig. Aiii[r].

[23] Lambley, *The Teaching and Cultivation of the French Language*, pp. 123–4, 405–9; several of these volumes, it should be noted, are actually reprints of earlier publications. On early French grammars more generally, see J.-C. Chevalier, *Histoire de la grammaire française* (Paris, 1994), pp. 13–28.

now no longer a vernacular of England.[24] Further acknowledgment of the non-
indigenous status of French comes in the identity of the Anglophones who
learned it. Both the proliferation of schools teaching French in sixteenth- and
seventeenth-century England, and the fact that French tutors remained common
features of English aristocratic households throughout this period, underscore
the decline of native speakers and also, therefore, of the language's new identity
within England's linguistic repertoire.[25] The increasing numbers of speakers who
sought to learn French not merely for cultural refinement but to conduct business
or travel in another nation likewise identifies the location of its primary utility
as abroad. And the foreignness of French in early modern England is also underscored by the early modern increase of unassimilated French loans, that is, of
loans that were not phonologically or morphologically reanalyzed in accordance
with English grammar.[26]

Earlier, I noted that Francophones do not seem to have dwelt on English and
its place – if any – in the French linguistic repertoire. The same is obviously not
true for Anglophones, who continued to invest French with sociolinguistic significance into the early modern period. Put simply, late medieval and early modern
England needed to account for French, sociolinguistically as well as politically,
in ways that France never needed to account for English. But just as important
as this persistence of French in the English linguistic repertoire is the fact that
the language's significance changed markedly through the course of the Middle
Ages. What to Edward I was a symbol of French perfidy and expansion, and what
could therefore itself be, in effect, a weapon as potent as pickaxe or mace, became,
as French was increasingly defined a foreign language, the mark of upstarts,
buffoons, and rapscallions. And this definition was projected onto earlier forms
of the language as well as its present form. In John Skelton's *Speke Parott*, the
bird does speak 'Dowche Frenshe of Paris', and in his *Logonomia* Gil once again
rehearses the legend of William the Conqueror's failed attempt to replace English
with French.[27] But already in Trevisa's translation of Higden's *Polychronicon*,
French serves as a proverbial way for the non-courtly and non-noble to mask
their origins and presume another social status. According to Caxton's 1482
print, 'vplondyssh men will counterfete and likene hem self to gentilmen and
arn besy so speke frensshe, for to be more sette by. Wherfor it is sayd by a comyn
prouerbe Jack wold be a gentilman if he coude speke frensshe'.[28] In his 1553 *Art of*

---

24 ('to speak and to write properly sweet French according to the practice of France'):
    Manières de langage, ed. Kristol, p. 81; this is a variant reading. Lusignan, *Parler vulgaire-
    ment*, pp. 101–2.
25 Lambley, *Teaching and Cultivation of the French Language*, pp. 114–54.
26 T. Nevalainen, 'Lexis and Semantics', in *The Cambridge History of the English Language*,
    vol. III: *1476–1776*, ed. R. Lass (Cambridge, 1999), p. 368.
27 J. Skelton, 'Speke Parott', l. 29 in *The Complete English Poems*, ed. J. Scattergood (New
    Haven CT, 1983); Gil, *Logonomia Anglica*, sig. B1r.
28 Trevisa, *Prolicionycion* [sic] (Westminster: Caxton, 1482), fol. lxvii v. There is consider-
    able incidental lexical variation in the transmission of this passage, and the proverb's
    inclusion seems to have originated with Caxton. See Trevisa, *Polychronicon Ranulphi*

hetorique, Thomas Wilson reverses the established complaint tradition of Anglo-
hones speaking French badly by describing the absence of both linguistic ability
nd self-awareness among visiting Francophones: 'He that cometh lately out of
rance, wil talke French English, & neuer blush at the matter.'[29] Far more expan-
ve are the comments of William Harrison who, in his 1587 additions about
ritain to Holinshed's *Chronicles*, brought together the earlier tradition of French
nguistic perfidy with later traditions of social climbing through French, and in
ffect rewrote not just the present of French in England but its past as well. In
'illiam the Conqueror's court, Harrison suggests, English

> grew into such contempt, that most men thought it no small dishonor to
> speake any English there. Which brauerie tooke his hold at the last likewise
> in the countrie with euerie plowman, that euen the verie carters began to wax
> wearie of there mother toong, & laboured to speake French, which as then was
> counted no small token of gentilitie. And no maruell, for euerie French rascall,
> when he came once hither, was taken for a gentleman, onelie bicause he was
> proud, and could vse his own language, and all this (I say) to exile the English
> and British speaches quite out of the countrie.[30]

From this identification of French with conniving nobles, upstart ploughmen,
nd con-artist immigrant rascals, it seems a small step of trivialization to the
irgely light-hearted whimsy at Katherine's expense in her French lesson in
enry V: 'De foot et de count! O Seigneur Dieu! Ils sont les mots de son mauvais,
orruptible, gros, et impudique, et non pour les dames d'honneur d'user: je ne
oudrai pronouncer ces mots devant les signeurs de France pour tout le monde.'[31]
lere, French neither symbolizes international treachery nor announces social
:heming and moral failure. In league with the parodied Welsh and Irish accents
f Fluellen and Macmorris in the same play, French has become a stage joke, only
ither more so than the Celtic examples. This joke turns not simply on Katherine's
mited command of English but also on the absurdity of French as a language
i which words as innocent as *foot* and *count* might be obscene, and on the irony
iat there might be anything racy enough to make a French nobleman blush.

Even as the role of French in England's linguistic repertoire shifted, then, the
inguage's sociolinguistic status increasingly became ameliorated or even seman-
cally bleached. Not the language of a conqueror, nor the language of social
resumption, nor even an English language at all, French had become, by the
eventeenth century, both a stage diversion and an international language, and
a neither case a language with a clear and significant role in England's linguistic

*Higden Monachi Cestrensis together with the English Translations of John Trevisa and an
Unknown Writer of the Fifteenth Century*, ed. C. Babington and J. R. Lumby, RS 41, 9 vols.
(London, 1865–86), 2, pp. 159 and 161.
Wilson, *The arte of rhetorique for the vse of all suche as are studious of eloquence, sette forth
in English* (London, 1553), fol. 86r.
R. Holinshed, *The First and Second Volumes of Chronicles* (London, 1587), pp. 13–14.
III.iv.48–52.

repertoire. But to return to a point I raised earlier, I would argue that this shi**
took place not because of a simple concerted struggle between English and Lati**
and French, or because these languages had, or were, something specific tha**
English wanted; if French were to serve as a model for English, it would nc**
have been presented as the language of fools and con-artists. The relative statu**
of French and English changed, rather, because of a more general reconfigura**
tion of the repertoire of English and England that was driven by the kinds c**
broadly based issues – ongoing and evolving responses to social pressures an**
other languages – that drive all such reconfigurations. For English and Englanc**
the expansion of markets, the growth of printing and literacy, political centraliza**
tion, the spread of schools, colonial aspirations, and nationalistic consolidatio**
all helped propel codification and standardization in ways that rendered Frencl**
largely irrelevant. When critics like Richard Mulcaster articulated beliefs in th**
intrinsic quality of English as a means of cultural identification, describing th**
contemporary version of the language 'to be the verie height thereof' and Englis**
as 'a tung of account' in 'matters of learning in anie kind' as well as in 'matter**
of war, whether ciuill or foren',[32] they effected not a replacement of French o**
Latin but a reidentification of a linguistic repertoire. While Latin, as the languag**
of humanism and university life, may have remained in this repertoire into th**
seventeenth and eighteenth centuries, of far greater account than French wer**
the languages that came into contact with English through colonial and busi**
ness activities: in England, Irish, Welsh, and Gaelic; in North America, Spanisl**
German, Swedish, and various African and Native American languages; in th**
South Pacific Maori, Hawaiian, and Aboriginal languages; and in Asia, Hind**
Punjabi, and Cantonese. And by extension, this same new linguistic repertoir**
came to include new varieties of English from North America, Africa, Australie**
and so forth. As English moved from the Middle Ages, through the early moder**
period, to the modern one, this reconfigured repertoire not only defined th**
language's changing status but determined the character of many of the sociolir**
guistic issues it embodied.

Through these kinds of contact, the ecology of English changed in two impo**
tant ways. First, it reflected a linguistic repertoire in which English no longe**
served as a Low language to the High languages of Latin and French. Englis**
itself, rather, came to be the dominant colonial language whose sociolinguisti**
identity depended, in part, on the subordination of indigenous African, Nort**
American, Asian, and Polynesian languages. And second, the ecology of Englis**
changed to include the systematic stratification of varieties of English, all arraye**
downwards from the increasingly codified standard. In this kind of ecolog**
English did not so much triumph over Latin or French as cease to compet**
against them in what had always been very much a struggle of its own inventio**

---

[32] R. Mulcaster, *The First Part of the Elementarie which entreateth chefelie of the right writin**
of our English tung (London, 1582; rpt Menston, 1970), pp. 159, 80–1.

28

Aristotle, Translation and the Mean: Shaping the Vernacular in Late Medieval Anglo-French Culture

Carolyn Collette*

One of the defining characteristics of late medieval Anglo-French court culture on both sides of the Channel is its attention to the importance of the mean expressed as interest in mediation and moderation in vernacular literature, chronicles, and governance texts. This culture did not invent intercession, a long-standing social and political practice in medieval Europe, but it valorized intercession as essential to good governance and, in developing the lexis of the mean and mediation, placed intercession within a newly widened network of terms and thought.[1] Late medieval Anglo-French ideas of the mean drew inspiration from a variety of sources, particularly from a renewed interest in classical philosophy. The choice of the vernacular for ideas that might earlier have fallen within the purview of Latin, the traditional language of governance and philosophy, marks a major shift. In both English and French, exposition of sociopolitical ideas was explicitly part of an ongoing discussion about the role of vernaculars in *translatio studii* – in disseminating valuable learning more widely than Latin could – and, by implication, in *translatio imperii*, a claim to inherit the cultural imperium associated with Rome and Latin.[2] Within these twin contexts

---

* I am grateful to Vincent DiMarco, Robert Edwards, Sara Maddox, Craig Taylor, and Jocelyn Wogan-Browne who read earlier drafts of this essay and offered helpful suggestions and advice.

1 See J. Krynen, *Idéal du prince et pouvoir royal en France à la fin du Moyen Age (1380–1440): étude de la littérature politique du temps* (Paris, 1981).

2 Anglo-French interest in the mean emerges during this period in large part from secular interest in Aristotle's writings on politics and ethics which, from the thirteenth century, gave rise to a plethora of handbooks for princes and nobles on how to achieve good governance of self, household, and polity. Charles V's and Charles VI's courts in France and Richard II's court in England were strongly influenced by the Neapolitan court culture of the Angevin dynasty at the beginning of the fourteenth century, a culture in which Robert of Naples' interest in Aristotle set a model for enlightened monarchy. For Aristotle's influence in England, see G. Mathew, *The Court of Richard II* (London, 1968), pp. 1–3, 6–9. See, too, S. Kelly, *The New Solomon: Robert of Naples (1309–1343) and Fourteenth-Century Kingship* (Leiden, 2003) on Robert of Naples' style of rule, strongly dependent on Giles of Rome's *De regimine principum*, and both Aristotle's *Ethiques* and *Politiques*.

of Anglo-French interest in translation and the existence of a shared vernacular discourse of the mean, this essay limns the outlines of an argument about how French and English translators self-consciously adapt and make vernacular Aristotelian ideas for contemporary audiences.

Vernacular: the changeable language

The master narrative of the history of English identifies the end of the fourteenth century as the time when the vernacular begins to express social, religious and political thought in a new public register. But by suggesting this is an isolated, national phenomenon, this narrative ignores the fact that linguistic confidence in England emerges in tandem with confidence in the vernacular particularly in France. Over the late fourteenth and fifteenth centuries, both languages simultaneously enlarge their vernacular lexicons of political and ethical discourse and they also theorize this development in remarkably similar terms.

To a great extent English expanded its abstract political vernacular by anglicizing French terms, as it had done for over a century. David Crystal estimates that of the 27,000 words that enter the English vocabulary between 1250 and 1450 22 per cent, or approximately 5,940, were words of French origin, and that over three quarters of these were nouns. The peak period of borrowing 'was the last quarter of the fourteenth century, when over 2,500 French words are identified'.[3] Although modern linguists often focus on this apparently intense appropriation, it seems to have gone unremarked by either English or French writers at the time.[4] But no less a medieval theorist of language than Dante in his *De vulgari eloquentia* shows that what is now marked as inter-linguistic borrowing could well be understood as a normal function of vernaculars, which were inherently unstable because they were responsive to changing circumstances, constantly adding and dropping vocabulary. For Dante, vernacular languages are not so much distinct in relation to one another as in their common difference from formal languages: they are constantly changing, while *grammatica*, the category of formal languages, is stable across geography and through time. While Dante's particular arguments about the vernacular may not have been directly known to Anglo-French court writers, his larger purpose, to call attention to the capacity

---

3   D. Crystal, *The Stories of English* (Woodstock, 2004), p. 155.
4   What is remarkable about the degree of borrowing of French abstractions into later medieval English is that none of them seems to be regarded as French, per se. A complete lack of self-conscious borrowing suggests the two languages were more nearly one than two even in the later fourteenth century. When Chaucer says the Prioress spoke French of Stratford atte Bowe, he acknowledges the existence of an indigenous form of the language in England. See W. Rothwell, 'Stratford atte Bowe and Paris', *MLR* 80 (1985), 39–54. The absence of comment stands in sharp contrast to well-known sixteenth-century anxiety about Latinate 'inkhorn' terms and their effect on English.

ıd potential of the vernacular, was widely echoed in vernacular texts well
ɔyond Italy.[5]

Because English borrowed vocabulary so intensely from French during the
ıtter Middle Ages, it can be tempting to see English as a lesser lexical partner.
ut such a perspective occludes the more important processes at work in the
ɔnstitution of vernacular as a language of politics on both sides of the Channel.
ırt of a broader European assertion of the importance and utility of the
ıother tongue, described by Dante as a language of change and growth, the
vo northern vernaculars present parallel internal developments of vocabulary
ıd of vernacular theory that encourage one to view their evolution during this
ɔriod as linked instances of the growing importance of the vernacular rather
ıan as examples of separate or separating languages.[6] The ultimate linguistic
ıstinction of late medieval England is not English from French, so much as an
ıignment of English with French as vernaculars that stand in opposition to Latin.

Late medieval English and French demonstrate change characteristic of
ɔrnaculars in the ways they expand their lexicons of political abstractions to
ɰpress the value of the mean. Both English and French create neologisms and
ıey both broaden the semantic range of words. The key terms that came to form
ıe discourse of the mean in both include *mene/moien* itself, as well as *governance,*
ʾudence, (at)temperaunce, reconciliation and *mediator.* All either made their first
ıtry or radically changed their existing profile in both English and French in the
ıte fourteenth century. Some of these terms had earlier careers: Anglo-Norman
ɰne and *prudence,* for example, are testified to in the thirteenth century. So, too,
ith earlier English borrowings from French: terms like *mediator* and *reconcile,*
ɪhich had been common in the religious discourse of Middle English developed
ırther meanings. *Mediator,* signifying an intermediary between God and man,
ɔuld now also signify, 'one who intervenes between two parties' particularly
ɪ 'effect reconciliation; an intercessor'. The verb *reconcilen* appears in late four-
ɪenth-century English signifying restoration of harmony and accord within the
ɪcular world, as well as a restoration of God's grace to humankind. This latter
ɔnnotation supplements the Anglo-Norman *reconciliacioun,* reunion of a person
ith the Church. The late Middle English verb appears to be a 're-borrowing'
ɔm later French, an example of a crossover from religious to secular discourse.
ı France *prudence* and *(ac)temperaunce,* previously reserved for moral treatises

---

Dante Aligheri, *De vulgari eloquentia,* ed. and trans. S. Botterill (Cambridge, 1996), pp.
21–3. Evidence for how well known this text was is not clear; three manuscripts exist,
and a printed edition of 1577. It is thought to have been written between 1302 and
1305.

Borrowings into a language occur either by appropriation or imposition; those words
appropriated tend to retain their original markers of pronunciation through their
spelling, remaining clear borrowings rather than naturalized forms whose spelling
reveals their absorption into what is termed the 'host' language. See M. Townend,
'Contacts and Conflicts: Latin, Norse, and French', in *The Oxford History of English,* ed.
L. Mugglestone (Oxford, 2006), pp. 61–85, esp. pp. 69–74.

or works on statecraft, develop new connotations,[7] particularly in Christine d
Pizan's extensive exposition of the topic of mediation and the role of the noble
woman as *moyeneresse* in *Le livre des trois vertus*, a text that employs the term
prudence, temperance, and *governaunce* to discuss strategies for managing both
household and polity.[8] In both English and French, *tempren*, and *temprer*, roc
forms for the nominalization *temperaunce*, develop a new connotation of resist
ance in the late fourteenth century.[9] Development of these terms as individua
words, and their interlocking and mutual association as a lexical set or colloca
tion, now occurs for the first time, so that it is only from this period that they ca
be said to become constituent elements of the discourse of the mean.[10]

French: a *language* noble and commun au gens de bonne prudence

In France, development of the political lexicon was a direct consequence c
Charles V's translation program.[11] He commissioned a spectrum of works t
support his project of providing his nobility with linguistically accessible poli
ical knowledge that would make them better men and better lords. One of th
chief theoreticians of Charles's program was Nicole Oresme, whose translation
of and commentaries on Aristotle's *Ethiques* and *Politiques* in the early 1370s offe
some of the earliest discussions of the meta-concept of the mean and its ke
terms *prudence* and *temperance*.[12] Oresme supports his larger project of expandin;

---

7   For the semantic shifts and lexical developments cited here, see OED, MED, ANI
     s.v. On the transformation and virtual re-gendering of the term *prudence* from a mal
     virtue associated with statecraft to a virtue of social action and social relationships, se
     J. D. Burnley, *Chaucer's Language and the Philosopher's Tradition* (Haverhill, 1979), pp
     51–7.
8   See further K. L. Forhan, *The Political Theory of Christine de Pizan* (Aldershot, 2002).
9   See C. C. Willard, 'Christine de Pizan's "Clock of Temperance"', *Esprit Créature*
     (1962), 148–54.
10   On the structure of collocations, see D. Burnley, 'Lexis and Semantics', in *The Cambridg*
     History of the English Language, vol. II: *1066–1476*, ed. N. Blake (Cambridge, 1992), pp
     409–99: 'Collocation, too, often reflects not contiguity of meaning, but reference t
     features of frequent situations of use or aspects of the user's world picture' (p. 451).
11   Charles V is known to have commissioned at least thirty translations of classical an
     medieval works as part of his project to create a royal library. For a discussion of th
     translations and translators, see F. Autrand, *Charles V: le sage* (Paris, 1994), pp. 728–3
12   Oresme, born in 1323, studied at the University of Paris where he was taught b
     Jean Buridan. He met Charles V when he was dauphin, and became his counselc
     and adviser when Charles became king. Charles appointed him tutor to his own so
     who would become Charles VI. In addition to holding several ecclesiastical office
     (including dean of the Cathedral of Rouen and bishop of Lisieux), he was a learne
     mathematician, philosopher, and translator who wrote on topics as varied as natura
     magic, judicial astrology, and the nature of money supplies.

the capacity of the vernacular to express complex political ideas by specifically providing glossaries of new and strange political terms in his translations.

Near the end of his *Proheme* to his translation of Aristotle's *Ethiques*, Oresme turns to the subject of translating Aristotle into French. He maintains that the French language, authorized by the king *pour le bien commun*, becomes the means through which previously inaccessible knowledge of the past becomes part of the common knowledge of the kingdom, the means through which French enters the larger discourse of human history:

> Mais pour ce que les livres morals de Aristote furent faiz en grec, et nous les avons en latin moult fort a entendre, le Roy a voulu, pour le bien commun, faire les translater en françois, afin que il et ses conseilliers et autres les puissent mieulx entendre, mesmement *Ethiques* et *Politiques*, desquels, comme dit est, le premier aprent estre bon homme et l'autre estre bon prince.
>
> (*Ethiques*, pp. 99–100)[13]

In the following *Excusacion et commendacion de ceste oeuvre*, Oresme considers how translation inevitably highlights the variability of individual languages. He notes the slippage between the original Greek lexicon and subsequent Latin translations of Aristotle, 'il appert par ce que encore y sont pluseurs moz grecs qui ne ont pas moz qui leur soient correspondens en latin' ('by this it seems that there are still more Greek words which do not have Latin equivalents', *Ethiques*, p. 100); similarly, he notes the slippage that occurs between Latin and French, and in so doing places French on a par with the great classical languages even as he concedes that French lacks Latin's extensive political vocabulary: 'latin est a present plus parfait et plus habondant langage que françois, par plus forte raison l'en ne pourroit translater proprement tout latin en françois' ('Latin is at present a more perfect and rich language than French, for this compelling reason it is not possible properly to translate all Latin into French', *Ethiques*, p. 100). But French, he asserts, is a language 'noble et commun à gens de grant engin et de bonne prudence' ('noble and shared by people of great intelligence and wise prudence', *Ethiques*, p. 101) sufficient to fill the lacunae translation creates; he recognizes it is necessary to use and develop a new French for the translations because even if the new terms 'ne sont pas communelment entendus ne cogneüs de chascun' ('are not commonly heard nor known by everyone', *Ethiques*, p. 100), French readers will welcome a revitalized French lexicon. As Greek was to Latin, so is Latin to French, poised to become the new Latin.[14]

---

[13] ('But because Aristotle's moral treatises were written in Greek, and we have them in Latin which is quite difficult to comprehend, the King has wished, for the common profit, to have them translated into French so that his counselors and others might better understand them, especially the *Ethics* and *Politics*, of which, it is said, the former instructs one in how to be a good man, the other in how to be a good prince'): *Maistre Nicole Oresme, Le Livre de Ethiques d'Aristote*, ed. A. D. Menut (New York, 1940), pp. 98–9.

[14] 'Or est il ainsi que pour le temps de lors, grec estoit en resgart de latin quant as Romains si comme est maintenant latin en regart de françois quant a nous. Et estoient

Oresme is keenly aware that translation is essentially oblique, an act of appropriation and transformation performed by successive generations, and that his translation can be no exception. He implies that the translator and the French language of his translations emerge as linguistic exemplars of mediation, designed to bring together courtly readers and ancient wisdom. In Oresme's form of *translatio studii*, the French language and the king's French translation project combine to establish French political theory as an expression of the capacity of French to create new registers of discourse and, still more importantly, to participate in a cultural alignment with the classical past. It is no accident that Oresme begins his *Proheme* by noting that Aristotle was 'docteur et conseillier du grant roy Alexandre' (*Ethiques*, p. 97), establishing an equation between the Greek king and his counsellor and the French king and himself.

Within the dialogue of past and present created by his accompanying commentary, Oresme's translations of Aristotle explore how the mean functions as an essential element in the virtuous and happy life and the prosperous community. His commentaries reveal how closely he interrogates Aristotle's meaning, adapting and re-thinking the philosopher's ideas in relation to French polity and the capacity of the French language to express his understanding. He uses various tones and verbal strategies. At times he is relatively concrete in his language. In the *Politiques* those who comprise *le moien* are a diverse group of citizens who act: 'gens qui conseillent et jugent', wealthy, powerful, but not necessarily noble.[15] Distribution of wealth in a city is expressed more abstractly, through a trope of music, compared to 'plusieurs sons ensemble', which comprise true musical *consonance*, a unity of modulated diversity. A society, like music, functions best when due proportion of multiple, diverse elements is established over the course of time (*Politiques*, p. 92).

In the *Ethiques*, *le moien* emerges as a highly complicated concept. Still central to the polity, it functions as a site of reconciliation between extremes, a site synonymous with right action that eschews both excess and deficiency and results in individual happiness and virtue. The need publicly to convey the dangers of excess generates new vocabulary. *Extreme*, one of the political neologisms that Oresme defines at the end of the *Ethiques* in his alphabetical list of political 'moz divers et estranges' unfamiliar to those 'qui ne sont pas exercitéz en ceste science', signifies deviancy from the mean of virtue, a word to denote 'habiz et operacions qui sont hors le moien de vertu ... la vertu est moienne et que les vices sont extremes' ('habits and behaviours which are outside the mean of virtue ... virtue is the mean in relation to which vices are extreme', *Ethiques*, p. 544).[16]

---

pour le temps les estudians introduiz en grec et a Romme et aillieurs, et les sciences communelment bailliees en grec; et en ce pays le langage commun et maternel, c'estoit latin. Donques puis je bien encore conclurre que la consideracion et le propos de nostre bon roy Charles est a recommender, qui fait les bons livres et excellens translater en françois' (*Ethiques*, p. 101).

15 *Ethiques*, p. 313.

16 In his introduction to his edition of the *Ethiques* Albert Menut lists several hundred

Using a discourse of resistance Oresme constructs the mean as dynamic, as a third way, to reconcile opposites into harmony.[17] He implies that the achievement of the mean is not the average of extremes, but the site from which extremes are modified. To convey this idea fully he turns to art as an alternative sign system in a program of illumination for the royal manuscripts of his translations of the *Ethiques*. Claire Sherman has shown that the illustrations Oresme devised and oversaw constitute a parallel visual text designed to shape interpretation of the verbal text.[18] Like neologisms, the images Oresme devised and oversaw augment his language. The mean appears as the image of a royal woman, a queen, positioned between grotesque figures (see Fig. 28.1). Although she is proportionately the mean between the outsized figure of *superhabondance* and the dwarfish image of *defaute*, the royal mean is different from the two figures of excess and deficiency in terms of gender, class, and aspect relative to the viewer. She looks forward out of the image, while the other figures are locked into the frame of the image. The image strongly implies that the mean is powerful yet opposed on two sides by difference.

In addition to visual metaphors Oresme also employs verbal metaphors to construct the mean as under constant threat. His translation of the *Politiques* allegorizes *polity* as a female who cares for the public good, employing a series of abstract nouns to define the semantic and ethical field the allegorized sign invokes, citing the 'industrie de sa prudence', 'balance ou poies de sa justice', constance et fermeté de sa fortitude', and the 'pacience de son attrempance' in order to provide 'medicine au salut de tous' (*Politiques*, p. 44). The discourse of the mean – constancy, fortitude, patience, prudence, and temperance – is called into play under pressure of an unstable dynamic that Oresme perceives to threaten the heart of polity: parties in natural opposition, like the rich and the poor 'qui sunt contraires', will cause disruption if the *moien*, the group who *conseillent et jugent* is small and therefore weak (*Politiques*, p. 92). Anxiety about the middle position inevitably raises the implication that just as a weak middle class threatens political disaster, so, too, inadequate language in a translation – the middle way between the original text and a new French expression of its *sentence* – threatens ideological as well as semantic failure.

words in contemporary use that Oresme coined in his translation of Aristotle's *Ethiques*; the list includes such familiar abstractions and adjectives as *aristocracie, communicacion, democracie, despotique, devocion, equivalente, expedient, incivile, injuste, inprudence, modereement, oligarchie, proporcionalité,* and *yconomie* (*Ethiques*, pp. 79–82).

[17] This discourse arises in part because Aristotle expresses his ideas through frequent metaphors of disease and the oppositional nature of curatives in medicine. Oresme combines the notion of opposition with the idea of the mean to construct the middle place as one of difference in kind from extremes of excess and deficiency.

[18] C. R. Sherman, *Imaging Aristotle: Verbal and Visual Representation in Fourteenth-Century France* (Berkeley, 1995). See also C. R. Sherman, 'Some Visual Definitions in the Illustrations of Aristotle's *Nichomachean Ethics* and *Politics* in the French Translations of Nicole Oresme', *The Art Bulletin* 59 (1977), 320–30.

Fig. 28.1: The Queen Virtu flanked by Superabondance and Defaute from *Les Ethiques d'Aristote*, Brussels, Bibl. Royale Albert Ier, MS 9505–06, fol. 24r

English for profyt of English men

Aristotle's *Ethics* and *Politics* were known in English court circles during the reign of Edward III, and Oresme's works came directly to England when the duke of Bedford took possession of the Louvre library in 1422 on Charles VI's death.[19] But thought about the mean also developed independently if concurrently in England. In English, first citations of the collocated vocabulary of the mean are of the works of Chaucer and of Gower, court poets who worked in a fully Anglo-French literary milieu, and, intriguingly, of the Wycliffe Bible translations of 1382 and 1384.[20] For the English, as for the French, the concept of the middle and its various dimensions of moderation, mediation, and measure is central to the ideal working of household and polity. Gower lays out his project in the *Confessio Amantis*, his 'boke for Engelond's sake' as a poem of the mean, as 'a middle wei',[21] a text 'between the vertu and the vice' that belong to the office of the wise and the great (*Confessio*, Prol. 70). Wise 'governance' that will appease the world and please the 'Godhed' (*Confessio*, Prol. 191) is his subject. So, too, Richard of Maidstone's *Concordia*, a narrative of reconciliation between Richard II and London, highlights the role of Queen Anne as she whose role, like the image of Queen Virtue in Oresme's manuscripts, is to reconcile the angry and powerful Richard and the repentant City. Chronicle narratives of the deeds of Anne of Bohemia enshrine both her actions and the paradigm of mediation they enact as ideal queenly comportment performed under difficult circumstances of tension and division.[22]

For English as for French writers, use of the vernacular is closely associated with the common *profyt* to be derived from translation. Like Oresme in his work of creating a vernacular useful for accomplishing Charles V's civic goals, the Wycliffite Bible translators saw the vernacular as a means of bringing necessary knowledge previously restricted to clerks and the learned tradition of Latin into the daily life of their culture. They affirm the value of the vernacular by

---

[19] See Richard de Bury, *Philobiblon*, trans. A. Taylor (Berkeley, 1948), pp. 69, 73 and passim. Richard de Bury was tutor to Edward when he was prince, and later his chancellor. On the fate of Charles V's library and its Oresme manuscripts, see J. Stratford, *The Bedford Inventories: The Worldly Goods of John, Duke of Bedford, Regent of France* (London, 1993), pp. 95–6; on Charles d'Orléans' acquisition of Oresme's translation of the *Ethiques* after Bedford's death in 1435, see P. Champion, *La librairie de Charles d'Orléans* (Paris, 1910), p. xxv.

[20] See MED, OED. Given the complexly interwoven history of English and Anglo-Norman as well as continental French, first citations must be regarded as indicative of increased or changed usage rather than definitive proof of entry into use or date of semantic change.

[21] John Gower, *Confessio Amantis*, eds. R. Peck and A. Galloway, 3 vols. (Kalamazoo MI, 2000–4), Prologue, 18–30. On Gower's interest in the middle way, or balance, see H. Cooper, '"Peised Evene in the Balance": A Thematic and Rhetorical Topos in the *Confessio Amantis*', *Medievalia* 16 (1993), 113–39.

[22] On Maidstone and Anne of Bohemia, see C. P. Collette, *Performing Polity: Women and Agency in the Anglo-French Tradition, 1385–1620* (Turnhout, 2006), pp. 99–121.

citing historical examples of *translatio studii* in terms that resonate with Oresme's implicit goal of positioning the French vernacular as cultural heir to Latin. They also make their case on the basis of language change, specifically the emergence of successive vernaculars, of which their form of English language is but one:

> Lord God! sithen at the bigynnyng of feith so manie men translatiden into Latyn, and to greet profyt of Latyn men, lat oo symple creature of God translate into English, for profyt of English men; for if wordli clerkis loken wel here croniclis and bokis, thei shulden fynde, that Bede translatide the bible, and expounide myche in Saxon, that was English, either comoun langage of this lond, in his tyme; and not oneli Bede, but also king Alured, that foundide Oxenford, translatide in hise laste daies. ... Also Frenshe men, Beemers, and Britons han the bible, and othere bokis of deuocioun and of exposicioun, translatid in here modir langage; whi shulden not English men haue the same in here modir langage, I can not wite ...[23]

Similarly, at the opening of *A Treatise on the Astrolabe* Chaucer describes himself as a 'lewd compilator of the labour of olde astrologiens' who has 'translatid in myn Englissh' the scientific text he is introducing. Like Oresme, he associates the vernacular with the king, praising him as 'lord of this langage'. And like his contemporary Bible translators he positions his project as part of the venerable and universal history of transmitting human knowledge in the vernacular:

> ... suffise to these trewe conclusions in Englissh as wel as sufficith to these noble clerkes Grekes these same conclusions in Grek; and to Arabiens in Arabik, and to Jewes in Ebrew, and to Latyn folk in Latyn; whiche Latyn folk had hem first out of othere dyverse langages, and writen hem in her owne tunge, that is to seyn, in Latyn. And God woot that in alle these langages and in many moo han these conclusions ben suffisantly lerned and taught, and yet by diverse reules; right as diverse pathes leden diverse folk the righte way to Rome.[24]

While the modern world thinks of Chaucer primarily as a literary genius, his own self-presentation was more closely aligned with the literary posture in the

---

[23] Prologue, *The Holy Bible ... from the Latin Vulgate by John Wycliffe and His Followers*, ed. J. Forshall and F. Madden, 2 vols. (Oxford, 1850), p. 59. For comment on this passage in the context of religious translation, see the essay by Watson in this volume.

[24] Geoffrey Chaucer, *A Treatise on the Astrolabe* in *The Riverside Chaucer*, ed. L. D. Benson, 3rd edn (Boston MA, 1987), pp. 661–83, line 30. It is notable that in addition to the familiar 'commonplaces' cited here, the opening of the *Treatise* also contains a theme of anxiety expressed in terms of usurpation and envy: 'And preie God save the king, that is lord of this langage, and alle that him feith berith and obeieth, everich in his degre, the more and the lasse. But considre wel that I ne usurpe not to have founden this werk of my labour or of myn engyn. I n'am but a lewd compilator of the labour of olde astrologiens, and have it translatid in myn Englissh oonly for thy doctrine. And with this swerd shal I sleen envie' (line 60). Chaucer seems to anticipate criticism of the translator as an appropriator of ideas. All citations of Chaucer's works are to this edition and will be identified by line number within the text.

ıssage above, consistently presenting himself as a borrower of topics, themes,
ıd a translator of others' thoughts into English. His numerous references to the
sufficiency of English in respect to vocabulary and rhyme echo throughout the
les and constitute a de facto apology for his extensive lexical appropriation.[25] In
ıe *Retraction* to the *Tales*, he refers to his works as his *translacions*; so too, in the
ʻologue to the *Legend of Good Women* the God of Love describes his work princi-
ılly as 'translacioun' (F. 324).[26] For Chaucer the role of translator is charged with
ıfluence, for the translator is a *mene*, the one who remembers and disseminates
ıd books and the wisdom they contain. So great is the translator's power that
ıe God of Love of the *Legend* castigates Chaucer's ability to sway his audience
.rough this art.

Through translation and adaptation of French vocabulary Chaucer interro-
ıtes ideals of moderation, temperance, and extremes. Some of the most memo-
ıble characters and scenes in the *Tales* centre in questions of moderation and
:cess: forms of *mesure, prudence* and *governaunce* recur in the *Clerk's Tale* where
ʻriselda embodies the strength of a life of virtuous measure that triumphs over
.e extreme of Walter's behaviour; the Parson, who opposes the excesses of sin
ıth advice about spiritual measure, invokes 'attemperaunce, that holdeth the
ıeen in alle thynges' in the remedy for gluttony (ParsT c.835); the *Nun's Priest's*
ʻle opens with the role of temperance in achieving the virtuous mean that leads
. a happy life, only to push it aside to focus on the *extreme* activities of Chanti-
ıeer's realm.

Nowhere is Chaucer's engagement with the ideals and paradoxes of the mean
. extensively displayed as in his story of *Prudence and Melibee*. His decision to
ıace the *Melibee* – with its protagonist *Prudence* and its themes of reconciliation
ıt the heart of the *Canterbury Tales* reveals his interest in the practice of media-
ın as well as his command of the Anglo-French discourse of the mean.[27] Forms
 attempraunce, mesure, governe/governaunce, and *reconcilen* recur throughout
.e tale. Moreover, the *Melibee* faithfully represents the Aristotelian doctrines of
ʻposites as a means to correct *extreme* situations at a crucial juncture in the tale
ʻhen Prudence counsels Melibee about why his idea of vengeance as an offering
ʻ violence for violence is mistaken:

> … wikkedness is nat contrarie to wikkednesse, ne vengeance to vengeaunce,
> ne wrong to wrong, but they been semblable./ And therefore o vengeaunce is
> nat warisshed by another vengeaunce, ne o wroong by another wroong,/ but
> everich of hem encreesceth and aggreggeth oother./ But certes … wikkednesse

The Man of Law's Tale 49,778; Squire's Tale, 37; The Second Nun's Tale 2, 87, 106, The
Parson's Tale c.869; see also, *The House of Fame* 510, *Astrolabe*, 27, 29, 51, 63, *Legend of Good Women* F 66.
See, too, *Legend of Good Women* F 329, 370, 425; G, 250, 255, 341, 350, 413.
On the language of the tale and its contributions to public civic discourse, see K. Taylor,
'Social Aesthetics and the Emergence of Civic Discourse from the *Shipman's Tale* to
Melibee', *The Chaucer Review* 39 (2005), 298–322.

shal be warisshed by goodnesse, discord by accord, werre by pees, and so forth of othere thynges. (*2475–80)

True opposites are essentially different and the difference of opposites is the ke to 'warisshing' – curing – excess.

Prudence's work of reconciliation places her between Melibeus and h enemies; the middle place she must mediate is not a melding of their attitude but a separate understanding to which each party must come independentl through the power of her words and her reasoning. The last hundred and fift lines of the tale include a narrative of the recurrent negotiations Prudence unde takes to bring about reconciliation, as well as her conversation with Melibee enemies in which both she and they reflect on the difficulties of achieving th middle place of peace, because it means putting oneself 'al outrely in the arb tracioun and juggement, and in the might and power' of one's enemies (*2940).

But while the *Melibee* presents the value of the mean in forestalling violenc and maintaining social and political harmony, Chaucer is elsewhere less clea less optimistic about the place of the middle. Arguably the most intriguing indeterminate site on which Chaucer explores ideas of mediation and the mea is in the *Legend of Good Women*. In the F Prologue to the *Legend of Good Wome* Chaucer casually invokes the *Ethiques* in reference to the reconciliation of lover asserting the social and political value of the *mene*: 'for vertu is the mene,/ A Etik seith ... And thus thise foweles, voide of al malice,/ Acordeden to love, an laften vice/ Of hate, and songen alle of oon acord' (F 165–169). As the Prologu to the *Legend* moves into the encounter among the God of Love, Alceste, an Chaucer, the mean, the place occupied by those who counsel, the intellectu space where extremes are reconciled and breaches healed, is a contested sit surrounded by emotion, misunderstanding, and enmity mixed with raw powe Alceste is the mediator who reconciles the powerful and angry God of Lov a figure of rich *superhabondance*, to Chaucer who is constructed as a figure defaute, termed a 'worm'. The mean that Alceste creates offers a site on whic both the God of Love and Chaucer can agree to a new relationship: Chaucer to make up for his insult to the God of Love, in writing of Criseyde's betrayal Troilus, by telling tales of how men have betrayed faithful women. In spite of th daisy poetic and the poetry of light that attend her, Alceste is idealized for th darkness and pain the middle may require; she is idealized for her courage i giving up her life – putting herself in the power of her enemies, as Prudence pu it – to save her husband.

Deschamps praised Chaucer as a great translator, and Hoccleve hailed him a a new Aristotle.[28] His themes, like his language, derive in part from French word and topics that were themselves shifting, changing, developing new semanti dimensions. The shared discourse of temperance, prudence, and reconcilia tion that attends exploration of the mean in both English and French suggest a degree of lexical unity in Anglo-French vernaculars that stems from share

---

[28] See *Chaucer: The Critical Heritage*, ed. D. Brewer, 2 vols. (London, 1978), I, 40, 63.

culture and several centuries of interwoven linguistic development. The common argument for the vernacular, articulated by Oresme, Chaucer, and the translators of the Wycliffe Bible, constructs an ideology of translation as an historical phenomenon of successive cultural appropriations, implying a human history of continual *translatio studii* and a continual need to reinvent language faithfully to replicate and to mediate the truths of *auctoritas* to successive generations. Just so, in *De vulgari eloquentia*, Dante envisions a glorious future for Italian vernacular as 'illustrious', a 'cardinal' political language central to the common profit of the Italian community because of its responsiveness to verbal need: 'Does it not daily make new grafts or prick out seedlings? What else do its gardeners do, if they are not uprooting or planting, as I said earlier? For this reason it has fully earned the right to deck itself out with so noble an epithet' (*De vulgari*, p. 43).

Whether Italian, French or English, medieval arguments for the vernacular transcend our notions of national boundaries. They build on a meta-cultural ideal like the human society Oresme envisions in the *Politiques*, one in which *consonance* and *symphonie* arise from multiple voices that blend to mediate between authority and audience in a variety of languages, spoken in the past and the present, a transnational and transhistorical phenomenon that Dante might have regarded as a linguistic shadow of the human unity that made it possible to build Babel. In thinking of medieval languages primarily as expressions of nationality we obscure the vision that underlies the borrowings, adaptations, and claims of living languages emerging as powerful tools of political expression and social imagination on both sides of the Channel.

29

Writing English in a French Penumbra: The Middle English 'Tree of Love' in MS Longleat 253

Julia Boffey*

In the Marquess of Bath's library at Longleat House, Warminster, is a small volume of 95 folios, now MS 253, whose medieval title appears to have been 'The book of knyghthode'.[1] It is best known to scholars for its inclusion (on fols. 2–75v) of a copy of the translation of Christine de Pizan's *Epistre d'Othea* made probably round about 1440 by Stephen Scrope (*c*.1396–1472) for his stepfather Sir John Fastolf (1380–1459), a text edited from this manuscript in 1904 by Sir George Warner, and collated by Curt F. Bühler for his 1970 Early English Text Society edition, which was based on the copy in Cambridge, St John's College H. 5.[2] Accompanying *The Epistle of Othea*, on fols. 76r–95v of MS Longleat 253, is a work that has received much less attention: in Warner's words, it is 'An English poem or series of poems, probably also translated from the French, in which love is compared with the growth of a tree.'[3] This work was not included

---

* I should like to express my gratitude to the Marquess of Bath for permission to consult this manuscript, and to Dr Kate Harris, Curator Longleat Historic Collections, for her advice and practical help.

1 The title appears on fol. 1r, a discoloured parchment leaf, which looks as if it might have once formed part of a loose wrapper for some or all of the manuscript.

2 *The Epistle of Othea to Hector*, ed. Sir G. Warner (London, 1904); *Stephen Scrope: The Epistle of Othea to Hector*, ed. C. F. Bühler, EETS OS 264 (1970). A further manuscript of the *Epistle*, now New York, Pierpont Morgan Library, MS M 775, contains a different dedication to an unidentified 'hye princesse'; this manuscript, owned by Sir John Astley (d. 1486) and in part duplicating London, British Library, MS Lansdowne 285, is described by G. A. Lester, *Sir John Paston's 'Grete Book': A Descriptive Catalogue, with an Introduction, of British Library MS Lansdowne 285* (Cambridge, 1984). Bühler's analysis of the manuscripts of the *Epistle* translation suggests the following chronology: (i) Scrope's hypothetical working copy (dated *c*.1440 because the preface to the translation talks of his carrying out the work when Fastolf was aged about 60); (ii) a copy presented to Fastolf, now lost, but represented in MS Longleat 253, the unfinished ornamentation of which would seem to indicate that it was not a presentation copy; (iii) a copy presented to Humphrey Stafford, duke of Buckingham (d. 1460), possibly St John's, MS H 5; (iv) a copy (presumably now lost) presented to a 'hye princesse', the preface to which accompanies the text in Morgan, MS M 775. Further details of all the *Epistle* manuscripts are supplied in A. I Doyle, 'Appendix B: A Note on St John's College, Cambridge, MS H. 5', in *Epistle*, ed. Bühler, pp. 125–7. On *Orthea* inEngland, see further the essay by Downes below.

3 *Epistle*, ed. Warner, p. ix.

ᵃ Carleton Brown's and Rossell Hope Robbins's *Index of Middle English Verse*, ᵃnd only vaguely outlined in the *Supplement* to this, in which it features as entry 3553.8: 'A poem to his mistress likening her to a tree in various seasons – about ᵗwenty folios; first leaf missing.' No folio numbers are given, no reference to an ᵈition, no description of verse form.[4] Bühler's edition of *The Epistle of Othea* ᵒffered a few more details, indicating that 'The second text (or texts) in the ᵛolume consists of rhymed couplets, in which love is likened to a tree, together ᵂith a debate between Reason and Love. This portion is incomplete at the end .'; but despite his commendation of the poem's technical merits ('the verse ᵢ infinitely better than what we find in the *Othea*'),[5] and its fairly substantial ᵉngth, it has apparently attracted no further scrutiny.

An exploration of this poem and of the context in which it was copied and ᵖresumably) read affords a rich opportunity to reflect on the nature of Anglo-ᶠrench cultural exchange in the fifteenth century. In particular, the likelihood ᵗhat the work itself was, in Warner's words, 'probably also translated from the ᶠrench', invites some meditation on the networks through which French texts ᵉached English readers at this period, and on the range of appropriations that ᵘch texts appear to have invited. Locating information about the origins and ᵃature of this unique, anonymous and unusually interesting poem, with its ᵉeming connections to the distinctively Francophile tastes of Fastolf and his ᵢrcle, is likely to offer some insight into what French literary culture signified in ᶠfteenth-century England. It also offers some ways of responding to one of the ᵠuestions that arises most pressingly from all that is known about what was, for ᵗhat place and time, the dominant form of cultural exchange: 'How might our ᵘnderstanding of seemingly monolingual compositions change if we locate them ᵢn a cultural environment saturated with translating activities?'[6]

First, some more details of the poem itself, for which *The Tree of Love* seems a ᵘuitable working title. It is copied in the manuscript following the *Epistle of Othea*, ᵃnd by the same scribe. Warner's contention that one or more leaves are lacking ᵗ the start is plausible, since the work currently starts on fol. 76r with no title or ᵢntroduction.[7] It begins with a couplet, 'These be the dwe techynges expresse / ᵗʰe whiche gyffeth yche state worthenes', immediately followed by a line intro-ᵈuced with a blank space where a decorated initial was obviously planned:

C. Brown and R. H. Robbins, *The Index of Middle English Verse* (New York, 1942); R. H. Robbins and J. L. Cutler, *Supplement to the Index of Middle English Verse* (Lexington KY, 1965).

Epistle of Othea, ed. Bühler, pp. xvii, xxiii.

M. R. Warren, 'Translation', in *Oxford Twenty-First Century Approaches to Literature: Middle English*, ed. P. Strohm (Oxford, 2007), pp. 51–67 (p. 51). I am grateful to Jocelyn Wogan-Browne for directing me to this essay.

Leaf and quire signatures, which are fairly regular in the earlier part of the manuscript, have been cropped away by this point.

[b]vt nowe herith wele the begynnyng
what that love dothe in his first taking
ffor who that so will take tent therto
wytte and fooly he may lerne bothe to.[8]

The work is in couplets throughout, copied at around 29 lines to the page, o
leaves which have been carefully ruled. It is structured around a comparison o
love to a tree: a tree that needs to be carefully planted by a gardener in goo
soil, and tended through the seasons as it grows and buds and flowers and bear
fruit. Details of this allegorical scheme are occasionally elaborated: things tha
help love to flourish, for example, are 'beaute', 'plesawnce' and 'courtesy'; th
tree's buds are love's kisses, and so on. Much is made throughout of the perils i
the way of love constituted by hard ground, rough winds, unseasonal change
of weather; much is made also of the value to the lover of good advice an
counsel. The narrator acknowledges his own need of this, and sketches in a littl
of his own hopelessness in love before launching into a formal debate betwee
the personifications Love and Reason. How this debate is resolved is not clear
at least one leaf seems to be missing near the end between fols. 92v and 93r – bu
by the point of its conclusion the narrator's take on love has turned a chillie
corner, and he stresses the inevitable disappearance of 'leaf' and 'flower':

For there is noon that may dure so longe
Ne kepe good weye ne other emong,
Ne in this worlde so mech noon ryot may
But be age he must nedes pase his way.
All we shall be at the lawe common
As vs shall lede the kyng of fortune,
For in no wyse noon may length his day
But that afors he must pase away. (fol. 93r)

Only God understands true love, and if we give ourselves to God as his fruit
we will become fruitful ourselves:

God as gardyner he is leche
The which as to his fruitfull trees
Hath gravnted vs lyfe & vitte also
Of the ioy that euer shall last now. (fol. 95v)

It is clear from the poem's layout that a fairly extensive illustrative schem
was intended. Gaps occur throughout the copy, at significant moments, for orna
mented or decorated initials, and these increase in number through the debat
section, to help differentiate the words of Love and of Reason. At least five half
or third-page miniatures also seem to have been planned for the opening part o

[8] In quotations from the manuscript, contractions have been silently expanded an
word division regularized. Thorn is represented in this transcription by 'th'.

the poem, preceding the debate, and the expected presence of these is acknowledged in the words of the text. The first illustration was seemingly expected to press home the equivalence between the lover's dedication to his lady and the gardener's to nurturing his tree: 'On hir he settyth now all his cure / As ye may se hir in portrature' (fol. 77v). The next space comes, without introduction, after a section on the perils of planting too early (fol. 80r). Shortly after this the reader is instructed 'Now takyth hede to the picture / Howe the tre buddyth aftir the wardure' (fol. 81r), and further on 'Now take hede to the picture / Which cordyth wele with the scripture / Howe freschely that the trees leveth' (fol. 83r). The last space present in the manuscript (we cannot know what was on the lost leaf or leaves) is prefaced by the lines 'Take hede aftur this to the picture / And that to yow shall shewe the nature / ffor as the tree is flowryd expresse / So fares owre love dowteles' (fol. 84v). What we seem to have here, very unusually, is a piece of verse writing programmed for illustration, whose author expected pictures to be supplied and was in a position to specify what they would contain.

This carefully constructed combination of text and image may well reflect aspects of the other item in the manuscript, the *Epistle of Othea*, which was provided in its original French version with a programme of copious manuscript illustrations,[9] and divided into sections that Scrope's translation renders as 'texte', 'allegorie' and 'glose'.[10] While the spaces left in MS Longleat 253 for illustrations to the English *Epistle* were left blank, varying numbers of illustrations are present in the other two copies of the English text, St John's College, MS H. 5 (208) and New York, Pierpont Morgan Library, MS M 775.[11] Scrope's guardian Fastolf, on whose commission the translation was made, owned a finely illustrated copy of the French original, now Oxford, Bodleian Library, MS Laud misc. 570, and may have owned another.[12] Illustrated and illuminated copies of various of Christine de Pizan's works were in English hands or known to English readers in the second half of fifteenth century (the date to which these *Epistle of Othea* manuscripts can be assigned), and in the context of these the planned

---

9 See S. Hindman, *Christine de Pizan's* Epistre d'Othéa: *Painting and Politics at the Court of Charles VI* (Toronto, 1986); G. Mombello, *La tradizione manoscritta dell'* Epistre Othea *di Christine de Pizan: Prolegomini all'edizione del testo* (Turin, 1967); M. A. Ignatius, 'Christine de Pizan's *Epistre Othea*: An Experiment in Literary Form', *Medievalia et Humanistica* n.s. 9 (1979), 127–42.

10 'And the seyde booke ys diuidyd in thre partys gederid in a summe of an C textys ... with an C commentys therevpon, called exposicyons or glosis vpon the seyde textys ... and vpon thies ... also an othyr C allegories & moralizacions'; see the prologue to the version of the *Epistle* in Longleat 253, transcribed in *Epistle of Othea*, ed. Bühler, pp. 121–4 (p. 123).

11 For descriptions and bibliography, see Scott, *LGM* II, 263–6 and II, 289–93 respectively.

12 C. F. Bühler, 'Sir John Fastolf's Manuscripts of the *Epitre d'Othéa* and Stephen Scrope's Translation of this Text', *Scriptorium* 3 (1949), 123–8; R. Beadle, 'Sir John Fastolf's French Books', in *Medieval Texts in Context*, ed. D. Renevey and G. Caie (London, 2008), pp. 96–112 (see especially pp. 97–8); Scott, *LGM* II, 264–5.

illustrations to *The Tree of Love* are not surprising.[13] There was also an extensive French tradition of illustrating love-allegories and *dits amoureux* encompassing both older works like *Le Roman de la Rose* and newer experiments such as René d'Anjou's *Livre du Cœur d'amours espris*.[14] It is extremely unusual, though, to find an English work of this kind with a planned programme of illustrations.

Although there is nothing explicit in the extant portion of *The Tree of Love* to suggest that it might be a translation, its survival alongside Scrope's translation in MS Longleat 253, and the illustrative potential common to both works, combine to suggest that a French source may be worth hypothesizing. Certain aspects of *The Tree of Love* complicate this search. Is anything missing at the start, for example – as Robbins and Cutler suggest by giving their *Supplement* number an asterisk? What is lacking, and how much of it, between fols. 92 and 93? One of the important consequences of these *lacunae* is their blurring of the tensions in the poem between more and less secular forms of love. While it is clear by the end that the poem recommends God as the only sure 'gardyner', its earlier portions seem (on the face of what survives) less preoccupied with this spiritual message and rather more concerned to advocate rules for courteous behaviour in the worldly conduct of a love affair. This is of a piece with the flavour of the *Epistle of Othea*, of course, designed for secular readers wanting to cultivate appropriately knightly modes of behaviour, and it rather interestingly positions the *Tree* as somewhere between love-allegories that aim to spark diversionary debate and those that use the genre as a vehicle for ethical, occasionally more explicitly spiritual, instruction. It might also indicate that the words 'The boke of knyghthode' that introduce MS Longleat 253 are designed to comprehend both the *Epistle* translation and its shorter companion-piece.[15]

This blurring between secular and spiritual also opens the way to speculating that *The Tree of Love* might have its source in something more along the lines of a spiritual allegory or a treatise of religious instruction, among the number of which it is not hard to find allegorical gardens and trees.[16] A convenient repre-

---

13 P. G. C. Campbell, 'Christine de Pizan en Angleterre', *Revue de littérature comparée* 5 (1925), 659–70; C. M. Meale, 'Legends of Good Women in the European Middle Ages', *Archiv* 144 (1992), 55–70. See also the essay by Downes in this volume.

14 Dated to 1457; see *King René's Book of Love (Le cueur d'amours espris)*, intro. and commentary F. Unterkircher, trans. S. Wilkins (New York, 1975).

15 'The Book of the ordre of chyualry or knyghthode' is also the title of Caxton's translation of a French version of the Catalan *Libre del orde de cavayleria*, by Raimon Lull.

16 See, for example, the many allegorical trees in *The Desert of Religion* (IMEV 672), in London, British Library, MSS Cotton Faustina B VI (ii), Stowe 39, and Addit. 37049; reproduced from the last in J. Hogg, ed., *An Illustrated Yorkshire Carthusian Religious Miscellany. British Library London Additional 37049. Volume 3: The Illustrations*, Analecta Cartusiana 95 (Salzburg, 1981), pp. 66–104; and the trees of virtues and vices in Oxford, Bodleian Library, MS Laud Misc. 156 (seemingly a model book for illustrations to Nicholas de Lyra, *Tituli quaestionum super Biblia*), described in *An Index of Images in English Manuscripts from the Time of Chaucer to Henry VIII, c.1380–c.1509: The Bodleian Library, Oxford. Fascicle II: MSS Dodsworth-Marshall*, ed. L. Dennison, M. W. Driver, A. Eljenholm Nichols and K. L. Scott (Turnhout, 2001), pp. 74–5 and fig. 15.

Writing English in a French Penumbra

sentative of this genre is the prose work called 'The Branches of the Appletree' (a Treatise that spekyth of the vertu & of the braunches of the appultree, which is expounded morally'),[17] extant in English in Wynkyn de Worde's printed compilation the *Tretyse of Loue* (STC 24234), and apparently deriving from, or closely connected with, a French tract of which one copy is to be found in Brussels, Bibliothèque Royale, MS 2292, copied by David Aubert in 1475 for Margaret of York.[18] Another example is the prose *deuout treatyse called the tree & xii frutes of the holy goost*, which survives in three manuscripts, and a later printed edition (STC 13608) from 1534/5.[19] Although both of these works are in prose, and entirely devotional in flavour, they suggest a general area for investigation of possible analogues to the verse *Tree of Love*.[20]

The closest analogue among the works I have consulted so far is a French text called variously *Le jardin de devotion* and *Le jardin amoureux de l'ame devote* and *Le jardin de vertueuse consolation*. It survives in at least seventeen continental manuscript copies and four early continental printed editions, and appears to have been known to at least some fifteenth-century English readers.[21] It is sometimes attributed to Jean Gerson, but seems more likely to be the work of Pierre d'Ailly (Petrus de Alliaco, 1350–1420), prolific author, prelate and Gerson's teacher for a time as chancellor of the University of Paris.[22] Its allegorical scheme is clearly outlined at the start:

> En ce mondain desert est le jardin d'amoureuse consolacion ou le vray Dieu d'amours habite; c'est le jardin gracieux ou habite le doulx Jesus et ouquel il appelle s'amie quant il dit ou livre des chansonettes amoureuses: *Veni in ortum meum, soror mea, sponsa mea* ...[23]

---

7 *The Tretyse of Loue*, ed. J. H. Fisher, EETS OS 223 (1951), pp. 108–18, with the French version (from Brussels, Bibliothèque Royale, MS 2292) on pp. 131–45.

8 *Tretyse*, ed Fisher, pp. xiv–xv; see also H. E. Allen, 'Wynkyn de Worde and a Second French Compilation from the *Ancrene Riwle* with a Description of the First (Trinity Coll. Cambridge MS 883)', in *Essays and Studies in Honor of Carleton Brown* (New York, 1940), pp. 182–220.

9 *A deuout treatyse called the tree & xii frutes of the holy goost*. *Edited from MS McLean 132, Fitzwilliam Museum, Cambridge*, ed. J. J. Vaissier (Groningen, 1960). Vaissier discusses the traditions of tree allegory on pp. lvi–lxxvii.

10 *The Orchard of Syon*, ed. P. Hodgson and G. M. Liegey, EETS OS 258 (1966), is a more extensive devotional treatment of the figure. For some other devotional and doctrinal trees see the essays by Watson and by Wogan-Browne in this volume (pp. 241–4, 349, and Figure 18.1). An interesting example of the use an allegorical tree in both secular and religious contexts is discussed by H. Phillips, 'Rewriting the Fall: Julian of Norwich and the *Chevalier des dames*', in *Women, the Book and the Godly: Selected Proceedings of the St Hilda's Conference, 1993*, ed. L. Smith and J. H. M. Taylor (Cambridge, 1995), pp. 149–56.

11 P.-Y. Badel, 'Pierre d'Ailly, auteur du *Jardin amoureux*', *Romania* 97 (1976), 369–81, offers much information about surviving copies.

2 The standard biography is L. Salembier, *Le Cardinal Pierre d'Ailly; chancelier de l'Université de Paris, Evêque du Puy et de Cambrai, 1350–1420* (Tourcoing, 1932).

3 'In the desert of this world there is the garden of loving consolation where the true God of love lives: that is the gracious garden where sweet Jesus lives and which he

The sixteen short chapters that follow describe in more detail the garden's construction, its 'grant beaute' (p. 147), the flowers, trees and fruits with which it is filled, and 'le precieux arbre de vie' at its heart. The chapters are rounded off with a verse 'chansonette amoureuse', exhorting lovers to see reflected in the natural world an image of God's 'noble pourtraicture' (p. 153).

One reason for pursuing this text in relation to the Middle English *Tree* is its survival in illustrated form. Paris, Bibliothèque nationale, f. fr. 1026 and f. fr. 22922, are both *de luxe* illustrated copies,[24] and although the first surviving printed edition has no illustration, the later ones have a number of woodcuts. A preliminary review of the manuscripts, many of which are now housed in French provincial city libraries, suggests that the work circulated in contexts comparable to the Scrope–Fastolf network, which seems the likeliest original environment of the *Tree of Love*. In Parma, MS Pal. 106, for example, the *Jardin* occupies 'les derniers feuillets d'un manuscrit ... daté de 1475, qui contient en outre deux ouvrages français. ... *Le Livre des bonnes mœurs* (Jacques Legrand) et *Somme le roi*'.[25] In The Hague, KB MS 71 G 61, it accompanies an illustrated complaint against death by Triboulet, jester to René d'Anjou, and in Brussels, Bibliothèque Royale, MS IV III, it is copied with other tracts attributed to Gerson and a copiously illustrated copy of Suso's *L'Horloge de sapience* that has connections with the Bedford Master.[26]

Owners and readers of the manuscript copies – secular aristocrats, royalty – seem in general terms similar to those who constituted Christine de Pizan's most ready audience. The edition of the *Jardin* printed for Vérard in 1506, for example, survives in a vellum copy with woodcuts over-painted by hand, and has associations with Louise de Savoie.[27] The earlier, manuscript copy, which is now Bibl.

calls his love when he says in the book of love songs: "Come into my garden, my sister, my spouse ..."' All quotations are (unless otherwise noted) from *Jean Gerson. Œuvres complètes*, ed. P. Glorieux, 10 vols. (Paris, 1960–73), VII (i), pp. 144–54. [It has proved impossible to consult *Œuvres françaises de Cardinal Pierre d'Ailly*, ed. L. Salembier, *Revue de Lille* 25 (1907).]

24 For a reproduction of one of the miniatures in Bibl. nat., f. fr. 1026, and some discussion of other work by the artist who has been identified as the Master of the *Jardin de vertueuse consolation*, see *Illuminating the Renaissance: The Triumph of Flemish Manuscript Painting in Europe*, ed. T. Kren and S. McKendrick (London, 2003), pp. 246–51.

25 Noted by P. Meyer, in *Romania* 34 (1905), 631–2, reviewing A. Roselli, *Le Jardrin* [*sic*] *de Paradis, tratello mistico in antico francese* (Parma, 1905).

26 See E. P. Spencer, '*L'Horloge de Sapience*. Bruxelles, Bibibliothèque Royale MS IV III', *Scriptorium* 17 (1963), 277–99; and 'Gerson, Ciboule, and the Bedford Master's Shop (Bruxelles, Bibl. Royale, MS IV. III, Part II)', *Scriptorium* 19 (1965), 104–8. In Paris, Bibl. nat., f. fr. 24865, the *Jardin* accompanies a number of saints' lives and devotional treatises that may well have formed reading for women; I am grateful to Emily Richards, Ph.D. student at the Centre for Medieval Studies, University of York, for this information.

27 Paris, Bibl. nat., Vél. 1759; M. B. Winn, *Anthoine Vérard, Parisian Publisher, 1485–1512: Prologues, Poems, and Presentations* (Geneva, 1997), pp. 169, 174; J. MacFarlane, *Antoine Vérard* (London, 1900), no. 265. There are also woodcuts in the Dutch translation printed in Antwerp by Gheraerdt Leeu in 1487, *Thoofkijn van devotien* (ISTC ia00478250).

nat., f. fr. 1026, came into the hands of Louis XII of France (d. 1515), having been originally copied for Louis de Gruuthuse (d. 1492), the Burgundian duke who was friend and host to Edward IV during his exile in Flanders in 1470–1 and created earl of Winchester in 1472 in recognition of this.[28] Louis de Gruuthuse's activities as a bibliophile are well known: his own library was extensive, and many volumes from it still survive;[29] furthermore, he seems to have advised Edward IV about his book acquisitions and perhaps sometimes acted as an intermediary.[30]

While Louis's associations with Edward IV might be implicated in the attention of English audiences to *Le jardin de devotion*, it is also the case that the printing of the text in Bruges in the 1470s (ISTC ia00478100) may testify to its widespread appeal and cultural cachet. Caxton's collaborator, Colard Mansion, chose this as the first book he printed there: 'Primum opus impressum per Colardum mansion. Brugis Laudetur omnipotens', as the colophon states (the book is undated but has on the evidence of its types been assigned to *c.*1475–6).[31] Mansion's decision to print this text suggests that he felt it likely to sell; and it is hard to believe that Caxton, quick to follow Mansion with English translations of some of his other early printed books, would not have known something of the *Jardin's* popularity and appeal.[32]

Of the rather vague set of connections between *The Tree of Love* and *Le jardin de devotion* that I am able to advance here, the most striking is that both works seem to emanate from contexts the Anglo-French cultural intersections of which involved cultivated readers, whose tastes (like those of Christine de Pizan and her patrons) were for spiritually informed instruction about the proper conduct of secular, often specifically aristocratic or knightly life. One further set of connections that seems to play around the English *Tree of Love* may strengthen these affiliations: connections with the massively influential *Somme le roi* written in

---

[28] Kren and McKendrick, *Illuminating the Renaissance*, p. 246.

[29] *Lodewijk van Gruuthuse, Mecenas en Europees Diplomaat, c.1427–1492*, ed. M. P. J. Martens (Bruges, 1992).

[30] J. Backhouse, 'Founders of the Royal Library: Edward IV and Henry VII as Collectors of Illuminated Manuscripts', in *England in the Fifteenth Century: Proceedings of the 1986 Harlaxton Symposium*, ed. D. Williams (Woodbridge, 1987), pp. 23–41; S. McKendrick, 'The *Romuléon* and the Manuscripts of Edward IV', in *England in the Fifteenth Century: Proceedings of the 1992 Harlaxton Symposium*, ed. N. Rogers (Stamford CA, 1994), pp. 149–69.

[31] W. and L. Hellinga, *The Fifteenth-Century Printing Types of the Low Countries*, 2 vols. (Amsterdam, 1966), I, 28–9; *Le cinquième centenaire de l'imprimerie dans les anciens Pays-Bas*, Exhibition catalogue, Brussels, Bibliothèque Royale Albert 1er (Brussels, 1973), pp. 212–13, 216–19.

[32] A rather surprising number of books, surely too many for coincidence, were printed both by Mansion at Bruges in French and by Caxton at Westminster in English: G. D. Painter, *William Caxton: A Quincentenary Biography of England's First Printer* (London, 1976), p. 80. Painter lists *Boethius, Cato, Dicts and Sayings, Art of Dying, Controversie de noblesse, Ovid.* Louis de Gruuthuyse's manuscript copy, Bibl. nat., f. fr. 1026, may postdate the printed edition, and even have been based on it.

1280 by the Dominican friar Laurent d'Orléans for King Philip III of France and circulating in both French and vernacular translations through the later medieval centuries.[33] Chapter 75 in this lengthy treatise on vices and virtues initiates an extended horticultural allegory in which God, 'the grete gardyner' (in Caxton's translation) nurtures individual human gardens through the agency of 'the tree of lyf' (Jesus) and trees of virtues: the allegory appears to have attracted illustration in copies of both the *Somme le roi* and derivative texts such as the *Miroir du monde*, translated into English as the *Mirroure of the Worlde* (and like the translation of the *Somme* printed by Caxton).[34]

A still closer link between the garden allegory of the *Somme le roi* and the context that produced *The Tree of Love* survives in a collection of materials annotated by William Worcester, Fastolf's secretary and eventual executor, now Cambridge, University Library, MS Add. 7870.[35] The contents of this manuscript, largely French works on the virtues, include on fols. 68r–71r a hitherto unidentified extract beginning 'La seinte escripture acomparage la vie du preudomme et de sa preude femme a vng bel jardin plain de verdure … cest jardin est plante de bon jardinier cest de dieu …': apparently an extract from *Somme le roi*, although not there noted as such.[36] The manuscript as a whole is the work of three scribes all writing hands influenced by French scripts, one of whom (not the copyist of the *Somme le roi* extract) has recently been identified as the Ricardus Franciscus who produced, among many other things, Scrope's *Epistle of Othea* in St John's, MS H 5 and the French *Epistre d'Othea* in Bodl., Laud Misc. 570.[37] This Fastolf circle, invoked in the prologue to *The Epistle of Othea* in MS Longleat 253, and including Worcester and Scrope, stands as a representative example of the contexts in which French texts might be circulated, read, copied and perhaps produced in new English versions: a likely environment for the generation of *The Tree of Love*, one might think.[38]

33 *Frère Laurent, La Somme le roi*, ed. É. Brayer, E. and A.-F. Labie-Leurquin, SATF (Paris, 2008); L. Carruthers, *La Somme le Roi de Lorens d'Orléans et ses traductions anglaises* (Paris, 1980). Caxton's translation (*The Royal Book*) is STC 24763.

34 Scott, *LGM* II, 352–5, who notes on fol. 99v 'Garden of Virtues, with Christ bandaging a tree'; Caxton's translation is STC 24762–3.

35 I would like to thank Dr Cath Nall for alerting me to the presence of this extract in the manuscript. Its contents, and Worcester's annotations, are discussed in D. Wakelin, *Humanism, Reading, and English Literature, 1430–1530* (Oxford, 2007), pp. 103–4.

36 'Holy Scripture compares the life of a worthy man and his wife to a beautiful garden full of greenery … this garden is planted by the good gardener, that is, by God …': cf. Caxton, *Royal Book* ch. 75, 'The holy scrypture sayth thus. The wyse man or wyse wo=//man hath a fayr gardyn ful of verdure & fayr trees … Thys //gardyn planted the grete gardyner / That is god the fader …'. Fastolf probably owned a copy of the *Somme*, listed in the 1448 inventory of his French books as 'Vices and Vertues', a title it was often given; Beadle, 'Sir John Fastolf's French Books', p. 105.

37 C. Nall, 'Ricardus Franciscus writes for William Worcester', *JEBS* 11 (2008), 207–12. On Franciscus, see further Driver in this volume.

38 P. G. C. Campbell, 'Christine de Pisan en Angleterre', *Revue de littérature comparée* 5 (1925), 659–71, notes that Worcester used parts of Christine's *Faits d'armes et de cheva-*

The account of Worcester's interest in French books relayed to John Paston II
y one of his correspondents *c.*1458 is couched in terms that equate the cultural
ppropriation of the French language and French books to the acquisition of land:

> I may sey to you that William hath goon to scole to a Lumbard called Karoll
> Giles, to lern and to be red in poetré or els in Frensh, for he hath byn with the
> same Karoll euery dey ij tymes or iij, and hath bought diuerse bokes of hym,
> for the which, as I suppose, he hath put hym-self in daunger to the same Karoll.
> I made a mocion to William to haue knoen part of his bisines, and he answered
> and said that he wold be as glad and as feyn of a good boke of Frensh or of
> poetré as my Maister Fastolf wold be to purchace a faire manoir ...[39]

he English circles in which many of the works mentioned in this discussion
ere transmitted appear to have constituted communities in which the literary
ctivities of appropriation and reappropriation, extracting and re-embedding,
anslating and rehandling, were familiar. The interests of these communities
ere wide-ranging but also notably long-lasting: the works of Christine de Pizan
nd to a lesser extent Alain Chartier), for example, retained their currency from
e very early fifteenth century through to the early sixteenth, and continued to
ispire the production of new translations for printing; and they served a variety
f appetites, whether for statecraft (*Othea*) or for military lore (the *Fais d'armes
de chevalerie*) or for 'the woman question' (the *Epistre de Cupide*, translated by
o less than Hoccleve). The famously illuminated copy of Christine's collected
orks that is now BL, MS Harley 4431 has a long and interesting history of
fteenth-century ownership that in fact draws together all the possible connec-
ons so far invoked in this attempt to construct a milieu in which *The Tree of
ove* might have come into being and found an audience. Put together early
i the century as a presentation manuscript for Queen Isabeau de Bavière, BL,
Iarley 4431 then came into the hands of the Duke of Bedford's wife Jacquetta of
uxembourg, as part of the movement of manuscripts from France to England
hich was seemingly to be so important to Fastolf's circle.[40] From Jacquetta it
assed to her stepson Anthony Woodville, Earl Rivers, who used it for the *Moral
roverbs of Christine*, printed by his friend Caxton.[41] After Woodville's death the

---

lerie in his *Boke of Noblesse* (pp. 662–3), while Wakelin, *Humanism*, p. 105, tracks the
appearance of extracts from Alain Chartier's works, first in Worcester's notebooks and
then incorporated into his own compositions.
Paston Letters and Papers of the Fifteenth Century, ed. N. Davis, EETS SS 20 and 21 (2004),
II, 175.
) S. L. Hindman, *Christine de Pizan's* Epistre d'Othéa, pp. 13–15, 18, 100–1. For illustrations from MS Harley 4431, see the British Library Catalogue of Illuminated Manuscripts at http://www.bl.uk/catalogues/illuminatedmanuscripts/introduction.asp.
A. E. B. Coldiron, 'Taking Advice from a Frenchwoman: Caxton, Pynson, and Christine
de Pizan's Moral Proverbs', in *Caxton's Trace: Studies in the History of English Printing*,
ed. W. Kuskin (Notre Dame IN, 2006), pp. 127–66. On Woodville and Caxton, see
L. Hellinga, *Caxton in Focus* (London, 1982), pp. 84–94.

manuscript came into the library of none other than Woodville's friend Louis de Gruuthuse, bibliophile and owner of a copy of *Le jardin de devotion*.

It may seem that there is little to be extrapolated from this series of illustrations of the connections between French and English texts and readers beyond the conclusion that most remain impossible to trace or define with precision. All that is possible to say about the sources of *The Tree of Love* at this stage is that it probably owes something to French texts such as the *Somme le roi* and *Le jardin de devotion*, and that it circulated in a milieu in which French works apparently came to readers' hands as easily as English ones. For every *Epistle of Othea*, whose dependence on a French source is explicit and can to some extent be mapped in the pattern of manuscript ownership, there are many other works – like *The Tree of Love* – whose French connections are more resistant to recovery. The very intractableness of such connections, though – leading us into circles where French and English books circulated together, where English readers copied French, made notes on and in it, translated it, and used it themselves – has its own point to make.

30

The French of English Letters:
Two Trilingual Verse Epistles in Context

Ad Putter

I would like to focus on a pair of remarkable trilingual poems from around 1400, which take the fictional form of a pair of letters. One of these, entitled *De amico ad amicam* in a Latin rubric, is from a lover to his lady and opens with the French verse *A celuy que plus eyme en mounde*; the other, which purports to be the lady's reply, is headed *Responcio*, and begins *A soun treschere et special*. The poems have been edited several times, most recently by Thomas Duncan, on the basis of the two manuscripts that were then known to exist: Cambridge University Library, MS Gg.4.27 [C] – an important early fifteenth-century anthology once owned by an East Anglian gentry family, and also containing the earliest and arguably best texts of the *Parliament of Fowls* and the *Legend of Good Women*[1] – and British Library, MS Harley 3362 [H], a codex containing mostly grammatical texts and probably a student textbook, with marginalia that connect it to the University of Oxford.[2] A few years ago a new manuscript witness came to light in the *Armburgh Papers* [A], a roll, Manchester, Chetham's Library, MS Mun. E.6.10 (4), consisting principally of letters and legal documents mostly in English related to the Armburgh family. This family originally came from East Anglia, and the roll records their efforts to enhance their 'worship' and their portfolio of real estate in the county of Warwickshire. The Armburghs' preoccupation with the acquisition of landed property, and their tireless involvement in litigation as a means to this end, are symptomatic of their class and age. Fortunately, a scribe filled up some of the roll with poems, three of them macaronic. The editor of the roll, Christine Carpenter,[3] was able to identify one of these as the poem *De amico ad amicam*. Although the Armburgh version is an incomplete and careless copy, it does occasionally contain readings that are superior to those of the other

---

[1] See M. B. Parkes and R. Beadle, *Poetical Works: A Facsimile of Cambridge University Library MS Gg.4.27*, 3 vols. (Cambridge, 1979–80).

[2] T. Duncan, ed., *Late Medieval English Lyrics and Carols: 1400–1530* (Harmondsworth, 2000). Citations from the poems will be from this edition, with relevant variants in square brackets and departures from Duncan justified in notes. For a discussion of the two manuscripts, G and H, and their associations with courtly and clerkly culture respectively, see J. Boffey, 'The Manuscripts of English Courtly Love Lyric in the Fifteenth Century', in *Manuscripts and Readers in Fifteenth-Century England: The Literary Implications of Manuscript Study*, ed. D. Pearsall (Cambridge, 1982), pp. 3–14.

[3] C. Carpenter, ed., *The Armburgh Papers* (Woodbridge, 1998).

manuscripts.[4] Another macaronic poem in French and English, unidentified by Carpenter, is in fact the poem 'Swetyng, I greet three'.[5] The remaining poems in the Armburgh roll appear to be unique copies. The most intriguing one is another trilingual love epistle, which begins:

A ele que ayme sur tout rien,	*To the woman I love above all else*
Of all tho that in this world beene,	
Corde meo dure fixa:	*Firmly fixed in my heart*
Enterement me commaunde de quere	*I commend myself to you with all my heart*[6]
As ye that ben to me most chere	
Intra mundi climata.	*In all the regions of the world*

In metrical form, this is the closest extant parallel to *De amico* and *Responcio*, and it provides intriguing evidence that the 'French of England' retained a valued place in later Middle English literary production.

How do we account for the vogue of trilingual love letters in later medieval England? I hope to answer this question by examining various relevant contexts. I shall begin with literary history. Macaronic verse had a distinguished pedigree in England,[7] and the two poems in question represent the culmination of a fine literary tradition. Another important context is that of historical socio-linguistics, and, having briefly placed the poems in their literary context, I would like to consider them in the context of letter-writing, a social practice in which French maintained its supremacy well into the fifteenth century. In the conclusion I shall try to draw together the literary and socio-linguistic dimensions by showing how the poet (or possibly poets) of *De amico ad amicam* and *Responcio* absorbed the linguistic conditions of his own culture into the structure and dynamics of his verbal artifice.

The first stanzas of *De amico ad amicam* illustrate the virtuosity of the poems as well as the linguistic challenges they pose for modern reader:

---

4   For example, it is clear from MS A, 'Ore a dieu que vous garde' ('Now I commend you to God; may he keep you') that 'O a dieu' (C & H and editions) is a scribal error, presumably owing to failure to expand an original abbreviation. Cf. the error *o* for *ore* in MS H, line 24. Citations from MS H are based on my transcription.

5   The identification is that of J. Boffey and A. S. G. Edwards, *A New Index to Middle English Verse* (London, 2005), no. 1998. The poem was edited by R. H. Robbins (ed.), *Secular Lyrics of the XIVth and XVth Centuries* (Oxford, 1952), no. 172. The identification disproves Carpenter's theory that the poems are 'linked with a named and identifiable person' (*Armburgh Papers*, pp. 2, 58), and that the opening line in MS A, transcribed by Carpenter as 'En Jehan roy soueraine', is addressed to Joan Armburgh. The correct reading (from MS Douce 95) is *En Jhesu roy souerayn*.

6   Cf. the formula in the salutation in the previous (English) poem: 'To yow... I recommende me with all myn hert.'

7   For discussion and further bibliography, see E. Archibald, 'Tradition and Innovation in the Macaronic Poetry of Dunbar and Skelton', *Modern Language Quarterly* 53 (1992), 126–94.

A celuy que plus eyme en mounde,	*To the one whom I most love in the world*
Of alle tho that I have found[e][8]	
Carissima,	*Dearest*
Saluz od treyé amour[9]	*Greetings with faithful love*
With grace and joye and alle honour	
Dulcissima.	*Sweetest (lady)*
Sachéz bien, pleysant et beele	*Be well assured, pleasing and beautiful one*
That I am ryght in good heele	*health*
Laus Christo!	*Praise be to Christ*
Et mon amour doné vous ay,	*And I have given you my love*
And also thin owene nyght and day	*as your own*
Incisto.[10]	*I persevere* (*De amico*, 1–12)

We have before us, then, a trilingual macaronic poem in the guise of a love letter. The stanza form is the very British tail-rhyme stanza, with the Latin placed in the *cauda*. This metrical separation of languages is traditional. The simplest and most common form is well illustrated by the following macaronic carol on the Annunciation:

Now syng we, syng we,	
'Regina celi, letare.'	*Queen of heaven, rejoice*
Gabryell, that angel bright,	
Bryghtter than the son light,	
From hevyn to erth he toke his flight;	
Regina celi, letare.	
In Nazareth, in that cyte,	
Before Mary he fell on kne	
And sayd, 'Mary, God ys with the;	
Regina celi, letare.	
'Hayle be thou, Mary, of mytes most,	*mightiest*
In the shall light the Holy Gost	

Duncan, following MS C, reads *found*; emendation to *founde*, supported by MS A (*founde*) and H (*fonde*), is indicated by the rhyme with *mounde*, which evidently takes final –*e* (see *Responcio*, line 28).

Duncan, following a suggestion by Spitzer (see n. 10) emends to *Saluz odtrey e amour* ('I grant you greetings and love'), but the MS reading is defensible (*od* = 'together with'; *treyé* = *trié*, 'proven'), and confirmed by MS A, *Salutez ad verray amour*, where *ad* presumably represents *od*. AND, s.v. *od*, records *ad* as a variant spelling (*Song of Dermot*, 1109).

[10] C & H: *In cisto*. L. Spitzer, in 'Emendations Proposed to *De Amico ad Amicam* and *Responcio'*, *Modern Language Notes* 67 (1952), 150–5, suggested that the MS reading represented a nonce-word *incisto* 'enshrine'. To Spitzer's credit, the verb he conjectured turns out to have existed (though recorded only once in a literal sense, 'to put into a chest': see *DMLBS*. MS A, however, indicates an easier solution: *As your own man nyght and day / Consisto*. Also in C & H = *as*; *incisto* = *insisto*. Note the similar spelling of <c> for <s> in *Responcio*.

To saue the sowles that were lost;
  Regina celi, letare'

Hayle be thou, Mary, maydyn shene,   *resplendent maiden*
From the fendes, that be so kene,
Thou kepe and save vs all from tene,   *harm*
  Regina celi, letare.[11]

Here, as in most macaronic carols, the two languages, Latin and English, have different functions in both form and content: the English tells the story, while the Latin gives the story scriptural authority, in this case by citing a line from the liturgy.[12] In the second and third stanzas, the Latin verse is attributed (by the editor's quotation marks) to the angel Gabriel, who said no such thing according to the Vulgate (Luke 1: 28–37), but the editorial problem of who speaks is of no concern to the poet. The point in this and other carols is that the Latin transcends the historical moment, just as the Latin verse formally transcends the triplets by initiating a different rhyme sound.[13]

Our two trilingual poems have a much more sophisticated design, but the prototype of the macaronic carol still remains relevant. Again the Latin has been separated out in the tail line, which rounds off the couplet and demarcates the space where the two vernacular languages cohabit. And even while the poet does not give us any scriptural quotation, he nevertheless manages to give his Latin a liturgical or scholastic ring, as in the following stanzas:

De moy, jeo pry, aves pyté,	*On me, I beg, have pity*
I falle so doth the lef on tre	
Tristando;	*With grieving*
Tot le mounde, longe et lé	*All the world far and wide*
I woldë leve and takë thee	
Zelando.	*With fervour*
Pur vostre amour, allas, allas,	*For love of you*
I am wersë than I was	
Per multa;	*By far*
Jeo suy dolorouse in tut manere,	*I am sad in every way*
Wolde God in youre armes I were	
Sepulta	*Buried* (*Responcio*, 25–36)

Zelare is pure ecclesiastical Latin: in the Vulgate the verb is often selected to express love of God, as in *quia zelatus est pro Deo suo* (Numbers 25: 13). *Per multa* 'by far', strikes me as a scholasticism. The verb *tristor*, as Leo Spitzer pointed

---

[11] R. L. Greene, ed., *The Early English Carols* (Oxford, 1935), no. 237B.
[12] As noted by Greene, *The Early English Carols*, p. lxxxv, the source is a hymn for the Eastertide service of the Blessed Virgin Mary.
[13] For another example of 'temporally transcendent' Latin, see carol no. 100 in Greene, *The Early English Carols*, where the liturgical phrase *Lapidauerunt Stephanum* is attributed to the Jews, regardless of 'tense' and 'historicity'.

out, is not classical Latin either but first occurs in the Bible. *Sepulta* is the inscription one would expect to find in a churchyard rather than a love poem.[14] The poem's Latin, as Spitzer put it, has its own 'linguistic climate',[15] and this climate reeks of Church and school. Other tail lines such as *notate, converto, laus Christo, memento*, also take us there – as, of course, does one of the poem's manuscripts, Harley 3362, probably the textbook of an Oxford University student.[16]

This special linguistic climate of Latinity is not just a matter of register but also of syntax. One of the delights of the poem is that the Latin *cauda* is closely integrated into the preceding clauses. It is continuous both semantically and syntactically, and in the realm of syntax the poet achieves high standards of grammatical correctness. For instance, verbs are conjugated as required by the preceding lines:

Tost serroy joyous et seyn,	*I would be instantly happy and well*
Yif thu woldest me serteyn	
Amare;	*Love*
Et tost serroy joious et lé,	*And I would be instantly happy and joyful*
There nys no thyng that shal me	
Grauare.	*Oppress* (De amico, 49–54)

Another example is the first stanza of *De amico* (cited above, p. 399), which constitutes the initial address to the lady, who must therefore be designated as *carissima* and *dulcissima* in the vocative. The only lapse of correctness occurs in *De amico*, 25–30, which in the manuscripts (C & H only) read:

Sachés bien, par verité	*Know well, in truth*
Yif I deye I clepe to þe	
Causantem;	*The one who caused it*
Et par ceo je vous ore ser: [C *creser*; H *oreser*][17] *And so I beg you, sweetheart*	
Love me well withoute danger,	
Amantem.	*As the one who loves you*

Amantem is perfect, syntactically parallel with *me* in English; but *causantem* is wrong after *to*: Duggan's emendation to *clepe þe* is daring but justified and the error is easily explained: *clepe* has historical final -*e*, but since that final -*e* was recessive, later scribes habitually omitted it. Scribal loss of final -*e* is demon-

---

14 Cf. Skelton's *Epitaphe*, lines 18–19, '*Sepultus est* among the wedes; / God forgeve hym his misdedes', ed. J. Scattergood, *John Skelton: The Complete Poems* (Harmondsworth, 1983), no. 8.
15 Spitzer, 'Emendations', p. 152.
16 The most interesting companion piece in Harley 3362 from this perspective is a Latin story of St Nicolas's miracles (*miracula nicolay*, beginning fol. 34v), which contains English glosses.
17 The C reading is nonsensical. Duncan emends unconvincingly to *treser* 'serve you greatly'. It seems preferable to follow H, and to construe *ser* as *suer* ('sister', but also a term of endearment): see *AND*, which also records the spelling variant *ser*, due to the levelling of /oe/ to /e/ in Anglo-Norman (I. Short, *Manual of Anglo-Norman*, ANTS OPS 7 (London: Anglo-Norman Text Society, 2007), §10.3).

strable elsewhere in the poem,[18] and it seems likely that in this instance the scribe tried to rescue the metre by adding a weak syllable (i.e. *to*) of his own making.

With grammatical correctness comes grammatical complexity. The Latin tail-lines impressed Spitzer with their epigrammatic terseness, and the Latin verses certainly pack a punch in very few words, yet not infrequently they spring a syntactical surprise on us. The following passage is illustrative:

Douce, belle, plesaunt et chere,	*Gentle, fair, pleasing and precious*
In all this land ne is thin pere	*equal*
Inventa;	*Found*
Claunchaunt ou[19] la clere note	*Singing with your clear tone*
Thow art in myn herte rote	*the depths of my heart*
Retenta.	*Held fast* (De amico, 43–8)

The audience who read, or more likely heard, this for the first time would have every reason to expect a redundant tag in the Latin, since the sense of the French and English lines is apparently complete ('There is no-one equal to you in all the land', 'Your place is in the depths of my heart'). In the event, however, the Latin tricks us with an unexpected layer of grammatical complexity: the verbs in 'ne is thin pere' and 'Thou art in myn herte rote' turn out to be not lexical verbs (in the existential sense of 'to be') but auxiliaries, with *inventa* and *retenta* as past participles. At other times grammatical complexity is added by syntactical flourishes. The use of the ablative gerund is a particular favourite of the poet's – *dolendo, florendo, zelando, ludendo, crescendo, jocundo*. Though economical in the Latin, these gerunds cannot be translated into English without wordy paraphrases of the kind provided by Duncan: 'with grieving', 'while blossoming', etc. This untranslatability is, I think, part of the poet's achievement. The Latin does what only Latin can do.

So much for the Latin: how about the 'French of England'? With this question we move away from one obvious context of trilingualism, the medieval classroom, to another, equally important setting: that of the local manor house and the gentry families who owned the Armburgh roll and CUL, MS Gg.4.27. Arguably the key to understanding the role of French in our poems lies in the fact that the poems were written as letters. In this particular discursive domain, English was a very late developer. There are no surviving letters in Middle English before the last quarter of the fourteenth century. The first English love letter seems to be Troilus' letter to Criseyde in Chaucer's *Troilus*, and, as Norman Davis pointed out,[20] it is hardly surprising that this precocious English letter shows, throughout, the influence of French conventions of polite correspondence. One might indeed

---

18 See n. 8 above.
19 The preposition is AN *ou(e)* = *avec*, not as Spitzer believed an error for *en*. See e.g. *Formularies*, ed. H. E. Salter, 2 vols. (Oxford, 1942), I, p. 86.
20 N. Davis, 'The *Litera Troili* and English Letters', *Review of English Studies* 16 (1965), 233–45.

rgue that Troilus' letter is vestigially multilingual. First, it is preceded by the
Latin rubric *Litera Troili*, just as our macaronic poems are rubricated with Latin
titles. And, second, Troilus signs off in French: 'Le Vostre T'. If the signature is
authorial (as the manuscript tradition would suggest), Chaucer presumably put
it there to give the letter a whiff of French authenticity, knowing that such letters
would normally have been written in French. In a discussion of similar French
language gestures' in English poems, Christopher Baswell raises an interesting
question: 'Is the reader invited to experience these poems primarily as English
or rather as French coded in a more accessible tongue that is nevertheless easily
penetrated, at intense moments, by its genuine voice?'[21] Troilus' letter gives rise
to the same question.

Setting aside rare exceptions (like Troilus' letter), the languages of English
letters before the fifteenth century were Latin and French. As Dominica Legge
observed, the choice between the two was generally determined by the kind of
business being transacted.[22] Latin was the normal choice for ecclesiastical and
academic affairs, while French was the obvious language for secular business
and the affairs of the noble household. French was therefore also the language
par excellence of the love letter, and in the domain of verse it had eclipsed Latin
by the end of the twelfth century, by which time 'the genre of the love letter
becomes increasingly marginal in Latin literature'.[23] A fascinating insight into
this important linguistic dimension of the medieval love letter is provided by the
correspondence from a fourteenth-century Norfolk abbot to his lover Margaret.
Drafts of his letters survive by accident on the final folios of what I take to be the
abbot's own copy of Innocent IV's *Decretals* commentary in Cambridge, Caius
College, MS 54.[24] The abbot composed his letters in amateurish Anglo-Norman
verse, with the occasional line in English. The first draft letter begins as follows:

> M., ma especiele
> Vus estes bone e bele;
> Gardez qu vus seez lele
> Aval la mamele,
> Ceo vus mand vostre abe de grant reverence.
> Loke nou that hit so be in obedience.

> (M., my special one, you are good and beautiful; be careful that you
> are loyal within your breast. This is what your abbot demands from
> you with great reverence. Now make sure that you do so in obedi-
> ence.)

---

[1] C. Baswell, 'Multilingualism on the Page', in Strohm, *Middle English*, pp. 38–50 (p. 43).

[2] *Anglo-Norman Letters and Petitions from All Souls MS 182*, ed. M. D. Legge, ANTS 3
(Oxford, 1941), p. ix.

[3] E. Ruhe, *De amasio ad amasiam: zur Gattungsgeschichte des mittelalterlichen Liebesbriefes*
(Munich, 1975), p. 91.

[4] The correspondence was edited by P. Meyer, 'Mélanges anglo-normands', *Romania* 38
(1909), 434–40. Quotations are taken from this edition; translations are my own.

The abbot's second draft letter develops into what is effectively a trilingual poem in which the abbot asks Margaret to prove her love for him in word *and* deed:

> Savez que dit seynt Escripture?
> *Dilectionis probatio est operis exhibitio,*
> D'amour la prove est de metre en ovre.
> Ceste proverbe recordez,
> Que vus la bien sachiez,
> Et de moy donkes remembrez.
> Si rein vers moy vus plest,
> Com a cely a ki plest, etc.
> Have Godday nou, Mergerete.[25]
> With gret love y the grete.
> Y wolde we miȝten us ofte mete
> In halle, in chambre and in the street,
> Withoute blame of the contre.
> God ȝeue that so miȝte hit be.

(Do you know what sacred scripture says? The test of love lies in putting it into action. Remember this proverb, so that you know it well, and then remember me. If anything pleases you about me, as a man who is pleased with you, etc. Now farewell, Margaret, with great love I hail you. I wish we could meet often, in hall, private room, and in the street without public shame. God grant that it might be so.)

The abbot uses French as the language of polite correspondence, Latin to ground a dictum in *seynt Escripture*, and finally switches to English for a last heartfelt plea. This final code-switch can be paralleled in a number of early fifteenth-century official letters, where, as Herbert Schendl has argued, the switch to English in the concluding postscript appears to have been motivated by the writer's wish to strike a more informal note.[26] In the case of the abbot's coda, this shift from the objective to the personal is clearly registered by the selection of pronouns: in English, Margaret is addressed informally with the non-deferential pronoun *thou*; in French she is addressed formally (*vous*). As we shall see, there are clear parallels here between the abbot's draft letters and our two macaronic love epistles, between the multilingualism of real life and that of high art.

In the field of letters, then, there was no fourteenth-century 'triumph of English', and the linguistic situation in this area might usefully be compared

---

25 M. Camargo, *The Middle English Verse Love Epistle* (Tübingen, 1991), pp. 29–32, thinks this is the start of a new letter, but this is unlikely. 'Have Godday nou' is not a salutation in Middle English but a farewell (see *MED s.v.* dai n. 10(d)). Camargo's argument that the letters are a literary game does not convince me either: the abbot recalls incidents (a dinner party at Fakenham, a joint visit to 'the Rood' [?Bromholm Priory]) that have only private significance.

26 H. Schendl, 'Code-Choice and Code-Switching in Some Early Fifteenth-Century Letters', in *Middle English from Tongue to Text: Selected Papers from the Third International Conference on Middle English*, ed. P. Lucas et al. (Frankfurt, 2002), pp. 247–62 (p. 258).

with the supremacy of French in the legal domain. The Statute of 1362 may have proscribed the use of English in law courts but, as William Rothwell has argued, the Statute did little to alter the hegemony of French, first, because it was concerned only with oral pleading and, second, because in practice English simply did not have the lexical resources to emancipate itself from French.[27] As he writes, 'only the syntactical framework of the language of pleading would be English rather than French: the grammatical or function words – adverbs, articles, conjunctions, prepositions, pronouns – along with some common verbs would be changed to English, but the legal vocabulary would have to remain French because ... there simply was not any alternative set of terms with English roots'. In this context, it is not surprising that good French continued to be indispensable to gentry families who sought recourse to the law.[28] John Barton famously remarked upon this in one of the earliest vernacular French grammars, *Donait francois* (1414):

> Pour ceo que les bones gens du Roiaume d'Engleterre sont enbrasez a scavoir lire et escrire, entendre et parler droit Francois afin qu'ils puissent entrecommunicer bonement ove lour voisins, c'est a dire les bones gens du roiaume de France, et ainsi pour ce que les leys d'Engleterre pour le graigneur partie et aussi beaucoup de bones choses sont misez en Francois, et aussi bien que prez touz les sires et toutes les dames en mesme roiaume d'Engleterre volentiers s'entrescrescrivent en romance – tresnecessaire je cuide estre aus Englois de scavoir la droite nature de Francois.[29]

> (Because the honourable people of the English kingdom are keen to learn to read and write, to understand and speak correct French so that they can communicate properly with their neighbours, that is to say, the honourable people of the kingdom of France, and also because most of the laws of England and also many other fine things are put in French, and also because almost all the lords and ladies in the said kingdom of England like to correspond in French – I think it is most essential for the English to know the correct nature of French.)

As many scholars have observed, these words testify to the continuing vitality of French in the legal arena. However, reading the passage in full, one is struck that Barton thought of letter-writing as a parallel discursive field where French reigned supreme.

There is another hint of the primacy of French in love-letters from a slightly later love lyric written in the form of an epistle by a lady to her lover, which ends as follows:

---

[27] W. Rothwell, 'English and French after 1362', *English Studies* 82 (2001), 539–59.

[28] It is noteworthy that the *paterfamilias* of the Armburghs, Robert Armburgh, was probably himself a lawyer.

[29] E. Stengel, ed., 'Die ältesten Anleitungsschriften zur Erlernung der französischen Sprache', *Zeitschrift für neufranzösische Sprache und Literatur* 1 (1870), 1–40 (p. 33). For a brief linguistic analysis of this passage, see the essays in this volume by Merrilees and Pagan, p. 118 and by Machan, p. 368.

> goo lyttle queare, & recommende me
>   Vnto my mastur with humble affectyon,
> Besechyng hym lowly, of mercy and petye,
>   Of my rude makyng to haue compassion.
>
> & as towchyng *þis letter of translatyon*
>   *owt of frenche*, how-so-euer þe englyshe be,
> all þis ys said vnder correctyon,
>   with the supportatyon of your benyngyte.
>   finis.[30]   (*To her lover*, 15–22)

It appears from the words I have italicized that this epistle was first written in French and then subsequently translated from French into English. These circumstances are implausible neither in the context I have described nor in view of the kind of English that the poet produces. The vocabulary – *recommende, correction, supportacyoun, benygnete* – suggests a work that has been only half-translated. Indeed, in this epistle, as in the legal pleading envisaged by Rothwell, the discourse is only 'grammatically' English, the lexical words being predominantly French. Even when fifteenth-century letter writers did venture to coin lexical words with English roots, their terms continue to acknowledge the prestige of French epistolary style through their conscious mimicry of romance equivalents. For example, the kinds of greetings that adorn Middle English letters in prose and verse – 'Right well beloved', 'my most entirely beloved' – are so obviously imitations of elegant French salutations – *tresamé, treschier*, etc. – as to seem no more than their placeholders.

These observations should put us in a better position to appreciate not only why *De amico* and *Responcio* begin in French, but also what is special and artful about their use of English, namely that the poet never attempts to make English do the work of French. On the contrary, each vernacular language performs a very different task. Consider the following lines:

> Ma tresduce et tresamé   My most sweet and most beloved
> Nyght and day for love of the
>   Suspiro.   I sigh
> Soyez permenant et leal,   Be constant and faithful
> Love me so that I it fele
>   Requiro.   (*De amico*, 13–28) I ask

The characteristic registers and morphological structure of the French and Latin could hardly be further apart. The poet's English is typically Germanic[31] and

---

30 Robbins, ed., *Secular Lyrics*, no. 207.
31 It might be objected that there are lines (e.g. *De amico*, 5, 'With grace and joye and alle honour') with French-derived lexis, but in the entire two poems I find only eleven romance words in the English. The French input in the poet's English lexis (*c*.10%) is thus remarkably small. The norm, represented by Chaucer, is around 35%, as shown by C. Cannon, *The Making of Chaucer's English* (Cambridge, 1998), pp. 61, 228.

monosyllabic, while the French is polysyllabic and the Latin trisyllabic. Strikingly, as in the abbot's correspondence, the French uses the deferential pronoun of address, *vous*, as reflected in the plural verb ending, while in the English, the same person is addressed as *thou*.[32] Similarly, where the French is pitched at the moral high ground, *Soyez permanent et leal*, the English is down-to-earth: *Love me so that I hit fele*. It is as if the English says what in French is only implied, as if the English monosyllables were closer to the realm of natural desire.[33] It is revealing in this context to recall Spitzer's fine observation that the similes drawing on the world of nature occur exclusively in the English language:

[Vostre amour] brenneth hote as doth the fyr (*De amico*, 41)
I were as lyght as the flour (*Responcio*, 23)
I falle so doth the lef on tre (*Responcio*, 26)

What kind of linguistic situation is portrayed by this play of languages? I think that the poet takes advantage of the fact that, for him and his audience, English is the mother tongue and French the language of acculturation. And although he refers to epistolary convention by opening with French, which naturally came first in that domain, he is nevertheless conscious of the primogeniture of the mother tongue (and makes us conscious of it) by making the English say directly what the French says indirectly. So in the following lines from *Responcio* –

De moy, jeo pry, avez peté
Turnëth youre herte and lovëth me   (40–1)

– what strikes us is not so much the difference in meaning but the difference in pragmatic force, in the degree of communicative directness. The English unpacks the French, so to speak, with the result that the French verses often appear as secondary elaborations of the English ones. What we have in these poems, then, is a play not just of three languages but of three registers: *by virtue of the poet's deliberate art*, the English is 'natural', the French sublimated, while the Latin performs a third form of elaboration, typically by taking the preceding couplet to a higher level of syntactical complexity.

Of course, the essays in the present collection provide overwhelming evidence that in real life the linguistic situation was not as simple as that, and it does not follow from my exposition that I think it was. Poetry, as everyone knows, is a

---

[32] This is consistent in *De amico* except in line 59, 'And in your herte taketh entent', where metre, too, supports emendation to 'And in thyn hertë take entent'. In *Responcio* such consistency is lacking.

[33] If we imagined ourselves as speakers of a primitive language, as Roger Bacon speculated in *De signis*, we would begin by expressing things of immediate importance in monosyllables, from which polysyllables could subsequently be derived to name things of secondary importance. See K. M. Fredborg, L. Nielsen and J. Pidborg, eds., 'An Unedited Part of Roger Bacon's *Opus Maius: De Signis*', *Traditio* 34 (1978), 75–136 (p. 131), and for further discussion, S. Lusignan, *Parler vulgairement: Les intellectuels et la langue française aux XIIIe et XIVe siècles* (Montreal, 1986), pp. 39–40.

stylized form of language. For example, at the level of sound, poets exploit and perfect the possibilities and tendencies of normal language. The best macaroni poets stylize the socio-linguistic relationships between co-existing (and in par co-extensive) languages in exactly the same way. This is the claim I would make for the poet (or poets) of *De amico* and *Responcio*. The art of these poems lies in the exaggeration of the linguistic and socio-linguistic differences between Latin French, and English, a stylization that leaves us with a purified flavour of each and an idealized impression of their interrelationships.

31

The Reception of Froissart's Writings in England: The Evidence of the Manuscripts

Godfried Croenen

The anonymous author of a rhetorical treatise known as *Les règles de la seconde rhétorique*, written in northern France sometime between 1411 and 1432, opened his work with a list of poets, in which he included Jean Froissart. He mentioned him as an important writer of poetry in French, but he reminded his readers that Froissart 'wrote all his works in honour of the English'.[1] Although principally meant as a remark about Froissart's poetic *œuvre*, the comment may also have been applicable to his historical output. Both Froissart's poetry and his *Chronicles* were begun in the 1360s when the young author considered himself to be in the service of the English Queen Philippa of Hainault.[2] Froissart crossed the Channel in 1362 to offer Philippa a manuscript of a chronicle in rhyme, after which he became 'her clerk and served her'.[3]

The queen's service seemed to have consisted mainly of the writing of poetry of various sorts, in both long narrative and short lyric forms, and Froissart's earliest surviving poetic works can indeed be dated to this period. Although the collection of historical information also seems to have occupied Froissart in the 1360s, none of his historical works, in the form in which they survive today, can be dated to this decade. The Amiens version of Book I of the *Chronicles* probably dates from 1378–9, and all the other versions of Book I – as well as the other Books of the *Chronicles* – must be more recent.[4] While the period of Froissart's English patronage seemed to have come to an end with Queen Philippa's death in August 1369, many of Froissart's later poems, including the *Joli buisson de jonece* of 1373, and different versions of the four books of the *Chronicles*, contain references to his earlier connections with the English court. Towards the end of his life, in the summer of 1395, Froissart undertook a last journey to England, of which he

---

1 *Recueil d'arts de seconde rhétorique*, ed. E. Langlois (Paris, 1902), p. 14: 'Moult furent d'aultres bons ouvriers, par especial messire Jehan Froissart, curé de Lestines en Haynault; mais il fist tous ses fais a l'onneur de la partie d'Engleterre.'
2 G. Croenen, 'Froissart et ses mécènes: quelques problèmes biographiques', in *Froissart dans sa forge : Colloque réuni à Paris, du 4 au 6 novembre 2004*, ed. O. Bombarde (Paris, 2006), pp. 9–32 (pp. 10–15).
3 Croenen, 'Froissart et ses mécènes', p. 12: 'à laquelle [roine] ... je fus clerc et la servoie de beaulx dittiers et traittiés amoureux'.
4 Froissart, *Chroniques, Livre I. Le manuscrit d'Amiens*, ed. G. T. Diller, 5 vols. (Geneva, 1991–8), I, ix–xxiii.

included a nostalgic and highly literary account in Book IV of his *Chronicles*, in which he contrasts the reign of Queen Philippa and King Edward III with that of their grandson Richard II.[5]

Froissart repeatedly claimed that his patronage situation did not influence his historical judgement and that he was able to report even-handedly the great deeds of arms performed on both sides by participants in the war between France and England. Nevertheless, any reader of the *Chronicles* could be forgiven for mistaking the laudatory comments about Philippa and her court, and about the chivalric achievements of her husband and eldest son the Black Prince, as indications of a pro-English bias in his accounts of the early phases of the Hundred Years' War. Later readers certainly took this view of the *Chronicles*. Sorel, writing in the seventeenth century, commented that it is unmistakable that Froissart favoured the English over the French.[6] More recently Ph. Contamine and L. Harf-Lancner have explained the relative paucity of manuscripts of Froissart's *Chronicles* in late medieval French royal and princely libraries by stating that the *Chronicles* were considered to be too pro-English and hence unsuitable to be included in these collections.[7]

As regards the manuscripts of Froissart's poetry, literary critics have often interpreted one of the two surviving contemporary manuscripts, Paris, Bibliothèque nationale de France, MS f. fr. 830, as having been copied for a French audience, in a language with more *francien* features, and containing a selection of texts from which those with a more obvious English connection were omitted.[8] The omitted texts are found in the twin manuscript, MS fr. 831, which contains clear evidence of having been in England as early as the fifteenth century. MS fr. 831 was very likely brought to England by Froissart himself in 1395, when he offered it to Thomas of Woodstock, duke of Gloucester.[9] Later it was owned by Richard Beauchamp, earl of Warwick, and Duke Humfrey of Gloucester. The original French owner of MS fr. 830 has not yet been identified, but it has recently been suggested that this copy of Froissart's collected poetic *œuvre* would have been very well suited for one of his most important – and often underestimated – patrons, Enguerrand de Coucy.[10]

Other manuscripts of Froissart's poetry have been lost but are known to have existed. Apart from Thomas of Woodstock's manuscript, Froissart also brought

5   M. Zink, *Froissart et le temps* (Paris, 1998), pp. 81–110.

6   C. Sorel, *La bibliotheque françoise* (Paris, 1667), p. 323.

7   L. Harf-Lancner, 'Image and Propaganda: The Illustration of Book I of Froissart's *Chroniques*', in *Froissart Across the Genres*, ed. D. Maddox and S. Sturm-Maddox (Gainesville FL, 1998), pp. 220–50 (p. 235).

8   K. M. Figg, 'The Narrative of Selection in Jean Froissart's Collected Poems: Omissions and Additions in BN MSS fr. 830 and 831', *JEBS* 5 (2002), 37–55.

9   G. Croenen, K. M. Figg and A. Taylor, 'Authorship, Patronage, and Literary Gifts: The Books Froissart Brought to England in 1395', *JEBS* 11 (2008), 1–42 (pp. 10–14).

10 Croenen, 'Froissart et ses mécènes', pp. 25–7.

nother, more lavish manuscript to England in 1395 and offered it to King Richard II, an occasion of which he has included a well-known account in his Book IV.[11] Two years earlier, in 1393, Froissart was paid by the Duke of Orleans for a manuscript containing poetry.[12] A document from the ducal archives mentions that this payment was for 'un livre appellé le dit royal'. This may have been a reference to a single long poem, otherwise unknown, but it is more likely to be a reference to a compilation manuscript of Froissart's poetry, similar to the surviving manuscripts copied in 1393 and 1394.

All four manuscripts discussed so far – two surviving and two lost – are directly connected to Froissart himself and were produced for him, and probably under his direction, in the 1390s in his native city of Valenciennes.[13] His preoccupation with collecting and organizing his own poetic *œuvre*, and assuring that it was distributed in its canonized form among a particular target audience, has clear reminiscences of how the manuscripts of the collected works of Guillaume de Machaut came about.[14] Slightly later, at the turn of the century, Christine de Pizan was also engaged in a similar enterprise to produce manuscripts containing collections of her own works.[15] Christine's manuscripts were usually personalized for specific patrons, but often the constituent parts were produced in advance and could potentially be used in more than one constellation to suit different dedicatees.

Froissart was profoundly influenced by Machaut, and it seems quite likely that, in the 1390s, he was doing something similar to Machaut and Christine de Pizan – looking back at his literary career, taking stock of his literary output, and trying to reap the benefit by offering copies of his collected works to old and new patrons.[16] It is therefore not unreasonable to suppose that Froissart also had further manuscripts of his poetic *œuvre* made, to offer them, for example, to the other patrons he mentions in connection to the preparation of his English journey of 1395: Albert of Bavaria, count of Hainault and Holland, his eldest son William of Ostrevant, Joan, duchess of Brabant, and the Hainault nobleman John, lord of Gommegnies.

Gommegnies clearly had strong English sympathies, having served both Edward III and Richard II, but the other patrons mentioned in 1395 were rather pro-French. If we are to include three or four hypothetical manuscripts in our

---

1 Croenen, Figg and Taylor, 'Authorship, Patronage, and Literary Gifts', pp. 1–2. The *Chronicles* describe the king's manuscript as having a binding with silver clasps, rather than the copper clasps of the binding of Woodstock's manuscript.

2 [L.] comte De Laborde, *Les ducs de Bourgogne. Études sur les lettres, les arts et l'industrie pendant le XVe siècle et plus particulièrement dans les Pays-Bas et le duché de Bourgogne*, 3 vols. (Paris, 1851), II, 69, no. 5557.

3 Croenen, Figg and Taylor, 'Authorship, Patronage, and Literary Gifts', pp. 14–18.

4 L. Earp, *Guillaume de Machaut: A Guide to Research* (New York, 1995), pp. 73–97.

5 J. Laidlaw, 'Christine and the Manuscript Tradition', in *Christine de Pizan: A Casebook*, ed. B. Altmann and B. McGrady (New York, 2003), pp. 231–49.

6 On this phenomenon in general, see J. Cerquiglini-Toulet, *La couleur de la mélancolie: La fréquentation des livres au XIVe siècle, 1300–1415* (Paris, 1993).

count, the distribution of the poetry manuscripts tips in favour of French or pro-French patrons, at the expense of the English or pro-English ones, but if we stick to the evidence of the surviving manuscripts – and of the two unambiguous references to lost manuscripts – then the evidence of the early ownership of these manuscripts remains remarkably balanced, with half of the manuscripts destined for, or offered to, English patrons, and the other half to French patrons. What is puzzling in all this, however, is that there is no evidence of any further manuscript transmission of Froissart's poetry in England, especially of his earlier works composed in the 1360s under the patronage of Philippa.[17] The only evidence we have of the circulation of these works in English royal circles is Froissart's own references to them.

The situation of the manuscript transmission of the *Chronicles* is quite similar in this respect to that of the poetry.[18] We only know about the offering of the rhymed chronicle to Philippa in 1362 through the prologue of the so-called A version of Book I of the *Chronicles*, which was written probably about twenty years later and which only survives in manuscripts that can hardly be older than the turn of the century. For a long time scholars have assumed that this rhymed chronicle had been completely lost, although Delisle tentatively identified a chronicle fragment as Froissart's lost work.[19] The recent discovery of another fragment of the same text makes this identification a bit more likely, but it does not add any evidence to the circulation of this text in England, as both fragments seem to originate from the same manuscript, which was copied and transmitted in mainland Europe.[20]

In contrast to the prominent place given to the lost chronicle and its presentation to the queen, Froissart makes no mention at all of another chronicle manuscript that he had apparently planned to present to her grandson, King Richard II, probably as a gift on the occasion of his marriage to Anne of Bohemia on 14 January 1382. There exists an unusually detailed, independent source that shows

---

[17] On the circulation of French poetry in England in the period *c.*1400, see M. Connolly and Y. Plumley, 'Crossing the Channel: John Shirley and the Circulation of French Lyric Poetry in England in the Early Fifteenth Century', in *Patrons, Authors and Workshops: Books and Book Production in Paris Around 1400*, ed. G. Croenen and P. Ainsworth (Leuven, 2006), pp. 311–32.

[18] I shall not discuss the two surviving manuscripts of Froissart's Arthurian romance, the *Meliador*, one of which is nearly complete and one a mere fragment, because nothing is known about their early history and ownership. Nevertheless it is worth pointing out that in terms of layout, format and scribal hands these two manuscripts have strong reminiscences of the two surviving poetry manuscripts, MSS fr. 830 and 831, and also of some of the earliest manuscripts of the *Chronicles*, in particular MSS fr. 6477–9.

[19] N. R. Cartier, 'The Lost Chronicle', *Speculum* 36 (1961), 424–34; L. Delisle, 'Fragment d'un poème historique du XIVe siècle', *Bibliothèque de l'École des Chartes* 60 (1899), 611–16.

[20] D. Stutzmann, 'Un deuxième fragment du poème historique de Froissart', *Bibliothèque de l'École des Chartes* 164 (2007), 573–80.

that in 1381 Froissart had a copy of his *Chronicles* prepared for Richard.[21] It is likely that this manuscript was copied under Froissart's supervision. It was still unbound when it was sent to be illuminated by the Parisian painter Guillaume le Bailly. On 12 December 1381, however, the manuscript was confiscated on the orders of the duke of Anjou on the grounds that it was intended to be offered to the enemy. Although this particular copy does not survive (or at least has not been identified) it may have been the archetype of an important part of the manuscript tradition of Book I of the *Chronicles*.[22]

Froissart's apparent reluctance to mention this incident, or to discuss in any way his intention to offer a manuscript of his *Chronicles* to Richard II, is puzzling, especially since he gives the presentation of the poetry manuscript to the same king in 1395 such a prominent place in the *Chronicles*. It may well be that, despite the affirmative statement to that effect in the register of Anjou's chancellor, it was not Froissart himself who was behind the aborted presentation in 1381–2. If the gift was indeed linked to Richard's marriage, then it may have been Froissart's main patrons in this period, Duke Wenceslaus of Luxembourg and his wife Joan of Brabant, who wanted to mark the occasion with the gift of a suitably luxurious manuscript of a text that would teach the young king about the valiant deeds of his grandfather, Edward III, and father, the Black Prince. The Brussels court played an important role in brokering the marriage of Richard to Anne of Bohemia who was, after all, Wenceslas's niece. When Simon Burley, the English ambassador sent to Germany to negotiate the marriage, passed through Brussels, the duke and duchess provided him with their letters of support. It was also at Brussels that Richard's wife-to-be waited for a month for a safe passage across the Channel.[23]

When Froissart travelled to England in 1395 it would probably have been inappropriate to offer the king a copy of his *Chronicles*. This work, after all, was mainly an account of the wars between France and England, while the author's journey to England in 1395 was precisely made possible because of a prolonged truce, the result of the peace negotiations at Leulinghen. Richard II himself was very much in favour of a permanent settlement to the conflict. His second marriage, to Isabella of France in November 1396, was part of his efforts to find a peace deal. The marriage was already being planned in 1395 and it was one of the issues that occupied the king while Froissart was trying to approach him to present him with his poetry manuscript. After two weeks of attempting to do so, Froissart finally got his chance on 25 July, when he was introduced into the royal

---

21 H. Moranvillé, *Journal de Jean Le Fèvre, évêque de Chartres, chancelier des rois de Sicile Louis Ier et Louis II d'Anjou*, 2 vols. (Paris, 1887), II, 7.

22 A. Varvaro, 'Il libro I delle *Chroniques* di Jean Froissart: Per una filologia integrata dei testi e delle immagini', *Medioevo Romanzo* 19 (1994), 3–36; G. Croenen, M. Mary and R. Rouse, 'Pierre de Liffol and the Manuscripts of Froissart's *Chronicles*', *Viator* 33 (2002), 261–93 (pp. 277–9).

23 Froissart, *Chroniques*, ed. S. Luce, G. Raynaud, L. Mirot and A. Mirot, 15 vols. published (Paris, 1869–1975), IX, 208–9; X, 165–9.

chamber by the duke of York, Richard Stury and Thomas Percy. When the king asked him what the beautifully bound book was about, Froissart's laconic reply was: 'Love'.[24] This was an obvious reference to the subject matter of the courtly poetry contained in the manuscript, but it may also have been meant to please the king by acknowledging his planned marriage as well as his desire for peace and love between the two warring countries.

Kervyn de Lettenhove suggested that, despite the reasons given above, in the summer of 1395 Froissart also brought with him some copies of his *Chronicles*. According to him Besançon, Bibliothèque municipale, MSS 864–5, may have been one of these manuscripts. He further cites Phillipps MS 3338 as proof of the success of Froissart's endeavours to ensure the distribution of the *Chronicles* in England.[25]

Apart from the fact that Froissart does not mention bringing manuscripts of his *Chronicles* to England in 1395, de Lettenhove's hypothesis is very unlikely for other reasons as well. The Besançon manuscript, which contains Books I–III, cannot have been brought to England in 1395, because it was produced in Paris after the author's death, in the second decade of the fifteenth century.[26] The Phillipps manuscript, now New Haven, Yale University Library, Beinecke MS 593, contains a heavily abridged version of Book I, which follows a *Brut Chronicle (Short Version)*.[27] It is the only known copy of Froissart's work copied in Anglo-Norman. Both Besançon MS 864 and Beinecke MS 593 contain the A redaction of Book I, which Froissart would probably not have preferred any more in 1395. By that time he had rewritten Book I into what is now known as the B redaction. The fact that the A redaction of Book I was much more widely distributed in the fifteenth century has probably nothing to do with a change of heart on the part of the author, or a preference for this earlier version among his readers. It must simply have been the result of the early phases of the manuscript transmission of this text. Around 1400 a single exemplar of the earlier A redaction of Book I seems to have been the only text available to the Parisian book trade, which went on to reproduce exclusively this version of Book I.[28]

Beinecke MS 593 is very modest, both in size and execution. The manuscript, which has been heavily trimmed by the binders, now measures 213 by 146 mm. It has no illuminations or illustrations, but red and blue pen-flourished initials mark the division of the text. The *Brut Chronicle* is copied by two fourteenth-century hands. At the end, a later, fifteenth-century hand has written the following rubric:

24 Croenen, Figg and Taylor, 'Authorship, Patronage, and Literary Gifts', pp. 1–2.
25 Froissart, *Œuvres. Chroniques*, ed. J. M. B. C. Kervyn de Lettenhove, 26 vols. (Brussels, 1867–77), I[II–III], pp. 84–5, 119.
26 Croenen, Mary and Rouse, 'Pierre de Liffol', pp. 269–75.
27 Dean no. 36 (p. 26). On the Anglo-Norman *Brut* and its manuscripts, see further the essay by Marvin in this volume.
28 This may have been the manuscript of the *Chronicles* confiscated by the duke of Anjou in 1381; see above note 22.

'Cy finoient les veulz chronikes d'Angleterre appellez le Brute jesqes au temps du roi Edward le secunde. Et y aprés ensuoient pluseurs autres novelles croniques dez guerres de France, d'Angleterre, d'Escoce, d'Espaigne et de Bretaigne faitz en le temps du noble roi Edward le tierce, et sount extraitez pour nobles cuers encoragier et eulx moustrer exemple et matiere dez faites d'armes et d'onneur.' (fol. 118v)

('Here end the old chronicles of England called *Brut* up to the time of King Edward the Second. And there follow afterwards new chronicles of the wars in France, England, Scotland, Spain and Brittany waged in the time of the noble King Edward the Third and they have been composed to encourage noble hearts and to show them the example and substance of deeds of arms and honour.')

The second half of the rubric is clearly copied after a rubric of a manuscript produced by the Parisian book trade.[29] The abridgment of Froissart's *Chronicles* (fols. 119r–202v) must itself also have been based on such a manuscript, as it repeats an interpolation for the years 1350–6 based on the *Grandes chroniques de France*, which is typical for the manuscripts of Froissart's *Chronicles* produced in the French capital in the first quarter of the fifteenth century. It is furthermore interesting to note that in the prologue the author of the *Chronicles* is called 'sire Jehan Froissart, croniqer fraunceis' (fol. 119r).

Despite Froissart's efforts, the reception and dissemination of his historical work in England at the end of the fourteenth and the beginning of the fifteenth century must have been minimal. The increased circulation of the *Chronicles* in England in the course of the fifteenth century cannot be directly linked with the author himself, but depended on the book trade in Paris where – after the author's death – during the second decade of the fifteenth century, a number of book people were engaged in the production of copies of the *Chronicles*.[30] One such manuscript dating from this period, containing Book I of the *Chronicles*, survives today as Stonyhurst College, MS 1. This book was produced under the direction of the *libraire* Pierre de Liffol.[31] Although it may have been originally designed with a French client in mind, the earliest owner's marks link it to the Arundel family, and the book was probably in England before the middle of the fifteenth century.[32] Brussels, Bibliothèque Royale, MS II 2552 (formerly Philipps MS 24258), which contains Book II of the *Chronicles*, may very well be the second volume of the Stonyhurst manuscript. This book was also made for Pierre de Liffol, and inscriptions show that it was already in England in the fifteenth

---

29 Cf. note 36 below.
30 Croenen, Mary and Rouse, 'Pierre de Liffol'.
31 Croenen, Mary and Rouse, 'Pierre de Liffol'.
32 Stonyhurst MS 1, fol. 160v and 197r. For the suggestion that this manuscript was intended for a French nobleman, see P. Ainsworth, 'Representing Royalty: Kings, Queens and Captains in Some Early Fifteenth-Century Manuscripts of Froissart's *Chroniques*', in *The Medieval Chronicle IV*, ed. E. Kooper (Amsterdam, 2006), pp. 1–20 (pp. 5–7).

century, where it was owned by the Stanley family, earls of Derby.[33] Selling French manuscripts to English clients must have been a normal activity for the Parisian booksellers. The documentation relating to the trial of Jean Fusoris shows that in August 1414 Regnaut Montet, one of the four principal *libraires* in Paris, sold various manuscripts to English ambassadors, including a second hand copy of Froissart's *Chronicles* owned by master Pierre de Liso, which was sold to Richard Courtenay, bishop of Norwich.[34]

Another contemporary Parisian manuscript, London, British Library, MS Arundel 67, contains the first three Books of the *Chronicles*. The opening folio of the second volume (fol. 7r) bears the heraldic achievement of an unidentified prince of Wales, but these were added in the second half of the fifteenth century.[35] Another addition is the genealogy of the last Capetians starting from Saint Louis, written in Anglo-Norman in an English hand on the last flyleaf of the third volume (fol. 314v). Although the opening folio of the first volume has been removed, the table still shows the original opening rubric of Book I as 'Croniques d'Angleterre' (fol. 1r). This is an unusual opening rubric: in Parisian manuscripts the opening rubrics normally mention both France and England and in that order.[36] All this makes it quite likely that this particular copy not only reached in England sometime in the fifteenth century, but also that it was made for an English, rather than a French client, even if it is impossible to identify him or her.[37]

Some of the other surviving manuscripts that were in England by the sixteenth or seventeenth centuries may already have been in the country before 1500, but all those that definitely were in England before the end of the fifteenth century

---

[33] The layout and format of the Brussels manuscript are identical to the Stonyhurst manuscript and its twins, MSS fr. 2663–4 and Besançon MSS 864–5, which contain Books I–II and Books I–III respectively. The same scribes (B and C) and miniature painter (the Giac Master) who worked on these other manuscripts can be found in Brussels MS II 2552, which has an English inscription on fol. 1r. On fol. 84r is inscribed in a large fifteenth-century English cursive hand the name 'Stanley'.

[34] L. Mirot, 'Le procès de maître Jean Fusoris, chanoine de Notre-Dame de Paris (1415–1416). Épisode des négociations franco-anglaises durant la Guerre de Cent Ans', *Mémoires de la Société de l'histoire de Paris et de l'Île-de-France* 27 (1900), 137–287 (pp. 186–92); M. Rouse and R. Rouse, *Manuscripts and Their Makers: Commercial Book Produ cers in Medieval Paris 1200–1500*, 2 vols. (Turnhout, 2000), I, 285–90.

[35] On the various identifications put forward, see James P. Carley, *The Books of King Henry VIII and his Wives* (London, 2004), p. 52; Ainsworth, 'Representing Royalty', pp. 10–13.

[36] Cf. Stonyhurst MS 1, fol. 1r: 'Cy commencent les croniques que fist sire Jehan Frois sart, lesquelles parlent des nouvelles guerres de France, d'Angleterre, d'Escoce d'Espaigne et de Bretaigne ...' Sir John Fastolf's list of French books mentions 'Chro nicles d'Angleterre'. This may have been a copy of Froissart's *Chronicles*: see Beadle 'Sir John Fastolf's French Books', in *Medieval Texts in Context*, ed. Caie and Renevey (pp. 103 and 111, note 44).

[37] On the *libraire* responsible for this manuscript, see G. Croenen, 'La tradition manus crite du Troisième Livre des *Chroniques* de Froissart', in *Froissart à la cour de Béarn l'écrivain, les arts et le pouvoir*, ed. V. Fasseur (Turnhout, 2009), pp. 15–59 (pp. 19–20).

are now part of the royal collections.[38] They form two illuminated sets, produced in Flanders between the late 1460s and early 1480s. Both sets contain all four books of the *Chronicles*, distributed into four or five volumes. They are mentioned in the list of books in Richmond Palace in 1535 and were already part of the library of King Edward IV, although several of the volumes show traces of earlier ownership by Lord Hastings and Thomas Thwaytes.[39] Boffey has suggested that the garrison of Calais functioned as a crucial transit point for the transmission of these manuscripts to England, but it is more likely that the English book collectors who owned them had multiple contacts with the European mainland and were able to source these books directly from Flanders.[40]

Further copies of the *Chronicles* do not survive outside the royal collections, but they must have existed: witness some references to lost copies in fifteenth-century inventories.[41] The inventory of the manor of Marks (Essex), compiled after the death of the lawyer Sir Thomas Urswick in 1479, mentions a number of books, including Froissart's *Chronicles*.[42] Another fifteenth-century lawyer, Thomas Kebell, serjeant-at-law and squire of Humberstone in Leicestershire, who died in 1500, also owned books in French, including Froissart's *Chronicles*,

---

[38] A Paris-made manuscript destined for Pierre de Fontenay, now New York, Morgan Library, MS M.804, was certainly in England by the sixteenth century, and may have been there earlier: P. Ainsworth, 'A Parisian in New York: Pierpont Morgan Library MS M.804 Revisited', *BJRL* 81 (1999), 127–51. A fragment of a manuscript of Book III, dating from the same period and copied by the Breton scribe Raoul Tainguy active in the Paris region, was later used as a flyleaf for another French manuscript, which was in England also in the sixteenth century (Cambridge, UL, MS Hh.3.16 (fol. VII), see Croenen, 'La tradition manuscrite', pp. 17, 19, 57). A later fifteenth-century French miscellany manuscript, which contains an extract of Book I, Oxford, Bodleian Library, Laud misc. 745 (fols. 1r–36r), has an inscription showing that it was part of the library of Sir Richard St George, Norroy king of arms in the first quarter of the seventeenth century, before it was acquired by Archbishop Laud.

[39] J. P. Carley, *The Libraries of King Henry VIII*, CBMLC 7 (London, 2000), pp. 7–8, no 7–11 [7–11], 13, no. 37 [39], 17, no. 56 [58]; J. Backhouse, 'Founders of the Royal Library: Edward IV and Henry VII as Collectors of Illuminated Manuscripts', in *England in the Fifteenth Century: Proceedings of the 1986 Harlaxton Symposium*, ed. D. Williams (Woodbridge, 1987), pp. 23–41 (pp. 29–30).

[40] J. Boffey, 'Books and Readers in Calais: Some Notes', *The Ricardian* 13 (2003), 67–74. D. Grummitt, in an unpublished paper 'The Calais Garrison: Military and Cultural Exchange between England, France and Burgundy in the Fifteenth Century' (Centre for Medieval Studies, University of York, 3 April 2005), has called into question the importance Boffey attaches to Calais in this respect.

[41] A lost manuscript owned by Robert Wodelarke and mentioned in a book-list of St Catherine's College, Cambridge as *Historie cronicales Anglie Francie et aliarum regionum*, which Genet tentatively identified as a copy of Froissart's *Chronicles*, must have been a different work as the second folio incipit clearly shows that it was a work in Latin. J.-P. Genet, 'Essai de bibliométrie médiévale: l'histoire dans les bibliothèques anglaises', *Revue française d'histoire du livre* 16 (1977), 531–68 (p. 534, n. 8); cf. P. D. Clarke, *The University and College Libraries of Cambridge*, CBMLC 10 (London, 2002), p. 602, no. 85.

[42] London, National Archives, E 154/2/2: 'Also a book of Frenche of *cronekles called Frosard*, prise VI s. VIII d.'

which was one of his more valuable books.[43] Kebell left it in his will to Lady Hungerford.

Some references in sixteenth-century wills and inventories could also refer to manuscripts of the *Chronicles*, but none are precise enough to exclude the possibility that they are referring to printed copies of the French text, or to printed copies of Lord Berners' English translation published in 1523–5.[44] One such ambiguous reference is found in the will of Thomas Benolt, of 24 April 1534, who bequeathed to Thomas Hawley, Carlisle Herald 'all my foure volumes of Frosard'.[45] Another is found in the will of the London mercer William Bromwell, of 28 November 1536, who left to 'Oliver Leder gentilman, the hole volume of Frosard'.[46] The *Chronicles* were first printed in Paris in 1498 or 1499 by A. Vérard, and this edition was reprinted several times in the first half of the sixteenth century. King Henry VIII owned more than one printed copy of the *Chronicles*, and it was the Vérard edition, or one of its reprints, that was used by Lord Berners for the English translation dedicated to Henry VIII.[47]

Conclusion

In France the perception among many readers was that Froissart was an English-biased author. This judgement probably originated in Froissart's work itself, which told the readers repeatedly about the author's English patrons. It is unlikely to have been a reflection of the medieval reception of Froissart's work across the Channel. Of the limited distribution of the poetry, only half of

---

[43] E. W. Ives, 'A Lawyer's Library in 1500', *Law Quarterly Review* 85 (1969), 104–16; idem, *The Common Lawyers of Pre-Reformation England – Thomas Kebell: A Case Study* (Cambridge, 1983), p. 427. The inventory describes the manuscript as 'a boke in Frenche of the *Coronycles* in parchement, price liijs. iiijd.' (p. 437).

[44] John Bourchier Lord Berners, *The first (second/third/fourth) volume of Sir Johan Froyssart of The chronycles of Englande, Fraunce, Spayne*, 2 vols. (London, 1523–5).

[45] A. R. Wagner, *Heralds and Heraldry in the Middle Ages* (London, 1939), p. 110.

[46] London, National Archives, PROB 11/27, fol. 14v (I owe this reference to Bethany Sinclair).

[47] Carley, *The Libraries of King Henry VIII*, p. 62, no. 207 [332], p. 108, no. 543 [858], p. 262, no. 99, 295, no. 190–9; idem, *The Books of King Henry VIII*, pp. 73–6, 89. For the base text of the translation, see A. Varvaro, 'Problèmes philologiques du Livre IV des *Chroniques* de Jean Froissart', in *Patrons, Authors and Workshops: Books and Book Production in Paris around 1400*, ed. G. Croenen and P. Ainsworth (Leuven, 2006), pp. 255–77 (pp. 271–2); Croenen, 'La tradition manuscrite', p. 16. There exists another English translation of the *Chronicles*, containing only Book IV, at Longleat House (MS 54, fols. 1r–154r). On the basis of Kennedy's dating of [1475–1525] it could have been made either using a manuscript exemplar or a printed edition: see E. D. Kennedy, *Chronicles and Other Historical Writing*, A Manual of the Writings in Middle English 1050–1500, vol. 8 (New Haven, 1989), pp. 2673–4, 2888. I have not yet been able to study the manuscript itself or read the Ph.D. thesis by L. Claverie, 'Edition et étude du manuscrit Longleat House 54, traduction en moyen anglais du Livre IV de Jean Froissart' (Ph.D. thesis, University of Poitiers, 2003).

he known manuscripts were intended for English patrons. Froissart's historical work had a much wider distribution, including in England, but one can hardly characterize it as a huge commercial success. Less than 10 per cent of the surviving copies (14 out of 146 known volumes) can be firmly linked to medieval English owners or patrons. The real success of Froissart in England started with the translation of his *Chronicles* into English by Lord Berners, which inaugurated a long series of full and abridged editions, and several new translations published in the nineteenth and twentieth centuries.[48]

---

[8] For a list of these translations, see G. Croenen, 'Bibliographie de Jean Froissart' (http://www.liv.ac.uk/~gcroenen/biblio.htm) [accessed 1 July 2008]. See also most recently S. Echard, *Printing the Middle Ages* (Philadelphia, 2008), pp. 162–3 and 171

32

'Me fault faire':
French Makers of Manuscripts for English Patrons

Martha W. Driver

The Hundred Years' War was a period when boundaries, particularly in France were more malleable than we now think of them as being. Warfare, moreover was accompanied by cross-cultural exchange that transcended geographic or national identity. Cities like Paris, Rouen and Calais were held for long periods by the English, and their wealthier English inhabitants commissioned books from local scribes and artists, some of whom later travelled to England to continue their careers writing and illuminating manuscripts. The manuscripts of the period were quite often copied by multilingual scribes and illuminated by peripatetic artists for patrons of different nationalities: in this milieu, the question of what it might mean to say that a manuscript is 'English' or 'French' is a complicated one. Catherine Reynolds, for instance, has distinguished several types of manuscript patron living in English-held areas of France during the Hundred Years' War, including 'English', 'English French' (by whom she means French people living under English rule), and 'French French' patrons all of whom 'turned to the same artists' in the fifteenth century to decorate and paint their books.[1] So too the careers and affiliations of scribes and artists are mobile and various.

The scribe Ricardus Franciscus and the illuminator called the 'Fastolf Master' appear together and separately in the creation of de luxe manuscripts during the Hundred Years' War. One of the best-known manuscripts on which they both worked is Oxford, Bodleian Library, MS Laud Misc. 570. This copy of Christine de Pizan's *Epistre d'Othea* and the *Livre des quatre vertus* was written in French in 1450 for Sir John Fastolf, the British landowner and campaigner who spent much of his military career in France. Ricardus has supplied inscriptions in the ascenders, a feature characteristic of his work. In this case 'Me fault faire' the French motto of Fastolf, is repeated throughout the text (Figure 32.1).[2] The

---

[1] C. Reynolds, 'English Patrons and French Artists in Fifteenth-Century Normandy', in *England and Normandy in the Middle Ages*, ed. D. Bates and A. Curry (London, 1994), pp. 299–313 (p. 311). Thanks are due to Jocelyn Wogan-Browne, midwife to this essay.

[2] Jocelyn Wogan-Browne has suggested (pers. comm., 23 April 2008) that 'fault' is a 'standard form in the French of England' and that the motto might mean 'I must do it' ('noblesse oblige'), which is one clear reading of it. For another nuance in meaning see the conclusion of this essay.

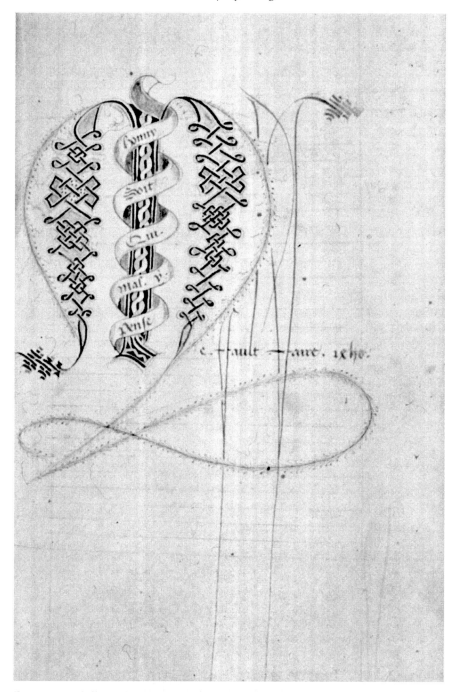

Figure 32.1: Calligraphic M, mottoes of Fastolf and Order of the Garter. Oxford, Bodleian Library, MS Laud Misc. 570, fol. 93, Christine de Pisan, *L'epistre d'Othea* and *Livre des quatre vertus*, in French, dated 1450

'Fastolf Master', himself named for this manuscript, is responsible for the illustrations and Ricardus has written and decorated the manuscript with strapwork and other pen flourishes.

Both scribe and artist seem to have been of French origin. Both were prolific and worked for the highest aristocratic circles in England. Jonathan Alexander's categories for the movement of books distinguish manuscripts that 'may have been specially commissioned abroad by owners who remained in or returned to England', or worked on by 'foreign illuminators [who] may have themselves migrated to work in England'.[3] Some combination of both of these seems at work in the careers of both the Fastolf Master and Ricardus, which can be partially reconstructed from the manuscripts they left behind. Several such manuscripts, including the three collaborations of the two men, will be the focus of this essay.[4]

In the case of the Fastolf Master, who worked in several cities over a span of about thirty years, there are currently some twenty manuscripts in which his hand has been detected or that are attributed to him.[5] It is generally accepted that the Fastolf Master began his career in Paris in the second decade of the fifteenth

---

3   J. J. G. Alexander, 'Foreign Illuminators and Illuminated Manuscripts', in *The Cambridge History of the Book in Britain, III: 1400–1557*, ed. L. Hellinga and J. B. Trapp (Cambridge, 1999), pp. 47–64 (p. 47).

4   A list of all manuscripts currently known to have been illuminated by the Fastolf Master or written by Ricardus, as well as those more tentatively attributed to them, is supplied in the Appendix, together with a time-line of relevant dates. Shelf marks are abbreviated where possible in the text, given in full in the Appendix. In the original form of this essay as a plenary address at the Eleventh York Manuscripts Conference, French in English Manuscripts and French Manuscripts in England (2007), fuller analysis of most of the known or tentatively ascribed work of the Fastolf Master and Ricardus was presented.

5   J. J. G. Alexander, 'A Lost Leaf from a Bodleian Book of Hours', *Bodleian Library Record* 8:5 (1971), 248–51, cites eighteen manuscripts (nine made for English use), along with one leaf in the City Museum and Art Gallery, Birmingham, that was once part of the eighteenth manuscript, Oxford, Bodleian Library, MS Auct. D. inf. 2. 11. His list draws on that of O. Pächt, 'Notes and News', *Bodleian Library Record* 4 (1952–3), 1. Another manuscript on this list, London, British Museum, Royal 15 E. VI, is later described by Alexander (in 'Foreign Illuminators') as by the Talbot Master (p. 55). Additions to Alexander's list include the Sobieski Hours (Windsor, Royal Library), described in E. P. Spencer, *The Sobieski Hours: A Manuscript in the Royal Library at Windsor Castle* (New York, 1977); Utrecht, Museum Catharijneconvent, MS ABM h4a, described in *Gothic Art for England 1400–1547*, ed. R. Marks and P. Williamson with E. Townsend (London, 2003), p. 228, item 92; and Paris, Bibliothèque de l'Arsenal, MS 575, identified in J. D. Farquhar, *Creation and Imitation: The Work of a Fifteenth-Century Manuscript Illuminator* (Fort Lauderdale FL, 1976), pp. 80, 82–8. König has identified the artist of *Le Livre du Chastel de Labour* (The Free Library of Philadelphia, Rare Book Department, MS Widener 1, *c.*1430–40) as the Fastolf Master, but Hindman, probably more accurately, ascribes the illumination to the Bedford Workshop. See *Das Buch vom Erfüllten Leben*, with commentary by E. König and G. Bartz (Lucerne: Faksimile Verlag Luzern, 2005), 2 vols., and S. Hindman, 'La Voie de Povreté ou de Richesse (Le Livre du Chastel de Labour)', in *Leaves of Gold: Manuscript Illumination from Philadelphia Collections*, ed. J. R. Tanis with J. A. Thompson (Philadelphia, 2001), item 70, pp. 202–5. Stylistic habits of the Fastolf Master do, however, appear in three of the illuminations, most notably the

century, then set up shop in about 1420 in Rouen (the English having taken that city in 1419) and subsequently followed his English patrons to England in the 1440s.[6] This move probably took place prior to the French reclaiming of Rouen in 1449 (see the appended Table 32.1). None of the Fastolf Master's surviving work is dated, though a few approximate dates can be reconstructed from internal evidence. We can, however, generally ascertain which of his books were made for French owners and which for English ones. Of the extant manuscripts, the majority have been made for English owners or come later into English hands.

Among the latter is a Book of Hours written in Latin and French (Cambridge, St Johns College, MS 264), for the use of Coutances, a suffragan of the Archbishopric of Rouen. This Hours lacks any English additions but was owned later by Lady Margaret Beaufort, countess of Richmond and Derby, who may have inherited it from her father, John Beaufort, duke of Somerset (d. 1444).[7] (Beaufort was knighted by Henry V at Rouen, then imprisoned in France after the Battle of Baugé until 1438, and subsequently served as a military leader in Normandy.) Lady Margaret gave this volume as a gift to Lady Anne Shirley on her marriage, personally inscribing it with: 'my good lady Shyrley pray for me that gevythe vow thys booke y hertely pray you / Margaret / modyr to the kynge'.[8]

A Sarum Hours written in Latin and French about 1430 for John, duke of Bedford (London, BL, MS Harley 1251), portraits of whom appear on three folios, is among the earliest illustrated by the Fastolf Master for an English patron. The miniature prefacing the Office of the Dead (Figure 32.2) has been adapted to represent the plan for Bedford's own funeral.[9] Given the style of the book and

---

representation of sculpted facial features and starry night skies (see *Leaves of Gold*, fig. 70–1, p. 204).

J. Plummer with G. Clark, *The Last Flowering: French Painting in Manuscripts, 1420–1530* (New York, 1982), p. 16, item 23; R. Wieck, *Painted Prayers: The Book of Hours in Medieval and Renaissance Art* (New York, 1997), p. 93, item 71, and passim. Farquhar, *Creation and Imitation*, p. 87, suggests that 'Although a number of [the Fastolf master's] manuscripts are connected with English patrons, this may be due to English occupation of Normandy rather than a period of activity in England.' Several manuscripts, however, may postdate Rouen's reclamation by French forces in 1449.

M. R. James, *A Descriptive Catalogue of the Manuscripts of St John's College, Cambridge* (Cambridge, 1913), pp. 311–13, item 264; J. Backhouse, 'Illuminated Manuscripts Associated with Henry VII and Members of His Immediate Family', in *The Reign of Henry VII: Proceedings of the 1993 Harlaxton Symposium*, ed. B. Thompson (Stamford CA, 1995), pp. 175–87 (p. 181); Reynolds, 'English Patrons', p. 308, and P. Binski and S. Panayotova, eds., *The Cambridge Illuminations: Ten Centuries of Book Production in the Medieval West* (London, 2005), pp. 204–5 (p. 205); M. K. Jones and M. G. Underwood, *The King's Mother: Lady Margaret Beaufort, Countess of Richmond and Derby* (Cambridge, 1992; repr. 1995), pp. 160, 298, cited in Alexander, 'Lost Leaf', p. 249.

Fol. 12v. Transcribed in James, *Descriptive Catalogue*, p. 311, and reproduced (illegibly) in Jones and Underwood, *King's Mother*, as plate 7 (between pp. 134 and 135).

A Catalogue of the Harleian Manuscripts in the British Museum, ed. R. Nares, T. H. Horne and F. Douce, rev. edn, 4 vols. (London, 1808–12), I, no pagination, item 1251; Alexander, 'Lost Leaf', p. 250; Scott, *LGM* I, 72, n. 19; II, 329, 331. Alexander, 'Lost Leaf', p. 250, cites this MS as for English use.

Figure 32.2: Funeral of John, duke of Bedford. London, British Library, MS Harley 1251, fol. 148, Hours of Eleanor Worcester, Sarum use, in Latin and French, *c.*1430

the many years Bedford spent in France (and his death in Rouen castle on 14 September 1435), it is likely that Harley 1251 was made in France.

Another Sarum Hours (New York, Pierpont Morgan Library, MS M. 105) illuminated early in the Fastolf Master's career, perhaps between 1420 and 1425, was made for Sir William Porter of Lincolnshire. Porter was knighted at Harfleur in 1415 and spent much of his military career in France; he took part in the siege of Rouen and fought at Patay. Attendant on Henry VI as a household knight, Porter returned to France in 1430 and died in England in 1434.[10] Porter's Book of Hours is illuminated with seventy-nine miniatures; at least another four illustrations are missing. Among English features is a table of contents supplied in English and Latin in a fifteenth-century hand. English saints predominate in the calendar, *memoriae* and litany, including Sts Cuthbert, Dunstan of Canterbury, Edmund of England, Erkenwald, John of Beverley, John of Bridlington, William of York, Winifred of Wales, Etheldreda and Frideswide. The artist has further supplied a lively scene of the murder of Thomas Becket.[11] Sir William Porter himself (Figure 32.3) is shown kneeling and supported by his guardian angel, his (Latin) speech scroll invoking all saints to pray for him perpetually. This very 'English' manuscript was in all probability made in France.[12]

The Fastolf Master's work further adorns the prayer roll of Henry Beauchamp, earl of Warwick (Utrecht, Museum Catharijneconvent, MS ABM h4a), dated to *c.*1440 and localized again to Rouen. Identified by his badge, Beauchamp is mentioned by name in prayers to Christ.[13] Not so readily identifiable English patrons appear in other prayer books associated with the Fastolf Master. One of these kneels by the tomb in a scene of Christ as the Man of Sorrows in a Sarum Hours (Cambridge, St John's College, MS 208), which has a calendar that includes feasts for Sts Dunstan, Augustine of Kent and Edmund Rich, the translation of Edward the Confessor and King Edmund, and an Office of the Dead for

---

[10] Plummer, *Last Flowering*, pp. 15–6, item 22; Alexander, 'Lost Leaf', p. 251; Wieck, *Painted Prayers*, p. 112, item 87; M. Driver and M. T. Orr, 'Appendix: Continental Manuscripts Made for the English Market', in *An Index of Images in English Manuscripts from the Time of Chaucer to Henry VIII, New York City: Columbia University-Union Theological* (London, 2007), pp. 70–3, item 76.

[11] Fol. 46. Morgan MS M. 105, 'Manuscript Descriptions', Corsair, available at http://corsair.morganlibrary.org.

[12] In most sources, including the Morgan catalogue, MS M. 105 has been localized to Rouen and assigned an early date. In a note in the Morgan file for this manuscript, Jonathan Alexander usefully blurs this matter-of-fact provenance: 'done in England or for Engl. use by Master of Sir John Fastolf' (see 'Manuscript Descriptions' cited in n. 11 above). Given Porter's career in France and his death in 1434, it seems likely his manuscript was made in France, as were most of those illuminated by the Fastolf Master early on.

[13] H. van der Velden, 'Prayer Roll of Henry Beauchamp, Duke of Warwick', in *Gothic Art for England 1400–1547*, ed. R. Marks and P. Williamson with E. Townsend (London, 2003), p. 228, item 92; A. Payne, 'The Beauchamps and the Nevilles', in *Gothic Art for England*, ed. Marks and Williamson with Townsend, pp. 219–21.

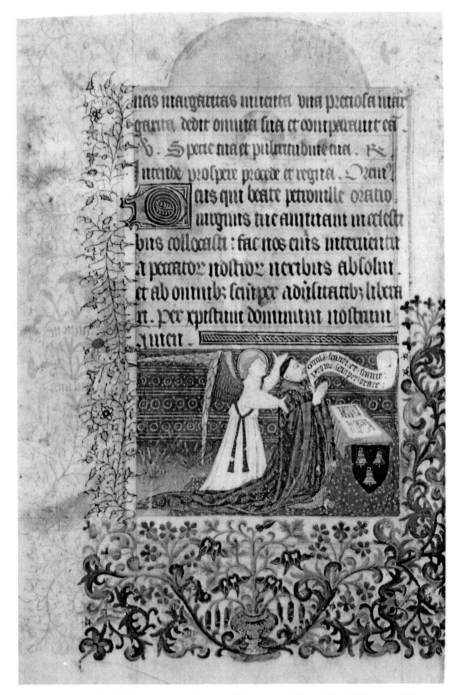

Figure 32.3: Sir William Porter with Guardian Angel. New York, Morgan Library and Museum, MS Morgan M. 105, fol. 84v, Kildare Book of Hours, Sarum use, in Latin with later English additions, *c.*1420–*c.*1425

arum use. References to Becket and the popes are erased. While the main text is Latin, prayers in English have been written over four pages. Once again, the categorization of the manuscript as French or English is problematic, though it has most recently become an 'English' manuscript.[14]

This mobility in the localization of manuscripts illuminated by the Fastolf Master occurs elsewhere in his *œuvre* and extends to fine detail. The Huntington Library catalogue places MS HM 47405, a copy of Walter Burley's Lives of Philosophers, in the middle of the fifteenth century and describes it as 'written in England, or perhaps in France where it may have received its historiated initial and marginal spray, but in England from an early date, as shown by the distinctly English decoration of the 2-line blue initials, and by the finding notes in the margins in an English hand'.[15] Another manuscript illuminated by the Fastolf Master and localized to England based on its English decoration is a Book of Hours for Sarum use (New York, Pierpont Morgan Library, MS Glazier 9) in Latin. John Plummer dates the manuscript to between 1440 and 1450, localizes it to either Northern France or England, and cites the artist's reliance on models originally supplied by the Boucicaut Master for much of the book's iconography. But Plummer also notes that 'the luxuriant borders are native', that is, made in England.[16] In her 1996 Survey, Kathleen Scott firmly places the production of this manuscript in England, calling it 'an outstanding product of the trend c.1450 to have Continental illuminators cross the Channel and work on books with native craftsmen'.[17]

Unlike the Fastolf Master, who served both French and English patrons, Ricardus Franciscus seems mainly to have been employed in copying books for English owners. Every work on his publication list (see Appendix) has English connections. Ricardus copied manuscripts in Latin, French and English for a number of known English patrons. These include John Fastolf, John Smert, Garter King of Arms, and later Edward IV and persons in his immediate circle.[18]

---

14 The Bodleian catalogue identifies this volume as French and dates it as mid-fifteenth century. Alexander and Temple include it under French manuscripts, again assigning a mid-fifteenth-century date (J. J. G. Alexander and E. Temple, *Illuminated Manuscripts in Oxford College Libraries, the University Archives and the Taylor Institution* (Oxford, 1985), p. 75, item 763). Ralph Hanna, however, localizes the manuscript to England and places it in the last quarter of the fifteenth century (R. Hanna with J. Griffiths, *Western Medieval Manuscripts of St. John's College, Oxford* (Oxford, 2002), pp. 308–9).

15 Walter Burley's *De vita et moribus philosophorum* (HM 47405), in Dutschke, *Guide to Medieval and Renaissance Manuscripts*, Digital Scriptorium, online at http://sunsite3.berkeley.edu/hehweb/HM47405.html [accessed 11 November 2008].

16 J. Plummer, *The Glazier Collection of Illuminated Manuscripts* (New York, 1968), p. 36, item 47; Plummer, *Last Flowering*, p. 16, item 23; Alexander, 'Lost Leaf', p. 251; K. L. Scott, 'A Mid-Fifteenth Century English Illuminating Shop and Its Customers', *JWCI* 31 (1968), 170–96 (p. 193, n. 130).

17 Scott, *LGM* II, 296–9 (p. 297), item 108.

18 M. Driver and M. Orr, *Index of Images*, pp. 40–4, item 32; Scott, *LGM* II, 322–5 (pp. 322–3), item 120.

Figure 32.4: Explicit Book I, Incipit Book II. New York, Morgan Library and Museum, MS M. 126, fols. 28v–29, John Gower, *Confessio amantis*, in English and Latin, *c.*1470

The style of calligraphy employed by Ricardus shows the influence of French *lettre bâtarde*. He often adorns ascenders and descenders with cadels and scroll-work (Figure 32.4).[19] As in the Laudian manuscript of Christine de Pizan made for Sir John Fastolf, these decorative spaces are sometimes filled in with inscriptions, which may be mottoes, names or lines of poetry. Several legal texts and documents have been signed (and sometimes dated) by Ricardus, including a statute copied in French during the reign of Edward IV. Because this document contains internal corrections made by the scribe, it has been suggested that Ricardus was fluent in Continental French and was French by birth.[20]

Ricardus is known to have worked in London with the artist William Abell; their work appears together, for example, in the Huntington Library's Statutes of the Archdeaconry of London, a text signed and dated 1447 by the scribe. Abell was a limner and stationer who was active in London from 1447 to 1474.[21] Ricardus wrote the grant of arms for the Tallow Chandler's Company of the City of London, a document with an initial 'A' supplied by Abell. The patent of arms, written in French and dated 24 September 1456, was granted and sealed by John Smert, Garter King of Arms. The hands of Ricardus and Abell are further found in a two-volume cartulary compiled by John Cok in the 1450s and 1460s. Ricardus wrote part of the text, and Abell supplied two historiated initials. These texts suggest that Ricardus may have been working in England from the 1440s.[22]

In the illuminated copy of John Gower's *Confessio amantis* in New York, Pierpont Morgan Library, MS M. 126, are twenty-one inscriptions supplied by the scribe. Some are recorded in the Morgan descriptive catalogue as 'Belle Lavine', 'Une le Roy' and 'Roy Lavine'.[23] These are misreadings in the Morgan catalogue, which overlook the playfulness of the scribe, who has written his inscriptions forwards, backwards, and even upside down. Correctly transcribed, the inscrip-

---

[19] M. B. Parkes, *English Cursive Book Hands 1250–1500* (Oxford, 1969), pp. xxi, 15, item 15.

[20] This according to the document's discoverer, Lisa Jefferson, who in her 'Two Fifteenth-Century Manuscripts of the Statutes of the Order of the Garter', in *English Manuscript Studies 1100–1700*, ed. P. Beal and J. Griffiths (London, 1995), V, 18–35, p. 19, cites thirteen manuscripts ascribed to Ricardus; R. Hamer, 'Spellings of the Fifteenth-Century Scribe Ricardus Franciscus', in *Five Hundred Years of Words and Sounds: A Festschrift for Eric Dobson*, ed. E. G. Stanley and D. Gray (Cambridge, 1983), pp. 63–73; C. M. Meale, 'Book Production and Social Status', in *Book Production and Publishing in England, 1375–1475*, ed. J. Griffiths and D. Pearsall (Cambridge, 1989), p. 202.

[21] J. Alexander, 'William Abell "Lymnour" and 15th-Century English Illumination', in *Kunsthistorische Forschungen Otto Pächt zu seinem 70. Geburtstag*, ed. A. Rosenauer and G. Weber (Vienna, 1972), pp. 166–72 (p. 166); C. P. Christianson, *A Directory of London Stationers and Book Artisans 1300–1500* (New York, 1990), pp. 59–60. Scott, *LGM* II, 319, lists eight manuscripts copied by Ricardus. M. D. Rust, *Imaginary Worlds in Medieval Books: Exploring the Manuscript Matrix* (New York, 2007), p. 166, says Ricardus copied nine manuscripts.

[22] Scott, 'Mid-Fifteenth Century English Illuminating Shop', p. 170, n. 3; Alexander, 'William Abell', p. 170.

[23] MS M 126, 'Manuscript Descriptions', Corsair, available at http://corsair.morganlibrary.org; see also Scott, *LGM* II, 323, item 120.

Figure 32.5: '*Vive La Belle quod Rycharde*'. New York, Morgan Library and Museum, MS M. 126, fol. 65v, John Gower, *Confessio amantis*, in English and Latin, *c.*1470

tions read 'Vive le roy' and 'Vive la belle'; these appear frequently, along with 'ave maria' and other Marian prayers, throughout the manuscript. The predominance of Marian prayers might indicate an aristocratic woman patron. Evidence of a female patron or owner may also be deduced from the first note to appear: 'I wold fayn please my lady.' Another proclaims, 'viue Le roy Edward IVe'. There are also several mottoes, including 'ma vie endure qd R'; 'prenes engre mon (coeur)' with a drawing of a heart; and 'a mon plesir qd R'. 'Prenes engre' perhaps derives from one of the lyrics of Charles d'Orléans, the line 'Take this with pleasure, I pray you' repeated as the refrain of a song. Known through the sixteenth century, the phrase closes John Skelton's *Garland of Laurel* dedicated to he countess of Surrey and her ladies.[24] The most important of these notations s found written upside down in an ascender on folio 65v, 'Vive la belle quod Rycharde' (Figure 32.5). Though the name 'Rycharde' seems jotted hurriedly, it s similar to the autograph in the document uncovered by Jefferson, as well as to he Huntington Statutes signature.

Marian prayers are repeated by Ricardus in ribbon-work flourishing in the script of the Rosenbach copy of John Lydgate's *Fall of Princes*, which, like New York, Pierpont Morgan Library, MS M. 126, has been dated to the third quarter of the fifteenth century.[25] Scott has found the hand of one of the two artists she identifies in the Rosenbach Lydgate, along with the border artist of M. 126, in an English translation of the *Quadrilogue* of Alain Chartier (MS 85), dated to about 1460 to 1475. This manuscript copied by Ricardus also has inscriptions in bande-roles throughout.[26] Close examination of several other manuscripts copied by Ricardus shows not only the use of inscriptions but connections between artists supplying initials and other aspects of decoration, which seems to imply the existence of a coterie of artists who, like the Fastolf Master and Ricardus, worked in the fifteenth century for a network of aristocratic patrons.

Two Middle English manuscripts copied by Ricardus return us to the Fastolf circle. London, BL, MS Harley 4012 was identified by Malcolm Parkes in 1977 as written by Ricardus.[27] Evidence that this is indeed the hand of Ricardus may be seen in various markers, for example, the use of *lettre bâtarde*, banderoles inscribed with mottoes, and the decorative use of hair-lines and ornamental capi-tals. This manuscript, a compendium of eighteen Middle English religious texts, was written for Anne Harling, the niece and wealthy ward of Sir John Fastolf in the 1430s. Her father, Sir Robert Harling, Fastolf's nephew, was killed at the siege of St Denis in 1435.

As Edward Wilson has pointed out, Anne signed this manuscript when married to her second husband: 'Thys ys the boke of Dame Anne Wyngefeld of

---

24 P. Champion, ed., *Charles D'Orléans: Poésies, I, La retenue d'amours, ballades, chansons, complaintes et caroles* (Paris, 1956), p. 222, chanson XXXI. See C. M. Meale, ' "Prenes: engre": An Early Sixteenth-Century Presentation Copy of *The Erle of Tolous'*, in *Romance Reading on the Book: Essays on Medieval Narrative Presented to Maldwyn Mills*, ed. J. Fellows, R. Field, G. Rogers and J. Weiss (Cardiff, 1996), pp. 221–36. The verse closes Skelton's *The Garland of Laurel* in editions printed by Richard Fawkes in 1523 (STC 22610) and Thomas Marshe in 1568 (STC 22608).

25 J. Krochalis, 'John Lydgate, *Fall of Princes'*, in *Sixty Bokes Olde and Newe: Manuscripts and Early Printed Books from Libraries in and Near Philadelphia*, ed. D. Anderson (Knoxville TN, 1986), pp. 105–9, says last third of the fifteenth century. Scott, *LGM* II, 320–2 (p. 320), item 119, provides the date c.1465–75 and repeats that date in her catalogue description (Scott, '*Fall of Princes* by John Lydgate', in *Leaves of Gold*, ed. Tanis with Thompson, item 72, p. 208).

26 Scott, *LGM* II, 318–20, item 118.

27 Parkes's dating is reported in E. Wilson, 'A Middle English Manuscript at Coughton Court, Warwickshire, and British Library MS. Harley 4012', *Notes & Queries* 24 (July 1977), 295–303 (p. 299).

Figure 32.6: Crucifixion. London, British Library, MS Harley 4012, fol. 109r, Middle English religious miscellany, *c.*1460–*c.*1470

ha[rl]ing.'[28] Anne Dutton has suggested the manuscript may have been copied when Sir Robert Wingfield went into exile with Edward IV in 1470; its pious contents are consolatory and reaffirm the sober, respectable reputation of its owner. The manuscript includes a humble pen-and-ink drawing of the Crucifixion that introduces an indulgence text (Figure 32.6), the only illustration in this volume and perhaps supplied by its scribe. Or the book might have been copied after Edward's return to England, when Wingfield was rewarded for his loyalty by 'becoming controller to the king's household 1471–81', placing this manuscript in the same court circles as Morgan M. 126.[29] Most interesting for

[28] Wilson, 'A Middle English Manuscript at Coughton Court', p. 301.

[29] A. M. Dutton, 'Piety, Politics and Persona: British Library MS Harley 4012 and Anne Harling', in *Prestige, Authority and Power in Late Medieval Manuscripts and Texts*, ed. F. Riddy (Cambridge, 2000), pp. 133–46 (p. 135), confuses the Fastolf Master with

the current study is the inscription 'ane' in the hand of the scribe written in an ascender on folio 15r (Figure 32.7), a direct reference by Ricardus to the name of the book's owner, Anne Harling.

One manuscript of Stephen Scrope's English translation of Christine's *Epistre d'Othea* (MS H. 5) was also copied by Ricardus. Scrope was Sir John Fastolf's stepson and a member of Fastolf's household.[30] Scrope's English text shares a common source with Oxford, MS Laud Misc. 570 (the French version of the *Othea* that Ricardus copied for Fastolf). The English text of the *Othea* made by Ricardus is illustrated with one colour and five grisaille miniatures.[31] Alexander and Scott agree that the illustrations in the St John's *Othea* are related to those in MS Laud Misc. 570. Alexander comments, 'Abell certainly knew the work of one foreign artist. This is proved by his copies of the miniatures by the so-called "Master of Sir John Fastolf" in the Laudian manuscript.'[32]

Knowing something now of the habits of both artist and scribe, let us turn to their three collaborations. The work of the Fastolf Master and the writing of Ricardus appear in a mid-fifteenth-century Sarum Hours (London, BL, MS Harley 2915), a collaboration first identified by Janet Backhouse in 1970.[33] Like New York, Pierpont Morgan Library, MS Glazier 9, this manuscript has striking acanthus borders executed in grisaille. The Fastolf Master works here in grisaille and semi-grisaille. The script shows the characteristic spikiness of Ricardus' *lettre bâtarde*, along with banderoles wrapped around ascenders, and the use of ornamental penwork. Though the original owner is unknown, a prayer composed for

Ricardus, incorrectly attributing the script of Harley 4012 to the Fastolf Master (p. 136). She also notes Norman Davis's comment (reported in Wilson, 'A Middle English Manuscript at Coughton Court', p. 299) 'that the hand resembles that of a scribe of Fastolf's in three letters dated from 1455 to 1456, written at Caister' (Dutton, 'Piety, Politics and Persona', p. 136).

[30] James, *Descriptive Catalogue*, pp. 238–40, item 208; C. F. Bühler, ed., *The Epistle of Othea*, translated from the French text of Christine de Pisan by Stephen Scrope, EETS (Oxford, 1970), pp. xiv–xv. See also 'Appendix B, A Note on St. John's College, Cambridge, MS. H. 5', by A. I. Doyle, ibid., pp. 125–7, for a description of the script. Binski and Panayotova, *The Cambridge Illuminations*, p. 270, item 126, describe Scrope's edition as 'the only one [of three independent English translations of de Pisan's *Othea*] to include illustrations'. This is incorrect, as Morgan MS M. 775 illustrates an English text of *Othea* with three half-page miniatures. See Driver and Orr, *Index of Images*, p. 56, item 50. Scrope's translation was later corrected by William Worcester, Fastolf's amanuensis and chronicler. See K. B. McFarlane, 'William Worcester: A Preliminary Survey', in *Studies Presented to Sir Hilary Jenkinson*, ed. J. Conway Davis (London, 1957), p. 215.

[31] All are attributed by Alexander to Abell ('William Abell', p. 168, item 19); Scott, however, has identified only the colour miniature as by Abell and says the grisaille illustrations are by 'a second hand of similar artistic stature' (Scott, *LGM* II, 264).

[32] Alexander, 'William Abell', p. 170; Scott, *LGM* II.

[33] *A Catalogue of the Harleian Manuscripts* II, ed Nares, Horne and Ellis, item 2915; Alexander, 'Lost Leaf', p. 250, n. 9; J. Backhouse, *Books of Hours* (London, 1985), pp. 30–1, fig. 26; J. Backhouse, *The Illuminated Page: Ten Centuries of Manuscript Painting in the British Library* (London, 1997), p. 175; Marks and Williamson, *Gothic Art*, pp. 344–5, item 224.

Figure 32.7: 'An[n]e'. London, British Library, MS Harley 4012, fol. 51r, Middle
English religious miscellany, c.1460–c.1470

John, duke of Bedford, occurs over several folios. Given the evidence, this Book
of Hours may have been made for an English aristocrat in the duke of Bedford's
circle. Reynolds suggests this was either Richard, duke of York or Edmund or
John Beaufort.[34] John Beaufort may also have owned the Book of Hours for the
use of Coutances (Cambridge, St John's College, MS 264) mentioned previously
as given by his daughter, Margaret, as a wedding gift to Lady Anne Shirley.

A second collaboration can be identified in another Hours for Sarum use (Los
Angeles, Getty Museum, MS 5), where Ricardus's more formal display script
features alongside the earlier recognized work of the Fastolf Master.[35] Again,
localizing the manuscript, and dating the work of artist and scribe have proven
to be complex.[36] The Getty Museum catalogue currently dates the manuscript to
between about 1430 and 1440 and cautiously locates its manufacture in either
'England or France'.[37]

Like several of the Sarum Hours discussed earlier, this book contains English
rubrics, and its calendar is marked by the inclusion of English saints, including
Edward the Confessor, Edmund, Thomas Becket, Botulph and Etheldreda.
Among the thirty-two full-page miniatures by the Fastolf Master is one of the
patron or owner, a layman who kneels before his guardian angel. As already
noted, in other manuscripts illuminated by the Fastolf Master there are often
donor portraits, though many of the patrons cannot now be identified. However,
the presence of an owner portrait in Getty MS 5 seems to discount Reynolds's

---

34 Reynolds in Marks and Williamson, *Gothic Art*, p. 345. Prayers for a woman have been
   added.
35 First cited by Alexander ('Lost Leaf', p. 251), his initial handlist (based on Otto Pächt's)
   of the seventeen examples of work by the Fastolf Master then known and listed as
   'whereabouts unknown'.
36 Sotheby's describes the manuscript as copied in London by Ricardus between 1440
   and 1450, and 'certainly written in England' (Catalogue of Western Manuscripts and
   Miniatures (London, Monday, 5 July 1976), pp. 51–3 (p. 51), item 80); H. P. Kraus gives
   a London provenance and dates Ricardus' copying of it to 1450 (*Illuminated Manuscripts from the Eleventh to the Eighteenth Centuries*: Catalogue 159 (New York, 1981), p.
   38, item 16, plate 16).
37 'Book of Hours, Sarum Use', *The J. Paul Getty Museum Journal* 13 (Malibu CA, 1985),
   202–3 (p. 202), no. 124.

assertion that 'the book would seem to have been intended for the open market'.[38] Michael K. Jones observed the notation 'Oxenford' beneath a miniature of St George and deduced that the first known owner of this book was most likely John de Vere, twelfth earl of Oxford (d. 1462), who, like Porter and Fastolf, was an active campaigner in France in the 1430s, travelled to France in 1441, and later in the 1440s became actively engaged in politics in Norfolk, working with Sir John Fastolf, among others, in 1450 to undermine the power of the duke of Suffolk's servants in Norfolk and Suffolk.[39] So the manuscript may have been made in France during the period in 1441 when de Vere travelled with the duke of York to Normandy. Or perhaps the manuscript was made later at some point during the association of de Vere in Norfolk with Sir John Fastolf.

Fastolf is certainly the patron of the third collaboration between the Fastolf Master and Ricardus, MS Laud Misc. 570, the French copy of Christine de Pizan's *Othea* and the *Livre des quatre vertus*, dated 1450 by the scribe and made in England.[40] In twenty-three banderoles wrapped around ascenders throughout the written text, Ricardus has supplied Fastolf's motto 'Me fault faire', along with the inscription 'A ma plaisance R F' on folio 23v and the motto of the Garter, 'Honi soyt qui mal y pense', at the end of the volume. While these playful inscriptions are employed by Ricardus elsewhere, as we have seen, in this case they are clearly owner-specific, his repeated motto referring directly to Fastolf as owner of the book and the Garter motto being included at the end of text perhaps to reassert Fastolf's claim to that title. (Made Knight of the Garter in 1426 following

---

[38] Reynolds, 'English Patrons and French Artists', p. 308. The anonymous patron is accompanied by a scroll with text from Psalm 16 (17), verse 8, '*custodi me ut pupillam oculi*'.

[39] Reynolds, 'English Patrons and French Artists', p. 308, n. 55, cites a communication from Jones identifying the owner as de Vere. John de Vere, twelfth earl of Oxford, not only fought and negotiated treaties in France but was active in Norfolk politics: 'In 1450, after the fall from power of William de la Pole, duke of Suffolk, Oxford took a leading role—together with John (VI) Mowbray, duke of Norfolk, and Sir John Fastolf—in attempts to undermine the local power of Suffolk's servants.' H. Castor, 'Vere, John de, twelfth earl of Oxford (1408–62)', *ODNB* http://www.oxforddnb.com/View/28213 [accessed 20 May 2007]. For de Vere's activities, see C. Richmond, *The Paston Family in the Fifteenth Century: Fastolf's Will* (Cambridge, 1996), pp. 118–21, 224–5, 233. There may also be a de Vere connection with St John's College, MS H. 5, Scrope's translation of Christine's *Othea*. Doyle, 'Appendix B', in Bühler, *The Epistle of Othea*, p. 126, comments: 'Anne, widow of Aubrey de Vere and Thomas Cobham, bequeathed to her sister-in-law, [Lady Margaret Beaufort] the Countess of Richmond "my boke with the pastilles of Othea",' which may, however, be any of several editions, either English or French, as Doyle further points out.

[40] O. Pächt and J. J. G. Alexander, *Illuminated Manuscripts in the Bodleian Library*, 3 vols. (Oxford, 1966–73), pp. 54–5, item 695; A. G. Watson, *Catalogue of Dated and Datable Manuscripts c.435–1600 in Oxford Libraries*, 2 vols. (Oxford, 1984), I, 100, comments on the discrepancy of date, misread in Bühler, 'Sir John Fastolf's Manuscripts of the *Epître d'Othéa*', *Scriptorium* 3 (1949), 123–8, as 1454. K. Chesney, 'Two MSS of Christine de Pisan', *Medium Aevum* 1 (1932), 35–41 (p. 39), first identified the motto '*Me fault faire*' as Fastolf's, found on 'a carving on the arch of a bow-window at Caister'.

Figure 32.8: Perseus and Andromeda. Oxford, Bodleian
Library, MS Laud Misc. 570, fol. 33v, Christine de Pisan,
L'epistre d'Othea and *Livre des quatre vertus*, in French,
dated 1450

successful campaigns in France, Fastolf later entered into protracted litigation after Sir John Talbot contested Fastolf's right to membership in the Order
following Fastolf's retreat from Patay. In the 1440s, Fastolf was vindicated after
rebutting the charge before the king and his peers, although the stigma of his trial
for 'conduct unbecoming' remained.[41]) The use of such 'owner-specific' mottoes

41 N. B. Warren, *Women of God and Arms: Female Spirituality and Political Conflict 1380–1600*
(Philadelphia, 2005), p. 69, comments, 'in the autumn of 1441 or the spring of 1442,
Fastolf had to "rebut a charge, laid before the king and his peers by the aggrieved
Lord Talbot, of conduct unbecoming a knight of the Garter at the battle of Patay"'.
The complex processes of 'The Degradation of a Knight Companion' are reported in
P. J. Begent and H. Chesshyre, *The Most Noble Order of the Garter: 650 Years with a
Chapter on the Statutes of the Order by Dr Lisa Jefferson* (London, 1999), pp. 269–76: 'the

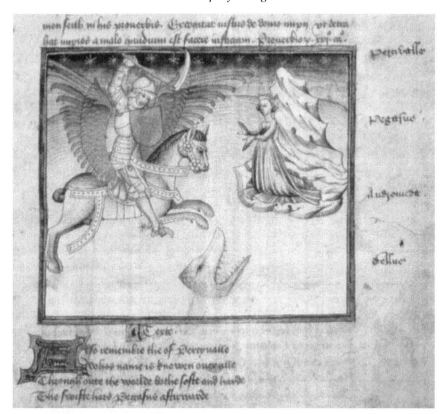

Figure 32.9: Perseus and Andromeda. Cambridge, St John's College, MS H. 5, fol. 9, Christine de Pisan, *The Epistle of Othea*, trans. Stephen Scrope, in English, c.1450–c.1460

in MS Laud Misc. 570 may further suggest that the bits of Marian prayers, 'prenes engre', and other inscriptions more usually found in books made by Ricardus may also point to specific patrons, particularly to Anne Harling, for example, in MS Harley 4012, or to an aristocratic female patron in the case of Morgan MS M. 126.[42]

questionable actions of Sir John Fastolf (KG 1426) which are said to have prompted Bedford temporarily to deprive Fastolf of his Garter, seem, when reviewed later by a committee of Knights Companions, to have been considered under a general accusation of "conduct unbecoming" rather than as a specific offense' (p. 269). See also L. Jefferson, 'MS Arundel 48 and the Earliest Statutes of the Order of the Garter', *EHR* 109 (1994), 356–85 (pp. 361–4, 374).

[42] For Elizabeth Woodville as a possible early owner of Morgan M. 126, see M. Driver, 'Women Readers and Pierpont Morgan MS M 126', in *John Gower: Manuscripts, Readers and Contexts*, ed. M. Urban (Turnhout, forthcoming), and Driver, 'Printing the *Confessio Amantis*: Caxton's Edition in Context', in *Revisioning Gower: New Essays*, ed. R. F. Yeager (Asheville NC, 1998), pp. 269–303 (pp. 282–5, n. 27, 28, 29, 30, 31).

The iconography of the images supplied by the Fastolf Master in the Laudian manuscript is very close to that seen later in the illustrations of the English translation by Scrope supplied by William Abell (or his English associate, if one follows Scott), with whom as earlier shown (p. 433 above), Ricardus Franciscus worked. Compare the illumination of Perseus and Andromeda by the Fastolf Master (Figure 32.8) with the grisaille example in the later English copy (Figure 32.9).[43] Examples like these suggest a complex network of influence among multilingual artists and scribes working within the Fastolf circle and beyond.

As many of these manuscripts attest, the Hundred Years' War (1337–1453) provided opportunities for cultural exchange from the early to mid-fifteenth century. English nobles fighting and governing in France developed a taste for French books. All the manuscripts copied by Ricardus have English associations or owners, and this is also the case with twelve of the surviving works made for English patrons illustrated by the Fastolf Master that have so far been identified. And as this survey shows, dating and localization, as Denis Muzerelle has pointed out so eloquently, are not exact sciences.[44] It is sometimes difficult to determine just what constitutes an 'English' manuscript in the fifteenth century. The careers of Ricardus Franciscus and the Fastolf Master suggest that French makers of manuscripts worked readily for English patrons and influenced, or perhaps one might say, educated the tastes of fifteenth-century English bibliophiles such as Sir John Fastolf. And in case the reader is wondering, one possible interpretation of the motto of Fastolf, 'Me fault faire', might be 'And there must I end'.[45]

---

[43] Jonathan Alexander comments on these cross-influences: 'native artists were influenced by the Fastolf Master, for example William Abell, who copied the illustrations of the *Epître d'Othée*'; Alexander, 'Foreign Illuminators', p. 49.

[44] D. Muzerelle, 'Dating MSS: What Is at Stake in the Steps Usually (but Infrequently) Taken?', *JEBS* 11 (2008), 167–80.

[45] Helen Swift, St Hilda's College (pers. comm., 23 November 2006), suggests this alternative reading of Fastolf's motto by translating *'fault'* (from *'falloir'*) as *'faut'* with the modern equivalent *'il me faut faire,'* with *'faire'* taking the direct object, and *'faire'* in the sense of 'to finish' (see Godefroy, *s.v.*), hence 'there must I end'.

Table 32.1: Movements of the scribe's and artist's patrons: timeline

419 Rouen seized by English forces

420 Paris taken by English forces; Sir William Porter present at the capture of Vernon

422 Sir William Porter serves in England as executor of Henry V's will

429 Porter and Sir John Fastolf fight at the Battle of Patay

430 Porter returns to France with Henry VI

434 Porter dies

435 Death of John, duke of Bedford

436 Paris reclaimed by the French

439 Fastolf returns to England

447 Statutes of the Archdeaconry of London written by Ricardus with initials supplied by William Abell, a member of the London Mistery of Stationers

449 Rouen reclaimed by the French

450 Christine de Pizan's *L'epistre d'Othea* and *Livre des quatre vertus*, written by Ricardus for Fastolf in French and illuminated by the Fastolf Master

459 Fastolf dies at Caister Castle, Norfolk

467 Statutes of the Order of the Garter, written in French, by Ricardus

Appendix

MSS Illuminated by or Attributed to the Fastolf Master
(* = Collaboration of the Fastolf Master and Ricardus Franciscus)

Cambridge, St John's College, MS 264, N. 24 (The Hours of Lady Margaret Beaufort), Book of Hours, use of Coutances, in Latin and French, *c*.1440, belonged formerly to John, duke of Somerset (d. 1444), illuminated by the Fastolf Master

Chicago, Newberry Library, MS 50.5 (Tripp Hours), Book of Hours, composite use (calendar, Hours of the Virgin, etc., for use of Rouen; Office of the Dead, Sarum use), in Latin and French, *c*.1450, illuminated by the Fastolf Master.

London, British Library, MS Harley 1251 (Hours of Eleanor Worcester), Book of Hours, use of Sarum, Latin and French, *c*.1430, illuminations by the Fastolf Master and assistant, for John, duke of Bedford (1389–1435), his portrait inscribed with his obituary.

*London, British Library, MS Harley 2915, Book of Hours, use of Sarum, in Latin and French, *c*.1440–*c*.1450, illuminated by the Fastolf Master and written by Ricardus Franciscus.

*Los Angeles, J. Paul Getty Museum, MS 5, 84 ML. 723 (Sotheby Hours), Book of Hours, Sarum use, in Latin with English rubrics, *c*.1430–*c*.1440, illuminated by the Fastolf Master and copied by Ricardus Franciscus possibly for John de Vere, earl of Oxford (d. 1462), whose signature occurs on folio 35v.

New York, Morgan Library and Museum, MS Glazier 9 (Berkeley Hours), Book of Hours, Sarum use, in Latin, *c*.1440–*c*.1450, illuminated by the Fastolf Master and a ?Netherlandish artist; borders, initials and spray work supplied by English artists.

New York, Morgan Library and Museum, MS M. 27, Hours of the Virgin, multiple use (calendar, Hours of the Virgin, Office of the Dead, use of Rouen 'under the English'; Suffrages include local saints of Coutances), in Latin, *c*.1423, illuminated by the Fastolf Master.

New York, Morgan Library and Museum, MS M. 105 (Kildare Book of Hours), Hours of the Virgin, Sarum use, in Latin with later English additions, *c*.1420–*c*.1425, illuminated by the Fastolf Master for Sir William Porter of Lincolnshire (d. 1434).

New York, Morgan Library and Museum, MS M. 1000, Book of Hours, Paris use, in Latin and French, *c.*1420, illuminated by Boucicaut Master, Master of Morgan 453 and the Fastolf Master, who contributed two illuminations only.

Oxford, Bodleian Library, MS Auct. D. inf. 2. 11, Book of Hours, use of Sarum, Latin and French, *c.*1440–*c.*1450, may have later belonged to Henry VII or Henry VIII, with forty-three miniatures by the Fastolf Master. Birmingham, City Museum and Art Gallery, P. 115, 55, a single leaf with a painting of the Annunciation, once belonged to this manuscript.

Oxford, Bodleian Library, MS Hatton 45, Psalter with London calendar, Latin, *c.*1450–*c.*1460, one historiated initial supplied by the Fastolf Master.

***Oxford, Bodleian Library, MS Laud Misc. 570,** Christine de Pizan, *L'epistre d'Othea* and *Livre des quatre vertus*, in French, dated 1450, illuminated by the Fastolf Master and written by Ricardus for Sir John Fastolf.

Oxford, Keble College Library, MS 38, Missal and Hours, Paris use, in French and Latin, *c.*1440, illuminated by the Fastolf Master.

Oxford, St John's College, MS 208, Office of the Dead, Psalms, Suffrages, Sarum use, Latin and English, *c.*1475, five illuminations by the Fastolf Master.

Paris, Bibliothèque de l'Arsenal, MS 560, Book of Hours, use of Coutances, in Latin, n.d., illuminated by the Fastolf Master.

Paris, Bibliothèque de l'Arsenal, MS 575, Book of Hours, use of Rome, in Latin, *c.*1440–*c.*1450, with three illuminations by the Fastolf Master, others by an artist or artists close to him and by the Arsenal 575 Master.

San Marino, Huntington Library, MS HM 1099, Book of Hours, composite use (calendar for use of Rouen, Hours of the Virgin for use of Paris, Office of the Dead for undetermined use), in French and Latin, *c.*1440–*c.*1450, illuminated by the Fastolf Master and workshop.

San Marino, Huntington Library, MS HM 47405, Walter Burley, *De vita et moribus philosophorum*, in Latin, *c.*1450, with historiated initial illuminated by the Fastolf Master; said to have been copied in England.

Utrecht, Museum Catharijneconvent, MS ABM h4a, prayer roll of Henry Beauchamp, duke of Warwick, in Latin and French, *c.*1440, miniatures attributed to the Fastolf Master.

Windsor, Royal Library, The Sobieski Hours, Book of Hours, use of Paris, in Latin and French, *c.*1420–*c.*1425, *c.*1440, illuminated by the Bedford Master, the

Master of the Munich *Golden Legend*, and the Fastolf Master (likely finishing earlier work by the aforementioned two artists).

Two further Fastolf MSS cited by Jonathan Alexander (1971) are **Cambridge, Fitzwilliam Museum, Marlay cuttings, Fr. 3** (from *Chroniques de France*?); and **Paris, Bibliothèque Ste Geneviève, MS 1015** (*Aegidius Romanus de regimine principum*). Kathleen Scott (1996) also cites **Biblioteca Apostolica Vaticana, Vat. Lat. 14938**, Hours, with a second artist. Eberhard König attributes **Philadelphia, Free Library, MS Widener 1** (*Le Livre du Chastel de Labour*), to the Fastolf Master but Sandra Hindman ascribes its illumination more generally to the Bedford circle (see note 5 above).

MSS Copied by or Attributed to Ricardus Franciscus
(* = Collaboration of the Fastolf Master and Ricardus)

Cambridge, St John's College, MS H. 5 (*olim* 208), Christine de Pizan, *The Epistle of Othea*, trans. Stephen Scrope, in English, *c*.1450–*c*.1460, illustrated by William Abell and perhaps another unnamed artist, copied by Ricardus.

*London, British Library, MS Harley 2915, Book of Hours, Sarum use, in Latin and French, *c*.1440–*c*.1450, illumination in color and semi-grisaille attributed to the Fastolf Master, copied by Ricardus.

London, British Library, MS Harley 4012, Middle English religious miscellany, *c*.1460–*c*.1470, identified as written in the hand of Ricardus (by Parkes, reported in Wilson, 'A Middle English Manuscript at Coughton Court').

London, British Library, MS Harley 4775, Jacobus de Voragine, *The Golden Legend*, in Middle English, date unknown, no known illustration, copied by Ricardus.

London, Hospital of St Bartholomew, Smithfield, Coks Cartulary, cartulary in two volumes, parts copied by Ricardus with two historiated initials supplied by William Abell.

London, the Worshipful Company of Tallow Chandlers, Grant of Arms, in French, dated 24 September 1456, signed and sealed by John Smert, Garter King of Arms, illustration in initial 'A' with portrait of Garter and Company's crest by William Abell, copied by Ricardus.

*Los Angeles, J. Paul Getty Museum, MS 5, 84 ML. 723 (Sotheby Hours), Book of Hours, Sarum use, in Latin with English rubrics, *c*.1430–*c*.1440, illuminated by the Fastolf Master and copied by Ricardus Franciscus possibly for John de Vere, earl of Oxford (d. 1462), whose signature occurs on folio 35v.

Nancy, Archives Départementales de Meurthe et Moselle, MS H 80, Statutes of the Order of the Garter, in French, dated 1467 and signed by Ricardus. Made possibly for Charles the Bold of Burgundy prior to his marriage with Margaret of York (Jefferson, 'Two Fifteenth-Century Manuscripts').

New York, Morgan Library and Museum, MS M. 126, John Gower, *Confessio mantis*, in English and Latin, c.1470, with 106 miniatures supplied by two Anglo-Flemish' artists, written by Ricardus.

Oxford, Bodleian Library, MS Ashmole 764, 'The first foundation of the office of arms', extracts from '*L'arbre de batailles*', '*Le songe du vergier*' and other heraldic texts, in Latin, English and French, c.1475, with three illuminations ascribed by Scott to the 'Three Kings' Master' and twenty items written by Ricardus.

Oxford, Bodleian Library, MS Ashmole 789, Writing exercises in English and Latin (fols. 1–5), c.1450, attributed to Ricardus.

Oxford, Bodleian Library, MS Laud Misc. 570, Christine de Pizan, *L'Epistre d'Othea and Livre des quatre vertus*, in French, dated 1450 by Ricardus and written by him, with ten illuminations by the Fastolf Master.

Oxford, University College, MS 85, Alain Chartier, *Quadrilogue*, the *Secretum secretorum, Good Governance of a Prince*, in English, c.1450, with two illuminations supplied by the 'Quadrilogue Master' and written by Ricardus.

Philadelphia, Rosenbach Museum and Library, MS 439/16 (olim Phillipps 1254), John Lydgate, *The Fall of Princes*, in English, c.1465–c.1475, with seven miniatures, the first perhaps by one artist (Scott says this is the 'Quadrilogue Master') and the rest by another; text by Ricardus.

San Marino, Huntington Library, MS HM 932, the Statutes of the Archdeaconry of London, in Latin, dated 1447, with two historiated initials by William Abell, written and signed by Ricardus.

Other possible documents copied by Ricardus include letters written from Caister by Fastolf to John Paston and Lady Whytyngham bound in with London, British Library, MS Additional 39848 (mentioned by Norman Davis as cited in Wilson, A Middle English MS at Coughton Court', p. 299); and the recent discovery by Catherine Nall of a hand very like that of Ricardus in a copy of the *Breviloquium* of John of Wales (Cambridge University Library, MS Add. 7870).

33

The French Self-Presentation of an English Mastiff: John Talbot's Book of Chivalry

Andrew Taylor

For that enthusiastic patriot Lieutenant-Colonel Alfred Burne, a military historian of the old school, the death of Sir John Talbot, earl of Shrewsbury, at the
Battle of Castillon in 1453 marked the end of the Hundred Years' War. Without
peerless Talbot, the English Achilles, all hope of regaining the land lost since
the coming of Joan of Arc faded. But what a death! His head adorned only by
a purple velvet cap (for, when ransomed three years earlier, he had sworn an
oath never again to wear armour against the French king), Talbot had brought
a small company by forced night march over the hills of St Emilion to take his
enemies by surprise, driven the first group of them out of town, and then hurled
his men against a wall of French cannons, hoping that once more his name alone
would put the French to flight. This time it did not, and Talbot was cut down
as he tried to rally his troops. The French leaders raised a tomb to their fallen
opponent; their chroniclers remembered him. As one put it, such was the end of
'ce fameux et renommé chef anglois qui depuis si longtemps passoit pour l'un
des fleaux le plus formidable et plus jurez ennemis de la France dont il avoit
paru estre l'effroy et la terreur' ('this famous and renowned English leader, who
for so long had been one of the most formidable scourges and most committed
enemies of France, which regarded him with terror and dismay').[1]

Being famous was part of Talbot's profession. He was a legend in both France
and England, renowned for his cruelty in one, and for his loyalty in the other,
and for his military ability in both. Burne writes of French towns that 'surrendered incontinently on the mere news that the great Talbot was approaching'.[2]
Talbot's more recent biographer, A. J. Pollard, shows why these towns did so. He
attributes to Talbot a deliberate policy of 'terror for military ends'.[3] Pollard notes
that after taking Jouy and Crépy in 1434, Talbot executed the garrisons, and after

---

[1] J. Chartier, *Histoire de Charles VI, roi de France et de son époque, 1403–1461*, ed. M. Vallet
de Viriville, 3 vols. (Paris, 1863–5), III, 7. Alfred H. Burne cites the passage in *The Agincourt War* (London, 1956), p. 342, but misattributes it to Mathew d'Escoucy.

[2] Burne, *Agincourt*, p. 274.

[3] A. J. Pollard, 'Talbot, John, first earl of Shrewsbury and first earl of Waterford (*c.*1387–
1453), soldier', *ODNB online* [accessed 14 May 2007]. But cf. Pollard's suggestion in *John
Talbot and the War in France, 1427–1453* (London, 1983), pp. 126–7, that Talbot gained
his reputation not because he was exceptionally vicious but rather because attitudes
to military brutality were changing.

taking Laval in 1428, he executed 65 men, some of them priests. Worse, at Lihons in 1440, when a group took refuge inside a church, Talbot burned it down over them. According to the Picardian chronicler Enguerrand de Monstrelet, 'thus there were killed and burnt most piteously a good three hundred or more people, both men, women, and children, and very few of those who were in the church escaped'.[4]

Talbot benefited from his reputation for ferocity and probably cultivated it deliberately, as one aspect of a complex public identity. In addition to his treatment of garrisons that had surrendered too slowly, he encouraged his identification with his Talbot hounds, large hunting dogs that not only served as his heraldic emblem, but also accompanied him everywhere as guard dogs and figured prominently in tapestries he commissioned.[5] Talbot was not just represented by these dogs but associated with their qualities. Through demotic appropriation this great nobleman became, in the popular verse of the time, 'oure gentill dogge' and 'our goode dogge', guarding England when other nobles betrayed her.[6]

It is tempting to see this staunch Englishman as a proto John Bull. There is no connection between the eighteenth-century figure and the fifteenth-century aristocrat, or between the stocky bull dog and the much larger talbot, or tracker hound, but Talbot and John Bull appeal to a similar national sense of identity; one that could see itself in a dog or dog-like man, a figure that is loyal, courageous and tenacious, but scarcely refined, and that is defined in specific opposition to the French. Talbot's use of the dogs to enhance his public image may have been a deliberate appeal to the stereotype that would only emerge fully a century later. To quote Pollard, a 'proto-nationalist dimension coloured [Talbot's] reputation in both France and England'.[7]

There are a few other indications that Talbot cultivated an identity as a stalwart Englishman. During the festivities at Calais to celebrate Richard's marriage to Isabella in 1396, Talbot (still in his teens) defeated all comers in wrestling and archery.[8] These were traditional village sports, and to excel in them Talbot must have practised assiduously. He would have done so in the company of the local men at one of the two family homes, Goodrich castle in the Dee valley on the Welsh border or Blackmere castle near Whitchurch in northern Stafford-

---

4   *La Chronique d'Enguerran de Monstrelet*, ed. L. Douët-d'Arcq, 6 vols. (Paris, 1861), V, 406 (trans. mine).

5   A. Claxton, 'The Sign of the Dog: An Examination of the Devonshire Hunting Tapestries', *JMH* 14 (1988), 127–79.

6   See, 'On the Popular Discontent at the Disasters in France', from MS Cotton Rolls ii 23, ed. T. Wright in *Political Poems and Songs*, 2 vols., RS 14 (London, 1859–61), II, 221–2, and V. J. Scattergood, *Politics and Poetry in the Fifteenth Century* (London, 1971), p. 160.

7   Pollard, *John Talbot*, p. 128.

8   H. Talbot, *The English Achilles: An Account of the Life and Campaigns of John Talbot, 1st Earl of Shrewsbury (1383–1453)* (London, 1981), p. 11.

shire, where Talbot recruited his personal bodyguard.[9] Talbot spent his life surrounded by men who, as a closely knit group, must have retained the local dialect. This area and its dialect, it should be remembered, had strong associations with manly courage and loyalty. Whitchurch lies close to the Cheshire boundary, and Cheshire was something of an English heartland in the popular imagination, its men renowned for their bravery. Richard II had drawn his bodyguard from Cheshire and, a century after Talbot's death, William Camden would write in his *Britannia* that no other province in England 'either brought more valorous Gentlemen into the field, or had more Families in it of Knights degree'.[10] The sense of regional identity was fostered by a tradition of alliterative verse that continued into the sixteenth century. Whitchurch, after all, is less than thirty miles from the Gawain country.[11] The figure of 'oure gentill dogge' Talbot, courteous but ferocious, may reach back to the same values and patterns of manly identity epitomized by the hearty but chivalric hunting lord, Sir Bertilak. It is the lesser known alliterative poems of the sixteenth century such as *Flodden Feilde* or *Scotish Feilde*, however, with their celebration of family connections among the local gentry and military triumphs over Scots and French, that provide a more direct sense of what it might mean to be a Stanley or a Lee in Cheshire or, by analogy, a Talbot in Staffordshire.[12] Some indication of how these strong regional bonds could be assimilated into an English patriotism comes from the challenge issued by the earl's grandson, Thomas Talbot, Viscount Lisle to William, Lord Berkeley in 1469. Thomas defied William to meet him either in individual combat or with his full army: 'I trust to God to mete you nere home with English men of my onw [sic] nation and neighbors – whereas ye by suttle craft have blowin about in divers places of England that I should intend to bring in Welshmen for to destroy and hurt my one nation and country.'[13]

If Talbot was indeed deliberately playing the bluff Englishman, then his reputation stands all the more sharply in contrast to what was arguably his most complex act of self-presentation, his gift of a massive chivalric anthology to Margaret of Anjou on the occasion of her marriage to Henry VI in 1445. This manuscript, now British Library, Royal 15 E VI, consists of 440 folios, beginning with genealogical tables setting out Henry's claim to the French throne, the prose *Roman d'Alexandre*, three *chansons de geste* of Charlemagne, the *Quatre fils Aymon*,

9 Talbot, *The English Achilles*, 8, drawing on G. A. Thevet, *Vrais portraits des homes illustres* (Book IV) (Paris, 1584).
10 William Camden, *Britain, or A chorographicall description of the most flourishing kingdomes, England, Scotland, and Ireland...* (London, 1637), p. 601.
11 A. McIntosh, 'A New Approach to Middle English Dialectology', *English Studies* 44 (1935), 1–11 (p. 5), locates the poem within 'a very small area either in SE Cheshire or just over the border in NE Staffordshire'.
12 I. F. Baird, ed., *Scotish Feilde and Flodden Feilde: Two Flodden Poems* (New York, 1981), and D. A. Lawton, 'Scottish Field: Alliterative Verse and Stanley Encomium in the Percy Folio', *LSE* n.s. 10 (1978), 42–57.
13 John Smyth, *The Lives of the Berkeleys*, vol. 2 of *The Berkeley Manuscripts*, ed. Sir J. Maclean, 3 vols. (Gloucester, 1893–5), pp. 109–11 (p. 109).

ve romances, including a prose version of *Guy de Warwik* and the *Chevalier au
ygne*, a chronicle of Normandy, political and military treatises including Honoré
ouvet's *Arbre des batailles*, Henri de Gauchi's *Le livre de politique* (a translation
f the *De regimine principum* of Aegidius Romanus), and Christine de Pizan's
ais d'armes, and finally the statutes of the Order of the Garter.[14] It is not just the
ize of the collection that is striking, however. As Craig Taylor has observed, a
ollection of chivalric treatises in a book commissioned by an Englishman was,
t this point, still very rare.[15] Copies of these treatises had circulated widely in
rance, and would do so England in the second half of the fifteenth century, but
part from the Henri de Gauchi translation, the Royal manuscript is the earliest
nglish manuscript to preserve any of the treatises. The combination of texts was
nusual as well. The *De regimine principum* did not normally circulate with chiv-
lric texts, for example. Such an ambitious and path-breaking collection must
urely have had a powerful *raison d'être*, but determining just what this was is
ot easy.

On the opening folio, there is a rondeau in which Talbot, using a personal
notto, 'mon seul desir', evokes his absolute loyalty to the king and queen:

> Mon seul desir
> Au Roy et vous
> E[s]t bien servir
> Jusqu'au mourir
> Ce sachent tous:
> Mon seul desir
> Au Roy et vous.

('My only desire, for the king and you, is to serve well until I die, as
all know, this is my only desire for the king and you.')

Above this there are introductory verses in which Talbot assures the royal
ouple of his loyalty and explains that this collection is being offered to ensure
he queen does not forget her French once she begins to speak English.

> Princesse tres exellente
> Ce liure cy vous presente
> De Schrosbery le conte.
> Ou quel liure a maint beau conte
> Des preux qui par grant labeur
> Vouldrent acquerir honnneur
> En France, en Angleterre,
> Et en aultre mainte terre.
> Esperant qu'a vostre loisir

---

4 G. F. Warner and J. P. Gilson, *Catalogue of the Western Manuscripts in the Old Royal
and King's Collection*, II (London, 1921), pp. 177–9. Anne D. Hedeman is preparing a
detailed description of the manuscript.

5 See C. D. Taylor, 'The Treatise Cycle of the Shrewsbury Book: BL MS Royal 15 E.VI'
(forthcoming). I thank Dr Taylor for sharing an early copy of this paper with me.

Vous vueillez prendre plaisir
En passant temps pour y lire
Pour oster ennuy qui nuire
Peult a toute creature.
Ou liure a une figure
Geneaulogie nommee
Par la quelle est tres bien prouuee
Verité demonstrant a plain
Que le roy nostre souuerain,
De vostre affye que dieux y gart,
Est venu de si noble part
Comme du bon Roy Saint Louys.
Si estes vous, certain en suys.
...
[Talbot] la fait faire ainsi que entens
Afin que vous y passez temps
Et lors que parlerez anglois
Que vous n'oubliez pas le françois.
Et que vous voyez les hystoires
Qui bien sont dignes de mémoire
Pour les tres haustes entreprinses
Qui ou dit liure sont comprinse.

('Most excellent princess, this book is here presented to you by the earl of Shrewsbury. In it are many fine stories about knights who, through great effort, wished to acquire honour in France, England, and elsewhere. Hoping that at your leisure you will take pleasure in spending time reading it to drive away boredom which can harm anyone. And in this book is a figure called a genealogical table which shows forth and plainly demonstrates that the king, our sovereign, and your fiancé – may God preserve him! – is descended from the same most noble lineage as good king Saint Louis, just as you are, I am certain. ... Talbot had this book made so that you could pass your time with it and so that, when you speak English, you will not forget French, and so that you could see the stories which are worthy of remembrance because of the most noble deeds which are contained within this said book.')

Facing this poem, on the recto of the first opening, there is indeed a genealogical table that traces Henry's descent from Saint Louis and Edward I, thus restating the English claim to the kingdom of France. This was familiar propaganda. A similar table was placed on display in Paris outside Notre-Dame in 1423.[16] As Catherine Reynolds notes, 'Talbot used his gift to ensure that Margaret understood her new position as not only Queen of England but also rightful Queen of

16 B. J. H. Rowe, 'King Henry VI's Claim to France in Picture and Poem', *The Library*, 4th series 13 (1933), 77–88.

France, an attitude that would make war inevitable.'[17] Despite the initial claim that the book was intended merely to ward off boredom, on its opening pages it makes a forceful political statement.

One of the chief difficulties in interpreting this volume is deciding to what extent it should be taken as essentially Talbot's own book, hastily reconfigured so that it could be offered to the queen as a rather unusual wedding gift, or whether it should be taken as essentially Margaret's book, a well-chosen gift for the woman who would become, it was hoped, mother of the next king of England. Reynolds has shown that the book's heraldic decorations, a series of banners in the margins, had been reworked in some haste. Several open spaces were originally left for large banners, but then filled in with innocuous decorative work.[18] The obvious explanation of these reworkings is that Talbot had already commissioned a personal collection, which was then modified to serve as a wedding present. Reynolds actually goes so far as to suggest that Talbot selected the manuscript as a gift because all the goldsmiths in Rouen were already working flat out, but this seems unlikely – surely the man who had terrorized the entire land could have intimidated a goldsmith in the town where he was commander in chief.

Michel-André Bossy, on the other hand, finds the Shrewsbury book a far more suitable present, one that subtly acknowledges Margaret but is primarily – and carefully – calculated to appeal to the hoped-for son. Bossy notes that Margaret was the daughter of one of the great bibliophiles of the age, René of Anjou, that on the genealogical page Margaret is 'translated into emblems', including a 'bouquet of marguerites' that is suggestively penetrated by her future husband, that the opening section, the *Roman d'Alexandre*, with its 'exotic adventures and their numerous illustrations' would have made it 'particularly appealing to a child' and that the first two *chansons de geste* 'offer a tacit salute to Margaret's lineage' for the first, *Simon de Pouille*, is set in Apulia, which was claimed by her father, while the second, the *Chanson d'Aspremont*, is set in Calabria, which was governed by her uncle.[19] From here the collection gradually works its way to more sober texts for a more mature political understanding, such as Henri Bouvet's *L'arbre de batailes* and Henri de Gauchi's translation of the *De regimine principum*, culminating in Christine de Pizan's *Livre des fais d'armes et de chevalerie*. Talbot would have taken satisfaction, Bossy argues, in offering a text for the use of the future heir to the English throne that had first been commissioned by John the Fearless, duke of Burgundy, for the Dauphin, especially if (as seems possible)

---

17 C. Reynolds, 'The Shrewsbury Book, British Library, Royal MS 15 E. VI', in *XII: Medieval Art, Architecture and Archaeology at Rouen, the British Archaeological Association Conference Transactions for the Year 1986*, ed. J. Stratford (London, 1993), pp. 109–16.

18 Fol. 86 for *Ogier*, fol. 273 for the *Chevalier au cygne*, fol. 266, and fol. 363 for the *Chroniques de Normandie*. Reynolds notes that the outlines of the planned banners are still visible in places (p. 110). A further sign of haste are the 'obvious insertions of omitted text in to *Ogier*, f. 153, and the *Quatre fils*, ff. 200–203' (p. 110).

19 M.-A. Bossy, 'Arms and the Bride: Christine de Pizan's Military Treatise as a Wedding Gift for Margret of Anjou', in *Christine de Pizan and the Categories of Difference*, ed. M. Desmond (Minneapolis, 1998), pp. 236–56 (pp. 245, 246, 247).

the version in the Shrewsbury book was copied directly from what had been intended as the Dauphin's personal manuscript.

Bossy makes a strong case for the suitability of the volume as a wedding present for Margaret, but the evidence of reconfiguration that Reynolds notes is important because it suggests that Talbot already had in train a major collection for himself, or perhaps for his wife. The inclusion of the prose *Guy de Warwik* and the *Chevalier au cygne* is suggestive. In 1425 Talbot had married Margaret Beauchamp, eldest daughter of Richard, earl of Warwick, and he was proud of the connection. As Ann Claxton has shown, to celebrate the marriage Talbot commissioned four magnificent hunting tapestries, the so-called Devonshire tapestries now in the Victoria and Albert Museum.[20] A large chivalric anthology would have made a fitting accompaniment. Richard Beauchamp had fostered the family's association with the legendary Guy of Warwick, purchasing the cave that was held to be Guy's hermitage from its monastic owners and founding a chapel there.[21] As John Frankis notes, the version of the prose *Guy* in the Royal manuscript, which appears to have been composed in the fifteenth century, may reflect the renewed local cult since, in contrast to the earlier Anglo-Norman version, which locates Guy's hermitage in a remote forest, the Royal text makes it clear that the hermitage lies near to Warwick castle.[22] The Royal prose *Guy* might well have been copied from a text that had been in the Beauchamp family and was acquired by Talbot through his marriage to Margaret or from one that he had commissioned or purchased himself because of this new family connection. The Beauchamps also claimed descent from the Swan Knight, Helyas, the legendary ancestor of Godfrey of Bouillon, whose magical transformation is told in the *Chevalier au cygne*. This connection would become so important to the family that by the late fifteenth century, when the chaplain Richard Rous came to trace the family's mythical lineage, it had completely eclipsed their relation to Guy of Warwick.[23] The Beauchamps were already claiming descent from the Swan knight by the time Talbot married into the family, however, since swans figure prominently in the Devonshire tapestries. The Royal collection, therefore, contained two works that were central to the Beauchamp family history (although Margaret of Anjou also claimed descent from the Swan knight, as did some two hundred titled houses in Europe).[24] Finally, in considering whether the book might originally have been intended to celebrate Talbot and his new kin, we should remember that Talbot's wife and Henry's queen conveniently had the same name, so the fields of marguerites on the borders of the pages would not have posed a problem if the book was to be redirected.

---

[20] See Claxton, 'Sign of the Dog'.

[21] J. Frankis, 'Taste and Patronage in Late Medieval England as Reflected in Versions of Guy of Warwick', *Medium Aevum* 66 (1997), 80–93 (pp. 85–6).

[22] Frankis, 'Taste and Patronage', p. 83.

[23] See S. Crane, *The Performance of Self: Ritual, Clothing, and Identity during the Hundred Years War* (Philadelphia, 2002), p. 116.

[24] This is the number suggested by Crane, *The Performance of Self*, p. 113.

Although two of the texts refer to the lineage of Margaret Beauchamp and three refer, rather less forcefully, to the lineage of Margaret of Anjou, the contents may still seem surprising. How are we to account for the presence of so many *chansons de geste* in a collection commissioned by such a determinedly English hero? Were *chansons de geste* really considered suitable reading for women? Would these works not have seemed bizarrely anachronistic by the mid-fifteenth century? The last objection is perhaps the easiest to address. Literary scholars have only rather belatedly accepted that the genre was not limited to the twelfth century and even those, such as Sarah Kay and Robert Stein, who have insisted that the *chanson de geste* is no earlier a genre than the romance have not had much to do with its late circulation.[25] The fourteenth- and fifteenth-century Middle French *remaniements*, modernizations, translations, and prose reworkings of Old French epic remain largely unstudied.[26] But there were plenty of them. Madeleine Blaess's suggestion that when Earl Beauchamp bequeathed his collection of romances and *chansons de geste* to Bordesley Abbey in 1305 he did so because he considered them too old-fashioned to be of interest, has been repeatedly challenged.[27] The theory proposed by André de Mandach that the monks of Saint Augustine's, Canterbury, were running a scriptorium committed to producing accurate copies of *chansons de geste* and that they provided the exemplars for those in the Royal manuscript does not stand up to close scrutiny, but the monks did have a large collection of *chansons de geste*.[28] Several of the texts in the Talbot anthology were in the collections of other late medieval English aristocrats. Thomas of Woodstock, duke of Gloucester, owned several French romances, including the *Le chevalier au cygne* and the *Roman d'Alexandre*, which appear in the inventory of his possessions taken after his murder in 1397.[29] Half a century later, when King Edward IV could no longer contain his passion for the beautiful but virtuous widow Elizabeth Grey, and married her, her father, Sir Richard Woodville, celebrated his ascension

---

[25] R. M. Stein, *Reality Fictions: Romance, History, and Governmental Authority, 1025–1180* (Notre Dame IN, 2006); S. Kay, *The Chansons de Geste in the Age of Romance: Political Fictions* (Oxford, 1995).

[26] An important exception in connection with the Royal manuscript is E. J. Mickel, Jr and J. Nelson, 'BM Royal 15 E VI and the Epic Cycle of the First Crusade', *Romania* 92 (1971), 532–56.

[27] M. Blaess, 'L'abbaye de Bordesley et les livres de Guy de Beauchamp', *Romania* 78 (1957), 511–18. For Anglo-Norman romances and *chansons de geste* through the fourteenth century, see K. Busby, *Codex and Context: Reading Old French Verse Narrative in Manuscript*, 2 vols. (Amsterdam, 2002), II, 500–9, and on *chansons de geste* in the fifteenth, see M. J. Burland, *Strange Words: Retelling and Reception in the Medieval Roland Textual Tradition* (Notre Dame IN, 2007).

[28] A. de Mandach, 'A Royal Wedding Present in the Making: Talbot's Chivalric Anthology (Royal 15 E VI) for Queen Margaret of Anjou and the "Laval–Middleton" Anthology of Nottingham', *Nottingham Mediaeval Studies* 18 (1974), 56–76. But see Busby, *Codex and Context*, I, 121.

[29] A. Goodman, *The Loyal Conspiracy: The Lords Appellant under Richard II* (London, 1971), pp. 97–81.

to the status of father-in-law to the king of England by purchasing a sumptuous copy of the *Roman d'Alexandre*, now Oxford, Bodleian Library, MS Bodley 264.[30]

The old stories of the deeds of knights could be read simply as entertainment, 'Pour oster ennuy qui nuire / Peult a toute creature', as the prologue to the Royal manuscript puts it (p. 448 above). In this capacity, they would have been heard by both men and women. They could also be read as courtesy literature and practical guides to chivalric protocol for knights. In the fifteenth century, French was still the language of chivalry. Any Englishman who wished to participate in jousts or tournaments or issue challenges outside the country would have needed to do so in French, which is why the heraldic texts in Sir John Paston's miscellany (British Library, MS Lansdowne 285) are in French.[31] When Margaret of Anjou used the aura of the Garter to try and coerce her fractious nobles, the rules of fellowship and loyalty she appealed to would have been in French.[32]

In the case of the Royal manuscript, however, the scope of Talbot's commission and the politically charged context of the volume suggest that the *chansons de geste* were seen as more than just good adventure stories told in the language of chivalry. Talbot would not have been the only one to attribute political force to such material. Keith Busby notes that into the fifteenth century various English monasteries, most notably Saint Augustine's, Canterbury, preserved and copied 'those *chansons de geste* which supported dynastic and territorial claims of the English royal family whom they served'.[33] For the French during the Hundred Years' War Charlemagne was 'the champion whose history revealed the role of the Franks as God's new chosen people'.[34] That Du Guesclin, the first French captain regularly to defeat the English, was on occasion hailed as a Tenth Worthy, joining Charlemagne and the other eight, as was Joan of Arc, is some indication of how the *matière de France* could be linked to the political travails of the kingdom of France six centuries later.

French books had become valued trophies for the English commanders, as seen most forcefully in John Duke of Bedford's purchase of a large part of the French royal library.[35] Whether, as seems likely, Bedford intended the books for the university he was establishing at Caen, or had other plans for the collection,

---

[30] See Busby, *Codex and Context*, I, 307–15. It has been suggested that the two books were the same, but see J. E. Krochalis, 'The Books and Reading of Henry V and His Circle', *Chaucer Review* 23 (1988), 50–77 (p. 70, n. 7).

[31] G. A. Lester, *Sir John Paston's 'Grete Boke', A Descriptive Catalogue, with an Introduction, of British Library MS Lansdowne 285* (Cambridge, 1984).

[32] D. Dunn, 'Margaret of Anjou, Chivalry and the Order of the Garter', in *St George's Chapel, Windsor, in the Late Middle Ages*, ed. C. Richmond and E. Scarff, Historical Monographs Relating to St George's Chapel, Windsor Castle 17 (Windsor, 2001), pp. 39–56.

[33] Busby, *Codex and Context*, I, 120–1.

[34] M. Keen, *Chivalry* (New Haven CT, 1984) p. 123, and R. Morrissey, *L'empereur à la barbe fleurie* (Paris, 1997).

[35] L. Delisle, *Recherches sur la librairie de Charles V*, 2 vols. (Paris, 1907), and L. Douët d'Arcq, ed., *Inventaire de la bibliothèque du roi Charles VI, fait au Louvre en 1423, par ordre du Régent duc de Bedford* (Paris, 1867).

its transfer was a political act, an assertion of the cultural authority of Bedford's master, Henry VI, and his claims to France.[36] For Talbot's part, one of his band, most probably Talbot himself, was careful to preserve at least one chivalric collection, the so-called Laval–Middleton MS,[37] which contains a number of romances and *chansons de geste*, including *Aspremont* (a text also found in the Royal manuscript), when Talbot took the castle from the Baroness de Laval in 1428.[38] Talbot's command that Rouen scribes assemble a large-scale collection of Charlemagne material, could, therefore be seen as an act of cultural appropriation, a *translatio studii* that reinforced a *translatio imperii*, laying claim to the glories of French heritage.

Presenting this massive volume to the new queen made a forceful and ambitious public statement, and one that was at least as much about Talbot as it was about the queen. Given Talbot's status as the symbol of the English hope in France, there would not actually have been that much difference between promoting his personal chivalric identity and promoting the welfare of the kingdom as he understood it, and the book does both. While it opens by restating the claims of the English royal line, it closes by stressing Talbot's distinguished career as Marshal of France. The book is framed by two images of a kneeling Talbot, shown, in the first, on the verso of the first opening, presenting the book itself to the king and queen; then, as the frontispiece to Christine de Pizan's *Fais d'armes*, the penultimate work, there is the often-reproduced scene of Talbot, kneeling before the king once more, this time to receive the sword of Marshal of France. The reversal of time here is striking: the book opens with a scene from the marriage and coronation of 1445, but closes with one that occurred ten years earlier. As Karen Fresco has suggested, the Book is an act of self-commemoration, and Talbot's life might be considered a book of the deeds of arms and chivalry.[39]

England had need of such a book, whether it was to be read by the king or by his future heir. By 1445, Henry VI was already twenty-four and had proved an alarming disappointment. He had come to France but once, in 1437, and he showed no signs of returning. His council in Normandy had been pleading with him for several years for greater support and complained that he had abandoned

---

36 See C. T. Allmand, *Lancastrian Normandy, 1415–1450: The History of a Medieval Occupation* (Oxford, 1983), pp. 105–20; also J. J. G. Alexander in 'Painting and Manuscript Illumination for Royal Patrons in the Later Middle Ages', in *English Court Culture in the Later Middle Ages*, ed. V. J. Scattergood and J. W. Sherborne (London 1983), pp. 141–62 (p. 161).

37 Nottingham University Library, MS Mi. LM. 6.

38 F. A. G. Cowper, 'Origins and Peregrinations of the Laval–Middleton Manuscript', *Nottingham Mediaeval Studies* 3 (1959), 3–18. De Mandach, 'Royal Wedding', assumes that it was Talbot himself who acquired the volume (p. 56), in part because he believes it acted as a model for the Royal manuscript (pp. 68–70). Both points seem strong possibilities but the evidence is not conclusive.

39 K. Fresco, comments made at 'Collections in Context: The Organization of Knowledge and Community in Europe (14th–17th centuries)', University of Illinois at Urbana-Champaign, 13–15 September 2007.

them, a ship without a captain.[40] His subjects in England were disappointed by his lack of military leadership and some may have already begun to question his psychological stability.[41] Henry VI did not actually go mad until 1453 – in fact it was the news of Talbot's defeat and death at Castillon that drove him over the edge – but he had been fragile for years. The year after his marriage to Margaret of Anjou, a London draper allegedly said that the king was not steadfast of wit.[42] Presumably, the draper was merely repeating what had been court gossip for some time. By the time Henry came to marry Margaret, it was clear to most of the English that there was an urgent need to inspire him with valour. If that proved impossible, all the greater need to inspire his heir.

The king and the queen both needed to be reminded of their rights, but the real target was more likely the future prince. Here, for Talbot, loyalty to the monarch, protection of England's rights and personal ambition would have worked hand in glove. In fact, Talbot could well have been angling for a specific job – not just Marshal of the English army in France but royal tutor. One of Talbot's chief models for his own chivalric career may have been his father-in-law, the earl of Warwick, whose reputation as a perfect knight led to his appointment as royal tutor to the young Henry VI.[43] Since the twelfth century, that role as chivalric exemplar for the prince had raised successful combatants with a flair for public relations to a seat in the highest council in the land; the great William Marshall even became regent. Did Talbot have such heights in mind? It seems not impossible. When the future king reached the age of six, and was delivered from his mother into the hands of some wise, virtuous, and courageous knight, who better to fill the role than Talbot, who had already assigned the prince his chivalric textbook?

The book, like the man who commissioned it, promotes England's claim to France. What then is its attitude to the French language? Two short texts in the anthology are directly linked to Talbot himself and may cast further light on this question. The first is the opening rondeau, which has been much criticized. Bossy, for example, remarks that 'The poem is a shaky rondeau: having committed a barbarism in the second line ['au roy' instead of 'pour le roy'], it stumbles grammatically in the third line and forgets to repeat the refrain in the middle of the poem.'[44] Bossy advances a daring hypothesis: 'One might almost think that the blemishes were intentionally left in, as if to convince the queen and others that those were truly Talbot's words, in his own version of French.'

Now there is little doubt that these lines are meant to be associated with Talbot. 'Mon seul desir' was some kind of personal motto, for it appears on Margaret's gown in one of the Devonshire tapestries. It is also quite likely that Talbot

---

[40] B. Wolffe, *Henry VI* (New Haven CT, 2001), p. 151.

[41] Wolffe, *Henry VI*, 17, 128; C. A. F. Meekings, 'Thomas Kerver's Case', *EHR*, 90 (1975), 331–46.

[42] PRO, K. B. 9/260/85, indictment of 11 January 1447, cited in Wolffe, *Henry VI*, p. 17.

[43] On Beauchamp's self-fashioning, see Y. Liu, 'Richard Beauchamp and the Uses of Romance', *Medium Aevum* 74 (2005), 271–87.

[44] Bossy, 'Arms and the Bride', p. 244, cf. Pollard, *John Talbot*, p. 128.

egarded the French language with some suspicion. And if the members of the
French delegation sighed as they were forced to keep step with the ponderous
chool French of their English counterparts, they would not have been the only
Frenchmen to do so.[45]

It would indeed be fascinating to imagine Talbot attempting to assure the court
of his simple English loyalty by deliberately writing bad French, but I doubt that
the case that he did so can be made on this rondeau, which is not perhaps quite as
bad as has been suggested. The absence of the refrain is not a major flaw. Copy-
sts often treated refrains in a cavalier fashion (the handling of the rondeau in
MSS of *The Parliament of Fowls* is a case in point).[46] Experienced amateur singers
could easily supply the missing lines just as they supplied the tune. As for the
grammar, the phrasing 'au roi' would not necessarily have been considered
ungrammatical at the time.[47] This leaves one unquestionable blunder, the failure
to write out 'est' in full, but since the resulting line makes no sense at all, and the
mistake could so easily have been rectified when the text was being copied, had
the scribe noticed it, it seems most likely that this was the scribe's blunder.

At the end we come back to the beginning, and to the introductory poem,
which tells the queen that Talbot has commanded the book so that she will be
able to keep up her French now that she has moved to the English court: 'Et
lors que parlerez anglois / Que vous n'oubliez pas le françois.' This time the
case that Talbot is engaged in elaborate self-deprecation seems stronger. Here,
in good French, Talbot presents a massive collection of French literature, at least
some of which he himself had read, all the while insisting that the queen has
come to a monolingual court, where she will speak nothing but English. The
book, with its profusion of elegantly copied texts, gives its own introduction the
lie.[48] This contradiction could be taken as playful courtly persiflage, meant to
reassure a young princess that the land where she had been cast up was not
as culturally desolate as she might have feared. Talbot and his wife had spent
nearly two months with Margaret and may have been personally sympathetic
to her and even known that she shared her father's love of books. But the lines,
as they might have been read aloud in the hall of Titchfield Abbey or Westminster, might also have conveyed a claim to imperium: here we speak English, but
we also speak French too. When Edward III launched his invasion in 1340, he

---

[45] Carol Harvey discusses a telling (though much earlier) triumph of French linguistic
sophistication over English provincialism in 'The Discourse of Characterization in
Jehan et Blonde', in *Speaking in the Medieval World*, ed. J. E. Godsall-Myers (Leiden,
2003), pp. 145–66.

[46] V. J. DiMarco, textual notes to *The Parliament of Fowls*, lines 680–92 in *The Riverside
Chaucer*, 3rd edn, ed. L. Benson (Boston MA, 1987).

[47] Godefroy, *s.v.* a I. 'spécialement au sens de pour, comme, en qualité de, a titre de'.

[48] D. J. Conlon, in his edition of *Le Roman de Guy de Warwik et de Herolt d'Ardenne* (Chapel
Hill NC, 1971), goes so far as to remark that 'the language of the scribe conforms so
closely to the language of the Ile de France that one is tempted to believe that it is
too good to be true' but finds some slight Anglo-French dialectical traces nonetheless
(p. 44).

told his barons to start learning French, but the letter that he addressed to his potential subjects stating his claims was written in Anglo-French. A century of struggle would teach the English the importance of such distinctions. Whether as a matter of diplomatic courtesy or as an implicit claim to cultural authority over the conquered land, the clerks of the English royal chancellery in Paris under the reign of Henry VI, even those with names such as Brouning or Parker, wrote not in Anglo- but in Parisian French.[49] So did the copyists working for Talbot.

Talbot was a proudly, perhaps even self-consciously, *English* hero, a scourge of the French, but his career culminated in the public presentation of a French anthology. It was not uncommon for an English aristocrat of his day to collect French romances and *chansons de geste*, and the volume to some degree depends on that familiarity. For those who could read it, French still seemed the natural language of aristocratic chivalry. Margaret would have been able to share the volume with her ladies in waiting. Talbot's commission of such a large collection of romances and *chansons de geste* was less common, however, and combining these literary texts with military and chivalric treatises still very uncommon indeed. This complex and unusual assemblage had at least a dual function to promote Talbot's public reputation and career and to promote the English claim to France. The attitude towards the French language at work in the Talbot anthology seems in keeping with this purpose. Like Bedford's acquisition of the French royal library, Talbot's assertion of control over French cultural heritage and the French language was aggressive, an act of cultural appropriation or *translatio imperii* that drives home the political aggression of the book's opening pages. The range of texts and the quality of the French showed that the English court could challenge Parisian cultural hegemony and that Talbot was no boorish soldier but a fitting member of this court, an exemplar of the international chivalric culture that England hoped to dominate. For other audiences Talbot cultivated other kinds of reputation, but through his gift he showed that he ruled French *lettrure* just as he hoped his sovereign would rule France.

---

[49] Some 1,400 letters and charters survive that were issued by this chancellery between 1424 and 1434. See Lusignan, *Langue des rois*, p. 248.

34

A 'Frenche booke called the Pistill of Othea': Christine de Pizan's French in England

Stephanie Downes

Christine de Pizan anticipated, actively encouraged and even occasionally oversaw the exportation and reception of her manuscripts throughout Europe. She specified, however, the importance of their dissemination in French:

> [P]arce que la dicte langue plus est commune par l'univers monde que quelconques autre, ne demourra pas pour tant vague et non utile nostre dicte oeuvre, qui durera au siecle sanz decheement par diverses copies.

> (Since French is a more common and universal language than any other, this work will not remain unknown and useless, but will endure in its many copies throughout the world.)[1]

For scholars of Christine's reception in England, English vernacular versions of her work have taken priority as the most informative, even inevitable, instances of the early English 'response' to Christine. A systematic examination of French manuscripts produced either in England or for English patrons, however, has not yet taken place, nor is a comprehensive list available. With few exceptions, the significance of French copies for Christine's reception in England has passed unobserved.

Christine's *Epistre d'Othea*, a letter from the fictional goddess Othea to the Trojan prince Hector, laid claim to a wide medieval audience.[2] Although three separate translations of the *Othea* (including one printed version) appeared in England during the fifteenth and sixteenth centuries, French manuscripts of the text circulated amongst English audiences in still greater numbers.[3] Five of the

---

[1] C. de Pizan, *Le livre des trois vertus*, ed. C. C. Willard and E. Hicks (Paris, 1989), p. 225, lines 19–21; C. de Pizan, *A Medieval Woman's Mirror of Honour: The Treasury of the City of Ladies*, trans. C. C. Willard (New York, 1989), p. 224.

[2] For a detailed description of the manuscripts, see G. Mombello, *La Tradizione Manoscritta dell'«Epistre Othea» di Christine de Pizan. Prolegomeni all'edizione del testo* (Turin, 1967). Referred to hereafter as the *Othea*.

[3] *The Epistle of Othea, Translated from the French text of Christine de Pisan by Stephen Scrope*, ed. C. F. Bühler, EETS OS 264 (London, 1970); *The Epistle of Othea to Hector ... Edited from the Harleian Manuscript 838*, ed. J. D. Gordon (Philadelphia, 1942); *Here foloweth the .C. Hystoryes of Troye*, trans. R. Wyer (London, c.1540).

eight French-language manuscripts of the *Othea* currently held in libraries in England reached their English audience no later than 1535, and of these at least three were produced by scribes and illustrators working in England or on the continent for English patrons.[4] This essay will consider in some detail two of these manuscripts, London, British Library, MS Harley 219, compiled by several English scribes in the mid-fifteenth century, and British Library, MS Royal 14 E II, a volume commissioned in Flanders for Edward IV of England between 1473 and 1483. Although produced several decades apart, both examples bear witness to the engagement of a French-speaking English audience with the work of a French woman, and provide an indication of the variety of uses for Christine's French in England throughout the century.[5]

Christine's account of her contacts with England is well known to modern scholars: in her autobiographical *Livre de l'advision Cristine*, the author details her acquaintance with John Montagu, the earl of Salisbury and the subsequent placement of her son, Jean, in his household in England in 1398.[6] When Salisbury's estate and belongings were forfeited to the Lancastrian crown following his execution for treason in 1400, Henry IV of England received among them the gifts – her *dittiez* and *livres* – that Christine had sent to Salisbury in friendship. Christine describes how the king himself issued her an invitation to travel to England and remain there as court poet. Paul Strohm asserts that the presence of a French poet like Christine might have answered Henry's need to secure the 'adherence of established figures' and the 'celebration of poets' in support of his

---

4   London, British Library, MS Harley 219 was executed in England; BL, MS Royal 14 E II was made before 1483 for Edward IV; BL, MS Harley 4431 was purchased by John of Lancaster, duke of Bedford, in 1425; BL, MS Royal 17 E IV appears in the 1535 catalogue of manuscripts at Richmond Palace (see H. Omont, 'Les Manuscrits Français des Rois d'Angleterre au Château de Richmond', in *Études romanes dédiées à Gaston Paris* (Paris, 1891), pp. 1–13); Oxford, Bodleian Library, MS Laud Misc. 570 was executed for John Fastolf (on whom see the essay by Driver in this volume) in 1450.

5   Douglas Gray explores the significance of the *Othea* in late medieval English culture, with specific reference to the English translations of the text, ' "A Fulle Wyse Gentyl-Woman of Fraunce": *The Epistle of Othea* and Later Medieval English Literary Culture', in *Medieval Women: English Texts and Contexts in Late Medieval Britain, Essays for Felicity Riddy*, ed. J. Wogan-Browne et al., Medieval Women: Texts and Contexts 3 (Turnhout, 2000), pp. 237–49.

6   For an edition of the full account in the original French, see *Le livre de l'advision Cristine*, eds. C. Reno and L. Dulac, Études Christiniennes 4 (Paris, 2001), p. 112. For a modern English translation, see *The Vision of Christine de Pizan*, trans. G. McLeod and. C. C. Willard with notes and interpretive essay by G. McLeod (Cambridge, 2005), pp. 106–7. See also J. C. Laidlaw, 'Christine de Pizan, The Earl of Salisbury and Henry IV', *French Studies* 36 (1982), 129–43. Laidlaw cites Christine's comment that Salisbury 'had seen' her writings as evidence that earlier manuscripts of her work had been produced and circulated in France prior to their meeting in 1398. None of these are extant: Laidlaw, 'Christine and the Manuscript Tradition', in *Christine de Pizan: A Casebook*, eds. B. K. Altmann and D. L. McGrady (New York, 2003), pp. 231–49 (p. 233).

aim to the throne.[7] Although Christine later declined the offer, over the next
two years she continued to send her works to the king to maintain his goodwill
and secure his protection of her son.[8]

Christine's presentation copies, including those originally addressed to Salisbury, have not survived, and it is difficult to discern precisely which works she
sent to England between 1398 and 1402, the putative date of her son's home-
coming. James Laidlaw has identified at least two texts that undoubtedly crossed
the Channel in this period, on the basis of their availability, suitability and, in
one case, on extant dedicatory evidence in a later, fifteenth-century copy.[9] One
the *Epistre au dieu d'amours* (1399), on which Thomas Hoccleve based his 1402
English adaptation; the other is the *Othea* (1400).[10] Because of its large number
of surviving manuscripts the *Othea* is often cited in studies of Christine's popularity, but it is worth noting that a range of Christine's works were known in
French in England from the first half of the century.[11] London, British Library, MS
Harley 4431, originally presented by Christine to the queen of France, Isabeau
of Bavaria, around 1413, was purchased by the Duke of Bedford in 1425 and
carried back to England. As well as the *Othea*, this collected edition contains a
number of Christine's books, *balades* and *rondeaux*.[12] Another well-documented
manuscript, now British Library, MS Royal 15 E VI, includes a customized adaptation of Christine's *Livre des fais d'armes et de chevaleric* for its intended recipient, Margaret of Anjou, on her marriage to Henry VI of England in 1445.[13] The
volume – entirely in French – is eminently suited to the instruction of the royal
children.[14] A passage on the treachery of the English in the original version is here
appropriately excised, presumably with Margaret and her eventual offspring in
mind.[15] British Library, MS Harley 4605 also contains a copy of the *Fais d'armes*,

P. Strohm, 'Saving the Appearances: Chaucer's Purse and the Fabrication of the
Lancastrian Claim', in *Chaucer's England: Literature in Historical Context*, ed. B. Hana-
walt (Minneapolis, 1992), pp. 21–40 (p. 35).
Vision, trans. McLeod and Willard, p. 107.
The prologue is partially printed in Laidlaw, 'Christine de Pizan', pp. 138–9; and in
full, though with an erroneous ascription of the dedication to Charles VI of France
in place of Henry IV, in G. Mombello, 'Per un'edizione critica dell' *Epistre Othea* di
Christine de Pizan', *Studi Francesi* (1965), pp. 1–12 (pp. 4–5).
Laidlaw, 'Christine de Pizan', pp. 135–40.
Mombello describes all forty-seven, *La tradizione manuscritta*, pp. 236–56 (pp. 246–7).
S. Hindman, 'The Composition of the Manuscript of Christine de Pizan's Collected
Works in the British Library: A Reassessment', *British Library Journal* 9 (1983), 93–123.
See also the online project *Christine de Pizan: The Making of the Queen's Manuscript*,
http://www.pizan.lib.ed.ac.uk/index.html [accessed 18 August 2008].
On this manuscript and Sir John Talbot, see further the essay by Taylor in this volume.
M.-A. Bossy, 'Arms and the Bride: Christine de Pizan's Military Treatise as a Gift for
Margaret of Anjou', in *Christine de Pizan and the Categories of Difference*, ed. M. Desmond
(Minneapolis, 1998), pp. 236–56 (p. 247).
G. Warner and J. P. Gilson, *British Museum Catalogue of Western Manuscripts in the Old
Royal and King's Collections*, 4 vols. (London, 1921), 2, 177–9.

written in 1434 by a French scribe in London.[16] Oxford, Bodleian Library, MS F
d. 5, which contains a copy of the *Livre des trois vertus* dating from the early 1440
displays an English scribal hand and miniatures,[17] while linguistic variants i
British Library, MS Royal 19 B XVIII, another text of the *Fais d'armes*, also poin
to English provenance.[18] A copy of Christine's *Epistre à la Reine* is preserved i
Oxford, All Souls MS 182, where it forms part of a letter-writing formulary fc
English government clerks and officials compiled around 1413.[19] Written record
provide evidence of the continuing circulation of Christine's French in Englanc
Alice Chaucer is known to have possessed a French copy of the *Cité des dame*
in the latter half of the century, while Lady Anne Scrope's will bequeaths '[t]
my lord of Surrey a Frenche booke called the Pistill of Othea' in 1498.[20] In th
absence of detailed colophons, dedications or other localizing apparatus, manu
scripts that were produced in England, by English scribes, or for English patron
are tricky to identify. The examples cited above, however, provide some furthe
evidence of the spectrum of Christine's French works that appealed to Englis
readers.

The popularity of the *Othea* in both France and England is often attribute
to its versatility: Sandra Hindman points out that by the mid-fifteenth centur
the work appeared in a variety of compilations based thematically on chivalr
morality, the virtues, classical mythology, or a combination thereof.[21] Christin
emphasizes that the work's primary intent was the tuition of noble adolescent

---

[16] London, British Library, MS Harley 4605, fol. 115r. It is this copy of the *Fais d'armes*, nc
MS Royal 15 E VI, as Francis Teague contends, that is the earliest known example i
England, the text not being present in MS Harley 4431. F. Teague, 'Christine de Pizan'
Book of War', in *The Reception of Christine de Pizan from the Fifteenth through the Nine
teenth Centuries: Visitors to the City*, ed. G. K. McLeod (Lewiston ME, 1991), pp. 25–4
(p. 25). For a brief description of MS Harley 4605, see P. G. C. Campbell, 'Christine d
Pisan en Angleterre', *Revue de Littérature Comparée* 5 (Paris, 1925), 659–71 (p. 664).

[17] C. C. Willard, 'The Manuscript Tradition of the *Livre des Trois Vertus* and Christine d
Pizan's Audience', *Journal of the History of Ideas* 27:3 (1966), 433–44 (p. 438).

[18] Campbell, 'Christine de Pisan en Angleterre', p. 664.

[19] *Anglo-Norman Letters and Petitions from All Souls MS 182*, ed. M. D. Legge, ANTS
(Oxford, 1941), pp. x–xi, 144–50; A. G. Watson, *A Descriptive Catalogue of the Medieva
Manuscripts of All Souls College Oxford* (Oxford, 1997), pp. 210–14 (p. 210).

[20] K. K. Jambeck, 'The Library of Alice Chaucer, Duchess of Suffolk: A Fifteenth-Centur
Owner of a "Boke of le Citee de Dames"', *The Profane Arts of the Middle Ages / Les art
profanes du moyen-âge* 7:2 (1998), 106–35; C. M. Meale suggests that Alice may also hav
owned a copy of Christine's *Dit de la pastoure*, 'Reading Women's Culture in Fifteenth
Century England: The Case of Alice Chaucer', in *Mediaevalitas: Reading the Middle Age*
ed. P. Boitani and A. Torti, The J. A. W. Bennett Memorial Lectures Series 9 (Cambridge
1996), pp. 81–101 (pp. 87–9). For Anne Scrope's will, see *Testamenta Eboracensia: or, Will
Registered at York*, ed. J. Raine, 6 vols. (London, 1868, 1836–1902), SS 53, 152.

[21] For the later appeal of the *Othea*, see S. L. Hindman, *Christine de Pizan's Epistre Othéa
Painting and Politics at the Court of Charles VI* (Toronto, 1986), pp. 138–42; S. Vierec
Gibbs, 'Christine de Pizan's *Epistre Othea* in England: The Manuscript Tradition o
Stephen Scrope's Translation', in *Contexts and Continuities: Proceedings of the IVt
International Colloquium on Christine de Pizan*, ed. A. J. Kennedy, R. Brown-Grant, J. C
Laidlaw and C. M. Müller (Glasgow, 2002), pp. 397–408.

The full title of the work, given by the author, describes it as a letter by 'Othea la deesse, que elle envoya a Hector de Troye quant il estoit en l'aage de quinze ans' ('the goddess Othea, which she sent to Hector of Troy when he was fifteen').[22] It has even been suggested that Christine may have written the text for the instruction of her own son: Jean would have been roughly the same age as the fictional recipient of the letter at the time of its composition c.1400.[23] Stephen Scrope's English translation and William Worcester's adaptation of sections from the *Fais d'armes* as the *Boke of Noblesse* both date from the middle decades of the fifteenth century and have come to epitomize the appropriation of Christine's writing for contemporary masculine narratives of English chivalry and identity.[24] Laurie Finke goes so far as to argue that the only extant manuscript of the *Boke of Noblesse*, MS Royal 18 B XXII, 'provides us with the best evidence of Christine's reception among fifteenth-century English readers'.[25]

The presence of the French *Othea* in MS Harley 219 extends the argument for Christine's appeal in England as primarily a writer of handbooks on chivalry. Here, the text is contained in what appears to be a didactic treatise for a young English noble, a recipient like the real-life Jean or the fictional Hector, with a specific emphasis on the fine-tuning of contemporary French language skills. The

---

[22] Christine de Pisan, *Epistre Othea*, ed. G. Parussa, Textes littéraires français 517 (Geneva, 1999), p. 197.

[23] Laidlaw, 'Christine de Pizan', pp. 137–8. Laidlaw overturns Becker's suggestion that the work may have been sent to England as a gift for Henry IV's son, who turned fifteen in 1402. See P. Becker, 'Christine de Pizan', *ZfSL* 54 (1931), 129–64 (p. 133).

[24] See, for example, C. Bühler, 'Introduction', in *The Epistle of Othea*, p. xxxii, n. 1; J. Hughes, 'Stephen Scrope and the Circle of John Fastolf: Moral and Intellectual Outlooks', in *Medieval Knighthood IV: Papers from the Fifth Strawberry Hill Conference 1990*, ed. C. Harper-Bill and R. Harvey (Woodbridge, 1992), pp. 109–46 (p. 136); or more recently, L. Finke, 'The Politics of the Canon, Christine de Pizan and the Fifteenth-Century Chaucerians', *Exemplaria* 19:1 (2007), 16–38. The argument is extended to include Brian Anslay's *Boke of the Cyte of Ladyes* (London, 1521), a translation of the *Livre de la cité des dames*, in J. Summit, *Lost Property: The Woman Writer and English Literary History, 1380–1589* (Chicago, 2000), pp. 93–107. The *Boke of Noblesse* was arguably written c.1450 by William Worcester, secretary to John Fastolf, and later revised by him in 1475, to commemorate Edward IV's invasion of France. See *The Boke of Noblesse Addressed to King Edward the Fourth on his Invasion of France in 1475*, ed. J. G. Nichols (London, 1860; reprinted New York, 1972) for an edition of the only extant text, British Library, MS Royal 18 B XXII. For the dates of Worcester's original composition and revisions, see C. Allmand and M. Keen, 'History and the Literature of War: The Boke of Noblesse of William Worcester', in *War, Government and Power in Late Medieval France*, ed. C. Allmand (Liverpool, 2000), pp. 92–105. The production of Scrope's *Boke of Knighthode*, which survives in three copies, is placed between 1440 and 1459 in *The Epistle of Othea*, ed. Bühler, pp. xviii–xxi. Several modern scholars place the date of the translation around 1450, presumably on the assumption that Bodleian, MS Laud 570, illuminated for Fastolf by Ricardus Franciscus in 1450, formed Scrope's base text. There is no strong evidence for this claim, as Bühler notes in the Introduction to his edition cited above. For a discussion of the work Franciscus produced for Fastolf, see further the essay by Driver in this volume.

[25] L. Finke, *Women's Writing in English: Medieval England* (London, 1999), p. 201.

manuscript dates from the mid-fifteenth century, and is without the miniatures frequently associated with the *Othea*.[26] The copy of the *Othea* it includes almost certainly descended from the manuscript Christine sent to Henry to bargain for her son's return to France, and is usually cited for the interest of its dedication to a 'prince excellent de haute renomee' ('excellent and highly renowned prince') and 'roy noble' ('noble king').[27] (This preface is the only example of a dedication penned by the author for a non-French monarch.[28]) As a result, perhaps, of the overwhelming attention paid to the text's prologue dedication, the Harley 219 *Othea* itself has not been adequately addressed in its mid-fifteenth-century English context. Gianni Mombello argues for this copy as an important stage in the literary transmission of the *Othea*; he dismisses it, however, for what he describes as numerous grammatical and orthographic errors.[29] Mombello's characterization of the text's linguistic specificities as spelling mistakes forecloses on this copy's ability to reveal something of the fifteenth-century milieu in which it was created, and what this suggests about how the *Othea* was read and interpreted by English audiences.

The manuscript contains an array of texts in both Latin and French, including romances, moral and didactic treatises, language dictionaries, prayers, numerous *essais de plume*, and even medicinal cures for troublesome eye diseases. Although some of these later additions do not contribute to the integrity of the whole, the four main works in the manuscript seem to have been assembled deliberately rather than haphazardly collated at a later date. The first of these is an assortment of the animal fables of Odo of Cheriton,[30] which is followed by a miscellany from the popular *Gesta Romanorum*, both in Latin.[31] The first French work in the manuscript, in a new hand, is the pseudo-Aristotelian *Secret des secrets, Livre du gouvernement des roys et des princes*, a text that purported to be for the instruction of Alexander the Great. Written in epistolary form, like the *Othea*, it outlines the qualities a king should and should not possess and tutors him in his comportment. The content of this work is a fitting introduction to Christine's instructional letter from Othea to Hector. The juxtaposition of these French epistles (the *Secret des secrets* a French translation from Latin), each of which functions as a *speculum* or mirror-for-princes, suggests that the compiler anticipated a dialogue between them. The *Othea* is the last of the four main works.

Christine's *Othea* is an appropriate crowning piece for the manuscript. In the style of an epistolary mirror-for-princes, the text speaks to the *Secret des secrets*

---

26 For a study of these, see Hindman, *Christine de Pizan's* Epistre Othéa.

27 Laidlaw, 'Christine de Pizan', pp. 138–9.

28 Parussa, 'Introduction,' in *Epistre Othea*, ed. Parussa, p. 107.

29 Mombello identifies examples such as 'pees' for 'paix, and 'chivalrie' for 'chevalrie'. He also cites sentences in which words have been slightly altered or are missing, changing the meaning of the line (Mombello, *Tradizione Manoscritta*, pp. 198–9).

30 For a French version of Odo's text, see L. Hervieux, *Les Fabulistes latins depuis le siècle d'Auguste jusqu'à la fin du moyen âge*, 5 vols. (Paris, 1893–9), IV.

31 A version of the *Gesta* text in Latin is available in an edition with notes in German, *Gesta Romanorum*, ed. H. Osterley (Berlin, 1872).

hat precedes it, while the anecdotal nature of the one hundred stories it tells
hroughout the 'glose' recalls the *Gesta Romanorum*. The *Othea* provides, further-
nore, a key to the understanding of the other texts in the volume: the popularity
f Christine's work for late medieval and early modern audiences lies partly in
ts three-tiered allegorical explanations of classical mythology. The structural
ivision of the work into text, gloss and allegory has been taken in modern schol-
rship as a model of late medieval reading practice and literary interpretation.[32]
n MS Harley 219, the 'texte' is written in a larger font, while the 'glose' wraps
round it on two or three sides, as if to draw out its meaning. The 'allegorie' is
hen inserted underneath, with the accompanying Latin moral rendered in red
nk. It is an integrated form of reading, which guides the reader's eye as it reveals
he semantic layers of the text.

A series of trilingual dictionaries begin on the final *Othea* folio, with head
words and phrases entirely in French, their equivalents given in either Latin or
Inglish. The original manuscript ends with a list, also in French, of the offices
hat fall under the management of the English Treasurer. The remaining folios
eature much sixteenth-century scribbling in English and Latin.[33]

The trilingual dictionaries offer the most salient assistance in reconstructing
he context and use of this manuscript. Although the Harleian Manuscript cata-
ogue describes the pieces after the *Othea* as having been added much later,[34]
e-examination suggests that the hand of the dictionary and the list of offices are
nore closely contemporaneous with that of the preceding *Othea*. Variation in the
and here does not necessarily indicate a later date, but possibly, and in keeping
vith the intended audience of the manuscript, a younger scribe. Added to the
inal folios of the manuscript, the neat script of the glossary and the alphabetiza-
ion of its terms suggest it was a considered addition to the collection, made a
hort time after its original assemblage.

The position of the glossary, its contents, and the nature of the treatises the
nanuscript contains, point to its use as a teaching or learning device. Definitions
rom French to English or Latin form a pattern that renders the lists an expedient
ool for a young English reader of French. The glossary's pedagogical nature is
urther underscored by the words defined within, which include basic French
prepositions such as *à* and *au*. On fol. 148v, for instance, there is a list of nouns:

2 R. Tuve, *Allegorical Imagery: Some Medieval Books and their Posterity* (Princeton, 1966),
p. 34.
3 In his description of the manuscript, Mombello identifies eight different hands
(Mombello, *Tradizione Manoscritta*, pp. 189–90).
4 See both the *Catalogue of the Harleian Manuscripts in the British Museum*, 4 vols. (London,
1808), 1, and the expanded entry in the British Library Online Catalogue of Manuscripts at http://www.bl.uk/catalogues/manuscripts/index.asp [accessed 15 August
2008].

> cousturer – a taillo[r]
> poign – a fist
> cheville – ancle
> livre – a book and a pound[35]

and on fol. 149, a long list of French verbs, for example:

> baverer – to debate
> chatiller – to tikele
> empoigner – to grype
> kaqueter – to kakele

Fol. 150 supplies a list of body parts, 'ma tete', 'ma gorge', which are all give in the possessive form, with equivalents in Latin or in English.

On fol. 151v we find a series of phrases translated from French into English The phrases themselves are of an everyday variety, similar to what one might expect in a modern-day phrasebook, and perhaps about as useful:

> torchez vos mains – whype yo[ur] hands
> mouchez v[ot]re nes – snyte yo[ur] nose
> mon cotel est voillie – my knyf is rusty
> il nest pas gab (mocquerie) – it is no iape [jape]
> cest chival de louwage – this is an hyred hors [this horse is a hack]
> je le fiz ennuis – I dyd it maug[e]r my teeth

The *passé simple* (as here, in 'je le *fiz*') occurs frequently throughout the text of the *Othea* in both the explanatory 'glose' and the 'allegorie'. An addition to the list of more domestic phrases given above, is the phrase 'tantdyz qul y feus – while he was there', in a different hand, which, with its more complicated imperfect subjunctive, is an inclusion that suggests a grammatical dimension to the lexicon.

In his 1920s study of Christine's reception in England, P. G. C. Campbell demonstrated the probability that the version of the *Othea* contained in M Harley 219 had been copied by an English scribe long before the identification of the dedication to the English king. Like Mombello, Campbell identified what he saw as a series of errors based on phonological anglophone readings of French sounds, such as 'Greek' for 'grec', 'uncore' for 'encore', 'taunt' for 'tant' 'lesson' for 'leçon' and 'Joeudy' for 'Jeudi'.[36] Sustained spellings of words such as 'pur' for the continental French 'pour', 'lour' for 'leur', 'beales' for 'belles' and 'merveillous' for 'merveilleux' are not necessarily evidence of a careless scribe o a poor grasp of the language, but indicate the practice of a copyist in an insula francophone environment, where the contemporary French in which the origina was written is flavoured with the incorporation of various localized elements o Anglo-Norman spelling.

---

[35] MS Harley 219, fol. 148v.
[36] Campbell, 'Christine de Pisan en Angleterre', p. 664.

The manuscript measures 243mm by 170mm and takes up 154 folios. It is a compact volume, roughly the size of a modern hardback novel, easily carried about and perused by a single reader. The vellum pages are well-thumbed. A number of annotations and manicules appear throughout the text of the *Othea* in the same hand as the dictionary, markers that reveal at least one reader's private attention to the text.

MS Harley 219 constitutes on the whole the kind of manuscript intended for a young English noble as a two-fold educational tool. Moral and didactic lessons are to be gleaned from the contents of the volume, specifically where it is concerned with the qualities of the good knight and able leader, but the book serves simultaneously as a handbook for the young student of French. In his early twentieth-century *Histoire de la langue française*, François Brunot notes that such manuals were often assembled as aids for the study and enjoyment of traditional and fashionable French treatises, and contained 'reminders' of French vocabulary along with major verbs and their forms.[37] Harley MS 219 falls demonstrably in this category.

Although produced some thirty years later, MS Royal 14 E II shows a comparable didacticism. Here, it is the edification not of any young noble, but specifically of the royal princes, Edward IV's sons:[38] the manuscript presents their arms on the opening folio, along with those of their father.[39] MS Royal 14 E II is one of several manuscripts Edward IV had copied at the end of his reign between 1473 and 1483 in Flanders, all of which were produced in French. It has been argued that, in the face of English defeat in the Hundred Years' War, the latter half of the fifteenth century witnessed a resurgence in the reproduction and translation of French chivalric writings, a trend that continued into the early Tudor period.[40] Margaret Kekewich views Edward's Flemish commissions in this vein, where a series of literary collections extolling chivalric virtue and military might formed 'a means of establishing a greater England and obliterating the dishonour of the defeat in France'.[41]

Edward was a prolific collector of manuscripts, and the store of volumes he brought together during his reign forms one of the foundations of the modern

---

[37] F. Brunot, *Histoire de la langue française, des origines à 1900*, 2 vols. (Paris, 1905), 1, 374–5 (p. 375, my translation).

[38] M. Kekewich, 'Edward IV, William Caxton, and Literary Patronage in Yorkist England', *MLR* 66 (1971), 481–7 (pp. 486–7).

[39] The princes' guardian, Anthony Woodville, the Earl Rivers, translated into English another work by Christine for the edification of the princes, the *Proverbes Moraux*, which was printed by Caxton in 1478. Woodville was once the owner of MS Harley 4431, the collection Christine presented to Isabeau of France. See *The Morale Proverbes of Crystyne*, trans. A. Woodville (London, 1478).

[40] See A. B. Ferguson, *The Indian Summer of English Chivalry* (Durham NC, 1960); Mervyn James, 'English Politics and the Concept of Honour, 1485–1642', *Past and Present*, Suppl. 3 (1978), 3, 10.

[41] Kekewich, 'Edward IV', p. 481.

British Library.[42] MS Royal 14 E II contains numerous royal badges of the house of York, predominantly the white rose *en soleil* set in a blue and gold lozenge, and the arms of the king on a shield surrounded by the Garter. The last badge included in the manuscript, complete with the royal motto, is in the border of the first folio of the *Othea*. Like the other manuscripts commissioned in Flanders by Edward, MS Royal 14 E II is an unwieldy volume. Given the size of the manuscripts in this collection, it is likely that they were intended to be read aloud from a lectern rather than for personal use, or even simply to display the wealth and status of their owner: the individual folios of the manuscript are still in pristine condition.

The complete manuscript contains five works in French. On fols. 1–294 is a copy of the *Chemin de vaillance*, or *Songe dor*, a long allegorical dream vision by Jean de Courcy, beautifully illuminated throughout. The *Chemin* is followed by Christine's *Othea* (the title of which appears as the *Traitte Othea* in the colophon); Alain Chartier's *Brevière des nobles*; and the *ix malheureux et les ix malheureuses* (complaints and laments attributed to various classical figures). The manuscript concludes with a French translation of Raymond Lull's prose treatise on war, originally written in Catalan, and given here as the *Livre de lordre de chevallerie*.

The border of the first folio is filled with royal insignia. Presented are two Yorkist badges, bounded by 'dieu et mon droit' in four royal blue semi-circles. The symbols form a royal genealogy: Edward IV's arms appear as a banner supported by a knight in the bottom right-hand corner, and again on a shield in the centre of the lower border, crowned and encircled with the Order of the Garter motto. In the middle of the right-hand side are the five martlets of Edward the Confessor, while in the upper corner are the three gold crowns of St Edmund, martyred Anglo-Saxon king and patron saint of the English monarchy.[43] The page is a fusion of diverse royal symbols, some a reflection of inherited French tradition, and some an evocation of the Anglo-Saxon past, which here converge to support Edward IV's Yorkist claim.

Of the sixteen sumptuous illustrations in the manuscript, fourteen are reserved for the *Chemin*. The remaining two mark the beginning of the *Livre de lordre de chevallerie*, and the beginning of the *Othea*. Unlike the usual miniatures that accompany the opening of the *Othea*, such as are to be found in the Queen's manuscript, BL, MS Harley 4431 or in Paris, Bibliothèque Nationale, MS f. fr. 606, MS Royal 14 E II does not depict an ethereal Othea who materializes before Hector on a cloud to deliver her letter.[44] Rather, the accompanying miniature styles Hector as a knight seated on a large chestnut destrier, flanked by two unmounted men. The knight's horse is positioned on a road that stretches into the distance through a lush green landscape. His body and his horse face the direction of the road, but his head is angled back towards a female figure.

[42] Kekewich, 'Edward IV', p. 481.

[43] The identification of these badges appears in the *British Museum Catalogue of Western Manuscripts*, ed. Warner and Gilson, 2, 139.

[44] Hindman, *Christine de Pizan's* Epistre Othéa, p. 139.

The woman holds no letter and her eyes are downcast, her arms and her left palm outstretched towards the knight. The scene depicted is highly suggestive of that section of the text in which Hector prepares to leave for war, despite his wife, Andromache's, prophetic dream of his death and consequent supplication that he refrain from the battle.[45] Its placement here, however, supplies no marker to link it directly with the Andromache episode. As a visual accompaniment to the text and the reader's first impression of the content of the work, the image foregrounds the notion of knighthood, with its armoured knight, his horse and his armour shaded with gold. Significantly, it is not a letter that passes between the two principal figures in the illumination, but a knight's helmet, which an attendant proffers on the tip of a sword, directly between Hector and the female figure. The illumination that introduces *Livre de lordre de chevallerie* depicts a scene of similar thematic import, in which a bearded hermit is engaged in the instruction of another knight.

English translations of the *Othea* suggest its reception chiefly as a manual of chivalry in the fifteenth century. For many modern scholars, the English title of Scrope's version, the *Boke of Knyghthode*, offers a case in point. MS Royal 14 E II, however, is thematically arranged around the idea of youth as well as that of knighthood. Jean de Courcy's *Chemin de vaillance* foregrounds youth in the manuscript, and the illuminations to the text accentuate this by marking the protagonist's progression from casually dressed adolescent, in his blue cloak and red cap, to fully armoured knight. The prologue emphasizes the youth of its narrator at the time that his dream occurred. Prouesse addresses him as '[b]eau filz' ('beautiful son') and stresses his 'jenne aage' ('youthful age') and 'jonnesse' ('youth'). She repeats that this dream is his 'commencement' ('beginning'), since 'en l'aage d'adolescence / [...] tu es de nouvel venu' ('you have just reached the time of your adolescence').[46] The narrator recounts the dream, however, from the vantage point of 'viel aage' ('old age') in a juxtaposition of youth with maturity and wisdom, which parallels the relationship between Hector and Othea, described by Christine as the goddess of the wisdom of women.[47]

The French copies of the *Othea* in the Harley 219 and Royal 14 E II manuscripts illuminate additional facets of Christine's reputation in England. In the former, the fact that the text is in French heightens the functionality of the volume as an educational tool; in the latter, the French vernacular lends the volume a foundation in French literary authority shared by the entire collection of Edward's Flemish commissions. The French *Othea* was a book read and interpreted in England, but equally suited to decoration and display. MS Harley 219 is portable and obviously well-read, MS Royal 14 E II is ornamented with genealogical symbols and texts whose reputations lend the volume as much value as its

45 *Epistre Othea*, ed. Parussa, pp. 324–5.

46 *Le Chemin de vaillance de Jean de Courcy e l'allegoria*, ed. S. Panunzio (Bari, 1979), pp. 142–3.

47 *Le Chemin de vaillance*, ed. Panunzio, p. 350; 'Othea, selon grec, peut estre pris pour sagece de femme,' *Epistre Othea*, ed. Parussa, p. 199.

embellished illuminations. In Bernard Shaw's *Saint Joan*, the generic English 'Nobleman' remarks:

> There is nothing on earth more exquisite than a bonny book, with well-placed columns of rich black writing in beautiful borders, and illuminated pictures cunningly inset. But nowadays, instead of looking at books, people read them.[48]

The evidence of the manuscripts themselves suggests that Christine's French was both 'looked at' and 'read' in England in the fifteenth century and that her works served not only as symbolic and political bearers of a French literary legacy but as practical manuals of instruction in language, chivalry and moral and social codes of behaviour.

Attention to the continuing demand on the part of English audiences for French language versions of Christine's works bears witness to the multilingual and multicultural practice of fifteenth-century manuscript production. English scribes can work for continental patrons, continental scribes for English patrons, and scribes, illuminators and patrons, like their books, can cross the Channel. So, too, Christine's English reception is not confined to a straightforward or predictable narrative of exportation and translation. Christine's English patron, the earl of Salisbury, had been a poet himself, and his poems, now lost, were reputedly written in French to satisfy the continental tastes of the Ricardian court.[49] The figure of Salisbury provides a pertinent reminder of the internationalism of medieval elites, while the manuscripts he patronized show that the history of the reception of Christine's French in England is also that of an audience appreciative of the literary merit of both languages. Christine called for the dissemination of her works in French, as a world-wide vernacular: the manuscript evidence demonstrates the accuracy of her prediction vis-à-vis England.

[48] G. B. Shaw, *Saint Joan* (1924), scene IV, lines 1–5.
[49] Salter, *English and International*, p. 244.

BIBLIOGRAPHY

Printed primary sources are listed under their authors' or editors' names below: for manuscripts and documents see the Index of Primary Texts and Manuscripts. Frequently cited works will be found in the list of Abbreviations, others under Secondary Sources below. Electronic databases are given under Online Resources below.

Primary Sources

Aelred of Rievaulx, *Vita sancti Edwardi regis et confessoris*, PL 195, 757–90.

Amt, E., ed., *The Cartulary of Godstow Abbey* (Oxford, forthcoming).

——, and S. D. Church, ed. and trans., *Dialogus de scaccario: The Dialogue of the Exchequer and Constitutio domus regis: The Establishment of the Royal Household* (Oxford, 2007).

The Anglo-Saxon Chronicle: A Collaborative Edition V: *MS C*, ed. K. O'Brien O'Keeffe, (Cambridge, 2001).

——, VII: *MS E*, ed. S. Irvine (Cambridge, 2004).

——, XVII: *The Annals of St Neots with* Vita prima sancti Neoti, ed. D. Dumville and M. Lapidge (Cambridge, 1983).

Anslay, B., trans., *The Boke of the Cyte of Ladyes* (London, 1521).

Aspin, I. S. T., ed., *Anglo-Norman Political Songs*, ANTS 11 (Oxford, 1953).

Augustine, *De civitate Dei*, ed. B. Dombart and A. Kalb, 2 vols. (Stuttgart, 1981).

Baird, I. F., ed., *Scotish Feilde and Flodden Feilde: Two Flodden Poems* (New York, 1982).

Barlow, F., ed., *The Life of King Edward Who Rests at Westminster: Attributed to a Monk of St Bertin* (London, 1962; 2nd edn Oxford, 1992).

Barratt, A., *The Knowing of Woman's Kind in Childing: A Middle English Version of Material Derived from the 'Trotula' and Other Sources*, Medieval Women: Texts and Contexts 4 (Turnhout, 2001).

Basile, M. E., J. F. Bestor, D. R. Coquillette and C. Donahue, eds., Lex Mercatoria *and Legal Pluralism: A Late Thirteenth-Century Treatise and Its Afterlife* (Cambridge, 1998).

Bately, J., ed., *The Old English Orosius*, EETS SS 6 (London, 1980).

Bateson, M., 'The Register of Crabhouse Nunnery', *Norfolk Archaeology* 11 (1892), 1–71.

——, *Records of the Borough of Leicester*, Selden Society 1 (London, 1899).

——, ed., *Borough Customs*, Selden Society 18 and 21 (London, 1904–6).

Baudri of Bourgueil, *Poèmes*, ed. J.-Y. Tilliette, 2 vols. (Paris, 1998–2002).

Bell, D. N., ed., *The Libraries of the Cistercians, Gilbertines and Premonstratensians*, CBMLC 3 (London, 1992).

Bellay, J. du, *The Defence and Illustration of the French Language*, trans. G. M. Turquet (London, 1939).

Benedeit, *The Anglo-Norman Voyage of St Brendan*, ed. I. Short and B. S. Merrilees (Manchester, 1979).

Benham, W. G., ed., *The Red Paper Book of Colchester* (Colchester, 1902).

——, ed., *The Oath Book or Red Parchment Book of Colchester* (Colchester, 1907).

Bennett, J. A. W., and G. V. Smithers, eds., *Early Middle English Verse and Prose* (Oxford, 1966; 2nd rev. edn 1982).

Benson, L. D., ed., *The Riverside Chaucer*, 3rd edn (Boston MA, 1987).

Bernard of Clairvaux, *In laudibus Virginis Matris*, Homilia II. 4. *Sancti Bernardi Opera*, 8 vols., ed. J. Leclercq, C. H. Talbot and H. Rochais (Rome, 1957–77).

Bickley, F. B., ed., *Little Red Book of Bristol*, 2 vols. (Bristol, 1900).

Bird, W. H. B., ed., *The Black Book of Winchester* (Winchester, 1925).

Blunt, J. H., ed., *Myroure of Oure Ladye*, EETS ES 19 (London, 1873).

Bolland, W. C., ed., *Select Cases in Eyre, AD 1292–1333*, Selden Society 30 (London, 1914).

Bond, E. A., and W. D. Selby, eds., *Chaucer Life Records*, Part III (London, 1886).

Boulton, M. B. M., trans., *Piety and Persecution in the French of England*, FRETS (forthcoming).

Boun, Rauf de, *Le Petit Bruit*, ed. D. Tyson, ANTS Plain Text Series 4 (London, 1987).

Bourchier, John, Lord Berners, trans., *The First (Second/Third/Fourth) Volume of Sir Johan Froyssart of The Chronycles of Englande, Fraunce, Spayne*, 2 vols. (London, 1523–25).

Bozon, Nicole, *Les contes moralisés de Nicole Bozon*, eds. P. Meyer and L. T. Smith, SATF 28 (Paris, 1889).

——, *Deux poèmes de Nicholas Bozon*, ed. J. Vising (Göteborg, 1919).

——, *Les proverbes de bon enseignement de Nicole Bozon*, ed. A. C. Thorn (Lund, 1920).

——, *Seven More Poems by Nicholas Bozon*, ed. M. A. Klenke (St Bonaventure NY, 1951).

——, *Three Saints' Lives by Nicholas Bozon*, ed. M. A. Klenke (St Bonaventure NY, 1947).

Brayer, É., E. and A.-F. Labie-Leurquin, eds., *Frère Laurent, La Somme le roi*, SATF (Paris, 2008).

Brereton, G., trans., Froissart, *Chronicles* (Harmondsworth, 1968).

Britnell, R. H., ed., *Records of the Borough of Crossgate, Durham, 1312–1531*, Surtees Society 212 (2008).

Brook, G. L., and R. F. Leslie, eds., *Laȝamon: Brut. Edited from British Museum MS Cotton Caligula A ix and British Museum MS Cotton Otho C xiii*, 2 vols. (London, 1963–78).

Brunner, K., ed., *Der mittelenglische Versroman über Richard Löwenherz* (Wien, 1913).

Bühler, C. F., ed., *The Epistle of Othea, Translated from the French text of Christine de Pisan by Stephen Scrope*, EETS OS 264 (London, 1970).

Burgess, G. S., with E. van Houts, trans., *The History of the Norman People: Wace's Roman de Rou* (Woodbridge, 2004).

Burley, Walter, *De vita et moribus philosophorum* (HM 47405), in Dutschke, *Guide to Medieval and Renaissance Manuscripts*, Digital Scriptorium, at http://sunsite3.berkeley.edu/hehweb/HM47405.html

Calendar of Inquisitions Miscellaneous: (Chancery) Preserved in the Public Record Office, 8 vols. (London, 1916–2003).

Calendar of Letters from the Mayor and Corporation of the City of London, A. D. 1350–1370 (London, 1885).

aley, J., and J. Hunter, eds., *Valor Ecclesiasticus*, 6 vols. (London, 1810–34).

amden, W., *Britain: or, a chorographicall description of the most flourishing kingdomes, England, Scotland, and Ireland, and the ilands adioyning, out of the depth of antiquitie / written first in Latine by William Camden; translated newly into English by Philémon Holland: finally, rev., amended, and enl. with sundry additions by the said author* (London, 1637).

ampbell, A., ed., *The Chronicle of Æthelweard* (London, 1962).

——, ed., *Encomium Emmae Reginae* (London, 1949), repr. with supplementary introduction by S. Keynes (Cambridge, 1998).

arley, J., ed., *The Libraries of King Henry VIII*, CBMLC 7 (London, 2007).

arpenter, C., ed., *The Armburgh Papers* (Woodbridge, 1998).

hambers R. W., and M. Daunt, eds., *A Book of London English, 1384–1425* (Oxford, 1931).

hampion, P., ed., *Charles d'Orléans : Poésies – I, La retenue d'amours, ballades, chansons, complaintes et caroles* (Paris, 1956).

haucer, Geoffrey, *A Treatise on the Astrolabe* in Benson, ed., *Riverside Chaucer*, pp. 661–83.

——, *Poetical Works of Geoffrey Chaucer: A Facsimile of Cambridge University Library MS Gg.4.27*, ed. M. B Parkes and R. Beadle, 3 vols. (Cambridge, 1979–80).

hristine de Pizan, *Epistre Othea*, ed. G. Parussa, Textes littéraires français 517 (Geneva, 1999).

——, *Le livre de l'advision Christine*, ed. C. Reno and L. Dulac, Études Christiniennes 4 (Paris, 2001).

——, *Livre de l'advision Christine*, ed. and trans. G. McLeod, and trans. C. C. Willard, *The Vision of Christine de Pizan* (Cambridge, 2005).

——, *Le livre des trois vertus*, ed. C. C. Willard and E. Hicks (Paris, 1989).

——, *A Medieval Woman's Mirror of Honour: The Treasury of the City of Ladies*, trans. C. C. Willard (New York, 1989).

hronicon Novaliciense, ed. C. C. Bethmann, MGH, SS 7 (Hanover, 1846).

lark, A., ed., *The English Register of Godstow Nunnery*, 3 vols., EETS OS 129, 130 and 142 (London, 1905–11).

larke, P. D., ed., *The University and College Libraries of Cambridge*, CBMLC 10 (London, 2002).

laverie, L., 'Édition et étude du manuscrit Longleat House 54, traduction en moyen anglais du Livre IV de Jean Froissart' (unpublished Ph.D. thesis, University of Poitiers, 2003).

obb, H. S., ed., *The Local Port Book of Southampton for 1439–40*, Southampton Records Series 5 (Southampton, 1961).

ohen, M., ed., *Mikra'ot Gedolot 'Haketer': Genesis II* (Ramat Gan, 1999).

onlon, D. J., ed., *Le Roman de Guy de Warwik et de Herolt d'Ardenne* (Chapel Hill NC, 1971).

oss, P. R., ed., *The Early Records of Medieval Coventry* (London, 1986).

oulton, G. G., ed., *Commentary on the Rule of St. Augustine by Robertus Richardinus* (Edinburgh, 1935).

ritall, E., 'Fragment of an Account of the Cellaress of Wilton Abbey, 1299', *Wiltshire Archaeological and Natural History Society* 12 (1956), 142–56.

ante Aligheri, *De vulgari eloquentia*, ed. and trans. S. Botterill (Cambridge, 1996).

——, *De vulgari eloquentia*, in W. Welliver, *Dante in Hell: The De vulgari eloquentia, Introduction, Text, Translation, Commentary* (Ravenna, 1981).

Davis, N., ed., *Paston Letters and Papers of the Fifteenth Century*, 2 vols. (Oxford, 1971-6).

Day, M., ed., *The English Text of the* Ancrene Riwle *Edited from Cotton ms. Nero A. XIV*, EETS OS 225 (London, 1957).

Dean, R. J., and M. D. Legge, eds., *The Rule of St. Benedict: A Norman Prose Version*, Medium Aevum Monographs 7 (Oxford, 1964).

Deluz, C., ed., *Jean de Mandeville: Le Livre des Merveilles du Monde* (Paris, 2000).

Depping, G.-B., ed., *Règlemens sur les arts et métiers de Paris rédigés au XIIIᵉ siècle et connus sous le nom du Livre des métiers d'Étienne Boileau*, Collection de documents inédits sur l'histoire de France (Paris, 1837).

Deschamps, Eustace, *Selected Poems*, ed. I. S. Laurie and D. M. Sinnreich-Levi, trans. D. Curzon and J. Fiskin (New York, 2003).

Devon, F., *Issues of the Exchequer, being a Collection of Payments made out of His Majesty's revenue, from King Henry III to King Henry VI* (London, 1837).

Dickins, B. and R. M. Wilson, eds., *Early Middle English Texts* (Cambridge, 1951; 3rd edn, 1956).

Dobson, E. J., ed., *The English Text of the* Ancrene Riwle *Edited from B. M. Cotton Ms. Cleopatra C. vi*, EETS OS 267 (London, 1972).

——, and F. Ll. Harrison, eds., *Medieval English Songs* (London, 1979).

Dobson, R. B., ed., *York City Chamberlains' Account Rolls, 1396–1500*, Surtees Society 192 (1980).

Douët-d'Arcq, L., ed., *La chronique d'Enguerran de Monstrelet*, 6 vols. (Paris, 1861).

——, ed., *Inventaire de la bibliothèque du roi Charles VI, fait au Louvre en 1423, par ordre du Régent duc de Bedford* (Paris, 1867).

Douglas, D. C., ed., 'Customs of Newcastle-upon-Tyne', in *English Historical Documents, II: 1042–1189* (Oxford, 1953), pp.1040–1.

Drost, M. A., ed., *Documents pour servir à l'histoire du commerce des Pays-Bas avec la France jusqu'à 1585, II, Actes notariés de Bordeaux 1470–1520* ('s-Gravenhage, 1989).

Dudo of St. Quentin, *De moribus et actis primorum Normanniæ ducum*, ed. J. Lair (Caen, 1865–72).

Dugdale, W., *Monasticon Anglicanum: A History of the Abbies and Other Monasteries, Hospitals, Frieries, and Cathedral and Collegiate Churches, with their dependencies, in England and Wales; also of all such Scotch, Irish, and French Monasteries as were in any manner connected with religious houses in England ...*, 6 vols., ed. J. Caley, H. Ellis and B. Bandinel, new edn (London, 1817–30).

Duncan, T., ed., *Late Medieval English Lyrics and Carols: 1400–1530* (Harmondsworth, 2000).

——, and M. Connolly, eds., *The Middle English Mirror: Sermons from Advent to Sexagesima*, Middle English Texts (Heidelberg, 2003).

Duwes, G., *An Introductorie for to Lerne to Rede, to Pronounce, and to Speake French trewly* (London, c.1532; rpt Menston, 1972).

Eckhardt, C. D., ed., *Castleford's* Chronicle, *or the Boke of Brute*, 2 vols., EETS OS 305 and 306 (Oxford, 1996).

Fisher, J. H., ed., *The Tretyse of Loue*, EETS OS 223 (London, 1951).

——, M. Richardson and J. L. Fisher, eds., *An Anthology of Chancery English* (Knoxville, KY, 1984).

Flodoard of Rheims, 'De triumphis Christi et SS. Palæstinæ libri tres, III 4: De Maria Ægyptiaca et Zosima', in *Flodoardi Canonici Remensis opera omnia*, PL 135, 541C-548C.

Flower, C. T., 'Obedientiaries' Accounts of Glastonbury and other Religious Houses', *St Paul's Ecclesiological Society* 7:2 (1912), 50–62.

Forshall J., and F. Madden, eds., *The Holy Bible ... from the Latin Vulgate by John Wycliffe and His Followers*, 2 vols. (Oxford, 1850).

Forshaw, H. P., ed., *Edmund of Abingdon, Speculum religiosorum and Speculum ecclesie*, Auctores Britannici Medii Aevi 3 (London, 1973).

Foster, B., ed., *The Local Port Book of Southampton, 1435–36*, Southampton Records Series 7 (Southampton, 1963).

Fouke le Fitz Waryn, ed. E .J. Hathaway, P. T. Ricketts, C. A. Robson and A. D. Wilshere ANTS 26–28 (Oxford, 1975).

Fowler, J., ed., *Extracts from the Account Rolls of the Abbey of Durham, 1303–1541*, 3 vols., Surtees Society 99, 100 and 103 (London, 1898–1901).

Foxe, J., *Acts and Monuments*, at http://www.hrionline.ac.uk/johnfoxe/transcript. html.

Fraser, C. M., ed., *Northern Petitions Illustrative of Life in Berwick, Cumbria and Durham in the Fourteenth Century*, Surtees Society 194 (Gateshead, 1981).

Fredborg, K. M., L. Nielsen, and J. Pidborg, eds., 'An Unedited Part of Roger Bacon's *Opus Maius: De Signis*', *Traditio* 34 (1978), 75–136.

Froissart, Jean, *Chroniques*, ed. S. Luce, G. Raynaud, L. Mirot and A. Mirot, 15 vols. (Paris, 1869–1975).

——, *Oeuvres de Froissart*, ed. J. M. B. C. Kervyn de Lettenhove and Auguste Scheler, 24 vols. (Brussels, 1867–77).

——, *Chroniques, Livre I. Le manuscrit d'Amiens*, ed. G. T. Diller, 5 vols. (Geneva, 1991–8).

Galbraith, V. H., ed., *The Anonimalle Chronicle, 1333–81* (Manchester, 1927).

Geffrei Gaimar, *L'estoire des Engleis*, ed. A. Bell, ANTS 14–16 (Oxford, 1960).

——, *Estoire des Engleis. History of the English*, ed. and trans. I. Short (Oxford, 2009).

Geoffrey of Monmouth, *The History of the Kings of Britain*, ed. M. D. Reeve, trans. N. Wright (Woodbridge, 2007).

Gerald of Wales, *Speculum duorum: or, A Mirror of Two Men*, ed. Y. Lefèvre and R. B. C. Huygen, trans. B. Dawson (Cardiff, 1974).

Gervase of Tilbury, *Otia imperialia: Recreation for an Emperor*, ed. and trans. S. E. Banks and J. W. Binns (Oxford, 2002).

Gidden, H. W., ed., *The Sign Manuals and the Letters Patent of Southampton to 1422*, I, Southampton Record Society 18 (Southampton, 1916).

Gilbert, J. T., ed., *Historic and Municipal Documents of Ireland (1172–1320), from the Archives of the City of Dublin*, RS 53 (London, 1870).

Gill, A., *Logonomia Anglica* (London, 1621, rept Menston, 1968).

Gilleland, J. R., 'Eight Anglo-Norman Cosmetic Recipes: MS. Cambridge, Trinity College 1044', *Romania* 109 (1988), 50–67.

Gilmore, G. D., 'Two Monastic Account Rolls', *Publications of the Bedfordshire Historical Record Society* 49 (1970), 41–55.

Girard d'Amiens, *Escanor: roman arthurien de vers de la fin du XIIIᵉ siècle*, ed. R. Trachsler, 2 vols., Textes littéraires français 449 (Geneva, 1994).

Giry, A., *Les Établissements de Rouen*, 2 vols. (Paris, 1883).

Given-Wilson, C., P. Brand, A. Curry, R. Horrox, G. Martin, J. R. S. Philips and M. Ormrod, eds., *Parliament Rolls of Medieval England* (CD ROM version, Leicester, 2005; print edition, 16 vols (Woodbridge 2005).

Glorieux, P., ed., *Jean Gerson. Oeuvres complètes*, 10 vols. (Paris, 1960–73).

Godden, M., and S. Irvine, eds., *The Old English Boethius* (Oxford, 2008).

Goolden, P., ed., *The Old English Apollonius of Tyre* (London, 1958).

Gordon, J. D., ed., *The Epistle of Othea to Hector ... Edited from the Harleian Manuscript 838* (Philadelphia, 1942).

Goscelin of St. Bertin, *Liber confortatorius*, ed. C. H. Talbot, *Analecta Monastica* series 3, 37 (1955), 1–117.

——, *Vita Edithae*, ed. A. Wilmart, 'La légende de Ste Édith en prose et vers par le moine Goscelin', *Analecta Bollandiana* 56 (1938), 5–101 and 265–307.

Gower, John, *Confessio amantis*, 3 vols., ed. R. Peck and A. Galloway (Kalamazoo MI, 2000–4).

Greatrex, J., ed., *Account Rolls of the Obedientiaries of Peterborough*, Northamptonshire Record Society Publications 33 (Northampton, 1984).

Greene, R. L., ed., *The Early English Carols* (Oxford, 1935).

Gregory, S., ed., *The Twelfth-Century Psalter Commentary in French for Laurette d'Alsace: an Edition of Psalms I–L*, 2 vols., MHRA Texts and Dissertations 29 (London, 1990).

Gross, C., *The Gild Merchant*, 2 vols. (Oxford, 1890).

Haas, E. de, ed., *Early Registers of Writs*, Selden Society 87 (London, 1970).

Hake, T. and A. Compton-Rickett, *The Life and Letters of Theodore Watts Dunton*, 2 vols. (London, 1916).

Hall, H., ed., *Select Cases Concerning the Law Merchant, A. D. 1239–1633, II: Central Courts*, Selden Society 46 (London, 1930).

Hamelius, P., ed., *Mandeville's Travels, translated from the French of Jean d'Outremeuse*, 2 vols., EETS OS 153 and 154 (London, 1919–23).

Hardy, T. D. and C. T. Martin, eds., *Lestorie des Engles solum la translacion Maistre Geffrei Gaimar*, 2 vols., RS 91 (London, 1888).

Harris, M. D., ed., *The Coventry Leet Book*, 4 vols., EETS OS 134, 135, 138 and 146 (London, 1907–13).

Harvey, B., ed., *Documents Illustrating the Rule of Walter de Wenlock, Abbot of Westminster, 1283–1307*, Camden 4th series 2 (London, 1965).

Haydon, F. S., ed., *Eulogium (historiarum sive temporis)*, 3 vols., RS 9 (London, 1858–63).

Hayward, C. T. R., ed. and trans., *Jerome's Hebrew Questions on Genesis* (Oxford, 1995).

Hector, L. C., 'Reports, Writs and Records in the Common Bench in the Reign of Richard II', in *Medieval Legal Records Edited in Memory of C. A. F. Meekings*, ed. R. F. Hunnisett and J. B. Post (London, 1978), pp. 267–88.

Henry of Grosmont, duke of Lancaster, *Le livre de seyntz medicines: The Unpublished Devotional Treatise of Henry of Lancaster*, ed. E. J. Arnould, ANTS 2 (Oxford, 1940).

——, *Le livre de seyntz medicines*, trans. C. Batt, *The Book of Holy Medicines* FRETS (forthcoming).

Henry of Huntingdon, *Historia Anglorum*, ed. D. A. Greenway (Oxford, 1997).

Herbert, J. A., ed., *The French Text of the* Ancrene Riwle *Edited from British Museum ms. Cotton Vitellius F. vii*, EETS OS 219 (London, 1944).

Hervieux, L., *Les fabulistes latins depuis le siècle d'Auguste jusqu'à la fin du moyen âge*, 5 vols. (Paris, 1893–99).

Higgett, J. with J. Durkan, eds., *Scottish Libraries*, CBMLC 12 (London, 2006).

Hildebert, *Hildebertus: carmina minora. Editio altera*, ed. A. B. Scott (Munich, 2001).

Hodgson, P., and G. M. Liegey, eds., *The Orcherd of Syon*, EETS OS 258 (London, 1966).

Hogg, J., ed., 'An Illustrated Yorkshire Carthusian Religious Miscellany. British

Library London Additional 37049. Volume 3: The Illustrations', *Analecta Cartusiana* 95 (Salzburg, 1981), pp. 66–104.

Iolden, A. J., ed., *Le Roman de Rou de Wace*, 3 vols., SATF (Paris, 1970–3).

——, *Protheselaus by Hue de Rotelande*, 3 vols., ANTS 47, 48 and 49 (London, 1991–8).

Iolinshed, R., *The First and Second Volumes of Chronicles* (London, 1587).

Iolmes G., et al., eds., *Foedera, conventiones, litterae, et cujuscumque generis acta publica inter reges Angliae ...*, 3rd edn, 10 vols. (The Hague, 1739–45).

Iopkins, A. W., ed., *Selected Rolls of the Chester City Courts, Late Thirteenth and early Fourteenth Century*, Chetham Society, 3rd series 2 (Manchester 1950).

Iorrox, R., ed., *Selected Rentals and Accounts of Medieval Hull, 1293–1528*, Yorkshire Archaeological Society Record Series 141 (1983).

Iouts, E. van, ed. and trans., *The Gesta Normanorum ducum of William of Jumièges, Orderic Vitalis and Robert of Torigni*, 2 vols. (Oxford, 1992–5).

Iowlett, R., ed., *Chronicles of the Reigns of Stephen, Henry II and Richard I*, 4 vols., RS 82 (London, 1884–9).

Iudson, W., ed., *Leet Jurisdiction in the City of Norwich during the XIIIth and XIVth Centuries*, Selden Society 5 (London, 1892).

—— and J. C. Tingey, eds., *The Records of the City of Norwich*, 2 vols. (Norwich, 1906–10).

Iunt, T., *Popular Medicine in Thirteenth-Century England: Introduction and Texts* (Cambridge, 1990).

——, 'An Anglo-Norman Treatise on the Religious Life', in *Medieval Codicology, Iconography, Literature, and Translation*, ed. P. Rolfe Monks and D. D. R. Owen (Leiden, 1994), pp. 267–75

——, *Anglo-Norman Medicine*, 2 vols. (Cambridge, 1994–7).

——, 'An Anglo-Norman Treatise on Female Religious', *Medium Aevum* 64 (1995), 205–31.

——, 'Anglo-Norman Rules for the Priories of St Mary de Pré and Sopwell', in Gregory and Trotter, *De mot en mot*, pp. 93–104.

——, *Three Receptaria from Medieval England*, Medium Aevum Monographs, New Series 21 (Oxford, 2001).

——, J. Bliss and H. Leyser, eds. and trans., *'Cher alme': Religious Practice and Devotion in Anglo-Norman Piety*, FRETS OPS 1 (forthcoming).

Iiescu, M., and D. Slusanski, *Du latin aux langues romanes. Choix de textes traduits et commentés (du IIe siècle avant J.C. jusqu'au Xe siècle après J.C.)* (Wilhelmsfeld, 1991).

Ian d'Arras, *Mélusine ou la noble histoire de Lusignan. Roman du xive siècle*, ed. J.-J. Vincensini (Paris, 2003).

Iean de Courcy, Le chemin de vaillance *de Jean de Courcy e l'allegoria*, ed. S. Panunzio (Bari, 1979).

Iefferson, L., ed., *Wardens' Accounts and Court Minute Books of the Goldsmiths' Mistery of London, 1334–1446* (Woodbridge, 2003).

Ierome, 'Prologue to the Pentateuch', *Biblia Sacra Iuxta Vulgatam Versionem*, ed. R. Weber (Stuttgart, 1983).

Ioseph, Kimhi, *Book of the Covenant*, trans. F. Talmage (Toronto, 1972).

IPS Hebrew-English Tanakh, Jewish Publication Society of America, 2nd edn (Philadelphia, 1999).

Iaeuper, R. W., and E. Kennedy, eds., *The Book of Chivalry of Geoffroi de Charny: Text, Context and Translation* (Philadelphia, 1996).

Kaye, M., ed., *Placita corone or La corone pledee devant justices*, Selden Society supple mentary series 4 (London, 1966).

Kershaw, I., and D. M. Smith (with T. N. Cooper), eds., *The Bolton Priory Compotu 1286–1325, together with a Priory Account Roll for 1377–1378*, Yorkshire Archaeolog ical Society Record Series 154 (York, 2000).

Kirk, R. E. G., ed., *Accounts of the Obedientiaries of Abingdon Abbey*, Camden Societ n.s. 51 (London, 1892).

Kitchin, G. W., ed., *Compotus Rolls of the Obedientiaries of St Swithun's Priory, Wincheste* Hampshire Record Society 18 (n. p., 1944).

Knighton, H., *Knighton's Chronicle 1337–1396*, ed. and trans. G. H. Martin (Oxforc 1995).

König, E., and G. Bartz, eds., *Das Buch vom Erfüllten Leben*, 2 vols (Lucerne: Faksimil Verlag Luzern, 2005).

Kowaleski, M., ed., *The Local Customs Accounts of the Port of Exeter 1266–1321*, Devo and Cornwall Record Society n.s. 36 (Exeter, 1993).

——, ed., *The Havener's Accounts of the Earldom and Duchy of Cornwall 1287–135* Devon and Cornwall Record Society n.s. 44 (Exeter, 2001).

Kristol, A. M., ed., *Manières de langage, 1396, 1399, 1415*, ANTS 53 (London, 1995).

Kunstmann, P., ed., *Adgar: 'Le gracial'* (Ottawa, 1982).

——, ed., *Miracles de Nostre Dame: tirés du Rosarius, Paris, ms. B. N. fr. 12483* (Ottawa 1991).

Lagarde, P. de, ed., Jerome's *Opera*, Pars I, 1, Corpus Christianorum Series Latina 7 (Turnhout, 1959).

Lage, G. R. de, ed., *Roman de Thèbes*, Classiques français du Moyen Age 94, 96, 2 vols (Paris, 1966–8).

Larsen, N., ed., *Hildeberti Cenomanensis episcopi Vita Beate Marie Egiptiace*, Corpu Christianorum Continuatio Medievalis 209 (Turnhout, 2004).

Le Blévec, D., ed., *Les cartulaires méridionaux* (Paris, 2006).

Leeu, G., *Thoofkijn van devotien* (Antwerp, 1487).

Legge, M. D., ed., *Anglo-Norman Letters and Petitions from All Souls MS 182*, ANTS (Oxford, 1941).

Levy B. J., and D. L. Jeffrey, eds. and trans., *The Anglo-Norman Lyric: An Antholog* (Toronto, 1990).

Liebermann, F., *Die Gesetze der Angelsachsen*, 3 vols. (Halle, 1903).

——, ed., *Quadripartitus, ein englisches Rechtsbuch von 1114* (Halle, 1892).

Longnon. A., ed., *Documents relatifs au comté de Champagne et de Brie, 1172–1361*, vols. (Paris, 1901–14).

Macaulay, G. C., ed., *The Complete Works of John Gower*, 4 vols. (Oxford, 1899–1902).

Maitland, F. W., ed., *Year Books of Edward II: 1 & 2 Edward II*, Selden Society 1 (London, 1904).

Mantou, R., *Documents linguistiques de la Belgique romane. 2, Chartes en langue français antérieures à 1271 conservées dans les provinces de Flandre orientale et de Flandre occi dentale* (Paris, 1987).

Marie de France, *Saint Patrick's Purgatory: A Poem by Marie de France*, trans. M. Curley (Binghamton NY, 1993).

Marsden, R. G., ed., *Select Pleas in the Court of Admiralty*, 2 vols., Selden Society 6 an 11 (London, 1894–7).

——, ed., *Documents Relating to Law and Custom of the Sea I: A. D. 1205–1648*, Nav Records Society 49 (London, 1915).

Martens, M. P. J., ed., *Lodewijk van Gruuthuse, Mecenas en Europees Diplomaat, c.1427–1492* (Bruges, 1992).

Martin, G. H., ed. and trans., *Portsmouth Royal Charters 1194–1974*, Portsmouth Record Series 9 (Portsmouth, 1995).

Marvin, J., ed. and trans., *The Oldest Anglo Norman Prose 'Brut' Chronicle: An Edition and Translation*, Medieval Chronicles 4 (Woodbridge, 2006).

McCarthy, A. J., ed., *Book to a Mother* (Salzburg, 1981).

Michel, F., *Libri Psalmorum versio antiqua gallica e cod. ms. in Bibl. Bodleiana* (Oxford, 1860).

Millett, B., with R. Dance, ed., Ancrene Wisse: *A Corrected Edition of the Text in Cambridge, Corpus Christi College, MS 402, with variants from other Manuscripts*, 2 vols., EETS 325 and 326 (Oxford, 2005–6).

Moon, H. M., ed., *The Lyfe of Soule: An Edition with Commentary* (Salzburg, 1978).

Morgan, N., with M. Brown, *The Lambeth Apocalypse: Manuscript 209 in Lambeth Palace Library*, 2 vols (London, 1990).

Moseley, C. W. R. D., trans., *The Travels of Sir John Mandeville* (Harmondsworth, 2005).

Mulcaster, R., *The First Part of the Elementarie* (London, 1582, rept Menston, 1970).

Murray, K. M. E., ed., *Register of Daniel Rough, Common Clerk of Romney 1353–1380*, Kent Records 16 (Ashford, 1945).

Mynors, R. A. B., R. H. Rouse and M. A. Rouse, eds., *Registrum Anglie de libris doctorum et auctorum veterum*, CBMLC 2 (London, 1991).

Nicolas, N. H., *Testamenta vetusta: Illustrations from wills, of manners, customs, &c from the reign of Henry the second to queen Elizabeth*, I (London, 1826).

Nichols, F. M., ed., *Britton: The French Text*, 2 vols. (Oxford, 1865).

Nichols, J., ed., *A Collection of All the Wills, now known to be extant, of the Kings and Queen of England, Princes and Princesses of Wales, and Every Branch of the Royal Blood, from the reign of William the Conqueror to that of Henry the Seventh, exclusive; with explanatory notes and a glossary* (London, 1780).

Nichols, J. G., ed., *The Boke of Noblesse Addressed to King Edward the Fourth on his Invasion of France in 1475* (London, 1860; rept New York, 1972).

Nigel de Longchamps, *Speculum stultorum*, ed. J. H. Mozley and R. R. Raymo (Berkeley CA, 1960).

Nobel, P., ed., *Poème anglo-normand sur l'Ancien Testament: édition et commentaire*, 2 vols. (Paris, 1996).

Nolan, E., and S. A. Hirsch, eds., *The Greek Grammar of Roger Bacon and a Fragment of his Hebrew Grammar* (Cambridge, 1902).

Noomen, W., ed., *Le Jeu d'Adam (Ordo representacionis Ade)* (Paris, 1971).

Odo, *Ysagoge in Theologiam*, in *Écrits théologiques de l'école d'Abélard*, ed. A. Landgraf (Louvain, 1934), pp. 63–289.

Olsen, B. M., ed., *Les Dits de Jean de Saint Quentin* (Paris 1978).

Orderic Vitalis, *The Ecclesiastical History of Orderic Vitalis*, ed. M. Chibnall, 6 vols. (Oxford, 1968–80).

Oresme, *Maistre Nicole Oresme, Le livre de éthiques d'Aristote, published from the Text of MS. 2902, Bibliotheque Royale de Belgique, with a Critical Introduction and Notes*, ed. A. D. Menut (New York, 1940).

——, *Maistre Nicole Oresme: Le livre de politiques d'Aristote: Published from the Text of the Avranches Manuscript 223*, ed. A. D. Menut, Transactions of the American Philosophical Society, n.s. 60 (Philadelphia, 1970).

Oschinsky, D., ed., *Walter of Henley and Other Treatises on Estate Management and Accounting* (Oxford, 1971).

Osterley, H., ed., *Gesta Romanorum* (Berlin, 1872).

Owen, D. M., ed., *The Making of King's Lynn: A Documentary Survey*, Records of Social and Economic History n.s. 9 (London, 1984).

——, ed., *William Asshebourne's Book*, Norfolk Record Society 48 (Norwich, 1981).

Pagan, H. J., 'The Anglo-Norman Prose *Brut* to 1332: An Edition' (unpublished Ph.D. dissertation, University of Toronto, 2006).

Parliament Rolls of Medieval England, see under Given-Wilson above and On-Line Resources below.

Paues, A. C., ed., *A Fourteenth Century English Biblical Version* (Cambridge, 1902).

Pierre de Peckham (d'Abernon de Fetcham), *Lumere as lais*, ed. G. Hesketh, ANTS 54–5, 56–7, 58 (London, 1996–9).

Pierre de Langtoft, *Chronicle of England*, ed. J.-C. Thiolier, *Edition critique et commentée de Pierre de Langtoft: Le règne d'Edouard Ier* (Créteil, 1989).

——, *Chronicle*, ed. T. Wright (London, 1866).

Pirenne, H., *Le soulèvement de la Flandre maritime de 1323–1328: documents inédits publiés avec une introduction par Henri Pirenne* (Brussels, 1900).

Postlewate, L., and D. Russell, trans., *Saint's Lives in the French of England: St George, St Faith and St Mary Magdalen, and the Legendary of Nicholas Bozon*, FRETS 6 (Tempe, AZ, forthcoming).

Prichard, M. J., and D. E. C. Yale, eds., *Hale and Fleetwood on Admiralty Jurisdiction*, Selden Society 108 (London, 1993).

Pugh, R. B., 'Fragment of an Account of Isabel of Lancaster, Nun of Amesbury, 1333–4', in *Festschrift zur Feier des zweihundertjährigen Bestandes des Haus-, Hof- und Staatsarchivs*, 1 Bd., ed. L. Santifaller (Vienna, 1949), pp. 487–98.

Raine, J., ed., *Testamenta Eboracensia: or, Wills Registered at York, Illustrative of the History, Manners, Language, Statistics &c., of the Province of York from the Year 1300 Downwards*, 6 vols. (London, 1836–1902).

Redstone, L. J., ed., 'Three Carrow Account Rolls', *Norfolk Archaeology* 29 (1946), 54–91.

Reginald of Durham, *Libellus de vita et miraculis S. Godrici, heremitae de Finchale*, ed. J. Stevenson, Surtees Society 20 (1847).

Register of Edward the Black Prince preserved in the Public Record Office. Part II (Duchy of Cornwall) A. D. 1351–1365 (London, 1931).

Register of Edward the Black Prince preserved in the Public Record Office. Part III (Palatinate of Chester), A. D. 1351–1365 (London, 1932).

René of Anjou, *King René's Book of Love* (Le cueur d'amours espris), introduction and commentary F. Unterkircher, trans. S. Wilkins (New York, 1975).

Renouard, J., ed., *Les coutumes de Beauvaisis* (Paris, 1842).

Richard de Bury, *Philobiblon*, trans. A. Taylor (Berkeley, 1948).

Richard of Saint Victor, *De Emmanuele libri duo*, in *Richardi Canonici Operum Pars Prima Exegetica*, PL 196, 601–66.

Richardson, H. G., and G. O. Sayles, eds., *Select Cases of Procedure without Writ under Henry III*, Selden Society 60 (London, 1941).

Riley, H. T., ed., *Munimenta Gildhallae Londoniensis: Liber Albus, Liber Custumarum et Liber Horn*, 3 vols., RS 12 (London, 1859–62).

——, *Memorials of London and London Life in the XIIth, XIVth, and XVth Centuries* (London, 1868).

obbins, R. H., ed., *Secular Lyrics of the XIVth and XVth Centuries* (Oxford, 1952).

obert Mannyng, *Chronicle*, ed. I. Sullens (Binghamton NY, 1996).

obert of Bridlington, *The Bridlington Dialogue: An Exposition of the Rule of St. Augustine for the Life of the Clergy*, trans. by a Religious of C. S. M. V (London, 1960).

oques, M., *Recueil général de lexiques français du moyen âge I : Lexiques alphabétiques*, 2 vols. (Paris, 1936–8).

otuli Parliamentorum, ed. J. Strachey et al., 6 vols. (London, 1767–77).

uelle, P., ed., *L'Ornement des Dames (Ornatus mulierum): Texte anglo-normande du XIIIe siècle. Le plus ancien recueil en français de recettes médicales pour les soins du visage, publié avec une introduction, une traduction, des notes et un glossaire* (Brussels, 1967).

ussell, D. W., *The Campsey Project* at http://margot.uwaterloo.ca/campsey/

ymer, T., *Foedera, conventiones, litterae, et cujuscumque generis acta publica inter reges Angliae ...*, ed. J. Caley, A. Clarke, F. Holbrooke, and R. Sanderson, 4 vols. (London, 1816–69); 3rd edn, ed. G. Holmes et al., 10 vols. (The Hague, 1739–45).

alembier, L., ed., 'Oeuvres françaises de Cardinal Pierre d'Ailly évêque de Cambrai 1350–1420', *Revue de Lille* 25 (1907).

alter, H. E., ed., *Chapters of the Augustinian Canons* (London, 1922).

——, ed., *Formularies*, 2 vols. (Oxford, 1942).

alverda de Grave, J.-J., ed., *Enéas: Roman du XIIe siècle*, 2 vols. (Paris, 1925).

amaran, C., 'Fragment d'une traduction en prose française du Psautier', *Romania* 55 (1929), 161–73.

ayles, G. O., ed., *Select Cases in the Court of King's Bench under Edward II*, Selden Society 74 (1957).

calacronica by Sir Thomas Gray, ed. A. King, *Scalacronica 1272–1363*, Surtees Society 209 (Woodbridge, 2005).

cattergood, V. J., ed., *John Skelton: The Complete Poems* (Harmondsworth, 1983).

chopp, J. W., ed., *The Anglo-Norman Custumal of Exeter*, History of Exeter Research Group 2 (Oxford, 1925).

earle, E., and B. Ross, eds., *Accounts of the Cellarers of Battle Abbey, 1275–1513*, Sussex Record Society 65 (Lewes, 1967).

ellers, M., ed., *York Memorandum Book*, 2 vols., Surtees Society 120 and 125 (Durham, 1912–15).

eymour, M. C., ed., *The Defective Version of Mandeville's Travels*, EETS OS 319 (Oxford, 2002).

hanks, E., ed., *Novae narrationes*, Selden Society 80 (1963).

harpe, R. et al., *English Benedictine Libraries: The Shorter Catalogues*, CBMLC 4 (London, 1996).

haw, G. B., *Saint Joan* (London, 1923).

hepherd, G., ed., *Ancrene Wisse* (Exeter, rev edn, 1991).

heppard, J. B., ed., *Literae Cantuarienses, the Letter Books of the Monastery of Christ Church, Canterbury*, 3 vols. (London, 1887–9).

hirley, W., ed., *Royal and other historical letters illustrative of the reign of Henry III, III: 1236–1272*, RS 27 (London, 1866).

hort, I., *La Chanson de Roland – The Song of Roland: The French Corpus*, gen. ed. J. J. Duggan, I, part 1: *The Oxford Version* (Turnhout, 2005).

keat, W. W., ed., *William of Palerne*, EETS ES 1 (1867).

kelton, John., *The Complete English Poems*, ed. J. Scattergood (New Haven CT, 1983).

mith, L. T., ed., *English Gilds*, EETS OS 40 (London, 1870).

Södergård, Ö., ed., *La vie d'Edouard le Confesseur: Poème anglo-normand du XIIe siècl* (Uppsala, 1948).

Spiele, I., ed., *Li romanz de Dieu et de sa mere d'Herman de Valenciennes* (Leiden, 1975)

Statutes of the Realm, ed. S. Raith, A. Luders and T. E. Tomlins, 11 vols. (London 1810–28).

Stockton, E. W., trans., *The Major Latin Works of John Gower:* The Voice of One Crying and The Tripartite Chronicle (Seattle, 1962).

Storey, C., ed., *La Vie de Saint Alexis* (Geneva, 1968).

Stracke, J. R., ed., *The Laud Herbal Glossary* (Amsterdam, 1974).

Stratford, J., *The Bedford Inventories: the Worldly Goods of John, Duke of Bedford, Regent of France* (London, 1993).

Stubbs, W., ed., *Select Charters and Other Illustrations of English Constitutional History from the Earliest Times to the Reign of Edward the First*, 9th edn, ed. H. W. C. Davi (Oxford, 1913).

Studer, P., ed., *The Oak Book of Southampton of c. A. D. 1300*, 3 vols., Southampton Record Society 10, 11 and 12 (Southampton, 1910–11).

——, ed., *The Port Books of Southampton or (Anglo-French) Accounts of Robert Florys Water-Bailiff and Receiver of Petty-Customs, A. D. 1427–1430* (Southampton, 1913).

Stutzmann, D., 'Un deuxième fragment du poème historique de Froissart', *Biblio thèque de l'École des Chartes* 164 (2007), 573–80.

Sullens, I., ed., *Handlyng Synne* (Binghamton NY, 1983).

Suter, H., A. Bjørnbo and R. Bestborn, eds., *Die astronomischen Tafeln des Muhammed ibn Musa Al-Kwarizmi in der Bearbeitung des Maslama ibn Ahmed al-Madjriti und de Lateinische Übersetzung des Athelhard von Bath* (Copenhagen, 1914).

Sutherland, R., ed., *'The Romaunt of the Rose' and 'Le Roman de la Rose': A Parallel-Text Edition* (Oxford, 1967).

Swift, E., ed., *The Obedientiary Rolls of Battle Abbey*, Sussex Archaeological Collections 78 (Lewes, 1938).

Tanquerey, J. F., *Recueil de lettres anglo-françaises 1265–1399* (Paris, 1916).

Taylor, J., ed., *The Kirkstall Abbey Chronicles*, Thoresby Society 42 (Leeds, 1952).

Thevet, G. A., *Vrais portraits des homes illustres*, IV (Paris, 1584).

Thomas, A. H., ed., *Calendar of Plea and Memoranda Rolls of the City of London, III 1381–1412* (Cambridge, 1932).

Trethewey, W. H., ed., *The French Text of the* Ancrene Riwle *Trinity College Cambridge MS R 14 7 with variants from Paris Bibliothèque nationale MS fonds fr 6276 & MS Bodley 90*, EETS OS 240 (London, 1958).

Trevisa, J., *Polychronicon Ranulphi Higden monachi Cestrensis Together with the English Translations of John Trevisa and an Unknown Writer of the Fifteenth Century*, ed C. Babington and J. R. Lumby, RS 41, 9 vols. (London, 1865–86).

Twiss, T., ed., *Monumenta Juridica: The Black Book of the Admiralty*, RS 55, 4 vols (London, 1871–6).

Vaissier, J. J., ed., *A deuout treatyse called the tree & xii frutes of the holy goost. Edited from MS McLean 132, Fitzwilliam Museum, Cambridge* (Groningen, 1960).

Valentine, E., 'An Edition of the Anglo-Norman Content of Five Medical Manuscripts of the Fourteenth and Fifteenth Centuries' (unpublished Ph.D. thesis, University of Exeter, 1990).

Viard, J., ed., *Les Grandes Chroniques de France*, Société de l'Histoire de France, 10 vols (Paris, 1920–53).

Wace, *Le Roman de Brut*, ed. I. Arnold, 2 vols. (Paris, 1938, 1940).

——, *Roman de Brut. A History of the British*, ed. and trans. J. Weiss, 2nd rev. edn (Exeter, 2002).

Walter Map, *De Nugis Curialium: Courtier's Trifles*, ed. and trans. M. R. James., C. N. L. Brooke and R. A. B. Mynors, Oxford Medieval Texts (Oxford, 1983).

Warner, G., ed., *The Buke of Iohn Maunduill* (Westminster, 1889).

——, ed., *The Epistle of Othea to Hector* (London, 1904).

Waters, E. G. R., ed., *The Anglo-Norman Voyage of St Brendan by Benedeit* (Oxford, 1928).

Watkin, H. R., ed., *Dartmouth, I: Pre-Reformation*, Parochial Histories of Devonshire 5 (Exeter, 1935).

Watson A. G., and T. Webber, eds., *The Libraries of the Augustinian Canons* CBMLC 6 (London, 1998).

Webster, A., *Mother and Daughter, an Uncompleted Sonnet-Sequence* (London, 1895).

Weiss, J., trans., *The Birth of Romance* (Everyman, 1996, rev. and republ. as *The Birth of Romance in England*, FRETS (forthcoming).

Whitelock, D., ed., with an appendix by C. Clark, *The Peterborough Chronicle (the Bodleian manuscript Laud misc. 638)*, Early English Manuscripts in Facsimile 4 (Copenhagen, 1954).

William of Malmesbury, *Gesta Regum Anglorum. The History of the English Kings*, ed. and trans. R. A. B. Mynors, completed by R. M. Thomson and M. Winterbottom, 2 vols. (Oxford, 1998–9).

Williston, J. H., ed., *Le Coutumier d'Oléron* (Poitiers, 1992).

Wilshere, A. D., ed., *Mirour de seinte eglise (St Edmund of Abingdon's* Speculum ecclesiae), ANTS 40 (London, 1982).

Wilson, T., *The arte of rhetorique for the vse of all suche as are studious of eloquence, sette forth in English* (London, 1553).

Wilson, W. V., trans., rev. N. Wilson van Baak, trans. as *John Gower, Mirour de l'omme (The Mirror of Mankind)*, with a foreword by R. F. Yeager (East Lansing MI, 1992).

Wimsatt, J. I. et al., eds., *'Le Jugement du roy de Behaigne' and 'Remède de Fortune' by Guillaume de Machaut*, Chaucer Library (Athens GA, 1988).

Wogan-Browne, J., N. Watson, A. Taylor, and R. Evans, eds., *The Idea of the Vernacular: An Anthology of Middle English Literary Theory, 1280–1520* (University Park PA, 1999).

Woodbine, G. E., ed., *Four Thirteenth-Century Law Tracts* (New Haven CT, 1910), pp. 53–115.

Woodville, Anthony, Earl Rivers., trans., *The Morale Proverbes of Cristyne* (London, 1478, republ. Early English Books Online).

Wooldridge, H. E., and H. V. Hughes, eds., *Early English Harmony: from the 10th to the 15th Century Illustrated by Facsimiles of MSS. with a Translation into Modern Musical Notation*, 2 vols. (London, 1897–1913).

Woolgar, C. M., ed., *Household Accounts from Medieval England*, British Academy Records of Social and Economic History n.s. 17 and 18 (Oxford, 1992–3).

Wright, T., ed., *The political songs of England: from the reign of John to that of Edward II* (London, 1839).

——, ed., *Political poems and songs relating to English history, composed during the period from the accession of Edward III to that of Richard III*, 2 vols., RS 14 (London, 1859–61).

——, ed., *The Anglo-Latin Satirical Poets and Epigrammatists of the Twelfth Century*, 2 vols., RS 59 (London, 1872).

Wright, W. A., ed., *The Metrical Chronicle of Robert of Gloucester*, RS 86 (London, 1887).

Wulff, F., and E. Walberg, eds., *Les vers de la mort par Hélinant, moine de Froidmont*, SATF (Paris, 1905).

Wyer, Robert, trans., *Here foloweth the .C. Hystoryes of Troye* (London, c.1540).

Yeager, R. F., ed., *John Gower: The Minor Latin Works* (Kalamazoo MI, 2005).

——, ed., *John Gower:* Cinkante Balades *and* Traitié pour les amantz marietz (forthcoming, 2009).

Ziolkowski, J., ed., *Jezebel: A Norman Latin Poem of the Early Eleventh Century* (New York, 1989).

Secondary Sources

Abulafia, A., *Christians and Jews in the Twelfth-Century Renaissance* (London, 1995).

Adams, J. N., *Bilingualism and the Latin Language* (Cambridge, 2003).

Aers, D., '*Vox populi* and the Literature of 1381', in Wallace, *Cambridge History of Medieval English Literature*, pp. 432–53.

Ainsworth, P., 'A Parisian in New York: Pierpont Morgan Library MS M.804 Revisited', *BJRL* 81/3 (1999), 127–51.

——, 'Representing Royalty: Kings, Queens and Captains in Some Early Fifteenth-Century Manuscripts of Froissart's *Chroniques*', in *The Medieval Chronicle IV*, ed. E. Kooper (Amsterdam, 2006), pp. 1–20.

Alexander, J. J. G., 'A Lost Leaf from a Bodleian Book of Hours', *Bodleian Library Record* 8:5 (June 1971), pp. 248–51.

——, 'William Abell "Lymnour" and 15th-Century English Illumination', in *Kunsthistorische Forschungen Otto Pächt zu seinem 70. Geburtstag*, ed. A. Rosenauer and G. Weber (Salzburg, 1972), pp. 166–72.

——, 'Scribes as Artists: the Arabesque Initial in Twelfth-Century English Manuscripts', in *Medieval Scribes, Manuscripts and Libraries: Essays Presented to N. R. Ker*, ed. M. B. Parkes and A. G. Watson (London, 1978), pp. 87–116.

——, 'Painting and Manuscript Illumination for Royal Patrons in the Later Middle Ages', in *English Court Culture in the Later Middle Ages*, ed. V. J. Scattergood and J. W. Sherborne (London, 1983), pp. 141–62.

——, 'Foreign Illuminators and Illuminated Manuscripts', in Hellinga and Trapp, *Cambridge History of the Book in Britain, III*, pp. 47–64.

—— and E. Temple, *Illuminated Manuscripts in Oxford College Libraries, the University Archives and the Taylor Institution* (Oxford, 1985).

Allen, H. E., 'Wynkyn de Worde and a Second French Compilation from the *Ancren Riwle* with a Description of the First (Trinity Coll. Cambridge MS 883)', in *Essays and Studies in Honor of Carleton Brown* (New York, 1940), pp. 182–219.

Allen, R., in T. Summerfield, with R. Allen, 'Chronicles and Historical Narratives', in Ellis, *Oxford History of Literary Translation*, pp. 332–63.

Allmand, C. T., *Lancastrian Normandy, 1415–1450: The History of a Medieval Occupation* (Oxford, 1983).

——, *Henry V* (London, 1992).

—— and M. Keen, 'History and the Literature of War: *The Boke of Noblesse* of William Worcester', in *War, Government and Power in Late Medieval France*, ed. C. Allmand (Liverpool, 2000), pp. 92–105.

Amer, S., 'Lesbian Sex and the Military: From the Medieval Arabic Tradition to

French Literature', in *Same Sex Love and Desire among Women in the Middle Ages*, ed. F. C. Sautman and P. Sheingorn (New York, 2001), pp. 179–98.

rchibald, E., *Apollonius of Tyre: Medieval and Renaissance Themes and Variations* (Cambridge, 1991).

——, 'Tradition and Innovation in the Macaronic Poetry of Dunbar and Skelton', *Modern Language Quarterly* 53:1 (1992), 126–49.

rmstrong, C. A., 'The Language Question in the Low Countries: The Use of Dutch by the Dukes of Burgundy and their Administration', in *Europe in the Late Middle Ages*, ed. J. R. Hale, J. R. L. Highfield and B. Smalley (Evanston IL, 1965), pp. 386–409.

rnould, E. J., *Le Manuel des péchés: étude de littérature religieuse anglo-normande* (Paris, 1940).

she, L., '"Exile-and-return" and Medieval English Law: The Anglo-Saxon Inheritance of Insular Romance', *Literature Compass*, April 2006, http://www.blackwell.compass.com/

——, *Fiction and History in England, 1066–1200* (Cambridge, 2007).

utrand, F., *Charles V: le Sage* (Paris, 1994).

very, M. E., 'The History of the Equitable Jurisdiction of Chancery Before 1460', *Bulletin of the Institute of Historical Research* 42 (1969), 129–44.

vril, F., 'Un chef-d'œuvre de l'enluminure sous le règne de Jean le Bon: la *Bible moralisée* manuscrit français 167 de la Bibliothèque nationale', in *Monuments et mémoires de la Fondation Eugène Piot* 58 (Paris, 1972), 91–125

——, *Les fastes du gothique: le siècle de Charles V* (Paris, 1981).

——, *L'art du temps des rois maudits: Philippe le Bel et ses fils* (Paris, 1998).

ackhouse, J., *Books of Hours* (London, 1985).

——, 'Founders of the Royal Library: Edward IV and Henry VII as Collectors of Illuminated Manuscripts', in *England in the Fifteenth Century: Proceedings of the 1986 Harlaxton Symposium*, ed. D. Williams (Woodbridge, 1987), pp. 23–41.

——, 'Illuminated Manuscripts Associated with Henry VII and Members of His Immediate Family', in *The Reign of Henry VII: Proceedings of the 1993 Harlaxton Symposium*, ed. B. Thompson (Stamford CA, 1995), pp. 175–87.

——, *The Illuminated Page: Ten Centuries of Manuscript Painting in the British Library* (London, 1997).

adel, P.–Y., 'Pierre d'Ailly, auteur du *Jardin amoureux*', *Romania* 97 (1976), 369–81.

ailey, M., *Medieval Suffolk: An Economic and Social History 1200–1500* (Woodbridge, 2007).

ainton, H., 'History between the Province and the Nation: Localising Gaimar's *Estoire des Engleis*' (MA dissertation, University of York, 2005).

aker, J. H., *Manual of Law French*, 2nd edn (Aldershot, 1990).

——, *The Common Law Tradition: Lawyers, Books and the Law* (London, 2000).

anham, D., 'A Millennium in Medicine? New Medical Texts and Ideas in England in the Eleventh Century', in *Anglo-Saxons: Studies Presented to Cyril Roy Hart*, ed. S. Keynes, A. P. Smyth and C. R. Hart (Dublin, 2006), pp. 230–42.

arber, C., *The English Language. A Historical Introduction* (Cambridge, 2002).

arkaï, R., *A History of Jewish Gynaecological Texts in the Middle Ages* (Leiden, 1998).

arnes, M., 'Norse in the British Isles', in *Viking Revaluations*, ed. A. Faulkes (London, 1993), pp. 65–84.

arratt, A., 'Dame Eleanor Hull: The Translator at Work', *Medium Aevum* 72 (2003), 277–96.

——, 'Keeping Body and Soul Together: The Charge to the Barking Cellaress' unpublished paper.

Bartlett, R., *The Making of Europe: Conquest, Colonization and Cultural Change, 950–135* (Harmondsworth, 1994).

Baswell, C., *Virgil in Medieval England: Figuring the Aeneid from the Twelfth Century t* *Chaucer* (Cambridge, 1995).

——, 'Latinitas', in Wallace, *Cambridge History of Medieval English Literature*, pp 122–51.

——, 'Multilingualism on the Page', in Strohm, ed., *Middle English*, pp. 38–50.

Bates, D., 'La Normandie et l'Angleterre de 900 à 1204', in *La Normandie et l'Angleterr au Moyen-Âge. Colloque de Cerisy-la-Salle (4–7 octobre 2001)*, ed. P. Boutet and V Gazeau (Caen, 2003), pp. 9–20.

Batt, C., D. Renevey and C. Whitehead, 'Domesticity and Medieval Devotional Liter ature', *LSE* 36 (2005), 195–250.

Baxter, S., 'MS C of the Anglo-Saxon Chronicle and the Politics of Mid-Eleventl Century England', *EHR* 122 (2007), 1189–1227.

Beadle, R., 'Sir John Fastolf's French Books', in *Medieval Texts in Context*, ed D. Renevey and G. Caie (London, 2008), pp. 96–112.

Becker, P., 'Christine de Pizan', *ZfSL* 54 (1931), 129–64.

Begent, P. J., and H. Chesshyre, *The Most Noble Order of the Garter: 650 Years with Chapter on the Statutes of the Order by Dr Lisa Jefferson* (London, 1999).

Bell, A., 'Gaimar's Patron, Raul le Fiz Gilebert', *Notes and Queries*, 12th series 8 (1921) 104–5.

——, 'Glossarial and Textual Notes on Gaimar's *Estoire des Engleis*', *MLR* 43 (1948) 39–46.

——, 'Gaimar's Early "Danish" Kings', *PMLA* 65 (1950), 601–40.

——, 'Further Glossarial and Textual Notes on Gaimar's *Estoire des Engleis*', *MLR* 4 (1954), 309–21.

Bell, D. N., 'Monastic Libraries: 1400–1557', in Hellinga and Trapp, *Cambridge Histor of the Book in Britain, III*, pp. 229–54.

——, 'The Libraries of Religious Houses in the Late Middle Ages', in Leedham-Gree and Webber, *Cambridge History of Libraries*, I, 126–51.

Belmon, J., and F. Vielliard, 'Latin farci et occitan dans les actes du XIe siècle', *Bibli othèque de l'École des Chartes*, 155 (1997), 149–83.

Bennett, A., 'A Book Designed for a Noblewoman: An Illustrated *Manuel des Péché* of the Thirteenth Century', in Brownrigg, *Medieval Book Production*, pp. 163–81.

Bennett, J. W., *The Rediscovery of Sir John Mandeville* (New York, 1954).

Bennett, M. J., 'Isabelle of France, Anglo-French Diplomacy and Cultural Exchange ir the Late 1350s', in *The Age of Edward III*, ed. J. S. Bothwell (York, 2001), pp. 215–25

——, 'Mandeville's *Travels* and the Anglo-French Moment', *Medium Aevum* 75 (2006) 273–92.

Bergamini, G., 'Un brevario francescano del XIV secolo nel Museo di Cividale de Friuli', *Le Venezie francescane: rivista semestrale di storia, arte e cultura* n.s. 3 (1986) 29–42.

Berger, S., *La Bible française au moyen âge: étude sur les plus anciennes versions de la Bibl écrites en prose de langue d'oïl* (Paris, 1884).

Bernard, J., *Navires et gens de mer à Bordeaux (vers 1400 – vers 1550)* (Paris, 1968).

Berndt, R., 'The Period of the Final Decline of French in Medieval England (14th anc early 15th centuries)', *Zeitschrift für Anglistik und Amerikanistik* 20 (1972), 341–69.

Berschin, H. and W., 'Mittellatein und Romanisch', *Zeitschrift für romanische Philologie* 102 (1987), 1–19.

Bevington, D., *Medieval Drama* (Boston, 1975).

Binski, P., 'Reflections on *La Estoire Seint Aedward le rei*: Hagiography and Kingship in Thirteenth-Century England', *JMH* 16 (1990), 333–50.

——, *Westminster Abbey and the Plantagenets: Kingship and the Representation of Power, 1200–1400* (New Haven CT, 1995).

——, and S. Panayotova, eds., *The Cambridge Illuminations: Ten Centuries of Book Production in the Medieval West* (London, 2005).

Blacker, J., *The Faces of Time: Portrayal of the Past in Old French and Latin Historical Narrative of the Anglo-Norman Regnum* (Austin TX, 1994).

——, '"Dame Cunstance la Gentil": Gaimar's Portrait of a Lady and her Books', in *The Court and Cultural Diversity: Selected Papers from the Eighth Triennial Congress of the International Courtly Literature Society*, ed. E. Mullally and J. Thompson (Cambridge, 1997), pp. 109–19.

Blaess, M., 'L'abbaye de Bordesley et les livres de Guy de Beauchamp', *Romania* 78 (1957), 511–18.

——, 'Les manuscrits français dans les monastères anglais au Moyen Age', *Romania* 94 (1973), 321–58.

Blake, N. F., 'Reynard the Fox in England', in *Aspects of the Medieval Animal Epic*, ed. E. Rombauts and A. Welkenhuysen (Leuven, 1975), pp. 53–65.

Blomefield, F., and C. Parkin, *An Essay Towards a Topographical History of the County of Norfolk*, 11 vols. (London, 1805–10).

Blurton, H., 'From *Chanson de Geste* to Magna Carta: Genre and the Barons in Matthew Paris's *Chronica majora*', *New Medieval Literatures* 9 (2007), 113–78.

Boffey, J., 'The Manuscripts of English Courtly Love Lyric in the Fifteenth Century', in *Manuscripts and Readers in Fifteenth-Century England: The Literary Implications of Manuscript Study*, ed. D. Pearsall (Cambridge, 1982), pp. 3–14.

——, 'Books and Readers in Calais: Some Notes', *The Ricardian* 13 (2003), 67–74.

Bolton, T., *The Empire of Cnut the Great: Conquest and Consolidation of Power in Northern Europe in the Early Eleventh Century* (London, 2009).

Bond, G. A., *The Loving Subject: Desire, Eloquence, and Power in Romanesque France* (Philadelphia, 1995).

Bond, J. C., 'Monastic Fisheries', in *Medieval Fish, Fisheries and Fishponds in England*, ed. M. Aston (Oxford, 1988), pp. 69–112.

——, 'The Fishponds of Eynsham Abbey', *The Eynsham Record: Journal of the Eynsham History Group* 9 (1992), 3–17.

Bonnard, J., *Les traductions de la Bible en vers français au Moyen Âge* (Paris, 1884, rept Geneva, 1967).

'Book of Hours, Sarum use, illuminated by the Master of Sir John Fastolf, England or France, ca. 1430–1440', *The J. Paul Getty Museum Journal* 13 (Malibu CA, 1985).

Bossuat, R., 'Traditions populaires relatives au martyre et à la sépulture de saint Denis', *Le Moyen Âge* 62 (1959), 479–509.

Bossy, M.-A., 'Arms and the Bride: Christine de Pizan's Military Treatise as a Wedding Gift for Margret of Anjou', in *Christine de Pizan and the Categories of Difference*, ed. M. Desmond (Minneapolis MN, 1998), pp. 236–56.

Bouchard, C. B., 'Monastic Cartularies: Organizing Eternity', in *Charters, Cartularies, and Archives: The Preservation and Transmission of Documents in the Medieval West*, ed. A. J. Kosto and A. Winroth (Toronto, 2002).

Bourcier, G., *An Introduction to the History of the English Language*, trans. C. Clark (Cheltenham, 1981).

Bourdillon, A. F. C., *The Order of Minoresses in England* (Manchester, 1926).

Boutemy, A., 'Deux poèmes inconnus de Serlon de Bayeux et une copie nouvelle de son poème contre les moines de Caen', *Le Moyen Âge* 48 (1938), 241–69.

Bowers, J. M., 'Chaucer after Retters: The Wartime Origins of English Literature', in Baker, *Inscribing the Hundred Years War*, pp. 91–125.

Brand, P., *The Origin of the English Legal Profession* (Oxford, 1992).

——, 'The Languages of the Law in Later Medieval England', in Trotter, *Multilingualism*, pp. 63–76.

——, 'Petitions and Parliament in the Reign of Edward I', in *Parchment and People: Parliament in the Middle Ages*, ed. L. Clark (Edinburgh, 2004), pp. 14–38.

Braunmüller, K., 'Communication Strategies in the Area of the Hanseatic League: The Approach by Semi-Communication', *Multilingua* 16:4 (1997), 365–73.

Bredehoft, T., *Textual Histories: Readings in the Anglo-Saxon Chronicle* (Toronto, 2001).

Brereton, G., 'Some Grammatical Changes Made by Two Revisers of the Anglo-Norman Version of *Des Grantz Geantz*', in *Studies in French Language and Mediæval Literature Presented to Mildred K. Pope by Pupils, Colleagues and Friends*, ed. anon. (Manchester, 1939), pp. 21–8.

Brewer, D., ed., *Chaucer: The Critical Heritage*, 2 vols. (London, 1978).

Brewer, E., 'The Sources of *Sir Gawain and the Green Knight*', in *A Companion to the Gawain-Poet*, ed. D. Brewer and J. Gibson, Arthurian Studies 38 (Cambridge, 1997), pp. 243–55.

Brewer, T., *Memoir of the Life and Times of John Carpenter* (London, 1856).

Britnell, R. H., 'The Oath Book of Colchester and the Borough Constitution, 1372–1404', *Essex Archaeology and History* XIV (1982), 94–101.

Brown, A. L., 'Parliament, *c.*1377–1422', in *The English Parliament in the Middle Ages*, ed. R. G. Davies and J. H. Denton (Manchester, 1982), pp. 109–40.

Brown, C., 'A Thirteenth-Century Manuscript at Maidstone', *MLR* 21 (1926), 1–12.

——, 'The Maidstone Text of the "Proverbs of Alfred"', *MLR* 21 (1926), 249–60.

Brownrigg, L.L., ed., *Medieval Book Production: Assessing the Evidence: Proceedings of the Second Conference of the Seminar in the History of the Book to 1500, Oxford, July 1988* (Los Altos Hills CA, 1990).

Bruneau, C., *Petite histoire de la langue française*, 2 vols. (Paris, 1955).

Brunel, C., 'Les premiers exemples de l'emploi du provençal dans les chartes', *Romania* 48 (1922), 335–64.

Brunot, F., *Histoire de la langue française, des origines à 1900*, 2 vols. (Paris, 1905).

Bühler, C. F., 'Sir John Fastolf's Manuscripts of the *Epitre d'Othéa* and Stephen Scrope's Translation of this Text', *Scriptorium* 3 (1949), 123–8.

Bullington, R., *Alexis in the Saint Albans Psalter: A Look Into the Heart of the Matter* (New York, 1991).

Buridant, C., *Grammaire nouvelle de l'ancien français* (Paris, 2000).

Burland, M. J., *Strange Words: Retelling and Reception in the Medieval Roland Textual Tradition* (Notre Dame IN, 2007).

Burne, A. H., *The Agincourt War* (London, 1956).

Burnett, C., *The Introduction of Arabic Learning into England* (London, 1997).

Burnley, D., 'Lexis and Semantics', in *The Cambridge History of the English Language, II: 1066–1476*, ed. N. Blake (Cambridge, 1992), pp. 409–99.

Burnley, J. D., *Chaucer's Language and the Philosopher's Tradition* (Haverhill, 1979).

——, 'French and Frenches in Fourteenth-Century London', in *Language Contact in the History of English*, ed. D. Kastovsky and A. Mettinger (Frankfurt, 2001), pp. 17–34.

Burwash, D., *English Merchant Shipping 1460–1540* (Toronto, 1947).

Busby, K., *Codex and Context: Reading Old French Verse Narrative in Manuscript*, 2 vols. (Amsterdam, 2002).

——, and A. Putter, eds., Introduction to *Medieval Multilingualism: The Francophone World and Its Neighbours*, ed. K. Busby and C. Kleinhenz, Texts and Cultures of Northern Europe (Turnhout, forthcoming).

Butterfield, A., '*Confessio amantis* and the French Tradition', in *A Companion to Gower*, ed. S. Echard (Cambridge, 2004), pp. 165–80.

——, ed., *Chaucer and the City* (Cambridge, 2006).

——, 'English, French and Anglo-French: Language and Nation in the *fabliau*', Special Issue of *Zeitschrift für deutsche Philologie: Mittelalterliche Novellistik im europäischen Kontext*, ed. M. Chinca, T. Reuvekamp-Felber and C. Young (Berlin, 2006), pp. 238–59.

——, *The Familiar Enemy: Chaucer, Language and Nation in the Hundred Years War* (Oxford, 2009).

——, 'Guerre et paix: l'anglais, le français et « l'anglo-français', *Séance publique annuelle du 20 juin 2008, Comptes Rendus de l'Académie des Inscriptions & Belles-lettres*, 9 (2009), forthcoming.

Caballero Navas, C., 'Algunos "secretos de mujeres" revelados: El *Šeʿar yašub* y la recepción y transmisión del *Trotula* en hebreo [Some "secrets of women" revealed. The *Sheʿar yašub* and the reception and transmission of the *Trotula* in Hebrew]', *Miscelánea de Estudios Árabes y Hebraicos, sección Hebreo* 55 (2006), 381–425.

Calin, W. W., *The French Tradition and the Literature of Medieval England* (Toronto, 1994).

Camargo, M., *The Middle English Verse Love Epistle* (Tübingen, 1991).

Camille, M., *Mirror in Parchment: The Luttrell Psalter and the Making of Medieval England* (London, 1988).

Campbell, J., 'Some Twelfth-Century Views of the Anglo-Saxon Past', in idem, *Essays in Anglo-Saxon History* (London, 1986), pp. 20–8.

Campbell, P. G. C., 'Christine de Pisan en Angleterre', *Revue de littérature comparée* 5 (Paris, 1925), 659–71.

Cannon, C., *The Making of Chaucer's English* (Cambridge, 1998).

——, 'Monastic Production', in Wallace, *Cambridge History of Medieval English Literature*, pp. 316–48.

——, 'The Form of the Self: *Ancrene Wisse* and Romance', *Medium Aevum* 70 (2001), 47–65.

Careri, M., T. Nixon, C. Ruby and I. Short, eds., *Catalogue illustré des manuscrits de la littérature française et occitane : le xii* siècle* (Rome, forthcoming).

Carley, J. P., *The Books of King Henry VIII and His Wives* (London, 2004).

Carlson, D. R., 'A Rhyme Distribution Chronology of John Gower's Latin Poetry', *Studies in Philology* 104 (2007), 15–55.

Carruthers, L., *La Somme le Roi de Lorens d'Orléans et ses traductions anglaises* (Paris, 1980).

Carruthers, M., *The Book of Memory: A Study of Memory in Medieval Culture*, 2nd edn (Cambridge, 2008).

Cartier, N. R., 'The Lost Chronicle', *Speculum* 36 (1961), 424–34.

Castor, H., 'Vere, John de, twelfth earl of Oxford (1408–1462)', *ODNB*, http://www oxforddnb.com/view/article/28213?docPos=11

Catalogue of the Harleian Manuscripts in the British Museum, commenced by H. Wanley and successively continued by D. Casley, W. Hocker and C. Morton, with an index by T. Astle, 4 vols. (London, 1808–12).

Catto, J., 'Written English: The Making of the Language, 1370–1400', *Past and Present* 179 (2003), 24–59.

Cavanaugh, S. H., *A Study of Books Privately Owned in England: 1300–1450*, 2 vols. (Ann Arbor, 1980).

Cerquiglini-Toulet, J., *La couleur de la mélancolie: la fréquentation des livres au XIV⁴ siècle, 1300–1415* (Paris, 1993).

Champion, P., *La librairie de Charles d'Orléans* (Paris, 1910).

Chapple, G. F., 'Correspondence of the City of London 1298–1370' (unpublished PhD thesis, University of London, 1938).

Chartier, J., *Histoire de Charles VI, roi de France et de son époque, 1403–1461*, ed. M. Vallet de Viriville, 3 vols. (Paris, 1863–5).

Chase, C., *The Dating of Beowulf* (Toronto, 1981).

Chaurand, J., *Nouvelle histoire de la langue française* (Paris, 1999).

Chesney, K., 'Two MSS of Christine de Pisan', *Medium Aevum* 1 (1932), 35–41.

Chevalier, J.-C., *Histoire de la grammaire française* (Paris, 1994).

Chibnall, M., *The Debate on the Norman Conquest*, Issues in Historiography (Manchester, 1999).

Christianson, C. P., *A Directory of London Stationers and Book Artisans 1300–1500* (New York, 1990).

Le Cinquième centenaire de l'imprimerie dans les anciens Pays-Bas, Exhibition catalogue, Brussels, Bibliothèque Royale Albert 1ᵉʳ (Brussels, 1973).

Clanchy, M. T., *England and its Rulers 1066–1272* (London, 1983).

——, *From Memory to Written Record: England, 1066–1307*, 2nd edn (Oxford, 1993).

Clark, R. L. A., 'Eve and her Audience in the Anglo-Norman *Adam*', in *Crossing Boundaries: Issues of Cultural and Individual Identity in the Middle Ages and the Renaissance*, ed. S. McKee (Turnhout, 1999), pp. 27–39.

Claxton, A., 'The Sign of the Dog: An Examination of the Devonshire Hunting Tapestries', *JMH* 14 (1988), 127–79.

Coldicott, D. K., *Hampshire Nunneries* (Chichester, 1989).

Coldiron, A. E. B., 'Taking Advice from a Frenchwoman: Caxton, Pynson, and Christine de Pizan's Moral Proverbs', in *Caxton's Trace: Studies in the History of English Printing*, ed. W. Kuskin (Notre Dame IN, 2006), pp. 127–66.

Cole, A., 'William Langland and the Invention of Lollardy', in *Lollards and Their Influence in Late Medieval England*, ed. F. Somerset, J. C. Havens and D. Pitard (Cambridge, 2003), pp. 37–58.

Coleman, Janet, *English Literature in History, 1350–1400: Medieval Readers and Writers* (London, 1981).

Coleman, Joyce, 'Handling Pilgrims: Robert Mannyng and the Gilbertine Cult', *Philological Quarterly* 81 (2004 for 2002), pp. 311–26.

Coletti, T., *Mary Magdalene and the Drama of Saints: Theater, Gender, and Religion in Late Medieval England* (Philadelphia, 2004).

Colish, M., *Medieval Foundations of the Western Intellectual Tradition: 400–1400* (New Haven CT, 1997).

Collette, C. P., *Performing Polity: Women and Agency in the Anglo-French Tradition, 1385–1620* (Turnhout, 2006).

Connolly, M., 'Shaking the Language Tree: Translating the Word into the Vernacular in the Anglo-Norman *Miroir* and Middle English *Mirror*', in *The Medieval Translator* 8, ed. R. Voaden, R. Tixier, T. S. Roura and J. R. Rytting (Turnhout, 2003), pp. 17–27.

——, and Y. Plumley, 'Crossing the Channel: John Shirley and the Circulation of French Lyric Poetry in England in the Early Fifteenth Century', in *Patrons, Authors and Workshops: Books and Book Production in Paris Around 1400*, ed. G. Croenen and P. Ainsworth (Leuven, 2006), pp. 311–32.

Constable, M., *The Law of the Other: The Half-Alien Jury and Changing Conceptions of Citizenship, Law and Knowledge* (Chicago, 1994).

Cooper, H., '"Peised Evene in the Balance": A Thematic and Rhetorical Topos in the *Confessio amantis*', *Medievalia* 16 (1993), 113–39.

Corrie, M., 'Harley 2253, Digby 89 and the Circulation of Literature in pre-Chaucerian England', in *Studies in the Harley Manuscript*, ed. Fein, pp. 427–44.

Cottle, B., *The Triumph of English* (London, 1969).

Cowper, F. A. G., 'Origins and Peregrinations of the Laval-Middleton Manuscript', *NMS* 3 (1959), 3–18.

Crane, S. (as S. Dannenbaum), *Insular Romance: Politics, Faith and Culture in Anglo-Norman and Middle English Romance* (Berkeley, 1986).

——, 'Anglo-Norman Cultures in England, 1066–1460', in Wallace, *Cambridge History of Medieval English Literature*, pp. 35–60.

——, *The Performance of Self: Ritual, Clothing and Identity during the Hundred Years War* (Philadelphia, 2002).

Crick, J., 'St. Albans, Westminster, and Some Twelfth-Century Views of the Anglo-Saxon Past', *ANS* 25 (2003 for 2002), 65–83.

Croenen, G., 'Froissart et ses mécènes: quelques problèmes biographiques', in *Froissart dans sa forge: Colloque réuni à Paris, du 4 au 6 novembre 2004*, ed. O. Bombarde (Paris, 2006), pp. 9–32.

——, 'La tradition manuscrite du Troisième Livre des *Chroniques* de Froissart', in *Froissart à la cour de Béarn: l'écrivain, les arts et le pouvoir*, ed. V. Fasseur (Turnhout, forthcoming), pp. 15–59.

——, M. Mary and R. Rouse, 'Pierre de Liffol and the Manuscripts of Froissart's *Chronicles*', *Viator* 33 (2002), 261–93.

——, K. M. Figg and A. Taylor, 'Authorship, Patronage, and Literary Gifts: The Books Froissart Brought to England in 1395', *JEBS* 11 (2008), 1–42.

Crook, D., *Records of the General Eyre*, Public Record Office Handbooks 20 (London, 1982).

Crosby, R., 'Robert Mannyng of Brunne: A New Biography', *PMLA* 57 (1942), 15–28.

Crystal, D., *The Stories of English* (Woodstock, 2004).

Cubitt, C., 'Virginity and Misogyny in Tenth- and Eleventh-Century England', *Gender and History* 12 (2000), 1–32.

Curry, A., '"A Game of Two Halves": Parliament, 1422–1454', in *Parchment and People*, ed. L. Clark (Edinburgh, 2004), pp. 73–102.

——, A. Bell et al., 'Languages in the Military Profession in Later Medieval England', in Ingham, *Anglo-Norman Language*.

Cuttino, G. P., 'King's Clerks and the Community of the Realm', *Speculum* 29 (1954), 395–409.

D'Aronco, M. A., 'How "English" is Anglo-Saxon Medicine? The Latin Sources for Anglo-Saxon Medical Texts', in *Britannia Latina: Latin in the Culture of Great Britain from the Middle Ages to the Twentieth Century*, ed. C. Burnett and N. Mann, Warburg Institute Colloquia 8 (London, 2005), 27–41.

Daniell, D., *The Bible in English: Its History and Influence* (New Haven CT, 2003).

Dashwood, G. H., 'Notes of Deeds and Survey of Crabhouse Nunnery, Norfolk', in *Norfolk Archaeology* (Norwich, 1859), pp. 257–62.

Davies, J. C., 'Common Law Writs and Returns, Richard I to Richard II', *Bulletin of the Institute of Historical Research* 26 (1953), 125–56 and 27 (1954), 1–34.

Davies, R. R., *Domination and Conquest: The Experience of Ireland, Scotland and Wales 1100–1300* (Cambridge, 1990).

——, 'The Peoples of Britain and Ireland, 1110–1400: IV Language and Historical Identity', *TRHS* 6th series 7 (1997), 1–24.

Davis, G. R. C., *Medieval Cartularies of Great Britain, A Short Catalogue* (London, 1958).

Davis, N., 'The *Litera Troili* and English Letters', *Review of English Studies* 16 (1965), 233–45.

Davis, R. H. C., *The Normans and their Myth* (London, 1976).

Deanesly, M., *The Lollard Bible and Other Medieval Biblical Versions* (Cambridge, 1920).

Deeming, H. L., 'The Songs of St Godric: A Neglected Context', *Music & Letters* 86 (2005), 169–85.

——, 'Music in English Miscellanies of the Twelfth and Thirteenth Centuries' (unpublished Ph.D. dissertation, 2 vols., Cambridge, 2005).

——, 'Observations on the Habits of Twelfth- and Thirteenth-Century Music Scribes', *Scriptorium* 60 (2006), 38–59.

——, *Miscellany Manuscripts and the Collecting of Texts: Scribes and Readers in Twelfth- and Thirteenth-Century Britain* (forthcoming).

Delachenal, R., *Histoire de Charles V*, 5 vols. (Paris, 1909–31).

Delisle, L., 'Fragment d'un poème historique du XIVᵉ siècle', *Bibliothèque de l'École des Chartes* 60 (1899), 611–16.

——, *Recherches sur la Librairie de Charles V*, 2 vols. (Paris, 1907).

Dennison, L., M. W. Driver, A. E. Nichols, and K. L. Scott, eds., *An Index of Images in English Manuscripts from the Time of Chaucer to Henry VIII, c.1380–c.1509: The Bodleian Library, Oxford. Fascicle II: MSS Dodsworth-Marshall* (Turnhout, 2001).

Déprez, E., *Études de diplomatique anglaise. De l'avènement d'Édouard Iᵉʳ à celui d'Henri VII (1272–1485). Le sceau privé, le sceau secret, le signet* (Paris, 1908).

Dickinson, J. C., *The Origins of the Austin Canons and Their Introduction into England* (London, 1950).

Diekstra, F. N. M., 'The Poetic Exchange between Philippe de Vitry and Jean de la Mote: A New Edition', *Neophilologus* 70 (1986), 504–19.

DiMarco, V. J., textual notes to *The Parliament of Fowls*, lines 680–92 in Benson, ed., *Riverside Chaucer*.

Dobson, E. J., *The Origins of* Ancrene Wisse (Oxford, 1976).

Dodd, G., *Justice and Grace: Private Petitioning and the English Parliament in the Late Middle Ages* (Oxford, 2007).

——, 'The Spread of English in the Records of Central Government, 1400–1430', in *Vernacularity in England and Wales, c. 1300–1550*, ed. E. Salter and H. Wicker (Turnhout, forthcoming).

——, 'Thomas Paunfield, the "heye Court of rightwisnesse" and the Language of

Petitioning in the Fifteenth Century', in Ormrod et al., eds., *Medieval Petitions*, pp. 222–41.

Donaldson, B. C., *Dutch: A Linguistic History of Holland and Belgium* (Leiden, 1983).

Donoghue, D., *Old English Literature: A Short Introduction* (Oxford, 2004).

Douët d'Arcq, L., ed., *Comptes de l'argenterie des rois de France au XIVᵉᵐᵉ siècle* (Paris, 1851).

Dove, M., *The First English Bible: The Text and Context of the Wycliffite Versions* (Cambridge, 2007).

Doyle, A. I., 'Book Production by the Monastic Orders in England (*c.*1375–1530): Assessing the Evidence', in Brownrigg, *Medieval Book Production*, pp. 1–19.

——, 'English Books In and Out of Court from Edward III to Henry VII', in *English Court Culture in the Later Middle Ages*, ed. V. J. Scattergood and J. W. Sherborne (London, 1983), pp. 163–81.

Driver, M., 'Printing the *Confessio amantis*: Caxton's Edition in Context', in *Re-Visioning Gower*, ed. R. F. Yeager (Ashville NC, 1998), pp. 269–303.

——, 'Women Readers and Pierpont Morgan MS M.126', in *John Gower: Manuscripts, Readers and Contexts*, ed. M. Urban (Turnhout, forthcoming).

——, and M. T. Orr, 'Appendix: Continental Manuscripts Made for the English Market', in *An Index of Images in English Manuscripts from the Time of Chaucer to Henry VIII, c.1380–c.1509* (London, 2007).

Dronke, P., *Women Writers of the Middle Ages* (Cambridge, 1984).

Duffy, E., *Marking the Hours: English People and Their Prayers 1240–1570* (New Haven CT, 2006).

Dumville, D., 'Kingship, Genealogies and Regnal Lists', in *Early Medieval Kingship*, ed. P. H. Sawyer and I. N. Woods (Leeds, 1977), pp. 72–104.

——, *Wessex and England from Alfred to Edgar: Six Essays on Political, Cultural and Ecclesiastical Revival* (Woodbridge, 1992).

Dunn, D., 'Margaret of Anjou, Chivalry and the Order of the Garter', in *St George's Chapel, Windsor in the Late Middle Ages*, ed. C. Richmond and E. Scarff, Historical Monographs Relating to St George's Chapel, Windsor Castle 17 (Windsor, 2001), pp. 39–56.

Dutton, A. M., 'Piety, Politics and Persona: MS Harley MS 4012 and Anne Harling', in *Prestige, Authority and Power in Late Medieval Manuscripts and Texts*, ed. F. Riddy (Cambridge, 2000), pp. 133–46.

Dyer, C., 'The Consumption of Fresh-Water Fish in Medieval England', in *Medieval Fish, Fisheries and Fishponds in England*, ed. M. Aston (Oxford, 1988), pp. 27–38.

——, *Standards of Living in the Later Middle Ages: Social Change in England, c.1200–1520* (Cambridge, 1989).

Earp, L., *Guillaume de Machaut: A Guide to Research* (New York, 1995).

Echard, S., 'Gower's Books of Latin: Language, Politics and Poetry', *Studies in the Age of Chaucer* 25 (2003), 123–56.

——, *Printing the Middle Ages* (Philadelphia, 2008).

Einhorn, E., *Old French: A Concise Handbook* (Cambridge, 1974).

Ellis, R., ed., *The Oxford History of Literary Translation in English, I: To 1550* (Oxford, 2008).

Evans, M. 'The *Ysagoge in Theologiam* and the Commentaries attributed to Bernard Silvestris', *JWCI* 54 (1991), 1–42.

——, 'An Illustrated Fragment of Peraldus' *Summa* of Vice: Haleian MS 2244', *JWCI* 45 (1982), 14–68.

Farquhar, J. D., *Creation and Imitation: The Work of a Fifteenth-Century Manuscript Illu-* *minator* (Fort Lauderdale FL, 1976).

Fein, S. G., ed., *Studies in the Harley Manuscript: The Scribes, Contents, and Socia* *Contexts of British Library MS Harley 2253* (Kalamazoo MI, 2000).

Fell, C., ed., *Edward, King and Martyr* (Leeds, 1971).

Fellows-Jensen, G., *Scandinavian Personal Names in Lincolnshire and Yorkshire* (Copen hagen, 1968).

——, 'Conquests and the Place-names of England, with Special Reference to the Viking Settlements', in T. Andersson et al., *Ortnamn och Språkkontakt* (Uppsala 1980), pp. 192–209.

Ferguson, A. B., *The Indian Summer of English Chivalry* (Durham NC, 1960).

Ferrante, J. M., 'The Bible as Thesaurus for Secular Literature', in *The Bible in th* *Middle Ages: Its Influence on Literature and Art*, ed. B. S. Levy (Binghamton NY 1992), pp. 23–50.

Field, R., 'Romance in England', in Wallace, *Cambridge History of Medieval Englisł* *Literature*, pp. 152–78.

——, 'Children of Anarchy: Anglo-Norman Romance in the Twelfth Century', in *Writers of the Reign of Henry II*, ed. Kennedy and Meecham-Jones, pp. 249–62.

——, 'Romance', in Ellis, *Oxford History of Literary Translation*, pp. 296–331.

Field, S., 'Reflecting the Royal Soul: The *Speculum anime* Composed for Blanche o Castile', *Medieval Studies* 68 (2006), 1–42.

——, 'From *Speculum anime* to *Miroir de l'âme*: The Origins of Vernacular Advice Literature at the Capetian Court', *Medieval Studies* (forthcoming).

Figg, K. M., 'The Narrative of Selection in Jean Froissart's Collected Poems: Omis sions and Additions in BN MSS fr. 830 and 831', *JEBS* 5 (2002), 37–55.

Finke, L., *Women's Writing in English: Medieval England* (London, 1999).

——, 'The Politics of the Canon, Christine de Pizan and the Fifteenth-Century Chaucerians', *Exemplaria*, 19:1 (2007), 16–38.

Fisher, J. H., *John Gower, Moral Philosopher and Friend of Chaucer* (New York, 1964).

——, *The Emergence of Standard English* (Lexington KY, 1996).

Fletcher, A. J., *Preaching, Politics and Poetry in Late Medieval England* (Dublin, 1998).

Foot, S., 'The Making of *Angelcynn*: English Identity before the Norman Conquest' *TRHS* 6th series 6 (1996), 25–49.

Forhan, K. L., *The Political Theory of Christine de Pizan* (Aldershot, 2002).

Francis, E. A., 'The Trial in Lanval', in *Studies in French Language and Medieval Literatur* *presented to Professor Mildred K. Pope by pupils, colleagues and friends* (Manchester 1939), pp. 115–24.

Frankis, J., 'Taste and Patronage in Late Medieval England as Reflected in Version: of Guy of Warwick', *Medium Aevum* 66 (1997), 80–93.

——, 'Languages and Cultures in Contact: Vernacular Lives of St Giles and Anglo Norman Annotations in an Anglo-Saxon Manuscript', *LSE* 38 (2007), 101–33.

Frappier, J., and R. R. Grimm, eds., *Grundriss der romanischen Literaturen des Mittela* *lters* VI (Heidelberg, 1968–70).

Fryde, N., *The Tyranny and Fall of Edward II 1321–1326* (Cambridge, 1979).

Fulk, R. D., and C. M. Cain, *A History of Old English Literature* (Oxford, 2003).

Gaunt S., and J. Weiss, eds., *Cultural Traffic in the Medieval Romance World, Journal o* *Romance Studies 4.3*, special issue (Winter 2004).

Genet, J.-P., 'Essai de bibliométrie médiévale: l'histoire dans les bibliothèque: anglaises', *Revue française d'histoire du livre* 16 (1977), 531–68.

Georgianna, L., 'Coming to Terms with the Norman Conquest: Nationalism and English Literary History', *Yearbook of Research in English and American Literature* 14, *Literature and the Nation*, ed. B. Thomas (Tübingen, 1998), 33–53.

Giancarlo, M., *Parliament and Literature in Late Medieval England* (Cambridge, 2007).

Gibson, M., T. A. Heslop and R. Pfaff, eds., *The Eadwine Psalter: Text, Image, and Monastic Culture in Twelfth-Century Canterbury*, Publications of the Modern Humanities Research Association 14 (London, 1992).

Gilbert, J., 'Men Behaving Badly: Linguistic Purity and Sexual Perversity in Derrida's *Le Monolinguisme de l'autre* and Gower's *Traitié pour essampler les amantz marietz*', *Romance Studies* 24:2 (2006), 77–89.

Gilchrist, R., *Contemplation and Action: The Other Monasticism* (New York, 1995).

—— and M. Oliva, *Religious Women in Medieval East Anglia: History and Archaeology c.1100–1540* (Norwich, 1993).

Gillespie, V., '*Doctrina* and *Predicacio*: The Design and Function of Some Pastoral Manuals', *LSE* n.s.11 (1980), 36–50.

——, '*Lukynge in haly bukes*: *Lectio* in some Late Medieval Spiritual Miscellanies', *Analecta Cartusiana* 106 (1984), 1–27, repr. in idem, *Looking in Holy Books: Essays on Late Medieval Religious Writing in England* (Cardiff, 2005).

Gillingham, J., 'Gaimar, the Prose *Brut* and the Making of English History', in *The English in the Twelfth Century*, ed. J. Gillingham (Woodbridge, 1995), pp. 113–22.

——, 'Henry of Huntingdon and the Twelfth-Century Revival of the English Nation', in *Concepts of National Identity in the Middle Ages*, ed. S. Forde, L. Johnson and A. Murray (Leeds, 1995), pp 75–101.

Given-Wilson, C., *Chronicles of the Revolution, 1397–1400* (Manchester, 1993).

Gneuss, H., 'The Origin of Standard Old English and Æthelwold's School at Winchester', *Anglo-Saxon England* 1 (1972), 63–84.

——, *Handlist of Anglo-Saxon Manuscripts: A List of Manuscripts and Manuscript Fragments Written or Owned in England up to 1100* (Tempe AZ, 2001).

Golden, J. K., 'Patronage and the Saints in the Devotional Miscellany British Library MS Egerton 745' (unpublished Ph.D. thesis, University of Pittsburgh, 2001).

——, 'Images of Instruction, Marie de Bretagne, and the Life of St. Eustace as Illustrated in the British Library MS Egerton 745', in *Insights and Interpretations*, ed. C. Hourihane (Princeton, 2002), pp. 60–84.

Goodman, A., *The Loyal Conspiracy: The Lords Appellant under Richard II* (London, 1971).

Goodman, J., 'Quidem de Sinagoga: The Jew of the *Jeu d'Adam*', in *Medieval Cultures in Contact*, ed. R. F. Gyug (New York, 2003), pp. 161–87.

Gransden, A., *Historical Writing in England c.550 to c.1307* (London, 1974).

Grassi, J. L., 'Royal Clerks from the Archdiocese of York in the Fourteenth Century', *Northern History* 5 (1970), 12–33.

Gray, D., '"A Fulle Wyse Gentyl-Woman of Fraunce": *The Epistle of Othea* and Later Medieval English Literary Culture', in *Medieval Women*, ed. Wogan-Browne et al., pp. 237–49.

Green, M. H., 'The Development of the *Trotula*', *Revue d'Histoire des Textes* 26 (1996), 119–203.

——, 'A Handlist of the Latin and Vernacular Manuscripts of the So-Called *Trotula* Texts. Part II: The Vernacular Texts and Latin Re-Writings', *Scriptorium* 51 (1997), 80–104.

——, 'Reconstructing the *Oeuvre* of Trota of Salerno', in *La Scuola medica Salernitana:*

Gli autori e i testi, ed. D. Jacquart and A. Paravicini Bagliani, Edizione Nazionale 'La Scuola medica Salernitana' 1 (Florence, 2007), 183–233.

——, *Making Women's Medicine Masculine: The Rise of Male Authority in Pre-Modern Gynaecology* (Oxford, 2008).

——, 'Rethinking the Manuscript Basis of Salvatore De Renzi's *Collectio Salernitana*: The Corpus of Medical Writings in the "Long" Twelfth Century', in *La 'Collectio Salernitana' di Salvatore De Renzi*, ed. D. Jacquart and A. Paravicini Bagliani, Edizione Nazionale 'La Scuola medica Salernitana' 3 (Florence, forthcoming 2009).

Grummitt, D., 'The Calais Garrison: Military and Cultural Exchange between England, France and Burgundy in the Fifteenth Century' (unpublished paper, Centre for Medieval Studies, University of York, 3 April 2005).

Gullick, M., and T. Webber, 'Summary Catalogue of Surviving Manuscripts from Leicester Abbey', in *Leicester Abbey: Medieval History, Archaeology, and Manuscript Studies*, ed. J. Story, J. Bourne and R. Buckley (Leicester, 2006), pp. 173–92.

Gumperz, J. J., 'Introduction', in *Directions in Sociolinguistics: The Ethnography of Communication*, ed. J. J. Gumperz and D. Hymes (New York, 1972).

Haeberli, E., 'Observations on the Loss of Verb-second in the History of English', in *Studies in Comparative Germanic Syntax. Proceedings from the 15th Workshop on Comparative Germanic Syntax*, ed. C. Zwart and W. Abraham (Amsterdam, 2002), pp. 245–72.

Hahn, T., 'Early Middle English', in Wallace, *Cambridge History of Medieval English Literature*, pp. 61–91.

Hamer, R., 'Spellings of the Fifteenth-Century Scribe Ricardus Franciscus', in *Five Hundred Years of Words and Sounds: A Festschrift for Eric Dobson*, ed. E. G. Stanley and D. Gray (Cambridge, 1983).

'Handlist of the Archives of Great Yarmouth Corporation' (unpublished typescript in the Norfolk Record Office, reproduced by the Historical Manuscripts Commission for the National Register of Archives, 1965).

Haney, K. E., *The Winchester Psalter: An Iconographic Study* (Leicester, 1986).

——, *The St. Albans Psalter: An Anglo-Norman Song of Faith* (New York, 2002).

Hanna, R., 'Augustinian Canons and Middle English Literature', in *The English Medieval Book: Studies in Memory of Jeremy Griffiths*, ed. A. S. G. Edwards, V. A. Gillespie and R. Hanna (London, 2000), pp. 27–42.

——, *London Literature 1300–1380* (Cambridge, 2005).

——, 'Some North Yorkshire Scribes and Their Context', in *Medieval Texts in Context*, ed. G. D. Caie and D. Renevey (London, 2008), pp. 167–91.

Hanna, R. with J. Griffiths, *Western Medieval Manuscripts of St John's College, Oxford* (Oxford, 2002).

Hanning, R. W., *The Individual in Twelfth Century Romance* (New Haven CT, 1977).

Harding, A., 'Plaints and Bills in the History of English Law, Mainly in the Period 1250–1350', in *Legal History Studies 1972*, ed. D. Jenkins (Cardiff, 1975), pp. 63–86.

——, *Medieval Law and the Foundations of the State* (Oxford, 2002).

Harf-Lancner, L., 'Image and Propaganda: The Illustration of Book I of Froissart's *Chroniques*', in *Froissart Across the Genres*, ed. D. Maddox and S. Sturm-Maddox (Gainesville FL, 1998), pp. 220–50.

——, 'Les romans d'Alexandre et le brouillage des formes', in *Conter de Troie et d'Alexandre*, ed. L. Harf-Lancner, L. Mathey-Maille and M. Szkilnik (Paris, 2006), pp. 19–27.

artung, A., ed., *A Manual of the Writings in Middle English, 1050–1500*, 12 vols. (New Haven CT, 1967–).

artzell, K. D., *Catalogue of Manuscripts Written or Owned in England up to 1200 Containing Music* (Woodbridge, 2006).

arvey, B., *Living and Dying in England, 1100–1540: The Monastic Experience* (Oxford, 1993).

—, *The Obedientiaries of Westminster Abbey and their Financial Records, c.1275 to 1540* (Woodbridge, 2002).

arvey, C., 'The Discourse of Characterization in *Jehan et Blonde*', in *Speaking in the Medieval World*, ed. J. E. Godsall-Myers (Leiden, 2003), pp. 145–66.

asenohr, G. and M. Zink, *Dictionnaire des lettres françaises: le moyen âge* (Paris, 1992).

askett, T. S., 'Country Lawyers? The Composers of English Chancery Bills', in *The Life of the Law*, ed. P. Birks (London, 1993), pp. 9–23.

askins, C. H., 'England and Sicily in the Twelfth Century', *EHR* 26 (Oxford, 1911), 433–47, 641–65.

augen, E., 'Dialect, Language, Nation', *American Anthropologist* 58 (1966), 922–35.

awkyard, A., 'Neville, George, third Baron Bergavenny (*c.*1469–1535)', in *ODNB*, http://www.oxforddnb.com/view/article/19935

eale, M., *The Dependent Priories of Medieval English Monasteries*, Studies in the History of Medieval Religion 22 (Woodbridge, 2004).

ellinga, L., *Caxton in Focus* (London, 1982).

—, and J. B. Trapp, eds., *The Cambridge History of the Book in Britain, III: 1400–1557* (Cambridge, 1999).

ellinga, W. and L. Hellinga, *The Fifteenth-Century Printing Types of the Low Countries*, 2 vols. (Amsterdam, 1966).

eslop, T. A. 'Decoration and Illustration', in Gibson et al., *The Eadwine Psalter*, pp. 25–61.

exter, R., *Ovid and Medieval Schooling* (Munich, 1986).

iatt, A., *The Making of Medieval Forgeries: False Documents in Medieval England* (London, 2004).

ickey, R., 'Assessing the Relative Status of Languages in Medieval Ireland', in *Studies in Middle English Linguistics*, ed. J. Fisiak (Berlin, 1997), pp. 181–205.

ill, B., 'British Library MS. Egerton 613–II', *Notes and Queries* 223 (1978), 492–501.

indman, S. L., 'The Composition of the Manuscript of Christine de Pizan's Collected Works in the British Library: A Reassessment', *British Library Journal* 9 (1983), 93–123.

—, *Christine de Pizan's* Epistre Othéa: *Painting and Politics at the Court of Charles VI* (Toronto, 1986).

—, 'La voie de povreté ou de richesse (Le livre du Chastel de Labour)', in Tanis, ed., *Leaves of Gold*, item 70, pp. 202–5.

irsch, J. C., 'Prayer and Meditation in Late Medieval England: MS Bodley 789', *Medium Aevum* 48 (1979), 55–66.

odgson, N. R., *Women, Crusading and the Holy Land in Historical Narrative* (Woodbridge, 2007).

ogg, R. M., N. Blake, R. Lass, S. Romaine, R. Burchfield, and J. Algeo, eds., *The Cambridge History of the English Language*, 6 vols. (Cambridge, 1992–2001).

ollis, S., *Writing the Wilton Women: Goscelin's Legend of Edith and* Liber Confortatorius (Turnhout, 2004).

Houts, E. van, 'Latin Poetry and the Anglo-Norman Court 1066–1135: The *Carmen Hastingae Proelio*', *JMH* 15 (1989), 39–62.

——, 'Women and the Writing of History in the Early Middle Ages: The Case Abbess Matilda of Essen and Aethelweard', *EME* 1 (1992), 53–68.

——, 'A Note on *Jezebel* and *Semiramis*: Two Latin Poems from the Early Eleven Century', *Journal of Medieval Latin* 2 (1992), 18–24.

——, 'The Flemish Contribution to Biographical Writing in England in the Eleven Century', in *Writing Medieval Biography: Essays in Honour of Professor Frank Barlo* ed. D. Bates, J. Crick and S. Hamilton (Woodbridge, 2007), pp. 111–28.

Huchon, M., *Le Français de la Renaissance* (Paris, 1988).

Hudson, A., 'Lollardy: The English Heresy?', in *Religion and National Identity*, e S. Mews, Studies in Church History 18 (Oxford, 1982), 261–83.

——, 'A Lollard Sect Vocabulary?', in A. Hudson, *Lollards and Their Books* (Londo 1985), pp. 164–80.

——, *The Premature Reformation: Lollard Texts and Wycliffite History* (Oxford, 1988).

Hudson, R. A., *Sociolinguistics* (Cambridge, 1980).

Hughes, J., 'Stephen Scrope and the Circle of John Fastolf: Moral and Intellectu Outlooks', in *Medieval Knighthood IV: Papers from the Fifth Strawberry Hill Confe ence 1990*, ed. C. Harper-Bill and R. Harvey (Woodbridge, 1992), pp. 109–46.

Hull, F., ed., *A Calendar of the White and Black Books of the Cinque Ports 1432–19* (London, 1966).

Huneycutt, L., *Matilda of Scotland: A Study in Medieval Queenship* (Woodbridge, 2003

Hunt, T., 'The Medical Recipes in MS. Royal 5 E. vi', *Notes and Queries* 231 (1986), 6–

——, *Plant Names of Medieval England* (Cambridge, 1989).

——, 'An Anglo-Norman Medical Treatise: The *Gardein du Cors*', in *The Editor and t Text*, ed. P. E. Bennett and G. A. Runnalls (Edinburgh, 1990), pp. 145–64.

——, *Teaching and Learning Latin in Thirteenth-Century England*, 3 vols. (Cambridg 1991).

——, 'Haymarus's *Relatio Tripartita* in Anglo-Norman', *Medieval Encounters: Jewis Christian and Muslim Culture in Confluence and Dialogue* 4/2 (1998), 119–29.

——, 'Old French Translations of Medical Texts', *FMLS* 35 (1999), 350–7.

——, 'Code-Switching in Medical Texts', in Trotter, *Multilingualism*, pp. 131–47.

——, 'Bibbesworth, Walter of (*b*. in or before 1219, *d*. in or after 1270)', in *ODN* http://www.oxforddnb.com/view/article/2340

——, 'Les Pronostics en anglo-normand: méthodes et documents', in *Moult obscur paroles: Études sur la prophétie médiévale*, ed. R. Trachsler, J. Abed and D. Exper Cultures et Civilisations Médiévales 39 (Paris, 2007).

Hyams, P. R., 'Henry II and Ganelon', *The Syracuse Scholar* 4 (1983), 23–35.

——, 'Warranty and Good Lordship in Twelfth-Century England', *Law and Histo Review* 2 (1987), 437–503.

Iglesias-Rábade, L., 'The Multi-Lingual Pulpit in England (1100–1500)', *Neophilolog* 80 (1996), 479–92.

Ignatius, M. A., 'Christine de Pizan's *Epistre Othea*: An Experiment in Literary Form *Medievalia et Humanistica* n.s. 9 (1979), 127–42.

Ingham, R., 'Negative Concord and the Loss of the Negative Particle *ne* in late Midd English', *Studia Anglica Posnaniensia* 42 (2006), 77–96.

——, 'On Two Negative Concord Dialects in Early English', *Language Variation a Change* 18 (2006), 241–66.

——, 'Syntactic Change in Anglo-Norman and Continental French Chronicles: W

There a 'Middle' Anglo-Norman?', *Journal of French Language Studies* 16:1 (2006), 25–49.

——, 'The Status of French in Medieval England: Evidence from the Use of Object Pronoun Syntax', *Vox Romanica* 65 (2006), 1–22.

——, 'Mixing Languages on the Manor', *Medium Aevum* 78 (2009), 80–97.

Ingledew, F., 'The Book of Troy and the Genealogical Construction of History: The Case of Geoffrey of Monmouth's *Historia regum Britanniae*', *Speculum* 69 (1994), 665–704.

Innes, M., 'Teutons or Trojans? The Carolingians and the Germanic Past', in *The Uses of the Past in the Early Middle Ages*, ed. Y. Hen and M. Innes (Cambridge, 2000), pp. 227–49.

Innes-Parker, C., 'The Legacy of *Ancrene Wisse*: Translations, Adaptations, Influence and Reading', in Wada, *Companion to* Ancrene Wisse.

Ives, E. W., 'A Lawyer's Library in 1500', *Law Quarterly Review* 85 (1969), 104–16.

——, *The Common Lawyers of Pre-Reformation England- Thomas Kebell: A Case Study* (Cambridge, 1983).

Iyeiri, Y., *Negative Constructions in Middle English* (Kyushu, 2001).

Jal, A., *Glossaire nautique: Répertoire polyglotte de termes de marine anciens et modernes*, 2 vols. (Paris, 1848), new edn, 6 vols. (Paris, 1970–2006).

Jambeck, K. K., 'The Library of Alice Chaucer, Duchess of Suffolk: A Fifteenth-Century Owner of a "Boke of le Citee de Dames"', *The Profane Arts of the Middle Ages / Les arts profanes du moyen-âge* 7:2 (1998), 106–35.

James, M., 'English Politics and the Concept of Honour, 1485–1642', *Past and Present*, Suppl. 3 (1978), 1–6.

James, M. K., *Studies in the Medieval Wine Trade* (Oxford, 1971).

James, M. R., *The Western Manuscripts in the Library of Emmanuel College: A Descriptive Catalogue* (Cambridge, 1904).

——, *A Descriptive Catalogue of the Manuscripts of St John's College, Cambridge* (Cambridge, 1913).

Jefferson, L., 'MS Arundel 48 and the Earliest Statutes of the Order of the Garter', *EHR* 109:431 (1994), 356–85.

——, 'Two Fifteenth-Century Manuscripts of the Statutes of the Order of the Garter', in *English Manuscript Studies, 1100–1700*: V, ed. P. Beal and J. Griffiths (London, 1995), pp. 18–35.

——, and W. Rothwell, 'Society and Lexis: A Study of the Anglo-French Vocabulary in the Fifteenth-Century Accounts of the Merchant Taylors' Company', *ZfSL* 107 (1997), 273–30.

Jeffrey, D. B., *The Early English Lyric and Franciscan Spirituality* (Lincoln NE, 1975).

Jenkinson, H., 'Mary de Sancto Paulo, Foundress of Pembroke College, Cambridge', *Archæologia*, 2nd series 16 (1915), 401–46.

Jessopp, A., 'Ups and Downs of an Old Nunnery', *Frivola* (London, 1896), pp. 28–82.

Johnson, C., ed., 'An Early Admiralty Case (A. D. 1361)', in *Camden Miscellany*, 15, 3rd series 41 (London, 1929), 1–5.

Jones, E. A., 'Literature of Religious Instruction', in *A Companion to Medieval English Literature and Culture c.1350–1500*, ed. P. Brown (Malden MA, 2007), pp. 407–22.

Jones, M. K., and M. G. Underwood, *The King's Mother: Lady Margaret Beaufort, Countess of Richmond and Derby* (Cambridge, 1992)

Jones, T., R. F. Yeager, T. Dolan, A. Fletcher and J. Dor, 'Did Richard Encourage the English Language?', in *Who Murdered Chaucer? A Medieval Mystery* (London, 2003).

Judge, A., 'French: A Planned Language?', in *French Today: Language in Its Social Context*, ed. C. Sanders (Cambridge, 1993), pp. 7–26.

Justice, S., *Writing and Rebellion: England in 1381* (Berkeley CA, 1994).

Kadens, E. E., 'The Vernacular in a Latin World: Changing the Language of Record in Thirteenth-Century Flanders' (Ph.D. dissertation, Princeton, 2001, to be published in the monograph series *Mediaevalia Lovaniensia*).

Kahane, R., and A. Tietze, *The Lingua Franca in the Levant: Turkish Nautical Terms of Italian and Greek Origin* (Urbana IL, 1958).

Kallel, A., 'The Loss of Negative Concord in English' (unpublished Ph.D. thesis, University of Reading, 2005).

Kay, S., *The Chansons de Geste in the Age of Romance: Political Fictions* (Oxford, 1995).

Kealey, E. J., *Medieval Medicus: A Social History of Anglo-Norman Medicine* (Baltimore, 1981).

Keats-Rohan, K. S. B., 'The Bretons and Normans of England 1066–1154: the Family, the Fief, and the Feudal Monarchy', *NMS* 36 (1992), 42–78.

Keen, M., *Chivalry* (New Haven CT, 1984).

Kehnel, A., 'Poets, Preachers and Friars Revisited: Fourteenth-Century Multilingual Franciscan Manuscripts', in Schaefer, *Beginnings of Standardization*, pp. 91–114.

Kekewich, M., 'Edward IV, William Caxton, and Literary Patronage in Yorkist England', *MLR* 66 (1971), 481–7.

Kelly, S., *The New Solomon: Robert of Naples (1309–1343) and Fourteenth-Century Kingship* (Leiden, 2003).

Kempshall, M. S., *Rhetoric and the Writing of History, 400–1500* (Manchester, forthcoming).

Kennedy, E. D., *Chronicles and Other Historical Writing: A Manual of the Writings in Middle English 1050–1500 VIII* (New Haven CT, 1989).

Kennedy, R., and S. Meecham-Jones, eds., *Writers of the Reign of Henry II: Twelve Essays* (Houndmills, 2006).

Ker, N. R., *Catalogue of Manuscripts Containing Anglo-Saxon* (Oxford, 1957).

Kibbee, D., *For to Speke Frenche Trewely: The French Language in England, 1000–1600: Its Status, Description and Instruction* (Amsterdam, 1991).

——, 'Emigrant Languages and Acculturation: the Case of Anglo-French', in Nielsen and Schøsler, *Origins and Development of Emigrant Languages*, pp. 1–20.

Kienzle, B. M., 'The Twelfth-Century Monastic Sermon', in *The Sermon*, ed. B. M. Kienzle, Typologie des sources du Moyen Âge occidental 81–3 (Turnhout, 2000), pp. 298–9.

Kiesselbach, T., 'Der Ursprung der rôles d'Oléron und des Seerechts von Damme', *Hansische Geschichtsblätter* (1906), pp. 1–60.

Kinoshita, S., *Medieval Boundaries: Rethinking Difference in Old French Literature* (Philadelphia, 2006).

Kitson, P., 'Lapidary Traditions in Anglo-Saxon England: Part I, the Background: The Old English Lapidary', *Anglo-Saxon England* 7 (1978), 9–60.

Klenke, M. A., 'Nicholas Bozon', *Modern Language Notes*, 69 (1954), 256–60.

Knowles, D., and R. N. Hadcock, *Medieval Religious Houses, England and Wales*, 2nd rev. edn (London, 1971).

Kok, A. de, *La place du pronom personnel régime conjoint en français. Une étude diachronique* (Amsterdam, 1985).

Kowaleski, M., 'The 1377 Dartmouth Poll Tax', *Devon and Cornwall Notes and Queries* 35:8 (1985), 286–95.

——, 'Gossip, Gender, and the Economy: The Origins of Scolding Indictments in Medieval English Towns' (unpublished paper given at the National Humanities Center, Research Triangle Park, North Carolina, October 2005).

——, '"Alien" Encounters in the Maritime World of Medieval England', *Medieval Encounters* 13 (2007), 96–21.

Kraus, H. P., *Illuminated Manuscripts from the Eleventh to the Eighteenth Centuries* (New York, 1981).

Kren, T., and S. McKendrick, eds., *Illuminating the Renaissance: The Triumph of Flemish Manuscript Painting in Europe* (London, 2003).

Krieger, K. F., *Ursprung und Wurzeln der Rôles de Oléron*, Quellen und Darstellungen zur hansischen Geschichte 15 (Köln, 1970).

Kristol, A. M., 'L'enseignement du français en Angleterre (XIIIᵉ–XVᵉ siècles): les sources manuscrites', *Romania* 111 (1990), 289–330.

——, 'Le ms. 188 de Magdalen College Oxford: une "pierre de Rosette" de l'enseignement médiéval du français en Angleterre', *Vox Romanica* 60 (2001), 149–67.

Krochalis, J., and R. J. Dean, 'Henry of Lancaster's *Livre de Seyntz Medicines*: New Fragments of an Anglo-Norman work', *The National Library of Wales Journal* 18 (1973), 87–94.

——, 'John Lydgate, *Fall of Princes*', in *Sixty Bokes Olde and Newe: Manuscripts and Early Printed Books from Libraries in and Near Philadelphia*, ed. D. Anderson (Knoxville TN, 1986), pp. 105–9.

——, 'The Books and Reading of Henry V and His Circle', *Chaucer Review* 23 (1988), 50–77.

Krynen, J., *Idéal du prince et pouvoir royal en France à la fin du Moyen Age (1380–1440): étude de la littérature politique du temps* (Paris, 1981).

Kuhn, S. H., 'The Vespasian Psalter Gloss: Original or Copy', *PMLA* 74:3 (1959), 161–77.

Kunstmann, P., 'Création et diffusion du relatif/interrogatif *lequel* en ancien français: Comparaison avec d'autres langues romanes', in *Actes du XVIIIᵉ Congrès International de Linguistique et de Philologie Romanes* (Tübingen, 1988), pp. 660–70.

——, *Le relatif-interrogatif en ancien français* (Geneva, 1990).

Laborde, L., marquis de, *Les ducs de Bourgogne: Études sur les lettres, les arts et l'industrie pendant le XVᵉ siècle et plus particulièrement dans les Pays-Bas et le duché de Bourgogne*, 3 vols. (Paris, 1851).

Laidlaw, J., 'Christine and the Manuscript Tradition', in *Christine de Pizan: A Casebook*, ed. B. K. Altmann and D. L. McGrady (New York, 2003), pp. 231–49.

——, 'Christine de Pizan, The Earl of Salisbury and Henry IV', *French Studies* 36 (1982), 129–43.

Lambley, K., *The Teaching and Cultivation of the French Language in England during Tudor and Stuart Times* (Manchester, 1920).

Langlois, E., ed., *Recueil d'arts de seconde rhétorique* (Paris, 1902).

——, *Les Manuscrits du Roman de la Rose. Description et Classement* (Lille, 1910, rept Geneva, 1974).

Lawrence, A., 'A Northern English School? Patterns of Production and Collection of Manuscripts in the Augustinian Houses of Yorkshire in the Twelfth and Thirteenth Centuries', in *Yorkshire Monasticism: Archaeology, Art and Architecture, from the 7th to the 16th Centuries*, ed. L. R. Hoey, British Archaeological Association Conference Transactions 16 (Leeds, 1995).

Lawrence-Mathers, A., *Manuscripts in Northumbria in the Eleventh and Twelfth Centuries* (Cambridge, 2003).

Lawson, M. K., *Cnut: The Danes and England in the Early Eleventh Century* (London, 1993).

Lawton, D. A., 'Scottish Field: Alliterative Verse and Stanley Encomium in the Percy Folio', *LSE* n.s. 10 (1978), 42–57.

Le Hir, Y., 'Sur les traductions en prose française du psautier', *Revue de Linguistique Romane* 25 (1961), 324–8.

Le Saux, F., *Laȝamon's Brut: The Poem and its Sources* (Cambridge, 1989).

Leckie, R. W. Jr, *The Passage of Dominion: Geoffrey of Monmouth and the Periodization of Insular History* (Toronto, 1983).

Leedham-Green, E. S., and T. Webber, eds., *The Cambridge History of Libraries in Britain and Ireland*, 3 vols. (Cambridge, 2006).

Legge, M. D., 'Anglo-Norman and the Historian', *History* 26 (1941–2), 163–75.

——, *Anglo-Norman Literature and its Background* (Oxford, 1963).

——, 'La précocité de la littérature anglo-normande', *Cahiers de civilisation médiévale* 8 (1965), 327–49.

——, 'Anglo-Norman as a Spoken Language', *ANS* 2 (1979), 108–17.

Lerer, S., 'Old English and its Afterlife', in Wallace, *Cambridge History of Medieval English Literature*, pp. 7–34.

Leroquais, V., *Les psautiers manuscrits latins des bibliothèques publiques de France* (Paris, 1940).

Lester, G. A., *Sir John Paston's 'Grete Book': A Descriptive Catalogue, with an Introduction of British Library MS Lansdowne 285* (Cambridge, 1984).

Lewis, R. E., and A. McIntosh, *A Descriptive Guide to the Manuscripts of The Prick of Conscience* (Oxford, 1982).

Liddy, C. D., *War, Politics and Finance in Late Medieval English Towns: Bristol, York and the Crown, 1350–1400* (Woodbridge, 2005).

Liebman, C. J., *Etude sur la Vie en prose de saint Denis* (New York, 1942).

Lindemann, M., *Zum Suffixwechsel von «-eresse » zu «-euse » und «-trice » im Französischen* (Tübingen, 1977).

Little, K. C., *Confession and Resistance: Defining the Self in Later Medieval England* (Notre Dame IN, 2006).

Liu, Y., 'Richard Beauchamp and the Uses of Romance', *Medium Aevum*, 74 (2005), 271–87.

Lodge, R. A., 'Language Attitudes and Linguistic Norms in France and England in the Thirteenth Century', in *Thirteenth Century England* 4, ed. P. R. Coss and S. D. Lloyd (Woodbridge, 1992), pp. 73–83.

——, *French: From Dialect to Standard* (London, 1993).

Löfstedt, L., 'Le Psautier en ancien français', in *Neuphilologische Mitteilungen*, 100 (1999), 421–32.

Loomis, R. S., 'Edward I, Arthurian Enthusiast', *Speculum* 28 (1953), 114–27.

LoPrete, K., *Adela of Blois: Countess and Lord (c.1067–1137)* (Dublin, 2007).

Loud, G. A., 'Il regno normanno-svevo visto dal regno d'Inghilterra', in *Il Mezzogiorno normanno-svevo visto dall'Europa e dal mondo mediterraneo: Atti delle tredicesime giornate normanno-sveve, Bari, 21–24 ottobre 1997*, ed. G. Musca (Bari, 1999), pp. 175–95.

Lowe, K. J. P., *Nuns' Chronicles and Convent Culture in Renaissance and Counter-Reformation Italy* (Cambridge, 2003).

Luscombe, D. E., 'The Authorship of the *Ysagoge in Theologiam*', *Archives d'Histoire Doctrinale et Littéraire du Moyen Age* 43 (1969), 7–16.

Lusignan, S., *Parler vulgairement: Les intellectuels et la langue française aux XIIIe et XIVe siècles*, 2nd edn (Paris, 1987).

MacCracken, H. N., 'Quixley's Ballades Royal (? 1402)', *Yorkshire Archaeological Journal* 20 (1909), 33–50.

MacCulloch, D. N. J., ed., *The Chorography of Suffolk* (Ipswich, 1976).

MacFarlane, J., *Antoine Vérard* (London, 1900).

Mac Niocaill, G., ed., 'Gnathaimh Bhaile Atha Cliath', *Na Buirgeisi XII–XIV Aois*, I (Dublin, 1964).

Machan, T. W., 'Language and Society in Twelfth-Century England', in *Placing Middle English in Context*, ed. I. Taavitsainen, T. Nevalainen, P. Pahta, and M. Rissanen (Berlin, 2000), pp. 43–64.

——, *English in the Middle Ages* (Oxford, 2003).

Madan, F., H. E. Craster et al., *A Summary Catalogue of Western Manuscripts in the Bodleian Library at Oxford*, 7 vols. in 8 (Oxford, 1895–1953).

Maddicott, J. R., *Simon de Montfort* (Cambridge 1994).

Mandach, A. de, 'A Royal Wedding Present in the Making: Talbot's Chivalric Anthology (Royal 15 E VI) for Queen Margaret of Anjou and the "Laval-Middleton" Anthology of Nottingham', *NMS* 18 (1974), 56–76.

'The Manuscripts of the Corporation of Rye', *Appendix to the Fifth Report of the Historical Manuscripts Commission, Part I* (London, 1876).

Marchello-Nizia, C., *La langue française aux XIVe et XVe siècles* (Paris, 1997).

Markey, D., 'The Anglo-Norman Version', in Gibson et al., *The Eadwine Psalter*, pp. 139–56.

Marks, R., and P. Williamson, eds., *Gothic Art for England 1400–1547* (London, 2003).

Martin, G., 'English Town Records', in *Pragmatic Literacy East and West, 1200–1330*, ed. R. H. Britnell (Woodbridge, 1997), pp. 122–5.

——, 'The Governance of Ipswich', in *Ipswich Borough Archives 1255–1835: A Catalogue*, comp. D. Allen, Suffolk Records Society 43 (Woodbridge, 2000).

Martin, R., 'Le préfixe A-/AD- en moyen français', *Romania* 119 (2001), 1–32.

Marvin, J., 'Albine and Isabelle: Regicidal Queens and the Historical Imagination of the Anglo-Norman Prose *Brut* Chronicles', *Arthurian Literature* 18 (2001), 143–91.

——, 'The Unassuming Reader: F. W. Maitland and the Editing of Anglo-Norman', in *The Book Unbound: Editing and Reading Medieval Manuscripts and Texts*, ed. S. Echard and S. Partridge (Toronto, 2004), pp. 14–36.

Marx, W., with R. Radulescu, eds., *Readers and Writers of the Prose* Brut, *Trivium* 36 special issue (Lampeter, 2006).

Matheson, L. M., *The Prose 'Brut': The Development of a Middle English Chronicle* (Tempe AZ, 1998).

——, 'Médecin sans Frontières? The European Dissemination of John of Burgundy's Plague Treatise', *American Notes and Queries*, 18:3 (2005), 17–28.

Mathew, G., *The Court of Richard II* (London, 1968).

Mathey-Maille, L., 'L'étymologie dans le *Roman de Rou* de Wace', in *De sens rassis. Essays in Honor of Rupert T. Pickens*, ed. K. Busby, B. Guidot and L. E. Whalen (Amsterdam, 2005), pp. 404–9.

——, *Écritures du passé. Histoires des ducs de Normandie* (Paris, 2007).

McFarlane, K. B., 'William Worcester: A Preliminary Survey', in *Studies Presented to Sir Hilary Jenkinson*, ed. J. Conway Davis (London, 1957), pp. 196–221.

McIntosh, A., 'A New Approach to Middle English Dialectology', *English Studies* 44 (1935), 1–11.

——, M. L. Samuels, M. Benskin, with M. Lang and K. Williams, eds., *A Linguistic Atlas of Late Medieval English*, 4 vols. (Aberdeen, 1986).

McKendrick, S., 'The *Romuléon* and the Manuscripts of Edward IV', in *England in the Fifteenth Century: Proceedings of the 1992 Harlaxton Symposium*, ed. N. Rogers (Stamford CA, 1994), pp. 149–69.

Meale, C. M., 'Patrons, Buyers and Owners: Book Production and Social Status', in *Book Production and Publishing in Britain, 1375–1475*, ed. J. Griffiths and D. Pearsall (Cambridge, 1989), pp. 201–38.

——, 'Legends of Good Women in the European Middle Ages', *Archiv* 144 (1992), 55–70.

——, '"Prenes : engre": An Early Sixteenth-Century Presentation Copy of *The Erle of Tolous*', in *Romance Reading on the Book: Essays on Medieval Narrative Presented to Maldwyn Mills*, ed. J. Fellows, R. Field, G. Rogers and J. Weiss (Cardiff, 1996), pp. 221–69.

——, 'Reading Women's Culture in Fifteenth-Century England: The Case of Alice Chaucer', in *Mediaevalitas: Reading the Middle Ages*, ed. P. Boitani and A. Torti, The J. A. W. Bennett Memorial Lectures Series 9 (Cambridge, 1996), pp. 81–101.

——, ed., *Women and Literature in Britain 1150–1500*, 2nd edn (Cambridge, 1996).

Meekings, C. A. F., 'Thomas Kerver's Case', *EHR* 90 (1975), 331–46.

Menger, L. E., *The Anglo-Norman Dialect* (New York, 1904).

Merrilees, B. 'Cambridge Psalter', in *Dictionary of the Middle Ages*, ed. R. J. Strayer, III (New York, 1983), p. 57.

——, 'Oxford Psalter', in *Dictionary of the Middle Ages*, ed. R. J. Strayer, IX (New York, 1987), p. 319.

——, «La simplification du système vocalique en anglo-normand», *Revue de linguistique romane* (1982), 319–26.

Mertes, K., *The English Noble Household, 1250–1600* (Oxford, 1988).

Meyer, P., 'Mélanges anglo-normands', *Romania* 38 (1909), 434–40.

——, 'Notice du Ms. Egerton 745 du Musée Britannique', *Romania* 39 (1910), [pt 1] 532–69; *Romania* 40 (1911), [pt 2] 41–69.

——, review of A. Roselli, *Le Jardrin [sic] de Paradis, tratello mistico in antico francese* (Parma, 1905), in *Romania* 34 (1905), 631–2.

Mickel, E. J., Jr and J. Nelson, 'BM Royal 15 E VI and the Epic Cycle of the First Crusade', *Romania* 92 (1971), 532–56.

Millett, B., with G. B. Jack and Y. Wada, *Ancrene Wisse, the Katherine Group, and the Wooing Group*, Annotated Bibliographies of Old and Middle English Literature (Woodbridge, 1996).

——, 'Women in No Man's Land: English Recluses and the Development of Vernacular Literature in the Twelfth and Thirteenth Centuries', in Meale, *Women and Literature in Britain*, pp. 86–103.

——, '*Ancrene Wisse* and the Conditions of Confession', *English Studies* 80 (1999), 193–215.

——, 'The Pastoral Context of the Trinity and Lambeth Homilies', in *Manuscript Geography of the West Midlands*, ed. W. Scase (Turnhout, 2007), pp. 43–64.

Milroy, J., *Linguistic Variation and Change* (Oxford, 1992).

Mirot, L., 'Le procès de maître Jean Fusoris, chanoine de Notre-Dame de Paris (1415–

1416). Épisode des négociations franco-anglaises durant la Guerre de Cent Ans', *Mémoires de la Société de l'histoire de Paris et de l'Île-de-France* 27 (1900), 137–287.

Mollat, M., 'La pêche à Dieppe', in *Etudes d'histoire maritime (1938–1975)* (Torino, 1977), pp. 1–42.

——, *La vie quotidienne des gens de mer en Atlantique (IXᵉ–XVIᵉ siècle)* (Paris, 1983).

Mombello, G., 'Per un'edizione critica dell' *Epistre Othea* di Christine de Pizan', *Studi Francesi* (1965), pp.1–12.

——, *La tradizione manoscritta dell'* Epistre Othea *di Christine de Pizan: Prolegomini all'edizione del testo* (Turin, 1967).

Mooney, L., 'Chaucer's Scribe', *Speculum* 81 (2006), 97–138.

Moore, A., 'A Barge of Edward III', *Mariner's Mirror* 6 (1920), 229–42.

Moore, J., '*Rex Omnipotens*: A Sequence Used in an Old English Ascension Day Homily', *Anglia* 106 (1988), 138–44.

Mora-Lebrun, F., *L'Enéide médiévale et la naissance du roman* (Paris, 1994).

Moran, J. A. H., *The Growth of English Schooling 1340–1548: Learning, Literacy, and Laicization in Pre-Reformation York Diocese* (Princeton NJ, 1985).

Moranvillé, H., *Journal de Jean Le Fèvre, évêque de Chartres, chancelier des rois de Sicile Louis Iᵉʳ et Louis II d'Anjou*, 2 vols. (Paris, 1887).

Morey, J., 'Peter Comestor, Biblical Paraphrase, and the Medieval Popular Bible', *Speculum* 68 (1993), 6–35.

——, *Book and Verse: A Guide to Middle English Biblical Literature* (Urbana IL, 2000).

Morgan, N. J., '49. Breviary', in *The Cambridge Illuminations: Ten Centuries of Book Production in the Medieval West*, ed. P. Binski and S. Panayotova (London, 2005), pp. 132–4.

——, 'Patrons and Their Devotions in the Thirteenth-Century English Psalters', in *The Illustrated Psalter*, ed. F. O. Büttner (Turnhout, 2005), pp. 309–22.

——, 'Books for the Liturgy and Private Prayer', in Morgan and Thomson, *Cambridge History of the Book*, II, 291–316.

——, and R. M. Thomson, *The Cambridge History of the Book in Britain, II: 1100–1400* (Cambridge, 2008).

Morrin, M. J., *John Waldeby, OSA, c.1315-c.1372: English Augustinian Preacher and Writer: With a Critical Edition of His Tract on the 'Ave Maria'*, Studia Augustiana Historica 2 (Rome, 1972–4).

Morrissey, R., *L'empereur à la barbe fleurie* (Paris, 1997).

Mortensen, L. B., 'Stylistic Choice in a Reborn Genre: The National Histories of Widukind of Corvey and Dudo of Saint-Quentin', in *Dudone di San Quintino*, ed. P. Gatti and A. Degl'Innocenti (Trent, 1995), pp. 77–102.

Mullally, E., 'Hiberno-Norman Literature and Its Public', in *Settlement and Society in Medieval Ireland: Studies Presented to F. X. Martin, O.S.A.*, ed. J. Bradley (Kilkenny, 1988), pp. 327–43.

Munby, J., R. Barber and R. Brown, *Edward III's Round Table and the Windsor Festival of 1344* (Woodbridge, 2007).

Murray, K. M. E., *The Constitutional History of the Cinque Ports* (Manchester, 1935).

Murray, K. S.-J., 'La mise en recueil comme glose? Le thème de la *translatio studii* dans le ms. Digby 23 de la Bibliothèque Bodléienne à Oxford', *Babel* 16 (2007), 345–55.

Muzerelle, D., 'Dating MSS: What Is at Stake in the Steps Usually (but Infrequently) Taken?', *JEBS* 11 (2008), 167–80.

Nall, C., 'Ricardus Franciscus Writes for William Worcester', *JEBS* 11 (2008), 207–12.

Nares, R., T. H. Horne and F. Douce, eds., *A Catalogue of the Harleian Collection c Manuscripts in the British Museum*, rev. edn, 4 vols. (London, 1808–12).

Nelson, J., 'Public Histories and Private History in the Work of Nithard', *Speculum* 60 (1985), 251–93.

——, 'History-writing at the Courts of Louis the Pious and Charles the Bald', in *Historiographie im frühen Mittelalter*, ed. A. Scharer and G. Scheibelreiter (Vienna 1994), pp. 435–42.

Neville, C. J., *Native Lordship in Medieval Scotland: The Earldom of Strathearn and Lenno. c.1140–1365* (Dublin, 2005).

Nicholas, D., *Medieval Flanders* (London, 1992).

Nicholson, P., *Love and Ethics in Gower's* Confessio amantis (Ann Arbor, 2005).

Nielsen, H.-F., and L. Schøsler, eds., *The Origins and Development of Emigrant Languages Proceedings from the Second Rasmus Rask Colloquium, Odense University, Novembe 1994*), (Odense, 1996).

Niles, J. D., *Old English Heroic Poems and the Social Life of Texts* (Turnhout, 2007).

O'Brien, B., 'Translating Technical Terms in Law-Codes from Alfred to the Angevins' in Tyler, *Conceptualizing Multilingualism*.

O'Brien O'Keeffe, K., 'Reading the C-Text: The After-Lives of London, British Library Cotton Tiberius B. I', in *Anglo-Saxon Manuscripts and Their Heritage*, ed. P. Pulsianc and E. M. Treharne (Aldershot, 1998), pp. 137–60.

Oliva, M., *The Convent and the Community in Late Medieval England: Female Monasterie. in the Diocese of Norwich, 1350–1540* (Woodbridge, 1998).

——, 'All in the Family? Monastic and Clerical Careers among Family Members ir the Late Middle Ages', *Medieval Prosopography* 20 (1999), 161–71.

Olszowy-Schlanger, J., *Les manuscrits hébreux dans l'Angleterre médiévale: étude histo rique et paléographique* (Louvain, 2003).

——, 'A Christian Tradition of Hebrew Vocalisation in Medieval England', in *Semiti. Studies in Honour of Edward Ullendorff*, ed. G. Khan (Leiden, 2005), pp. 126–45.

Omont, H., 'Les manuscrits français des rois d'Angleterre au château de Richmond' in *Études romanes dédiées à Gaston Paris* (Paris, 1891), pp. 1–13.

O'Neill, P. P., 'The English Version', in Gibson et al., *The Eadwine Psalter*, pp. 123–38

Orchard, A., *Pride and Prodigies: Studies in the Monsters of the Beowulf-Manuscrip* (Cambridge, 1995).

Ormrod, W. M., 'Edward III's Government of England, c.1346–1356' (unpublishec Ph.D. thesis, University of Oxford, 1984).

——, 'On – and Off – the Record: The Rolls of Parliament, 1337–1377', in *Parchmen and People*, ed. L. Clark (Edinburgh, 2004), pp. 39–56.

——, G. Dodd and A. Musson, eds., *Medieval Petitions: Grace and Grievance* (York 2009).

——, 'Murmur, Clamour and Noise: Voicing Complaint and Remedy in Petition: to the English Crown, c.1300–c.1460', in Ormrod et al., eds., *Medieval Petitions* pp. 135–55.

Oschinsky, D., review of Karl-Friederich Krieger, *Ursprung und Wurzeln der Rôle: d'Oléron*, *EHR* 87 (1972), 857.

Otter, M., 'La Vie des deux Offa, l'Enfance de Saint Edmund, et la logique des "ante cedents"', in *Médiévales: Langue, Textes, Histoires* 38 (2000), 17–34.

——, *Inventiones: Fiction and Referentiality in Twelfth-Century English Historical Writing* (Chapel Hill NC, 1996).

Pächt, O., 'Notes and News', *Bodleian Library Record* 4 (1952–3).

——, C. R. Dodwell and F. Wormald, eds., *The St. Alban's Psalter (Albani Psalter)* (London, 1960).

——, and J. J. G. Alexander, *Illuminated Manuscripts in the Bodleian Library*, 3 vols. (Oxford, 1966–73).

Page, C., 'A Catalogue and Bibliography of English Song from Its Beginnings to *c.*1300', *R. M. A. Research Chronicle* 13 (1976), 67–83.

——, '*Angelus ad Virginem*: A New Work by Philip the Chancellor?', *Early Music* 11 (1983), 139–44.

Page, W., ed., *Victoria County History, London*, I (London, 1909).

Painter, G. D., *William Caxton. A Quincentenary Biography of England's First Printer* (London, 1976).

Palazzo, E., *A History of Liturgical Books from the Beginnings to the Thirteenth Centuries*, trans. M. Beaumont (Collegeville MN, 1998).

Paradisi, G., '"Par muement de langages": Il tempo, la memoria e il volgare in Wace', *Francofonia* 45 (2003), 27–45.

Parkes, M. B., *English Cursive Book Hands 1250–1500* (Oxford, 1969).

——, 'The Palaeography of the Parker Manuscript of the *Chronicle*, Laws and Sedulius, and Historiography at Winchester in the Late Ninth and Tenth Centuries', *Anglo-Saxon England* 5 (1976), 149–71.

——, 'The Date of the Oxford Manuscript of *La Chanson de Roland* (Oxford, Bodleian Library, MS Digby 23)', *Medioevo Romanzo* 10/2 (1985), 161–75.

——, *Pause and Effect: An Introduction to the History of Punctuation in the West* (Berkeley, 1993).

Parsons, D., 'How long did the Scandinavian Language Survive in England? Again', in *Vikings and the Danelaw*, ed. J. Graham-Campbell et al. (Oxford, 2001), pp. 299–312.

Paterson, L., 'La médecine en Occitanie avant 1250', *Actes du premier congrès international de l'Association Internationale d'Études Occitanes*, ed. P. T. Ricketts (London, 1987), pp. 383–99.

——, 'Military Surgery: Knights, Sergeants, and Raimon of Avignon's Version of the *Chirurgia* of Roger of Salerno (1180–1209)', in *The Ideals and Practice of Medieval Knighthood II*, Papers from the 3rd Strawberry Hill Conference, ed. C. Harper-Bill and R. Harvey (Woodbridge, 1988), pp. 117–46.

Patterson, L., *Negotiating the Past: The Historical Understanding of Medieval Literature* (Madison WI, 1987).

Payne, A., 'The Beauchamps and the Nevilles', in *Gothic Art for England 1400–1547*, ed. R. Marks and P. Williamson with E. Townsend (London, 2003), pp. 219–21.

Payne, T. B., '*Aurelianis civitas*: Student Unrest in Medieval France and a Conductus by Philip the Chancellor', *Speculum* 75 (2000), 589–614.

Pearsall, D., *Old English and Middle English Poetry* (London, 1977).

——, 'Gower's Latin in the *Confessio amantis*', in *Latin and Vernacular: Studies in Late-Medieval Texts and Manuscripts*, ed. A. J. Minnis (Cambridge, 1989), pp. 13–25.

——, *The Life of Geoffrey Chaucer: A Critical Biography* (Oxford, 1992).

——, 'Chaucer and Englishness', *Proceedings of the British Academy* 101 (1998), 77–99.

——, 'The Rede (Boarstall) Gower: British Library, MS Harley 3490', in *The English Medieval Book*, ed. A. S. G. Edwards, V. Gillespie and R. Hanna (Oxford, 2000), pp. 87–99.

Pearson, M., 'Coastal Communities and Maritime History', *History in Focus: The Sea* 9 (2005), at http://www.history.ac.uk/ihr/Focus/Sea/articles/pearson.html.

Pépin, G., 'Petitions from Gascony: Testimonies of a Special Relationship', in Ormrod et al., eds., *Medieval Petitions*, pp. 120–34.

Pfister, M., 'Die sprachliche Bedeutung von Paris und der Ile-de-France vor dem 13. Jh.', *Vox Romanica* 32 (1973), 217–53.

Phillips, H., 'Rewriting the Fall: Julian of Norwich and the *Chevalier des dames*', in *Women, the Book and the Godly. Selected Proceedings of the St Hilda's Conference, 1993*, ed. L. Smith and J. H. M. Taylor (Cambridge, 1995), pp. 149–56.

Phythian-Adams, C., 'Environments and Identities: Landscape as Cultural Projection in the English Provincial Past', in *Environments and Historical Change: The Linacre Lectures 1998*, ed. P. Slack (Oxford, 1999), pp. 118–46.

Pickering, O., 'South English Legendary Style in Robert of Gloucester's *Chronicle*', *Medium Aevum* 70 (2001), 1–18.

Pickwoad, N., and T. Webber, 'Codicology and Palaeography', in Gibson et al., *The Eadwine Psalter*, pp. 4–24.

Plummer, J., *The Glazier Collection of Illuminated Manuscripts* (New York, 1968).

——, with G. Clark, *The Last Flowering: French Painting in Manuscripts, 1420–1530* (New York, 1982).

Pollard, A. J., *John Talbot and the War in France, 1427–1453* (London, 1983).

——, 'Talbot, John, first earl of Shrewsbury and first earl of Waterford (*c*.1387–1453), soldier', *ODNB*, http://www.oxforddnb.com/view/article/26932?docPos=9

Pope, M. K., *From Latin to Modern French with especial consideration of Anglo-Norman* (Manchester, 1934; rev. edn 1952).

Porter, D. W., 'The Earliest Texts with English and French', *Anglo-Saxon England* 28 (1999), 87–110.

Postles, D., 'The Learning of Austin Canons: the Case of Oseney Abbey', *NMS* 29 (1985), 32–43.

Postlewate, L., 'From Preaching to Storytelling: The *Metaphors* of Nicole Bozon', in *Framing the Text: Reading Tradition and Image in Medieval Europe*, ed. K. L. Boardman, C. Emerson and A. Tudor, *Medievalia* 20 (Binghamton NY, 2001), pp. 73–91.

——, 'Preaching the Sins of the Ladies: Nicole Bozon's "Char d'Orgueil"', in *Cultural Performances in Medieval France*, ed. E. Doss-Quinby, R. Krueger and E. J. Burns (Cambridge, 2007), pp. 195–202.

Pouzet, J.-P., 'Quelques aspects de l'influence des chanoines augustins sur la production et la transmission littéraire vernaculaire en Angleterre (XIIIe–XVe siècles)', *Comptes Rendus de l'Académie des Inscriptions & Belles-Lettres* 2006 (for 2004), 169–213.

——, 'Southwark Gower – Augustinian Agencies in Gower's Manuscripts and Texts' (forthcoming).

Power, E., *Medieval English Nunneries* (Oxford, 1921).

Powicke, F. M., *The Loss of Normandy 1189–1204* (Manchester, 1913).

Prestwich, M., 'Turberville, Sir Thomas de (*d.* 1295), soldier and traitor', *ODNB*, http://www.oxforddnb.com/view/article/38079?docPos=15

——, *Edward I* (London, 1988).

Putter, A., and J. Jefferson, eds., *Multilingualism in Later Medieval Britain: Sources and Analysis* (Turnhout, forthcoming).

Ramsay, N., 'Scriveners and Notaries as Legal Intermediaries in Later Medieval England', in *Enterprise and Individuals in Fifteenth-Century England*, ed. J. Kermode (Stroud, 1991), pp.118–31.

Rankin, J. W., 'The Hymns of St Godric', *PMLA* 38 (1923), 699–711.

Ray, R. D., 'Medieval Historiography Through the Twelfth-Century', *Viator* 5 (1974), 33–59.

Rector, G., *'En sa chambre sovent le lit: Otium* and the Pedagogical Sociabilities of Early *Romanz* Literature (*c.*1100–1150)' (forthcoming).

Revard, C., 'Courtly Romances in the Privy Wardrobe', in *The Court and Cultural Diversity: Selected Papers from the Eighth Triennial Congress of the International Courtly Literature Society,* ed. E. Mullally and J. Thompson (Cambridge, 1997), pp. 297–308.

——, *'The Papelard's Priest* and the Black Prince's Men: Audiences of an Alliterative Poem, *c.*1350–1370', *Studies in the Age of Chaucer* 23 (2001), 359–406.

——, 'Four Fabliaux from London, British Library MS Harley 2253, Translated into English Verse', *Chaucer Review* 40 (2005), 111–40.

Reynolds, C., 'The Shrewsbury Book, British Library, Royal MS 15 E. VI', in *XII: Medieval Art, Architecture and Archaeology at Rouen, the British Archaeological Association Conference Transactions for the Year 1986,* ed. J. Stratford (London, 1993), pp. 109–16.

——, 'English Patrons and French Artists in Fifteenth-Century Normandy', in *England and Normandy in the Middle Ages,* ed. D. Bates and A. Curry (London, 1994), pp. 299–313.

Riché, P., *Les Écoles et l'enseignement dans l'Occident chrétien de la fin du Ve siècle au milieu du XIe siècle* (Paris, 1979).

Richmond, C., *The Paston Family in the Fifteenth Century: Fastolf's Will* (Cambridge, 1996).

Richter, M., *Sprache und Gesellschaft im Mittelalter: Untersuchungen zur mündlichen Kommunikation in England von der Mitte des elften bis zum Beginn des vierzehnten Jahrhunderts* (Stuttgart, 1979).

Riddy, F., '"Women talking about the things of God": A Late Medieval Subculture', in Meale, *Women and Literature in Britain,* pp. 104–27.

Rigg, A. G., *A History of Anglo-Latin Literature 1066–1422* (Cambridge, 1992).

Ringrose, J., 'The Foundress and Her College: Marie de St Pol', in *Pembroke College Cambridge: A Celebration,* ed. A. V. Grimstone (Cambridge, 1999).

Robbins, R. H., 'The "Arma Christi" Rolls', *MLR* 34 (1939), 415–20.

——, 'Geoffrey Chaucier, poète français, Father of English Poetry', *Chaucer Review* 13 (1978), 93–115.

——, 'The Vintner's Son: French Wine in English Bottles', in *Eleanor of Aquitaine: Patron and Politician,* ed. W. W. Kibler (Austin TX, 1976), pp. 147–72.

——, and J. L. Cutler, *Supplement to the Index of Middle English Verse* (Lexington KY, 1965).

Robinson, D. M., *The Geography of Augustinian Settlement in Medieval England and Wales,* 2 vols. (Oxford, 1980).

Robinson, P. A., 'A Study of Some Aspects of the Transmission of English Verse Texts in Late Medieval Manuscripts' (unpublished B. Litt. dissertation, Oxford, 1972).

——, 'The "Booklet": A Self-Contained Unit in Composite Manuscripts', *Codicologica* 3 (1980), 46–69.

Rodger, N. A. M., *The Safeguard of the Sea: A Naval History of Britain, I: 660–1649* (London, 1997).

Rogers, C. J., *War Cruel and Sharp: English Strategy under Edward III, 1327–1360* (Woodbridge, 2000).

Rohlfs, G., *From Vulgar Latin to Old French: An Introduction to the Study of the Old French Language,* trans. V. Almazan and L. McCarthy (Detroit MI, 1970).

Romaine, S., *Bilingualism* (Oxford, 1989; 2nd edn, 1995).

Rosenthal, C. L., 'A Possible Source of Chaucer's *Booke of the Duchesse – Li Regrete de Guillaume* by Jehan de la Motte', *Modern Language Notes* 48 (1933), 511–14.

Rothwell, W., 'The Teaching of French in Medieval England', *MLR* 63 (1968), 37–46.

——, 'The Role of French in Thirteenth-Century England', *BJRL* 58 (1976), 445–66.

——, 'A quelle époque a-t-on cessé de parler français en Angleterre?, in *Mélanges de philologie romane offerts à Charles Camproux*, ed. R. Lafont et al., 2 vols. (Montpellier, 1978), II, 1075–89.

——, 'Anglo-French Lexical Contacts, Old and New', *MLR* 74 (1979), 287–96.

——, 'Language and Government in Medieval England', *ZfSL* 93 (1983), 258–70.

——, 'From Latin to Modern French: Fifty Years On', *BJRL* 68 (1985), 179–209.

——, 'Stratford atte Bowe and Paris', *MLR* 80 (1985), 39–54.

——, 'Chaucer and Stratford Atte Bowe', *BJRL* 74 (1992), 3–28.

——, 'The "faus franceis d'Angleterre", Later Anglo-Norman', in Short, *Anglo-Norman Anniversary Essays*, pp. 309–26.

——, 'Adding Insult to Injury: The English who Curse in Borrowed French', in Nielsen and Schøsler, *Origins and Development of Emigrant Languages*, pp. 41–54.

——, 'Playing "follow my leader" in Anglo-Norman Studies', *Journal of French Language Studies* 6:2 (1996), 177–210.

——, 'English and French in England after 1362', *English Studies* 82 (2001), 539–59.

——, 'Henry of Lancaster and Geoffrey Chaucer: Anglo-French and Middle English in Fourteenth-Century England', *MLR* 99 (2004), 313–27.

Round, J. H., *The Commune of London* (Westminster, 1899).

Rouse, R. H. and M. A., *Manuscripts and Their Makers: Commercial Book Producers in Medieval Paris 1200–1500*, 2 vols. (Turnhout, 2000).

Rowe, J. H., 'King Henry VI's Claim to France in Picture and Poem', *The Library*, 4th series 13 (1933), 77–88.

Ruhe, E., *De amasio ad amasiam: Zur Gattungsgeschichte des mittelalterlichen Liebesbriefes* (Munich, 1975).

Runyan, T. J., 'The Rolls of Oléron and the Admiralty Court in Fourteenth Century England', *American Journal of Legal History* 19 (1975), 95–111.

Russell, D., 'The Campsey Collection of Old French Saints' Lives: A Re-Examination of its Structure and Provenance', *Scriptorium* 57:1 (2003), 51–83.

Rust, M. D., *Imaginary Worlds in Medieval Books: Exploring the Manuscript Matrix* (New York, 2007).

Salembier, L., *Le Cardinal Pierre d'Ailly; chancelier de l'Université de Paris, Eveque du Puy et de Cambrai, 1350–1420* (Tourcoing, 1931).

Saltman, A., 'Gilbert Crispin as a Source of the Anti-Jewish Polemic of the *Ysagoge in Theologiam*', in *Confrontation and Coexistence*, ed. P. Artzi (Ramat Gan, 1984), pp. 89–99.

Salverda de Grave, J. J., *L'influence de la langue française en Hollande d'après les mots empruntés* (Paris, 1913)

Sanborn, F. R., *Origins of the Early English Maritime and Commercial Law* (New York, 1930).

Sandahl, B., *Middle English Sea Terms*, 3 vols. (Uppsala, 1951–82).

Saul, A., 'The Herring Industry at Great Yarmouth, c.1280–1400', *Norfolk Archaeology* 38 (1981), 33–43.

Saunders, H. W., *An Introduction to Obedientiary and Manor Rolls of Norwich Cathedral Priory* (Norwich, 1930).

Sawyer, P. H., *Anglo-Saxon Lincolnshire* (Lincoln, 1998).

Sayers, J., *Innocent III: Leader of Europe 1198–1216* (London, 1994).

Sayers, W., 'Chaucer's Shipman and the Law Marine', *Chaucer Review* 37 (2002), 145–58.

——, 'Ships and Sailors in Geffrei Gaimar's *Estoire des Engleis*', *MLR* 98 (2003), 299–310.

Scarfe, N., *The Suffolk Landscape* (Bury St Edmunds, 1987).

Scase, W., *Literature and Complaint in England, 1272–1553* (Oxford, 2007).

Scattergood, V. J., *Politics and Poetry in the Fifteenth Century* (London, 1971).

Schaefer, U., ed., *The Beginnings of Standardization: Language and Culture in Fourteenth-Century England* (Frankfurt, 2006).

Scharer, A., 'The Writing of History at King Alfred's Court', *EME* 5 (1996), 177–206.

Schendl, H., 'Linguistic Aspects of Code-switching in Medieval English Texts', in Trotter, *Multilingualism*, pp. 77–92.

——, 'Code-Choice and Code-Switching in Some Early Fifteenth-century Letters', in *Middle English from Tongue to Text: Selected Papers from the Third International Conference on Middle English*, ed. P. Lucas et al. (Frankfurt, 2002), pp. 247–62.

Schmolke-Hasselmann, B., trans. M. and R. Middleton, *The Evolution of Arthurian Romance from Chrétien to Froissart* (Cambridge, 1998).

Schøsler, L., *La déclinaison bicasuelle de l'ancien français, son rôle dans la syntaxe de la phrase, les causes de sa disparition*, Etudes romanes de l'Université d'Odense 19 (Odense, 1984).

Scott, K. L., 'A Mid-Fifteenth Century English Illuminating Shop and Its Customers', *JWCI* 31 (1968), 170–96.

——, '*Fall of Princes* by John Lydgate', in Tanis, ed., *Leaves of Gold*, item 72, p. 208.

Seymour, M. C., 'The Scribal Tradition of Mandeville's *Travels*: The Insular Version', *Scriptorium* 18 (1964), 34–48.

——, *Sir John Mandeville* (Aldershot, 1993).

Sharpe, R., *A Handlist of the Latin Writers of Great Britain and Ireland Before 1540*, Publications of the Journal of Medieval Latin 1 (Turnhout, 2001).

——, 'The Medieval Librarian', in Leedham-Green and Webber, *Cambridge History of Libraries*, I, 218–41.

——, 'Library Catalogues and Indexes', in Morgan and Thomson, *Cambridge History of the Book in Britain*, II, 197–218.

Shepherd, G., 'English Bible Versions Before Wycliffe', in *The West from the Fathers to the Reformation*, *The Cambridge History of the Bible*, II, ed. G. W. H. Lampe (Cambridge, 1963), pp. 362–87.

Sherman, C. R., 'Some Visual Definitions in the Illustrations of Aristotle's *Nichomachean Ethics* and *Politics* in the French Translations of Nicole Oresme', *The Art Bulletin* 59 (1977), 320–30.

——, *Imaging Aristotle: Verbal and Visual Representation in Fourteenth-Century France* (Berkeley, 1995).

Shippey, T. A., and A. Haarder, eds., *'Beowulf': The Critical Heritage* (London, 1998).

Short, I., 'On Bilingualism in Anglo-Norman England', *Romance Philology* 33 (1979–80), 469–79.

——, 'Gaimar et les débuts de l'historiographie en langue française', in *Chroniques nationales et universelles*, ed. D. Buschinger (Göppingen, 1990), pp. 155–62.

——, 'Literary Culture at the Court of Henry II', in *Henry II: New Interpretations*, ed. C. Harper-Bill and N. Vincent (Woodbridge, 2007), pp. 335–61.

——, *Manual of Anglo-Norman*, ANTS OPS 7 (London, 2007).

——, ed., *Anglo-Norman Anniversary Essays*, ANTS OPS 2 (London, 1993).

Signori, G., 'Muriel and Others ... or Poems as Pledges of Friendship', in *Friendship in Medieval Europe*, ed. J. Haseldine (Stroud, 1999), pp. 199–212.

Sirat, C., 'Paléographie Hebraïque Médiaévale', in *Rapports sur les conférences de l'École Pratique des Hautes Études*, IVe section (Paris, 1975), pp. 559–74.

Skeat, W., *The Place-Names of Suffolk* (Cambridge, 1913).

Smalley, B., *The Study of the Bible in the Middle Ages* (1952; rept Notre Dame IN, 1964).

Smith, H. P., 'Poole's Ancient Admiralty Court', *Proceedings of the Dorset Natural History and Archaeological Society* 49 (1928), 126–7.

Smith, J. J., 'The Use of English: Language Contact, Dialect Variation and Written Standardization during the Middle English Period', in *English in Its Social Contexts: Essays in Historical Sociolinguistics*, ed. T. W. Machan and C. T. Scott (Oxford, 1992), pp. 47–68.

Smyth, J., *The Lives of the Berkeleys, The Berkeley Manuscripts*, 3 vols., ed. J. Maclean, II (Gloucester, 1893–5).

Sneddon, D., 'The Anglo-Norman Psalters: A Note on the Relationships between the Oxford and Arundel Psalters', *Romania* 99 (1978), 395–9.

Solopova, E., 'English Poetry of the Reign of Henry II', in *Writers of the Reign of Henry II*, ed. Kennedy and Meecham-Jones, pp. 187–204.

Somerset, F., and N. Watson, eds., *The Vulgar Tongue: Medieval and Postmedieval Vernacularity* (University Park PA, 2004).

Sorel, C., *La bibliotheque françoise* (Paris, 1667).

Sparks, H. F. D., 'Jerome as Biblical Scholar', in *The Cambridge History of the Bible*, 3 vols., ed. P. R. Ackroyd and C. F. Evans (Cambridge, 1970), I, 510–41.

Spence, John, 'Anglo-Norman Prose Chronicles and Their Audiences', in *English Manuscript Studies, 1100–1700: XIV, Regional Manuscripts*, ed. A. S. G. Edwards (London 2008), pp. 27–59.

Spencer, E. P., 'L'Horloge de Sapience: Bruxelles, Bibibliothèque Royale MS IV III', *Scriptorium* 17 (1963), 282–3.

——, 'Gerson, Ciboule, and the Bedford Master's Shop (Bruxelles, Bibliothèque Royale, MS IV. III, Part II)', *Scriptorium* 19 (1965), 104–8.

——, *The Sobieski Hours: A Manuscript in the Royal Library at Windsor Castle* (New York, 1977).

Spiegel, G. M., 'The Cult of Saint Denis and Capetian Kingship', *JMH* 1 (1975), 43–69.

Spitzer, L., 'Emendations Proposed to *De Amico ad Amicam* and *Responcio*', *Modern Language Notes* 67 (1952), 150–5.

Städtler, T., ed., *Zu den Anfängen der französischen Grammatiksprache: Textausgaben und Wortschatzsdudien* (Tübingen, 1988).

Stafford, P., *Queen Emma and Queen Edith: Queenship and Women's Power in Eleventh-Century England* (Oxford, 1997).

Staley, L., 'Gower, Richard II, Henry of Derby, and the Business of Making Culture', *Speculum* 75 (2000), 68–96.

Stein, R. M., *Reality Fictions. Romance, History and Governmental Authority, 1025–1180* (Notre Dame IN, 2006).

——, 'Multilingualism', in Strohm, ed., *Middle English*, pp. 23–37.

Steiner, E., *Documentary Culture and the Making of English Literature* (Cambridge, 2003).

——, and C. Barrington, ed., *The Letter of the Law: Legal Practice and Literary Production in Medieval England* (Ithaca NY, 2002).

Stengel, E., ed., 'Die ältesten Anleitungsschriften zur Erlernung der französischen Sprache', *Zeitschrift für neufranzösische Sprache und Literatur* 1 (1870), 1–40.

Stephenson, R., 'Byrhtferth's *Enchiridion*: The Effectiveness of Hermeneutic Latin', in Tyler, *Conceptualizing Multilingualism*.

Stevenson, J., 'Anglo-Latin Women Poets', in *Latin Learning and English Lore: Studies in Anglo-Saxon Literature for Michael Lapidge*, ed. K. O'Brien O'Keeffe and A. Orchard, 2 vols. (Toronto, 2005), II, 86–107.

Stöber, K., *Late Medieval Monasteries and their Patrons: England and Wales, c.1300–1450* (Woodbridge, 2007).

Stone, L., W. Rothwell, T. B. W. Reid et al., eds., *Anglo-Norman Dictionary*, seven fascicles (London, 1977–92), 2nd edn S. Gregory, W. Rothwell and D.A. Trotter with M. Beddow, 2 vols., A-C, D-E (London, 2005).

Stoneman, R., 'The Medieval Alexander', in *Latin Fiction: The Latin Novel in Context*, ed. H. Hofmann (London, 1999), pp. 238–52.

Stones, A., 'The Stylistic Context of the *Roman de Fauvel*, with a Note on *Fauvain*. Appendix B: The Stylistic Subgroups surrounding the Fauvel Master', in *Fauvel Studies: Allegory, Chronicle, Music, and Image in Paris, Bibliothèque nationale de France, MS fonds français 146*, ed. M. Bent and A. Wathey (Oxford, 1998), pp. 529–67.

Strohm, P., 'Saving the Appearances: Chaucer's Purse and the Fabrication of the Lancastrian Claim', in *Chaucer's England: Literature in Historical Context*, ed. B. Hanawalt (Minneapolis, 1992), pp. 21–40.

——, ed., *Middle English: Oxford Twenty-First Century Approaches to Literature* (Oxford, 2007).

Studer, P., *The Study of Anglo-Norman*. Inaugural Lecture delivered before the University of Oxford on 6 February 1920 (Oxford, 1920).

——, and J. Evans, *Anglo-Norman Lapidaries* (Paris, 1924).

'Suffolk: Dates of Commencement of Registers for Parishes Formed before 1832', *Genealogical Aids* 32 (Canterbury, 1983).

Summerfield, T., 'The Political Songs in the *Chronicles* of Pierre de Langtoft and Robert Mannyng', in *The Court and Cultural Diversity*, ed. E. Mullally and J. Thompson (Cambridge, 1997), pp. 139–48.

——, *The Matter of Kings' Lives: The Design of Past and Present in the Early Fourteenth-Century Verse Chronicles by Pierre de Langtoft and Robert Mannyng* (Amsterdam, 1998).

——, 'The Testimony of Writing: Pierre de Langtoft and the Appeals to History, 1291–1306', in *The Scots and Medieval Arthurian Legend*, ed. R. Purdie and N. Royan, Arthurian Studies 61 (Cambridge, 2005), pp. 25–42.

——, 'Kings and Gentlemen, Saints and Saracens: Language Variety in Middle English Romances', in Putter and Jefferson, *Multilingualism in Later Medieval Britain*.

Summit, J., *Lost Property: The Woman Writer and English Literary History, 1380–1589* (Chicago, 2000).

Swan, M., and E. M. Treharne, eds., *Rewriting English in the Twelfth Century* (Cambridge, 2000).

Swiggers, P., 'Le Donait françois: la plus ancienne grammaire française', *Revue des langues romanes* 89 (1985), 235–51.

Symes, C., 'Prescription, Proscription, Transcription, Improvisation: Assessing the Written and Unwritten Evidence for Pre-Modern Performance Practice', in *Scripted Orality*, ed. D. Pietropaolo (Toronto, forthcoming).

511

Talbot, H., *The English Achilles: An Account of the Life and Campaigns of John Talbot, 1ˢᵗ Earl of Shrewsbury (1383–1453)* (London, 1981).

Tanis, J. R., ed., with J. A. Thompson, *Leaves of Gold: Manuscript Illumination from Philadelphia Collections* (Philadelphia, 2001).

Taylor, A., 'Was There a Song of Roland?', *Speculum* 76 (2001), 28–65.

——, *Textual Situations: Three Medieval Manuscripts and Their Readers* (Philadelphia, 2002).

Taylor., C. D., 'The Treatise Cycle of the Shrewsbury Book: BL ms Royal 15 E.VI' (forthcoming).

Taylor, K., 'Social Aesthetics and the Emergence of Civic Discourse from the *Shipman's Tale* to *Melibee*', *Chaucer Review* 39 (2005), 298–322.

Teague, F., 'Christine de Pizan's Book of War', in *The Reception of Christine de Pizan from the Fifteenth Through the Nineteenth Centuries: Visitors to the City*, ed. G. K. McLeod (Lewiston ME, 1991), pp. 25–41.

Thiolier, J.-C., 'Pierre de Langtoft: historiographe d'Edouard Iᵉʳ Plantagenêt', in Short, *Anglo-Norman Anniversary Essays*, pp. 379–94.

——, 'L'itinéraire de Pierre de Langtoft', in *Miscellanea Mediaevalia: Mélanges offerts à Philippe Ménard*, ed. J.-C. Faucon, A. Labbé and D. Quéruel (Paris, 1998), II, 1329–53.

Thomas, H. M., *The English and the Normans: Ethnic Hostility, Assimilation and Identity, 1066–1220* (Oxford, 2003).

Thompson, J. J., *Robert Thornton and the London Thornton Manuscript: British Library MS Additional 31042* (Cambridge, 1987).

Thompson, S., *Women Religious: The Founding of English Nunneries after the Norman Conquest* (Oxford, 1991).

Thomson, R. M., 'The Library of Bury St. Edmunds Abbey in the Eleventh and Twelfth Centuries', *Speculum* 47 (1972), 617–45.

——, 'Minor Manuscript Decoration from the West of England in the Twelfth Century', in *Reading Texts and Images: Essays on Medieval and Renaissance Art and Patronage in Honour of Margaret M. Manion*, ed. B. J. Muir (Exeter, 2002), pp. 19–34, rev. in idem, *Books and Learning in Twelfth-Century England: The Ending of* 'Alter Orbis' (Walkern, Herts, 2006).

Tilliette, J.-Y., '*Troiae ab oris*: Aspects de la révolution poétique de la seconde moitié du XIᵉ siècle', *Latomus* 58 (1999), 405–31.

Tillotson, J., *Marrick Priory: A Nunnery in Late Medieval Yorkshire*, Borthwick Papers no. 75 (York, 1989).

Toswell, M. J., 'The Late Anglo-Saxon Psalter: Ancestor of the Book of Hours?', *Florilegium* 14 (1995–6), 1–24.

Townend, M., 'Contacts and Conflicts: Latin, Norse, and French', in *The Oxford History of English*, ed. L. Mugglestone (Oxford, 2006).

——, 'Norse Poets and English Kings: Skaldic Performance in Anglo-Saxon England', *Offa* 58 (2001), 269–75.

Treharne, E. M., 'The Production and Script of Manuscripts Containing English Religious Texts in the First Half of the Twelfth Century', in *Rewriting Old English in the Twelfth Century*, ed. Swan and Treharne, pp. 11–40.

——, 'English in the Post-Conquest Period', in *A Companion to Anglo-Saxon Literature*, ed. P. Pulsiano and E. Treharne (Oxford, 2001), pp. 403–14.

——, 'Periodization and Categorization: The Silence of (the) English in the Twelfth Century', *New Medieval Literatures* 8 (2006), 247–73.

Trend, J. B., 'The First English Songs', *Music and Letters* 9 (1928), 111–28.

Trotter, D. A., 'The Anglo-Norman Inscriptions at Berkeley Castle', *Medium Aevum* 59 (1990), 114–20.

——, 'Walter of Stapledon and the Premarital Inspection of Philippa of Hainault', *French Studies Bulletin* 49 (1993), 1–4.

——, 'L'anglo-français au pays de Galles: une enquête préliminaire', *Revue de linguistique romane* 58 (1994), 461–87.

——, 'Language Contact and Lexicography: The Case of Anglo-Norman', in Nielsen and Schøsler, *Origins and Development of Emigrant Languages*, pp. 1–39.

——, '"Mossenhor, fet metre aquesta letra en bon francés": Anglo-French in Gascony', in Gregory and Trotter, *De mot en mot*, pp. 199–222.

——, 'The Anglo-French Lexis of the *Ancrene Wisse*: a re-evaluation', in Wada, *Companion to* Ancrene Wisse, pp. 83–101.

——, 'L'anglo-normand: variété insulaire ou variété isolée?', *Grammaires du vulgaire. Médiévales* 45 D (2003), 43–54.

——, 'Not as Eccentric as It Looks: Anglo-French and French French', *FMLS* 39 (2003), 427–38.

——, '*Oceano vox*: You Never know Where a Ship Comes From', in *Aspects of Multilingualism in European Language History*, ed. K. Braunmüller and G. Ferraresi (Amsterdam, 2003), pp. 15–33.

——, 'Langue et transmission du savoir artisanal: la construction navale en Angleterre au Moyen Âge', in *La transmission des savoirs au Moyen Âge et à la Renaissance I: du XIIe au XVe siècle*, ed. P. Nobel (Besançon, 2005), pp. 319–29.

——, 'Language Contact, Multilingualism, and the Evidence Problem', in Schaefer, *Beginnings of Standardization*, pp. 73–90.

——, 'Language and Law in the Anglo-French *Mirror of Justices*', in *L'Art de la Philologie: Mélanges en l'honneur de Leena Löfsted*, ed. J. Härmä, E. Suomela-Härmä and O. Välikangas (Helsinki, 2007), pp. 257–270.

——, 'Translation and the Development of Scholarly and Scientific Discourse: Early Medical Translations and Multilingual Lexicography', *International Encyclopedia of Translation Studies*, ed. H. Kittel et al. (Berlin, 2007), pp. 1073–81.

——, '*Tutes choses en sapience*: la transmission du lexique biblique dans les psautiers anglo-normands', in *Gouvernement des hommes, gouvernement des âmes: Mélanges Charles Brucker*, ed. V. Bubenicek et al. (Nancy, 2007), pp. 507–15.

——, 'Words, words, words ... but what exactly is a "word" in Anglo-Norman?', in *Essays in Honour of Brian Merrilees*, « *Queil boen professeur, mult enseinné, queil boen collegue* » : *Mélanges offerts à Brian Merrilees*, ed. C. Harvey, *Florilegium* 24 (2007), 109–23.

——, '*Pur meuz acorder en parlance E descorder en variaunce*: convergence et divergence dans l'évolution de l'anglo-normand', in *Sprachwandel und (Dis-)Kontinuität in der Romania*, ed. S. Heinemann and P. Videsott (Tübingen, 2008), pp. 87–95.

——, 'Intra-textual Multilingualism and Diaphasic/Diastratic Variation in Anglo-Norman', in Tyler, *Conceptualizing Multilingualism*.

——, 'Bridging the Gap: The (Socio)linguistic Evidence of some Medieval Bridge Accounts', in Ingham, *Anglo-Norman Language*.

Turville-Petre, T., 'Humphrey de Bohun and *William of Palerne*', *Neuphilologische Mitteilungen* 75 (1974), 250–2.

——, *The Alliterative Revival* (Cambridge, 1977).

——, 'Politics and Poetry in the Early Fourteenth Century: The Case of Robert Manning's *Chronicle*', *Review of English Studies* n.s. 39 (1988), 1–29.

——, *England the Nation: Language, Literature, and National Identity, 1290–1340* (Oxford, 1996).

Tuve, R., *Allegorical Imagery: Some Medieval Books and Their Posterity* (Princeton, 1966).

Tyler, E., 'Fictions of Family: The *Encomium Emmae Reginae* and Virgil's *Aeneid*', *Viator* 36 (2005), 149–79.

——, 'Talking about History in Eleventh-Century England: the *Encomium Emmae Reginae* and the Court of Harthacnut', *EME* 13 (2005), 359–83.

——, 'The *Vita Ædwardi*: The Politics of Poetry at Wilton Abbey', *ANS* 31 (2009), 135–56.

——, 'Crossing Conquests: Polyglot Royal Women and Literary Culture in Eleventh-Century England', in Tyler, *Conceptualizing Multilingualism*.

——, *Crossing Conquests: Women and the Politics of Literature in Eleventh Century England* (forthcoming).

——, 'Trojans in Anglo-Saxon England: Precedent without Descent', in *Troy and the European Imagination*, ed. E. Archibald and J. Clarke (Cambridge, forthcoming).

Underhill, F. A., *For Her Good Estate: The Life of Elizabeth de Burgh* (New York, 1999).

Uselmann, S., 'Women Reading and Reading Women: Early Scribal Notions of Literacy in the *Ancrene Wisse*', *Exemplaria* 16:2 (2004), 369–404.

Vale, J., *Edward III and Chivalry. Chivalric Society and its Context 1270–1350* (Woodbridge, 1982).

Vale, M., *The Princely Court: Medieval Courts and Culture in North-West Europe, 1270–1380* (Oxford, 2001).

——, *The Ancient Enemy: England, France and Europe from the Angevins to the Tudors 1154–1558* (London, 2007).

Valente, C., 'Simon de Montfort, Earl of Leicester, and the Utility of Sanctity in Thirteenth-Century England', *JMH* 21 (1995), 27–49.

Valls, H., 'Studies on Roger Frugardi's *Chirurgia*' (unpublished Ph.D. thesis, University of Toronto, 1995).

Van Deusen, N., ed., *The Place of the Psalms in the Intellectual Culture of the Middle Ages* (Albany NY, 1999).

Vance, E., *Mervelous Signals: Poetics and Sign Theory in the Middle Ages* (Lincoln NE, 1986).

Varvaro, A., 'Il libro I delle *Chroniques* di Jean Froissart: Per una filologia integrata dei testi e delle immagini', *Medioevo Romanzo* 19 (1994), 3–36.

——, 'Problèmes philologiques du Livre IV des *Chroniques* de Jean Froissart', in *Patrons, Authors and Workshops: Books and Book Production in Paris around 1400*, ed. G. Croenen and P. Ainsworth (Leuven, 2006), pp. 255–77.

Vaughan, M. F., 'The Prophets of the Anglo-Norman *Adam*', *Traditio* 39 (1983), 81–114.

Velden, H. van der, 'A Prayer Roll of Henry Beauchamp, Duke of Warwick', in *Gothic Art for England 1400–1547*, ed. R. Marks and P. Williamson with E. Townsend (London, 2003).

Vielliard, F., and J. Monfrin, *Manuel bibliographique de la littérature française du moyen âge de Robert Bossuat*, 3ᵉ supplément 1960–1980 (Paris, 1986–91).

Viereck Gibbs, S., 'Christine de Pizan's *Epistre Othea* in England: The Manuscript Tradition of Stephen Scrope's Translation', in *Contexts and Continuities: Proceedings of the IVth International Colloquium on Christine de Pizan*, ed. A. J. Kennedy, R. Brown-Grant, J. C. Laidlaw and C. M. Müller (Glasgow, 2002), pp. 397–408.

ince, A., 'Lincoln in the Viking Age', in *Vikings and the Danelaw*, ed. J. Graham-Campbell et al. (Oxford, 2001), pp. 157–79.

incent, N., 'Aigueblanche, Peter d'[Peter de Aqua Blanca] (*d.* 1268), bishop of Hereford and royal councillor', *ODNB*, http://www.oxforddnb.com/view/article/22015.

oigts, L. E., 'What's the Word? Bilingualism in late-Medieval England', *Speculum* 71 (1996), 813–26.

'ada, Y., ed., *A Companion to Ancrene Wisse* (Woodbridge, 2003).

'agner, A. R., *Heralds and Heraldry in the Middle Ages* (London, 1939).

'ake, J., and W. A. Pantin, 'Delapres Abbey, Its History and Architecture', *Northamptonshire Past and Present* 2 (1958), 225–42.

'akelin, D., *Humanism, Reading, and English Literature, 1430–1530* (Oxford, 2007).

'ansborough, J. E., *Lingua franca in the Mediterranean* (Richmond, 1996).

'ard, J., 'St Pol, Mary de, countess of Pembroke (*c.*1304–1377)', *ODNB*, http://www.oxforddnb.com/view/article/53073?docPos=2.

Jard, R. M., 'A Surviving Charter-Party of 1323', *Mariner's Mirror* 81 (1995), 387–401.

——, 'The Earliest Known Sailing Directions in English: Transcription and Analysis', *Deutsche Schiffahrtsarchiv* 27 (2004), 357–8.

——, *The World of the Medieval Shipmaster: Law, Buiness, and the Sea, c. 1350–1450* (Woodbridge, 2009).

Jarner, G. F., and J. P. Gilson, *Catalogue of Western Manuscripts in the Old Royal and King's Collections*, 4 vols. (London, 1921).

Jarren, M. R., *History on the Edge: Excalibur and the Borders of Britain* (Minneapolis, 2000).

——, 'Translation', in Strohm, ed., *Middle English*, pp. 51–67.

Jarren, N. B., *Women of God and Arms: Female Spirituality and Political Conflict, 1380–1600* (Philadelphia, 2005).

Jartburg, W. von , et al., *Französisches Etymologisches Wörterbuch* (Tübingen, 1948–).

Jaters, D. W., *The Rutters of the Sea: The Sailing Directions of Pierre Garcie* (New Haven CT, 1967).

Jatson, A. G., *A Descriptive Catalogue of the Medieval Manuscripts of All Souls College Oxford* (Oxford, 1997).

——, *Catalogue of Dated and Datable Manuscripts c.435–1600 in Oxford Libraries*, 2 vols. (Oxford, 1984).

Jatson, N., 'Censorship and Cultural Change in Late-Medieval England: Vernacular Theology, the Oxford Translation Debate, and Arundel's *Constitutions* of 1409', *Speculum* 70 (1995), 822–64.

——, 'The Politics of Middle English Writing', in *The Idea of the Vernacular*, ed. Wogan-Browne et al. (University Park PA, 1999), pp. 331–52.

——, 'Fashioning the Puritan Gentry-woman: Devotion and Dissent in *A Book to a Mother*', in *Medieval Women*, ed. Wogan-Browne et al., pp. 169–84.

——, 'Vernacular Apocalyptic: On *The Lanterne of Light*', *Revista Canaria de estudios Ingleses* 47 (2003), 115–28.

——, *Balaam's Ass: Vernacular Theology and the Secularization of England, 1050–1550* (forthcoming).

—— and J. Wogan-Browne, 'The French of England: the *Compileison*, *Ancrene Wisse*, and the Idea of Anglo-Norman', in Gaunt and Weiss, eds., *Cultural Traffic in the Medieval Romance World*, 35–59.

Waugh, S. L., 'Marriage, Class and Royal Lordship in England under Henry III', *Viator* 16 (1985), 181–207.

Webber, T., 'Monastic and Cathedral Book Collections in the Late Eleventh and Twelfth Centuries', in Leedham-Green and Webber, *Cambridge History of Libraries* I, 109–25.

Wenzel, S., *Verses in Sermons* (Cambridge MA, 1978).

——, *Preachers, Poets and the Early English Lyric* (Princeton, 1986).

——, 'Sermon Collections and their Taxonomy', in *The Whole Book: Cultural Perspectives on the Medieval Miscellany*, ed. S. G. Nichols and S. Wenzel (Ann Arbor, 1997), pp. 7–21.

White, W., 'Norfolk: Wiggenhall St. Mary Magdalen', in *William White's History, Gazetteer, and Directory of Norfolk* (Sheffield, 1845).

Wieck, R., *Painted Prayers: The Book of Hours in Medieval and Renaissance Art* (New York, 1997).

Wilkins, N., 'Music and Poetry at Court: England and France in the Late Middle Ages', in *English Court Culture in the Later Middle Ages*, ed. V. J. Scattergood and J. W. Sherborne (London, 1983), pp. 183–204.

Wilkinson, B., 'The Seals of the Two Benches under Edward III', *EHR* 42 (1927), 397–401.

Willard, C. C., 'Christine de Pizan's "Clock of Temperance"', *Esprit Créature* 2 (1962), 148–54.

——, 'The Manuscript Tradition of the *Livre des Trois Vertus* and Christine de Pizan's Audience', *Journal of the History of Ideas* 27:3 (1966), 433–44.

Williams, D., *The French Fetish from Chaucer to Shakespeare* (Cambridge, 2004).

Williamson, D. M., 'Ralf son of Gilbert and Ralf son of Ralf', *Lincolnshire Architecture and Archaeological Society Reports and Papers* 5 (1953), 19–26.

Wilson, E., 'A Middle English Manuscript at Coughton Court, Warwickshire, and British Library MS. Harley 4012', *Notes & Queries* 222 (1977), 295–303.

Wilson, R. M., 'English and French in England 1100–1300', *History* 28 (1943), 37–60.

Wimsatt, J. I., *Chaucer and the French Love Poets: The Literary Background of the Book of the Duchess* (Chapel Hill, NC, 1968).

——, 'Guillaume de Machaut and Chaucer's Love Lyrics', *Medium Aevum* 47 (1978), 66–87.

——, 'Chaucer, Fortune, and Machaut's *Il m'est avis*', in *Chaucer Problems and Perspectives: Essays Presented to Paul E. Beichner*, ed. E. Vasta and Z. P. Thundy (Notre Dame IN, 1979), pp. 119–31.

——, *Chaucer and the Poems of 'Ch' in University of Pennsylvania MS French 15*, Chaucer Studies 9 (Cambridge, 1982).

——, *Chaucer and his French Contemporaries. Natural Music in the Fourteenth Century* (Toronto, 1991).

Windeatt, B., 'Geoffrey Chaucer', in Ellis, *Oxford History of Literary Translation*, pp. 137–48.

Winn, M. B., *Anthoine Vérard, Parisian Publisher, 1485–1512: Prologues, Poems, and Presentations* (Geneva, 1997).

Wiseman, T. P., *The Myths of Rome* (Exeter, 2004).

Wogan-Browne, J., '"Clerc u lai, muïne u dame": Women and Anglo-Norman Hagiography in the Twelfth and Thirteenth Centuries', in Meale, *Women and Literature in Britain*, pp. 61–85.

——, *Saints' Lives and Women's Literary Culture c.1150–1300: Virginity and its Authorizations* (Oxford, 2001).

——, 'Dead to the World? Death and the Maiden Revisited in Medieval Women's Convent Culture', in *Guidance for Women in Twelfth-Century Convents*, ed. V. P. Morton (Cambridge, 2003), pp. 157–80.

——, 'How to Marry Your Wife with Honour and fin'amour: Forming Men for Marriage in Anglo-Norman England', in *Thirteenth Century England*, ed. R. Britnell, M. Prestwich and R. Frame (Woodbridge, 2003), pp. 131–50.

——, 'Powers of Record, Powers of Example: Hagiography and Women's History', in *Gendering the Master Narrative: Women and Power in the Middle Ages*, ed. M. Erler and M. Kowaleski (Ithaca NY, 2003), pp. 71–93.

——, 'Virginity Always Comes Twice: Virginity and Romance, Virginity and Profession', in *Maistresse of My Wit: Medieval Women and Modern Scholars*, ed. L. d'Arcens and J. Ruys (Turnhout, 2004), pp. 335–69.

——, '"Our Steward, St Jerome": Theology and the Anglo-Norman Household', in *Household, Women, and Christianities in Late Antiquity and the Middle Ages*, ed. A. Mulder-Bakker and J. Wogan-Browne (Turnhout, 2005), pp. 133–66.

——, 'Women's Formal and Informal Traditions of Biblical Knowledge in Anglo-Norman England', in *Saints, Scholars, and Politicians: Gender as a Tool in Medieval Studies: Festschrift in Honour of Anneke Mulder-Bakker on the Occasion of Her Sixty-Fifth Birthday*, ed. M. van Dijk and R. Nip (Turnhout, 2005), pp. 85–109.

——, 'Time to Read: Pastoral Care, Vernacular Access and the Case of Angier of St Frideswide', in *The Literature of Pastoral Care and Devotion in Medieval England: Essays in Honour of Bella Millett*, ed. C. Gunn and C. I. Parker (York, forthcoming).

——, and R. Voaden, A. Diamond, C. M. Meale, A. Hutchison, L. Johnson, eds., *Medieval Women: Texts and Contexts in Later Medieval Britain: Essays for Felicity Riddy*, Medieval Women Texts and Contexts 3 (Turnhout, 2000).

Woledge, B., and H. P. Clive, *Répertoire des plus anciens textes en prose française depuis 842 jusqu'aux premières années du XIIIe siècle* (Geneva, 1964).

Wolffe, B., *Henry VI* (New Haven CT, 2001).

Wolfram, H., 'Political Theory and Narrative in Charters', *Viator* 26 (1995), 39–51.

Woodbine, G. E., 'The Language of English Law', *Speculum* 18 (1943), 395–436.

Woolgar, C., 'Diet and Consumption in Gentry and Noble Households: A Case Study from around the Wash', in *Rulers and Ruled in Late Medieval England: Essays Presented to Gerald Harriss*, ed. R. E. Archer and S. Walker (London, 1995), pp. 17–31.

Wormald, F., *The Winchester Psalter* (London, 1973).

——, and C. E. Wright, eds., *The English Library before 1700: Studies in Its History* (London, 1958).

Wormald, P., 'Archbishop Wulfstan and the Holiness of Society', in *Legal Culture in the Early Medieval West* (London, 1999), pp. 225–51.

——, *The Making of English Law: King Alfred to the Twelfth Century, I: Legislation and Its Limits* (Oxford, 1999).

Wright, L., *Sources of London English: Medieval Thames Vocabulary* (Oxford, 1996).

——, 'The Records of the Hanseatic Merchants: Ignorant, Sleepy, or Degenerate?', *Multilingua* 16 (1997), 335–50.

——, 'Trade between England and the Low Countries: Evidence from Historical Linguistics', in *England and the Low Countries in the Late Middle Ages*, ed. C. Barron and N. Saul (Stroud, 1998), pp. 169–79.

——, 'Bills, Accounts, Inventories: Everyday Trilingual Activities in the Business World of Later Medieval England', in Trotter, *Multilingualism*, pp. 149–56.

——, 'Some Morphological Features of the Norfolk Guild Certificates of 1388/9: an Exercise in Variation', in *East Anglian English*, ed. J. Fisiak and P. Trudgill (Cambridge, 2001), pp. 79–162.

——, 'Models of Language Mixing: Code-Switching versus Semicommunication in Medieval Latin and Medieval English Accounts', in *Language Contact in the History of English*, ed. D. Kastovsky and A. Mettinger (Frankfurt, 2001), pp. 363–76.

——, 'On London Mixed Language Business Writing and the Singular Definite Articles *le* and *la*', in Ingham, *Anglo-Norman Language*.

Wright, R., *Late Latin and Early Romance* (Liverpool, 1978).

Yeager, R. F., 'Did Gower Write Cento?', in *John Gower: Recent Readings*, ed. R. F. Yeager (Kalamazoo MI, 1989).

——, *John Gower's Poetic: The Search for a New Arion* (Cambridge, 1990).

——, 'Politics and the French Language in England During the Hundred Years' War: The Case of John Gower', in Baker, *Inscribing the Hundred Years' War*, pp.127–57.

——, 'John Gower's Audience: The Ballades', *Chaucer Review* 40 (2005), 81–105.

——, 'Gower's French Audience: The *Mirour de l'Omme*', *Chaucer Review* 41 (2006), 111–37.

Zink, M., *Froissart et le temps* (Paris, 1998).

Zupitza, J., 'Cantus beati Godrici', *Englische Studien* 11 (1888), 401–32.

Zupko, R., *A Dictionary of Weights and Measures for the British Isles: The Middle Ages to the Twentieth Century* (Philadelphia, 1985).

Online Resources

Ancient Petitions (*Medieval Petitions: A Catalogue of the 'Ancient Petitions' in the National Archives*), dir. W. M. Ormrod
http://www.nationalarchives.gov.uk/catalogue/default.asp

Anglo-Norman Hub
www.anglo-norman.net

Bodleian Library Catalogues of Western Manuscripts to *c*. 1500
http://www.bodley.ox.ac.uk/dept/scwmss/wmss/medieval/medieval.htm

British Library Catalogue of Manuscripts
www.bl.uk/catalogues/manuscripts.htm

British Library Catalogue of Illuminated Manuscripts
www.bl.uk/catalogues/illuminatedmanuscripts/

Bibliographie de Jean Froissart, Godfried Croenen
http://www.liv.ac.uk/~gcroenen/biblio.htm

The Campsey Project, D. W. Russell
http://margot.uwaterloo.ca/campsey/cmphome_e.html

Christine de Pizan: The Making of the Queen's Manuscript
www.pizan.lib.ed.ac.uk/index.html

Corsair - the Online Research Resource of the Pierpont Morgan Library
http://corsair.morganlibrary.org

Digital Scriptorium
http://www.scriptorium.columbia.edu/

lish Monastic Archives
vww.ucl.ac.uk/history2/englishmonasticarchives
ich of England at Fordham
ittp://www.fordham.edu/frenchofengland
de to Medieval and Renassiance Manuscripts, Digital Scriptorium
.unsite.berkeley.edu/scriptorium/hehweb/HM47405.html
tory in Focus: The Sea
ittp://www.history.ac.uk/ihr/focus/sea
gining History project list of publications
ittp://www.qub.ac.uk/imagining-history/outputs/index.htm
· Incunabula Short Title Catalogue
ittp://www.bl.uk/catalogues/istc/index.html
ex of Descriptions of the ME Prose *Brut*
www.qub.ac.uk/imagining-history/resources/short/index.php
oduction to the On-Line AND, 'Anglo-French and the AND', W. Rothwell,
ittp://www.anglo-norman.net/sitedocs/main-intro.hml
guage Transmission, Richard Ingham
www.richardingham.com
nuscripts of the Bibliothèque Ste Geneviève and of the Bibliothèque Mazarine
liberfloridus.cines.fr/textes/biblio_fr.html
· National Archives on-line Catalogue
www.nationalarchives.gov.uk/catalogue
· National Archives Documents Online
www.nationalarchives.gov.uk/documentsonline
tional Register of Archives
www.nationalarchives.gov.uk/nra/
ford Dictionary of National Biography
www.oxforddnb.com/
· *Parliament Rolls of Medieval England*, ed. C. Given-Wilson et al.
http://www.sd-editions.com/PROME/home.html
· Pierpont Morgan Library Online Research (see also under Corsair)
http://www.themorgan.org/research/corsair.asp
· *Production and Use of English Manuscripts 1060–1220*
www.le.ac.uk/ee/em1060to1220
e St. Alban's Psalter
www.abdn.ac.uk/stalbanspsalter/english/index.shtml
·sor de la langue française
http://atilf.atilf.fr/tlf.htm
e Soldier in Later Medieval England
http://www.medievalsoldier.org/

INDEX OF PRIMARY TEXTS AND MANUSCRIPTS

Manuscripts

INDEX OF PRIMARY AUTHORS

GENERAL INDEX: PERSONS AND PLACES, SUBJECTS

(authors mentioned in the text are listed in the **Index of Primary Authors**)

Subjects

YORK MEDIEVAL PRESS: PUBLICATIONS

od's Words, Women's Voices: The Discernment of Spirits in the Writing of Late-Medieval Jomen Visionaries, Rosalyn Voaden (1999)

ilgrimage Explored, ed. J. Stopford (1999)

iety, Fraternity and Power: Religious Gilds in Late Medieval Yorkshire 1389–1547, David J. F. Crouch (2000)

ourts and Regions in Medieval Europe, ed. Sarah Rees Jones, Richard Marks and ..J. Minnis (2000)

reasure in the Medieval West, ed. Elizabeth M. Tyler (2000)

Junneries, Learning and Spirituality in Late Medieval English Society: The Dominican 'riory of Dartford, Paul Lee (2000)

rophecy and Public Affairs in Later Medieval England, Lesley A. Coote (2000)

he Problem of Labour in Fourteenth-Century England, ed. James Bothwell, P. J. P. ;oldberg and W. M. Ormrod (2000)

Jew Directions in later Medieval Manuscript Studies: Essays from the 1998 Harvard 'onference, ed. Derek Pearsall (2000)

:istercians, Heresy and Crusadse in Occitania, 1145–1229: Preaching in the Lord's 'ineyard, Beverly Mayne Kienzle (2001)

;uilds and the Parish Community in Late Medieval East Anglia, c. 1470–1550, <en Farnhill (2001)

he Age of Edward III, ed. J. S. Bothwell (2001)

"ime in the Medieval World, ed. Chris Humphrey and W. M. Ormrod (2001)

"he Cross Goes North: Processes of Conversion in Northern Europe, AD 300–1300, •d. Martin Carver (2002)

Jenry IV: The Establishment of the Regime, 1399–1406, ed. Gwilym Dodd and)ouglas Biggs (2003)

Youth in the Middle Ages, ed. P. J. P. Goldberg and Felicity Riddy (2004)

The Idea of the Castle in Medieval England, Abigail Wheatley (2004)

Rites of Passage: Cultures of Transition in the Fourteenth Century, ed. Nicola ?. McDonald and W. M. Ormrod (2004)

:reating the Monastic Past in Medieval Flanders, Karine Ugé (2005)

5t William of York, Christopher Norton (2006)

Medieval Obscenities, ed. Nicola F. McDonald (2006)

The Reign of Edward II: New Perspectives, ed. Gwilym Dodd and Anthony Musson (2006)

Old English Poetics: The Aesthetics of the Familiar in Anglo-Saxon England, Elizabeth M. Tyler (2006)

The Late Medieval Interlude: The Drama of Youth and Aristocratic Masculinity, Fiona S. Dunlop (2007)

The Late Medieval English College and its Context, ed. Clive Burgess and Martin Heal (2008)

The Reign of Henry IV: Rebellion and Survival, 1403–1413, ed. Gwilym Dodd and Douglas Biggs (2008)

Medieval Petitions: Grace and Grievance, ed. W. Mark Ormrod, Gwilym Dodd and Anthony Musson (2009)

St Edmund, King and Martyr: Changing Images of a Medieval Saint, ed. Anthony Bale (2009)

The Royal Pardon: Access to Mercy in Fourteenth-Century England, Helen Lacey (2009)

Texts and Traditions of Medieval Pastoral Care: Essays in Honour of Bella Millett, ed. Cate Gunn and Catherine Innes-Parker (2009)

The Anglo-Norman Language and its Contexts, ed. Richard Ingham (2010)

Parliament and Political Pamphleteering in Fourteenth-Century England, Clementine Oliver (2010)

The Saints' Lives of Jocelin of Furness: Hagiography, Patronage and Ecclesiastical Politics, Helen Birkett (2010)

The York Mystery Plays: Performance in the City, ed. Margaret Rogerson (2011)

Wills and Will-Making in Anglo-Saxon England, Linda Tollerton (2011)

The Songs and Travels of a Tudor Minstrel: Richard Sheale of Tamworth, Andrew Taylor (2012)

Sin in Medieval and Early Modern Culture: The Tradition of the Seven Deadly Sins, ed. Richard G. Newhauser and Susan J. Ridyard (2012)

Socialising the Child in Late Medieval England, c. 1400–1600, Merridee L. Bailey (2012)

Barking Abbey and Medieval Literary Culture: Authorship and Authority in a Female Community, ed. Jennifer N. Brown and Donna Alfano Bussell (2012)

Christians and Jews in Angevin England: The York Massacre of 1190, Narratives and Contexts, ed. Sarah Rees Jones and Sethina Watson (2013)

Reimagining History in Anglo-Norman Prose Chronicles, John Spence (2013)

Henry V: New Interpretations, ed. Gwilym Dodd (2013)

York Studies in Medieval Theology

I   *Medieval Theology and the Natural Body*, ed. Peter Biller and A. J. Minnis (1997)

II *Handling Sin: Confession in the Middle Ages*, ed. Peter Biller and A. J. Minnis (1998)

III *Religion and Medicine in the Middle Ages*, ed. Peter Biller and Joseph Ziegler (2001)

IV *Texts and the Repression of Medieval Heresy*, ed. Caterina Bruschi and Peter Biller (2002)

York Manuscripts Conference

Manuscripts and Readers in Fifteenth-Century England: The Literary Implications of Manuscript Study, ed. Derek Pearsall (1983) [Proceedings of the 1981 York Manuscripts Conference]

Manuscripts and Texts: Editorial Problems in Later Middle English Literature, ed. Derek Pearsall (1987) [Proceedings of the 1985 York Manuscripts Conference]

Latin and Vernacular: Studies in Late-Medieval Texts and Manuscripts, ed. A. J. Minnis (1989) [Proceedings of the 1987 York Manuscripts Conference]

Regionalism in Late-Medieval Manuscripts and Texts: Essays celebrating the publication of 'A Linguistic Atlas of Late Mediaeval English', ed. Felicity Riddy (1991) [Proceedings of the 1989 York Manuscripts Conference]

Late-Medieval Religious Texts and their Transmission: Essays in Honour of A. I. Doyle, ed. A. J. Minnis (1994) [Proceedings of the 1991 York Manuscripts Conference]

Prestige, Authority and Power in Late Medieval Manuscripts and Texts, ed. Felicity Riddy (2000) [Proceedings of the 1994 York Manuscripts Conference]

Middle English Poetry: Texts and Traditions. Essays in Honour of Derek Pearsall, ed. A. J. Minnis (2001) [Proceedings of the 1996 York Manuscripts Conference]

Manuscript Culture in the British Isles

I *Design and Distribution of Late Medieval Manuscripts in England*, ed. Margaret Connolly and Linne R. Mooney (2008)

II *Women and Writing, c.1340-c.1650: The Domestication of Print Culture*, ed. Anne Lawrence-Mathers and Phillipa Hardman (2010)

III *The Wollaton Medieval Manuscripts: Texts, Owners and Readers*, ed. Ralph Hanna and Thorlac Turville-Petre (2010)

IV *Scribes and the City: London Guildhall Clerks and the Dissemination of Middle English Literature, 1375–1425*, Linne R. Mooney and Estelle Stubbs (2013)

Heresy and Inquisition in the Middle Ages

Heresy and Heretics in the Thirteenth Century: The Textual Representations, L. J. Sackville (2011)

Heresy, Crusade and Inquisition in Medieval Quercy, Claire Taylor (2011)

CPSIA information can be obtained
at www.ICGtesting.com
Printed in the USA
FFOW02n2015041016
28189FF